THESE
UNITED
STATES

ALSO BY GLENDA ELIZABETH GILMORE

Defying Dixie:
The Radical Roots of Civil Rights,
1919–1950 (2008)

Who Were the Progressives?
(2002, editor)

Jumpin' Jim Crow:
Southern Politics from Civil War to Civil Rights
(2000, co-editor)

Gender and Jim Crow:
Women and the Politics of White Supremacy
in North Carolina 1896–1920 (1996)

ALSO BY THOMAS J. SUGRUE

Not Even Past:
Barack Obama and the Burden of Race (2010)

Sweet Land of Liberty:
The Forgotten Struggle for Civil Rights
in the North (2008)

The New Suburban History (2005, co-editor)

W.E.B. DuBois, Race, and the City:
The Philadelphia Negro and Its Legacy
(1998, co-editor)

The Origins of the Urban Crisis:
Race and Inequality in Postwar Detroit (1996)

THESE UNITED STATES

A Nation in the Making, 1890 to the Present

Glenda Elizabeth Gilmore

Thomas J. Sugrue

W. W. NORTON & COMPANY

Independent Publishers Since 1923

NEW YORK • LONDON

For information about permission to reproduce selections from this book, write to Permissions, W. W. Norton & Company, Inc., 500 Fifth Avenue, New York, NY 10110

For information about special discounts for bulk purchases, please contact W. W. Norton Special Sales at specialsales@wwnorton.com or 800-233-4830

Manufacturing by Quad Graphics Fairfield
Book design by BTDnyc
Production manager: Julia Druskin

ISBN: 978-0-393-23952-2

W. W. Norton & Company, Inc.
500 Fifth Avenue, New York, N.Y. 10110
www.wwnorton.com

W. W. Norton & Company Ltd.
Castle House, 75/76 Wells Street, London W1T 3QT

1 2 3 4 5 6 7 8 9 0

To Ben,
my *anam cara*.

and

To Brittany

I do not look upon these United States as a finished product.
We are still in the making.

—FRANKLIN DELANO ROOSEVELT, 1936

CONTENTS

CHAPTER 13

"A SEASON OF DARKNESS":
THE TROUBLED 1970S • 495

CHAPTER 14

THE NEW GILDED AGE, 1980–2000 • 536

CHAPTER 15

UNITED WE STAND, DIVIDED WE FALL,
SINCE 2000 • 589

ILLUSTRATIONS FOLLOW PAGES 200 AND 360

LIST OF MAPS

"WE ARE STILL IN THE MAKING"

THE THIRTY-SECOND PRESIDENT of the United States, Franklin Delano Roosevelt, spoke on the radio from his childhood home at Hyde Park, New York, on February 23, 1936. It was Brotherhood Day, an event sponsored by the National Conference of Christians and Jews as a time for Americans to honor their common interests and values. "I am happy to speak to you from my own home on the evening of a Sabbath Day," the president told a nation shivering in single-digit temperatures over much of its expanse. His voice warmed them. "I like to think of our country as one home in which the interests of each member are bound up with the happiness of all." He assured his listeners, who had endured years of economic hardship, that they would not be abandoned: "the welfare of your family or mine cannot be bought at the sacrifice of our neighbor's family . . . our wellbeing depends, in the long run, upon the wellbeing of our neighbors." With public confidence at a low ebb, FDR promised that the government would act to restore prosperity. "I do not look upon these United States as a finished product," he told his audience. "We are still in the making."[1]

It is safe to say that most of the nation was listening that night, since Roosevelt regularly captured an audience of up to 70 percent of Americans when he spoke in his intimate fashion to them. Saul Bellow, the novelist, recalled an occasion when he was "walking eastward on the Chicago Midway on a summer evening. . . . drivers had pulled over, parking bumper to bumper, and turned on their radios to hear Roosevelt. They had rolled down the windows and opened the car doors. Everywhere the same voice, its odd Eastern accent. . . . You could follow without missing a single word as you strolled by."[2]

From the depths of the Depression, Roosevelt and his listeners could see that the American dream of expanding opportunity was not the inevitable result of markets and elections. It took work, legislation, organization, and planning, to build a strong democracy. The twentieth century as a whole, however, permits different perspectives on the dynamics of American democracy. From the Progressive era to the Great Society, with the exception of the Great Depression, the United States established a solid, prosperous middle class that perpetuated its ability to make life better for each succeeding generation. By the 1950s, many observers considered it inevitable that this achievable dream would extend to almost all Americans. Poverty would diminish, affordable educational institutions would flourish, and social conflict would become a vestige of the past.

But this was not to be. *These United States* starts and ends in periods of massive inequality. Experts conclude that the arc of inequality in the United States over the long twentieth century resembles an upside-down bell curve: the maldistribution of income starts out high in the 1890s, dips in the midcentury, and begins rising again in the 1970s.[3] In 1900, the top 10 percent of earners took home about 41 percent of the nation's income. The figure rose to a high of 45 percent in 1930, but the Great Depression, New Deal measures, and the economic leveling of World War II reduced the top decile's share to 33 percent in 1950, where it stayed for the next twenty years.[4]

Contemporary economists predicted that this equalization of income would continue. They attributed the maldistribution of income and wealth at the beginning of the century to the shock of rapid industrialization in the United States. In the 1950s and 1960s, they reasoned, the mature industrial economy would deliver consistent growth, which would in turn ameliorate income disparities and expand the middle class. The American dream would inexorably unfold.[5] In the immediate post–World War II decades, the country seemed on track to fulfill their rosy predictions.

Instead, income inequality began to grow after 1970. The top 10 percent, who took home 34 percent of the wages in 1970, collected almost 48 percent in 2010, a higher share than at any time in the twentieth century. The strong middle class built during the midcentury period began to weaken after 1970 as the percentage of wages claimed by the top 10 percent rose by a steady 5 percent per year through the end of the century.[6] The share of wages claimed by the top 1 percent of earners is even more striking: 18 percent in 1910, 8 percent in 1970, and 18 percent in 2010.[7]

Many of those who listened to FDR over the radio in February 1936 had lost their homes; others had saved them through New Deal programs such as the Home Owners' Loan Corporation or the Emergency Farm Mortgage Act. Their children would purchase homes through Veterans Administration loans or with help from the Federal Housing Administration. Some of their great-grandchildren would lose their homes in the 14 million foreclosures that took place during the Great Recession of 2007–2009.[8] The twentieth-century history of the United States raises the question of whether the American dream of an expanding middle class was a historical accident, the contingent result of an industrial nation coming of age, the growth of a federal social safety net, and the spending on the military-industrial complex that began in World War II.

Roughly one out of every ten people who listened to Roosevelt that night was African American. Since they occupied the lowest-paying jobs, the Great Depression hit black Americans harder overall than white Americans. Seven months after FDR's speech, they would abandon the Republican Party en masse to vote for the Democrats' New Deal. *These United States* opens in the 1890s as African Americans mount a vigorous movement to fight Jim Crow segregation and the loss of the voting rights that Reconstruction had guaranteed them. The book ends with an African American in his second term as president. During his first run for the presidency in 2008, on the anniversary of Martin Luther King, Jr.'s, death, Senator Barack Obama quoted King, himself paraphrasing a white abolitionist in 1853: "the arc of the moral universe is long, but it bends towards justice." Obama added, in an echo of FDR, "But here is the thing; it does not bend on its own. It bends because each of us in our own ways put our hand on the arc and we bend it in the direction of justice."[9]

From Jim Crow to Ferguson, *These United States* chronicles African Americans with their "hand[s] on the arc." A long civil rights movement spans our pages. We meet a young black woman, Ida B. Wells, handing out brochures in protest of African Americans' exclusion from the nation's 1893 World's Columbian Exposition; a young couple, William and Daisy Myers, facing jeering white protesters as they integrated Levittown, Pennsylvania, in 1957; and John Lewis, the son of sharecroppers, in a Nashville jail cell in 1960, speaking from the rostrum at the presidential inauguration in 2009. Like an expanding middle class, the drive for racial equality gives us another measure of America's success in developing a strong democracy across the twentieth century. In *These United States*, we present African American history not as a separate story but as American history itself.

The long twentieth century was also pivotal for this nation of immigrants. Debates over immigration policy consumed voters and elected officials repeatedly over the century. Politics, prejudice, and labor demands usually drove these debates, which often flared into violence. Anti-Chinese actions in the West culminated in exclusion laws once the foundation for the nation's railroads had been laid. And when fears of immigrant radicalism outweighed the need for unskilled labor, Congress adopted laws to curb immigration from southern and eastern Europe in 1924. During the 1930s, the government limited Mexican immigration, but when it needed workers during World War II and into the 1960s, authorities brought them into the country through the bracero program. In 1965 immigration reform lifted the 1924 quotas and led to a strong increase in newcomers from Latin America, the Caribbean, and Asia. By 1990, 20 million legal immigrants lived in the United States. Millions more came without documentation. In 1990 the United States removed 30,039 "inadmissible or deported aliens" from the country. By 2000, that number had grown to 188,467; by 2010, it reached 383,031.[10] In a rapidly globalizing world, citizenship issues and immigration policies continue to divide communities and political parties.

By the time FDR spoke on Brotherhood Day, Eleanor Roosevelt was the "foremost political woman in the United States."[11] Twenty-five years earlier, her husband's endorsement of woman suffrage had surprised her. She believed that women could implement social change without the ballot. After women won the right to vote in 1920, she became a politician in her own right. By 1980, women who reported voting outnumbered men by 6.4 million. By 2012, that gap had grown to 10.3 million.[12] Through traditional party politics and social movements, women expanded American democracy over the long twentieth century.

The patterns of women's work also changed over the period. When *These United States* opens, most Americans, including many women, thought that working women took jobs away from men who needed to support entire families. This idea of the "family wage" and the lone male breadwinner eroded over the century. The female component of the labor force, 17 percent in 1890, grew to 47 percent in 2010.[13] During World War II and afterward, women organized to improve working conditions, increase their wages, and get the support that they needed to raise families while bringing home paychecks. In the 1940s a young labor journalist, Betty Friedan, argued that unionization would provide economic security for women workers, and in the 1960s she helped found the National Organization for Women to push for equal pay for equal work and to prevent discrimination by sex in the workplace. There has been progress on this front, though a gap remains still to close: in 1979 women working full time earned 62 percent of men's earnings; in 2012 they earned 81 percent. [14]

Other women activists called for a stronger safety net to help young mothers stay at home and raise their children, and they fought against stereotypes, proffered by the New Right, that they were nothing but "welfare queens." Beginning in the 1970s, feminist activists calling for women's reproductive freedom faced a formidable challenge from other women who argued for the preservation of the "traditional family." The struggle over family, morality, and sexuality shaped everyday life and national politics in the last quarter of the twentieth century and beyond.

Most of Roosevelt's 1936 listeners looked to the New Deal—and hence to the federal government—for access to their country's political, economic, and social promise. They grappled, as we do, with the responsibility of the government to its people. In 1890 the federal government was small, with unenforceable antitrust regulations. The Progressive era and the New Deal expanded the role of the federal government, which now acted to regulate commerce, support decent working conditions and workers' rights, and build programs such as Social Security to protect people from hardship. By midcentury, the federal government had the tools to manage the economy and regulate financial institutions.

During the post–World War II years, as federal regulation and the sheer size of government grew, a well-funded and well-organized conservative insurgency rose to challenge the New Deal state and liberalism. Business leaders like General Electric's Lemuel Boulware and his spokesman, actor Ronald Reagan, celebrated free enterprise and argued that social welfare sapped Americans' work ethic, while regulation and taxation endangered individual liberty. They were joined by a growing group of religious conservatives who saw godliness as the antidote to Communism. Opponents of civil rights joined the cause, on the grounds that antidiscrimination laws represented government intrusion into individual rights to freedom of association.

By the 1960s, that New Right had become a major insurgent movement within the Republican Party. Fueled by opposition to urban riots and black power in the 1960s and by growing unease at new norms regarding personal sexuality unleashed by the liberation movements of the period, the New Right gained adherents. By the late 1970s and 1980s, those insurgents pushed aside moderate Republicans, turning the GOP rightward and leading many Democrats to reinvent liberalism. Democratic and Republican presidents embraced deregulation, arguing that government rules on food production, air traffic control, banking, and home mortgage lending impeded competition and growth. Ronald Reagan promoted supply-side economics on the theory that cutting taxes and regulatory controls would increase corporate profits, which would "trickle down" to poor and middle-class Americans. By the end of the century, the mainstream of the Democratic Party had accepted much of the conservative critique of the New Deal and called for less government and lower taxes, although they held their ground on the questions of reproductive rights and individual liberties. Ideological arguments hardened, producing a weaker state, less effective commercial regulation, a frayed social safety net, and deeper inequality.

Less than two weeks after FDR's Brotherhood Day address, Adolf Hitler ordered German troops into the Rhineland, violating the terms of the Versailles Treaty that had ended World War I. The U.S. Congress, dominated by isolationist sentiment, passed a series of neutrality acts designed to keep the nation out of developing conflicts. Differences over the nation's interests abroad have buffeted American foreign policy since 1898, when the Spanish-American War raised issues of interventions in foreign conflicts. Indeed, after 1914, as war spread through Europe, many Americans opposed U.S. intervention for the sake of markets or empire. President Woodrow Wilson changed the tenor of that debate by asserting the U.S. responsibility to "make the world safe for democracy." In 1917 he used this sense of mission to persuade a reluctant public to enter the war. After the Central Powers' defeat, the isolationists in Congress refused to accept Wilson's global mission and declined to join the League of Nations. Isolationism kept the country from intervening against Nazi aggression until the Japanese attack at Pearl Harbor in 1941. The last war's lessons often overshadow the realities of later confrontations.

The American troops who achieved victory in World War II believed that they were indeed making the world safe for democracy. After the "good war," the founding of the United Nations, the successful occupation of

Japan, and the rebuilding of Europe, most Americans believed that they had a duty actively to export democracy, in part to ensure national security. This belief in triumphant democracy infused Americans with the will to challenge the USSR throughout the Cold War. The Korean conflict and the Vietnam War represented tangible commitments to that belief: U.S. security depended, many thought, upon stopping Communism in far-flung nations. During the Vietnam War, massive resistance at home grew and even spread to the military itself, forcing President Richard Nixon to announce a program of Vietnamization of the war and simultaneously a pullout of American troops. The loss in Vietnam brought to the forefront questions not only about the country's purpose but also about its ability to perpetuate its global power. Conversely, the 1991 fall of the Soviet Union inspired new hope that the United States could proceed to democratize the world.

Our current debates are driven by the legacies of decades of intervention in the Middle East. From Eisenhower's decision to back a coup in Iran in 1953 to the oil crises after the Yom Kippur War of 1973, the United States has been diplomatically, militarily, and economically entangled with the region. In the 1980s the United States intervened in the Iraq-Iran War, empowering Saddam Hussein, and provided military and economic aid to Afghan rebels fighting the Soviet Union. Many of them were Islamic fundamentalists who later became active in the terrorist group Al Qaeda. For twenty-five years, beginning in 1991, the United States paid the price of those interventions in two wars against Iraq (1991 and 2003–11), a war in Afghanistan (2001–14), and struggles against extremist organizations throughout the region.

The attacks on the United States on September 11, 2001, and the Bush administration's war on terror, raised questions of intervention, human rights, and national security to high relief. In a moment of intense fear and moral outrage, the United States created clandestine prisons, tortured suspected terrorists, and rejected many of the conventional laws of war in the name of a national emergency. But the targets of the war on terror proved to be elusive, and the costs considerable. Many Americans now argue that, with limited resources and growing problems of domestic inequality, military intervention endangers the country as never before. Economic globalization, with its attendant costs to the domestic prosperity, threatens the United States' ability to sustain itself as a global power.

Throughout *These United States*, we track the connections between grassroots actions and elite power. Woman suffragists confronted President Woodrow Wilson through mass demonstrations in the streets of the capital. Their promise to help mobilize for the Great War secured his commitment to support a national suffrage amendment. Civil rights demonstrators produced clashes across the South that helped persuade President Lyndon Johnson to sponsor the Civil Rights Act of 1964. The electoral victories of activists on the right helped shape the agenda of Congress and presidents from Nixon to Obama. Rights and access won by one movement laid legal, structural, and aspirational foundations for the next. The debates of the twentieth century remain the debates of the twenty-first.

Finally, in the spirit of FDR's observation, we share a commitment to the individual lives, well known and unknown, who join together to make history. You will meet some unforgettable characters in the pages that follow. William Frank Fonvielle, a hopeful African American college student, sets off on a trip through the South in 1893 to report on the strange new phenomenon of segregation. Lew Sanders, in 1936 a bored radio salesman, learns to fly and leads a heroic band of college-age men through every major air battle of the Pacific theater during World War II. Lawrence James Merschel, the all-American son of a World War II veteran, lands in Vietnam twenty days after the Tet Offensive and a month before Lyndon Johnson decides to pull back his commitment to the war. Betty Dukes, a black California woman, discovers the limits of race and gender equality when she tries to advance in Wal-Mart, the world's largest corporation. Through these and many more twentieth-century lives, we root the broad history of the United States in the intimacy of personal experience. Here we find a nation in the making.

THESE
UNITED
STATES

CHAPTER 1

ORIGINS OF THE AMERICAN CENTURY

FRIEND PITTS WILLIAMS packed his brand-new diary as he set out with his dad on a high school graduation trip to visit the World's Columbian Exposition in Chicago in August 1893. The exposition honored the four hundredth anniversary of Christopher Columbus's "discovery" of America, and its designers planned it to demonstrate the modern and powerful nation that the United States had become. Called "the greatest event in the history of the country since the Civil War," it became the greatest event in Friend Williams's life so far.[1]

The country's most prominent architects—Frederick Law Olmsted, Daniel Burnham, and Louis Sullivan—had designed a fairground on Chicago's southern lakefront to be a city in itself, one fit for a thriving, democratic nation and industrial powerhouse. They hoped that the exposition's architecture, especially the collection of Roman and Greek marble buildings that they called the White City, would uplift and inspire visitors. The 1893 World's Columbian Exposition celebrated the country's post–Civil War industrial and technological revolution and announced that it was one of the most powerful nations in the world. It shaped public perception of what the United States was and forged expectations of what it could be.

Even as it touted the United States' successes, the exposition inadvertently exposed its shortcomings. Since the Civil War, an industrial revolution had changed daily life in profound ways. Fueled by a cheap workforce of European and Asian immigrants, the U.S. economy generated extreme wealth for a narrow sector of industrial and financial leaders. Most observers attributed the nation's rapid economic growth to an unregulated business climate and believed that it rewarded the strong over the weak. A serious recession began even as the exposition opened and gave impetus to a budding labor movement. Some unions questioned the basis of capitalism itself, but the American Federation of Labor, founded in 1886, accepted capitalism and worked to improve working conditions and pay. It grew to be the country's largest labor union. The economy, tied to a global gold standard, disadvantaged the majority of Americans who continued to farm the land and limited credit for agricultural improvements. Farmers fought back, first by joining in a national alliance and then by forming a third party, the People's Party. Discrimination against African Americans kept an impoverished farm labor force in place, and in the South, where 80 percent of black Americans lived, states moved to strip them of the civil rights they had gained in Reconstruction. Much had been accomplished in the United States since the Civil War, as the exposition testified, but much had been sacrificed for those triumphs.

THE WORLD'S COLUMBIAN EXPOSITION

Boarding the evening train in Buffalo, New York, one evening about nine p.m. Friend Williams slept all night, arrived in Chicago by eleven the next morning, and "set out to see the big show." It cost him fifty cents to get in, a price he felt cheap for the "grand sight."[2] Williams's first grand sight was the White City itself on the shores of Lake Michigan: rows of neoclassical buildings up and down two broad boulevards with a lake in the middle. At one end was a colossal statue—*The Republic*—a toga-clad woman, holding aloft an eagle perched on a globe signifying the U.S. role in spreading democracy. *The Republic* might have mixed America's metaphors, but the nearby Peristyle mangled them. Commemorating Columbus's voyage, a colonnade marked the Peristyle's perimeter and surrounded Christopher Columbus himself, who was portrayed as charging, for some inexplicable reason, on a horse-drawn Roman chariot.

Celebrating the Nation's Grandeur

The grand architecture of the White City was meant to awe the 27 million people who visited it. It marked a departure for a nation that had long celebrated its humble beginnings, one where presidents boasted of growing up in log cabins. The White City's palaces certainly awed Williams, who marveled at the elevated electric train running around its 215 buildings. The

Palace of Electricity, with a moving sidewalk and thousands of lights, boasted that the United States "eclipsed by her dazzling light every other nation."[3] Thomas Edison, who had started his own laboratory in 1876, served as an example of what one gifted man could do. He invented the phonograph and the motion picture camera, and he perfected the incandescent light bulbs that dazzled Williams. Close by stood Machinery Hall, stuffed with new inventions. In the Horticulture Building, a huge globe turned, surrounded by American-made farm machinery, the kind that many southern and midwestern farmers had already gone into debt to buy. The fair represented agriculture as an industry rather than as the small farmer's husbandry.

Williams inspected the replica of Columbus's *Santa María*, scrambled over one of the U.S. Navy's new battleships, and boarded a Viking vessel that had actually sailed to Chicago from Norway. Elsewhere people boarded a mock ocean liner, where they fancied themselves sailing around the world. The India Building with its rajas and the Swedish Building with its gymnasium dazzled Williams. Suddenly the rest of the world seemed very close. The United States was taking its place among the global powers. In 1893 the country had not followed European nations into settler colonialism in Africa and Asia, but the exposition portrayed it as capable of doing so.

The markedly more prosaic exhibitions in the Women's Building promoted a role for women in the commercial world. Its Board of Lady Managers included 117 women, representatives from each state, who planned the exhibitions. The board members were almost all elite white women who did not work outside the home, but the exhibits demonstrated women's practical skills. The board chair defended women's right to work for wages. The prevailing family wage concept dictated that women should stay in the home, to reserve wages for male heads of households, but the chair countered that "there is, unfortunately, not a home for each woman to preside over; most men are unable to maintain one."[4]

Frederick Law Olmsted's Dream

Three men named Fred—Frederick Law Olmsted, Frederick Douglass, and Frederick Jackson Turner—embodied the exposition's energy and themes. Frederick Law Olmsted saw the nation's future as a triumph of planning and design. Frederick Douglass, born in slavery, fought for fairer representation of African Americans at the exposition. The historian Frederick Jackson

Turner argued that the closure of the frontier in 1890 had brought to an end the opportunity to attain a family farm, which would change the country's character and perhaps threaten democracy.

As Olmsted watched people like the Williams mill about the White City, he noticed that they seemed overwhelmed and ill at ease. Observers described visitors as "shy, very much overdressed," or contained in "a quiet uncomfortable dignity." The exhibits conveyed a "scholastic formality" that "took all the life out of sight-seeing."[5] Far from being uplifted by their country's grandeur, the crowds seemed bored. The architects had built palaces to celebrate the nation, but such grandiosity simply distanced the people from their own role in democracy. It made them dull spectators.

The People's Pleasures

The adjacent Midway Plaisance dashed the White City's lofty cultural ambitions and foretold the hold of a new, robust—and less lofty—global culture. Much to Olmsted's chagrin, the crowd came alive when it exited the White City for the Midway. Restaurants, shops, theaters, and displays stretched out a mile long. If the White City was white, the Midway decidedly was not. It was foreign, chaotic, crowded, and dirty—and much more interesting to Williams and most of the other visitors. Crowds packed the World Congress of Beauty, which boasted women from 140 nations. Most of the beauties were probably locals, many of them African Americans.

The Midway surpassed P. T. Barnum's circuses, and the people loved it. The longest lines formed in front of the Persian Palace of Eros, where Little Egypt performed the dance that soon swept the nation, the hootchy-kootchy. The Ferris wheel ran second in popularity. Designed by George W. G. Ferris for the exposition, this triumph of U.S. ingenuity operated solely for fun. Williams pronounced it the "most satisfactory thing on the Midway."[6]

But it was not the only thing he saw there, since he talked his dad into walking through the Midway each night as they made their way back to their hotel. "Some will call it a wild scene as they walk down it at night," he confided to his diary. It was always "thronged" until midnight. "Several nationalities are planted side by side in this one street until nearly all the great countries of the world have a spot ornamented with some building typical of its native land." Music and strange languages assaulted Williams's senses, and here visitors formed "a jolly crowd."[7] An Irish village flourished alongside a Blarney Castle replica, and 125 Javanese occupied a mock village. Samoans danced at the South Sea Theater. Cairo's Arab street replicated sixty-two shops and hosted two parades each day and a "Danse du Ventre" every night. Egyptians juggled. Africans drummed. Hungarian Gypsies told fortunes. The Turks built a mosque; the Algerians a bazaar. At the Dahomey Village, West Africans sang, danced, and reenacted battles, led by women warriors. Buffalo Bill's Wild West Show, set up adjacent to the exposition, reminded visitors that the Wild West had moved from reality to fantasy.

Frederick Douglass's Dream Deferred

Seventy-five-year-old African American Frederick Douglass found both the Midway and the White City troubling. An ex-slave who had escaped to freedom to become a leading abolitionist, Douglass had been U.S. ambassador to Haiti and now served as the island nation's representative to the fair. He noticed at once that the White City contained exhibits from United States, Central and South America, and Europe, relegating Africa to the Midway. The Republic of Haiti sponsored a building, but African Americans were not represented in the White City at all. As for the Midway's Dahomey Village, Douglass charged that exploiters had brought "African savages here to act the monkey."[8]

Ida B. Wells, a young black woman, urged African Americans to boycott the exposition's promotional "Colored People's Day," since African Americans held only menial jobs on the exposition staff and the exhibitions excluded them. The previous year Wells had been teaching and working as a journalist in Memphis; she had then fled whites who threatened her life because of a column she wrote protesting the lynching of three friends. Now internationally known, Wells argued that foreign visitors would ask, "Why are not the colored people, who constitute so large an element of the American population, and who have contributed so large a share to American greatness, more visibly present and better represented in this World's Exposition?" In answer, Douglass and Wells coauthored a brochure entitled "The Reason Why the Colored American Is Not in the World's Columbian Exposition."[9] It documented U.S. racism.

Instead of boycotting "Colored People's Day," Douglass spoke on the portico of the Haitian Building. White men at the back of the crowd began heckling him. He looked up from his text, fixed them in his glare, and said,

"Men talk of the Negro problem. There is no Negro problem. The problem is whether the American people have loyalty enough, honor enough, patriotism enough, to live up to their own constitution."[10] Douglass allowed Wells to set up a desk at the Haitian Building, from which she handed out ten thousand copies of their brochure.

Frederick Jackson Turner's Vanishing Frontier

As the exposition banished African Americans, it also erased Native Americans from American history. Frederick Jackson Turner, a young historian, addressed a new organization of professional historians, the American Historical Association, which met in Chicago in conjunction with the exposition. His topic, "The Significance of the Frontier in American History," became one of the most famous speeches by a historian and one of the most influential interpretations of American history. Turner told his mostly male, white audience that the line of American settlement—the frontier—had reached its end at the Pacific Ocean three years earlier, in 1890. Since the frontier had operated as a social safety valve for the young country, its end marked a turning point in American history. Thomas Jefferson had predicted that small farmers who owned their own land—yeomen—would maintain their economic and political independence and ensure a democratic country. Now without the frontier, Turner argued, future generations of Americans would have to find other ways to keep democracy alive.

But the American West through which Turner's frontier moved had not been an empty wilderness. Historians' and ethnologists' estimates of the numbers of Native Americans in the continental United States vary widely—from 1.8 million to 18 million upon European contact. Decades of warfare, peaking in the 1860s and 1870s, had decimated the Plains Indians, and white settler attacks had wiped out many California Indian tribes. The Dawes Act of 1887 cut across tribal authority and allowed Native Americans to keep small, often arid landholdings if they would give up tribal ties and become American citizens. The government settled others on reservations. In 1890, the same year cited by Turner as marking the end of the frontier, the Indian wars culminated in the massacre by U.S. troops of more than 150 Lakota, mostly women and children, at Wounded Knee Creek in South Dakota. By 1900 only 250,000 American Indians lived in the United States.

While Turner's thoughts lingered on the loss of a vital source for American democracy, young men like Friend Williams did not pause to mourn the frontier's passing. Williams believed that the country's industrial might would raise living standards and propel the United States to global greatness. Some argued that Americans would have to look abroad to find new markets, now that the country had settled all available land. Perhaps the United States should export new democracies to faraway places.

BUILDING AN INDUSTRIAL NATION

The White City at the World's Columbian Exposition touted one side of an industrial revolution that had reordered the nation's economy since 1863. Some Americans had become very rich, and a few had garnered the unflattering nickname "robber baron." The country that had repudiated European aristocracy suddenly seemed have its own commercial aristocracy. The writers Mark Twain and Charles Dudley Warner dubbed the nineteenth century's last three decades the "Gilded Age." The name stuck.

The independent farmer, beholden to no one and voting his conscience, gave way to a generation of employees—wage slaves, some thought. Some wondered how the political system—a republic with powers derived from the consent of the governed—could stand up to the concentration of wealth among the few. Although most Americans still expected future presidents to arise from the ranks of rough, knobby boys who came of age splitting logs in the heartland, some feared that presidents might be drawn exclusively from the ranks of the pampered elite.

The Self-Made Man: Andrew Carnegie

To counter this fear, Americans clung to the idea that theirs was a country in which anyone who had enough initiative could become a millionaire. The stories of three exceptional boys—Dick, Andrew, and John—demonstrate the possibilities of the self-made man in this period. Andrew and John had grown up in the boom and bust economy of the mid-nineteenth century, with minimal business regulation and abundant natural resources.

But Dick never grew up at all. He existed only in Horatio Alger novels and in the imaginations of Alger's millions of readers. Dick's full name was Ragged Dick. He was born so poor that he could not support a last name, and by depriving Dick of one, Alger implied that elite family ties mattered little. Alger's 120 books reached more than 17 million people in the last thirty years of the nineteenth century. His characters tended to be orphans, cast out onto uncaring city streets as prepubescent boys, to live by their own wit. They made their own luck, often through acts of bravery or by demonstrating exceptional honesty, usually in the presence of a millionaire who himself turned out to be a self-made man. The millionaire who discovered Ragged Dick on the streets proclaimed that "in this free country poverty is no bar to a man's advancement."[11]

If Dick lived only in fiction, Andrew and John lived in the real world. The extraordinary lives of Andrew Carnegie and John Davison Rockefeller reinforced the mythology that any boy could make it in America. Less desperate than Ragged Dick's impoverished beginnings, their nonetheless humble origins belied—or perhaps foretold, depending on whether you embraced the self-made-man myth—their later success. Carnegie struck out at the age of thirteen; Rockefeller left home at fifteen. Carnegie did not graduate from high school; Rockefeller graduated but did not go to college—instead, he took a short commercial course. Their extraordinary success sprang in part from the moment in which they lived. Carnegie was born in 1835 and Rockefeller in 1839.

When Carnegie's family emigrated from Scotland to Allegheny City, Pennsylvania, near Pittsburgh, in 1848, the thirteen-year-old went to work in a factory. His first break came two years later, when he landed a job as an office boy in a telegraph company. Samuel Morse had invented the telegraph eleven years earlier, and wires now hummed up and down the East Coast, carrying messages in Morse code. Operators listened, wrote down on paper dots and dashes, and then translated those odd marks into letters and words. As Carnegie went about his duties—fetching supplies, sharpening pencils, and emptying rubbish—the *click click click* of Morse code filled his ears. Soon he realized that he could instantly translate the clicks into words, without writing them out first. He became a blisteringly fast telegraph operator and worked his way up in the firm. He saved every nickel and invested his savings. In 1861, Carnegie and a partner bought a Pennsylvania farm where oil seeped up in the fields. They channeled it into a depression called Carnegie's Pond, expecting the pond to fill up a couple of times before the supply exhausted itself. But the oil kept bubbling up for over a century. During the Civil War, Carnegie coordinated Union rail transportation and bought a steel mill that produced railroad ties.

In the West, railroads became the symbol of the age, iron rivers that

created, rather than answered, consumer demand. In Nebraska, a vast open plain before the rails came through, railroad officials jumped off the train every few miles and founded "towns," naming them alphabetically from east to west. Settlers followed. Rails stretched across wide-open spaces, so managers needed systems and communications that would extend their oversight up and down the lines. All this would have been impossible without the telegraph, whose lines spanned the country by 1861. The railroads never functioned as purely capitalistic enterprises: they required government support at every stage. Building railroads took enormous capital, a cheap labor force, and above all, land. The federal government donated 129 million acres in land grants, made loans, and executed favorable land leases for the privately owned railroads.

All this came at a cost. Many railroads failed and lost their investors' money. Railroad lawyers obliterated landowners' opposition, and railroad lobbyists bribed politicians at the state and federal levels. The writer Henry Adams quipped that his generation was "mortgaged to the railroads."[12] The first transcontinental line reached California in 1869, following existing connections from the Midwest. In 1870 the United States had 35,000 miles of track, and by 1900 mileage exceeded 200,000. On the East Coast, the rails linked communities, moved raw materials and labor, and sped products to markets. They created the commercial infrastructure that brought the West into the national economy and accelerated industrial growth.

The iron and steel industry grew dramatically, partly because of railroad construction, and Andrew Carnegie became the nation's richest man by 1900. By 1890 his Edgar Thomson Steel Works, twelve miles from Pittsburgh, was the country's largest steel mill. In 1892 the empire acquired two more mills, including the famous Homestead.

Carnegie also owned a plethora of companies that cornered, extracted, supplied, and produced everything that a steel mill might need. He described making steel this way:

> The eighth wonder of the world is this: two pounds of iron-stone purchased on the shores of Lake Superior and transported to Pittsburgh; two pounds of coal, mined in Connellsville and manufactured into one and one-fourth pounds of coke and brought to Pittsburgh; one half pound of limestone mined east of the Alleghenies and brought to Pittsburgh; a little manganese ore,

mined in Virginia and brought to Pittsburgh, and these four and one half pounds of material manufactured into one pound of solid steel and sold for one cent! That's all that needs be said about the steel business.[13]

Controlling production from start to finish—known as a vertical trust—helped make a one-cent pound of steel profitable. Carnegie owned the coal mine, the coke manufacturing facility, the limestone and manganese mines, and the Pittsburgh mill. Someone observed that "such a magnificent aggregation of industrial power has never before been under the domination of a single man."[14] Carnegie's accumulation of wealth was astonishing. Then he began giving it away.

When Andrew Carnegie turned sixty-two, he sold his business interests for more than $300 million and spent the rest of his life as a philanthropist. He donated money to towns and colleges across the English-speaking world to build more than 2,500 libraries, and he established the Carnegie Endowment for World Peace in 1910. Denouncing inherited wealth as a corrupting force, he argued that "the lot of the skilled workman is far better than that of the heir to an hereditary title, who is likely to lead an unhappy wicked life."[15] Horatio Alger could not have said it better. But most industrialists lacked Andrew Carnegie's fear of inherited wealth.

The Self-Made Man: John D. Rockefeller

While Carnegie perfected the vertical trust, Rockefeller specialized in the horizontal trust, combining competitors into one company to monopolize a type of business and control a market. For Rockefeller, that business was oil refining. When the sixteen-year-old completed his ten-week business course in Cleveland, Ohio, a head for figures was his only asset. Starting off as a bookkeeper, he then began his own produce company, which turned out to be small potatoes compared to oil refining. Like Carnegie, Rockefeller worked for the Union during the Civil War and bought oil fields close to Carnegie Pond. In 1863 he built an oil refinery in Cleveland. There, by 1870, he consolidated several companies under the name Standard Oil. With the rapid growth of the railroads, Rockefeller could ship oil and kerosene across the country quickly. Because he was a high-volume shipper, he negotiated low rates. John D. Rockefeller and Standard Oil became household names. By 1882 he had subsumed forty companies' stock under the

Standard Oil Trust, which by 1900 controlled 90 percent of the nation's oil refineries and made more than $45 million a year. Dubbed Wreck-a-feller by other oil refiners, Rockefeller set his own prices below cost until his competitor's customers vanished. Facing bankruptcy, the competitor often agreed to sell his company to Standard Oil. After eliminating the competition, Rockefeller would raise prices again.

With a fortune of a billion dollars in 1913, Rockefeller outdistanced Carnegie as the richest man in America. Unlike Carnegie, Rockefeller passed down his wealth to his children, and his son, John D. Rockefeller, Jr., persuaded his father to found the Rockefeller Foundation. The very magnitude of the foundation meant that Rockefeller philanthropy shaped U.S. social policy for decades in some sectors, for example, education and medicine. Within the realms that it funded, the foundation could set policies that states followed.

By 1900 many of the corporations that would grow to be the largest in the twentieth century already existed: Goodyear Tire, General Electric, Nabisco, Coca-Cola, and DuPont. Competition disappeared when subjected to an oil trust, a steel trust, a sugar trust, and a leather trust. A reporter quipped, "The average citizen was born to the profit of the milk trust and dies to the profit of the coffin trust."[16] In 1902 Ida Tarbell, a Pennsylvanian, wrote nineteen articles in *McClure's Magazine* that exposed Rockefeller's business methods. The federal government had only lightly regulated business in the past, and Tarbell's evidence of Rockefeller's business tactics enraged citizens.

Regulation, Laissez-Faire, and Social Darwinism

The federal government had little motivation to introduce reform in any sector. The Republican Party had held the White House and controlled Congress for thirty-five years after 1869, with the exception of the eight years when Democrat Grover Cleveland served two nonconsecutive terms. Captains of industry and midwestern farmers alike were Republicans, and during elections the party constantly invoked the great sacrifices of Union soldiers for Republican principles, a tactic called "waving the bloody shirt." The Democratic Party claimed some support among northern workers, especially immigrants, along with the unwavering allegiance of southern ex-Confederates. Thus Republican officials glided into power easily with only a few positive programs.

Sometimes scandals interrupted the pattern. Cleveland won the presidency in 1884 when it was revealed that his Republican opponent, James G. Blaine, a wheeler-dealer congressman from Maine, had granted railroads special favors. Blaine denied misconduct, but the publication of his letter to a business executive showed him to be an unctuous dissembler comfortably inhabiting the pockets of the rich. The best part was that he wrote on the bottom: "Burn this letter!" Across the country, little girls skipped rope to the rhyme:

> *James G. Blaine, James G. Blaine,*
> *Continental liar from the State of Maine!*
> *Burn this letter.*

When politicians did propose mild business regulation, the conservative Supreme Court thwarted them. Business regulation fell to the states, and in 1886 alone the court struck down 230 state commercial laws. Unable to regulate, the federal government turned to fact-finding. Moved in 1882 by labor unrest, Congress organized the Blair Committee to explore relations between capital and labor, and the federal government established the Bureau of Labor Statistics in 1884. President Cleveland and Congress bent to pressure to curb the railroads' power and established the Interstate Commerce Commission (ICC) in 1887, based on the explicit constitutional provision of federal power to regulate commerce among states. The ICC ended large shippers' railroad discounts, tied rates to distance, and ordered the publication of railroad fares. Farmers and small businessmen began to pay lower shipping rates as railroad prices became tied to distance, not to volume.

Cleveland then lost the 1888 presidential election to Republican Benjamin Harrison, who worked with Congress to pass the Sherman Antitrust Act in 1890. It outlawed "every contract, combination . . . or conspiracy in restraint of trade or commerce." Congressmen characterized the act as consumer protection: "preventing arrangements designed to advance the cost of the consumer." The vague language—"restraint of trade" and "arrangements designed"—described intentions rather than concrete actions and made it difficult to define or prosecute malfeasance. Lawsuits that tested the Sherman Act only confused the matter.

Cleveland regained the presidency in 1893, becoming both the twenty-second and twenty-fourth president, the only one to serve nonconsecutive terms. Using the Sherman Antitrust Act, he directed the Department of Justice to break up the American Sugar Refining Company trust, which controlled 98 percent of U.S. sugar manufacturing. However, the Supreme Court ruled in *United States v. E. C. Knight Co.* (1895) that the Constitution's commerce clause allowed federal regulation only of the distribution of goods, not of their manufacture. Celebrating the ruling, one New York banker proposed a toast to "the Supreme Court of the United States— guardian of the dollar, defender of private property, sheet anchor of the Republic."[17] After that debacle, the Sherman Antitrust Act remained largely untested for years.

Like many others in business and politics, the New York banker who toasted the Supreme Court believed that a healthy economy needed no government interference. Lack of regulation, or laissez-faire economics (translated as "leave it alone") became at this time an intellectual principle undergirding the argument that democracy and free enterprise depended on each other. Economists reasoned that in a democracy the people ruled themselves; so it followed that commerce must regulate itself. Laissez-faire advocates celebrated two Supreme Court rulings in 1886 and 1888 that extended citizens' rights in the Fourteenth Amendment (designed to make freed people citizens) to corporations.

There were links between laissez-faire economics and a new cultural strain, Social Darwinism, an offshoot of Charles Darwin's work in biological evolution. According to Social Darwinists, society progresses by accumulating wealth, rewarding a few deserving people, and weeding out the weak. When a man became rich, it proved that the biological principle of survival of the fittest worked in society. The strongest citizens formed a talented aristocracy to lead the rest up civilization's ladder. Poverty and its trappings—child labor or slums—represented sad but inevitable, even necessary, conditions. Hard times would winnow the masses by limiting their ability to have children or bringing about an early death. A few worthy poor individuals—Ragged Dick, perhaps—would rise to the top through Darwin's principle of natural selection. As the weak withered and died, the ranks of the poor would diminish.

William Graham Sumner, a Skull and Bonesman as a student at Yale and later a professor there, saw himself as one of the fittest, despite the fact that he had started on top. Sumner argued in 1883:

Certain ills belong to the hardships of human life. They are natural. . . . The fact that my neighbor has succeeded in this struggle better than I constitutes no grievance for me. . . . The aggregation of large fortunes is not at all a thing to be regretted. On the contrary, it is a necessary condition of many forms of social advance. . . . Society . . . does not need any care or supervision.

When Sumner wrote that the "right to the pursuit of happiness is nothing but a license to maintain the struggle for existence," he was right on one thing: laborers had little time to pursue happiness outside their struggle for existence.[18] In 1894 the novelist Hamlin Garland wondered how the rules of Social Darwinism were working out at Carnegie's Homestead Steel Mill. He reported, "Everywhere [at Homestead] . . . were pits like the mouth of hell, and fierce ovens giving off a glare of heat . . . horrible stenches of gases . . . steam sissed and threatened." In intense heat, men worked twelve hours a day, six days a week. Unskilled laborers, many of them new immigrants, brought home an average of $1.70 per day (or about $42.00 currently). Homestead's skilled workers could make an average of $5.50 a day (about $130 today), a large sum compared to other skilled professions, at $3.57. Despite the skilled workers' good wages, one observer commented, "you don't notice any old men here." The young men seemed "discouraged and sullen." As for the town, "everywhere the yellow mud of the streets lay kneaded into a sticky mass, through which groups of pale, lean men slouched in faded garments."[19] Within a single month, Homestead Steel reported seven deaths. Perhaps natural selection actually did eliminate the weak. But it is less clear that the fittest rose at Homestead.

In 1910 at least 35,000 American workers died on the job. In Pittsburgh's steel and iron mills, 195 workers died in a single year. Other dangers lurked in the shadows. Most physicians understood that inhaling coal dust or using dangerous chemicals on the job would bequeath workers long, slow deaths. Exhaustion also contributed to the annual death toll. In 1910 the average industrial employee worked six days a week and more than nine hours a day. Advocates of laissez-faire economics taught that a person had a right to work as many hours as he or she chose. They called it "liberty of contract." State-mandated caps on hours would limit individual decision making, they argued.

The state courts and the U.S. Supreme Court repeatedly honored liberty of contract and struck down laws limiting hours. Often state legislatures had drafted those laws to protect certain occupations—for example, bakers, who had to begin work in the predawn hours. However, the Supreme Court in *Lochner v. New York* (1905) found bakers' demands for an eight-hour day to be unconstitutional. The justices declared that limiting working hours was "mere meddlesome interferences with the rights of the individual."[20]

Chinese Immigration and the Exclusion Acts

Employers could draw on an abundant supply of cheap labor and fire workers at will because of the continual influx of immigrants. Chinese immigrants, mostly male, began coming to the American West in the 1840s during the Gold Rush. Driven by crushing poverty and an indenture system, some 300,000 people had left China for the United States by 1882. Upon arrival, the Chinese also faced discriminatory hurdles. In 1854 California classed Chinese men with African Americans and Native Americans to forbid them to testify in court against white men. Black Californians protested, to no avail, that they were citizens and deserved fair judicial process. After the Civil War, the Central Pacific Railroad found the California Chinese laborers to be such hard workers that they went directly to China to bring back thousands more. For the most part, they did not rise and prosper but remained segregated in the worst jobs.

In the 1870s northern California's economic growth slowed, and another set of immigrants, Irish laborers in San Francisco, many of whom had worked on the Union Pacific Railroad, began to complain that Chinese labor depressed wages for everyone. The Chinese, they argued, did not have to support families (they were mostly single males) and accepted terrible working and living conditions. Having been victims of discrimination themselves did not deter Californians from making immigration restriction a political issue. By 1880, 75,000 Chinese people lived in the state. In 1882, Congress passed the Chinese Exclusion Act, which drastically restricted Chinese immigration. Australia and Canada passed similar laws, and Congress renewed the act in 1892. Ten years later Congress voted to extend the Chinese Exclusion Act permanently.

The Exclusion Act specifically prohibited only "skilled and unskilled laborers and Chinese employed in mining," so a few Chinese professionals, teachers, students, and merchants, became U.S. residents. Wong Fay, a

thirty-year-old doctor and druggist, obtained permission to live in Red-
lands, California, sometime after 1892. His immigration card noted that he
was "other than laborer."

In 1905 the federal government established an immigration station on
Angel Island in the San Francisco Bay to process Pacific immigrants. Angel
Island operated as a fortified gate, not as an open door. Officials detained
eligible immigrants for weeks and interrogated them, searching for the
slightest discrepancy in their records. In 1916, when Louie Gar Fun, a merchant who had immigrated earlier, traveled from Boise, Idaho, to meet his
wife and son at Angel Island, immigration officials kept them there for three
months. They interrogated the family about life in China (to prove that they
were actually married) and required copious documentation from Boise (to
prove that he was an upstanding merchant).[21] The exclusion of Chinese
around the Pacific Rim by English-speaking countries owed a good deal to
racism, but it also reflected the growing interconnectedness of the global
economy in an industrial age. Growth required cheap, movable labor, but it
had to be the right kind at the right time.

European Immigration on the East Coast

Between 1860 and 1880, some 13.5 million people entered the United States
through East Coast ports, most of them from northern Europe and the British
Isles. In 1892 the federal government opened an immigration station on Ellis
Island in New York harbor. When fourteen-year-old Annie Moore boarded
the steamship *Nevada* in Cork City, Ireland, she had no idea that fifteen days
later—on New Year's Day 1893—she would be the first immigrant processed
through Ellis Island. Perhaps she earned the honor because she was a "rosy-
cheeked Irish girl"; perhaps because she was sympathetic, journeying with her
younger brothers to join their parents in New York. She alighted on Ellis
Island amid a cacophony of ships' whistles on a transport decked out in bun-
ting. An immigration official presented her with a ten-dollar gold piece.

In the subsequent decades, between 1892 and 1930, 19 million more
emigrants, many from Scandinavia and southern and eastern Europe, followed Annie Moore. One million arrived each year between 1900 and 1906.
Four million Italians came before 1924, along with three million Russians,
many of them Jews. Eastern immigration peaked as 1,285,349 new Americans went through Ellis Island in the twelve-month period that ended in
June 1907. After the Chinese Exclusion Act of 1882, unrestricted Mexican

immigrants arrived to work on the railroads to replace Chinese workers, and their numbers reached 100,000 by 1900. By 1920, 478,000 Mexican citizens resided in the United States.

European immigrants fled their farms as their countries moved to large-scale agricultural production and free trade across national borders. Governments eliminated common land, and landlords drove away tenants. Some immigrants—for example, eastern European Jews and Irish Catholics—left their homes because of religious persecution. Others fled compulsory national military service. They traveled on new, fast steamships at low fares.

Upon their arrival in America, these "uprooted peasants" mostly lived in cities. By 1910 the population of the country's twelve largest cities comprised 40 percent first-generation immigrants and 20 percent second-generation immigrants. First-generation immigrants included more men than women, and the majority were fifteen to forty-five years old. Two-thirds of East Cost immigrants settled in the Northeast and the mid-Atlantic states. Chicago became their midwestern center. Far fewer made their way to the South, but Scandinavians settled on the Great Plains, where inhospitable land remained affordable.

Urban immigrants clustered in neighborhoods and worked in industries with their fellow country people, enabling them to circumvent language barriers, find employment, and learn the ropes. In early twentieth-century New York, Jews made up 70 percent of garment workers. Slavs worked in Pennsylvania coal mines. The immigration wave from 1890 to 1924 transformed the country from a mostly Protestant nation to a nation of Protestants, Catholics, and Jews. In cities like Buffalo, Cleveland, Chicago, and Milwaukee, Catholic immigrants and their children approached a majority of the population. The kind of nativism—fear of immigrants—that Californians had reserved for the Chinese in the 1880s became directed at other ethnic groups. Speaking and reading languages other than English at school or at work was often banned. Protestants feared that Catholic candidates for public office would owe allegiance to the church over American law.

Women and Children at Work

For all the labor power that industry gained from immigrant men, the new industrial working class included many other sorts of people. Women found work in dressmakers' shops, food preparation, textile mills, and garment factories, and as sales clerks in burgeoning retail stores. In garment factories, working ten to twelve hours a day, women lost wages for misplacing needles, using too much thread, or taking too much time in the bathroom. One woman recalled that her co-worker had lost three hours' pay for talking: not for talking too much but for talking at all. She remembered, "It was my first real job and I was afraid of losing it, so I tried to keep silent. But for a lively girl like me to keep her mouth shut for eleven hours is torture; it almost drove me wild!"[22]

From 1870 to 1900 one of every six workers was a woman, 85 percent of them unmarried. Often immigrants or their daughters, the five million women who worked in 1900 earned less than men, even for the same job, and few people saw anything wrong with that. Most believed that employers should pay a higher "family wage" to a man to support his dependents. Some reasoned that wage-earning women, especially those who lived on their own, took jobs away from male household heads. The concept that women should live within family units was so strong that the census counted women on their own as "women adrift." For women adrift—grown daughters, widows, or married women who had been deserted by their husbands—the family wage ideal sentenced them to poverty. They crowded into shabby boardinghouses. A survey of 210 prostitutes in one city found that 140 of them had previously tried to support themselves at factory work or as saleswomen; when they could not, they had turned to prostitution. The office workforce became feminized only after 1910. Before that time, men monopolized bookkeeping and clerk positions.

Among ten-to-fifteen-year-old children, one in every six held a full-time job. In southern textile mills, one-third of the workforce was commonly under thirteen. For example, in North Carolina in 1903, it was legal for a child of twelve to work all night and sixty-six hours a week. States in the South lacked birth certificates and took the parents' word for their children's ages. In the North immigrant parents could claim whatever age they wished for their foreign-born children. Child labor worked to the advantage of factory owners in two ways. First, it depressed adult workers' wages by establishing low base pay for entry-level tasks; it was an anchor that pulled down all wages. Second, young laborers grew up to be a captive workforce of low-paid adults, uneducated and unprepared for anything else.

Despite their exploitation, women and children who worked in factories often considered themselves more fortunate than those who worked at home. In Chicago alone, nearly eleven thousand people worked at home, paid for each item that they produced rather than for their time. Very young children could be pressed into service for piecework. A social worker uncovered a typical case: a family of eight living in a three-room flat where the father, mother, two daughters, and a cousin made trousers. They earned sixty-five cents for a dozen pairs of pants, and they worked seven days a week on a board atop the kitchen table.

The abundant supply of labor, stoked by immigration and supplemented by women's and children's labor, kept wages low and made workers expendable. "I regard my people," one manager declared, "as I regard my machinery. So long as they can do my work for what I choose to pay them, I keep them, getting out of them all I can."[23]

MOBILIZING FARMERS: THE POPULIST MOVEMENT

Against this industrial backdrop, many farmers found growing hardship on the land. The Chicago exposition itself implied a threat to farming as a way of life. Everything was becoming so enormous, so fast, so technical, and so expensive. The agricultural machinery on display seemed too costly for a typical farm family. The Midway's pleasures verified farmers' suspicions that cities begat vice. The differences between urbanites like Friend Williams and rural people become a yawning gap. The perspectives of farmers and city slickers, agriculturalists and industrialists, debtors and creditors grew farther apart in the last two decades of the nineteenth century.

A Crisis on the Farm

Many rural people in the late nineteenth century defined their goal as self-sufficiency, invoking the ideal of the independent yeoman farmer whom Thomas Jefferson had seen as the nation's backbone. They clung to the belief that leaving the farm for wage labor signified failure. To southern and western Protestants, the farm held moral worth because there people lived as God intended them to, in tune with a natural bounty. The man-made city represented evil because there people lived under bosses. Self-sufficiency guaranteed economic and political independence. They condemned as immoral those who managed others, profited through passive investment, or lived on other people's squabbles. But as the nation grew more urban, managers, investors, and lawyers multiplied.

Other farmers, particularly the more prosperous ones who produced marketable cash crops, stood ready to sacrifice self-sufficiency if the market economy became more advantageous to agricultural producers. They saw themselves as small businessmen who deserved a level playing field to produce and market their crops. But in the early 1890s, the economy favored their suppliers, transporters, and crop brokers.

A perfect storm of problems had coalesced in the last fifteen years of the century to devastate farmers. Bad luck accounted for some disasters; the new industrial capitalism with its global scope accounted for more. It seemed as if some remote power structure had stacked the deck. The agricultural economy had structural problems, particularly in the South, which had been left in economic shambles after the Civil War. Everywhere money remained in short supply, and land was unequally distributed.

In the South landowners, who had little money, and landless freed people adopted sharecropping as a halfway measure. Theoretically sharecropping constituted a cooperative venture: the landowner lent the land, tools, and seed; the farm family worked hard, raised the crop, and shared the harvest and profit. Some sharecroppers succeeded, and 25 percent of black farmers owned their land by 1900. More often sharecropping disadvantaged farm laborers. If the family provided their own mule, plow, and seeds, they might keep one-half of the crop value; if they came with only their hands, and the landowner furnished them with tools and fed them all year, they might find themselves in debt postharvest. [24]

Sharecropping ranks increased as southern and midwestern small farmers fell into debt. The more prosperous ones could mortgage the farm, but banks charged southern and southwestern farmers prohibitively high interest. Those who could not mortgage their land mortgaged their ungrown crop. The "furnishing merchant" who took the crop lien provided supplies. If the farmer could not pay off the crop lien at harvest time, the merchant took the land, and the former landowner became a sharecropper elsewhere.

This credit system flourished without the slightest regulation. Furnishing merchants often charged 50 percent interest. Moreover, the sharecropper or indebted farmer had to pay the furnishing merchant's high prices for supplies, since he served as both their bank and their store. The national distribution of banks two years after the World's Columbian Exposition illustrates the problem. Nationally in 1895, there was a bank for every 16,000 people. But in Texas, for example, there was one bank for every

58,130 people. In many counties there was no bank at all. In the South 25 percent of farmers were tenants in 1880, but by 1900, 49 percent were.

The smart thing to do, if you were a sharecropper or a farmer with a crop lien, was to plant a cash crop for market. There wasn't much money in green beans, squash, or tomatoes, and a poor transportation infrastructure made it difficult to market them. In the South and Southwest, the cash crops were cotton and in some places tobacco—marketable crops that did not rot and brought the highest return. In the Midwest and the Great Plains, wheat was the cash crop. Two things happened when everyone planted the same crop: overproduction lowered the price, and one-crop agriculture exhausted the land. However, the furnishing merchant often insisted, "No cotton, no credit." With overproduction, cash crop prices fell. A bale of cotton brought 17 cents per pound in 1870 but only 6 cents in 1894. Midwestern farmers' wheat fell in price from 95 cents per bushel in 1880 to 51 cents in 1895.[25] Falling prices meant that many landowners who had been secure in 1880 resorted to crop liens and lost their farms by 1890.

Farmers in a Capitalist World

The nation's commercial structure compounded farmers' problems. For example, before the Interstate Commerce Commission's reforms in 1887, railroads charged more per mile for short hauls than for long hauls, a burden that fell heavily on midwestern farmers who had to ship their wheat to Chicago. Southern and southwestern farmers sold their cotton at the local gin, but a global market determined its price. It was twice as expensive to ship North Carolina–grown cotton to New York than to ship Egyptian-grown cotton there. Moreover, without an income tax, a poor farmer might pay more tax on his farm property than a wealthy industrialist paid on his profits.

To make things worse, many farmers paid artificially high prices for necessary supplies, because trusts monopolized particular resources. No governmental regulation prevented cornering the market on a commodity and then raising its price; indeed, these agricultural trusts operated as legitimate businesses. For example, as the W. R. Grace Company gained control of the guano industry off of Peru, farmers who depended on guano for fertilizer suddenly found the price sky high. Another trust bought up all the Mexican jute, used to make burlap to wrap cotton bales, and tripled the price.

Finally, from 1870 until the early 1890s, the entire country experienced a deflationary spiral—a continual drop in prices. This depressed income and made debts harder to pay back. If you borrowed one hundred dollars to buy the Derring Pony Binder shown at the Chicago exposition—"saves horses, saves grain, saves time, saves twine"—repaying the loan became more difficult each year because your crop sold for less. Deflation occurred in part because the United States, along with most other industrial countries, was on the gold standard. Since the 1873 Coinage Act, the government could issue only as much money as it could back up with gold. With little gold discovered between 1873 and the mid-1890s, the currency remained static as the population rapidly increased. There was less money per person in the 1890s than in 1873, lowering wages and restricting credit worldwide. Few banks would lend to farmers, but all sought to profit by lending to their monopolistic suppliers.

The most compelling solution was for Congress to legislate bimetallism, using silver as well as gold to back the monetary system. Since silver was more plentiful than gold, it would make a more flexible foundation for the currency. Advocates of bimetallism proposed monetizing silver at a value of 16 to 1: sixteen ounces of silver could equal one ounce of gold.

The Wonderful Wizard of Oz *and the Farmers' Alliance*

If the implications of the gold standard sound abstract and confusing, we can seek understanding in *The Wizard of Oz*, the landmark 1939 film based on the novel, *The Wonderful Wizard of Oz* by L. Frank Baum, published in 1900.[26] Dorothy, Auntie Em, the Tin Man, the Scarecrow, and the Cowardly Lion represent figures who loomed large in farmers' imaginations in the 1890s. The Wicked Witch of the West, the Munchkins, and the Winged Monkeys all played dark roles in the western farmers' plight. The silver shoes (turned ruby red for Judy Garland in the film), the yellow brick road, and Oz himself offered the only hope.

Dorothy cannot understand why Auntie Em and Uncle Henry seem as depressed and gray as the prairie itself. They represent the farm family's despair over the agrarian crisis. When a vicious storm uproots Dorothy and the family's crops, she finds herself wearing silver shoes walking down a yellow brick road toward Oz. In Oz, 16 oz. (ounces) of silver will finally equal 1 oz. of gold. The monetary system baffled real-life farmers, which is why, when Dorothy meets the Scarecrow, he lacks a brain. Farmers, like the Scarecrow, need to wise up, Baum thought, and lobby for bimetallism. Plentiful silver, used for coinage, would loosen credit and raise crop prices and wages. Their slogan became "free silver."

As Dorothy and the Scarecrow set off down the yellow brick road toward Oz, they meet the Tin Man. He has accidentally chopped off his own arms and legs in industrial accidents and replaced them with tin parts, until he has become the factory owner's dream: a machine that lacks a heart. Representing a factory worker who earns ever-decreasing wages, the Tin Man has sold his humanity to capitalists, but Oz can remedy his plight and raise his wages. The Wicked Witch of the East, who dies when Dorothy's house lands on her, calls forth the eastern factory owners who have kept "the Munchkins in bondage for many years, making them slave for her night and day."[27] The Wicked Witch of the West, who has exhausted farmland and created a desolate prairie, can be vanquished with water. The Winged Monkeys, who do her bidding, are the Plains Indians, who will vanish as prosperous cultivators advance.

Scarecrows (and farmers) wised up when they joined the Farmers' Alliance, an organization that explained the politics of agricultural trusts, rapacious railroad tactics, and the gold standard, all in plain language. Founded around 1875 in Texas, the Alliance expanded in the late 1880s. It functioned as a school for farm families through a system of traveling lecturers, who met in local chapters throughout the South and West. Alliance lecturers condemned the adoption of the gold standard, which they called the "Crime of '73," railed against the trusts, and taught farmers how to start cooperative stores to eliminate furnishing merchants. A cooperative could pool farmers' crops at the end of the season, sell them at higher prices, and negotiate a better rate with the railroad. Farmers began to realize that their descent into poverty sprang not from their own shortcomings but from their country's political economy. As they rushed to join the movement, an Alliance lecturer compared them to ripe fruit: "You can gather them by a gentle shake of a bush."[28]

Farmers in Nebraska began to see themselves as sharing economic interests with farmers in North Carolina: their common goals spanned the Civil War's divides. As Alliance president and North Carolinian Leonidas L. Polk told Dorothy's Kansas neighbors in 1890, "The farmer of North Carolina, Georgia, Texas, South Carolina is your brother."[29] The white farmers of the Alliance realized that they needed African American support, but integrating them into their own Alliance was a step too far. More than one million black farmers joined the segregated Colored Farmers' Alliance. If the two organizations were segregated, their principles were not.

The Alliance also reached out to industrial laborers. Farmers' and laborers' concerns overlapped most obviously on the gold standard, which was depressing both crop prices and industrial wages. They also agreed on immigration restriction to curb cheap labor and population growth. Both laborers and farmers called for government ownership of the railroads, and both supported a progressive income tax, one with rates that increased with income level.

The People's Party

At first the Alliance tried to get Republican and Democratic candidates to endorse their principles. With their typical gift for simplification, the group's representatives laid out the "Alliance Yardstick"—a platform of demands— by which to measure candidates. Office seekers had to promise to support free silver, railroad regulation, and something called the subtreasury, a plan for the federal government to build warehouses where farmers could store their crops as collateral for government loans. When the price was right, farmers would sell their crop to repay the loans. The subtreasury would mitigate the harshness of market forces, such as low prices when crops flooded the market. It would loosen credit and ease transportation costs.

Six gubernatorial and more than fifty congressional candidates promised to follow the Alliance Yardstick if elected in 1890; once in office, however, they sometimes voted against Yardstick principles. The subtreasury proved the major sticking point. Some called it "communism" or, worse, a "hideous abortion of demagogy and fanaticism."[30] Midwestern Republicans refused to support free silver because they were the party of big business and the banks, the "sound money" party. Disappointed that officials abandoned the Yardstick, some Alliance members argued that political power required party organization. However, not all Alliance members embraced a third party; the more prosperous often remained committed to the traditional parties.

The Alliance called a convention in Omaha in July 1892, where its members formed the People's Party and began to call themselves Populists. The Omaha Platform combined the Yardstick's measures with others designed to win industrial laborers' votes. To their goals of free silver, government ownership of the railroads, a progressive income tax, and the subtreasury, the People's Party added the demand for a federal law to establish an eight-hour day, abolition of the private police forces that industrialists used to break unions, and immigration limits. The platform also called for states to adopt a voting reform known as the referendum, which provided for citizen votes on legislation, and the initiative, which allowed citizens to propose legislation by petition.

Populism took the South and West by storm. Since almost all white southerners were Democrats and most midwesterners were Republicans, an alliance of southern and midwestern farmers would create a voting bloc that could win local elections and combine nationally with either Republicans or Democrats as a swing vote. Midwesterners had already flirted with third parties, but white southerners had fought and died in the Civil War for the Democratic Party's white supremacist principles. Leaving the party of their fathers took courage. Despite the formidable barriers to joining a third party, farmers crossed party lines to forge an interregional coalition.

Alliance president Leonidas Polk died three weeks before the Omaha convention. If he had lived and been nominated for president, westerners might have borne the shock of voting across regional lines more successfully than southerners did. The People's Party nominated an ex-Union general from Iowa, James B. Weaver, for president and an ex-Confederate major from Virginia, James G. Field, for vice president. Voting for a former Union general proved too much for many white southerners. When Weaver and his wife campaigned for the Populist ticket in Georgia, one man reported that bystanders pelted the Weavers with so many eggs, they looked like walking omelets.[31]

Nonetheless the national election of 1892 demonstrated Populist power. The Democrat Grover Cleveland defeated the incumbent, Republican Benjamin Harrison, by less than half a million votes. The midwestern share of the one million votes won by Populist James B. Weaver might have been enough to elect Harrison. Three states elected Populist governors, thirteen Populists went to the House of Representatives, and North Carolina and Nebraska elected Populist senators. Although he was a Democrat, Cleveland's election represented a defeat for free silver, since he clung to the gold standard despite the support in his party for bimetallism.

William Jennings Bryan and Free Silver

In 1893, as Friend Williams and 27 million others toured the World's Columbian Exposition, the worst depression since the Civil War was gaining steam. As the economy collapsed, President Cleveland's hard money policy lost southern Democratic support. The disastrous economy swept many congressmen out of office in 1894, even those who supported free silver. Among them was William Jennings Bryan, an idealistic young Democratic Nebraskan. For the next three years, Bryan traveled across the country speaking for free silver, a cause, as he described it, "as holy as the cause of liberty."[32]

At the 1896 Democratic Convention, Bryan accepted the presidential nomination with a fiery speech. "Burn down your cities and leave our farms," he roared, "and your cities will spring up again as if by magic; but destroy our farms, and grass will grow in the streets of every city in the country." A huge man, Bryan stood before the crowd and stretched out his arms like the crucified Jesus Christ: "We will answer their demand for a gold standard by saying to them: You shall not press down upon the brow of labor this crown of thorns, you shall not crucify mankind upon a cross of gold."[33] The Democratic Party platform adopted the Populist call for the free coinage of silver at a ratio of 16 ounces to 1 ounce of gold. Bryan's roar earned him a permanent place in children's hearts as the Cowardly Lion. Courage! That's what the Cowardly Lion needs to reach the Emerald City, named for the plentiful dollar bills that will pave the streets and cover the buildings after adopting free silver. Courage—and votes.

In 1896 the Democratic Party platform supported free silver, snatching away the People's Party's main issue. The Republicans nominated William McKinley, a gold standard supporter. His commitment to higher tariffs on imported goods to protect American manufacturing drew industrial workers into the Republican Party. The Populists met with the Democrats, argued among themselves, and also nominated Bryan as their candidate. He did not accept their nomination. The free silver issue now obscured all others on the Populist agenda. With the Democratic nomination of Bryan and its free silver endorsement, southern white Populists could return to the Democratic Party. In the West, just before Election Day, the price of wheat rose, weakening Bryan's support. He received 6,467,000 votes to McKinley's 7,035,000. McKinley had reinvigorated the Republican coalition of the Northeast and Midwest.

Perhaps the People's Party's worst enemy was good times: economic conditions began to improve after 1896. From 1897 to 1914, worldwide gold discoveries—from South Africa to Alaska—increased the money supply by

7.5 percent. Credit loosened, and farm commodity prices and wages rose. Many of those who remained on their farms adopted more conservative politics. By then hundreds of thousands of Populists had lost their land and moved to cities to become wage laborers. Like Dorothy, they sometimes dreamed about Populism, but mostly they hardened their hearts as they left their farms to become Tin Men in an industrial capitalist society. Despite the failure of the People's Party, it nonetheless set a reform agenda that other parties would adopt in bits and pieces during the Progressive era, the first two decades of the twentieth century.[34]

BUILDING AMERICAN UNIONS

The Chicago exposition displayed American inventions and manufactured goods as triumphs of capitalism, but it omitted the producers of that bounty. Workers had few rights and an uncertain future in industrial America. Frederick Jackson Turner predicted that the end of the frontier would reduce Americans to employees who would lose control over their independence and impoverish democracy. Frederick Douglass asked where African Americans fit into the new industrial age.

The issue of labor's rights was one of the key conundrums of the late nineteenth and early twentieth centuries. As the industrial workforce expanded from 1880 to 1920, no one championed a country that was filled with wage slaves dependent upon a few robber barons, but disagreements abounded on how to reform work and the workplace. Horatio Alger, William Graham Sumner, and the Social Darwinists believed that the system would fix itself through individual spunk or social evolution. Others believed that workers should unite to even the playing field between employers and employees. Some among those who sought workers' unity debated whether workers should attempt to reform capitalism or try to overthrow it altogether.

The 1893 Depression: Coxey's Army and Debs's Socialism

The Depression of 1893 left two million workers without jobs, and the nation's cities teemed with idle men roaming the streets. Charities, all of which were private, failed to stem the crisis. The *New York World* newspaper gave away more than a million loaves of bread. Populists blamed the gold standard for the crisis, socialists blamed capitalism, others attributed it to the trusts, and many disparaged government for favoring factory owners at workers' expense.

In Ohio a group of men began to organize—not a union, not a socialist party, but a public outcry, a "petition in boots"—to force Congress to create jobs and pay workers in paper currency that was not backed by gold. Chief organizer Jacob Coxey, a wealthy businessman, seemed an unlikely leader of an unemployed march, but he passionately believed in abandoning the gold standard and printing enough legal tender to reinvigorate the economy. He even named his youngest son Legal Tender Coxey. Calling themselves the Commonweal of Christ, Coxey's Ohio army set out for Washington in the spring of 1894. Other men came (albeit part of the way by rail) from Los Angeles and San Francisco. Contingents marched south from Boston through New Haven, where twenty-six men from the Connecticut division joined the fifty-eight Bostonians. An African American contingent from Indiana met them in Washington.

They arrived in the capital on May 1 only to starve at their encampments, trying to live on blackberries and scorned by the federal government. Congressmen called them tramps, hoboes, and vagabonds. Coxey's Army dissolved in defeat, but not before it had graphically raised the question of the federal government's responsibility to its working citizens.

Some of the European immigrants who arrived carrying few possessions were heavily endowed with socialist ideals. The Social Democratic Workingmen's Party of the United States, founded in 1874, advocated that workers should own factories. Members argued over whether they could achieve worker control through democratic means—voting in unions and electing government officials—or whether only revolution would abolish capitalism. Because socialist immigrants came from different European intellectual traditions, they rarely agreed among themselves. In 1877 the Workingmen's Party, composed mostly of German immigrants, renamed itself the Socialist Labor Party (SLP); it had 2,500 members by 1880. In 1892 the New York socialist Daniel De Leon became editor of the SLP newspaper. Born in Dutch Curaçao, off the coast of Venezuela, and educated in Germany and the United States, De Leon promoted a socialist revolution.

The 1893 depression prompted a native-born American from Terre Haute, Indiana, Eugene V. Debs, to form the American Railway Union. Debs had previously believed that workers and employers toiled in a cooperative venture for the common good, but as industries grew large and gained power over workers, he turned to unions to right the balance. The next year three thousand fabricators of sleeping cars walked out when George Pullman cut their wages, and they asked Debs's union to strike in sympathy. In the summer of 1894 American Railway Union workers boycotted lines that ran Pullman cars and halted national rail traffic. President Grover Cleveland invoked the little-used Sherman Antitrust Act, arguing that the strikers interfered with interstate commerce. Citing the need to move the mail, he called in U.S. marshals and roughly fourteen thousand regular army troops, who fought with and arrested strikers in Chicago. When Debs refused to obey an injunction to end the strike, the federal government sent him to prison.

Two years later Debs emerged from prison a socialist. He announced in the *Railway Times*, "The issue is Socialism versus Capitalism. I am for Socialism because I am for humanity."[35] To Debs, socialism represented the ideal that he had forged in Terre Haute: a cooperative venture between workers and managers. In 1897 he founded the Social Democratic Party, which drew members from Daniel De Leon's Socialist Labor Party.

Debs ran for president five times, beginning in 1900. More than 400,000 people voted for him in 1904 and again in 1908. Many urban immigrants supported the Social Democratic Party, and some former Populists did too. Oklahomans, who had supported Populism in large numbers, made up the largest state organization and elected six socialists to the state legislature. The Kansas-based socialist newspaper *Appeal to Reason* reached half a million people. The Social Democratic Party promoted a "long ballot" that allowed people to vote on issues as well as candidates. One voter said, "I'm a socialist because it's the only way out of our miserable mess, and because the old parties are flim-flamming us all the time."[36]

The Knights of Labor and the American Federation of Labor

Workers had been organizing into unions ever since industrialists such as Carnegie and Rockefeller had begun building their industries. The first substantial national labor union, the Knights of Labor, began in Philadelphia in 1869. It grew quickly in the 1880s and spread to every corner of the country. The Knights pioneered many of the concepts that the People's Party incorporated into the Omaha Platform—for example, the progressive income tax. And like the Farmers' Alliance, they sought to reform the capitalist market through cooperative ventures; they proposed to replace wages with profit sharing. More than 700,000 workers joined, and some members turned to politics in the late 1880s. But the large organization, loosely structured into six thousand locals, could not instill discipline in its members, and strikes and violence undermined its strength before 1890.

In 1886 the founding of the American Federation of Labor (AFL) presented an alternative for those who feared socialism or the Knights of Labor's cooperative vision. Led by Samuel L. Gompers, a Jewish immigrant from London, the AFL accepted the permanence of capitalism and wage labor. On the assumption that the wage system represented the future, workers had to expand their rights and power.

The AFL grew to be the nation's largest union by organizing craft workers. About one in six male workers qualified: they were skilled, performing a specific craft, such as baking or weaving, that required training, independent judgment, and often special tools. In 1904 a skilled craftsman could earn as much as $800 a year, compared to the manufacturing worker's average of $477. The estimated annual survival wage for a family of four was $500. Skilled workers tended to be descendants of northern European immigrants and were often native born. Since fathers taught their trade only to friends, sons, or neighbors, craftsmen maintained ethnic monopolies in their work. Unskilled laborers who were easily replaced and lacked bargaining clout were unwelcome in the AFL.

Samuel Gompers himself worked as a cigar maker before mechanization prevailed. He cut and blended tobaccos and rolled them into cigars. To bear this tedious and repetitive work, cigar workers hired men to read newspapers to them while they worked. Machines began rolling cigars around 1870, and Gompers began organizing workers around 1873. Unionism consumed him. Late in life he could not remember whether he had ten or twelve children.[37]

Steering clear of politics in its early years, the AFL offered "pure and simple unionism" in which workers joined to pursue specific workplace goals.[38] Higher wages came first, and achieving them depended on preserving the family wage concept, limiting immigration to stabilize the labor force, and excluding women from industry.[39] Nonetheless the number of women workers doubled from four million in 1890 to eight million in 1910. Only 1 percent of these women belonged to a union. The AFL avoided organizing women in earnest until after 1910.[40]

In addition to pay hikes, the AFL negotiated for better conditions and fewer hours. To achieve those goals, it supported the right to collective bargaining, which meant that when a majority of employees in a certain craft at a company voted for the union, it spoke for all workers there in that craft, even those who had voted against joining. Collective bargaining seemed undemocratic to many, but the AFL argued that the factory was hardly a democracy. Workers did not elect their bosses or factory owners, and only through unity would workplace standards rise. If employers acted collectively, so should workers. Collective bargaining limited employers' ability to undermine unionism by pressuring individuals and firing union sympathizers. Apart from advocating legislation for union rights, the AFL remained nonpartisan so that its members could chart their own political alliances.

As the AFL won improvements in working conditions, its numbers grew. From 200,000 in 1890, membership soared to 548,000 by 1900 and to more than 1.5 million by 1910. By the time the United States entered World War I in 1917, three million had joined, and membership reached four million in 1920. Several factors contributed to the AFL's phenomenal success. Most skilled workers apprenticed workers in their trades, and they taught unionism alongside their craft. AFL unions supported their members during hard times through strike benefits, insurance policies, and loans.

Perhaps the greatest reason for the AFL's success was the prosperity that began after 1896 and continued until around 1914. An increased money supply and new markets abroad, opened through trade and imperialism, spurred the economy. As the demand for laborers increased, employers negotiated more willingly with unions.

The Industrial Workers of the World

A socialist union, the Industrial Workers of the World (IWW), grew alongside the more conservative AFL. Founded in 1905 by socialist Eugene V. Debs and labor leader Big Bill Haywood, the Wobblies, as members were called, made up "one big union." They welcomed any worker, man or woman, child or adult, skilled or unskilled, who disavowed capitalism. Born in 1869 in Salt Lake City, Haywood had been a hard-rock miner when he was fifteen. He had first joined a union at an Idaho silver mine. By thirty, he had worked across the country and endured the worst treatment that employers could muster.[41] Shortly after his fortieth birthday, in 1911, Haywood disavowed Debs's Social Democratic Party, calling its members "step-at-a-time people," and urged more radical direct action through the IWW.

Employers and the government recognized the IWW's opposition to capitalism and fought the Wobblies with everything they had. The preamble of the union's constitution read:

> The working class and the employing class have nothing in common. . . . Between these two classes a struggle must go on until the workers of the world organize as a class, take possession of the means of production, abolish the wages system, and live in harmony with the Earth. . . . Instead of the conservative motto, "A fair day's wage for a fair day's work," we must inscribe on our banner the revolutionary watchword, "Abolition of the wage system."[42]

After 1911 the IWW assumed that class warfare was inevitable, and it organized accordingly. "Strikes are mere incidents in the class war," announced an IWW pamphlet. The union flourished in the toughest industries, such as lumbering and mining in the West. It is hard to pin down how many Wobblies there were at any given time: perhaps 12,000 in 1912, or as many as 100,000 during World War I. Regularly facing violent opposition from companies' hired securities, Wobblies were toughened fighters. When the organizer of a Utah copper strike, Joe Hill, faced a firing squad for a murder he swore he did not commit, he telegraphed Big Bill Haywood: "Don't waste time mourning—organize!"[43]

State Protection of Workers

Pressure from unions and citizens' concern about the violence that surrounded strikes gave rise to movements to reform state employment laws. Reformers argued that if the government protected employers' private property, it also had a role in protecting workers through wage, hours, and safety laws. In a 1908 decision, *Muller v. Oregon*, the Supreme Court held that state interest in protecting women could override liberty of contract. The Boston attorney Louis D. Brandeis had filed a brief in *Muller*, written with the help of his sister-in-law Josephine Goldmark of the National Consumers League, that used new statistics about women's health to argue for protection. The court agreed because "healthy mothers are essential to vigorous offspring, the physical well-being of women becomes an object of public interest . . . to preserve the strength and vigor of the race."[44] By 1917 eleven states had set minimum wage laws for women and children. No minimum wage laws existed for adult male workers in the United States, despite the adoption of such a law in Great Britain in 1909.

In theory, workers could sue their employers over injuries sustained on the job. In practice, most injured workers had a difficult time navigating the courts, lawsuits continued for years, and many feared that suing their employers would prompt firing. Only one in four such suits resulted in any payment at all. Governmental action could protect workers while limiting employers' damages.

In 1910 New York State passed legislation to pay workers for injuries, while capping employers' damages and prohibiting lawsuits. Using employers' contributions, the state administered workers' compensation for injuries and death. Riskier industries paid higher contributions into the pool, and the collective funding meant that no individual company would be devastated by a payout. By 1920 forty states had adopted workers' compensation laws.

If man functioned like a machine, then his parts could be given a price. According to the 1916 New York rates, the loss of both feet amounted to a payment of $6,083.16 to the footless worker. Loss of vision in both eyes netted the blind employee $5,842.08.[45] In practice, the administration of workers' compensation could pit powerful employers and company doctors against lone injured employees, but it nonetheless established a system for workers' redress.

Renewed prosperity after 1896, the growing power of the AFL, and a civic awareness that the state should set standards for working conditions combined to give workers more choices in 1910 than they had had in 1880. The progress, however, was limited by region, type of industry, sex, and race.

THE COLOR LINE

As Frederick Douglass and Ida B. Wells-Barnett handed out pamphlets to protest the exclusion of African Americans from the World's Colombian Exposition, African Americans in the South were fighting an epic battle against the theft of their civil rights. Until then they had continued to vote in the South, elected some black officials, and mostly avoided segregation by law. North Carolina and Virginia had black state legislators in the 1880s, and North Carolina elected a black congressman in 1898. A white Virginian described conditions in 1885: "Nobody here objects to sitting in political conventions with Negroes. Nobody here objects to serving on juries with Negroes. In both branches of the Virginia legislature, Negroes sit, as they have a right to sit." Another white man observed in the same year, "In Virginia, blacks may ride exactly as white people do and in the same cars."[46]

In the summer of 1893, as Friend Williams traveled by train to Chicago and the exposition, William Frank Fonvielle boarded a train in Salisbury, North Carolina, for a summer road trip through the South. An African American student at Livingstone College in North Carolina and editor of his college newspaper, he promised to report back on racial progress and oppression. He took his trip at a crucial moment.[47]

Progress and Restraint

In the Deep South, Mississippi had ratified a new constitution in 1890. It required a voter to pass a literacy test: to "be able to read any section of the Constitution, or be able to understand the same when read to him, or to give a reasonable interpretation thereof." The "understanding clause" requiring a "reasonable interpretation" opened the way for white local registrars to administer the literacy test unfairly. The new rules also required a person to pay a poll tax in order to be eligible to vote. A court case, *Williams v. Mississippi*, immediately followed to challenge the law's constitutionality, and most African Americans expected the federal courts to void it.

In addition to wanting to see firsthand a state that would disfranchise him, Fonvielle looked for the new forms of segregation that were springing up on public transportation and in public space. He had heard that some railway stations had separate black and white waiting rooms, and that sometimes trains stopped at a state line for conductors to force black passengers into a separate car. They called it the Jim Crow car, naming it for a white minstrel who performed in blackface before the Civil War. "Jim Crow" first became a nickname for African Americans; then African Americans appropriated it as shorthand for white oppression, disenfranchisement, and segregation.[48]

The year before Fonvielle's trip, 1892, had been incredibly violent in the South: at least 230 people been lynched, 69 white and 161 black. With almost one thousand lynching victims in the past decade, Fonvielle hoped that the bloody record had peaked.[49] Most of the black victims were men, but some were women. Groups of white southerners, particularly in the Deep South, lynched African Americans who were accused of crimes, as well as those who asserted their rights in business or politics. To persuade white men to vote Democratic, white supremacists argued that black political power would turn African American men into rapists who coveted white women. A vote for a People's Party candidate—or worse, a Republican—would undermine white supremacy, limit white men's ability to protect their wives and daughters, and embolden black men to ravage some and marry others.

When Fonvielle's train crossed into South Carolina, which lynched fifteen black people that year and had a reputation for violence, he hung out the window, eager to see a white man. When one appeared, Fonvielle described him: "He had on but one suspender, a cotton shirt, a frying pan hat, a pair of pantaloons. . . . I wondered if . . . this specimen of South Carolina manhood had ever helped lynch anybody."

Fonvielle's generation of African Americans had poured into the South's new black educational institutions, many of them, like Livingstone, coeducational. Black literacy rates rose rapidly, from an estimated 5 or 10 percent under slavery to 50 percent in 1910. Among those born after 1860, literacy percentages were even higher.[50] Moreover, many blacks demanded first-class educations, the kind that white men were getting. Fonvielle read Latin. While waiting at the station in Carlisle, South Carolina, he sat reading a brand-new best-selling novel. A white man came up and asked if he were not afraid to read so many novels. Fonvielle responded that it depended on the novel. The white man, amazed at this educated black man, began to quiz him: Have you read Dickens? *Ben-Hur?* Shakespeare? William Fonvielle pulled a volume of Shakespeare from his suitcase and offered to lend it to his questioner.

By the time he got to Spartanburg, South Carolina, Fonvielle's education began in earnest. "'When I arrived at Spartanburg—which is a pretty town—I was reminded that I was in the South by the appearance of two sign boards at the station: 'This room is for colored people. This room is for white people.' . . . Those signs perplexed me, for I had never seen anything like them before." After sleeping on the train, Fonvielle woke up in Atlanta. He reported, "Upon first glance, Atlanta reminds one of a

Northern city; but a five minutes stay will be sufficient to knock all such silly notions out of your head." Hungry for breakfast, he found himself barred from the station restaurant. Atlanta, he told his readers, was a "mean hole . . . chained down with prejudice." A new city ordinance ordered African Americans to sit in the back of streetcars, and black riders boycotted. Fonvielle could not believe his eyes. He marveled, "The Negroes are taxed to help keep up the city parks, [but] the council will not permit them nor the dogs to enter."

The imposition of rigid segregation was gradual. It had started in the lower South with Louisiana's Separate Car Act of 1890 and moved north. Fonvielle's journey took him south to meet it. Leaving Atlanta, he had to travel on the Jim Crow car. He asked, "Did you ever see a 'Jim Crow' car? If you haven't, let me describe it to you. . . . It is divided into two compartments. The end next to the baggage car is the 'Crow' car . . . the other end is a smoker." Black passengers sat amid white passengers' tobacco smoke, engine smoke, and coal dust, packed in with luggage. African Americans paid as much as whites, who sat "on cushioned seats." As he toured Montgomery, Mobile, and New Orleans, Fonvielle found Jim Crow everywhere. Shaken, he continued to believe that these ridiculous restrictions would be temporary. As he traveled north into Tennessee, Jim Crow disappeared. "I lay back on the beautiful plush rests, in a nice chair car, . . . [and when I saw] the Smoky Mountains . . . I thought of heaven." A decade later, by 1903, the conditions that Fonvielle had observed as curiosities would be law throughout the South, even in his own beloved North Carolina.

Segregation and Disenfranchisement

When Louisiana imposed its Separate Car Act in 1890, New Orleanians of color formed a citizens' committee to fight the law. They recruited Homer Adolph Plessy, a man "white enough to gain access to the train and black enough to be arrested for doing so." The East Louisiana Railroad Company supported them because the act "saddled their employees with the burden of becoming the state's race policemen."[51] When Plessy boarded the whites-only car, he intended to spark a test case and win it. But in 1896 the Supreme Court ruled in *Plessy v. Ferguson* that segregation was legal, as long as the accommodation provided for blacks was equal to that provided for whites. In practice, that equality was a fiction.

Legal segregation went hand in hand with a movement to push African Americans out of politics. It started with the Mississippi voting law. A more robust black political tradition existed in the upper South, where the People's Party had succeeded in drawing white men from the Democratic Party to "fuse" with black Republicans. That shook Democrats in that region and inspired them to follow the Mississippi example.

The Fifteenth Amendment had enfranchised African Americans, so states could not pass laws explicitly to prohibit black voting. Instead, they legalized racially neutral requirements that were aimed disproportionately at black voters. In 1898 the U.S. Supreme Court ruled Mississippi's "understanding clause" constitutional, and other southern states passed similar laws. Since many northern states responded to the influx of immigrants by passing state laws to make their voting more difficult, they found it difficult to condemn southern black disenfranchisement.

DISENFRANCHISEMENT BY LEGISLATION OR STATE CONSTITUTIONAL AMENDMENT

Mississippi	1890
South Carolina	1895
Louisiana	1898
North Carolina	1900
Virginia	1902
Alabama	1902
Georgia and Texas	1908[52]

But many white people worried about their own ability to pass a literacy test, so some states included a grandfather clause in their requirements. A white man could declare that his grandfather had voted, the registrar duly recorded his name in the "Grandfather Book," and the grandson could skip the literacy test. The Supreme Court found the grandfather clause unconstitutional in 1915, but not before the test had driven most black people from the polls. Some states nominated candidates in a whites-only primary, arguing that the Democratic Party was a private club. After 1900 in the southern states, winning the Democratic primary meant winning the general election. There was no point for a black person to risk his life to vote for a preordained slate of white men.

The poll tax completed disenfranchisement's bag of tricks. It required African Americans and whites to pay two to four dollars every year for the privilege of voting. The tax had to be paid prior to the election, and the person had to furnish receipts to register. Often the poll tax was cumulative for three years. If you missed a year or lost a receipt in a three-year period, you could not vote in the fourth year. The poll tax depressed both black and white voting in the South, and voter turnout became very small. This meant that a few whites held disproportionate power, that southern congressmen represented far fewer voters than did other congressmen.

As tough as these laws were, white southerners needed more than literacy tests and poll taxes to eradicate black voting completely: they backed up the laws with violence. In 1898 a prominent white man in Wilmington, North Carolina, proclaimed that he would drive African Americans out of politics, even if he had to "chok[e] the Cape Fear River with the bodies of [N]egroes."[53] His party lost the next election, whereupon he made good on his promise and led a mob that shot black citizens down in the streets. Then he ousted city officials and seized the mayor's office for himself.

Black southerners quickly realized that the federal government would not help them. A witness to the Wilmington massacre wrote to the U.S. attorney general, begging him for protection. "Is this the land of the free and the home of the brave?" she asked. "How can the Negro sing my country 'tis of thee?"[54] Roughly one million black southerners had left the region by 1920 to escape Jim Crow's dangers. From a safe distance, they participated in northern politics and hoped someday to bring national political pressure to bear against Jim Crow back home.

Black Strategies in White America

By 1905 those African Americans who stayed in the former Confederacy found themselves virtually banished from local elections, but that didn't mean that they weren't political actors. In his famous 1895 Atlanta Exposition speech, Tuskegee College president Booker T. Washington recommended vocational training rather than classical education for African Americans. The former slave implied that black southerners would not seek social integration, but he did demand that southern factories hire black people: "The opportunity to earn a dollar in a factory just now is worth infinitely more than the opportunity to spend a dollar in an opera-house."

He looked forward to the near future when the African American third of the southern population would produce and share in one-third of its industrial bounty.

His white listeners heeded only his concessions—for example, his abdication of the kind of classical higher education that whites pursued. In its stead, Washington promoted black "uplift" through vocational education. According to him, if southern African Americans obtained a practical education, they could support themselves and lead sober lives marked by achievement. Surely then white southerners would recognize their contributions and capabilities, and white supremacy would wither. Outwardly compliant with white supremacy, he fought behind the scenes against disenfranchisement. Washington remained active in national Republican Party politics until his death in 1915.

The northern-born black sociologist W. E. B. Du Bois positioned himself as Washington's nemesis. A graduate of Tennessee's Fisk University, Du Bois was the first African American to earn a Harvard Ph.D. He believed that Washington had conceded too much and said so in his 1903 book *The Souls of Black Folk*. Any man, he insisted, should be able to have a classical education. Moreover, accepting segregation meant abdicating all civil rights by acknowledging that black people were not equal to whites. "The problem of the Twentieth Century is the problem of the color line," Du Bois warned. In 1905 he founded the Niagara Movement, the forerunner of the National Association for the Advancement of Colored People (NAACP), which was begun in 1909 to fight for political and civil rights.

William Frank Fonvielle watched in despair as whites stole his civil rights. His optimism dwindled as his classmates migrated north, and he worried about his future. In the months that followed his own disenfranchisement in 1900, he wrote this poem:

Somewhere

Is there a place that hides from sight
Where daytime never turns to night?
Somewhere, somewhere?
There must be, else we could not bear
The pain, the anguish we have here.

For his part, inspired by the dazzling technology that he witnessed at the World's Columbian Exposition, Friend Pitts Williams became a civil engineer. He introduced sanitary sewers and city water to Amsterdam, New York, and joined the American Society of Civil Engineers in 1909. As a modern, rational expert who worked for the public good, Williams became a part of the progressive reform movement that would reorder the United States in the first two decades of the twentieth century.

CHAPTER 2

"TO START TO MAKE THIS WORLD OVER":

IMPERIALISM AND PROGRESSIVISM, 1898–1912

ELIJAH BANNING TUNNELL felt the ship roll beneath his feet as he stirred the big pots on the stove. On that day in May 1898, the sea breeze coming off Cuban waters felt warmer than it might have in his native Virginia. He had grown up on the Eastern Shore, among sailors, oystermen, and wild ponies. He loved the salt smell and gentle touch of sea spray, and he especially loved this sleek, fast new boat on which he worked. Tunnell had come aboard the *USS Winslow* two months before, as it docked in Norfolk, Virginia, in March, a month after his twenty-fifth birthday.[1] The *Winslow* was five months old, just over 160 feet long, and carried four officers and twenty sailors. It could sail at twenty-five knots, fire torpedoes at enemy targets, and zip away. At least, that was the plan. If the *Winslow* couldn't fire, turn, and run, then it would be a sitting duck: it had no armor.

Shortly before Tunnell joined the crew of the *Winslow*, on February 15, 1898, the battleship *USS Maine* had exploded in the harbor at Havana, Cuba. The blast blew a hole in the ship's side and cost 266 men their lives. President William McKinley had dispatched the *Maine* to Havana in response to Congress's agitation to do something about the unrest in Cuba, ninety miles off the U.S. shore. American investment there totaled over $50 million. Struggles against Spanish colonial rule had raged off and on for three decades, only recently becoming a full-fledged War of Independence in 1895. José Martí led the nationalist movement that encouraged all of the island's people to think of themselves as Cubans, put aside racial differences, and throw out their Spanish rulers. Spain's General Valeriano Weyler, aka "the Butcher," hoped to quell unrest by moving rural Cuban families into concentration camps. At least 200,000 people died in them.

By 1823, when the Monroe Doctrine discouraged European countries from interfering in the western hemisphere, most Central and South American countries had gained independence. In 1898 Spain retained only two colonies there: Puerto Rico and Cuba. Weyler's cruelty contributed to the American perception that Spain was an autocratic throwback to a feudal time, and liberating Cuba became a humanitarian imperative. African Americans in particular hoped for the establishment of a "Negro republic" on the island.[2]

Republican businessmen and bankers urged a reluctant McKinley to protect their Cuban commercial interests, predominantly in the sugar sector. The Democrats, a minority in both houses of Congress, pushed for war to establish democracy in Cuba, even though they feared an ongoing occupation would disadvantage U.S. labor and flood the South with Catholic mixed-race Cubans. The recently defeated Democratic presidential candidate William Jennings Bryan saw entering the Cuban conflict as a way to fulfill the country's Christian imperative—its manifest destiny—to bring democracy to the oppressed. The sinking of the *Maine* proved the catalyst that solidified U.S. public opinion and persuaded McKinley to ask Congress to declare war.

Once American forces were on the ground in Cuba, the Philippines, and Puerto Rico, powerful Republican business interests persuaded Congress and McKinley to stay in those places. Cuba chafed at the lost promise of independence, and the Philippines revolted against U.S. occupation. The outcome confounded Democrats, who deplored the country's new imperial role. The Spanish-American War brought the United States territories in the Atlantic and Pacific. By 1904 the nation found itself embroiled in foreign affairs on an unprecedented scale.

Some argued that U.S. foreign involvement—many called it an empire—diverted attention from societal problems at home. They had in mind the chaos of urban living that defined the lives of more and more Americans. The list of problems was long: sanitation, industrial working conditions, corrupt municipal governments, the lack of woman suffrage and other limits on the vote, powerful trusts, and a mostly unregulated financial system that brought booms and busts. In the years from 1900 to World War I, many Americans came to understand these as problems that could be solved by rational means, which is why we now know this period as the Progressive era.

In large part, the technological and scientific advances of the last two decades of the nineteenth century generated innovations and methods to solve age-old issues in new ways. Improved statistical means for fact-finding documented the sources and extent of problems. Journalists and social scientists exposed and analyzed societal woes—from political corruption to poverty—so that the public could rationally understand the challenges that lay before them.

Experts provided data and problem-solving methods, and average citizens organized themselves to confront challenges. Religious groups used progressive methods to root out what they referred to as sin. Idealistic young people set up urban settlement houses to Americanize immigrants. Scientific managers applied new efficiency methods to old production problems in industry. The women who lobbied cities to create sanitary water and sewer systems called their activism "municipal housekeeping." Temperance groups such as the Woman's Christian Temperance Union employed new sociological studies to support their decades-long campaign to prohibit the sale of alcohol. Public health practitioners brought medical breakthroughs to neighborhood clinics.

Progressivism began on the local level and moved to state government. It rose to the national level when President Theodore Roosevelt tested new methods of business regulation and sponsored environmental initiatives. By the 1912 presidential election, progressive reform issues dominated both the Republican and Democratic political agendas and spawned to a short-lived third party, the Progressive Party. From 1898 until the election of Woodrow Wilson in 1912, the United States imposed its will on its new territories abroad and reorganized domestic government to better serve its people at home.

THE SPANISH-AMERICAN WAR

Ostensibly, President McKinley had sent the *Maine* to make a friendly call on Havana, but everyone knew that the battleship symbolized U.S. naval power over Cuba. Most likely, the *Maine*'s boilers exploded, but most Americans believed that Butcher Weyler had ordered it blown up. "Remember the

Maine; to hell with Spain," became the rallying cry on the streets and in the halls of Congress. William Randolph Hearst's growing newspaper chain sensationalized the ship's sinking to boost circulation and portrayed it as among the greatest crimes ever perpetrated. A naïve public believed what they read in the newspaper.

In addition to assuaging moral outrage, sending American troops to Cuba was good business. As industry matured, Americans looked for new investment opportunities abroad. An 1891 agreement lowered tariffs on sugar coming from the Dominican Republic into the United States and eliminated them on U.S. products going into the Dominican Republic. In the three years before Elijah Tunnell found himself on the *Winslow*, the unrest of the Cuban civil war had cut U.S.–Cuban trade by $100 million, and American manufacturers began to pressure President McKinley to intervene. In addition to being important markets for the United States, Central American and Caribbean countries welcomed enormous U.S. investments. The United Fruit Company owned large swaths of Costa Rica, Honduras, and Guatemala. In the Pacific, U.S. investors in Hawaii had supported the overthrow of the monarchy there in 1893, but President Cleveland thwarted their hope that the United States would annex the islands. The Hawaiians established a republic, and U.S. investors continued to press for annexation.

A "Splendid Little War" for the Victors

When Congress declared war on Spain on April 25, 1898, the *Winslow* positioned itself in a blockade of the Cuban coast. A twenty-four-year-old white man, Worth Bagley, who had formerly served on the *Maine*, guided the *Winslow* as it cut through Cuban waters. Cheating death on the *Maine* represented only the most recent chapter in Bagley's charmed life. His grandfather, Jonathan Worth, had been governor of North Carolina, his father had been a Confederate major, and he had attended the U.S. Naval Academy when he was only fifteen years old. He flunked out, but two years later Bagley returned and led Navy to victory in the first Army-Navy football game. He celebrated his twenty-fourth birthday on the *Winslow* in Key West.

The *Winslow*'s crew constituted a floating fraternity of national reconciliation thirty-three years after the Civil War. Tunnell and Bagley, who had been born a year and 250 miles apart, now hovered off the Cuban coast together. Despite all they shared, it was what separated them—race and rank—that would determine their fame. Tunnell was the black cabin cook on the *Winslow*. Ensign Bagley, a white man, served as second-in-command on the vessel.

Tunnell, the son of slaves, and Bagley, the son of a Confederate major, shared their quarters with Fireman First Class George Burton Meek, the son of a Union private. A month younger than Tunnell, Meek grew up in Sandusky, Ohio, an important stop on the Underground Railroad, the northern system of safe houses for fugitive slaves. On board the *Winslow*, Worth Bagley and George Meek likely discussed the last war even as they braced for the next one. If so, they probably discovered how closely connected their families' fates had been in the Civil War. George Meek's father, John F. Meek, had been a private in Company I, 177th Ohio Infantry Regiment, which had forced Bagley's grandfather out of Raleigh, North Carolina, as he evacuated crucial state records. Bagley, the son of a rebel, Meek, the son of a Yankee, and Tunnell, the son of a slave, now found themselves fighting together for the liberation of a nation of mixed-race people and the protection of U.S. commercial interests.

The Spanish-American War took its first American lives on May 11, 1898. That morning the *Winslow* and the revenue cutter *Hudson* accompanied the *Wilmington* into the harbor at Cárdenas, east of Havana. The captain of the *Wilmington* meant to put up a show of force, but embarrassingly, the large gunboat immediately ran aground. The three vessels had to wait until just after noon for high tide to float the ship. As the tide crested, Elijah Tunnell was cooking lunch aboard the *Winslow*, George Meek was stoking one of the two engines, and Worth Bagley was navigating. As the *Wilmington* floated off the bottom of the harbor, the Americans spotted a moored Spanish gunboat. Action at last! The *Winslow* set its torpedoes and cruised within fifteen hundred feet of the Spaniards to investigate.

Suddenly, the gunboat and a heretofore hidden shore battery fired on the *Winslow*, destroyed the steering, and turned the ship broadside to the shore. Another shell pierced the hull, killed George Meek, and exploded one of the ship's engines. Worth Bagley ran up to the deck to relay directions to the engineers who were trying to move the *Winslow*, hampered by the broken steering mechanism. They succeeded in floating the ship about four hundred yards offshore. On Bagley's last sprint up to the deck, a shell exploded and killed him. When Tunnell ran up from the galley to help, another shell blew his legs off. Bleeding to death as his mates carried him on board the *Wilmington*, Tunnell asked, "Did we win the fight boys?" Upon hearing that they had won what came to be called the Battle of Cárdenas, Tunnell's last words were: "Then I die happy."[3]

Nine years later, amid great fanfare, throngs watched the unveiling of a monument to Worth Bagley beside the state capitol building in Raleigh, North Carolina. The governor declared that the occasion of Bagley's death was "the day on which the breach of sectionalism had been healed and union had been cemented in the blood of Worth Bagley." The base read "First Fallen, 1898," but Bagley wasn't the first to fall—he was the first *officer* to fall.[4] One can find the first to fall in a cemetery in Clyde, a small town in Sandusky County, Ohio, where a statue of George Meek towers above the other gravesites. He appears jaunty in his sailor's uniform, one hip cocked as if ready to step off his pedestal. Carved into the base are these words: "George Burton Meek . . . The first to be killed in the service of U.S. in the war with Spain."[5] There is no monument to Elijah Tunnell.

The Cuban conflict quickly became a global one. As American ships blockaded Cuba, the U.S. Asiatic Squadron languished in Hong Kong. In 1898 the Asiatic Squadron consisted of just nine vessels under the command of Commodore George Dewey, who received a telegram from Washington on April 24, 1898:

> **Dewey, Hongkong:**
>
> **War has commenced between the United States and Spain. Proceed at once to the Philippine Islands. Commence operations at once, particularly against the Spanish fleet. You must capture vessels or destroy. Use utmost endeavors. LONG.**[6]

When Dewey opened that telegram, he was a vigorous sixty-one-year old. His naval career had taken off during the Civil War when he displayed strategic brilliance in the battle of Fort Fisher, North Carolina, which had allowed George Meek's father to commence the Campaign of the Carolinas and sent Worth Bagley's grandfather fleeing from Raleigh. The Spanish-American War provided common ground on which the northerners and southerners could meet, put aside differences, and unite against a common enemy.

Dewey's small fleet made it from Hong Kong to Manila in three days. The Spanish, with thirteen ships, expected them. One Spanish general predicted that there would be little trouble since Dewey commanded a "squadron manned by foreigners" who had "neither instruction nor discipline."[7] He implied that they were ruffians who had come to rob the Spanish. As a precaution against attack, the Spanish moved their fleet into Manila Bay, a natural harbor that billowed out from a narrow, heavily mined entrance with batteries on both sides. The U.S. Asiatic Squadron located the Spanish fleet within twenty-four hours of its arrival. The Spanish counted on sinking U.S. ships as they entered the narrows of the harbor, but in the dead of night, the Asiatic Squadron sneaked in, withstood a barrage from the shore batteries, skirted the mines in the channel, and sank the Spanish fleet—all before its admiral awoke.

When President McKinley got the news back in Washington, he had to look at a map to figure out where the Philippines were. They turned out to be in a handy place. The Asiatic Squadron, which would become the U.S. Pacific Fleet, had taken a port between China, Indonesia, and mainland Southeast Asia. After Dewey took Manila, a land battle with the Philippines' Spanish rulers ensued.

On the ground in Cuba, Theodore Roosevelt, a rambunctious, Harvard-educated, thirty-nine-year-old New Yorker, emerged as a hero after he led the First U.S. Volunteer Cavalry, nicknamed the Rough Riders, in a charge up San Juan Hill on July 1, 1898. Wearing cowboy hats and bandanas, these skilled riders had been recruited from Arizona, Texas, New Mexico, and Oklahoma. The U.S. troops had been milling around the bottom of the Spanish-held hill for hours when Roosevelt emerged from the woods on horseback and yelled out for everyone to join him or get out of his way. Startled by this short white man with a brushy mustache wearing a sombrero rimmed with a blue polka-dot bandanna, fifteen hundred African American Buffalo Soldiers nearby sprang into action. Those from the Ninth and Nineteenth Cavalry charged the hill, and the Twenty-fourth and Twenty-fifth Infantry fell in to attack the fortifications. If the Spanish had slaughtered the Americans, Roosevelt might have faced a court-martial for the irregularity of his charge, but with its success he became a national hero. In his memoirs, he bragged so immodestly about his Cuban service that one humorist quipped that Roosevelt should have called the autobiography *Alone in Cuba.*[8] Frederic Remington, the celebrated artist of the West, painted the scene, but he omitted the black soldiers.

African Americans knew that Roosevelt had not been alone. Across the country, black men and women hung prints of an anonymous artist's depiction of "the famous charge of the colored troops up San Juan Hill."[9]

Designing the American Empire

The short war, with its episodic and far-flung fighting, would cast a long shadow over U.S. foreign affairs in the twentieth century. During the war almost 2,500 U.S. troops died of tropical diseases, but fewer than 400 perished in the fighting. Republican Secretary of State John Hay dubbed the affair a "splendid little war." It was the first foreign war for the United States since the Mexican-American War in 1846–48. Dewey's defeat of the Spanish fleet at Manila represented the first battle ever fought by the United States outside the western hemisphere.

The three-month-long war came to an official conclusion with the 1899 Treaty of Paris, signed by the United States and Spain. Congress had annexed Hawaii in June 1898, and the United States now controlled Puerto Rico, Guam, and part of Samoa as territories. The Spanish ceded the Philippines, whose people had hoped for independence, to the United States for $20 million. America extended guardianship over the Cuban government. The treaty's sticking point in the Senate was the provision that made the Philippines an American colony. Most Republicans and some southern Democrats supported it, but faced with the prospect of managing an empire, doubts arose in Congress. Anti-expansionist Democrats and two Republicans almost blocked Senate approval of the treaty but finally approved it by only one vote over the required two-thirds majority.

U.S. FOREIGN ENGAGEMENT
AT THE TURN OF THE CENTURY

Between 1895 and 1915, the United States transformed itself from an isolationist country to a world empire with commercial interests and territories in the Atlantic and the Pacific. It exerted active influence on—indeed, it interfered in—the affairs of China and South American countries. Democrat William Jennings Bryan at first supported ratification of the Treaty of Paris, but he and others who had supported intervention for the sake of democracy began openly to oppose U.S. imperialism when a treaty amendment failed to pass that would have guaranteed freedom and stability for the Philippines. Anti-expansionist sentiment grew as those who had initially supported the war felt betrayed by U.S. occupation of the Philippines. They argued that it undermined the United States' founding principles to rule over other nations, exposed the country to needless risk, and corrupted Americans themselves.

Debates over Empire and Freedom

The empire became a fact before most Americans had time to reckon with its implications, but a few immediately saw it as the country's manifest destiny. Republican congressional leaders Albert Beveridge of Indiana and Henry Cabot Lodge of Massachusetts created an imperialist faction in the Senate. Beveridge declared: "God has marked the American people as His chosen nation to finally lead in the regeneration of the world. This is the divine mission of America, and it holds for us all the profit, all the glory, all the happiness possible to man." Never one to exude modesty, he continued, "We are the trustees of the world's progress, guardians of its righteous peace."[10] Led by a Republican majority in Congress and by Republican presidents from 1896 until 1912, Americans reconsidered their conception of the Atlantic and Pacific as enormous moats protecting an isolated land and began to see those oceans as highways for the country's goods, people, and military might.

Commercial navigation and military sea power proceeded together. The U.S. Navy had found its champion in 1890 when Alfred Thayer Mahan published *The Influence of Sea Power upon History, 1660–1783*. Mahan concluded that industrial growth mandated new markets that could be reached only by sea. The United States needed a two-ocean navy—covering the Atlantic and the Pacific separately—because those oceans would be strategic highways for commerce and defense. The larger Pacific navy would need more coaling and telegraph stations, such as the one on Midway Atoll, which the United States had claimed in 1856 to harvest guano.

What persuaded the majority of Americans to support such a far-flung and antidemocratic adventure? When historians try to explain the strong public support, they often minimize imperial forethought and regard the acquired territories as an "accidental empire." In this view, President William McKinley was unable to stand up to the public outcry for revenge for the *Maine*, and then the country found itself saddled with poor and helpless people who needed help. The United States could not abandon them.

Other historians think the war was less accidental than opportunistic.

As Secretary of State William H. Seward had predicted thirty-two years earlier, the United States increasingly sought markets for its rapidly growing industrial production. In 1870 the United States made 23.3 percent of all the world's products; in 1900 it made 30.1 percent, more than any other country. U.S. agricultural potential seemed unlimited, and its domestic territory had been tamed. Californians looked to Hawaii's agribusiness in sugar as a model for making farming pay, and Americans invested in extractive industries and plantation agriculture in Mexico and Central America, looking for the next frontier. The country might mitigate the effects of recessions and depressions by creating foreign markets to channel surplus production. Moreover, with the growing population of the continental United States, investors looked abroad for cheap goods to import to the domestic market.

As the party of business and the majority party in Congress, Republicans generally backed expansion abroad. They worried that new imperial powers—for example, Japan and Germany—had recently joined the old empires of Britain and France to seize territory and markets in Asia and Africa. Moreover, European commercial powers pressed into Mexico, Central, and South America with schemes that would thwart the United States' economic designs there if nothing was done. Republicans interpreted the Monroe Doctrine as discouraging European economic colonialism in addition to settler colonialism. One historian has called the changing national political mood a move from "continentalism to globalism."[11]

But to attribute the motivation for intervening in Cuba simply to commerce and markets overlooks the more altruistic thinking of vast swaths of the American public, from recent Democratic presidential candidate William Jennings Bryan to the Woman's Christian Temperance Union, educators, doctors, and missionaries, at the beginning of the war. Americans had set about fixing things at home: implementing prohibition on the local level, teaching new practical subjects in schools and educating the general population, and instituting sanitary practices that saved lives. They hoped to take this wealth of knowledge abroad to those who needed it. If they could export order, stability, and efficiency where there had been chaos, disruption, and backwardness, then the world could solve its problems. The strong would lead the weak into the light.

When Theodore Roosevelt returned to New York from Cuba, his admiring friend, the British poet Rudyard Kipling, forwarded one of his poems to him. Kipling urged Americans to stay the course in the Philippines and rule the natives just as the British ruled India. He told Roosevelt to "put all the weight of your influence into hanging on permanently to the whole Philippines. America has gone and stuck a pickaxe into the foundations of a rotten house and she is morally bound to build the house over again from the foundations or have it fall about her ears."[12] When TR forwarded a copy to his friend Senator Henry Cabot Lodge (R-MA), he called Kipling's effort "poor poetry" but thought it "made sense from the expansionist standpoint." Lodge, an imperialist himself, pronounced it "better poetry than you say."[13]

The poem appeared a few months after the Spanish cease-fire in *McClure's* and became wildly popular:

> *Take up the White Man's burden,*
> *Send forth the best ye breed,*
> *Go bind your sons to exile*
> *To serve your captives' need;*
> *To wait, on heavy harness,*
> *On fluttered folk and wild*
> *Your new-caught sullen people*
> *Half devil and half child.*[14]

Heretofore this "White Man" had been European, but now his American cousin muscled in. After all, the United States had recently settled its own race problem through disenfranchisement and segregation and had demonstrated its strength to shoulder the "White Man's burden." Americans would Christianize the natives, teach them democracy, and of course, sell them things. Who were these "people half devil and half child"? They were Cubans and Filipinos, both peoples who had set out to throw off their colonial rulers—just as the American colonists had done to the British—and had ended up under U.S. domination. No wonder they were "sullen." The confusion of Social Darwinism and the idea that the "White Man" had evolved beyond all other races came through loud and clear. U.S. intervention in the 1898 war upended the Cuban and Filipino independence struggles, and it came to be known as the Spanish-American War, a name that excluded Cuba and the Philippines and reflected the hubris of empire.

Managing the New Empire

When the United States declared war against Spain the previous April, the Teller Amendment to that declaration had promised that "the United States hereby disclaims any . . . intention to exercise sovereignty, jurisdiction, or control" over Cuba. Senator Henry Teller (R-CO) headed a group of a few Republican and many Democratic senators who could support entering the war only if the United States left "the government and control of the island to its people" upon victory.[15] Teller had been a Democrat but had switched parties in 1896. His home state produced sugar from beets, and Coloradans feared that relaxed trade barriers or outright annexation would bring them into competition with Cuban sugarcane imports. Some southern Democrats, who feared a close association with Catholic and racially mixed Cuba, joined with Teller to pass the amendment.

Yet in direct contradiction to the Teller Amendment, peace found Republican congressmen and businessmen arguing, along with Rudyard Kipling, that they must stay and teach the Cubans democracy. U.S. investors sent back from Cuba reports of a floundering country in need of economic and diplomatic supervision. The United States made Cuba a military protectorate in 1898. General Leonard Wood, the military governor of Cuba, told Secretary of War Elihu Root, "The people ask me what we mean by a stable government in Cuba. I tell them that when money can be borrowed at a reasonable rate of interest and when capital is willing to invest in the Island, a condition of stability will have been reached."[16]

In 1901 Senator Orville Platt (R-CT) sponsored an amendment to an army appropriations bill that required U.S. approval of all treaties that Cuba made and gave the United States the right to intervene to ensure domestic tranquility. The United States forced the Cubans to incorporate the Platt Amendment into their new constitution in 1901. The 1903 Cuban-American Treaty of Relations incorporated the right of intervention and treaty approval and limited Cuba's borrowing authority. It leased permanently the land around Guantánamo Bay to the United States for its use as a naval base. The United States gained a Caribbean naval station, but the Cuban people protested that they had been cheated out of their independence.

Puerto Rico fared no better. The Foraker Act of 1900 declared it a U.S. territory and made its people citizens of Puerto Rico, not of the United

States. It could not apply for statehood. In the next four years, the Supreme Court ruled that the U.S. Constitution did not apply in U.S. territories. In 1917 Congress made the Puerto Ricans U.S. citizens, but the island remained a territory, without the rights of a state.

After cooperating with Admiral Dewey to defeat the Spanish, Philippine president Emilio Aguinaldo led the Filipinos into a war for independence against American occupiers. Dewey had promised Aguinaldo that the islands would be independent, perhaps under an American protectorate as imposed on Cuba. But when the United States paid Spain $20 million for the Philippines, it decided to make the territory a colony.

Outright Philippine resistance caused even some formerly bellicose Republicans to rethink the costs of American imperialism. The author Henry Adams wrote to Theodore Roosevelt expressing his alarm that "we must slaughter a million or two of foolish Malays in order to give them the comforts of flannel petticoats and electric railways."[17] Mark Twain, one of the founders of the American Anti-Imperialist League, condemned the occupation. Democrat William Jennings Bryan roared: "What is our title to the Philippine Islands? Do we hold them by treaty or by conquest? Did we buy them or did we take them? Did we purchase the people? If not, how did we secure title to them? Were they thrown in with the land?"[18]

Opposition to fighting Philippine independence crossed party lines and included Social Darwinists such as William Graham Sumner, who deplored the introduction of colonists into the body politic, as well as Progressive reformers who would have preferred democracy abroad. They joined in 1898 to found the American Anti-Imperialist League and invoked President Abraham Lincoln: "No man is good enough to govern another man, without that other's consent. . . . When the white man governs himself, that is self-government; but when he governs himself, and also governs another man, that is more than self-government—that is despotism."[19]

Lincoln had had domestic slavery in mind when he railed against despotism, but the American Anti-Imperialist League borrowed his words in 1899 to condemn the empire that the Spanish-American War had bequeathed.[20]

Some African Americans had originally supported the war because of the terrible things that Butcher Weyler had done to Cubans, many of whom were people of color, and because they hoped Cuban independence would prove the democratic capacity of people of color. But as young black men from the southern United States fought in Cuba and the Philippines, their home states in the South disenfranchised and segregated them. They soon realized that the United States would administer an empire, using race as a rationale to rule over others. Some black soldiers in the Philippines deserted and joined the resistance. Here is a black man's riff on Kipling's poem, published two months after the original appeared in *McClure's*:

> *Pile on the Black Man's Burden*
> *His wail with laughter drown*
> *You've sealed the Red Man's problem,*
> *And will take up the Brown.*[21]

After the Second Battle of Manila in 1899, Aguinaldo and his troops drew U.S. soldiers deep into the Filipino countryside, where the Filipinos proved difficult to subdue. American soldiers captured Aguinaldo in 1901, but groups of Filipinos fought on for another decade. In 1902 the United States declared victory in the Philippine-American War and managed to install a puppet government in the Philippines at a dear cost: the death of at least 200,000 Filipinos, 75 percent of them noncombatants.[22] Deceptively simple, amazingly short, and extremely fruitful, the Spanish-American War and its aftermath made the United States a colonial power and a global force.

A New Man for a New Century: Teddy Roosevelt

At the turn of the twentieth century, the sons of Civil War veterans embraced a new style of manhood, one that emphasized masculine adventure, "muscular Christianity," and a paternal obligation to teach democracy to the "child races" of the world. Isolationism no longer seemed prudent; it seemed weak. Theodore Roosevelt embodied the new manly image as a man of action, not hesitation; one who believed that problems could be solved yet wanted to use existing societal structures to solve them. A curious combination of New England and the West, of new and old, of reformer and obstructionist, Theodore Roosevelt represented the country's confusion and yearning for change.

Born in 1858, Roosevelt came of age after the Civil War. The son of a banker, he developed childhood asthma that forced him to avoid exercise and be educated at home. As a teenager, he took long walks, rode horses, and began boxing lessons to build his stamina. He graduated from Harvard with good marks but without much direction in life. He married a woman whom he loved inordinately, and he dabbled in state politics as a legislator in Albany. On a single night in 1884, his wife Alice died at home while bearing their only child, as two floors up his mother died of typhoid fever. The baby lived. Roosevelt grieved so profoundly that he could never bring himself to mention his wife again. The young widower fell into a deep depression and grew frustrated with state politics. He moved to North Dakota to become a rancher for three years, an experience that left him fit and with a passion for conservation.[23] Ten years after he moved back to the East, he won an appointment as assistant secretary of the navy in 1897, a post from which he organized the Rough Riders and jumped into the Spanish-American War. A Republican by heritage and a member of the most elite New York social class, he capitalized on his fame to win the governorship of New York in 1898.

Day in and day out, Roosevelt behaved oddly enough to earn himself an army of detractors. He swam naked in the icy Potomac River and took jujitsu lessons. He was five feet eight inches tall and weighed two hundred pounds, which gave him the appearance of a fireplug. He jumped and jerked around, unable to sit still, and interrupted everyone's conversations. When he gave a speech, his arms waved, his speech raced, and his face contorted. He made everyone uncomfortable. One New York Republican boss confided, "I do not particularly like Theodore. He has been a disturbing element in every situation to which he has been a party."[24]

In 1900 President McKinley faced reelection as he rode the high tide of good feeling that followed the Spanish-American War. Meanwhile some New York State Republicans dreaded Governor Roosevelt's reform zeal and worried that he would direct it toward business. They wanted him out of the governor's mansion and urged McKinley to name him vice president on the 1900 Republican ticket. The job was a thankless one; everyone knew it was where politicians went to be shut up. Roosevelt accepted the nomination but objected to being kicked upstairs. He resolved to abandon politics, after his term ended, and become a history professor. McKinley easily won reelection, and Roosevelt suddenly found himself in the ill-fitting job of vice president.

The Panama Canal

On September 6, 1901, President McKinley visited the Pan-American Exposition at Buffalo, New York. It had been a turbulent eight years since the 1893 World's Columbian Exposition. The Populists had risen and fallen. The currency question had faded. The United States had emerged from isolationism and reinvented itself as an empire, much to the discomfort of small-d democrats at home. That September day in Buffalo was warm as the president bent over to offer a little girl a red carnation. Then he turned to shake the hand of Leon Czolgosz, an unemployed anarchist, who shot him in the stomach. McKinley was gravely injured, but after a week Roosevelt thought him to be "coming along splendidly."[25] TR used the moment of respite to take his family camping in the Adirondacks, twelve miles from any telephone or telegraph. Once settled in, Roosevelt was astonished to see a man running into camp. The messenger informed him that McKinley would not live through the night. At forty-two, Theodore Roosevelt became the youngest president in American history.

The view from San Juan Hill focused Roosevelt's perspective from the Oval Office. His first major objective after he became president was to build a canal through Central America to connect the Atlantic and Pacific, a longtime dream of commercial interests and those who supported military sea power. In 1900 McKinley had benefited from a $60,000 campaign contribution from William Nelson Cromwell, a New York lawyer for a French company, Compagnie Nouvelle du Canal Interocéanique, that owned the rights to a passage through the Colombian jungle and some rusty digging equipment left over from a failed canal-building attempt two decades earlier. Before the Spanish-American War, such a passage would have simply been commercially advantageous, but now it served a vital military purpose as well, connecting the Atlantic and Pacific fleets and facilitating communication among the territories. Roosevelt's ballooning ambitions for the canal drew the interest of powerful Republican bankers but few others. The U.S. government owned no land in Central America; moreover, a treaty signed in the 1850s with Britain, the Clayton Bulwer Treaty, stipulated that Great Britain and the United States must build such a canal together if one were built at all.

First, Roosevelt ascertained that Britain would not press the treaty. Second, he set about finding the auspicious spot in Central America on which to impose his canal. Two factors pointed toward Nicaragua: flat countryside and a natural lake, both of which would save money in construction. But nine factors stacked up against Nicaragua: the country's eight volcanoes and Cromwell, the New York lawyer working for the Compagnie Nouvelle du Canal Interocéanique to lobby Congress to choose a Columbian route. To discredit Nicaragua, Cromwell publicized its volcanoes and enlisted powerful Senator Mark Hanna (R-OH), who had managed McKinley's presidential campaigns. The minor eruption of Pelée, one of the eight volcanoes, in 1902, and Cromwell's circulation of a Nicaraguan stamp with smoke coming from volcanic Mount Momotombo persuaded Congress to vote for the Columbian route. Then the United States offered $10 million to the Colombian government to buy a swath of land six miles wide running through the Columbian state of Panama. But the Colombian Senate rejected the offer.

Going around Congress in 1903, Roosevelt indicated to a group of Columbian businessmen that the United States would support a rebellion if the state of Panama seceded from Colombia. When five hundred Colombians began to fight for Panamanian independence, an American gunboat, the *Nashville*, appeared off the coast of Panama to prevent Colombian reinforcements from joining the battle. Roosevelt later bragged of sending the *Nashville* and arming the rebels, "I took the Canal Zone and let Congress debate."[26]

He needn't have worried about congressional opposition. The U.S. Senate recognized the independence of Panama forty minutes after the revolution began. Roosevelt officially recognized the new Panamanian government three days later. Within two weeks, Panama and the United States signed the Hay–Bunau-Varilla Treaty, which gave the United States the right to build the canal, increased the width of the zone to ten miles, and allowed the United States to maintain it in perpetuity. Building the canal was an immense task that imported workers from around the Caribbean and the United States, in addition to employing Panamanians. It would take eleven years to build, and it would become vital to American industry and defense.

The Roosevelt Corollary

In his annual speech to Congress in 1904, Roosevelt served notice on the world that the United States would not tolerate instability in Central and South America; nor would it allow European powers to exercise influence there. His declaration became known as the Roosevelt Corollary to the

Monroe Doctrine. He began by denying that the United States had "any land hunger." "All that this country desires is to see the neighboring countries stable, orderly, and prosperous," he argued. He promised that "any country whose people conduct themselves well can count upon our hearty friendship." But woe to the country that did not behave itself: "Chronic wrongdoing . . . which results in a general loosening of the ties of civilized society, may in America, as elsewhere, ultimately require intervention by some civilized nation." If that wrongdoing occurred in the western hemisphere, the Roosevelt Corollary gave the United States the duty to "exercise international police power."[27] In other words, Roosevelt's corollary claimed U.S. power to intervene by force in Latin American affairs.

Roosevelt's was no idle threat. To protect American sugar investments, U.S. troops entered Santo Domingo in 1904 and 1905. The Dominican Republic agreed to allow U.S. customs officials to manage its import and export taxes to reduce the nation's debt. U.S. soldiers intervened in Cuba in 1906 and 1908 and in Nicaragua in 1912. William Howard Taft, who succeeded Theodore Roosevelt in 1908 for one term, tried to emphasize long-term investments over armed intervention. He called his policy "dollar diplomacy," but even he moved to protect those investments in Nicaragua through intervention in 1912. When riots broke out in Haiti in 1916, Woodrow Wilson, Taft's successor, sent U.S. troops, who remained until 1934, and dispatched U.S. bureaucrats to administer Haiti's police force, health care, and schools.

Empire in the Pacific

Now in possession of Hawaii and the Philippines, the United States could have expanded its influence in the Pacific, but opportunities were limited because other powers had already carved up much of Asia. China had lost a war with Japan in 1895, and now Japan, Russia, Britain, Germany, and France, all with holdings in China, wanted to set aside "spheres of influence" where each imperial power could do business unchallenged by the others. The Germans used naval power to occupy a strategic Chinese bay, around which they constructed the city of Tsingtao, which became a trading center and the home of very good German beer. But local challenges abounded; for example, the British had taken the lead in putting down the Boxer Rebellion in China, which sought to expel foreigners from 1898 to

1900. Nearby, France colonized Indo-China, which is today Vietnam, Laos, and Cambodia. Britain held Hong Kong, Malaya, Burma, and India.

The Americans came so late to the party that they could not hope to elbow in to profit from a weak China, so U.S. diplomats reversed, at least on paper, the policies that embroiled the country in empire in the Philippines and the Caribbean. Beginning in 1899, McKinley's secretary of state, John Hay, sent a series of letters that outlined the U.S. position and became known as the Open Door Notes. The United States warned the other imperial powers to maintain China's territorial integrity and to stop establishing economic spheres of influence. Further, there must be an open door for all countries to trade with China. The Open Door Notes postured more than they threatened. They feigned U.S. resolve to prevent the building of structures that already existed. Yet they asserted U.S. interest in the region. If the United States couldn't send troops or bankers to China, thousands of American Christian missionaries settled there, many of them women. They founded schools and Young Women's Christian Associations, and they staffed hospitals.

With global involvement came responsibilities that the United States could neither foresee nor execute consistently. Members of the American Anti-Imperialist League understood that a country could not simultaneously proclaim democracy and practice authoritarianism. To William Jennings Bryan, the nation's very character had changed. Before 1900 Americans had stood up for "those who were struggling for the right to govern themselves, to proclaim the interest which our people have, from the date of their own independence, felt in every contest between human rights and arbitrary power."[28] The United States had transformed itself from a shining anticolonial ideal into a tarnished arbitrary power.

THE ROOTS OF PROGRESSIVISM

Americans launched international adventures in part because they believed themselves to be solving many of the problems that vexed their own neighborhoods, cities, and nation. As Thomas Edison, the man who invented the phonograph and perfected the electric light bulb, pondered the mess that America faced, he wrote to the man who manufactured the Model T, his friend Henry Ford: "In a lot of respects we Americans are the rawest and crudest of all. Our production, our factory laws, our charities, our relations between capital and labor, our distribution—all wrong, out of gear. We've stumbled along for a while trying to run a new civilization in old ways, but we've got to start to make this world over."[29]

New ways of thinking and growing scientific knowledge promised to provide solutions to centuries-old problems. People began to face up to societal challenges, and everywhere they looked they saw possibilities. Despite the immense tasks that Americans faced, most believed, along with Edison, that they could start to make the world over. From about 1895 through 1920, people sought political, social, economic, and cultural remedies for the ills of a rapidly industrializing and urbanizing society. Historians have termed it the Progressive era.

Progressivism was broadly based and rooted in the group of educated people who formed a growing urban middle class. After the Panic of 1893 and the easing of the currency supply beginning in 1896, the nation experienced steady inflation. Despite a short-lived recession in 1907, workers' hourly wages increased from fifteen cents per hour to twenty, while average working hours fell. Companies added managerial staff, and urban growth provided opportunities for entrepreneurship, especially in retail sales. These white-collar jobs paid fixed salaries. The bank assistant manager, the department store window dresser, and the life insurance salesman represented occupations that promised security for middle-class families. They had a stake in bringing order and efficiency to the cities in which they lived, and they connected across geographical lines to form associations that shared ideas. Urban families increasingly bought rather than produced household essentials, and as consumers they experienced first hand the high cost of living that inflation brought. The key to maintaining a middle-class life would be maintaining a balance between rising prices and wages. Regulating business made sense to them.

Ultimately a national Progressive Party formed and ran candidates in 1912; it had emerged from a rather inchoate reform spirit. As a constellation of reform impulses rather than a specific program for change, Progressivism resembles the later civil rights movement more closely than it does Populism. In Progressivism, varieties of individual groups with overlapping ideals came together to push a wide-ranging program of solutions—some political, some not—to reform society through rational, scientific, and organized means.

If Progressivism is so difficult to pin down, why is it so important? During the Progressive era, Americans put into place many of the safety valves that protect citizens today: the Food and Drug Administration, the secret ballot, the direct election of senators, women's right to vote, wage and hour regulation such as overtime, occupational safety rules, educational reform, social service agencies, professional city management, and the income tax, among others. Progressivism adjusted excesses, curbed chaos, and outlined a system of best practices that enabled the United States to continue on the path of robust capitalism. Ultimately, its moderate reforms may have prevented a more radical reordering of American society.

Problems in a Laissez-Faire Society

It is difficult to convey how filthy urban areas were. The sidewalks were slick with spit, spreading tuberculosis: men chewed tobacco and women dipped snuff, and all spat on the sidewalks. In warm weather, flies swarmed. Mothers covered children in fly netting when they put them out to play. If someone was ill, another had to stay at the bedside and constantly fan away the flies. Flies carried typhoid fever and many other diseases, and the death rate rose sharply in summer. Yet urban homes, shops, and bakeries lacked window screens. Why were there so many flies? They bred in the two kinds of waste in the streets, animal and human. Until the turn of the century in many cities, the "night soil" wagon came once a week and pumped out the open troughs into which outhouses emptied. Only the wealthiest citizens in larger cities had running water and sanitary sewers. It was extraordinary that anyone made it down the street and lived to tell about it. These problems were too much for individuals to solve; they demanded government oversight.

From 1900 to 1915, voters in many cities shifted the power to run municipalities from popular elected leaders to appointed professional managers who had been educated in government, engineering, or public service. Previously, officials may or may not have had qualifications to run what were becoming complicated services. With inefficiency came corruption. Whether the sewer line reached one's home might depend on a bribe, and a job in the police department hinged on whom one knew rather than what one knew about policing. The mayors, aldermen, and commissioners who supervised the work often lacked managerial experience.

The majority of people in large cities in the North and Midwest were either immigrants or children of immigrants. Since 1880 the United States had opened its borders to 15 million new Americans who settled in urban areas with populations greater than 50,000.[30] In addition to the language, educational, and cultural problems that this presented, it also meant simply that there were huge numbers of recently arrived poor people. Crowded into unsanitary tenements, these immigrants sought help from settlement houses and taxed city resources.

Most urban reform began east of the Mississippi. Of the seventy-eight cities with populations over 50,000 in 1900, sixty-seven were east of Kansas, the geographical center of the country. Growing cities such as Atlanta and Omaha adopted Progressive ideas as they expanded. Educated young men and the first numerous generation of college women founded settlement houses to provide immigrants with the resources that they needed to help them thrive in a confusing new place, to give them health care and leisure opportunities, and to educate their sons and daughters on American ways. The most famous was Chicago's Hull House, founded by Jane Addams. Urban reformers worked with doctors and public health officials who embraced the late nineteenth-century research proving that germs spread diseases: living conditions in the slums could contaminate an entire city, rich and poor alike.

The *New York Sun* reporter Jacob Riis had exposed the degradation of life in *How the Other Half Lives*, published first as a long magazine piece in 1889 and then as a book in 1890. The work captured the imagination of young people, who pledged to clean up the slums. Riis followed with hard-hitting articles on water quality, city corruption, and other social problems. In 1895, when Theodore Roosevelt served as president of the board of commissioners of the New York City Police Department, Riis and Roosevelt prowled the city together at night. Riis inspired in Roosevelt an awareness of social problems and began TR's education in Progressivism.

Moreover, a chaotic national economy, with labor disruptions across the country in the 1880s and 1890s, convinced even the most avaricious business leaders that a new kind of efficiency was needed to break the cycle of "boom and bust." Part of that solution might even involve some sort of government oversight of the economy. The skilled laborers organized by the American Federation of Labor agreed. Some voters grew so sick of politics as usual that they sought alternatives. In 1911 the Socialist Party won mayoral elections in thirty-eight towns and cities. All told, more than eleven hundred Socialists held office. The public felt a sense of crisis and looked outside traditional politics to find solutions to shared problems.

Cities and Towns That Elected Socialists

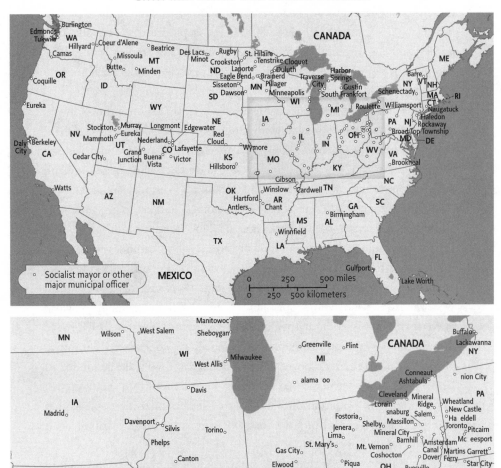

Who Were the Progressives?

Citizen reformers built a structure of progressive expectations around which politicians would later mold their platforms. Around the world, industrialized countries faced many of the same problems, and Americans borrowed solutions from England, Germany, and other European nations. Many of these civic reformers belonged to the old middle class, among them professionals such as ministers whose influence was seeping away in an industrial society. Some, particularly in mid-America, had been Populists and continued to push parts of their legislative agenda, such as a progressive income tax and the eight-hour day.

Since many Progressive issues involved the family and working women's rights, women's interests meshed with Progressive politics. Existing organizations such as the Woman's Christian Temperance Union (WCTU) and the National American Woman Suffrage Association (NAWSA) made women's working conditions, municipal health and sanitation regulation, and immigrant education part of their work. Urban women staffed settlement houses and organized to get public parks and neighborhood clean-up days. The WCTU maintained that alcohol was at the center of a multitude of problems, from poverty to vice. A fast-growing alliance of men, the Anti-Saloon League, joined the WCTU after 1895 to promote prohibition as a Progressive reform.

The issue of birth control came to public attention through the work of Margaret Sanger, who campaigned to overturn state laws that forbade dispensing information about contraception. Birth control could improve public health and reduce poverty, and poor women were desperate for it. Upper-class women generally could obtain information from their doctors, so prohibiting information on birth control devices hurt the poor. Sanger founded her own clinics in New York to dispense not just information but birth control devices as well.

Male Progressives belonged to a new middle class made up of factory owners, salespeople, lawyers, and merchants eager to get a piece of the expanding economic pie. They organized themselves into professional associations to share ideas and control access to their professions. These business Progressives believed that the clashes between labor and capital in the nineteenth century had been growing pains in a society that did not yet understand how to fine-tune its industrial machine. Labor and management, they argued, shared the same goal: prosperity. To achieve that mutual end, industrialists must design both mechanical and personnel systems that maximized productivity. The guru of business Progressives was an industrial engineer named Frederick Winslow Taylor, who believed that production could be planned to avoid human error: "The shop, and indeed, the whole works, should be managed, not by the manager, superintendent, or foreman, but by the planning department."[31]

Experts initiated an educational revolution as well. Led by educator John Dewey, a movement developed to emphasize practical goals and maximize student development. Dewey, a Vermont-born philosopher who earned his Ph.D. at Johns Hopkins, became famous for espousing pragmatism, first at the University of Chicago and then at Columbia University. Dewey saw the school as the incubator of good citizens. The job of the teacher, therefore, was not to fill the student with knowledge but to teach the student how to think and therefore how to live. As Dewey put it, "I believe that every teacher should realize . . . that he is a social servant set apart for the maintenance of proper social order and the securing of the right social growth."[32] Experiential learning—learning by doing—taught the individual to exercise his or her own intrinsic rationality. The only abstract subjects that Dewey advocated studying were history, with an emphasis on economics, and science, with an emphasis on evolutionary principles. The rest of the curriculum should impart practical knowledge and useful skills. Dewey's educational philosophies traveled far and fast through the normal schools, or teachers' institutions, that grew at a fantastic rate under Progressive state legislatures. By 1920 one could walk into just about any school in the country and find teachers who followed Dewey's philosophy.

Progressivism began as the educated classes' effort to instruct those less fortunate, but before it finished, the less fortunate took up its methods to make their own demands on the polity. If immigrants found themselves the objects of social workers' attentions, they quickly banded together to form their own social service organizations. If society expected women to safeguard their children in an interdependent urban environment, then women demanded a vote in municipal affairs. If southern black women followed new sanitary regimes as domestics in white women's homes, then they called upon their cities and states to help them provide the same services to black neighborhoods. If politics was to be democratic, then the ballot must be secret and the people should be able to directly elect their senators.

PROGRESSIVE ERA REFORM

What began as small groups of middle-class experts experimenting with reform became a shared set of expectations about democracy that most Americans ultimately embraced. Democracy no longer meant freedom from regulation, as it had in the late nineteenth century; now regulation became a path toward democracy. Strategic regulation evened the playing field enough to let everyone participate in the game. For example, state and municipal requirements to pasteurize milk gave mothers confidence that milk would not kill their babies, even as it restored their faith in the market as well. The reformers and the reformed merged as everyone began to expect government oversight, social services, and protection from exploitation. In a rapidly changing world, Americans sought to rationalize their choices and to introduce systematic fairness in commerce, government, and the workplace.

One thing that all Progressives could agree on was that the first step toward solving problems was to expose them to the light and air of public opinion. This involved two main routes: investigative journalism and scientific surveys. Newspapers and magazines infiltrated the underside of city and state governments. Reporters got themselves committed to lunatic asylums in order to report on conditions; they went inside corporate structures to expose anticompetitive practices, and they alerted people to dangers that lurked in their food, water, air, and homes. The Socialist Upton Sinclair wrote *The Jungle* to awaken the public to the plight of labor in the Chicago meat-packing industry, but he succeeded in terrifying the public about food production itself. "I aimed at the public's heart and by accident hit its stomach," he declared ruefully.[33]

Although Theodore Roosevelt thought of himself as a Progressive, he deplored the extent to which this reporting fed on the lurid and attacked businessmen. He named sensational journalists "muck-rakers," because they uncovered the "vile and debasing" parts of life, when they should be looking at more "lofty" things.[34] But Roosevelt's criticism scarcely bothered muckrakers such as Sinclair.

The scientific survey constituted the second interpretative channel that promoted Progressive ideas. The Progressives were crazy about statistics, even if they had only rudimentary ideas about how to deploy them. Across the country, people began counting everything, from the number of deaths from tuberculosis in New York City (237 of every 100,000 deaths in 1900) to the number of railroad workers' deaths (103 of 366,742 workers in 1900). Measurement mattered because it could be used to describe problems, track the effects of interventions, and document solutions when a problem declined. Two challenges limited the application of Progressives' findings: so little sound data preceded their studies that they could not properly evaluate their findings, and the general public had no idea how to interpret them.

Urban Prostitution: A Case Study in Progressive Problem Solving

Applying Progressive methods to vice began when a grand jury investigation in 1910 in New York City sought out the facts on the sex trade. Leading citizens sat on the grand jury, including John D. Rockefeller, Jr., the idealistic young son of the great nineteenth-century robber baron. Reformers called prostitution the "white slave trade," gathered statistics, and drew up elaborate charts about how individual prostitutes made profits for brothel owners, whom they called "white slavers." Prostitution, the grand jury argued, resulted from unregulated capitalism rather than from individual moral failings. Women were victims. Entire sections of cities—red-light districts—were given over to prostitution, where local landlords profited from high rents and the underworld connections they fostered there. In Chicago, investigators estimated that prostitution brought in $15 million in profits in 1911.

Most large cities began their own investigations and set up "vice commissions" to eradicate the menace of the "Vice Trust."[35] They shared information through a national group, the American Social Hygiene Association. A formerly taboo subject now engaged the best young men in the country. They found that most young women became prostitutes after being seduced by a man, who deserted them; afterward they could not support themselves by working at low-wage jobs. The vice commissions' scientific investigations removed the blame from the young women and put it on economic forces.

Christian leaders in Atlanta decided to purge the city of prostitution in 1912. By tackling one of the world's oldest problems with some of its newest methods, they embodied the hopes, methods, and limitations of Progressivism. The Atlanta men became muckrakers through advertising. "The Houses in Our Midst," screamed the headline of the "Men and Religion Forward Bulletin" printed on July 15 in the *Atlanta Constitution*. Young girls, the bulletin argued, had become commodities, "fodder for the houses of prostitution that lined Mechanic Street."[36] The Men and Religion Forward (MRF) Movement was a national organization that sought to bring men back into the Protestant churches by giving them opportunities to carry out practical social reforms in Christ's name.[37] It planned to bring commercial methods to Christ's work and Christ's teachings to commercial work. They wanted to file down capitalism's rough edges.

The preeminent writer among Social Gospelers such as those who joined the MRF Movement was Walter Rauschenbusch, who argued in

Christianity and the Social Crisis (1907) that the "social crisis" resulted from industrialization.[38] *Collier's* magazine announced that the movement's leaders had "taken hold of religion, and are boosting it with the fervor and publicity skills which a gang of salesmen would apply to soap that floats or suits that wear." They were "going after souls in just the same way that the Standard Oil Company goes after business."[39]

Before it ran its first advertisement, Atlanta's MRF Movement had begun its campaign against prostitution with a thoroughly Progressive tool: it conducted a scientific survey of conditions. Most cities tolerated prostitution in "segregated districts," poor neighborhoods, often near the railroad tracks; in Atlanta the men toured forty-four brothels and interviewed the prostitutes and madams. Then, armed with data, the MRF called upon the mayor to set up a formal committee to investigate conditions like those already known to exist in Chicago, Syracuse, St. Louis, and New York. When the vice commission spent several weeks doing nothing, the MRF went over its head to the people and ran the first advertisement.

The MRF spoke of prostitution using a new language of social hygiene derived from science. It employed blunt medical descriptions to demonstrate prostitution's danger to everyone. Using scientific evidence on venereal disease, they argued that segregated districts for prostitutes accomplished nothing because their customers carried disease all over town. They persuaded Police Chief James Beavers to raid the houses of prostitution, but they forewarned the madams and prostitutes that they would be shut down. The MRF members took the displaced prostitutes into their own homes. The day after the raid, one woman stabbed herself in the heart and left a note that read, "Damn Chief Beavers." But prostitute Belle Summers, so bold that she listed herself in the Atlanta city directory as a madam, donated her life savings of $2,500 to the MRF to open a rescue home for prostitutes. Summers left Atlanta for Nyack, New York, entered a Christian Missionary School, and became a social worker. If the first part of her life provided a model for young Atlantan Margaret Mitchell's madam, Belle Watling, in *Gone with the Wind*, the second part was stranger than fiction. The MRF Movement broke up the segregated district, but they did not chase vice out of Atlanta.

Reforming Government

The volunteerism and rational methods in which the Progressives placed so much faith sometimes failed them, and they realized that governments—

municipal, state, and federal—must become better models of efficiency and fairness to serve citizens in constructive ways. They wanted governments to have enough power to broker competing interests while remaining accountable to the public will. They wanted to get government *into* citizens' lives to accomplish things that lay beyond the reach of individuals.

Yet their goal was not simply to protect; it was also to serve. Once good management prevailed, then there must be clear channels to inform the public of governmental action and to respond to public opinion about that action. The entire system depended on citizens having the right to know what government did and the right to tell government what they wanted it to do. Progressives set about reforming government from the local level up.

At the turn of the twentieth century, political "machines" ran some of the largest cities in the country. Machines ruled by personalized networks that rewarded friends with jobs, a practice called the spoils system. The spoils system turned graft into a high art. Machines organized immigrant communities by ethnicity through trusted community leaders to control "the Irish vote" or "the Italian vote." In New York, the machine was Tammany Hall. In Memphis, Boss Crump ran the machine. To expose the workings of such urban political machines, a young muckraker named Lincoln Steffens published a series of investigative articles in *McClure's Magazine*. Born in California in 1866, Steffens exemplified the skepticism of tradition characteristic of his post–Civil War generation.

Steffens's articles, gathered into a book in 1904 entitled *The Shame of the Cities*, exploded the myth that immigrants were responsible for the mismanagement of cities. One New Yorker told Steffens that "the Irish Catholics were at the bottom" of city mismanagement, but Steffens called this "the foreign element excuse" and termed it "one of the hypocritical ideas that save us from the clear sight of ourselves."[40] It was not that he did not find corrupt Irishmen or Italians in large cities; it was that he also found corrupt Scottish Presbyterians, corrupt Scandinavians, and corrupt New Englanders there.

Steffens also attacked the image of the businessman as hero—that businessmen were smarter and more capable than others and so made the best officials. The typical businessman, he wrote, was a "self-righteous fraud," because he was "busy with politics, oh, very busy and very businesslike . . . buying boodlers . . . defending grafters . . . originating corruption . . . sharing with bosses . . . deploring reform . . . and beating good government with corruption funds." The successful businessman did not have time for politics.[41]

New ideas for managing urban growth sprang up in unlikely places, in small and midsize cities in the hinterlands. Emerging under names like the "Des Moines Idea" (for a city commission to limit mayoral power), fifty cities adopted some sort of commission government in the first six months of 1911. Reformers meant to make city governments more efficient and less partisan, able to benefit from oversight by experts. Many variations on the theme emerged. Citywide elections for councilmen diluted the ward power concentrated in neighborhood enclaves. To strip elected mayors of their personal power, some cities turned to appointed city managers who had received an education in planning and administration. Others turned to appointed commissions. Most wrote job descriptions for paid managerial positions and then required qualifications, instead of political connections, to fill them. Reform swept the nation as the National Municipal League, the American Civic Association, and the Chamber of Commerce publicized solutions to municipal problems.

Once a new kind of city government was in place, it often turned first to regulating the companies that provided public services. Competition and free enterprise worked poorly when it came to picking up trash, providing water, and turning on electricity. Certain city services naturally demanded coordination and large-scale operations to be cost effective for consumers. Previously, many utility companies had bribed city officials with votes or money to sell them service franchises. The private franchisee decided how high rates should be or where streetcar tracks would go.

Reforming cities and states sought to oversee public services by choosing either public ownership or public regulation. In many places today, the city or state still owns vital services, called public utilities. For example, the Los Angeles Department of Water and Power, established in 1909, was in 2011 the nation's largest municipal utility. In New York, Governor Charles Evans Hughes strengthened the state oversight commission that set utility rates and standards of service, and even limited profits, while allowing the service provider to remain under private or shareholder management. Utility companies regulated by the states prospered, and customers could rely on their services.[42]

Municipal reform experiments went hand and hand with reform of state government. Across the nation, voters elected men who pledged to clean up politics in the state capital, change state laws, and amend state constitutions. Progressive governors who became nationally famous included

Hiram Johnson in California, Charles Evans Hughes in New York, Robert La Follette in Wisconsin, and Woodrow Wilson in New Jersey. These governors set about making their state's voting laws more democratic.

Suffrage

Reform of state suffrage laws both limited and extended democracy. Southern states disfranchised African Americans, northern states disfranchised immigrants, and western states disfranchised Asian immigrants by using complicated registration requirements, literacy tests, and sometimes simply flat-out denials of the vote. Progressives found it easy to support such measures because they wanted a better-educated electorate more than they wanted a larger electorate. Many of those who supported woman suffrage argued that by giving native-born white women the right to vote, they could outnumber less desirable voters. Even as Progressives narrowed the electorate, they gave the individual vote more power. They made ballots available to all who qualified and made sure a fair count took place. They reduced officials' term lengths and enabled voters to impeach them. Wisconsin governor Robert La Follette led a drive for woman suffrage in state elections.

In many states Progressives campaigned to open up state governments to more popular input, adopting, for instance, the direct primary that Governor Woodrow Wilson introduced into New Jersey. The idea was to put the voter in closer touch with the action, requiring government to be more responsive to the people's will. Some states avoided many of these reform measures, but most adopted the secret, or Australian, ballot. Before its adoption, one had to be given a ballot, mark it, and hand it back to an official, who then saw how you had voted. The secret ballot diminished vote buying.

No state underwent more radical reform than did California under the direction of the liberal Republican governor Hiram Johnson. The state adopted the secret ballot, but it did not stop there. Article 2 of the California constitution mandated that voters, not back-room party regulars or state legislators, choose nominees for public office. It also required nonpartisan elections for certain high-competency elected positions, like judges, school board members, and county and city officials. It gave voters the power of the initiative to make their own laws. All citizens had to do was present to the proper state official a petition with the text of a "proposed statute or amendment to the Constitution . . . signed by 5 percent of the voters [based on the gubernatorial vote in the last election] in the case of a statute, and 8 percent in the case of an amendment to the constitution." Then all Californians would vote on the initiative at the next election, and if they approved it, it would become law. The state went still further. Voters could also "reject statutes or parts of statutes" by calling a referendum on an existing law in the same way they could call an initiative. This meant that citizens could overturn laws that state legislators had passed. Finally, California gave voters the ultimate second chance: recall, or the option of removing an elected official for any reason. The mechanism of recall meant that after election an official had to keep public opinion in mind or be relieved of office. In California, it took 12 percent of the number who originally voted for an official to sign a petition in order to force another vote on that official.[43]

The initiative, referendum, and recall extended to voters serious responsibilities that went along with their rights to know what government did and to tell government what they wanted it to do. It took a majority to elect a governor, but only a small minority was needed to set in motion a recall. Minority groups who felt strongly about an issue could impose their version of statutes on complacent majorities. The initiative, referendum, and recall put state government directly into citizens' hands, for better or worse. Through initiatives in 1912 in California, voters amended the state constitution, passed a statute, and voted in three referendums. These citizen initiatives reformed the workings of state government and taxation and approved Proposition 7, to outlaw bookmaking and establish state regulation of horse racing. With these reforms, citizens themselves took on the work of democracy.

FEDERAL PROGRESSIVISM

Reforming the federal government would be much harder and its results more limited. It would depend on strengthening the office of president, and Theodore Roosevelt was fit for the fight. When Roosevelt moved from his camp in the Adirondacks to 1600 Pennsylvania Avenue, he understood that his own Republican Party would not put out the welcome mat for him. The accidental president set about building a personal power base. Senator Mark Hanna (R-OH) and House Speaker Joseph G. Cannon (R-IL), both powerful conservative Republicans with antiregulation records, controlled Congress. Disempowering Hanna and Cannon would not be enough, however.

Roosevelt believed that Congress itself had grown too strong, upsetting the balance of powers in the federal government. He wanted to increase the importance of the presidency and make the federal administration strong enough solve the biggest problems that faced America.

Apart from promulgating these lofty ideals, Roosevelt was not sure what to expect from himself. At first he did little but follow careful conservative practices that protected the status quo. But he grew into a Progressive in the Oval Office. In his initial address to Congress, he spoke vaguely, venturing that we should do something about trusts, such as Standard Oil, that stifled competition and raised prices, but we should not get carried away. Labor needed more power, but it must not abuse that power. He said it best in the introduction to his autobiography: "We of the great modern democracies must strive unceasingly to make our several countries lands in which a poor man who works hard can live comfortably and honestly, and in which a rich man cannot live dishonestly nor in slothful avoidance of duty."[44] It was not that Roosevelt loved the poor and hated the rich; it was that he loved duty and hated sloth. But his admonitions fell short on the details.

To Roosevelt, power was a fact of life, but its exercise must be moral. "I believe in corporations; I believe in trade unions. Both have come to stay. . . . But where, in either one or the other, there develops corruption or mere brutal indifference to the rights of others, and short-sighted refusal to look beyond the moment's gain, then the offender, whether union or corporation, must be fought."[45] The federal government lacked the power to do any of that fighting or even to referee the match. Roosevelt itched to get the government into the ring to ensure a "Square Deal" for all. Heretofore businessmen had largely ignored the weak federal government. While grassroots reforms built stronger cities and states, national politics responded to Progressivism; it did not initiate it. Without the historical accident of Roosevelt's presidency, it might not have responded at all.

Regulating Industry and Finance

Having the federal government referee the competing interests of business and the public proved difficult and brought criticism from all sides, particularly from big business and Wall Street, two constituencies that thought they had the Republican Party in their pockets. McKinley had been their man, and his death shocked them. On the day McKinley died, as the powerful Republican banker and railroad magnate J. Pierpont Morgan "received the news on his way to his yacht," an excited pack of newspapermen surrounded him. One shouted: "Mr. Morgan, President McKinley is dead." Silent for a moment, Morgan then responded, "This is sad, sad, very sad news. It is very sad news, very sad."[46] Morgan had good reason to be sad, apart from his regard for McKinley. He had counted on his close friendship with McKinley's campaign manager, Senator Mark Hanna, to create a laissez-faire business climate for his banking and railroad ventures.

Now he would have to deal with Theodore Roosevelt. Five years earlier Morgan's Northern Pacific Railway and Minnesotan James J. Hill's Great Northern Railway had formed an alliance—a combination—to fight off competition. In 1901 they joined with a rival, Edward Harriman, head of the Union Pacific Railroad. Morgan, Hill, and Harriman acted secretly, paid off the directors of their former companies, and set themselves up in a new holding company, Northern Securities, capitalized at $400 million. Northern Securities controlled all the country's rail freight between the Mississippi River and the Pacific Ocean. Where previously the Great Northern, Northern Pacific, and Union Pacific had competed with one another, now three men monopolized almost half of the nation's transportation system. Roosevelt asked his attorney general, Philander C. Knox, to investigate Northern Securities as a possible violation of the Sherman Antitrust Act, which prohibited "a combination in restraint of interstate or international trade." Northern Securities amounted to the largest combination the nation had ever seen. The Justice Department filed suit in *Northern Securities Co. v. United States* in 1902.

When the Justice Department filed suit, an astonished and angry Morgan told Roosevelt that if he wanted something of him, he should have come to him and asked. But the idea of the president of the United States going to Wall Street as a supplicant galled Roosevelt. Morgan, Harriman, and Hill believed themselves to be above the presidency. Hill said he was "damned" if he was going to break up his company because of "political adventurers who have never done anything but pose and draw a salary." If Morgan, Hill, and Harriman felt outrage, Mark Hanna was beside himself with embarrassment, since he was a close friend of Hill and the railroad's biggest promoter in the Congress.[47] Hanna, the master fixer, had been left out of the loop. With one stroke, Roosevelt had wounded two enemies: the railroad trust and the leader of the Republican Party.

Morgan eventually deigned to go to Washington, where he told Roosevelt and his attorney general that they had erred—and acted crassly—by going public with a lawsuit. Morgan explained to them how power worked: "If we have done anything wrong, send your man to my man and they can fix it up." Roosevelt's attorney general responded, "We don't want to fix it up, we want to stop it."[48] Northern Securities fought the case to the U.S. Supreme Court, which found in favor of the government in 1904. Justice John Marshall Harlan wrote for the majority: "No scheme or device could more certainly come within the words of the [Sherman Act] . . . or could more effectively and certainly suppress free competition. . . . If such a combination be not destroyed, . . . the entire commerce of the immense territory . . . will be at the mercy of a single holding corporation."[49]

As TR regulated trusts, he also intervened in labor issues. In May 1902, 100,000 anthracite coal miners struck in West Virginia and Pennsylvania for shorter working hours. When the strike continued into October, Roosevelt appointed a commission to resolve it and called management and labor to Washington to forge a solution. Business was outraged that the federal government had inserted itself into an industrial matter and given workers a seat at the table. But with winter coming, the situation was dire. Ultimately the commission mediated an agreement that called for compromise on both sides. The mine owners stopped short of recognizing the United Mine Workers, but from then on an ongoing arbitration board would settle disputes. Government intervention on an unprecedented scale had succeeded.

Protecting the Public

As usual, Roosevelt savored the victory. The public loved him more than ever, and the press nicknamed him "The Trustbuster." One popular magazine opined that "corporations deriving their existence from the hands of the people must submit to regulation by the people."[50] Roosevelt's Justice Department would bring forty-two more suits under the Sherman Antitrust Act. *Northern Securities* had proved the principle that the federal government could regulate commerce, and government intervention in management-labor disputes would continue.

A landslide returned Roosevelt to the White House in 1904. With a tamer Congress and the courts on his side, he focused on consumer protection and environmental policy. Progressives had tried to regulate food and drugs at the local and state level, but they lacked the reach to compel companies to change. Tremendous problems existed with just about anything that one purchased to ingest. Children's medications contained cocaine and opium. Most remedies for the common cold contained morphine, and women regularly became addicted to it. Ayer's Sarsaparilla promised to "treat the blood" to make people feel better—which it certainly did, at least temporarily, at 26 percent alcohol. Whiskol, at an even higher alcohol percentage, advertised itself as a "non-intoxicating stimulant."[51] As far as food went, Upton Sinclair's exposé of meat-packing in *The Jungle* turned out to be just the tip of a very nasty iceberg.

In 1906 Roosevelt pushed the Pure Food and Drug Act and the Meat-Inspection Act through Congress with the help of Progressive interest groups ranging from physicians to mothers. The Pure Food and Drug Act required the labeling of ingredients and prohibited some products from being sold without a prescription, placing them in the category of federally controlled substances. The secretary of agriculture could fine or imprison those who sold contaminated drugs, and every manufacturer had to label his products honestly. The Meat-Inspection Act empowered officials from the Department of Agriculture to go into processing centers to inspect meat. Large, well-organized companies accepted regulation calmly, since it would increase consumer confidence and win customers away from local butchers and homemade remedies.[52] The two acts enabled people to trust national brands. Through the acts, the federal government assumed the power to protect a nation that was coming to define itself by its consumption.

Preserving the Environment

Roosevelt's environmentalism began during his ranching years in North Dakota. Environmentalists were split into two camps; conservationists, who wanted to use natural resources wisely, and preservationists, who wanted to maintain the wilderness in its natural state. TR was a conservationist, but he greatly admired the country's leading preservationist, the Scottish-born naturalist John Muir. An eccentric genius, Muir had taken botany classes at the University of Wisconsin, walked a thousand miles from Indiana to Florida, and worked as a shepherd in Yosemite, a California wilderness in the Sierra Nevada. For years he lived alone in a small cabin there, writing articles calling for the area's preservation and founding the Sierra Club in 1892. Muir wanted Congress to designate Yosemite a federal national park, as it had Yellowstone in 1872. Instead, the final legislation designated the land a park but left it under California's control. In 1903 Roosevelt made a pilgrimage to Yosemite to camp out with Muir.

Roosevelt remembered his visit to Muir as the grandest day of his life and reported he was "as happy as a boy out of school." For his part, Muir lectured Roosevelt, an avid hunter, about the "boyishness of killing things."[53] Roosevelt and Muir hatched a plan to take Yosemite Valley and Mariposa Grove, outside state park boundaries, into federal protection, which Congress did in 1906. California transferred the rest of Yosemite to the National Parks Service in 1916.

The idea of wide-open spaces had been vital to the American ideal of a free, robust citizen, as historian Frederick Jackson Turner had argued in 1893. For Muir, natural preservation was a spiritual quest. Others feared that if settlement tamed open spaces, generations of Americans would never know real freedom. Americans looked anxiously at Europeans, hemmed in by their environment and complacent with class hierarchy. Americans needed room to stretch out.

More tangibly, environmental protection would guarantee the raw materials that the United States needed to maintain its industrial power. Thousands of years of deforestation had devastated parts of Europe; now the French meticulously managed their forests. Throughout the nineteenth century, Americans had felled trees as if there were an inexhaustible supply. Gifford Pinchot was born in Connecticut into a family that had made some of its wealth from lumbering. Gifford's father, an early conservationist, urged his son to study forestry abroad, and he went to France after graduation from Yale in 1889. He returned as the country's first professionally trained, American-born forester, and his family bequeathed to Yale a forestry school. Pinchot believed that "the earth and its resources belong of right to its people."[54] His head was in the treetops, but his feet were firmly rooted in practical matters. He believed that regional conservation plans would never suffice; rather, he pushed for a national conservation plan for forests.

Pinchot's philosophy brought together Roosevelt's aims to conserve the environment and to increase federal power. The men had become friends when Roosevelt was governor of New York. As president, Roosevelt appointed him head of the U.S. Forest Service, and together they sought to make the government's western holdings into parks, preserves, and national forests. The two wealthy, energetic, and visionary Yankees talked every day. During his presidency, Roosevelt added 148 million new acres of forest reserves to the existing 40 million acres. In 1905 Congress transferred control of those reserves to the Forest Service, over which Pinchot presided.

Mining operators, ranchers, and large farmers quickly came to deplore the fact that the federal government held large swaths of land, paying no state taxes, preventing the damming of rivers, and controlling mineral and grazing resources. Bipartisan support among western congressmen slowed the momentum for land preservation, requiring congressional approval to set aside any more land in Oregon, Washington, Montana, Colorado, and Wyoming. Roosevelt could have vetoed the bill, but he did not. Instead, he and Pinchot stayed up all night on the eve of the day it would become law. Down on their hands and knees, they searched maps for new forest reserves to create. By dawn, they had created twenty-one more reserves, preserving 16 million acres.

PROGRESSIVISM AT HIGH TIDE

Roosevelt's handpicked successor, William Howard Taft, had been his secretary of war and, previously, the first governor-general of the Philippines. In his first run for any public office in 1908, the Republican Taft defeated the perennial Democratic candidate William Jennings Bryan in his third bid for the presidency. Taft had graduated from Yale, where he wrestled in the heavyweight intramural competition. At 355 pounds when he entered the White House, he was the anti-Roosevelt: sedentary, calm, and cautious.

Roosevelt Haunting Taft

When Taft took office in 1909, Roosevelt left for a big game safari in Africa. Taft filed ninety antitrust lawsuits against corporations, including the American Tobacco Company, which had engaged in predatory pricing. He helped fulfill the dream of the Populists and labor alike by supporting the passage of the Sixteenth Amendment, which introduced a progressive income tax. Rather than military intervention, Taft followed a policy of "dollar diplomacy" that federally guaranteed private U.S. investors' loans in countries in Central and South America.

Meanwhile Roosevelt and his son Kermit trooped across Africa, accompanied by 250 porters and guides. They shot more than five hundred large animals. John Muir must have rolled his eyes. Roosevelt loved the adventure and returned with eleven hundred specimens for the Smithsonian Institution.[55] He followed Taft's presidency from afar.

Upon Roosevelt and Kermit's return, Gifford Pinchot met them at the boat with the news that Taft had fired him as head of the Forest Service. Pinchot's archrival, Republican secretary of the interior and former Seattle mayor Richard Ballinger had begun his tenure as secretary by abolishing federal protection on some western land and leasing it out to businessmen to build hydroelectric dams. He sold several million acres of public land in Alaska with rich coal deposits to some Seattle businessmen, who promptly sold it to Roosevelt's nemesis, banker J. P. Morgan. It was when Pinchot complained publicly about Ballinger's performance that Taft had fired him. Roosevelt believed that Taft was in the pockets of big business and had destroyed much of his administration's progress. In Roosevelt's wildest dreams, he could not have imagined a more perfect betrayal by Taft. His favorite cause, his best friend, and his worst enemy had all converged in an immoral exercise of power.

A Republican Split

Roosevelt challenged the big-business wing of the Republican Party when he announced that he would take on Taft for the 1912 presidential nomination with these unforgettable words: "My hat is in the ring! I am stripped to the buff and ready to fight!"[56] As the election of 1912 approached, Taft faced a bloody battle with the metaphorically naked Roosevelt. Taft called Roosevelt "a demagogue"; Roosevelt shot back that Taft was a "fathead."[57] When Taft won the Republican nomination, Roosevelt immediately formed his own party, the Progressive Party. The Republican Party had proved an awkward home for TR's pro-regulation Progressivism, and Taft had moved back into the traditional Republican pro-business stand.

Roosevelt took up a cudgel that he called the New Nationalism, a program that combined Progressive reform and old Populist proposals into a strong federal government that would regulate private greed. The New Nationalism called for the states to ratify the federal income tax amendment, and it endorsed an inheritance tax, a national law prohibiting child labor, an eight-hour workday, and the passage of woman suffrage. Roosevelt set himself above party politics. He proclaimed, "We stand at Armageddon, and we battle for the Lord."[58] Asked by a reporter if he was fit enough to run for president, Roosevelt bragged that he was "fit as a bull moose." At that point, most people began referring to the Progressive Party as the Bull Moose Party.

As Roosevelt campaigned in Milwaukee, an assassin, vowing that no one deserved three terms, shot him in the chest. His folded-up speech and the glasses case in his breast pocket slowed the bullet. Roosevelt stood mute for a moment before he announced, "The bullet is in me now, so I cannot make a very long speech." He protected the assassin from the crowd's wrath, finished the speech, and went to the hospital for a week.[59] If he was no longer as fit as a bull moose, he had the courage of one.

The formation of the Progressive Party wove together the separate strands of Progressivism at the national level, but the weave was rough and frayed easily. By 1912 Progressivism represented too many agendas forged separately and brought together by too many people with conflicting ideologies to succeed for very long. That year's campaign represented the high tide of the Progressive era and helped move the Democrats into Progressive ranks. In the national election, Taft and Roosevelt lined up to fight each other and the Democratic candidate Woodrow Wilson. All three claimed to be progressive. The Socialist Party candidate, Eugene V. Debs, did not stand a chance of winning the presidency, but his presence in the race could draw votes from Roosevelt and Wilson.

The 1912 Presidential Election

Woodrow Wilson had surprised many party regulars by winning his party's nomination. He was a liberal Democrat, with a reputation as a Progressive governor in New Jersey, but he was born in the South and came of age there. The robust battle that pitted TR, Taft, and Wilson against one another focused on their ideas about how to use federal power and the proper role of the executive branch in doing so.

Newcomer Wilson proved a formidable foe. Son of a Presbyterian minister, he grew up in Virginia, Georgia, South Carolina, and North Carolina. He graduated from Princeton and attended law school at the University of Virginia but did not graduate. After passing the Georgia bar exam, he briefly practiced in Atlanta, hated it, and quit to earn a Ph.D. in history at Johns Hopkins University. His classmates included many southerners, for example, Thomas Dixon, who would write the novels that became the film *The*

Birth of a Nation. The film was a fictionalized account of white southerners rising up against the purported outbreak of criminality that northerners and African Americans had unleashed against them during Reconstruction. Wilson ultimately returned to Princeton as a professor of history and political science. In 1902 he became the university's president and embarked on a campaign to democratize the school, targeting the elite eating clubs for elimination. In 1910 he ran as an outside candidate for governor against the machine faction of the New Jersey Democratic Party and won. Two years later he took on "the demagogue" and "the fathead" as the Democrats' presidential candidate.

In the campaign of 1912, Wilson ran on a Progressive platform called the "New Freedom." Wilson recruited a young lawyer, Louis Brandeis, to help him outline the program. The New Freedom favored small government and held that federal intervention should be a last resort. The goal should be to increase liberty and competition, which would naturally result in an ordered economy and society. True to his southern roots, Wilson emphasized states' rights over federal power, which he thought had become too strong. The New Freedom advocated many of the Progressive Party's causes, for example, recognition of the right to unionize.

On the stump, the three parties' platforms tended to meld into indistinguishable Progressive panaceas. Wilson's New Freedom seemed vague about how it would stand up to big business without using big government. The Socialist Party candidate Eugene V. Debs offered a leftist alternative, and Taft promised to take the more moderate Republican votes from Roosevelt. In the end, Roosevelt barely beat his archenemy Taft, but he lost to Wilson by more than two million votes. The Democrats rushed in to grab the mantle of reform, the Republicans descended into chaos, and the Socialists rejoiced that Debs had received 900,000 votes. The old Bull Moose was crushed, a man without a party or a public.

Despite the loss, during his terms Roosevelt had succeeded in strengthening the office of the presidency, and newfound federal power had changed national politics forever. The public now expected action from the federal government, and Progressive reform would continue during Wilson's terms. Nonetheless, public attention would be drawn away from domestic problems when war broke out in Europe in August 1914. The United States' retention of international possessions after the

Spanish-American War had solidified its role as a global power. American companies traded globally, and the country managed the Philippines as a colony, Hawaii and Puerto Rico as territories, and Cuba as a protectorate. But those foreign adventures would pale compared to what awaited Americans in the great war to come.

CHAPTER 3

REFINING AND EXPORTING PROGRESSIVISM:

WILSON'S NEW FREEDOM AND THE GREAT WAR, 1913–1919

WOODROW WILSON'S TRAIN pulled into Washington's Union Station a day before his inauguration on March 3, 1913. The generally taciturn Wilson could barely contain the excitement that had built up during the trip. Such high emotions felt unfamiliar to him. Generally, he described himself as "reserved," "shy," and "fastidious." If people did not warm to him, he told himself that was the way he wanted it. He mused, "I have a narrow, uncatholic taste in friends, I reject the offer in almost every case—and then am dismayed to look about and see how few persons in the world stand near me and know me as I am."[1] His education—the Ivy League college, the law school, the Ph.D.—made him secretly, and sometimes not so secretly, consider himself smarter than those around him.

Now he could use that superior intellect to instruct the American people. After years of the emotionally voluble Theodore Roosevelt and the florid William Taft, this thin, bespectacled professor imagined that his calculated rationality would be a welcome relief to the nation. The people and their president would move forward together in a measured way to mop up unsolved economic problems and create a system that ran smoothly. Wilson would strike a balance between government regulation and capitalist freedom. Tomorrow, in his inaugural speech, he would declare that "government may be put at the service of humanity." But he warned: "We shall deal with our economic system as it is and as it may be modified, not as it might be if we had a clean sheet of paper to write upon."[2]

Passion had no place at 1600 Pennsylvania Avenue. He would reason with the people, and they would see it his way. Even before he had much leadership experience, he theorized about it in his work. "Men are as clay in the hands of the consummate leader," he reckoned.[3] As the steam engine gave its last sigh of relief, Wilson steeled himself, rose from his seat, ducked his head under the compartment door, fixed a smile on his face, and stepped out to greet—no one. "Where are all the people?" an aide blurted out to a policeman.

A few blocks away from Union Station, twenty-eight-year-old Alice Paul looked out at all the people. Half a million of them—mostly men—jostled each other on the sidewalks of Pennsylvania Avenue. Five thousand more—almost all women—clogged the street. That morning those women broke every rule. They marched in public, snarled at men who threw curses at them, pushed back when the men tried to shove them, and stole Woodrow Wilson's limelight. It was all for their cause: women's right to vote. Back at Union Station, the policeman answered the aide's question on where everyone was: "Watching the suffrage parade."[4]

The fight for woman suffrage became an organized movement in Wilson's presidency, but victory would be deferred until after the Great War. First President Wilson set about implementing his New Freedom platform through economic legislation. He wanted to foster business competition in the long run and eliminate the need for governmental interference in it in the short run. He worked with the American Federation of Labor to improve working conditions, but he fought more radical unions. A southern white supremacist by upbringing, he limited African American participation in the federal government, while southern discrimination prompted African Americans to move North in great numbers to seek jobs and more freedom.

War broke out in Europe in 1914 as empires, entangled in alliances that pitted them against one another, sought to gain military primacy over the Continent and around the world. While most Americans sought to stay out of the war, Wilson began to ease the country toward involvement, and the United States entered the war in 1917. Wilson hoped to end the imperial power balances that dominated Europe, enable ethnic groups within those empires to govern themselves, and export democracy. He dreamed of perfecting international relations through establishing a governing consortium of major powers, including the United States. He would fail.

THE FIGHT FOR WOMAN SUFFRAGE

Alice Paul, a twenty-eight-year-old woman with luminous large black eyes, dark hair, and a dreamy expression that belied her resolve, had first imagined and then organized the woman suffrage parade. Already she had been to hell and back for her belief in woman suffrage—enduring prison, hunger strikes, and forced feeding in Britain. If she eclipsed Woodrow Wilson on that one day, she knew that she, and the suffrage cause, would endure darker days to come.

Wilson must have felt disgust when he heard about the parade. His entourage routed itself around the demonstration to save him from what he described as "the chilled, scandalized feeling that always comes over me when I see and hear women speak in public."[5] Four years later Alice Paul made sure that when Wilson awakened and raised his blinds to let the morning sun stream in, the first thing he saw a would be a woman suffragist picketing in front of the White House.

Alice Paul's Right to Vote

Three years earlier Paul had returned to the United States after working in the British suffrage campaign. She had graduated from Swarthmore, earned an M.A. at the University of Pennsylvania, and spent a year working in a New York settlement house. She went to Britain to study and pursue social work. The first time she was arrested there, she dressed up as a charwoman to get into the Guild Hall where Prime Minister Herbert Asquith was scheduled to speak the next day. Unnoticed, she spent the night. She recalled, "The Prime Minister made a most eloquent speech, and I listened, waiting for a chance to break in. At last there came a pause. Summoning all my strength, I shouted at the top of my voice: 'How about votes for women?'" Chaos ensued. "You would have thought I had thrown a bomb," she said.[6] Arrested twice more, she went on hunger strikes, and British authorities force-fed her for a month through a tube that went down her throat and into her stomach. Her reputation as a daring leader preceded her return to the States.

Paul's nonviolent direct action techniques fit with her Quaker background, but her courage and determination pushed her to the forefront of any crowd. When she proposed to the National American Woman Suffrage Association (NAWSA) that it stage a parade the day before Wilson's inauguration, it approved—if she could raise the money. She raised $15,000, propelled American suffragists into the national press, and took the nation's women to the streets.

Two women on horseback led the parade, with NAWSA president Anna Howard Shaw and other officers walking behind them. Shaw was a licensed Methodist minister and a medical doctor. From 1886, she had chaired the Woman's Christian Temperance Union (WCTU) suffrage department. The WCTU took up suffrage work in part because its members believed that women would vote for prohibition. Frances Willard, president of the WCTU from 1879 until her death in 1898, argued that the organization could achieve temperance by empowering women and adopted the slogan "Do Everything." Because the WCTU ran a thriving journalistic enterprise, marched on the polls, visited prisoners, and participated in antivice crusades, its members developed political savvy, which they brought with them to the suffrage campaign. Shaw began volunteering for NAWSA in the 1890s. The immediate past president of NAWSA, Carrie Chapman Catt, had also worked in the WCTU. She would succeed Shaw in that office, for a second term, in 1915.

Shaw could tolerate a suffrage parade, but she disapproved of the militant tactics that Alice Paul had learned from the British suffragists. As Shaw marched, nine bands, twenty-four floats, and five thousand marchers followed. At the head walked women representatives from countries such as Australia and Finland that had already adopted woman suffrage. Groups of professional women followed, with state and foreign delegations behind them.

Splits in the Woman Suffrage Movement

One of the women who marched that morning was four months short of her sixtieth birthday, and she had every right to feel exhausted. It had been twenty years since Ida B. Wells-Barnett had stood day after day in front of the Haitian Exhibition handing out her pamphlet "The Reason Why the Colored American Is Not in the World's Columbian Exposition." In March 1913 she took the train to Washington at her own expense. Back home in Chicago, she had founded the Alpha Suffrage Club, continued her campaign against lynching, and organized a settlement house in her neighborhood. Perhaps the most famous black woman in the United States at the time, she had come a long way—metaphorically and actually—to join the battle for suffrage. March organizers had told her that the white southern suffragists opposed her marching with the white Illinois women; she and the other Alpha Suffrage Club members would have to go to the back of the parade and march with a segregated group of black women suffragists. Wells-Barnett waited among the spectators until the Illinois delegation marched past and jumped into line with them, successfully integrating the parade.

The success of the march obscured disputes between militants and more conservative suffragists over tactics and ideology, just as Wells-Barnett's action presaged the political problems that the passage of woman suffrage would pose for the southern states. NAWSA had allowed Paul to orchestrate the parade but afterward distanced itself from her militant approach. Paul split from NAWSA later the same year to form the Congressional Union, which became the National Woman's Party (NWP), dedicated to applying unrelenting political pressure to officials. It targeted male politicians who refused to support woman suffrage and worked to defeat them regardless of party affiliation. Its members paraded, demonstrated, and went to prison for suffrage. On the other hand, NAWSA worked nonconfrontationally within the political system to organize women to persuade male voters and office-holders to help the suffrage cause.

The differences between the moderate NAWSA women and those who followed Alice Paul ran deeper than tactics. The NWP stuck to the argument that women had the natural right to vote, a position that had formed the bedrock of the suffrage movement for the previous sixty years. On the other hand, NAWSA saw an opportunity to argue that woman suffrage would contribute to good government. With this argument, NAWSA felt that it no longer needed to convince people of woman's natural rights. NAWSA could table divisive issues of equality and women's natural rights until suffrage passed; then women could use the ballot to achieve equality.

NAWSA maintained that without the vote women could not be successful progressive citizens. For example, they could not run a safe and efficient home without also becoming involved in municipal housekeeping—the suffragists' term for cleaning up the democratic process and electing pro-family officials. One suffrage brochure outlined the problems that homemakers faced daily, such as tainted food, unhealthy tenements, and rampant vice. Then it intoned, "Alone, she cannot make these things right. Who or what can? The city can do it, the city government that is elected by the people, to take care of the interests of the people. . . . Do the women elect them? No, the men do." Abandoning nineteenth-century woman suffragist Susan B. Anthony's argument that "woman was made first for her own happiness, with the absolute right to herself," NAWSA suffragists now argued, "Women are by nature and training, housekeepers, let them have a hand in the city's housekeeping, even if they introduce an occasional house-cleaning."[7] Natural rights had given way to progressive utilitarianism.

The difference between the NWP's rights argument and NAWSA's expediency argument was stark. Alice Paul's NWP used the language of republicanism, invoking antityranny and equality. NAWSA used the language of Progressivism, invoking women's usefulness in municipal housekeeping and drawing on a long-standing WTCU claim to female moral authority. The NWP asked for much more than the vote—it asked for equality under the U.S. political and legal system. NAWSA members unified around getting the vote and put more controversial issues of equality aside.

A National Coalition

In the years before Wilson's inauguration, the woman suffrage movement had progressed on three fronts. First, the public reacted negatively to the vociferous antisuffrage lobbying conducted by liquor dealers, textile manufacturers, and antireform politicians, and to their predictions that women would vote for temperance laws, higher state minimum wages for the female workforce in cotton mills, and the ouster of corrupt officials. Second, facing political opposition, male Progressives began to recognize the need to empower their female allies. In 1912 Teddy Roosevelt's Progressive Party endorsed woman suffrage and promised women "an equal voice with men in every phase of party management."[8] Third, educated, practical women who had gained experience in working for progressive reform now transferred their organizational skills to the suffrage campaign. After 1900 NAWSA began to emphasize grassroots organizing for suffrage over vague national appeals to natural rights. For example, the Boston Equal Suffrage Association canvassed door to door.

The vast majority of suffragists who marched in March 1913 were middle-class, white, native-born women who followed NAWSA and positioned themselves as potential voters for good government. From their elite perspective, they believed that women would form an educated, responsible electorate to counter immigrants' radicalism and to flush out corruption. The entire strategy assumed that women would vote collectively to champion forward-looking social programs and to guard women's individual rights.

Four western states—Utah, Wyoming, Colorado, and Idaho—had granted full woman suffrage by 1900. Careful organization won suffrage in five more western states by 1912: Washington, California, Arizona, Kansas, and Oregon.[9] Montana and Nevada followed in 1914, bringing the total to eleven before the first eastern state—New York—enfranchised women in 1917. In the West men so outnumbered women that women's votes there counted for less than in the East, perhaps making enfranchising them more palatable. Moreover, western farms and ranches operated as family economic units, making it more likely that women would vote as their husbands did. Some historians have suggested that pervasive hardship fell on western women and men alike, creating a more egalitarian political climate. Moreover, new state governments in the West may have been less dominated by vested interests and hence more open to new ideas.

States with majority Democratic voters tended to be slower to initiate

State Adoption of Woman Suffrage to 1914

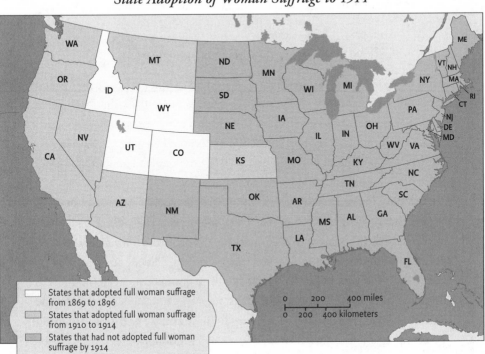

woman suffrage on the state level, for two opposing reasons. As the "wet" party, most Democrats, excluding those in the South, opposed prohibition. Since enfranchising women might lead to prohibition, northeastern and western Democrats, many of them Catholic, feared it. In the South, Democrats would have welcomed prohibition but worried that enfranchising women would bring federal scrutiny that would restore the vote to African Americans.

Some states and cities allowed partial suffrage—for example, women could vote for school boards or in temperance campaigns. As more states ratified suffrage, moderates worried that Paul's militant tactics would erode their growing support. Despite progress on the state level, both the NWP and NAWSA understood that only a constitutional amendment would guarantee suffrage in federal elections and across the nation. Passage of such an amendment would become more likely as women in western states elected sympathetic congressmen who would back it.

Woodrow Wilson did not care about suffrage as a political issue, and Alice Paul and the NWP resolved to target him until he did. As Wilson gave the state of the union speech in December 1916, suffragists in the congressional balcony unfurled a banner that screamed, "Votes for Women."[10] Nonetheless, NAWSA grew more quickly than the NWP and claimed two million members by 1917, on the eve of U.S. entry into the Great War.

WILSON'S ECONOMIC REFORMS

After his 1913 inauguration, Wilson continued to ignore the suffragists and focused on enacting the New Freedom platform. In 1912 the Progressive Party had drawn voters away from Republican candidates, and Democrats gained sixty-one seats in the House for a majority. They held a Senate majority for the first time in two decades. With a cooperative Congress in place, Wilson set about reshaping federal policy.

Wilson's New Freedom called for the federal government to set in place a few general principles to govern the economy and then step back. Once implemented, the rules would allow competition, and hence capitalism, to flourish without government intervention in specific situations. Wilson quickly tackled what he saw as the major problems: eliminating high tariffs that protected Republican industrialists' interests, rationalizing the chaotic banking system, inscribing labor's right to unionize, and strengthening weak antitrust laws. Wilson wanted to avoid Theodore Roosevelt's interventions at moments of crisis, such as in the Northern Securities case or the anthracite coal confrontation. He hoped to eliminate dramatic, ad hoc interventions in business affairs, increase commercial efficiency, and smooth the business cycle—without increasing the size of government.

New Freedom in Action: Tariffs and Taxes

Lower tariffs on imported goods would bring lower prices to consumers and more competition to U.S. industries. High tariffs had long been good politics for two reasons. First, Republicans, who represented the more industrial states in Congress, tended to support them to protect the manufacturers in their home states. These industries, such as cotton mills and furniture factories, could maintain higher prices and sell more products without foreign competition. Second, since 1896, industrial workers had voted Republican in support of tariffs, thinking that higher prices and more sales on domestic goods translated into higher wages and more jobs. But people outside industrial cities, particularly in the South and the West, along with the growing middle class in urban areas, wanted lower tariffs so that they could buy cheaper goods in an inflationary period. Working with a congressional Democratic majority, Wilson could dare to lower the tariff because he owed his election more to consumers than to industrialists.

If Congress lowered the tariff, however, it would have to provide a way to replace the shortfall in government revenue. A solution was already in the works: a federal income tax. The government had imposed an income tax during the Civil War, but the courts overturned two later attempts to reinstate it. The historical roadblock had been several constitutional provisions that required federal taxation on individuals to be proportioned among the states by percentage of national population within each state. In 1910, for example, roughly 92 million people lived in the United States, 2.5 percent in California and 10 percent in New York. It was a political impossibility that New York would agree to pay 10 percent of the nation's income tax.

In 1909 Congress eliminated proportionality with the Sixteenth Amendment. It read, "The Congress shall have power to lay and collect taxes on incomes, from whatever source derived, without apportionment among the several States, and without regard to any census or enumeration." By the 1912 election, thirty-four of the required thirty-six states had ratified it, and Taft, Roosevelt, and Wilson all supported ratification. When West Virginia and Delaware ratified early in 1913, the Sixteenth Amendment became law, giving the federal government the power to impose an income tax directly on individuals.

The Revenue Act of 1913, also known as the Underwood-Simmons Act, combined a federal income tax with a lower tariff. The income tax was progressive; in other words, the highest earners paid more tax. Those rare individuals who earned more than $500,000 per year paid 7 percent, and anyone who earned from $3,000 to $20,000 paid 1 percent. Income under $3,000 was exempt. At a time when average income amounted to $750 a year and professionals earned roughly $3,000 per year, most people would not pay any federal income tax at all. In 1914 they had to complete the new tax Form 1040 as a practice run; they did not actually have to pay taxes until 1915.

Reforming the Banking System

Wilson then pursued banking reform. From the distance of the twenty-first century, the chaos of the banking system in 1913 is difficult to imagine, even considering the flaws in banking today. If, in our time, voters hold the president accountable for managing the economy, in 1913 the president lacked the tools to influence the economy very much at all. The period from 1870 to 1910 comprised repeating cycles of boom and bust, punctuated by financial panics. These panics could stem from many factors, but groups of wealthy bankers, whom the public dubbed the "money trust," often contributed to these financial catastrophes through reckless behavior. New York banks, for example, exacerbated the Panic of 1907 with their failed speculations in copper. Once the panic began, banks quickly faced liquidity crises as depositors attempted to withdraw their funds all at once. This triggered sudden bank failures and provoked some of the largest New York banks to use private, unauthorized clearinghouse loan certificates in place of gold-backed currency. A major crisis in 1907 was averted when J. P. Morgan formed a group of wealthy individuals who pledged personal loans to back up the banks.

The chaos of the Panic of 1907 convinced many politicians, bankers, and average citizens that the nation needed centralized control over the money supply to spread risk and prevent bank failures. New York speculators could damage the entire banking system. Individual banks simply could no longer manage credit and currency in a modern industrial nation nor could the nation count on wealthy individuals to bail out banks. Even if they did so, the practice gave a small, wealthy elite too much power over the country's money supply. An efficient and sound banking system demanded central management.

In December 1913, after several years of reports and debate, Congress passed the Federal Reserve Act. The act required all nationally chartered banks to purchase stock in the Federal Reserve. It set up a main branch in Washington to provide some supervision over bank behavior and to serve as a liquidity provider of last resort. Twelve regional Federal Reserve banks cleared checks and provided local bank oversight. The Department of Treasury printed Federal Reserve notes to serve as legal tender backed by gold. The regional Federal Reserve banks would circulate the notes, which even today read: "This note is legal tender for all debts, public and private."

Regulating Business

The Clayton Antitrust Act incorporated several Populist demands regarding the regulation of monopolies. Passed in 1914, the act tried to make up for the weaknesses of the 1890 Sherman Antitrust Act, which could provide punitive measures enforced through the courts only after the fact. The Sherman Act did not even define monopolistic practices.

The Clayton Act exempted labor unions from antitrust laws and stipulated certain business practices as illegal. Among those prohibited were charging different rates to different customers, a practice the Populists had condemned in railroad pricing. The act outlawed anticompetitive pledges, such as agreements to trade exclusively between firms and quid pro quo buying schemes. It outlawed mergers and acquisitions in which the resulting combination would discourage competition, and it prohibited a single individual from simultaneously serving on the boards of competing companies.

Congress created the Federal Trade Commission (FTC) in 1914 to enforce the act's provisions. FTC rulings on business practices would be challenged in court, which created a body of law on corporate regulation. The process embodied the New Freedom concept of smoothing the path to competition without burdensome bureaucratic restrictions. Wilson said, "It is our purpose to destroy monopoly and maintain competition as the only efficient instrument of business liberty."[11] His trust prevention replaced Roosevelt's trust busting.

Wilson and Organized Labor

Wilson agreed that labor had a right to organize and considered the American Federation of Labor a reasonable model. He mistrusted the Industrial Workers of the World, however, partly for its socialist goals, and partly for its intent to organize unskilled as well as skilled workers and welcome women and racial and ethnic minorities.

Early in 1912 the IWW had supported working women's issues in the "Bread and Roses" strike at the American Woolen Company in Lawrence, Massachusetts. Half the workers were "unskilled" women, and most were eighteen and under—people whom the AFL would never have organized. The IWW organized skilled and unskilled workers together, women as well as men. In January the mill owners cut workers' wages. Polish women workers spontaneously walked off their jobs and out of the mill, shouting, "Short pay! Short pay!" A few days later 3,500 Italian and Jewish women followed them. The IWW arrived to organize the women who were still working. Within a few days, 25,000 workers struck at mills in Lawrence, representing twenty-five nationalities.[12]

The strikers asked for restoration of their wages, a fifty-four-hour week, and double pay for overtime. The women marched in front of the mill in moving picket lines, an innovation. One reporter noted the "strange sudden fire of the mingled nationalities" when the picketers began to sing.[13] When police on the roof of the mills attacked the women pickets below with water hoses, the general public became outraged.

The women's plight moved reformers in ways that the harsh working conditions for men never had, and the public began to connect employers' treatment of women workers to broader social issues. Appalled by the loss of 146 women in a fire at New York City's Triangle Shirtwaist Factory in 1911, the public embraced James Oppenheim's poem "Bread and Roses," published in *American Magazine* the month before the Lawrence strike.

BREAD AND ROSES

As we come marching, marching in the beauty of the day,
A million darkened kitchens, a thousand mill lofts gray,
Are touched with all the radiance that a sudden sun discloses,
For the people hear us singing: "Bread and roses! Bread and roses!"

As we come marching, marching, we battle too for men,
For they are women's children, and we mother them again.
Our lives shall not be sweated from birth until life closes;
Hearts starve as well as bodies; give us bread, but give us roses![14]

Oppenheim captured real and enduring problems: the exploitation of women workers and the future of democracy in a country where factory owners treated laborers as machines.

Elizabeth Gurley Flynn, an IWW organizer, brought the striking women together across ethnic divides. Flynn had been a Socialist and suffragist since she entered the labor movement at sixteen. Her fearless action on the picket line inspired IWW organizer Joe Hill to write the song "The Rebel Girl" about her.

That's the Rebel Girl, that's the Rebel Girl!
To the working class she's a precious pearl.[15]

The women's unity, sustained by the contributions that Flynn raised among sympathetic elite New York women, brought the American Woolen Company to the table. The mill offered raises, as well as time and a quarter for overtime, and it promised to let the strikers return to work. Most did.

Although the Bread and Roses strike was the IWW's most famous campaign, the AFL far outdistanced the IWW in membership in the years that followed. The federation's membership rose from 2.7 million in 1918 to over four million in 1920. AFL president Samuel Gompers bargained adeptly with power and forged an alliance with Wilson. Gompers argued that unions must strive to win "at the hands of government what they could accomplish by their own initiative and activities."[16] His goals, if achieved, would provide a chance for unionized skilled workers to enjoy safe and satisfying lives, but unskilled workers would be left to fend for themselves.

CIVIL RIGHTS AND THE NEW FREEDOM

Wilson's systematic vision of how the nation should work did not encompass a role for African Americans. With Democrats controlling Congress and the executive branch, southern white men enjoyed more power than they had at any time since secession. Many of Wilson's appointees were white southerners who had supported his election campaign, and they brought the stain of segregation with them to Washington and to federal employment. In the 1880s the District of Columbia had passed municipal ordinances prohibiting segregation in public accommodations, but private clubs and the city's schools had been segregated since Reconstruction. Federal jobs, especially in the Postal Service and the Treasury Department, remained open to African Americans, and a black middle class grew up in the capital. Republicans—the party of Lincoln—had been appointing African Americans to federal positions for four decades. President Roosevelt had dinner in the White House with Booker T. Washington, an event Wilson would have found unthinkable.

Segregating the Federal Government

Wilson stocked his cabinet with southerners. His secretary of the navy, Josephus Daniels of North Carolina, owned the largest newspaper in the state and had masterminded the 1898 white supremacy campaign there. Wilson's admiration of Daniels sprang from that campaign, and in Wilson's 1902 textbook, *A History of the American People*, he lauded white supremacists' recent action to rid the South of "the incubus of that ignorant and hostile [Negro] vote."[17] Once in Washington, Daniels saw himself as a symbol of reconciliation between Union and Confederacy. Worth Bagley, the first officer killed in the Spanish-American War, was his brother-in-law. Prior to his appointment as secretary of the navy, Daniels's main strength lay in journalistic race baiting, and he had no naval or military experience. Other southerners in the cabinet were Texan Albert S. Burleson who served as postmaster general, and William G. McAdoo, secretary of the treasury, born in Georgia.

In addition to appointing southerners to his cabinet, Wilson depended on southern point men in Congress. Oscar Underwood (D-AL), as majority leader of the House, worked with Senator Furnifold Simmons (D-NC), another architect of white supremacy, to sponsor the tariff bill. Carter Glass of Virginia chaired the House Banking Committee and backed the Federal Reserve Act. Representative Henry D. Clayton (D-AL) sponsored the antitrust act. The Democratic congressional surge of 1912 had long-lasting effects on politics. Because Democrats had suppressed voter participation in the South with the literacy test and the poll tax, a proportionately small number of voters would reelect these congressmen to term after term, allowing them to gain seniority and chair powerful committees. Carter Glass represented Virginia in the House and Senate from 1902 until 1946.

Postmaster Burleson first proposed segregation as policy just five weeks after the inauguration. He told the cabinet that the Post Office employed many black men on the trains that carried the mail; they worked side by side with white mail clerks. They were left over from Republican administrations, which had rewarded political loyalty with jobs. Burleson demanded that they be removed from the trains, arguing that it was "almost impossible to have different drinking vessels and different towels, or places to wash" on the cars, and that "segregation was best for the negro and for the service."[18]

The second problem that Burleson broached extended to all federal departments: how could they avoid hiring African Americans, and how could they separate, demote, transfer, and fire the black people already at work? At first Wilson demurred, but Burleson pressed and cited departments in which white women worked under black male supervisors. In Washington seven black clerks worked in the public Post Office building. Postmaster Burleson transferred them all to the dead letter department, where the public would not see them.

In McAdoo's Treasury Department building, they first segregated the lavatories, then the cafeteria, then the workspace, then the jobs. African Americans who supervised whites found themselves demoted. The assistant secretary of the treasury ordered white employees to omit the words "Sir," "Madam," and "Respectfully Yours," when writing to the African American staff. Federal agencies with southern offices, such as the Internal Revenue Service in Atlanta, fired all of their black employees. W. E. B. Du Bois, editor of the NAACP's magazine *The Crisis*, protested that federal agencies treated African Americans like "lepers," and his publicity campaign slightly slowed the segregation campaign.

The Great Migration

During Wilson's presidency, southern African Americans continued the great migration to the North that disfranchisement and segregation had begun at the turn of the century. In 1900, 90 percent of African Americans lived in the South. Those who left during the first decade of the twentieth century tended to be more prosperous, better educated, and from states in the upper South. One in thirteen black North Carolinians left the state in that decade. That trickle turned into the largest migration of an ethnic group in peacetime in American history. From 1916 until 1930, one million African Americans left the South at a rate of 16,000 each month, or 500 people every single day. Between 1916 and 1970, six million African Americans migrated. Many left because they feared for their physical safety, others for jobs after segregation took hold, some because they could not live without civil and political rights, and some because whites had taken their farms through violence or fraud. Despite the racism that they encountered in the North and West, which limited job opportunities and housing options, in spite of the unfamiliar freezing winters and bleak neighborhoods into which they were forced, still they went. The East Coast migrant trail led from Virginia, North Carolina, South Carolina, and Georgia to Philadelphia and New York. The midwestern trail ran from the Mississippi Delta to Chicago and Detroit. The boll weevil cotton infestation that began in 1892 in Texas spread inexorably northward and increased the pace by driving tenants in the Deep South off their farms. The Great War accelerated it by opening up northern jobs vacated by whites gone to war and by shutting off immigration.

AFRICAN AMERICAN MIGRATION TO NORTHERN CITIES

| | Black Population (rounded) | | |
	1910	1920	% increase
New York City	91,700	152,000	66%
Chicago	44,100	109,500	148%
Detroit	5,700	41,000	611%

Did those white southerners who had been so eager to segregate and oppress black southerners cheer their departure? Perhaps at first, but they quickly realized the loss of their cheap labor. In the Deep South, white plantation owners banned northern black newspapers, stopped trains and pulled black people off them, prohibited agents from recruiting southern African Americans for northern jobs, and even talked of suspending the mail service to prevent African Americans from hearing about northern opportunities. For their parts, the northern migrants registered to vote and began to have some influence in politics once again. Best of all was their new freedom. One man remembered crossing the Ohio River as his train headed north to Chicago. He left what had been designated the "Jim Crow" car and entered the "white people's coach." To his astonishment, "Here I was sitting beside a white man, and he said nothing. He did not try to make me get up or in any way embarrass me."[19]

Stonewalling Woman Suffrage

Wilson continued to overlook woman suffrage for the first three years of his term, but by mid-1916 avoidance became impossible. That summer both the Republican and the Democratic party conventions adopted platform planks that endorsed woman suffrage but did not stipulate the method by which it should be enacted. Some argued that woman suffrage should proceed on a state-by-state basis. Others supported a constitutional amendment that would have to be ratified by two-thirds of the states. In September 1916, following the party conventions, NAWSA president Carrie Chapman Catt called a convention in Atlantic City and invited President Wilson. He came and lent his support for suffrage, adding, "We will not quarrel in the long run as to the method of it."[20]

When Wilson left, Catt called together NAWSA leaders and outlined her strategy to make Wilson's long run NAWSA's short run. She came up with a "winning plan" for a "new deal." First, in the eleven states where women already voted, she proposed to lobby state legislatures to pass and send resolutions to Congress demanding that it draft and pass a federal amendment. Second, NAWSA would step up its work in states where suffrage legislation was pending and in states that seemed likely to ratify a federal amendment. Third, in states where suffrage did not seem likely to pass, NAWSA supporters would initiate referenda to secure suffrage in presidential elections only. Fourth, in the South, where many white men and women opposed woman suffrage because they believed that it would bring disfranchised African Americans back to the polls, suffragists should try to secure women's right to vote in the already segregated party primaries. Catt's methodical approach excluded Alice Paul and the NWP's direct protest methods.

THE GREAT WAR

Despite pervasive concern about European instability, the suddenness with which war broke out there in 1914 astonished the world. Conflict was commonplace in some of the European nations' far-flung colonies. The British and the French maintained large empires, and the Spanish, Dutch, Italians, and Portuguese also held colonies. On the European continent, however, the tottering antidemocratic regimes stood: the Hapsburg Austro-Hungarian Empire; the Hohenzollern Empire in Germany and Prussia with Kaiser Wilhelm II at its head; and the Romanovs in Russia.

The European powers had competed against one another for decades, spending lavishly on arms and naval races. Members of the ruling families that headed the European powers were often related. Kaiser Wilhelm of Germany, for instance, was the grandson of Britain's Queen Victoria. These powers allied with one another through binding treaties that proved dangerous fuel for the match of violence. Great Britain, France, and Russia formed the Triple Entente, while Germany and Austria-Hungary termed their alliance the Central Powers. France and Germany retained enmity from the Franco-Prussian War of 1870, and Austria feared Russia's territorial ambitions. The rivalry between Britain and Germany led to the British alliance with France and Russia.

Launching a "Great War"

Moreover, European imperial nations had annexed—sometimes by force—historically homogeneous ethnic nations and provinces to expand their own borders. The Serbs, of Slavic origin, had settled in what is today Bosnia-Herzegovina and neighboring Serbia in the seventh century. The weak Ottoman Empire had controlled Serbia until 1876, when the Serbs broke away and declared independence for Serbia and Bosnia, only to be thwarted when the Austro-Hungarian Empire took over Bosnia two years later. The Bosnian Serbs retained hopes of joining independent Serbia and establishing a pan-Slavic nation, perhaps with Russia's help.

Unrest at home, expensive arms races, and entangling alliances all contributed to the war, but so did European nations' rulers unquenchable thirst for colonies. They anticipated that war at home would result in the winners gaining the losers' overseas territories. A decisive war could redraw the map of the world.

What would become known as the Great War began with a single event on June 28, 1914. In Sarajevo, Bosnia-Herzegovina's capital, a young Serbian nationalist assassinated the Austro-Hungarian archduke Franz Ferdinand. Ferdinand was the nephew of Emperor Franz Josef, ruler of the empire, which controlled Bosnia-Herzegovina. The Austro-Hungarian

Empire declared war on Serbia on July 23, 1914. Kaiser Wilhelm II of Germany, a close friend of Ferdinand, declared war on Serbia.

Treaties, public and secret, ignited a chain reaction across all of Europe. Honoring its treaty obligations to the Austro-Hungarian Empire, Germany declared war on Serbia. To preempt Russia, whose secret treaty with Serbia now came to light, Germany also declared war on Russia and France, a Russian ally. Germany overran Belgium and threatened to enter France. Because Great Britain had a treaty with France, it warned Germany to preserve Belgian neutrality.

Britain declared war on Germany on August 4, 1914. Within thirty-six days, one shot and one death had plunged Europe into a total war that would result in 16 million deaths. The Central Powers included Germany, the Austro-Hungarian Empire, the Ottoman Empire, and Bulgaria. The former Entente of Britain, France, and Russia joined with Romania, Serbia, Italy, and twenty-four other countries to form the Allied Powers. They waged war over heavily populated land. Germany set up forward lines in Belgium, and British troops poured into France. Almost at once the British and French on one side, and the Germans on the other, dug into trenches facing each other.

Technology had outstripped human conceptions of war. Trenches had been used in the past for refuge after battles on land, but now the machine gun made trench warfare a bloody massacre of little strategic value. Troops who left the trenches to advance a few yards were mowed down by machine guns and long-range artillery in the killing fields between the trenches. Poison gas from both sides permeated the air and first sickened soldiers and then left them with permanent neurological damage.

The result was a stalemate from 1914 to late 1916, a stalemate with an enormous loss of life. The Siege of Verdun in France began in February 1916 and ended five months later with 330,000 dead Germans and 350,000 dead Frenchmen. At the Battle of the Somme, from July to October 1916, one million people died without either side gaining any geographical advantage.[21] The British poet Wilfred Owen commented on the hopelessness of war in the trenches:

Bent double, like old beggars under sacks,
Knock-kneed, coughing like hags, we cursed through sludge . . .
Men marched asleep. Many had lost their boots
But limped on, blood-shod. All went lame; all blind.[22]

The American Reaction

On August 4, when Britain declared war on Germany, Woodrow Wilson warned that "every man who really loves America will act and speak in the true spirit of neutrality"; he mandated neutrality as the official U.S. position. Most Americans had only the haziest idea of why Europe had exploded and wanted to stay out of the war. As a nation of immigrants, the United States had ties—historic, familial, and commercial—to both sides of the conflict. Sympathy tended toward Britain, where the most U.S. investments were, but substantial numbers of Americans favored Germany and had invested there. Many Irish Americans hated Britain, which occupied Ireland, and hoped that a German victory would result in Irish independence. German Americans had prospered in the United States for decades while maintaining German cultural ties. There were twenty-four German newspapers in 1914 in Texas alone, and culturally Milwaukee had as much in common with Munich as it did with Miami.

The United States, following the Roosevelt Corollary, was preoccupied with the security of American interests in Latin America. In 1914 Wilson occupied Veracruz, Mexico, for seven months, ostensibly to intervene after local authorities insulted U.S. Marines but actually to position troops amid the unrest that accompanied the Mexican Revolution, begun in 1910. He sent U.S. troops to Haiti in 1915 to quell violence that threatened U.S. investments. The Mexican rebel Francisco "Pancho" Villa, a former ally, attacked U.S. troops in New Mexico in March 1916, and Wilson ordered an expeditionary force to chase him throughout northern Mexico. With its small army and navy, the United States could ill afford to join European wars.

Old Populist and Democrat William Jennings Bryan, who served as Wilson's secretary of state, supported neutrality. Bryan believed that preserving American values depended on avoiding foreign entanglements. Democrats in Congress who represented the agrarian South followed the Populist tradition of isolationism; they controlled the House Military Affairs Committee. Western and midwestern Republicans in Congress generally advocated neutrality as well. Senator William Borah (R-ID) was an even stronger isolationist than Bryan. Progressive senator Robert La Follette (R-WI) leaned toward pacifism and advocated U.S. disarmament.

On the other hand, Senator Henry Cabot Lodge (R-MA) began pushing for the United States to mobilize for war to protect Britain. Northeastern Republicans joined him and urged preparedness out of an affinity for Britain and concern for U.S. investments there. Teddy Roosevelt simply itched for a fight. Some Democrats with roots in the business-oriented New South, such as Josephus Daniels, secretary of the navy, were sympathetic to transnational involvement.

For his part, Woodrow Wilson believed that the outbreak of war in Europe posed a threat to the United States. He thought Kaiser Wilhelm II headed an authoritarian and militaristic regime with a thirst for power. Germany had come late to the race for empire and had designs on Africa and Asia. When they gained a foothold, they proved to be ruthless colonial masters. Wilson foresaw a Europe subordinated to a victorious Germany as a monstrous risk to the United States. He knew, however, that his party leaned toward strict neutrality, and he gave no indication in 1914 and early 1915 that he would support involvement.

The War on the Seas

After Britain declared war on Germany in August 1914, British ships moved to blockade the ports of its foe. The Germans had developed an effective submarine, which they called the *Unterseeboot* (Undersea Boat) and nick-named it the U-boat. As the war began, Germany did not know how well the submarine would work against a blockade. The rules of naval warfare required an attacking vessel to warn that a ship would be sunk and to take on board the enemy sailors, neither of which a submarine could do. Sneaky and deadly, U-boats struck terror in the hearts of British seamen, who called them "damned un-English weapons."[23] Moreover, U-boat captains could neither be sure of the nationality of the ship that they had in their sights, nor distinguish noncombatant vessels.

A February 1915 German declaration made "all the waters around Great Britain and Ireland, including the whole of the English Channel, a war zone." Hence U-boats would try to "destroy every enemy ship found in that war zone." They acknowledged that this would "threaten neutral persons and ships"; the only way to escape danger was to stay clear.[24] Wilson decided to allow armed British merchant vessels into American ports. Moreover, Americans sailed on British ships and American ships traded with Britain in the war zone. Wilson warned the Germans that they would be held strictly accountable for American lives.

Rumors of war were only whispers to Rosina Leverich as she anxiously awaited the arrival of her passport in April 1915. The twenty-eight-year-old New Orleans heiress and her mother had left the Garden District and came to New York to prepare for a visit to her brother in London. Young William Edward Leverich was taking his place in the family's international cotton trade. Sixty years earlier the Leverichs had planted family outposts in New Orleans, New York, and London. For Rosina it would be the trip of a lifetime. Their passports arrived on April 21, in time for their May 1 sailing to Liverpool. They had booked in on the "largest and fastest" steamer of the British-owned Cunard Line, the *RMS Lusitania*, an ocean liner in which the British had built a secret compartment to ship arms. The British had reclassified the ship as an armed merchant cruiser.

The Leverichs arrived early for the ten a.m. sailing, only to find that chaos reigned on the pier. The passengers buzzed with gossip about a small advertisement in that morning's *New York Times*. "NOTICE!" it began. "Travellers intending to embark on the Atlantic voyage are reminded that a state of war exists between Germany and her allies and Great Britain and her allies; that the zone of war includes the waters adjacent to the British Isles; that, in accordance with formal notice given by the Imperial German Government, vessels flying the flag of Great Britain, or any of her allies, are liable to destruction in those waters." The signature read: "Imperial German Embassy, Washington DC."[25]

Reporters swarmed, interviewing the *Lusitania*'s passengers and crew. No more than the usual number, it seemed, had canceled their bookings. Dewar's distillery general manager and passenger Alexander Campbell scoffed, "I think it is a lot of tommy rot for any Government to do such a thing. . . . The *Lusitania* can run away from any German submarine." It is not clear whether the passengers knew that the *Lusitania* carried a large store of arms, but they realized that Canadian soldiers made up the preponderance of passengers.[26]

Rosina and her mother settled into their second-class cabin, mingled with the other 140 Americans aboard, and watched the hundreds of Canadian troops muster and mill about. On their second day at sea, they learned that a German submarine had torpedoed an American ship, the *Gulflight*, resulting in two American deaths. Six days out, on May 7, they caught sight of the Irish coast. By two-thirty that afternoon, the *Lusitania* came about eight miles off the picturesque sailing port of Kinsale.

First they saw the submarine, then the streaming path of a torpedo.

The second torpedo exploded the munitions. Rosina's mother reached for her jewelry and stuck it down into her whalebone corset as they ran from their cabin. The ship sank in eighteen minutes, but bodies washed up on Kinsale's beaches for days.

William Leverich identified his mother by the jewelry that remained wedged between the corset's whalebones and her bones. Almost twelve hundred people drowned that day; Rosina's body remained forever missing.[27]

Remember the Maine*! Remember the* Lusitania*!* Theodore Roosevelt certainly remembered both. Using the honorific "colonel" rather than "president," Roosevelt railed against the sinking of the *Lusitania* as "an act of piracy."[28] Secretary of State Bryan sent the official U.S. protest five days later. He asserted that "American citizens act within their indisputable rights in taking their ships and in travelling wherever their legitimate business calls them upon the high seas." The protest called on the Germans to abandon submarine warfare against merchant ships of any nation, demanded a "repudiation" of the act, and insisted on reparations. The German government replied that it had been mistaken in its attack on the *Gulflight* but justified its attack on the *Lusitania* because it carried Canadian troops and "no less than 5,400 cases of ammunition destined for the destruction of brave German soldiers."[29]

Wilson continued to launch protests, but Bryan resigned as secretary of state because he wanted the president to disavow the British practice of accepting American civilians on its armed ships. Wilson should ban such travel, Bryan thought, and his failure to do so resembled "putting women and children in front of an army."[30] Bryan suspected that the president's failure to protest to the British reflected a covert plan to bring the United States into the war. If Bryan found Wilson bellicose, Roosevelt considered his protests too weak and called for universal military training. Wilson instituted voluntary training instead, whereupon Roosevelt exploded that Wilson used "weasel words" that "sucked all the meaning" out of a commitment to prepare for war.[31]

In May 1916 Germany temporarily resolved the submarine issue with the Sussex Pledge. It promised that if the United States would put pressure on England to lift its blockade, the Germans would not attack merchant ships without prior clear warning. When submarines did attack, they would make every effort to rescue passengers and crew.

A Conflicted Neutrality

During 1916 and 1917 Americans remained deeply divided about their country's role in the war; they fell roughly into four camps whose popularity shifted as events unfolded. First, the pacifists were a considerable group, many of them Socialists and Progressives; they would never support war. Second, the isolationists, who wanted to keep the country out of war, were split between those like Bryan and the agrarian southern Democrats, who would fight only if America were directly threatened, and those who gradually became persuaded that Germany had to be stopped in Europe. Third, many Republicans and urban Democrats supported preparedness from the outset and would go to war to protect America's interests abroad. Fourth, interventionists such as Anglophile northeastern Republicans sought to prepare and enter the war on the Allies' side as soon as possible.

The issue made for strange bedfellows and broke up old friendships. Many of Roosevelt's allies in the Progressive Party, such as settlement house founder Jane Addams, strongly opposed entering the war. Suffragists and feminists flocked to the Woman's Peace Party. In November 1915 pacifist automaker Henry Ford reserved an entire ocean liner to take Americans to a peace conference in Europe. On the other hand, Roosevelt pushed for preparedness and intervention whenever he had a forum.

Conservative interventionists joined the National Security League, which stressed civil defense, vilified Germans, and began to link interventionism with patriotism. Those who opposed intervention came under increasing pressure after 1915, as Americans became increasingly invested in an Allied Powers' victory over Germany. By April 1917 U.S. bankers had loaned $2.3 billion to the Allies, and trade with them had increased 184 percent in the same period. The United States had exported over $1 billion in arms to the Allies by 1917. During the same period, trade with Germany had totaled only $27 million.[32]

The U.S. Entry into War

The election of 1916 turned on the issue of U.S. involvement in the Great War. Roosevelt wanted the Republican nomination, but that party snubbed him because of his 1912 defection to the Progressive Party. Instead, the Republicans nominated Charles Evans Hughes, an old-fashioned Progressive, ex-governor of New York, and a sitting Supreme Court justice when nominated. The Progressive Party nominated its old bull moose, but Roosevelt declined the nomination, knowing that a tripartite contest would surely hand Wilson another term; the party then endorsed Hughes. Roosevelt did the same. Both Hughes and Wilson avowed preparedness, but eschewed war itself. Hughes argued that Wilson's vacillation had drawn the country into European affairs and promised to be firm with both sides in the conflict. He also endorsed woman suffrage by federal amendment, a version of which was already circulating and was named the Susan B. Anthony Amendment for the tireless nineteenth-century suffragist. Wilson ran on the slogan "He Kept Us Out of War." The election turned out to be the closest since 1876: Wilson received 277 electoral votes to Hughes's 254.

On January 31, 1917, Germany announced the resumption of unrestricted submarine warfare, gambling that the move would topple Britain before the United States could mobilize. But Germany didn't count on the Russian Revolution, which broke out in March, removing Wilson's objections to joining Britain and France in an alliance with the antidemocratic Czar Nicholas II. In the first six months of the Russian Revolution, Alexander Kerensky's republican government seemed to be a liberal state. By entering on the side of Britain, France, and Russia, the United States could now side with democracy instead of German autocracy. Moreover, Woodrow Wilson desperately wanted a seat at the peace table when the fighting ceased, even if the Allies lost. To be there, the United States had to enter the war. All Wilson needed was a catalyst.

He found it in the Zimmermann telegram, a January 19, 1917, message from German state secretary for foreign affairs Arthur Zimmermann to the German ambassador in Mexico; it was sent from Germany through Galveston, Texas to Mexico. British intelligence intercepted the telegram, which seemed to be rows and rows of numbers. The Germans risked sending it because they did not realize that the British had cracked their code. Zimmermann directed the ambassador to enlist Mexican cooperation to invade the United States. When decoded, the chilling message began, "We intend to begin on the first of February unrestricted submarine warfare. We shall endeavor in spite of this to keep the United States of America neutral. In the event of this not succeeding, we make Mexico a proposal of alliance on the following basis: make war together, make peace together, generous financial support and an understanding on our part that Mexico is to reconquer its lost territory in Texas, New Mexico, and Arizona."[33] When the telegram became public, the Mexican government quickly disavowed any interest in joining the Germans. Nonetheless, the specter of German-armed Mexicans pouring over the border threw Americans into a frenzy. The scenario proved so provocative that some said Wilson had faked the telegraph to push the country into war.

"Militant Americanism was dominant in Washington today," *The New York Times* reported in response to Wilson's announcement of the telegram. "By one bold strike President Wilson had emboldened the timid, scattered his enemies, and brought honest critics to his side. . . . Germany's enmity is now clearly revealed." If Wilson wanted a declaration of war against the Central Powers, his chance had arrived: "Patriotic zeal was at a fever heat in the House of Representatives" and "pacifist qualms faded in the Senate."[34] The German resumption of submarine warfare two weeks later occasioned a rash of *Lusitania*-like incidents, although none with heavy casualties.

The large U.S. investment in an Allied victory, the outrage over submarine warfare, and the provocation of the Zimmermann telegram moved Americans toward war, yet these factors furnished only a laundry list of catalysts rather than a call to arms that resounded with moral purpose. If the United States entered the horrible conflict, Americans would know what they were fighting against, but what would they be fighting for?

Wilson answered that question in his April 2, 1917, address to a joint session of Congress, when he presented his resolution for war. Members of Congress had to fight their way into the building that day, since police could not hold back the pacifist protesters who attacked pro-war Senator Henry Cabot Lodge and even occupied the vice president's office. The precept that the president articulated to the joint session came to be known as Wilsonianism: the idea that the growth of democracy abroad makes the United States more secure at home.

Wilson argued that world peace "can never be maintained except by a concert of the democracies of the world." Weak nations that cannot stand up to imperial power depend on the United States to give them a chance to be independent and democratic. The United States will fight to "make the world free." Congress several times interrupted his speech with loud cheers and yelling, but when he uttered the sentence that would become most famous—"The world must be made safe for democracy"—the members sat still until a lone senator began to applaud, "gravely and emphatically." One by one, others followed until a "great roar" rose. Americans had found their cause. Wilson coupled this high ideal with a request that Congress approve "universal service"—in other words, a draft.[35]

Finally, on April 6, after over sixteen hours of debate, the House voted on Wilson's war resolution. Pacifist Jeanette Rankin (R-MT), the only woman in Congress, sat tortured by the decision before her. She believed that "peace is a woman's job."[36] The sergeant-at-arms had to call for her vote three times before she responded with these words: "I want to stand by my country, but I cannot vote for war. I vote"—and here her voice broke into a sob—"No!" as "big tears" spilled over. She was one of fifty who voted no; 373 voted for war.[37]

Safe for Democracy

Wilson's vision of spreading democracy to Europe propelled the United States into a powerful, if yet imaginary, role in world affairs. The pacifists, the isolationists, and even many of those who supported preparedness would not have agreed with Wilson's idea that the United States had an urgent state interest in European affairs. Fewer still would have argued that the United States had an obligation to ensure that weak European states or colonial territories of strong European states should be able to count on America to fight for their right to democracy. But recent events inflamed public opinion against the Germans, and Wilson's higher purpose for declaring war provided an uplifting rationale. It also set the United States on a course to global power and responsibility.

With his speech, Wilson remapped U.S. interests to construct a geopolitical formation that would become known as "the West": a theoretical democratic zone that unified the interests of the United States and Europe. At a stroke, he extended the Declaration of Independence to the world's peoples as he called for "the vindication of right, of human right."[38] If human rights applied to Europe, could they not also extend to colonized peoples? African Americans quickly began speaking of the application of Wilson's democratic principles to Africa. Nationalists in colonized countries around the world, such as in French Indochina, took hope.

U.S. INVOLVEMENT IN THE GREAT WAR

Lofty intellectual plans to extend democracy did not have much bearing on the United States' readiness to fight in Europe. Poorly equipped and lacking in ships, the American military stood at only 127,000 men. Dwight David

Eisenhower, a young infantry officer charged with moving supplies domestically, found his task difficult because of the poor state of highways in the South and parts of the West. The country had declared war, but it would not fight for many months.

Marshaling Troops and Organizing the Home Front

One reason Wilson demanded a draft was to overcome divided loyalties among Americans. Many Irish Americans and German Americans remained opposed to entering the war. Wilson deplored their attitudes: "There are citizens of the United States . . . born under other flags but welcomed under generous naturalization laws to the full freedom and opportunity of America, who have poured the poison of disloyalty into the very arteries of our national life."[39] The draft would stanch disloyalty. Moreover, Wilson knew that only a massive commitment of troops would give the United States any influence at the peace table. Draft boards operated community by community; thus they were subject to local politics. A board in Fulton County, Georgia, for example, exempted 526 out of 815 white people but only 6 out of 202 African Americans.

The Socialist Party and its leader, Eugene V. Debs, characterized the fray as a war for empire, to be won on the backs of the drafted working class. The day after the United States declared war, the Socialist Party argued that the declaration was a "crime against the people of the United States" and called for "vigorous resistance" to the draft.[40] On the other hand, AFL president Samuel Gompers had come out for preparedness in 1916, bargaining that union support for the war would give labor power in a wartime government. After he pledged that AFL unions would not strike during wartime, Wilson appointed him to the advisory commission of the Council of National Defense.

Wilson would have to rally groups that he had previously ignored or suppressed, including woman suffragists and African Americans. Carrie Chapman Catt, president of NAWSA since 1915, had been a member of the Woman's Peace Party, but she now pledged NAWSA to the war effort. Like Gompers, Catt foresaw power for the suffrage organization and made a deal with Wilson to leave the issue of suffrage aside for the duration of the war. NAWSA members helped Councils on Preparedness in every state and recruited women to work in food production, the American Red Cross, and aid to soldiers stationed stateside.

Before the United States entered the war, most black leaders had seen it as a consequence of the European imperialist ambition that had conquered and divvied up all of Africa. W. E. B. Du Bois, Harvard educated with a German Ph.D., wrote in the NAACP's *The Crisis* magazine, "Well, civilization has met its Waterloo. . . . The civilization by which America insists on measuring us and to which we must conform our natural tastes and inclinations is the daughter of that European civilization which is now rushing furiously to its doom."[41]

Yet a year later Du Bois, like Catt, changed his position. He thought that African Americans, led by black officers, could prove themselves in combat and claim full citizenship after the war. The federal government started the first-ever training camp for "colored officers" in Des Moines, Iowa. Glad that black officers would lead black troops but disappointed at the segregated facility, Du Bois argued that African Americans should not be forced to choose "between the insult of a separate camp and the irreparable injury of strengthening the present custom of putting no black men in positions of authority."[42]

Ultimately, Du Bois accepted an army commission and worked in Washington. He published a powerful editorial in *The Crisis* making the case for African Americans to support the war, entitled "Close Ranks." He urged, "Let us not hesitate. Let us, while this war lasts, forget our special grievances and close our ranks shoulder to shoulder with our white fellow citizens and the allied nations that are fighting for democracy. We make no ordinary sacrifice, but we make it gladly and willingly with our eyes lifted to the hills."[43] Of the roughly 385,000 African Americans who served in the war, 200,000 went abroad with the American Expeditionary Forces (AEF), as the units that went to Europe were named. Forty thousand of them served as combat troops.

Some 4,743,826 Americans served during the war, of whom four million were part of the AEF. The shortage of ships meant that it took months to get them to Europe. From the outset, the U.S. military did not want to engage in the disastrous trench warfare that had already cost so many so much in return for so little. General John Joseph "Black Jack" Pershing, who had chased Pancho Villa through Mexico and now commanded the AEF, insisted that his troops first be trained stateside. He opposed sending them to fight in the French trenches, although they ultimately fought there. Roosevelt's favorite and youngest son, Quentin, transferred his motorcycle-tinkering skills to airplanes, learned to fly a Nieuport fighter plane, and served in France under the legendary Captain Eddie Rickenbacker, in the Ninety-fourth Aero Squadron.

This small group of flying aces overcame the trench war standoff as they flew over enemy lines to strafe those on the ground. The Germans also unleashed air squadrons, but they stayed mostly behind German lines, while British, French, Canadian, and American pilots crossed into German airspace to engage in dogfights, firing machine guns. The pilots were astonishingly vulnerable. France produced 68,000 airplanes during the war and lost 52,000 of them.

The Threat to Civil Liberties

In June 1917, as draft boards conscripted men and the military geared up, Congress responded to Wilson's fear of disloyalty among Americans by passing the Espionage Act. This far-reaching act restricted dissemination of military information, from code books to blueprints to photographs of bases, on risk of punishment by death, and established a $10,000 fine and up to 20 years imprisonment for obstructing military operations in wartime.

The Espionage Act's most controversial section restricted freedom of speech. Anyone who shall "promote the success of its [the United States] enemies . . . shall willfully cause or attempt to cause insubordination, disloyalty, mutiny, refusal of duty, in the military or naval forces of the United States, or shall willfully obstruct the recruiting or enlistment service" faced punishment.[44]

Abhorring the deal that NAWSA made with Wilson to subordinate the cause of woman suffrage to the war effort, Alice Paul and the National Woman's Party picketed the White House and walked right into the Espionage Act. She and other suffragists were arrested for the "making of untrue statements which interfered with the conduct of the war," by carrying banners with "treasonous and seditious" words. Police were terribly embarrassed when it turned out that the words on the banners quoted Wilson's own speeches, albeit in the spirit of irony, since the suffragists carried them. For example, one "treasonous" banner quoted Wilson's war resolution: "We shall fight for the things which we have always held nearest our hearts—for democracy, for the right of those who submit to authority to have a voice in their own governments."[45] Befuddled police realized that the president's resolution for war could not be charged under the Espionage Act and that picketing itself was legal, so they charged sixteen women with obstructing traffic and sent them to jail for sixty days.

The imprisoned suffragists declared themselves political prisoners, went on hunger strikes, and refused to get dressed or to leave their beds. The government responded by putting them in solitary confinement and force-feeding them. When Wilson pardoned them, they promptly returned to picketing, jail, and more force-feeding. Anne Martin, chair of the NWP's legislative committee, explained their campaign this way: "It's unpatriotic, we are told to complain of injustice now. We believe that it is unpatriotic not to complain. We have no right to allow our own representatives to act basely—to preach freedom abroad, and to deny freedom at home."[46]

Postmaster General Albert Burleson used the Espionage Act to monitor the publications of ethnic groups, labor unions, and the Socialist Party, and censored and confiscated newspapers and magazines. The many foreign-language publications across America had to translate any article that referred to the government or the war. Before the war, industrious and generally prosperous German Americans had been one of the most respected immigrant groups, but now people hounded them, banned the German language, and renamed sauerkraut "victory cabbage." Across the nation, mobs set upon Germans and beat them, even lynching one. Burleson banned most Socialist material, and the Socialist leader Eugene V. Debs received a ten-year prison sentence for giving an antiwar speech.

Wilson had learned about the power of the press from progressive journalism, and now he reached out to old muckrakers to build a pro-war propaganda machine inside the government. Journalist George Creel headed the Committee on Public Information (CPI), which the secretaries of state, war, and the navy saw as a way to involve average citizens in a "feeling of partnership" with the government.[47] But the partnership soon became one-sided. The CPI created clubs of Four-Minute Men across the country to give pro-war speeches on food conservation, purchasing war bonds known as Liberty Bonds, and patriotism. The Four-Minute Men captured the stage whenever they could, even between reel changes at the movies. The CPI produced pamphlets in foreign languages and created Loyalty Leagues in ethnic neighborhoods to distribute them.

As the war continued, the CPI strategy shifted from educating immigrants to repressing dissent. The clubs became surveillance mechanisms to denounce neighbors whose patriotism was in question. Intolerance increased, and 100 percent Americanism became the watchword. The volunteer American Protective League swelled to 250,000 members who reported on their neighbors to the Department of the Attorney General.

In May 1918 Congress passed an amendment to the Espionage Act, called the Sedition Act, that prohibited "any disloyal, profane, scurrilous, or abusive language about the form of government of the United States, of the Constitution of the U.S., of the flag of the U.S., or the uniform of the Army or Navy," or any language that might bring those institutions "into contempt, scorn, . . . or disrepute." The Sedition Act went even further than the Espionage Act, criminalizing criticism of the war. Now one could not criticize the government at all. The act gave local federal attorneys broad discretion to determine whom they would prosecute. Oddly enough, Wilson thought the Sedition Act provided the government a way to protect critics from the lynch mobs he had empowered under the CPI: by sending them to jail.

During the war, the Justice Department raided 48 Industrial Workers of the World meeting halls, arrested 165 IWW leaders, put 101 of them on trial for sedition, and won convictions against them all. Big Bill Haywood got a twenty-year sentence and fled the United States to avoid imprisonment. He hoped to find "a new society in which there will be no battle between capitalist and wage earner" in the Soviet Union.[48] He died there in 1928 and was interred in two places: in the wall of the Kremlin in Moscow and near a monument to labor martyrs in Chicago.

Charles T. Schenck, prosecuted under the Espionage Act for distributing Socialist literature urging men to resist the draft, took his case to the Supreme Court, which in 1919 upheld his criminal conviction under the act. Justice Oliver Wendell Holmes argued that the First Amendment did not extend to "falsely shouting fire in a theatre and causing a panic." The justices ruled that the government could restrict speech in wartime when it presented "a clear and present danger."[49]

Over There

The first U.S. troops reached France in June 1917 but did not join the front until October. So far the Allies had thrown everything they had against the German lines and achieved little. The first U.S. forces acted as ancillary forces to the dug-in French, British, Canadians, and Australians. It took four months to build the U.S. force to one million, and three million followed over the next year. The Germans had attempted a series of knockout blows in the spring and early summer of 1918. They met with success but not enough to overwhelm the Allies. In early 1918 four U.S. divisions assumed battle lines with the French and British troops, and by May they began to battle the Germans directly. In September half a million Americans mounted an operation to overwhelm the Germans. Culminating in the

Military Action in the Great War

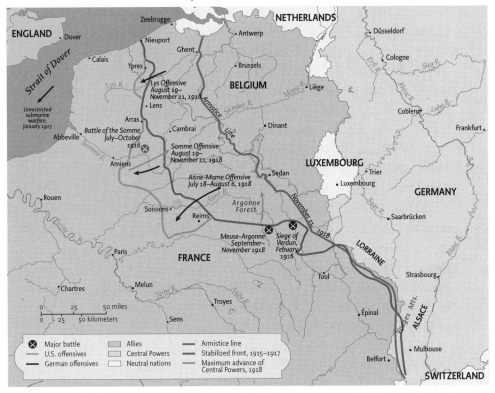

Battle of Argonne, one million American and French troops retook more than two hundred square miles of French territory.

Germany's rapid fall came as a profound shock to the German people, who had thought they were winning the war. On November 11, 1918, Germany signed an armistice. Some 126,000 Americans had died in the war, more than half from disease. Over six million Allies and four million Germans died in combat. Despite the disparity in casualties and deaths, the U.S. effort won Wilson the place at the peace table that he had so coveted.

If the United States provided the tipping factor in the war, the war itself provided the basis for the modern U.S. armed forces. By its end, almost five million men had served. But for the thirteen thousand Americans who served with a multinational Allied force of over 100,000 in the new Russian Soviet Federative Socialist Republic, the war did not end there. The March 1917 Russian Revolution had deposed Romanov czar Nicholas II and instituted the Russian Provisional Government. Its leaders vowed to keep fighting the Germans, a highly unpopular stance. In October 1917 a group of

Russian Marxists, the Bolsheviks, deposed the Provisional Government. Led by Vladimir Lenin, the group quickly won public support. Russians flocked to join the Bolshevik Red Army, defeated the White Russians who remained loyal to the Provisional Government, and took over several former territories of the Russian Empire. In March 1918 the Bolshevik government signed a separate peace treaty with the Central Powers. While fighting continued in Europe, Allied troops, including Michigan soldiers who made up the Polar Bear Unit, entered northern Russia to link up with stranded Czechoslovakian legions and to secure Allied supplies that the Bolsheviks were confiscating for use in their own civil war.

After the German surrender, Allied forces, including Americans, continued to fight against the new Communist state. They hoped to win the support of the local people against the Bolsheviks but failed completely. Spread out across the vast area that would become the Soviet Union, the 100,000 troops had little chance of holding territory, much less of vanquishing the popular Bolsheviks. In 1920 Allied troops withdrew, leaving behind a legacy of resentment among the new Soviets.

THE TREATY AND THE LEAGUE

Like the college professor he had been, Wilson went to the Versailles Peace Conference armed with lecture notes to instruct Britain's David Lloyd George and France's Georges Clemenceau. Lloyd George had become Britain's prime minister in December 1916, and Clemenceau took over that role in France in November 1917.

Wilson's Fourteen Points

Wilson had articulated his program, called the Fourteen Points, before a joint session of Congress in January 1918; it promised nothing less than an end to war forever. Six of the points spoke broadly to international peace. First, Wilson demanded that the peace conference produce "open covenants, openly arrived at," making every agreement and provision in the treaties public, to avoid the secret alliances that had led European countries into war. Second, he remembered the *Lusitania* and perhaps the *Maine*, two naval tragedies that had propelled the United States into wars, and called for "absolute freedom of navigation upon the seas," anywhere, anytime, even in war.

His third point struck at the trade imbalances that caused international tension when he called for "the removal of all economic barriers and . . . an equality of trade conditions" among parties to the peace. Fourth, he proposed disarming all nations "to the lowest point consistent with domestic safety." His fifth point was potentiality the most far reaching, yet it was the most opaque: "impartial adjustment of all colonial claims . . . [and] the interests of the populations concerned must have equal weight with the equitable claims of the government whose title is to be determined."[50]

Putting this fifth point together with eight other points that dealt with restoring territory and sovereignty to combatants and weak European states, Wilson articulated what came to be called the "self-determination of nations." Instead of the traditional balance of power between European empires dangerously suspended in opposing blocs, Wilson argued that sustainable peace depended upon recognizing each nation's right to exist and that each nation's government should be based on its people's will. But self-determination's devils lay in its application.

Finally, the fourteenth point, the linchpin of the entire peace project, was the formation of an international organization of nations "for the purpose of affording mutual guarantees of political independence and territorial integrity to great and small states alike."[51] The proposal embodied Wilson's lifelong dream of an international superparliament. It would be named the League of Nations, and its fate would break Woodrow Wilson's heart.

The idealistic Fourteen Points clashed with the punitive terms of the Versailles Treaty. The Allies forced Germany to pay war reparations based on complicated formulas. No one knew how high Germany's bill would go, but estimates put it over $33 billion, an impossible debt to repay. Germany's economy collapsed completely. Britain and France had suffered economically and lost a generation of young men.

The treaty redrew the map of Europe by shrinking Germany and the Austro-Hungarian Empire. From its southern part, joined with the former Serbia and Montenegro, the treaty created Yugoslavia. Romania gained large parts of the empire's eastern territory. Czechoslovakia became a nation, carved out of southwestern Germany and northern Austro-Hungarian territory. The Poles, who had rebelled against Germany in 1918, became an independent country on land formerly in northeastern Germany, as did Lithuania, Latvia, and Estonia. France would occupy the Saar Basin and the

Rhineland, western areas that represented Germany's industrial strength, and it reclaimed Alsace Lorraine, which had been lost to Germany in the Franco-Prussian War.

British and French opposition on the ground in the Middle East thwarted Wilson's efforts to aid leaders there supporting an Arab state amid the crumbling Ottoman Empire. France and Britain simply drew a "line in the sand" and issued mandates that gave France control of Lebanon and Syria and that awarded Britain southern Syria, Iraq, and Palestine. Self-determination did not extend to the Middle East.

Nor did it extend to those hopeful colonial subjects who came to Versailles to lobby for democracy. Ho Chi Minh, a young Vietnamese man who had already lived in New York, Boston, and Paris, lobbied the American delegation for the self-determination of French Indochina. Unsuccessful, he joined the French Communist Party in 1920. W. E. B. Du Bois convened a Pan-African Conference alongside the Versailles talks. Leading African Americans met with colonized people from the Caribbean and the few who attended from Africa. They asked that European African colonies be put under the protection of the League of Nations. Democracy should be introduced gradually, but the pan-Africanists did not seek immediate self-determination. Political leaders at Versailles ignored them, but Du Bois remained hopeful that the league would give people of color an international political voice.

The Treaty of Versailles, the official settlement of the "war to end all wars," planted the seeds of new wars that stretched into the twenty-first century.

The Congressional Debate

Humidity bathed Washingtonians on September 3, 1919, as Woodrow Wilson set out on a twenty-two day, eight-thousand-mile train trip around the United States to persuade Americans to support the League of Nations. His jaunty look—white shoes, white pants, and a white straw boater with a navy blue blazer—masked his worries. He waved goodbye to a few constituents as his train car pulled out of Union Station. Only six years had passed since he had arrived at the same station for what he hoped would be a triumphant arrival as president-elect, only to be greeted by thousands of antagonistic woman suffragists intent on stealing his thunder. This morning he deserved a triumphant departure. He had led the country through the Great War, rescued Europe, and crafted a peace treaty that promised to end all wars.

Wilson could not celebrate, however, because the Senate threatened to scuttle his pride and joy, the Treaty of Versailles and its provision for a League of Nations. Wilson thought that if he took the issue directly to the American people, they would press their senators to ratify the treaty. Popular opinion favored it, but fully one-third of the Senate defied their constituents and called for modification of the treaty.

Senators blocked the treaty for a variety of reasons, and opposition leader Senator Henry Cabot Lodge pounded home their points with a fervor born of his hatred for Wilson. The blueblood Republican "Slim" Lodge thought the treaty to be exceptionally reckless. He believed that Wilson's idealistic venture into statecraft would constrain the United States' ability to defend itself, even as it became entangled in European affairs.

Moreover Lodge argued that the Covenant of the League of Nations, part of the treaty, threatened to limit U.S. interventions in the western hemisphere under the Roosevelt Corollary to the Monroe Doctrine as well as destabilize the country's economic interests abroad. The covenant guaranteed "political independence and territorial integrity to great and small states alike."[52] Lodge wondered if that fool Wilson had forgotten that he had sent troops to occupy independent Haiti in 1915 when unrest threatened American business interests there. The U.S. military still occupied Haiti as the Senate debated a treaty that would have forbade their deployment in the first place.

Lodge feared that when conflict arose in the future, Wilson's league would snatch Roosevelt's big stick out of presidential hands and shuffle the United States off to a diplomatic version of time out: a six month cooling-off period mandated for members in conflict with one another. If, as a league member, the United States chose not to cool off, its only other option was to submit to binding arbitration through the league. Lodge argued that that provision alone would hand over U.S. sovereignty to the forty-four (of a potential forty-six) countries that had already signed the covenant, including thirteen recent enemies during the Great War. Joining the league, in Lodge's view, would eviscerate Congress's right to declare war, as Lodge put it, "without asking anybody's leave."[53]

Alongside Lodge's sovereignty concerns lay the mutual protection pledge in article 10 of the covenant. Members would pledge to "preserve . . . against external aggression the territorial integrity and existing political independence of all Members of the League."[54] Senator Lodge believed that this promise knotted the United States into the center of a web of entangling European alliances.

Finally, the treaty's representation of other nations' sovereignty as inviolate—self-determination as a guiding principle for nation-states— seemed to many senators unworkable. Some thought that certain nations had progressed down the evolutionary track to self-government at a more rapid pace than others, and weak nations needed guidance from more evolved countries such as the United States. The Roosevelt Corollary gave the United States a rationale for sorting out the affairs of its southern neighbors. It seemed to Lodge that smaller and poorer countries needed U.S. direction. When Wilson had called for "self-determination," weak nations, even some colonies, gained hope that they might someday be freed of domination by stronger nations.

During August 1919, Lodge successfully pulled together congressional opposition and demanded changes in the treaty before Senate ratification. Wilson refused to compromise a jot. It had been eighteen months since he had first broached to Congress the idea of a league. After the Paris Peace Conference, he had returned to the United States in July to tell the Senate that it now had the responsibility to maintain the peace through the League of Nations.

Opposition to ratification developed quickly upon Wilson's return and fell into two camps: maybe and never. Lodge led the maybes, a group that would accept the treaty only after amendments—or reservations— modified it. Those twenty senators saw themselves as reservationists. Another fifteen—the irreconcilables—would not ratify under any circumstances. This group included William Borah (R-ID), who had been a strong isolationist before the war, and Robert La Follette (R-WI), who leaned toward pacifism. Many of the irreconcilables were Progressive domestic leaders who loathed the idea of the country becoming contractually embroiled in foreign affairs. David I. Walsh (D-MA) led a group of anti-British Irish Americans who thought the treaty gave Britain too much power because its colonies had equal voting power to sovereign nations such as the United States. Together the reservationists and the irreconcilables, at thirty-five of ninety-six senators, might combine to deprive the treaty of the two-thirds majority required to ratify. First-term senator

Joseph T. Robinson (D-AR) led the ratification forces. The Democrats publicly supported Wilson, but many Democrats from the rural South held secret reservations about article 10.

Campaigning for the League

Wilson had to pull only three or four senators into his camp to get the votes he needed. Perhaps he should have stayed in Washington and tried to win over a few senators, rather than depart on a speaking tour to win over thousands of people. Heady with the power he had gained in world affairs when the United States helped win the war and flush with his vision of himself as peacemaker, Wilson held himself above compromise. Establishing the league had become a missionary undertaking for him, and its promise blinded him to practical politics. He set off to convince the American people of the league's righteousness.

As the capital vanished behind him, Wilson and his wife Edith greeted the twenty journalists and one motion picture cameraman on board the train. His personal secretary, Joseph Tumulty, tightly orchestrated the trip. Wilson expected he would parade into each town, win over local officials, and then give a speech at a large local venue. His appearance, he thought, would personally persuade the thousands in attendance to support ratification, increasing the pressure on their senators back in Washington. Since the league proved the treaty's sticking point, Wilson's speeches focused on the covenant's details.

For all of Tumulty's planning, few showed up that first gray, rainy day in Columbus, Ohio, but the crowds got thicker as the president headed from Indianapolis to St. Louis. There Wilson taunted senators to make good on their promises to enumerate revisions to the treaty; it was a "put up or shut up" speech, the *Chicago Daily Tribune* said.[55] He grew even testier and more combative in Kansas City. By the time he reached Des Moines, the Senate had attached four reservations to the treaty. Wilson denounced them in Omaha on September 8 and in Seattle on the thirteenth.

On September 16, Lodge sent the treaty, with fourteen amendments, to the Senate floor. Lodge's fourteen reservations seemed deliberately to mock Wilson's Fourteen Points. One provided for U.S. withdrawal from the League at any time. Another repudiated the obligation to uphold other members' territory and independence. The amendments declared the United States' right to conduct foreign affairs as it pleased, almost to the point of taunting Europe about the Monroe Doctrine: "said doctrine is to be interpreted by the United States alone and is hereby declared to be wholly outside the jurisdiction of said League of Nations."[56]

The next day enormous crowds turned out for Wilson in San Francisco. He irrationally accused the reservationists and irreconcilables of pro-German sentiment. Leaving California, he told the crowd in Salt Lake City that the "spectre of bolshevism" hung over the Senate. But in the Salt Lake heat, Edith Wilson and Joe Tumulty noticed that he faltered and grasped for words.

In Pueblo, Colorado, on September 25, Wilson complained that he had a splitting headache. It faded as he mounted the podium, where he gave voice to his fury against the Senate and accused unnamed senators of disloyalty to the United States. He stirred up the same fears he had cultivated during the Great War, arguing that someone who extolled his ethnic identity, for example, by calling himself Irish American, was a "man who carries a hyphen around with him." That hyphen amounted to "a dagger that he is ready to plunge into the vitals of this Republic." He would not compromise with reservationists: "We go in on equal terms or we do not go in at all; and if we do not go in, my fellow citizens, think of the tragedy of that result." Treaty ratification and league membership would "lead us, and through us the world, out into pastures of quietness and peace such as the world never dreamed of before."[57] Many in the Pueblo audience cried.

Wilson's Collapse

Wilson's horrible headache returned after the Pueblo speech, and Edith called for the doctor on board. Wilson had probably been suffering transient ischemic attacks—small strokes—and that night he suffered a major stroke. Tumulty reported him as paralyzed on his left side; his doctor thought he might not live through the night. But Wilson could still speak, and he told Tumulty that he would lose the League of Nations if he disrupted the speaking tour. The doctor insisted that he return to Washington. Once there, on September 28, Wilson felt good enough to walk out of Union Station and into a waiting car, but four days later he suffered another stroke, a major incident that left him permanently paralyzed on his left side. Edith Wilson and Joseph Tumulty whisked him from public view. As Wilson recovered a bit, he appeared at ceremonial events and signed bills, but he never again fulfilled a full slate of presidential duties.

Despite his inability to fight robustly for the treaty, Wilson stubbornly urged Democrats to stand firm against amendments. When the Senate rejected it on November 19, even Edith urged him to accept the reservations. He replied, "Little girl, don't you desert me; that I cannot stand. Can't you see I have no moral right to accept any change in a paper I have signed without giving every signatory, even the Germans, the right to do the same thing?"[58] More months of debate followed. Wilson's opposition to amendment resulted in the unusual situation of the Democrats, who supported the treaty without reservations, voting with the irreconcilables to defeat a treaty with amendments. The Senate voted again on March 19, 1920. This time the Democrats voted for it but fell short of the required two-thirds vote. The Senate never ratified the Treaty of Versailles. Seven months later the Norwegian Nobel Committee awarded Wilson the Nobel Peace Prize.

Wilson had given his word to his European counterparts that the United States would ratify the treaty that they had all signed, and that he would brook no changes to it. But Wilson lacked the authority to bind the country to the document, and he lacked the foresight to involve the opposition Republicans in his ambitions for U.S. power abroad or for peace. Ultimately, his resort to the propaganda tour broke his health and killed the faint hope of ratification. Wilson longed to save the world, and he had a worthy cause, but his hubris clouded his vision.

The United States never joined the League of Nations. Twenty-one years later it entered a second world war from which a new United Nations emerged. If Wilson's conception of the president as the arbiter of international affairs failed him, the concept began to appeal to Americans in the coming decades.

CHAPTER 4

PROSPERITY'S PRECIPICE:

THE PARADOXES OF THE 1920S

The day he became an American citizen, June 7, 1918, must have been the proudest day in twenty-two-year-old William Joseph Hushka's life. He recruited two fellow soldiers from Camp Funston in Kansas to witness the ceremony. Hushka would have worn his brand-new private's uniform, since he had enlisted in the army only eight days earlier. With his 1913 arrival in the United States from Russian-occupied Lithuania in mind, he proudly swore to uphold the Constitution of the United States, and he became an American. He had emigrated to join his brother Charles, who had arrived in 1907, and they looked forward to other Lithuanian relatives joining them. In keeping with President Woodrow Wilson's hopes for national self-determination, in February 1918 Lithuania had thrown off Russian rule and declared itself an independent state.

Hushka treasured his freedom enough to fight for his new country, even as he celebrated the liberation of his old one. Private Hushka became a private first class in November 1918, the month the Great War ended. He witnessed from afar Woodrow Wilson's peacemaking efforts at Versailles. In the early fall of 1919, as he worked in a shipyard in Philadelphia, he hoped that the establishment of the League of Nations would allow Lithuania to stay independent, but his new country had troubles enough.

The Great War's aftermath and Wilson's incapacitation contributed to the domestic tumult in 1919. Americans had suffered from an influenza pandemic, spread by troop movements around the country. In 1918 and

1919, 675,000 people died. African Americans who returned from war met white supremacist mobs across the South and in major northern cities determined to subordinate them. Labor demands, pent up during the war, came to the surface, and workers struck for wage gains as inflation gripped the nation. The successful Bolshevik Revolution in Russia sparked fear of domestic Communism, and many saw postwar strikes as Communist-inspired. A series of anarchist bombings contributed to the panic. In the 1919 Red Scare the federal bureaucracy turned from chasing German spies to chasing domestic Communists.

After a chaotic year of rampant inflation and worker protests, economic growth brought prosperity, and prompted the development of a strong consumer culture. Republican Presidents Warren G. Harding and Calvin Coolidge stepped back from the activism of the previous two decades and promoted business expansion as a panacea for lingering problems. The nation embraced "normalcy" and a return to traditional values while curbing immigration and promoting discrimination through a new Ku Klux Klan.[1]

The 1920s marked the decade when Americans became thoroughly modern. New technology brought radios and electronic appliances into homes, and people paid for them on credit. A national entertainment culture developed over the airwaves and in film. Cities grew, and with them new freedoms arose. Women dumped chaperones, shortened their skirts, and frequented nightclubs. African Americans found spaces in northern cities to develop literature, theater, and music that testified to their subordinated past and imagined a "New Negro" with a bright future.

In the late 1920s the dancing stopped to reveal the economic problems of a mature industrial society, unfinished Progressive-era challenges, and a shaky European economy. Following a stock market crash in 1929, the recent prosperity vanished and economic indicators plummeted. As conditions remained dire through 1932, President Herbert Hoover firmly avoided direct governmental interference in the economy. A great debate broke out over the government's role in such a catastrophe, and Democratic presidential candidate Franklin Delano Roosevelt promised to act if elected. Desperate Americans embraced his New Deal, even if they had no idea what it would deliver.

DOMESTIC POLITICS IN THE AFTERMATH
OF THE GREAT WAR

Many in Congress and the attorney general's office interpreted the serious domestic upheavals that rocked the country in 1919 as Socialist or Communist plots. The Espionage and Sedition Acts passed during the Great War gave the government powerful tools to use against dissenters. The Bureau of Intelligence, under Attorney General A. Mitchell Palmer and headed by J. Edgar Hoover, wielded domestic surveillance and repressive measures against protesters. The few Americans who actually became Communists in the period went underground by 1920. That year, in response to the governmental threat to civil liberties, free speech advocates organized the American Civil Liberties Union to protect freedoms guaranteed by the Bill of Rights.

The Red Scare

Black soldiers returned from Europe echoing W. E. B. Du Bois's vow to win civil rights at home: "We return. We return from fighting. We return fighting. Make way for democracy!"[2] But self-determination did not extend to Wilson's America. White men attacked uniformed black servicemen in southern cities, and in Bisbee, Arizona, police attacked the African American Tenth U.S. Cavalry stationed there. Twenty-six riots heated up the summer of 1919.[3] In Elaine, Arkansas, white landowners massacred black sharecroppers who formed a union. In late July in Chicago, a white man stoned a black boy who was swimming in Lake Michigan, and he drowned, prompting days of racial violence during which whites tried to burn down the black neighborhood on Chicago's South Side. Ultimately twenty-three African Americans and fifteen white people died.

Labor trouble erupted as well, as postwar inflation spread and robust wartime employment weakened. Moreover, since the American Federation of Labor had promised not to strike during the war, bottled-up grievances now overflowed. In 1919 one out of every five workers struck, a total of four million people. Coal, steel, and railroad workers walked off their jobs. Thirty-five thousand Seattle shipyard workers, dealing with rising prices and a housing shortage, struck on January 21, 1919. Two weeks later the city's Central Labor Council voted for a general strike—an action for all workers, even those in essential services such as the police—to support the shipyard strikers. Sixty thousand more people went on strike, much to the consternation of AFL president Gompers, who denounced the tactic of the general strike. Seattle mayor Ole Hanson requested federal troops, called the strikers "red revolutionists," and broke the strike in four days.[4] National newspapers warned that the Communists might have started their U.S. revolution in Seattle.

In September the AFL voted for a national steelworkers' strike, after a series of repressive measures by employers the previous spring. Workers struck from Colorado to New York, totaling 50 percent of steelworkers. Most of the more than 350,000 strikers were immigrant workers, who struck for better pay and an eight-hour day. Employers stoked fears of alien influences and Communism and succeeded in turning public opinion against the strike. Native-born workers began to return to work, chafing under charges of anti-Americanism. The strike collapsed in January 1920.

The 1917 Bolshevik Revolution and the subsequent establishment of the Soviet state had unnerved many, who interpreted the Seattle and steel strikes as part of a worldwide Communist revolution. Certainly, the Communists who had formed the new Soviet Union hoped for that result. In March 1919 in Moscow, they established an international organization, the Comintern, to promote revolution abroad. In April a full-blown Red Scare exploded in the United States, beginning on April 28 when a bomb arrived by mail at Mayor Hanson's office in Seattle. A day later a bomb exploded at the home of an anti-immigration senator and mangled the hands of his domestic servant as she opened it. Mail inspectors subsequently found thirty-four more bombs around the nation, including one posted to Attorney General A. Mitchell Palmer. By June the bombers had taken to the streets, and explosions in eight cities killed two people. One device went off in front of Palmer's Washington home.

The perpetrators were not Communists but Italian-born anarchists. Their leader, Luigi Galleani, believed in "propaganda of the deed."[5] He saw killing those who oppressed workers not as murder but as a political act. Unable to fix blame for the bombings, Attorney General Palmer arrested Communists and radicals on the left. Despite the fact that anarchists, not Communists, had mounted the bombing campaign and that actual Communists were few on the ground, Attorney General Palmer used the opportunity to eradicate the fledgling Communist Party in the United States. The Pennsylvanian had been a progressive Democrat in Congress, had supported woman suffrage and legislation against child labor, and had been reluctant to enter the Great War. He believed that fighting Communism fit into his Progressive agenda.

Palmer terrified the nation when he predicted that a Bolshevik Revolution in the United States would take place on May 1, International Workers' Day. When it failed to materialize, people began to suspect that he had exaggerated the danger, but he continued to fight Reds. He raided meetings and headquarters and arrested several hundred radicals without regard for civil liberties. The Alien Act of 1918 gave him the power to deport noncitizens without a trial. In December, he sent 249 radical aliens to the Soviet Union on a ship nicknamed the "Soviet Ark."

Palmer's right-hand man, twenty-four-year-old J. Edgar Hoover, had worked during the war deporting suspicious aliens, and afterward he took over the General Intelligence Agency within the Bureau of Investigation. Hoover believed African Americans were especially vulnerable to radical recruitment. From the start, he amalgamated racism and anti-Communism. The press asked, "Have the Blacks turned Red?"[6]

By 1920, 591 people had been deported, five duly elected Socialists had been expelled from the New York state legislature, and the two competing Communist Parties had gone underground. Hoover's surveillance of black activists and left-wing groups would continue for more than fifty years. Galleani's bombs, instead of fulfilling his anarchist ambitions, helped make the domestic intelligence measures of the Great War a permanent part of the federal government. Those Americans who considered Palmer and Hoover's tactics unconstitutional built on a small wartime organization that protested the Espionage and Sedition Acts, and in 1920 they founded the American Civil Liberties Union. Headed by Roger Baldwin, a young Progressive social worker, members worked to shore up the Bill of Rights' guarantees of free speech, a free press, the right to assemble, and fair judicial procedures.

The fervor for change and the confidence in the country's competence that had defined Progressivism suffered under the Red Scare. Some Progressive tides began to recede; for example, unions lost two million workers in the early 1920s. Socialists, who had been comfortably elected to office in many places across the country, now became castigated as Communists, ending the Socialist Party's hope of playing a viable political role in the United States. Civil liberties sustained repeated blows. The most American of impulses—the urge to work within a democratic society to change it—could now be portrayed as anti-American.

The Nineteenth Amendment and the States

By 1919 the nation's new concerns about radicalism made enfranchising native-born white women less controversial than ever. National American Woman Suffrage Association president Carrie Chapman Catt had kept her prewar deal with Wilson to curtail suffrage activity and diverted the organization's resources to war efforts. In June Wilson then kept his promise and supported congressional passage of the Nineteenth Amendment, enfranchising women. Wyoming ratified the Susan B. Anthony Amendment first, and most northern and western state legislatures followed quickly. But by July 1920 it stalled as legislators in states of the former Confederacy adamantly opposed it. These whites-only state governments had disfranchised black men, and many white men feared that a woman suffrage amendment would direct federal scrutiny to their voting rights restrictions. Some argued that enfranchising women would bring black women to the polls, soon to be followed by black men. Ten southern states either tabled the amendment or voted outright against it. By August 1920 thirty-five states outside the region had approved.

Ratification would take one more state, and that state would have to come from the solid South. After North Carolina tabled the amendment in early August, ratification depended on the Tennessee state legislature. Debate raged for weeks in the capital city of Nashville as roses scented the air. Suffrage supporters wore yellow roses. Antisuffragists poured into the city wearing red roses, many of them Tennessee whiskey lobbyists who deplored women's temperance campaigns.

Spectators in the Tennessee house chamber watching the amendment debate probably noticed three things about State Representative Harry Thomas Burn: he wore a red rose, he looked like a teenager (as the youngest member of the general assembly, at twenty-four), and he was handsome. But no onlooker could have discerned his emotional agony on August 18, 1920. Twice, a motion to table the amendment came up, and twice Burn voted to table. Both votes resulted in a 48-to-48 deadlock. Burn felt guiltier with each vote. He could feel in his pocket the crumpled letter that he had received the night before from his suffragist mother back home in the tiny railroad junction of Niota.

Dear Son, . . . Hurray and vote for Suffrage and don't keep them in doubt. I noticed Chandlers' speech, it was very bitter. I've been waiting to see how you stood but have not seen anything yet. . . . Don't forget to be a good boy and help Mrs. Catt with her "Rats." Is she the one that put rat in ratification, Ha! No more from mama this time. With lots of love, Mama.[7]

After the two deadlocked votes to table the amendment, the antisuffragists believed they had enough votes to kill it and introduced a motion calling the question: an up-or-down vote for or against suffrage. Burn realized that he might be able to explain to his widowed suffragist mother why he had voted to table the amendment, but he could never explain to her voting against it. His antisuffragist red rose would die tomorrow; his mother's disappointment would live forever. Burn, still wearing the red rose, voted for the Susan B. Anthony Amendment, and it passed 49 to 47. As he explained the next day, "I knew that a mother's advice is always safest for her boy to follow."[8] With his single vote, American women won the right to vote.

The Embrace of Mediocrity

As the nation recovered from the Red Scare and adjusted to the close call that resulted in the enfranchisement of women, the 1920 presidential election loomed. Wilson's health continued to fail, and he played a negligible role in the selection of the Democratic candidate. Left without a prominent leader, the Democrats nominated James M. Cox, a loyal Ohio congressman who had supported signing the Treaty of Versailles. A thirty-seven-year-old New Yorker, Franklin Delano Roosevelt, joined the ticket as the vice-presidential candidate. The Republicans had no obvious presidential candidate. Theodore Roosevelt had died brokenhearted on January 6, 1919, six months after he learned of the death of his youngest son Quentin, a World War I aviator, shot down behind German lines.

The Republicans nominated an obscure man from Marion, Ohio, Warren Gamaliel Harding. He owned the local newspaper there, and none of his neighbors thought him to be smart or ambitious. But he had married a smart woman, Florence Kling DeWolfe, whose father loathed him. Perhaps the old man hated him because rumor had it that Harding was part African American—not such a far-fetched story, as many "white" Ohioans had once been "black," passing over the color line when the state harbored escaped slaves. Or perhaps his wife's father disliked Harding's gambling or his heavy drinking. Or he might have heard of Harding's mistresses, who appear to have been numerous. Whatever the source of his dislike for Warren, Florence's father did not speak to the couple for eight years. Florence Harding ran the newspaper and touted her husband's capabilities. She made him run for Senate; after he won, he was absent as much as he was present.

After the tumult of war and the massive social and political change of the Progressive era, by 1920 voters seemed to want peace and quiet. Harding promised both in his call for "a return to normalcy." He intoned, "America's present need is not heroics, but healing; not nostrums but normalcy; not revolution, but restoration." Normalcy, according to Harding, was not "the old order, but a regular steady order of things."[9] The Republican Harding beat his fellow Ohioan Cox, winning over 66 percent of the national vote.

Republicans found it easy to win elections in the 1920s despite weak candidates. A decade of economic growth brought many urban families abundance unknown to their parents. Rising wages, credit buying, and domestic labor-saving devices lulled Americans into complacency. The ratification of the Eighteenth Amendment in 1919 that mandated Prohibition had settled one of the major issues that had long divided the wet Democrats and the dry Republicans. The ratification of woman suffrage in 1920 had settled another. Most voters, weary of war, grew more isolationist in the wake of the League of Nations debacle.

In lieu of pressing issues, voters' party affiliations, which were often based on their cultural and religious identities, remained as they had been since the Civil War. Republicans commanded the majority of the electorate. They tended to be Protestant, descended from native-born parents, traditional, and middle or upper class; they outnumbered the Catholics, new immigrants, radicals, white southerners, and working-class people who voted Democratic at the polls. Immigrants in urban enclaves worked through ethnic power brokers rather than through grassroots involvement in party politics and tended to vote Democratic. Of course, some issues crossed party lines. While many working-class Catholics in the North and West joined the Democratic Party, southern Democrats were as anti-Catholic as any midwestern Republican. People in both parties supported immigration restriction.[10] After 1921 political participation fell dramatically as northern legislatures followed southern ones and approved the use of literacy tests to dissuade new citizens from voting.

Poker Politics

If Republican popularity outside the South ensured Harding's election, the man himself quickly disclaimed his capability for the job: "I don't seem to grasp that I'm President."[11] He appointed his gambling buddies to responsible positions and held weekly poker games in the White House. Some called his cronies the poker cabinet. Now that he was in the public eye, keeping two mistresses seemed dangerous, so he would just have one. The Republicans sent one to Japan and moved the other to Washington. Rumors of an illegitimate daughter swirled up and down Pennsylvania Avenue, but neither the mistresses nor the offspring became general public knowledge.

Harding's friends proceeded to enrich themselves illegally. Charles R. Forbes, director of the Veterans Administration (VA), took a personal cut from the sale of VA hospital supplies stockpiled during the war. Harding demanded his resignation but allowed him to escape prosecution. Two private companies bribed Albert Fall, the secretary of the interior, for leases of oil rights on national parkland at Teapot Dome, Wyoming. Traveling in Alaska and California in the summer of 1923, Harding dodged reports of corruption in his administration. In San Francisco on August 2, he dropped dead.

As Vice President Calvin Coolidge assumed office, politicians predicted, "Teapot Dome is going to be a heavy load for Mr. Coolidge to carry."[12] Coolidge seemed a ghost beside the colorful Harding. Born in Plymouth, Vermont, he had gone to Amherst College and made a career as a lawyer and public official in Massachusetts. He had been governor before becoming vice president, and he believed that the best government was small government. Famous for breaking a police strike in Boston, Coolidge was deemed by voters a law-and-order candidate, capable of curtailing the sort of labor trouble that had disrupted Seattle. After his unelected year as president, Coolidge accepted the Republican nomination in 1924. His Democratic opponent, John William Davis from West Virginia, lacked public recognition and won only 29 percent of the vote.

AFFLUENCE AND ITS DISCONTENTS

The country's industrial infrastructure had matured by 1920, manpower needs slacked, and factory jobs increasingly demanded skilled labor.

With states disfranchising recent immigrants, the federal government now decided to restrict immigration, hoping to eliminate certain nationalities altogether. Congressman Albert Johnson (R-WA) and Senator David Reed (R-PA) sponsored a bill to mold the rest of the nation to their own "Anglo Saxon" images. The Immigration Act of 1924 reflected the mature labor market as well as the anti-alien wartime hysteria and fears of working-class radicalism. As Senator Ellison DuRant Smith (D-SC) put it, "The time has arrived when we should shut the door. We have been called the melting pot of the world . . . we had allowed influences to enter our borders that were about to melt the pot in place of us being the melting pot."[13]

Immigration "Reform"

William Joseph Hushka would have disagreed with Ellison DuRant Smith. In 1920 Hushka moved from Philadelphia to Chicago, where he joined his brother Charles as a butcher in a Chicago meat market. The Hushkas lived on a block with only a few native-born neighbors. Soon he met seventeen-year-old Frances, a fellow Lithuanian American. The next year, as he held their daughter, Loretta, in his arms, Hushka had every reason to believe that his adopted country would make good on the promising future that he imagined for their family. When Loretta was three, Congress shut the door on her European relatives.

The Immigration Act of 1924 incorporated the latest thinking from a strain of pseudoscience known as eugenics. Eugenicists argued that character was inheritable and that some ethnicities had evolved more slowly than others. At the Carnegie Institute for Experimental Evolution in Cold Spring Harbor, New York, scientists maintained a Eugenics Record Office to trace traits they believed were hereditary, such as "feeble mindedness" and mental illness. Congressmen relied on the Cold Spring scientists and on Madison Grant's 1916 book *The Passing of the Great Race* to draft the legislation. New York attorney Grant had imbibed William Graham Sumner's Social Darwinism at Yale. Grant, not surprisingly an Anglo-Saxon himself, grouped the Anglo-Saxons along with other northern Europeans into a category called the Nordic races. He believed that southern European Catholics would soon outnumber Nordic Protestants in the United States. Senator DuRant Smith praised Grant's book and stated, "Thank God we have in America perhaps the largest percentage of any country in the world of the pure, unadulterated Anglo-Saxon stock."[14] Eugenics reached its high tide in the mid-1920s in the United States, and its ideas greatly influenced Adolf Hitler.

White supremacists in the South found vindication in eugenics and saw their regimes as models for good government elsewhere. For example, in 1924 Virginia passed the Racial Integrity Act, prohibiting marriage between a white person and anyone descended from an African American or a Native American. When some elite Virginians protested that they descended from Pocahontas and English colonizer John Rolfe, the General Assembly passed an amendment allowing intermarriage if someone had *less* than one-sixteenth Indian blood. A state functionary policed all this, busily trying to determine if a bride or groom's great-grandmother had been a Chickahominy. Thus northeastern Republicans who wanted to limit immigration by national origin found bipartisan support in southern Democrats.

The Immigration Act of 1924 limited the total number of immigrants who could annually enter the United States. It followed the precedent of the Chinese Exclusion Act of 1882 but went much further. It reached back to 1890, before large numbers of southern and eastern Europeans had arrived (indeed, before William Hushka had arrived from Lithuania), to calculate the ideal ethnic makeup of Americans. The yearly immigration quota would be no more than 2 percent of what the U.S. total for each nationality had been in 1890. Congress hoped that the law would freeze ethnic composition at least at 1924 levels and perhaps gradually return the country to the more homogenously Nordic days of 1890. The law did not limit immigration within the western hemisphere, however, because huge Californian agribusinesses lobbied to maintain a seasonal Mexican labor force.

The chart below demonstrates the effect of the law. Asia did not even get a separate category—it is subsumed under "All Others" and limited to 1,900 people annually, cutting off most of the exceptions to the Chinese Exclusion Act. Moreover, the law drastically cut southern and eastern European immigration. Four million Italians had entered the United States from 1880 to 1900, followed by another two million between 1900 and 1920. Now fewer than 4,000 Italians could enter in any year. Some 540,000 Greeks had immigrated to the United States between 1890 and 1924. Under the new law, one hundred would be admitted each year.

THE IMMIGRATION ACT OF 1924

Northwest Europe & Scandinavia	Quota	Eastern & Southern Europe	Quota	Other Countries	Quota
Germany	51,227	Poland	5,982	Africa (other than Egypt)	1,100
Great Britain and Northern Ireland	34,007	Italy	3,845	Armenia	124
Irish Free State (Ireland)	28,567	Czechoslovakia	3,073	Australia	121
Sweden	9,561	Russia	2,248	Palestine	100
Norway	6,453	Yugoslavia	671	Syria	100
France	3,954	Romania	603	Turkey	100
Denmark	2,789	Portugal	503	Egypt	100
Switzerland	2,081	Hungary	473	New Zealand & Pacific Islands	100
Netherlands	1,648	Lithuania	344	All others	1,900
Austria	785	Latvia	142		
Belgium	512	Spain	131		
Finland	471	Estonia	124		
Free City of Danzig	228	Albania	100		
Iceland	100	Bulgaria	100		
Luxembourg	100	Greece	100		
Total (Number)	**142,483**	**Total (Number)**	**18,439**	**Total (Number)**	**3,745**
Total (%)	**86.5**	**Total (%)**	**11.2**	**Total (%)**	**2.3**

(Total Annual immigrant quota: 164,667)

Source: *Statistical Abstract of the United States* (Washington, D.C.: Government Printing Office, 1929), 100.

The 344 Lithuanians who would be allowed into the country in any given year could probably have all fit into a single dance hall in William Hushka's southwest Chicago neighborhood.

A National Ku Klux Klan

As some white Americans worried about the rising tide of color, they joined the recently revived Ku Klux Klan. The 1915 Atlanta-based reincarnation of the Reconstruction Klan swept the nation, adding anti-Catholicism and anti-Semitism to its program of racial hatred. The second Klan incorporated the violence and racism of the first but focused on ethnic and religious differences and a broad fear of cultural change.

The new Ku Klux Klan found the old Midwest to be particularly fertile recruiting ground. Middle-class families embraced the KKK's slogan, "America for Americans." More than half a million women joined, hoping to gain power over errant husbands and community morality in small-town America. Divorce was on the rise, even in the conservative South, and after Prohibition the illegal use of alcohol abounded. Men who had belonged to the Justice Department's American Protective League during the Great War now used the Klan as a sort of action-packed voluntary association to advocate 100 percent Americanism. Many Democratic politicians embraced the KKK as an organization that exercised local moral authority.

Despite its "Invisible Empire" tagline, the modern KKK operated in public view. On a hot July 4 in Kokomo, Indiana, in 1923, more than 100,000 people drove their flag-draped family cars to Melfalfa Park for a rally; some had traveled across the country.[15] A welcoming cadre of eight hundred men and women in purple-hooded Klan robes cheered as a small plane circled the park bearing the letters "KKK" on its underside. Upon landing, the Grand Dragon for the Invisible Empire for the Realm of Indiana, David Curtiss Stephenson, alighted and announced, "It grieves me to be late. The President of the United States kept me unduly long counseling upon vital matters of state."[16] The crowd gasped at hearing how powerful their leader was; it did not seem to dawn on them that President Harding was in Alaska that day, not in Washington. At that moment almost a third of Kokomo's residents belonged to the Klan. By Thanksgiving, Indiana claimed 350,000 members, more than any other state. Four million joined nationwide.[17]

Certainly the KKK despised African Americans, but it also focused its efforts on stripping political, moral, and civic power from Catholics, Jews, and recent immigrants whom it believed were "trying to control the country."[18] The Klan developed cells in western Canada to discourage Catholic and African American immigration, and it spread to Mexico and even to New Zealand.[19] The export provoked international criticism of American racism. A Japanese newspaper declared, "Lynching is possible in the United States because the spirit of America is in favor it. If this were not true, this foul crime would never have grown to its present proportions."[20] U.S. Klansmen founded Der Deutsche Orden des Feurigen Kreuzes (The German Order of the Fiery Cross) in Berlin in 1925, but the mainstream German press condemned its members as "ill-balanced and romantic youths."[21]

The United States seemed ripe for a version of the fascism that would soon grip Europe, but instead the Klan began to self-destruct. Indiana's Grand Dragon Stephenson proved to be an emotionally disturbed and power-hungry man who kidnapped, raped, and mutilated a young woman. She poisoned herself to escape him. Convicted of second-degree murder, from prison Stephenson began releasing proof that the KKK had bribed Indiana state officials. Politicians everywhere distanced themselves from the KKK. Its membership had dwindled to thirty thousand by 1930, but hatred continued to smolder in those ashes.

A Fundamentalist Turn

Religious fundamentalism attracted people in rural communities and urban settings who yearned for tradition in rapidly changing times. Millions read *The Fundamentals: A Testimony to the Truth*, a collection of essays published from 1910 to 1915 that argued that the Bible taught unchanging truths. Essays such as "The Certainty and Importance of the Bodily Resurrection of Jesus Christ from the Dead" demanded a literal understanding of the Bible, not to be challenged by science, technology, or culture.[22] Fundamentalism appealed to members of certain Protestant denominations, such as the Baptists, who had always followed strict scriptural interpretations. The Pentecostal and Holiness sects, new branches of Protestantism that emerged after 1900, combined fundamentalism with the belief that God's spirit entered people and caused them to speak in tongues: to burst forth in unrecognizable language when the Spirit baptized them. Emotive, inclusive, nonhierarchical, and racially integrated, Pentecostal and Holiness churches grew rapidly in the 1920s, particularly among the poor and working class.

Taking the Bible literally meant believing all of it—for example, that the world was built in seven days. For decades many people had been privately skeptical of Charles Darwin's evolutionary theory in *On the Origin of Species*, published in 1859. But now fundamentalism posed the choice in stark terms: if one accepted the Bible, then one could not allow teaching evolution to one's children. Five southern states outlawed the teaching of evolution by 1925. In that year the Dayton, Tennessee, high school football coach and science teacher John Thomas Scopes agreed to mount a legal challenge to his state's ban. Dayton businessmen chose him for the test not because he was a crusading rebel fighting the antiscience forces of darkness but because he was an amiable and modern young man. Their goal was to test the law's constitutionality and to prove that their city was forward-looking. Scopes could not remember what he had said in class about evolution.

William Jennings Bryan, the old Populist and Democrat, brought his personal fundamentalist views to court as an attorney for the state. Clarence Darrow, America's greatest trial lawyer and civil libertarian, represented Scopes. The trial took place during a hot spell, and Bryan and Darrow soaked their shirts with sweat and fanned themselves after arguments. Bryan reduced evolution to the claim that humans were descended directly from monkeys, a common misinterpretation of Darwin's argument. The rest of the nation mocked the ignorant hillbillies who banned the teaching of evolution. The understanding gap was not only geographical, educational, and religious; it was generational as well. Tennessee grandmas told their grandchildren that while *they* might believe they were descended from monkeys, their grandmas certainly were not. The jury convicted Scopes for teaching evolution, but the trial slowed the trend to ban it. Fifteen states had pending legislation to do so, but only Arkansas and Mississippi passed bans. William Jennings Bryan dropped dead five days after the trial ended. He had always stood for rural folks against city slickers, for the farm versus the corporation, and for the power of simplicity over complexity.

The Balm of Prosperity and the People's Entertainment

An upsurge of prosperity in the mid-1920s dissipated much of the yearning for prewar normalcy. Since 1914 the cost of living and wages had both risen dramatically, but for three heady years, from mid-1925 to mid-1928, wages rose faster than living costs, giving employees more disposable income than ever before.[23] Simultaneously, average working hours began falling, affording families more leisure time to spend their money. Consumer goods got cheaper, and with credit, working families could afford durable goods such as new electric appliances. By 1929 half of all families owned an automobile. Housing construction boomed, and for the first time, average Americans began investing in the soaring stock market, blinded to risk. The Progressive era's reforms seemed to have produced a system in which labor and capital could cooperate. One Harvard economist called the new economic situation "our peaceful revolution."[24]

Part of this revolution was the extension of credit to workers. In the past, without collateral, lenders did not routinely extend credit to wage laborers because they could be fired or laid off. Now stores selling consumer goods encouraged the housewife to put a down payment on a new stove, take it home, and pay a small amount each month on the installment plan. This sort of credit grew out of the automobile industry in the 1910s, when Henry Ford realized that he could sell more cars by making them affordable through installment buying. Of course, installment plans charged interest, but by the mid-1920s almost everyone expected sustained employment and higher earnings each year. The system purported to be a serendipitous loop: if workers purchased more goods, factories could produce more, earn more, and employ more. The image of the robber baron and bloated plutocrat receded, and the businessman emerged as an American hero on a patriotic mission. Calvin Coolidge put it this way: "After all, the chief business of the American people is business. They are profoundly concerned with producing, buying, selling, investing and prospering in the world."[25] In late 1926 the president of the National Automobile Chamber of Commerce attributed the record boom year for auto purchases to credit and argued, "It is sound economics to provide credit facilities for the consumer as for the producer." He compared credit buying to a forced savings plan.[26]

Of course, some observers discouraged the consumer binge and condemned the credit system that fueled it. One critic argued that hitherto people had borrowed money only to invest in something that would make them more money, like the farmer who takes a loan for a tractor that helps produce more crops to sell. Now people borrowed money not to produce but to consume goods that would generate no revenue. Credit buying was a bet on the future that would come due over time. The critic concluded that "building production through an artificial stimulation of consumption can not be permanent."[27] Easy credit led manufacturers into overproduction because they expected an ever-growing consumer base. And it led consumers to spend money they did not have. But by 1926 there was already a sign that the bill might be coming due: used car sales equaled those of new cars, casting a shadow over this key industry.

In their newfound leisure time, Americans increasingly listened to the radio, beginning with the first broadcast from Pittsburgh's KDKA in 1920. That year there were four radio stations in the entire country, but by 1922 there were 600. A radio in a standing case could cost $150, and stores sold them on the installment plan. But many people bought or built cheaper, less powerful, sets. By 1930, 12 million homes had radios. People in the other 18 million homes crowded into their neighbors' living rooms or rocked on their front porches at night listening to drama, music, and comedy broadcast by 50,000-watt stations with amazing range. Even smaller stations had reach: San Francisco's KERC, a 50-watt station, broadcast live jazz performances that New Zealanders could listen to. When Chicago's WLS broadcast the Art Kahn's Orchestra's "Lucky Kentucky," Nebraskans and North Carolinians danced in step.

Radio created a space for new religious leaders to reach wide audiences. Preachers with good radio voices founded their own churches and broadcast their message across the country. In 1923 Aimee Semple McPherson founded the International Church of the Foursquare Gospel in Los Angeles, which drew a congregation of ten thousand; she then took her message of faith healing and personal miracles to the airwaves. She supported William Jennings Bryan during the Scopes Trial, married three times, and faked her own kidnapping, none of which diminished her radio following in the 1920s.

In 1925 movie theaters sold 50 million tickets each week, equivalent to 40 percent of the U.S. population. Luxurious cinemas sprang up to dazzle moviegoers on and off the screen. In 1927 in Los Angeles, Sid Grauman opened the extravagant Chinese Theatre with 2,258 seats. When a silent screen actress accidentally stepped in the wet concrete on the sidewalk out front, a tradition was born. He invited the biggest stars to leave a handprint, footprint, or signature in cement on what became the Hollywood Walk of Fame. Mickey Mouse, born in 1928, could do none of those things, but on his fiftieth birthday in 1978, he became the first animated character awarded a star on the Walk of Fame.

Los Angeles provided space and good weather for filming, and in 1919 the star Charlie Chaplin built his own studio there in an orange grove. He produced major hits that spanned the era from silent films to sound, from *The Kid* in 1921 to *The Great Dictator* in 1940. In 1930 twenty studios produced hundreds of films each year. Hollywood's Warner Bros. Studio introduced sound in cinema in 1926, and spoken dialogue with *The Jazz Singer*. The script centered on a Jewish immigrant who broke with his family to pursue a career as a jazz pianist. Al Jolson starred in the talkie, which was still largely silent, except for six songs and three hundred words. In the final scene, Jolson appeared in blackface, heavy black makeup with white lipstick that white stage actors regularly used to impersonate African Americans to sing "Mother of Mine, I Still Have You." At the time African Americans rarely appeared in white-produced films; black characters were played by white actors in blackface. Black performers endured the obvious racist connotations of Jolson's use of blackface because he fought segregation and pioneered hiring black actors in film.

A segregated movie industry grew up as well, and the Hollywood Production Code banned the depiction of interracial couples. The first black talkie was King Vidor's *Hallelujah*, which proved by its meager box office receipts that whites were uninterested in realistic movies with all-black casts. However, they flocked to films that portrayed the black grotesque, such as the 1933 *The Emperor Jones*, in which singer and actor Paul Robeson plays a Pullman porter and murderer who escapes to the Caribbean and sets himself up as an emperor. Black film producer Oscar Micheaux's thirty-nine films spanned the silent-talkie divide and starred African Americans. In segregated balconies and black-owned theaters, African Americans watched black heroes in action.

A NATION ON THE MOVE

Prosperity in America's cities drew migrants from farms and small towns. Despite the curb on immigration, the nation's largest cities grew, and the country's population moved north and west. In 1925 more than 17 million cars crisscrossed the country on improved state highways, the result of a Good Roads Movement that began in 1916. The necessity of moving troops and matériel during the Great War encouraged federal highway legislation to aid states in building macadam roads. Cities sometimes used concrete to pave roads, and in more remote rural areas, even a graded gravel road represented an improvement. For southern African Americans, the growth of northern and western cities promised opportunity, and the pace of the Great Migration quickened.

Urbanizing America

Western cities gained population at the expense of older eastern metropolises. Philadelphia, the nation's third-largest city in 1930, peaked at 1.9 million that year and then began to lose population. In the 1930s cities like Cleveland, Pittsburgh, and Boston shrank as well. Small towns such as Albuquerque, at 15,000 in 1920, grew 75 percent to 26,000 by 1930. Dallas grew from almost 159,000 to 269,000 in the same period.

Los Angeles, the nation's thirty-sixth largest city in 1900, became the fifth largest by 1930, with 1.2 million people. After Los Angeles annexed the San Fernando Valley in 1915, the city spread eastward, and new highways enabled it to sprawl farther. The Mulholland Highway, built in 1924, made it easier for suburbanites in the Hollywood Hills to commute. The city core faded as a focal point, as merchants began to build satellite stores in suburbs like Bel Air.

Western cities such as Denver benefited from new technology that connected them to the rest of the nation. Engineers could now tunnel through what had seemed to be impossible obstacles, including the Rocky Mountains. In 1928 the city of Denver completed the Moffat Tunnel to bring it 176 miles closer to the Pacific by rail. But the connectors with the greatest potential in the West were the new passenger airlines and airports. By the late 1920s the wood and fabric boxlike frames of Great War aircraft gave way to molded wooden fuselages, then to metal frames in the early 1930s. Boise, Idaho, opened an airport in 1926, and the airline that flew out of it became United Airlines. Denver built what it claimed was the best airport in the West in 1929. Los Angeles began operations at what is now LAX in 1930. By 1932, 474,000 people flew annually. A young pilot from Minnesota, Charles Lindbergh, set the record for a cross-country flight from Los Angeles to New York in 1930: fourteen hours and forty-five minutes.

New York, Chicago, Detroit, and their suburbs continued to grow. New York expanded from 5.5 million people in 1920 to almost 7 million by 1930. Chicago added almost a million people, bringing its numbers to 3.4 million. Detroit went from just under 1 million to 1.5 million. Parkways took New York's middle class to their homes in Scarsdale and on Long Island, and buses sped commuters to the city's other boroughs. Brooklyn, annexed in 1898, gained more than a half-million residents in the 1920s, many traveling on the subway lines that opened in 1915. New York improved and extended those lines throughout the 1920s. Detroit built an eight-lane highway to Pontiac, twenty-four miles away, and auto executives drove to work on it in forty minutes. Even small southern towns experienced rapid growth, as African Americans and poor white people abandoned rural areas and fled sharecropping.

As middle-class families began to move out of central cities into suburbs, immigrants who had arrived in the 1910s and early 1920s moved into their former homes. Clustered in particular neighborhoods, Irish, Italian, Polish, and African American families found some autonomy and political power by electing their own ward representatives. Urban politicians brokered contracts, protected constituents from the larger city, and often tolerated or participated in bribery and business favoritism.

These neighborhoods sometimes became incubators for organized crime. The ratification of the Prohibition amendment in 1919 did not dampen Americans' appetite for alcohol. Making illegal alcohol available to thirsty consumers was a crime that some considered worth the risk. Many ethnic cultures embraced social drinking, but now the beer garden and pub were illegal. Gambling offered not only excitement but also hope. Organized crime seemed to provide a path to power and employment for urban young men. In Chicago a study of the leaders of crime organizations in the late 1920s found 31 percent to be Italian, 29 percent Irish, 20 percent Jewish, and 12 percent African American.[28] Organized crime produced national networks and bosses. The gangster Al Capone started in Chicago as a bootlegger, a person who made illegal alcohol, and made a tax-free fortune with his distribution network.

The Great Migration quickened in the 1920s. New York's black population more than doubled during the decade, from 152,000 to 328,000. Chicago's did as well, counting 109,500 African Americans in 1920 and 234,000 ten years later. Detroit had roughly 41,000 African Americans at the beginning of the decade and 120,066 at the end. In that single decade, more than 700,000 southern African Americans left the South. They moved to find jobs, to escape Jim Crow and its violence, and because their kin had moved before them. When they arrived in northern cities, they settled among other African Americans, often near family members and church congregations that included neighbors from home.

Tensions between immigrant communities and African American neighborhoods ran high. Lithuanian-born William Joseph Hushka lived in southwest Chicago during the decade when 125,000 African Americans moved into the city, many settling on the South Side, in a neighborhood adjacent to his. Segregation existed in the North, often enforced by covenants in deeds that forbade a white person to sell a home to a black person. African Americans set up businesses and professional services, such as barbershops, funeral homes, and law firms that served their communities. Black women's clubs, NAACP branches, and YMCAs developed. A new organization, the Urban League, helped migrants find jobs and learn how to fit into city life in places like New York's Harlem, which was becoming African American.

At Home Abroad: Garveyism

As African Americans abandoned the South, some looked even farther away to find freedom. Echoing Woodrow Wilson's principle of self-determination, many hoped for the liberation of Africa from European rule. Some hoped for the chance to live in a free African country, where they could create their own nation. In 1916 a twenty-nine-year-old Jamaican, Marcus Mosiah Garvey, arrived in New York determined to provide that opportunity. As a racial separatist and pan-African nationalist, he inspired the largest mass movement in black U.S. history in 1914 when he founded the Universal Negro Improvement Association and African Communities (Imperial) League (UNIA). Everything that Garvey proposed—from his African vision to the uniforms that he created for members—was as elaborate as the movement's name. By the early 1920s there were seven hundred UNIA branches in thirty-eight states, and 200,000 subscribed to the organization's newspaper. Black nationalistic schemes and organizations had been a strand of African American political thought since 1817, but no one had previously built such a mass movement.

From New York, Garvey accused NAACP leaders like W. E. B. Du Bois, who fought segregation, of perpetrating "a scheme to destroy the Negro race" through integrating African Americans into white American life.[29] He despised the idea of racial intermarriage and argued that black progress would be limited until an African republic could protect members of the African diaspora abroad. Subsequently black Americans could point to African democratic success, use African diplomacy, and if they met with failure in Indiana or Iowa, return to their home country, as Italian and Irish

Americans did. The UNIA's "Declaration of Rights of Negro Peoples of the World" echoed Wilson's Fourteen Points: "by the principle of Europe for the Europeans and Asia for the Asiatics; we also demand Africa for the Africans at home and abroad."[30]

Poor and working-class black people flocked to the UNIA. Twenty thousand Garveyites marched boldly down Harlem streets in 1920 while others met more quietly in Houston barbershops. Garvey established scores of branches in Central America, in the Caribbean, and in Africa itself. He sold stock in his steamship company, the Black Star Line, which owned three ships to take emigrants to Africa. Some African Americans thought the UNIA misled people into turning their backs on the United States to pursue an elusive dream of repatriation. Among UNIA's few white allies were Ku Klux Klan members who shared its philosophy of racial separatism.

The federal government examined the UNIA's records and found that funds had been diverted to other business ventures that enriched Garvey personally. Attorney General A. Mitchell Palmer began investigating Garvey in 1919, and the Harding administration successfully prosecuted him for mail fraud in 1923. Garvey served four years of a five-year sentence and was deported to Jamaica upon release. The movement splintered as Garvey later tried to lead it from London, but its nationalistic ideas inspired a generation of African Americans who felt excluded from the mostly middle-class NAACP, the radicalism of the Communist Party, and white labor unions. The idea that Africa should be free of European rule became mainstream by the 1940s, and the UNIA left a legacy of black nationalism that radicals tapped into during the civil rights movement of the 1950s and 1960s.

The Harlem Renaissance

African Americans gained grassroots political power within the established black neighborhoods in northern cities, where they could register and vote. With the ratification of woman suffrage in 1920, black women became a political force in their own right. Harlemite Bessye Bearden, who had migrated with her family from North Carolina in 1914, organized a Democratic women's club, and local white politicians rewarded her with a government position in the Internal Revenue Service. In Chicago, Ida B. Wells-Barnett's Alpha Suffrage Club went from organizing for suffrage to organizing for black candidates. In 1929 with Wells-Barnett's help, Oscar de Priest (R-IL) became the first black person elected to Congress from a nonsouthern state and the first black man elected to Congress in the twentieth century.

Congressman de Priest's family history illustrates the causes of the Great Migration and its effects on northern politics. His family had fled Florence, a small place on the Tennessee River in Alabama's red clay hills. A rough town, Florence had been scarred by divided loyalties in the Civil War, with violence always at a simmer. Just a decade before the de Priests left, three black men had been lynched there after whites accused them of burning down the white female academy. The city fathers left their bodies hanging for a week. Rising racial animosity persuaded the de Priests to leave the South in 1877 for Dayton, Ohio.

Their migration pattern fit that of many other black families who went first to nearby larger cities, then to northern urban areas. Oscar de Priest moved to Chicago in 1889, where he became a real estate baron as black southern migrants poured into the city. Chicago had a ward system, and the predominantly black second ward elected de Priest its alderman in 1915. De Priest's local power persuaded the mayor to appoint him to a vacant congressional seat in 1928, and in 1929 he won election to Congress.

In the North, African Americans found the cultural opening to write, perform, and make art. Dubbed, somewhat misleadingly, the *Harlem* Renaissance, an efflorescence of artistic production resulted from the heady freedom that northern urban life afforded young African Americans. The renaissance was not confined to Harlem. In Chicago, Detroit, Los Angeles, and every city of size in between, black artists and writers inscribed a "New Negro": assertive, brilliant, creative, and full of hope about the future while drawing on the black folk tradition.

The folk music of black southerners would soon take the nation by storm. The year the de Priests left Florence, Alabama, William Christopher Handy was two years old. His parents always kept time from the seminal event in their lives, Lee's surrender to Grant, so he knew he was born "eight years after the surrender" in 1873. Handy first made music by standing behind his uncle while he fiddled, reaching over his left shoulder, and beating time across the violin strings. Handy rubbed a nail over a dead horse's jawbone, sang through a fine-tooth comb, and hollered with his thumb against his Adam's apple, which he called his "goozle."[31] He whistled trains on the harmonica. When his dad said that he would rather see him dead in a hearse than alive playing the blues, Handy left Florence with a traveling band, singing and playing the cornet. He moved to New York City in 1917.

Handy brought the music with him. Calling himself "The Father of the Blues," he launched a wildly successful sheet music publishing business that he later turned into the Handy Record Company. That first year he wrote a string of hits, including "St. Louis Blues." The blues and jazz took white metropolitans by storm. In 1925 Bessie Smith sang Handy's "St. Louis Blues" to the accompaniment of twenty-four-year-old Louis Armstrong's cornet, and Columbia Records had the hit of the decade on its hands.

Celebrating black folk culture and contesting white representations of black life came easy to young Harlemites who created literature, art, and music on their own terms. Countee Cullen, a Harvard-educated black poet, could imagine no better place to be than Harlem:

> *What would I do in heaven, pray?*
> *I with my dancing feet.*[32]

A party at Harlem's Witoka Club on 145th Street on a raw early March evening in 1932 illustrates why Cullen would choose Harlem over heaven. Everyone was gathered to celebrate his new novel, *One Way to Heaven*. Former North Carolinian Bessye Bearden, correspondent for the *Chicago Defender*, wrote that "a number of literati and their guests" chatted in one room, while in another a band played and Cullen "danced every dance." Paul Robeson, the Rutgers University All-American football player, singer, and actor, arrived fresh from the London stage to prepare to film *The Emperor Jones*. West Indian Harold Jackman, "the handsomest man in Harlem," danced a lot with Cullen, as did Fredi Washington, film star and dancer from Savannah, Georgia.[33] A former Floridian, the talented sculptor Augusta Savage chatted with renowned artist Aaron Douglas from Kansas, who had collaborated with Wallace Thurman from Utah on a Harlem literary magazine, *Fire!* Mrs. Edward Ellington came, although her husband Duke, who grew up in Washington, D.C., could not. The most famous jazz musician in the country, Ellington was holding down his gig at the nearby Cotton Club, where he played for white New Yorkers who came up to Harlem to hear him. On that night, as on many others in Harlem, it was bliss to be young, gifted, black, and far away from Jim Crow. As writer and anthropologist Zora Neale Hurston, from Florida, put it, "Sometimes I feel discriminated against, but it does not make me angry. It merely astonishes me. How can anyone deny themselves the pleasure of my company?"[34]

Young white southerners fled to the nation's largest cities as well, and there they glimpsed the future. Thomas Sigismund Stribling, a white graduate of Florence Normal School, a few years younger than de Priest and Handy, wrote a novel set in their hometown about a young black Harvard graduate who returns to the South. *Birthright*, published in 1922, chronicles the South's Jim Crow system and depicts the Great Migration. Stribling's novels outsold William Faulkner's in the 1920s, and he won a Pulitzer Prize. In 1928 Stribling stood dumbstruck on a sidewalk in Harlem. Out of the shadow of Jim Crow, everything changed: "It is unbelievable that black folks on 125th St. act precisely like white folks on 42nd St." The freedom that surprised Stribling liberated him as well. He marveled, "It is a curious thing that in the south no black man and white man discuss the race question, but the moment they set foot on the neutral north they immediately begin to ask each other questions . . . they have held in their hearts all their lives." [35]

THE POLITICS OF PROSPERITY

The revolution in manners and morals that burst forth in the 1920s had been long in the making. The number of working women living away from their nuclear families had steadily increased in the past three decades. As office work feminized in the 1910s and department stores hired female sales clerks, women with modest incomes and leisure hours filled the streets. In a startling reversal of *Muller v. Oregon*, the 1908 case that had allowed states to set maximum hours to protect working women, in 1923 the Supreme Court ruled in *Adkins v. Children's Hospital* that women no longer deserved special treatment, because they could vote.

Women's Issues

"Women adrift" in the 1890s became "jazz babies" in the 1920s. College girls and daughters of well-to-do families joined them in movie theatres, jazz clubs, and speakeasies. In 1915 most middle and upper-class young women had to have chaperones in public places; by 1925 they ventured out alone on "automobile dates" with men. Women's clothing changed dramatically as hems rose and dresses loosened. In 1915 most public pools required suits with long sleeves and leggings to plunge in, but by 1925 women's bathing suits were tank tops that ended in shorts or skirts that left the thighs uncovered. In jazz clubs and dance halls, young women shook their bodies as black jazz singer Eva Taylor sang, "I wish I could shimmy like my sister Kate. / She shimmies like jelly on a plate. / My mama wanted to know last night, / what makes the boys think Kate's so nice?"[36]

Had Carrie Chapman Catt and her legions fought for this? Certainly not explicitly, but within the woman's movement, there had always been those who advocated personal freedom and an end to the double standard that required women to be pure while men indulged themselves in sexual liaisons. The double standard did not end in the 1920s, nor were most women jazz babies, but some women gained the freedom to have a little fun.

After suffrage, women expanded their political roles as well. They extended the definition of municipal housekeeping, for example, through improved sanitation, pure food and drug laws, public transit, and new parks. But they also advocated for unemployment compensation, the eight-hour workday, and protective labor laws for women and children. In these areas, they pushed maternalism into the legal system.

But they did so within the confines of their Republican or Democratic Party membership. After Harry Burn put the "rat" in ratification, many assumed that women would cross party lines to vote on women's issues, but for the most part, they did not. This should not have been surprising, given that suffragists came from different class and regional backgrounds. The majority of women, it turned out, voted for the party that their fathers, husbands, and sons joined, which reflected their class interests.

The significance of woman suffrage came not from women voting for women's issues but from their entrance into political office and the party organizations. The numbers of women who ran for office were often small, but large numbers of women organized to elect candidates, such as Ida Wells-Barnett in Chicago and Bessye Bearden in Harlem. Women tended to be on the side of good government and reform in either party. In Texas, for instance, white Democratic women worked together in 1927 to elect a reformer, thirty-three-year-old Attorney General Dan Moody, governor over a woman incumbent, Miriam A. (Ma) Ferguson, wife of an impeached governor, James E. Ferguson. Moody fought Ferguson's corrupt machine, defeated Ma in a runoff election, and then appointed women to several important posts in state government. Other governors across the nation did the same. At first largely invisible in journalistic accounts of politics at the time, these women worked in women's auxiliaries of their state party organizations. They also came together at the national level in parties' women's divisions.

Eleanor Roosevelt and Public Service

Eleanor Roosevelt was one such woman. Her activism in the 1920s represents the degree to which the Progressive reformers influenced state government in a period of conservative Republican control in Washington. Moreover, her political style represents that of most women after suffrage in 1920: she became active in the party to which the men in her family belonged. She worked for male candidates, focused on reform in state governance, and served on the national level in the women's division of the national party.

Eleanor's father, Elliott, was Theodore Roosevelt's younger brother, an alcoholic who shamed the family. Orphaned by the age of seven, Eleanor was shuffled off, to be brought up by her rigid aunts. They soon sent her to an English boarding school, Allenswood. There teachers cultivated a social consciousness among upper-class women, taught them to argue for just causes, and instilled in them the courage of their convictions—and to do all that in French. Eleanor looked back on her time at Allenswood as "the happiest years of my life."[37] She returned to New York to work at the College Settlement House on the Lower East Side, where she taught physical fitness.

Eleanor soon fell in love with her wealthy distant cousin Franklin Delano Roosevelt, not an easy feat given that Franklin's mother Sarah rarely let him out of her sight. Brought up on a Hudson River estate, FDR came from two wealthy and distinguished families. His Delano grandfather had made a fortune in the opium trade in China in the nineteenth century, and Theodore Roosevelt was his fifth cousin. His young mother Sarah had married a much older man. When Franklin was nine, his father was sixty-two. FDR learned to assume a placid countenance to placate his frequently ill father and never to admit that anything was wrong. He went to prep school at Groton, then to Harvard College, where his mother moved to be near him. When he decided to attend Columbia Law School in 1904, Sarah left Cambridge for New York. When Eleanor and Franklin's love blossomed into marriage in 1905, they moved into a duplex townhouse in New York City. Sarah moved into the other side of it. Eleanor had five children in ten years of marriage, all under Sarah's watchful eye.

Their quiet married life ended in 1910 when the Democratic Party asked Franklin to run for state senate. Most elite New York families were Republicans, but Franklin's father had supported Democrat Grover Cleveland, whose fiscal austerity appealed to him. Nonetheless Franklin had surely supported his Republican cousin Theodore. When the Democrats came to him with the idea of running for state senate, Franklin replied that he had to ask Sarah first. A Democratic boss said, "Frank, the men are waiting for your answer. They won't like to hear that you had to ask your mother." FDR answered, "I'll take it"—probably the first decision he ever made without asking his mother and the one that most affected his life.[38] When Franklin came out for woman suffrage in 1911, his decision shocked Eleanor, who had not joined NAWSA.

In 1913 Woodrow Wilson appointed FDR assistant secretary of the navy, a position that TR had once held. Eleanor and Franklin moved to Washington. Roosevelt worked under the secretary of the navy, Josephus Daniels, a strict moralist, and Eleanor helped his wife set up the Naval Red Cross. In 1918 Eleanor discovered that Franklin was having an affair with her social secretary, Lucy Mercer. She offered him a divorce, but FDR knew that Daniels would fire him if he divorced. Being fired by Daniels was nothing compared to Sarah's threat to disinherit him. His political advisers told him his career would be over if he divorced. Franklin ardently wanted to stay with Eleanor for all those reasons. He ran as Democrat James M. Cox's vice-presidential candidate in 1920. But Eleanor felt as if the "bottom dropped out" of her world.[39] She pulled herself together and forged a new partnership with FDR. Their partnership never again included a marital relationship, but it freed her to do what she wanted to do. And what she wanted to do was politics.

Franklin's subsequent misfortune—he contracted polio in 1921—ironically propelled Eleanor into public life. He would never walk again, but he always held out hope that he would. Both Eleanor and Franklin played out a fantasy in which he would someday be cured of polio; Eleanor told him that she was entering Democratic politics only until he was able to return himself. She also set herself up as an independent woman, spending one night a week with women friends active in the League of Women Voters. With other women, she purchased a girls' school in New York City, where she taught three days a week.

After building this base outside her home, Eleanor joined a pioneering generation of women who worked for the traditional parties. She did not work in a nonpartisan way for women's issues; rather, she sought to persuade New York State women to vote Democratic. Louis Howe, a Democratic political operative who had advised FDR before he contracted polio, now functioned as ER's adviser. He made her into a politician, just as he had made FDR into one. By 1924, ER was powerful in her own right, but she always told FDR that she was his "temporary stand-in" in those years. From these beginnings, she became, as her biographer described her, "the foremost political woman of the twentieth century."[40]

Eleanor Roosevelt expanded her power base in the fall of 1924, when she campaigned for Alfred E. Smith for governor of New York against her first cousin, Teddy Roosevelt, Jr. She traveled the state with a steam-spouting teapot on the hood of her car to signify the Republicans' crookedness in the Teapot Dome Scandal. She called her cousin a "young man whose public service record shows him willing to do the bidding of his friends," bestowing on him the kiss of death since Teapot Dome and other Harding-era scandals originated with the president's cronies.[41]

Alice Paul's National Woman's Party proposed an Equal Rights Amendment (ERA) in 1923, and thereafter in every congressional session, that read: "Equality of rights under the law shall not be denied or abridged by the United States or by any State on account of sex." But Eleanor Roosevelt saw herself as a difference feminist. Women aren't the same as men, she argued, but they are equal to men in political rights. She fought for the legal protection of working women. By 1928 Eleanor directed the bureau of women's activities of the Democratic National Committee and headed the woman's advisory committee for New York governor Al Smith's presidential campaign. She worked sixteen-hour days and headed a loyal staff.

New York Democratic operatives wanted to nominate Franklin for governor to succeed Smith in 1928, but he demurred because he hoped that two additional years in rehabilitation would enable him to walk again. During their state convention, the Democrats tried all day to reach him by telephone, but he refused to take their calls. That night when Eleanor called home, FDR told her "with evident glee" that he had avoided all calls from politicians. She replied that she was with those politicians, handed the telephone to Al Smith, and rushed from the room to hear Smith booming out, "Hello, Frank."[42] She did not call FDR back and in the morning learned that her husband had accepted the Democratic nomination for governor. Franklin had avoided all politicians that day except the most astute one: his wife. Running as a reform Democrat, FDR won by a little over 25,000 votes out of a total that exceeded four million. With Franklin in the governor's mansion in Albany, Eleanor commuted to New York City to teach, and she remained a political operative in her own right.

Hoover Versus Smith

In 1927 President Calvin Coolidge handed his secretary a one-sentence note to release to the press: "I do not choose to run for President."[43] The Republicans turned to Coolidge's secretary of commerce, Herbert Hoover, whom virtually everyone, regardless of party affiliation, regarded as an extremely competent administrator. A Stanford-educated engineer, Hoover had practical experience in Australia and China and emerged from the Great War as the quintessential can-do American expert. Wilson named him head of the Food Administration, charged with implementing food conservation at home and engineering food delivery to the Allies abroad. After the war, Hoover headed the American Relief Administration to Europe and Russia. He was the consummate manager, recruiting volunteers, inspiring workers, and directing the huge and successful effort. To many people, he seemed to be the person best qualified to maintain pro-business governmental policies, eliminate graft and waste, and use resources efficiently.[44] His wife, Lou Henry Hoover, was the first woman geology major to graduate from Stanford and remains the only first lady ever to speak fluent Chinese. Modern women did not confine themselves to Eleanor Roosevelt's Democratic Party.

Of course, the Roosevelts supported the Democratic presidential candidate, Alfred Smith, Franklin's predecessor as governor of New York. In New York State, Smith enacted Progressive-era reforms, represented urban dwellers and immigrants, and appealed to blue-collar workers. The first Catholic to seek the presidency, he wanted to repeal Prohibition, arguing that it spurred lawlessness and robbed states of alcohol sales taxes. Both his Catholicism and his wet politics stirred great opposition. Smith failed to win his home state of New York and ended up with the electoral votes of only seven states, six in the Democratic Deep South. Smith won only 16.5 percent of the Electoral College vote and 40.8 percent of the popular vote. But the trouncing belied the Democratic Party's growing urban support; in Chicago and New York City, many African Americans abandoned the Republican Party to vote for Smith.

THE GREAT DEPRESSION

Hoover's honeymoon with the America people was short. Calvin Coolidge announced just before he left office that stocks were "cheap at current prices," and most agreed with him. Even Americans of modest means invested in stocks. In an interview in the *Ladies' Home Journal*, the chief financial officer for General Motors, who was also the chairman of the Democratic National Committee, recommended that women encourage their husbands to buy stocks.[45] It seemed that Americans expected prosperity forever. Perhaps they believed that Progressive-era reforms had muted the business cycle's extremes through labor reform and currency and corporate regulation. Herbert Hoover's lived experience taught him that good planning and efficient business methods should yield prosperity—if not in the immediate future, then soon enough. He was wrong. Nothing had prepared him to deal with a protracted depression.

The Stock Market Crash

Things seemed to go swimmingly until September 1929, when the stock market began to waver. Share prices fell and failed to recover quickly. But financial analysts and institutional investors remained bullish. Hoover minimized an 11 percent market drop on October 24, arguing that "the fundamental business of the country . . . is on a very sound and prosperous basis."[46] Then on October 28, Black Monday, stocks closed down almost 13 percent more. Black Tuesday followed on the twenty-ninth, when heavy selling in a declining market congested ticker tape reports to those outside Wall Street; the reports ran two hours late. Waiting to hear even worse news, investors panicked and sold, and the market lost an additional 12 percent in value. Things leveled off a bit on Thursday and Friday. When the markets reopened on Monday, November 4, prices continued to tank, and on Tuesday investors unloaded whatever they could. Sell orders still climbed on Wednesday and continued. By November 13 the Dow had lost 39 percent of its value.[47] Hoover announced, "Any lack of confidence in . . . the basic strength of business in the United States is foolish."[48]

Several conditions contributed to the collapse. First, some of the investors who began the run on the market had bought stock on margin, betting that stock prices would rise before their margin payments came due. When prices began to fall, these investors sold quickly in order to stem their losses. Second, there had been large new stock offerings in August and September to which investors had not responded warmly. This resulted in more stock in circulation at lower prices and sparked a nagging sense that buyers were growing cold. Third, investors pulled money out of the stock market for interest-bearing investments. Fourth, a series of business failures in Great Britain and Europe just before the crash and a declining stock market there prompted foreign investors to pull their money out of U.S. banks for use at home.

A Constellation of Economic Catastrophes

A crash in the stock market, even one that devalued stocks by almost 40 percent, did not necessarily foretell a Great Depression. Some indicators remained strong. Hoover reminded Americans that factories ran full force, unemployment seemed manageable, and consumers continued spending.[49] Since Hoover, like most businesspeople and economists, believed that governmental intervention in the markets would shake confidence further, he decided to keep to a hands-off policy and remain positive. The spring of 1930 brought a slight resurgence. In March 1930 Hoover intoned, "All the evidence indicates that the worst effects of the [stock market] crash upon unemployment will have . . . passed during the next sixty days."[50] Two months later he continued to beat the same drum: "I am convinced we have now passed the worst and with continued unity of effort we shall rapidly recover."[51]

Nonetheless, even before the stock market crash, cracks in the economy had become visible. Earnings in mature industries, such as railroads, coal mining, and textiles had declined, but their stock remained overpriced. Farm prices fell throughout the 1920s by as much as 60 percent, at a time when over 20 percent of Americans worked in agriculture. Credit buying had prompted manufacturing overproduction, and consumer demand had leveled off in 1926. When the spending stopped, companies found themselves with huge, unsold inventories. They began to fire workers, which depressed spending even more. The gross domestic product plummeted by one-third from 1929 to 1932.

During the remaining months of Hoover's presidency, the stock market crash turned slowly into a Great Depression after the summer of 1930. Certainly the market fall contributed to a spending retraction because it wiped out much of the country's wealth. The Dow Jones Industrial Average, from a pre-crash high of 381.17 in early September 1929, hit bottom on July 8, 1932, at 41.22.

Moreover, the country's adherence to the gold standard, as any old Populist would have warned, exacerbated the Depression and contributed to the broad fall in prices and wages. Gold was like an anchor tied to the drowning economy. It limited any expansion in the money supply, which in turn curtailed credit, investments, and purchases, contributing to unemployment and deflation.

The Great Depression was a global economic crisis. Europe had entered a recession in 1929, in part prompted by Germany's inability to pay 8.5 billion marks in reparations to the Allies, a condition of the Treaty of Versailles. Other European nations never recovered their industrial strength or commercial growth after World War I, and with Germany's default, France and Britain could not repay their debts to U.S. banks. Not only could they not enforce the treaty's terms on Germany, Britain and France experienced inflation and low manufacturing output. Throughout his presidency and beyond, Hoover held to the theory that the Depression had resulted from the chaotic effects of the Great War and from what he called "an orgy of speculation" on the stock market.[52]

Companies fired workers wholesale. By spring 1930 four million Americans were unemployed, and that number grew to five million by 1931. By 1932 unemployment reached 23.6 percent nationwide, and industrial cities suffered the most. Cleveland faced 50 percent unemployment, and in Toledo an amazing 80 percent of the workforce sat idle.[53] Those who remained at work saw their wages cut. Unemployment and lower wages made personal earnings fall nationwide from $87 billion to $40 billion between 1929 and 1933.

Devastation swept the country. Some five thousand banks failed between 1929 and 1933, and with no federal government deposit insurance, people lost their life savings. Breadlines appeared in large cities filled with homeless people. New York City authorities anchored abandoned boats in the Hudson and allowed people to sleep on them. Thousands of men thronged city parks all day and all night. Young people dropped out of school, moved back in with their families, and postponed marriage. Child-birth rates plummeted. Women supported 33 percent of families completely, and another third received 25 percent to 99 percent of their support from women. In 1932 85 percent of single women worked, along with 30 percent of married black women and 10 percent of married white women. To reserve scarce jobs for men, employers and economists campaigned to keep married women out of the workforce. Moreover, the Depression hit harder in the male sectors of the economy, particularly mining and heavy industry. Faced with changing gender roles and no longer able to support their families, men blamed themselves and left home, often just traveling around, searching for work. Entire families moved back to the farms they had escaped, reversing urbanizing trends for a time. In 1933, 45 percent of farm mortgages were delinquent, and many also lost their farms to foreclosure. People doubled up and lived together, sharing space with relatives and friends. Urbanites grew food in the cities and traded goods and services.

WHAT SHOULD GOVERNMENT DO?

People looked for help to the federal government in general and to Herbert Hoover in particular. Economists argued for federal spending to stimulate the economy and employ people on public works projects. One labor leader noted, "When private enterprise fails, public enterprise is our only resource."[54] Hoover believed that the nation's future depended on a balanced federal budget, and he believed that public relief to citizens would make them dependent and undermine free enterprise.

Hoover's Ideology

As Hoover hesitated to use federal power to intervene directly in the economy, people began to see him as Nero, who famously fiddled while Rome burned. Unemployed men called the shantytowns that they lived in Hoovervilles and the newspapers that covered them while they slept on park benches became Hoover blankets. In September 1932 one of the nation's leading business magazines outlined the hopelessness of it all:

You are a carpenter. Your last cent is gone. They have cut off the gas. The kid is white and stupid-looking . . . you can't get a job now for love nor money. What do you do? In some, but by no means all cities you can get a meal at the Salvation Army . . . but that's no use now: So you go to the cop. He pulls out his directory and sends you to one of the listed charitable societies. You are a white collar man. You have a wife and two children. What do you do? You do as the carpenter did.[55]

Hoover supported his conviction that the federal government should remain aloof from the situation by pointing out that European governments had failed to halt their depression after increasing spending and implementing public works programs. He remained true to the principle that government aid would weaken individual and national character. He noted, "I have insisted upon a balanced budget as the foundation of all public and private financial stability and of all public confidence."[56]

Hoover's principles made room for government relief to business. In 1929, taking a page from the Populist playbook, he created a subtreasury of sorts, the Federal Farm Board (FFB), to buy up farm surpluses in hopes of stopping the decline in prices. The plan backfired. Finding a new market in the FFB, starving farmers actually increased their production and produced more surpluses, driving down prices even further. The FFB had the authority to extend $500 million in twenty-year loans to the nation's farmers, but that sum proved a drop in the bucket. In 1930 Congress passed the Smoot-Harley Tariff to protect American industry, which Hoover reluctantly signed. Since no one was buying foreign goods anyway, it had little domestic effect, but Europeans retaliated by raising tariffs, reducing U.S. exports.

Hoover did sanction direct federal aid, mostly to corporations, in 1932. The Reconstruction Finance Corporation operated as an independent federal agency that made $2 billion available to banks to lend to large businesses. The Federal Home Loan Bank system underwrote bank loans to mortgage holders to avoid foreclosure. Instead of using the federal money to ease credit, however, the weakening banks used the money to save themselves. Just before he left office, Hoover directed $113 million of a previously authorized $300 million in loans to the states to fund relief for individuals and families, on the condition that the loans be repaid within thirty days.

The diminished percentage of what had been authorized and the short repayment period infuriated desperate citizens. Hoover must have recognized the paucity of his relief, since in 1930 Pennsylvania had appropriated $100 million in relief funds and ran out of money in three months. States dispersed $547 million in emergency relief in 1930 and 1931, but hunger and homelessness rose.

Hoover believed that the business of relief should be conducted on a voluntary basis, hearkening back to the operation that he directed to send food from the United States to starving Belgians during the Great War. For Hoover, the lesson of that war was the mobilization of volunteers. He was not the only politician who drew his lessons from his formative governmental experience in the war: Franklin Delano Roosevelt's stint as assistant secretary of the navy during wartime mobilization taught him the value of centralized planning orchestrated by the federal government. Both men drew on those experiences when they faced off in the 1932 presidential election.

Roosevelt's Nomination

In June 1932, three years into the deepening depression, the Democratic Party representatives met in Chicago to select a candidate to defeat Herbert Hoover. After several ballots, the convention voted to nominate New York governor and rising political star Franklin Roosevelt. FDR had initiated successful relief programs at the state level and had pioneered radio broadcasts to keep New Yorkers apprised of what the state was doing to help them. In past party nominating processes, likely candidates had not attended the convention, and nominees often waited several weeks to accept the tap. This time the nominee jumped into a trimotor plane and flew all night from Albany to Chicago, reflecting his decisive style and symbolizing the urgency of the situation.

On July 2 the stunned convention delegates heard FDR begin his acceptance speech by offering his apologies in a way that cemented his daring and vigor: "I regret that I am late, but I have no control over the winds of Heaven." Next, in one gesture, he brought the country out of nineteenth-century politics-as-usual and foreshadowed the strong executive that he would become: "The appearance before a National Convention of its nominee for President, to be formally notified of his selection, is unprecedented and unusual, but these are unprecedented and unusual times." His personal acceptance of the nomination signaled his desire to break "the absurd traditions." He promised to do the same as president: "We will break foolish traditions and leave it to the Republican leadership, far more skilled in that art, to break promises."[57] The crowd went wild.

Then FDR outlined a new approach to solving the Great Depression. He criticized the Republican policy as what we would call today a trickle-down one: "a favored few are helped and hopes that some of their prosperity will leak through, sift through, to labor, to the farmer, to the small business man." FDR promised that instead the Democrats would be "a party of liberal thought, of planned action, of enlightened international outlook, and of the greatest good to the greatest number of our citizens." He blamed the Depression on "a vast cycle of building and inflation" during the 1920s that drove up consumer prices and ultimately lowered production, and a taxation policy that benefited wealthy corporations. The resulting "enormous corporate surpluses" went into overproduction and financial speculation. The Hoover administration had failed to discipline corporate provocateurs and had punished working Americans for elite businessmen's mistakes. The government bore responsibility to the poor because "never in history have the interests of all the people been so united in a single economic problem."[58] He promised to lead a fight to repeal Prohibition so that the states could tax alcohol and to institute transparent regulation of the securities industry. He proposed public works employment programs that would eventually become self-sustaining by reclaiming farmland and building infrastructure. He pledged enlightened farm support. He would reduce the tariff.

The details of those programs mattered less than the complete reorientation that FDR promised of government's role in the crisis. Roosevelt assured the country that, unlike Herbert Hoover, he would put people first: "Our Republican leaders tell us economic laws—sacred, inviolable, unchangeable—cause panics which no one could prevent. But while they prate of economic laws, men and women are starving. We must lay hold of the fact that economic laws are not made by nature. They are made by human beings." The federal government would "assume bold leadership in distress relief." He won the nation's heart when he accused the Republicans of having "failed in national vision, because in disaster they have held out no hope, they have pointed out no path for the people below to climb back to places of security and of safety in our American life." As for himself, Roosevelt promised, "I pledge you, I pledge myself, to a New Deal for the

American people." The organ cranked out "Happy Days Are Here Again."[59] But they weren't.

The Bonus Expeditionary Force

For William Joseph Hushka, the Great War veteran and Chicago butcher, the summer of 1932 arrived after a series of personal calamities. His young wife Frances had left him, taken their daughter Loretta, and married another man. Both he and his brother Charles lost their jobs at the meat market, and William crowded with his brother's family in an apartment above a store in southwest Chicago. Thirty-five years old in 1932, William felt washed up. He could barely recall how high his spirits had been back in June 1918 when Private Hushka had become an American citizen.

When he heard of the Bonus Expeditionary Force (BEF), an organization of veterans of the Great War who would go to Washington and lobby for the government to pay them their promised pensions now, he joined them. To tell the truth, he didn't have any other options. Roosevelt's acceptance speech that summer did little to lift Hushka's spirits as he and seventeen thousand other Great War veterans whiled away their days in a massive encampment in Washington, D.C. The BEF, which some called the Bonus Army, had begun arriving in the capital in late spring of 1932. They came for what was theirs: bonuses for their war service, authorized by Congress in 1924. The World War Adjusted Compensation Act had provided honorably discharged veterans with a certificate of service that entitled them to one dollar a day for each day of wartime domestic service and $1.29 for each day that they served abroad, along with compound interest from 1924. The only problem was that the veterans came to claim their due fifteen years early: the certificates could not be redeemed until 1945. Initial legislation allowed individuals to take out a loan from the government for 22.5 percent of their certificate's face value, but so many of them did so that in 1931 Congress cut the amount that they could borrow to 22.5 percent of *half* of the face value. Certainly the government had little money, but neither did the veterans, and the 50 percent cut in their only lifeline prompted them to action. They formed the BEF to march on Washington and demand not just the restoration of the ability to borrow 100 percent of the face value, but also immediate payment of the full amount with interest.

Many vets brought their families; 43,000 people lived in Camp Marks on Anacostia Flats in southeast Washington, which the veterans ran like a military facility. Some families occupied nearby empty federal buildings. With no job, no family, and no prospects, William Hushka could only hope that the rumor that Congress was considering awarding the full bonus sooner was true. The House passed a bill on June 15 to move forward the payment date, but as the Bonus Army massed outside the Capitol to hear the results of the vote, the Senate rejected it. Hoover opposed the bill on the grounds that it "breaks barriers of self-reliance and self-support in our people."[60]

Hoover and General Douglas MacArthur, chief of staff of the U.S. Army, harbored deep suspicions about the Bonus Expeditionary Force. Instead of seeing it as a group of as patriots and deserving veterans, Mac-Arthur thought Communists controlled it. A few Communists did participate in the March, but the vast majority of the veterans, who had been busy serving in the U.S. Army during the Bolshevik Revolution, saw themselves as 100 percent Americans. Hoover and MacArthur borrowed trouble by expecting the worst. They assumed that the metropolitan police would not control the crowd, so they marshaled mounted troops and ordered an armored car and a rapid-fire gun to control the crowd. There seems to have been little discussion of the wisdom of using the U.S. military against civilians, except from the district police chief himself, who called it the "Hoover Administration's attempt to make political capital out of hunger, misery, and despair."[61]

When Congress adjourned in mid-June, the government offered the veterans and their families transportation costs home, and all but five thousand demonstrators took the offer. William Hushka knew nothing of MacArthur's plans, but then he had no barriers of self-reliance left to break. He decided to stay until the bitter end.

On the evening of July 28, MacArthur's mounted troops, riding with drawn bayonets and armed with tear gas, paraded to Camp Marks, where the veterans, thinking that the army had arrived to honor them, welcomed them with shouts. As darkness fell, the mounted troops set upon the campers, lit their shanties and pup tents ablaze, and rounded up cowering veterans like cattle. Reporters photographed and filmed it all. Troops and police entered the occupied public buildings to clear out the families there, and someone shot and killed two unarmed men. The next morning Hoover deceptively claimed, "The mobs which were defying the municipal government were dissolved without the firing of a shot or the loss of a life."[62] The two wounded veterans died at once, and fifty-five other people were injured, some of whom died in the aftermath.

One of the two unarmed veterans whom troops killed was William Joseph Hushka. Two days later he was buried in Arlington National Cemetery, exercising in death one of the few veterans' rights that remained to him in life. His ex-wife Frances and her new husband attended the service, and his brother came. Trailing behind them, looking lost and alone, walked his nine-year-old daughter Loretta. Dressed like child star Shirley Temple with a big white ribbon in her hair and a fluffy white dress, she held up the rear of William Joseph Hushka's last parade.

Hoover's proudest moment—routing disorder in the nation's capital—quickly became a disgraceful nail in his political coffin as newsreels in every movie theater around the country showed soldiers on towering horses knocking over women and children with bayonets while burning their possessions. Audiences watched the film with jeers and boos directed not at the veterans but at the army and MacArthur, who had personally participated while mounted on horseback. MacArthur's military assistant, a young officer who had served in the Great War, had cautioned the general not to get involved. Dwight Eisenhower put it bluntly: "I told that dumb son-of-a-bitch not to go."[63]

Afterward one marcher declared, "I used to be a hundred-percenter," referring to Wilson's 100 percent Americanism during the Great War. But "now I'm a Red radical. I had an American flag, but the damned tin soldiers burned it. Now I don't ever want to see a flag again. Give me a gun and I'll go back to Washington."[64] Following the debacle, Franklin Roosevelt condemned Hoover's actions as those of a coward: "There is nothing inside the man but jelly. Maybe there never was anything else. Why didn't Hoover offer the men coffee and sandwiches, instead of turning Doug MacArthur loose?"[65]

The Happy Warrior

FDR took his presidential campaign across the country in the late summer and fall of 1932. In Topeka, he promised "a definitive policy looking to the planned use of the land" but gave no details.[66] In Salt Lake City, he hinted that he might abandon the gold standard and quoted from the Democratic platform, "We favor a sound currency to be preserved at all hazards and an international monetary conference . . . to consider the rehabilitation of silver and related questions."[67] There he proposed to aid—and regulate—the railroads.

With Eleanor sometimes at his side, sometimes campaigning elsewhere, Roosevelt earned his nickname, the Happy Warrior, as he appeared exuberant: "I am having . . . a glorious time . . . never have I met people more cordial, more interested, more enthusiastic in their hospitality." He construed his warm welcome as "an expression of the hope that people have that a new deal will mean better and happier days for all of us."[68] Already he had masterfully transferred ownership of that new deal from the government to the people.

His promises covered all possible bases. After advocating aid to the railroads in Salt Lake, he pledged regulation of public utilities in Portland. In Seattle, he pointed out that the tariff had hurt farmers and failed to help manufacturers. Canada, for example, had in retaliation set high tariffs on U.S. peaches and asparagus. FDR vowed to reform the tariff on March 4, 1933, his first day in office. In San Francisco, he called for "an economic constitutional order," and "the development of an economic declaration of rights," for business.[69] He was long on promises and short on details. As a Roosevelt biographer put it, the ghostwritten speeches "slashed and pummeled the Hoover administration."[70]

Roosevelt's hopeful but vague campaign made him the president of a country in the throes of a Great Depression. He won 22,814,539 popular votes, and Hoover garnered 15,759,930. Hoover's loss resembled Smith's just four years earlier: Republicans carried only Pennsylvania, Delaware, Connecticut, Vermont, New Hampshire, and Maine. The new Senate would be Democratic 59 to 37, and the new House would be Democratic 312 to 123. Roosevelt carried forty-two states and helped elect a Democratic Congress that would work with him to implement the New Deal. Happy days would have to wait four months, however, since Hoover remained president until the inauguration on March 3, 1932. That delay only increased the public's misery.

Franklin Delano Roosevelt had won a mandate, but no one, not even Franklin himself, knew what he would do with it. For her part, Eleanor Roosevelt announced that as first lady she would remain "plain, ordinary Mrs. Roosevelt."[71]

CHAPTER 5

A TWENTIETH-CENTURY PRESIDENT:

FRANKLIN DELANO ROOSEVELT'S FIRST TERM, 1932–1936

NINETEEN-YEAR-OLD WALT'S muscles ached from felling trees to clear a break for the fires raging up on Dead Horse Ridge. As he read his camp newspaper, *Happy Days*, and dug into the free lunch in the mess tent, he marveled at the thirty pounds he had gained in a few short months. The weight gain filled out his face, oddly haggard for a teenager. In Montana, he climbed Glacier Park's mountains and cut through undergrowth in Flathead National Forest. Sometimes he planted trees. Sometimes he cut them down. He carved out trails that snaked up the Rockies and built fire lookout towers. He learned to love the outdoors, the food, and the work. Like most boys of his generation, Walt had been hustling for as long as he could remember. When he graduated from high school in New York in 1934, there were no jobs. He joined the federal government's Civilian Conservation Corps (CCC), where a young man could put a canvas roof over his head, eat three meals a day, make $30 a month, and send $25 of it home to his family. The contrast between the streets of New York and the trails of Montana could not have been starker.[1]

Unlike Walt, Ray didn't bother to finish high school in California before joining the CCC. He knew that a diploma didn't count for much when there was no work available. His single mom's music store had gone bankrupt. When the tall and rather austere teenager was sixteen, the CCC taught him the "meaning of hard work, the joy of a job well done, while being paid for it." Like Walt, Ray gained weight and his body became "hardened . . . and [his] sense of self-respect returned." He learned carpentry and construction techniques and built a fire tower and bridges on Mount Shasta. "Mostly, I learned about this great country of ours," Ray recalled.[2]

Bob chose to join the CCC because he had run out of choices. The son of a Norwegian immigrant widow living in Bridgeport, Connecticut, by the time he was fifteen he had been thrown out of three schools in three states. He took to the road, hoboed around the country, and ended up digging ditches for the CCC.[3] Bob may not have lived in the glorious wilderness that Walt experienced or developed the deep love for America that Ray did, but his enlistment in the CCC probably kept him out of jail. One Chicago judge reckoned that the CCC had accounted for a more than 50 percent drop in juvenile crime in his city. And the CCC changed Bob's life too, since his stint landed him in California, where he turned his smoldering good looks and bad boy persona into a career.

Civilian Conservation Corps workers Walt, Ray, and Bob—Walter Matthau, Raymond Burr, and Robert Mitchum—became three of Hollywood's biggest stars. The CCC saved a generation of young men—it represented the New Deal's effort to put Americans back to work.

The New Deal faced the greatest economic challenge in the country's history by expanding the federal government's economic role. In 1933 the U.S. financial system—banking, investments, and currency—was collapsing. One in four Americans was unemployed. Factories shut, and farmers starved. In the spring and early summer of 1933, termed the First Hundred Days, Roosevelt worked with Congress during its first session to pass a series of emergency measures. After two years, in 1935, the Depression had lifted slightly but remained dire. Unemployment had dropped from 25 percent to 20 percent, while personal income had risen but remained 20 percent below what it had been in 1929.

In 1935 and 1936 the president and Congress tried to ease the Depression's grip by implementing bold economic plans and social safety nets. The Social Security Act positioned the government as the protector of individuals. Union membership grew. Just as FDR realized that the New Deal was not working fast enough to end the Depression, the Supreme Court began to find its programs unconstitutional.

Throughout Roosevelt's first term, the threat from European fascism became more urgent. Alongside Roosevelt's inauguration in the spring of

1933, Adolf Hitler consolidated his power in Germany, and Benito Mussolini experimented with an authoritarian state in Italy. Fascist governments' total economic control and increased military spending eased unemployment there. In those early days, many Americans admired their efficiency. Others worried that the federal government was too weak to stand up to the growing fascist threat, while still others thought that FDR emulated fascism by expanding the state. A variety of homegrown crackpot economic solutions abounded in America. Actual fascist and Communist movements surfaced, and their leaders urged Roosevelt to take stronger action during his first term. Roosevelt attempted to steer a middle course.

In the election of 1936, African Americans and northern working-class whites left the Republican Party to join with white southerners in the Democratic Party and reelected Roosevelt. This odd combination, called the New Deal coalition, would hold for three decades and make the Democrats the majority party. Most Americans accepted the fact that the federal government bore responsibility for the public's economic well-being. In one term, Roosevelt recast the role of the federal government in American public life and made the office of the president a powerful force.

BETWEEN ELECTION AND INAUGURATION

Roosevelt's campaign promises of a New Deal had lifted spirits, but Americans could not eat promises for the four months of unparalleled economic suffering between the November election and the March inauguration. Average personal income bottomed out during those four months. Three out of four people who were still employed faced wage and hour cuts. President Herbert Hoover grew distraught as Roosevelt refused to cooperate on stopgap measures. To calm the financial markets, Hoover wanted FDR to promise to retain the gold standard and balance the budget. Roosevelt refused, even after two excruciating meetings during which Hoover lectured him on the financial crisis. Roosevelt remained genial and rather vague. Hoover observed that the president-elect was a "very ignorant . . . well-meaning young man."[4]

The well-meaning Roosevelt may have seemed ignorant to Hoover because he did not have a systematic plan to address the chaos. Instead, he held conflicting economic beliefs, had few preconceived ideas about federal power, and adhered to no particular constitutional philosophy. He was determined to apply the practical remedies that he had learned in Progressive-era wartime Washington and as governor of New York.

Roosevelt's most urgent tasks would be to prevent the collapse of the financial system and to reduce unemployment. He had to restore Americans' faith in the financial system by fixing its most egregious faults. He had to stimulate industry and agriculture at the same time that he reformed those sectors' worst practices.

The Banking Crisis

Between the election and the inauguration, thousands of banks failed, a term inadequate to describe the horror and devastation that bank failure brought on communities. Life savings vanished; there was no deposit insurance. People lined up at their local banks to withdraw their money. These runs on banks left them insolvent, without enough money to pay the depositors. A bank employee would lock the front door, sling a "closed" sign on the window, and slink out the back door. Outside "people were lined up and screaming and crying and mad and everything." After a run on the bank in Gresham, Nebraska, the local bank president drove three miles out of town and shot himself.[5] Almost fifteen hundred banks failed in 1932, and four thousand failed in 1933, most of them by the end of March.[6]

Surviving banks took "holidays," closing for a period during which depositors couldn't access their money. In Detroit, 400,000 people, almost 25 percent of the population, were unemployed, and the two largest banks stood on the verge of collapse. When Michigan regulators asked Henry Ford, the largest depositor in both banks, to lend the money to insure their solvency, he threatened instead to pull his deposits out. The governor declared a statewide banking holiday on Valentine's Day, leaving Michigan citizens for weeks with only the cash in their pockets and under their mattresses. On February 18 Hoover sent Roosevelt a ten-page handwritten letter predicting a financial apocalypse and blaming it on FDR's refusal to cooperate. Roosevelt left the letter unanswered for two weeks. He was determined to start fresh to escape Hoover's legacy.

By inauguration eve, March 3, 1933, twenty-eight states had declared banking holidays. Merchants set rules for doing business without cash. Some permitted people with current accounts to charge goods. Some accepted checks for purchases, hoping to cash them when the banks reopened. If a customer brought in a payroll check from his or her employer, the merchant might exchange store credit for the total but would not give any cash back. Few had any cash anyway.

On Hoover's last day in office, Federal Reserve Board and Treasury officials drafted an executive order to enact a nationwide banking holiday. This would freeze accounts, prevent bank runs, and prohibit investors from converting more currency into gold. Traditionally, the outgoing president invites the incoming president and his family to the White House for dinner on the inauguration's eve. The graceful gesture remained beyond Hoover's reach; instead of dinner, he invited Eleanor and Franklin Roosevelt to afternoon tea. Hoover lit into Roosevelt, blaming investors' two-month-old gold buying spree on FDR's refusal to endorse the gold standard. Hoover asked Roosevelt to cosign the emergency executive order; he refused.[7] The question on Inauguration Day was not whether Roosevelt would depart from Hoover's approach but how he would do so.

Confidence and Fear

Despite the crises that surrounded him, Roosevelt focused on one task in his inaugural speech: restoring public confidence. This he could do. As the boy who had reassured his sickly father and calmed his overprotective mother, and later as the physically handicapped politician who had portrayed his campaign tour as a buoyant exercise in chatting with the American people, FDR inspired hope because he never admitted defeat.

In his inaugural address, Franklin Delano Roosevelt spoke directly to the people: "This is preeminently the time to speak the truth, the whole truth, frankly and boldly." His acknowledgment of the disaster helped listeners in Gresham, Nebraska, think that their family's misery might not be unique. He reassured them, "This great Nation will endure as it has endured, will revive and will prosper." Hoover had constantly pointed out the dangers that waited to assail the country, but Roosevelt calmly intoned, "Let me assert my firm belief that the only thing we have to fear is fear itself—nameless, unreasoning, unjustified terror which paralyzes needed efforts to convert retreat into advance."[8]

Some leaders achieve greatness because of their grasp of complex problems, but Roosevelt was not among them. He did not know a lot about finance, industry, or agriculture. His genius lay in his ability to frame problems in simple and constructive ways. His solutions assumed that most Americans were people of good will; if they understood a problem, they would jump right in to solve it. Supreme Court justice Oliver Wendell Holmes described FDR as a man with a "second-class intellect" and a "first-class temperament."[9] But Holmes was wrong about his intellect.

Unlike presidents before him, Franklin Roosevelt had a twentieth-century mind. Free of philosophical allegiances, unfettered by ideological cant, possessing only the mildest religiosity, unencumbered by historical ghosts, he was a contemporary man. He lacked Wilson's sense of divine mission and Harding and Coolidge's capitalistic faith. Unlike his cousin Theodore Roosevelt and the generation that came of age just after the Civil War, Franklin looked forward, not backward. FDR knew plenty about human nature and politics. It was said that you could draw a line across the United States at any angle, and FDR could tell you the counties that lay along it. His coming of age in the Progressive era taught him that problems had solutions. His working experience was organizational: he ran naval logistics during World War I, and he organized New York State politics. A savvy negotiator and a charismatic presence, Roosevelt believed himself capable of fixing things. His country desperately needed a fixer.

Roosevelt simplified the crisis by focusing on unemployment and banking reform. "Our greatest primary task is to put people to work," he argued. "It can be accomplished in part by direct recruiting by the Government itself . . . accomplishing greatly needed projects to stimulate and reorganize the use of our natural resources." Then FDR outlined government responsibility for financial regulation, declaring, "There must be a strict supervision of all banking and credits and investments; there must be an end to speculation with other people's money, and there must be provision for an adequate but sound currency."[10]

The Emergency Banking Relief Act

The next morning, March 5, 1933, Roosevelt declared a four-day national bank holiday and called Congress into special session on March 9. The Emergency Banking Relief Act awaited legislators. With this first bill, FDR began the New Deal practice of sending bills from the executive branch to Congress, a reversal of the customary origination of legislation. The act extended the bank holiday for three more days. Individual banks could reopen only when the government examiners deemed them safe, and the controller of the currency could seize troubled banks' assets. The Federal Reserve could provide emergency currency to banks without regard to the gold reserve. Only eight hours passed between the introduction of the bill and its passage.

With the banks temporarily closed, Roosevelt talked to the people about what to do next. Ninety percent of American homes had radios, and most of them tuned in on Sunday evening, March 12, to hear what Roosevelt billed as a fireside chat. This would be the first of thirty such chats, in which FDR shared a problem with the American people, assumed their sound reasoning, and asked for their cooperation. That first night FDR's carefully crafted message reassured citizens whose money languished in a closed bank. He started with the basics: "First of all, when you put your money in a bank, the bank does not deposit your money in a safe deposit vault . . . the bank puts your money to work to keep the wheels of industry and agriculture turning around." Over the past six weeks, the bank runs meant that even "the soundest banks" couldn't meet this "spur of the moment" drain. The banking holiday, FDR told the people, was not a panicked response to the crisis but the "first step in the Government's reconstruction of our financial and economic fabric." The second step was Congress's "patriotic" approval of the holiday by passing the act to allow banks to reopen when the government pronounced them sound.

The whole thing, the president continued, had been a "great inconvenience" to the American people, but their patience had given the Fed the chance to "supply the currency necessary to meet the situation." All that new currency was "backed by actual, good assets," he said. He did not say that it was backed by gold. "I can assure you that it is safer to keep your money in a reopened bank than under the mattress," he said. The president and Congress had tackled the whole complicated affair with gusto: "It was the Government's job to straighten out this situation and do it as quickly as possible—and the job is being performed." Now that FDR had done his job, Americans must do theirs and redeposit their money. He challenged them, "We have provided the machinery to restore our financial system; it is up to you to make it work. . . . Together we cannot fail."[11] On March 13 a thousand banks reopened, and deposits outnumbered withdrawals. The process of closing, auditing, and reopening banks signified government backing of the banks. The process worked as "*de facto* 100 percent deposit insurance."[12]

In reality, the situation was grimmer than that. Government officials cursorily reviewed the banks and tried to reopen every one possible. A month later the banks that had accounted for 90 percent of deposits before the holiday had reopened, but 4,215 remained closed. Many small, underfunded banks merged with others. Some never reopened, and those depositors lost their money. But the country had a functional banking system again. The stock market rallied modestly.

THE FIRST HUNDRED DAYS: EMERGENCY MEDICINE

The banking holiday restored public confidence, but the currency remained imperiled. Between the election and the inauguration, bankers and investors had traded currency for gold, fearing that Roosevelt might devalue the dollar or abandon the gold standard or both. The gold standard had already eroded internationally and domestically. The 1913 Federal Reserve Act required retaining gold equivalent to 40 percent of currency in circulation. But in March the New York branch of the Fed held only 24 percent of its currency value in gold.[13]

Lacking a coherent economic philosophy, FDR simultaneously embraced cutting the budget to send the signal that the government was tightening its belt. In mid-March, at Roosevelt's urging, Congress passed the Economy Act and cut $500 million in spending from the federal budget. The reduction contributed to higher unemployment and an economic contraction.

Stimulants

In the month before the inauguration, Congress had done little to stem the financial crisis, but on February 20 it had voted to repeal Prohibition and sent the Twenty-first Amendment to be ratified in special conventions by three-fourths of the states. Roosevelt decided that the country needed a beer immediately and that the government needed to tax it. Congress, two days after it slashed the federal budget, passed Roosevelt's Beer-Wine Revenue Act to tax alcohol. Suddenly Americans could buy a 3.2 percent alcohol beer and wine, except in places where state-level prohibition had preceded the Eighteenth Amendment. "Well, it's off!" FDR exclaimed when he signed the bill, and brewers rushed to apply for permits. At 12:01 a.m. on April 7, a crowd cheered as a beer delivery truck drove up to the White House. Restaurants had laid in a supply of beer and wine the day before and opened at midnight. "The waving of steins" continued until dawn.[14] On December 5, 1933, the Twenty-first Amendment achieved ratification by thirty-six states and became law.

On March 21, FDR sent the bill to Congress that created the Civilian Conservation Corps, arguing that it would provide "simple work not interfering with normal employment, and confining itself to forestry, the prevention of soil erosion, flood control and similar projects."[15] By July, almost fifteen hundred camps with 250,000 workers had opened. A special branch set 28,000 Great War veterans to work, and 14,000 Native Americans worked on reservations. CCC men created thirteen state forests in Minnesota alone and built the Appalachian Trail in Georgia, North Carolina, and Virginia. CCC members restored totem poles in Alaska and built the Red Rocks Amphitheatre in Colorado. The twenty-five dollars that CCC men sent home each month stimulated local economies. The CCC accustomed a generation of men to government rules and organization, acclimatizing them to a structure that would help mobilize the country quickly when World War II arrived. The national wealth that they created remains a treasure today. Not every New Deal program succeeded so spectacularly.

By mid-April, Congress turned to currency reform as the dollar continued to fall against foreign currencies. Representatives of southern and western farmers argued for the Populists' dream: bimetallism, using silver to back currency. Roosevelt wanted to loosen the money supply to inflate falling prices, but he did not want to be tied to bimetallism. The country had not adhered to the gold standard since the banking holiday, and European countries had abandoned it months earlier. On April 19, FDR asked Congress for emergency powers to regulate the currency, and he banned the use of gold for foreign exchange. The dollar rose against the British pound, and most bankers agreed with the move. The president's actions effectively abandoned the gold standard without adopting bimetallism. In a literal sense, the currency might be less valuable, but the country's faith in it rose.

The Brains Trust

Roosevelt's lack of entrenched economic ideology allowed him to explore divergent approaches. A widely told, perhaps apocryphal, tale involved a bright-eyed young reporter who asked FDR, "'Mr. President, are you a Communist?' FDR replied, 'No.' 'Are you a capitalist?' 'NO.' 'Are you a Socialist?' 'NO.' 'Well, what is your philosophy then?' 'Philosophy?' asked a puzzled

FDR. 'I am a Christian and a Democrat. That's all.'"[16] One of FDR's campaign speechwriters commented that FDR followed only one principle: "Government should achieve the subordination of private interests to collective interests, [and] substitute cooperation for the mad scramble of selfish individualism."[17]

Roosevelt recruited people into his administration to provide the in-depth knowledge that he realized he lacked. Many advisers had been with him since the presidential campaign, and some dated back to his gubernatorial years. Roosevelt brought together experts, described a problem to them, and refereed their solutions. For the most part, those experts had come of age during the Progressive era and served in the armed forces or worked in wartime government. Most were not politicians. A reporter dubbed them the Brains Trust.

Roosevelt appointed Henry A. Wallace of Iowa as secretary of agriculture. Ironically, Wallace was the son of the secretary of agriculture under Harding and Coolidge when the farm depression began. Brains Truster Rexford Tugwell, a Columbia University professor, advised on agricultural economics as assistant secretary. The late 1920s depression in farm prices had presaged the stock market crash, and many, including Tugwell and Roosevelt, thought that the nation's agricultural system contributed to the boom and bust cycles.

Harry Hopkins, head of New York's Temporary Emergency Relief Administration, joined the Brains Trust to extend direct monetary relief to the unemployed. Raymond Moley, one of FDR's campaign speechwriters, became assistant secretary of state. Frances Perkins, who had headed New York's Industrial Commission, became secretary of labor.

Roosevelt listened agreeably to various advisers while searching for compromises among different viewpoints. One historian termed his style "congenial evasiveness."[18] Moley reported, "He is wholly conscious of his ability to send callers away happy and glowing and in agreement with him and his ideas."[19] FDR's availability proved to be a marvelous antidote to Hoover's reclusiveness. However, FDR incorporated conflicting ideas to such an extent that his advisers complained that he sometimes eviscerated a program's intellectual coherence.

Adviser Louis Howe honed FDR's open personality into a political force. The president could stay on the sunny side with his interlocutors because the omnipresent Howe and other advisers would shape the final decision. Howe had managed FDR's New York state senate campaign, been with him in the Department of the Navy during World War I, and seen him through polio. Howe had devoted every day of his life since to electing FDR to public office, first as governor and then as president. It was Howe who worried about the quagmire of details surrounding decisions. Howe called himself Roosevelt's "no man," and Roosevelt needed him so much that Howe moved into the Lincoln Bedroom in the White House.[20] *The New York Times* called Howe "the President's Other I."[21]

The First Lady as Politician

The president's wife was another I. Eleanor Roosevelt traveled outside Washington to bring the country to FDR, who found it physically difficult to leave the White House. Howe taught ER to speak in public, and he managed her image as closely as he managed the president's. After the election, forty-eight-year-old Eleanor felt great trepidation about the role of first lady. To allay her anxiety, she wrote a book between the election and the inauguration entitled *It's Up to the Women*. The economic emergency gave her an unprecedented chance to rally women to fight the Great Depression.

During the presidential campaign, Lorena Hickok, an Associated Press reporter, had fallen in love with Eleanor, and her emotional support gave the new first lady the confidence she needed move into her new life. As Franklin told the nation that the only thing they had to fear was fear itself, a fearful Eleanor sat, head down, twirling a sapphire and diamond ring that Hick had given her, thinking that she ached to hold Hick. Soon Hickok moved into the White House, and the two women traveled around New England in the summer of 1933 in a blue convertible, to the astonishment of the motel owners on whom they dropped in without reservations. The relationship never became as complete as Hick wished, but it began to fill the vast emotional emptiness that had engulfed Eleanor after Franklin's affair with Lucy Mercer.[22]

As first lady, Eleanor Roosevelt held press conferences for women reporters only and gave them hard news rather than domestic trivia. She knew that this would lead news outlets to employ more women reporters. She promoted the appointment of more than one hundred women to prominent positions throughout the administration. A woman appointee who had worked in the trenches to elect Democratic candidates celebrated the political patronage heretofore reserved for men: "The change from women's status in government before Roosevelt is unbelievable." Another remembered that before the New Deal, all the women in federal government could have dined together in a small room, but by 1934 it would take a hall to hold them.[23]

FDR began to dispatch his wife to investigate the Depression that he could not see firsthand, given his limited mobility. "Watch people's faces," he told her. "Look at the conditions of the clothes on the wash lines." One Gloucester fisherman said, "She ain't dressed up, and she ain't scared to talk."[24] She traveled so much that a *Washington Post* headline announced: "First Lady Spends Night in White House." In the summer of 1933, the first lady began to write a monthly column in the magazine *Woman's Home Companion* entitled "I Want You to Write to Me," and 300,000 people did.

Frances Perkins

Roosevelt appointed deeply committed and well-informed people, including the first woman to serve in a presidential cabinet, Frances Coralie Perkins. She grew up in Worcester, Massachusetts, and was senior class president at Mount Holyoke College, a cradle of Progressive-era women leaders. She volunteered at Chicago's Hull House and worked for a Philadelphia organization that rescued prostitutes. She took graduate courses in economics at the University of Pennsylvania and earned an M.A. in political science at Columbia University. She joined the Progressive Party in 1912.

Through Perkins, women who had come of age in the Progressive era found a voice in the White House. Perkins had headed the New York branch of the National Consumers League, an organization that promoted better working conditions for women. One day while having tea on New York's Washington Square, Perkins heard fire bells. She rushed across the square to the Triangle Shirtwaist Factory, where smoke billowed out of the windows. As she watched, women held on to windowsills until they lost their strength and dropped to the pavement. Other women simply jumped to their deaths. After the Triangle Shirtwaist Factory fire of March 25, 1911, Perkins never doubted the importance of improving working conditions for everyone.

In 1918 Perkins supported Al Smith for governor, and he appointed her to the oversight board for the Industrial Commission. His successor as governor, Roosevelt, appointed Perkins to chair the Industrial Commission. She traveled to England to study an unemployment insurance program and enacted a version in New York. She persuaded FDR to support a statewide old age pension plan. In her spare time, she alerted the press to errors in Herbert Hoover's unemployment calculations.

Perkins provided the programmatic focus and know how behind FDR's diffuse inclinations to improve citizens' lives. She had experience in worker health and safety, statistical expertise on both employment and consumption, and knowledge of women's and children's issues. She plunged into unpleasant tasks and often managed men who were reluctant to work for a woman. Perkins furnished the brains and energy behind the New Deal's most revered and lasting programs.[25]

THE FIRST HUNDRED DAYS: LASTING REFORM

By late April 1933, Roosevelt turned from emergency management to more lasting reform. Legislation in March and April—the Emergency Banking Act, the Economy Act, the Beer-Wine Revenue Act, and the CCC—had stopped the country's free fall. In the six weeks between May 1 and the end of the special congressional session, on June 16, the administration wrote and Congress passed ten more acts. They focused on reforming the financial sector, extending credit to homeowners and farmers, restructuring the farm commodity market, reorganizing industry on a more cooperative basis, and encouraging workers to join unions. African Americans began to have input into federal programs in unprecedented ways.

Relief for the People

In May and June two acts were passed to protect investors and small depositors. The Truth in Securities Act required full disclosure of facts pertinent to the issuance of stock. The act gained enforcement mechanisms the next year, when Congress created the Securities and Exchange Commission. The second major financial regulation, the Banking Act, separated consumer and investment banking. Referred to by the names of its sponsors, Senator Carter Glass (D-VA) and Congressman Henry Steagall (D-AL), the act ended banks' speculation in stocks and real estate using individual depositors' money, which many of the failed banks had done. The act prohibited banks from owning firms that sold securities. It also created a separate agency, the Federal Deposit Insurance Corporation, to insure personal deposits in federal banks so that people would never again lose their savings in bank failures. Both acts benefited bankers by restoring public faith in the financial sector, and they offered individual depositors unprecedented protection.

In May and June FDR and Congress turned to unemployment. Unlike Hoover, who abhorred direct relief, FDR believed that the severe crisis called for the government to provide emergency funds to citizens. Private, municipal, and state relief was a mishmash of failed remedies, with some states providing small stipends to the unemployed for limited periods. On May 22, Congress appropriated $500 million to create the Federal Emergency Relief Administration (FERA) and sent $250 million to state public charity offices, many of them headed by women. To encourage states to appropriate additional funds, FERA then added an additional federal dollar for every three that the states contributed. FDR appointed Harry Hopkins, a Social Gospel Progressive and former settlement house worker, to head FERA. Hopkins vowed to feed 22 million people and carry out FDR's observation that government should try to provide its citizens "a more abundant life." From his desk stuck in a hallway, Hopkins distributed $5 million in his first two hours on the job.[26]

Relief for Farmers

The decade-long farming depression contributed to the economic crisis. Roosevelt saw agriculture as a chaotic sector with too many farmers, too much exhausted land, and too little planning. Farmers clung to unproductive land, eking out a living by overproducing cash crops, driving farm prices down. Farmers' isolation made it difficult to extend electricity or telephones to them; bad roads hampered marketing crops. Even when mechanization triumphed, things went awry. The 1892 invention of the gasoline-powered tractor rapidly expanded the land under cultivation in the Great Plains and exhausted topsoil. The farm crisis worsened when drought struck. In the summer and fall of 1933, high winds carried topsoil into the air, and huge dust storms spread from South Dakota across the Great Plains. Over the next two years, scores of dust storms turned the region into the Dust Bowl.

Farm crises from the 1880s to the Dust Bowl convinced New Dealers that only governmental intervention would stop agriculture from periodically undermining the entire economy. The administration developed both short- and long-term plans for the reorganization of agriculture, many of them suggested by Brains Truster Rexford Tugwell, assistant secretary of agriculture, and endorsed by his boss, Henry Wallace.

In the spring of 1933, Congress passed two acts to address the immediate farm crisis and two to reorganize the relationship between the government and agriculture. The Emergency Farm Mortgage Act extended loan repayment periods and allocated $200 million that ultimately refinanced one out of five farm mortgages and allowed families to keep their land. The Farm Credit Act established a system of lending institutions to provide short-term credit for agricultural production. Neither of these measures would matter much unless farmers could realize higher crop prices.

The Agricultural Adjustment Act (AAA), passed on May 12, 1933, attacked low prices by attacking overproduction. Had Congress passed it in February or March, it could have avoided the chaos that followed by preventing annual planting and breeding cycles. That first summer the AAA paid farmers to kill their squirming piglets to drive up the price of bacon, to pour out gallons of milk, and to plow under fragile seedlings, all to drive up commodity prices. Even the Populists, who understood that overproduction caused problems, would have balked at such destruction while people starved. In subsequent years, the AAA would pay landowners cash subsidies to thin their livestock and *not* to plant. New Dealers hoped that government planning could aid the strongest farmers while easing out the weakest.

A government-engineered dam near Muscle Shoals, Alabama, on the Tennessee River, inspired the fourth agricultural program launched in the First Hundred Days. Built during the Great War, the dam had stood unused during the 1920s, while southern farmers, especially mountaineers, had no access to electricity. For example, only 2.1 percent of farm families in Arkansas had electricity.[27] Senator George Norris (R-NE) had taken FDR to Muscle Shoals before the inauguration to persuade him to use the idle dam to generate electricity. FDR saw the opportunity to build other dams, employ more people, and extend electricity through the region. Congress chartered the Tennessee Valley Authority (TVA) in May 1933, making it the first regional planning authority. The dams followed a broad swath down Virginia's Shenandoah Valley into the Great Smoky Mountains of Tennessee, North Carolina, and Georgia, turning west to follow the Tennessee River through Alabama and western Tennessee, then turning upward to Paducah, Kentucky. Many objected that the TVA put the government into competition with private industry, but the difficulty of profitably electrifying such a remote region had long deterred private enterprise. Moreover, FDR believed that unequal development in the United States, especially in the poverty-stricken South and the drought-ridden Dust Bowl, created soft spots in the national economy that inhibited overall recovery. In 1935 Roosevelt established the Rural Electrification Administration (REA) to bring power to the 80 percent of the nation's farms that lacked electricity. By 1945 the REA's publicly owned cooperatives had electrified 90 percent of them.[28]

Electrification changed the South forever. Women could use washing machines to wring clothes without hand cranking. They could stop bringing in wood and adopt electric stoves that glowed red with a flip of the dial. Outside the house, farm families could buy milking machines and corn grinders. On Saturday nights, people could tune their radios to the 50,000-watt Nashville station WSM and listen to Roy Acuff sing "Great Speckled Bird" on the Grand Ole Opry. Down in the Mississippi Delta, sharecroppers could go to a juke joint on Saturday night, put a nickel in the new electric Rock-Ola, and hear a long-gone neighbor singing the Chicago blues. Industry could move into remote communities and offer people alternatives to farming.

The New Deal changed land management and farming in the West as well. Work began in 1933 on Grand Coulee Dam on the Columbia River in Washington to provide electricity. By 1935, Congress provided for Grand Coulee to be built even higher to irrigate crops. Technology combined with hard labor in New Deal programs to make the United States the world's engineering leader.

Relief for Business

The most far-reaching act of the First Hundred Days, the National Industrial Recovery Act (NIRA), signed by FDR on June 16, 1933, centralized business planning. Leaders in a sector—for example, the steel industry—would meet yearly to plan production, employment, and even wages. If cooperative planning succeeded in reviving industry and sustaining the workforce, then increased consumer spending should follow. The act might smooth the business cycle.

The act melded the voluntary trade association of the 1920s with the kind of centralized governmental planning that many New Dealers had learned during the Great War.[29] FDR sent Raymond Moley to consult with the Chamber of Commerce and the bankers, while Frances Perkins gathered various plans to limit working hours. Business leaders such as Charles

Schwab, chair of Bethlehem Steel, helped draft the legislation. But critics saw little difference between consultation and collusion and believed that the act violated federal antitrust laws. A few likened it to the state power of Italian fascism or Soviet collectivism.

The act created the National Recovery Administration (NRA), headed by Hugh Samuel Johnson. As a brigadier general during the war, Johnson had managed military purchasing and supplies. Most large businesses endorsed the NRA, hoping that it would enable them to raise prices and hold down payroll. Even the conservative National Association of Manufacturers supported it. The act ordered each industry to draw up fair competition codes, but because of concerns about antitrust laws, participation was voluntary. Nonetheless, if a business did not join its trade association, it could not put the NRA logo—a Blue Eagle—in its window or on its products. Since the government advised consumers to shop only for goods with the Blue Eagle, the NRA virtually legalized price and wage fixing.

Small businesses quickly complained that the "big boys in the industry" dictated the codes and the "little fellows weren't being consulted," making it impossible for small firms to adhere to industry standards.[30] In addition, while some industries—for example, auto manufacturing—could produce codes that fit the entire sector, smaller and more variable ones could not. The NRA finally exempted peripheral industries from the act after the burlesque theater industry proudly announced that it had adopted a fair trade practice to limit each production to four strips during the show.[31]

The NIRA sweetened the deal through an appropriation of $3.3 billion for public works to be loaned to private industry, a provision that Frances Perkins had persuaded Roosevelt to include as an economic stimulus. The appropriation created the Public Works Administration (PWA), which under Secretary of the Interior Harold Ickes completed 34,000 projects. PWA projects created roads, bridges, tunnels, airports, dams, and schools and put people back to work. Its funds built the Blue Ridge Parkway and the Grand Coulee Dam. The PWA stimulated the economy as it built the nation's modern infrastructure.

Relief for Labor

While drafting the NRA, Frances Perkins hoped to strengthen labor unions. She conferred with William Green, president of the AFL, who wrote a few sentences into a section of the NIRA that enshrined labor's rights in federal law. Section 7(a) encouraged workers "to organize and bargain collectively through representatives of their own choosing" and were to be "free from the interference, restraint, or coercion of employers." It marked the first time that the federal government formally recognized the right to organize. It also required employers to abide by "the maximum hours of labor, minimum rates of pay, and other conditions of employment, approved or prescribed by the president"—the first time the federal government claimed the right to set a minimum wage. Perkins reflected that the wording of 7(a) was "almost an accident . . . the labor movement at the time was dead."[32] Since business had little fear of strikes, even antiunion Cotton Textile Institute representatives agreed to 7(a).

"The President wants you to join the union!" trumpeted the AFL as it seized on Section 7(a). In large industries, such as steel, unions became a part of the NRA planning process. But in nonunionized industries and smaller companies, managers hated Section 7(a). Many refused to abide by it, and the summer after the NIRA's passage, 1934, became one of the bloodiest in labor history. A West Coast longshoremen's strike, led by organizer Harry Bridges, resulted in two deaths, and a general sympathy strike followed. Bridges was a former IWW member, and some thought him to be a Communist. Also in 1934 a Minneapolis trucking strike shut down the city and brought armed conflict to the streets. Southern textile manufacturers posted their Blue Eagles and ignored the working hours and wage requirements. At South Carolina's Langley Cotton Mills, a striker complained that the mill flew the Blue Eagle but hired scabs to strike-break. Mill owners brutally suppressed a general textile strike that spread across the East Coast in 1934. Textile mills from Maine to Georgia shut down. Sheriff's deputies fired into a crowd of three hundred strikers at Chiquola Mill in Honea Path, South Carolina, killing seven. Ten thousand people showed up at the funeral.

Despite opposition, nonunion workers began to organize themselves. For example, Filipino lettuce pickers, unaffiliated with the AFL, successfully struck in Salinas, California. Strikers often expanded their actions beyond the workplace. A striker at the Toledo, Ohio, Auto-Lite Company recalled that in the summer of 1934: "Toledo was in the grip of a tremendous popular upsurge of anger at the greedy bosses. . . . It was a strike won on the picket line by a community uprising."[33] Labor's hopes in the United States coincided with a calendar of desperation around the world: too many people had been unemployed for too long.

Unions and industries seized the NRA opportunity, but its head, Hugh Johnson, ran the agency more as a patriotic rally than as a business endeavor. He secretly feared that the Supreme Court would find the NRA unconstitutional, so he focused on the hoopla of volunteerism. He failed to implement any enforcement committees, and when many industry codes proposed inflationary price increases, he left them unchallenged.

The NRA's problems quickly became evident. Wages and hours did not rise with prices. Therefore, as prices rose, consumption fell—a disastrous result. Then in July 1934, in a rare enforcement gesture, the NRA took the A.L.A. Schechter Poultry Company in New York City to court for wage and hour violations, sloppy paperwork, and selling live chickens that did not meet the poultry health code. It came to be called the sick chicken case. Upon their conviction, Schechter appealed and challenged the NRA's constitutionality. FDR fired Johnson, and the government prepared to defend the NRA as the Schechter case wound its way to the Supreme Court.

Hope for African Americans

When the Depression began, African Americans held the lowest-paid industrial jobs, worked as debt-ridden sharecroppers, or owned small farms on exhausted land. Their economic plight became a bellwether for FDR as he tried to navigate out of the crisis. He quietly sent out word to abolish Woodrow Wilson's segregation of government offices, which had stayed in place through the Republican administrations of the 1920s, and he appointed more African Americans to high positions than any president at that point. In August 1933 he announced the end of the U.S. occupation of Haiti, a move that delighted African Americans, who had lobbied for it since Wilson's invasion in 1915.

Franklin Roosevelt knew that endemic black poverty hurt both the South and northern cities. He also understood that African Americans who had migrated north could vote, not just in Chicago, Detroit, or New York but also elsewhere in tight congressional races. By the early 1930s, black voters in the North were beginning to abandon the Republican Party and register as Democrats. The Republicans had done little to help their black constituency while in power in the 1920s, and Roosevelt presented an alternative.

In 1933 Roosevelt publicly condemned lynching as murder, prompting praise from W. E. B. Du Bois. Eleanor Roosevelt stepped up as a forceful advocate for African Americans. By 1935 she believed in full civil rights but declined to advocate for integration because she thought it would be impossible to legislate.

Appointing African Americans to meaningful jobs became a New Deal hallmark. In 1933 Roosevelt named Washington, D.C., native William H. Hastie assistant solicitor in the Department of the Interior, which influenced housing policy, and later appointed him to the federal bench. An Amherst graduate, Hastie had made the *Harvard Law Review*. North Carolina native Robert Vann practiced law and published the *Pittsburgh Courier*. His endorsement of Roosevelt in 1932 reached over 100,000 black voters. Roosevelt appointed him assistant to the attorney general in 1933.

As administrative agencies grew, African American managers came on board to represent black interests. One such advocate was Robert C. Weaver, who entered the administration upon receiving his Ph.D. in economics from Harvard in 1934. He became the assistant to the Farm Security Administration's Will Alexander, a white southern man who had founded the Atlanta-based Commission for Interracial Cooperation. Weaver worked closely with Ralph Bunche, another Harvard-educated black man, who headed the political science department at Howard University. Bunche and his colleagues used their proximity to Congress to draw attention to black issues. In 1935 they hosted a conference on "The Position of the Negro in Our National Economic Crisis" and identified sharecropping as a threat to agricultural prosperity.[34] When the Department of the Interior began to build public housing, Robert Weaver made sure that black tenants were included.

Of the roughly fifty African Americans in upper-level jobs in the Roosevelt administration, Mary McLeod Bethune cultivated the most significant public profile. The youngest of fifteen children and the first born in freedom, Bethune had never used a fork or climbed a flight of stairs when she arrived as a teenager in the early 1890s as a scholarship student at Scotia Seminary for Negro Girls in Concord, North Carolina. In the 1930s Bethune began to convert her experience in black women's organizations into political capital. As president of the National Association of Colored Women's Clubs, she established the NACWC headquarters in Washington. Coolidge and Hoover had appointed her to child welfare commissions, but Bethune changed her registration from Republican to Democrat upon FDR's election. She turned her natural gifts—a quick mind, an imposing physical presence, and raw courage—into the political persona of the formidable black woman. She walked around Washington with a cane, not because she needed it but because she said it gave her "swank."[35]

Roosevelt appointed Bethune to the board of the National Youth Administration (NYA), a WPA department that trained and employed young people. She quickly complained to Roosevelt that the WPA and the NYA discriminated against African Americans. The president created a position for her as director of the NYA's Division of Negro Affairs. He admired Bethune because she was, like him, a practical politician. He said, "Mrs. Bethune is a great woman. She has her feet on the ground; not only on the ground, but deep down in the ploughed soil."[36] Bethune brought black New Dealers together into the Federal Council of Negro Affairs in 1936, which became known as the Black Cabinet. Bethune's relationship with Eleanor was exceptionally close. They wrote and met often, and ER took Bethune's concerns to the president. When Bethune wanted William Hastie and Hubert Delaney to be appointed as federal judges, ER wrote to Franklin, "How about these requests? The young lawyer [whom Bethune] wants as judge made a very good impression at the Urban League Dinner."[37]

The New Deal's tentative inclusion of African Americans broke with the past in other ways as well. White and black New Deal administrators worked directly with black Americans as participants in federal programs, often bypassing the local white people who managed them to be sure that aid and services reached black southerners. Moreover, New Deal policy making took African Americans into account as citizens: fighting the Depression meant including all the people, at least as economic units. In 1936, when FDR went to Howard University to dedicate a new building, he said, "As far as it was humanly possible, the Government has followed the policy that among American citizens there should be no forgotten men and no forgotten races. It is a wise and truly American policy."[38] One historian has argued that the New Deal represented "days of hope" for black Americans.[39]

The New Deal Through 1934

When the special session of Congress ended on June 16, 1933, the body had passed fifteen bills in one hundred days, the most productive legislative period in congressional history. Journalist Anne O'Hare McCormick described the atmosphere: people "are vivified by a strong undercurrent of wonder and excitement. . . . You never saw before in Washington so much government." McCormick reported that the New Dealers "set about reorganizing agriculture, reflating the currency, reforming the structure of business and industry."[40]

In the following session that began in January 1934, Congress established the Federal Communications Commission to regulate telephone service and radio, created the Securities and Exchange Commission to police Wall Street, and passed the National Housing Act, which established the first public housing and the Federal Housing Administration (FHA). The FHA set standards for interest rates, terms, and down payments for home mortgages and insured some private mortgages. By the winter of 1934, 20 million Americans drew a little more than twenty dollars each month from Harry Hopkins's Federal Emergency Relief Administration, which people referred to as the dole.

The Democrats gained nine congressional seats in the November 1934 elections, in spite of growing criticism on the right. Conservative Republicans and Democrats had organized the American Liberty League the preceding August. The Liberty League professed to be non-partisan and dedicated itself to stopping the New Deal. Al Smith, the Roosevelts' old patron, became the Liberty League's spokesperson. He equated New Deal economic interventions with socialism. Many prominent league leaders were, like Smith, anti-New Deal Democrats, including a former head of the Democratic National Committee. These conservatives found allies in southern congressmen who opposed New Deal programs that threatened white supremacy by including African Americans.

RADICAL SOLUTIONS FOR
AN INTRACTABLE DEPRESSION

After the First Hundred Days, the depression remained overwhelming. Over the summer and fall of 1933, the economic indicators had moved in the right direction but not by much. Unemployment had crested at almost 25 percent in 1932; it fell to 20 percent by 1934. One out of five people remained unemployed. Stocks doubled in value from late 1932 to 1934, but that brought prices only to 1925 levels. Conditions seemed to be improving, but glacially and from the bottom of a very deep trough.

A prolonged depression caused people to question themselves, their government, and the economic system itself. Desperate for change, some turned to fascism and some to Communism. Fascist governments in Europe continued to gain power by crushing opposition and scapegoating Jews and Communists. Many people embraced the simple solutions that popular leaders like Louisiana senator Huey Long, Detroit priest Father Coughlin, and Californian Francis Townsend offered.

Desperation and Daily Life: The Politics of Hunger

The duration of the Depression exhausted family resources. "Dear Chief Executive," wrote a St. Louis man after the First Hundred Days, "In the past three years, my salary has been on a constant decline." As he earned less and less, he had borrowed small sums from loan companies. The high interest rate meant that he paid the loan sharks back more than he had borrowed. "These people keep hounding me night and day," he said, begging FDR for "help, advice or information."[41] Even the employed had begun to sink. Those who had pieced things together through temporary work, credit at the store, or selling their possessions now found themselves penniless.

An outpouring of letters to the Roosevelts demonstrated that people believed that the federal government could and should help them. One woman who wrote to FDR described herself as the "mother of seven children and utterly heartbroken, in that they are hungry, have only 65 cents in money, The father is in L.A. trying to find something to do,—provisions all gone. . . . O, President, my heart is breaking."[42] A Philadelphia woman had no money for heat in 1932, so her pipes burst, and her family went without water for a year. She had saved her house with a mortgage through the Home Owners' Loan Corporation but now faced eviction. They had "no money, no home, and no wheres to go," she wrote.[43] One expectant mother sent FDR a shopping list for her unborn baby. The First Hundred Days had saved the financial system, stabilized mortgages and farm credit, reorganized industry and agriculture, and put some people back to work. But it had not ended the Great Depression.

The politics of hunger brought protesters out into the streets. Beginning in 1930, Communist and Socialist unemployed councils had organized hunger marches in which hundreds of thousands demonstrated in the streets across the nation. Black teenager Angelo Herndon joined a Communist-sponsored unemployed council in Alabama. He marveled that he had "found organizations in which Negroes and whites sat together, and worked together and knew no difference of race or color. . . and come out . . . for the rights of the workers. . . . It was like all of a sudden turning a corner on a dirty, old street and finding yourself facing a broad, shining highway."[44]

Marches of the unemployed became relief riots by 1933, when cities and states ran out of resources and faced hungry crowds as the promise of federal relief raised expectations. Not all unemployed demonstrations were Communist sponsored: in Kansas City, two thousand unemployed people sang hymns outside the courthouse until the city voted relief appropriations. Atlanta's municipal government dispensed relief to 23,000 families in 1932, but by the time that FERA relief reached there in July 1933, only 11,000 families qualified under the federal rules; the other 12,000 would have to go hungry. When Angelo Herndon led an integrated march of one thousand in protest, an Atlanta court convicted him of sedition, which carried the death penalty. He appealed, and the U.S. Supreme Court struck down the state sedition law in 1937.

Fascism at Home and Abroad

The politics of hunger also attracted many people to fascist organizations that promised to solve the country's economic problems. In 1934 the number of domestic fascist organizations topped one hundred. From the Silver Shirts in Los Angeles (who built survivalist bunkers in the hills) to the Black Legion in Detroit (whose members planned to gas synagogues), these organizations thrived on hard times. Only one or two of them had direct ties to the National Socialist German Workers' Party, but Hitler thought it would be easy to use them to take over the United States. To him, the nation's response to the Great Depression symbolized its weaknesses. He pointed to *The Grapes of Wrath*, John Steinbeck's book about displaced Dust Bowl farmers, to argue that such degraded "peasants" sapped America's strength.[45]

In April 1933 Roosevelt had invited Hitler to the United States to negotiate the German war debt, but the freshly installed German chancellor had declined. The U.S. ambassador to Germany, William E. Dodd, confided to FDR that Hitler inspired in him a "sense of horror." For his part, Hitler called Dodd "an old imbecile."[46] African Americans immediately recognized the danger that Hitler posed. In March 1933, when amid an anti-Communist panic the Reichstag passed an Enabling Act to allow Hitler to rule by decree, the Baltimore *Afro-American* ran the headline "Adolf Hitler, K.K.K."[47] The next month Hitler threw all Jews, except war veterans, out of the civil service. When Hitler became chancellor, 30 percent of the

Germans were unemployed; within a year he had halved that number through authoritarian planning and rising militarism.

In July 1933 Hitler sent Communists to Dachau, a concentration camp for political prisoners. Nazi street violence against Jews escalated in 1934 as Hitler declared himself Führer in addition to the constitutional offices of president and chancellor. By the end of the year, Roosevelt pushed Ambassador Dodd to influence Hitler to moderate Nazi persecution of the Jews, but there was little the ambassador could do.

In his first term, FDR refused to take a public stand against Germany's attacks on the Jews, on the basis that he could not interfere in another nation's internal affairs. In the Roosevelt administration, Jews represented 15 percent of the top appointees, but they only made up 3 percent of the U.S. population.[48] Jewish New Dealers worked with little success to prompt a stronger government response. The continuing restrictions on the immigration of German Jews into the United States proved tragic. The immigration quota for Germany was large, but American consuls required proof that immigrants would be self-supporting before they granted them visas. FDR could have loosened this policy, either directly or through Dodd, but he did not do so until 1938. As a result, in 1935, just 20 percent of the German immigration quota was used. "Tens of thousands of German Jews" tried to enter the United States, but only 5,201 received visas.[49]

If many private citizens knew of Hitler's persecution of the Jews from the beginning, why did so few Americans act to stop it? Discrimination against Jews existed across the United States. Moreover, no one expected that Hitler would try to exterminate the Jews. White Americans flinched from intervening in German discrimination, especially since the Great War had left Americans wary of European involvement. At first some Americans even admired the Nazis because Hitler had arrested and imprisoned Communists, who had opposed him at every turn.

Homegrown Radicals: Huey Long, Francis Townsend, and Father Coughlin

Somewhere between unemployed Communists in the streets and fascists hiding in L.A. bunkers lay vast numbers of hungry Americans who believed that if the Depression continued, something must be wrong with the government. Complicated solutions had failed; to some, simple solutions seemed more compelling. Three men—Louisiana senator Huey Long,

Father Charles Coughlin, a Detroit priest with a radio show, and a California doctor, Francis Townsend—offered simple solutions. None of the three hewed to strict ideological lines, and none of their plans would have worked, but they traded in dreams, not in reality.

As governor of Louisiana, Long had taxed the rich to benefit the poor. In turn, the poor adored the man they called the Kingfish. Long had grown up in northern Louisiana's piney woods, while most Louisiana elites came from plantation country to the south. Called the "Messiah of the Rednecks," Long inspired worship. "They do not merely vote for him. They worship the ground he walks on. He is part of their religion," a reporter wrote.[50] FDR privately pronounced Long "one of the two most dangerous men in the country," even as he dined with him.[51] (The other was General Douglas MacArthur.) Senator Long hated bankers, and he opposed emergency financial legislation because it shored up the banking industry, but he supported programs such as the CCC. He voted against the National Industrial Recovery Act, arguing that it gave industry too much power.

Late in 1934 Senator Long announced a radical economic program, the Share Our Wealth Plan. It would effectively cap a single individual's wealth at $4 million and guarantee everyone an annual income of $2,500. It would provide free college tuition, $5,000 to each household, old age pensions, and a shorter working week, all through taxing the wealthy. After someone earned a million dollars annually, the government would keep the rest. Long probably knew that his plan wouldn't work. He did not divulge how he might reclaim cash from the wealthy, or how he might confiscate real estate or stocks. But even if he could redistribute wealth, the plan could not have recovered enough money to alleviate poverty. Nonetheless Long claimed 27,000 Share Our Wealth clubs nationwide.

In Long Beach, California, Francis Townsend looked out his bathroom window one morning and saw three old women rummaging around for food in the garbage cans out back. This was the last straw for the doctor, who wrote to his local newspaper in September 1933, shaming the United States for its treatment of the elderly poor and proposing a solution. Townsend suggested that the government give a two-hundred-dollar monthly stipend to the elderly, provided that they spent it every month or be fined. Townsend could not explain how the government would police the expenditures, or levy and collect the fines. To boost employment among younger workers, the mandatory retirement age would be sixty. A national sales tax would tap the upsurge in spending by the elderly and in turn fund old-age pensions.

Townsend had identified an enormous problem. Most urban workers had not saved for retirement, and many had lost money in bank failures or bankrupt pension plans. Moreover, older people stayed in the workforce to the detriment of young workers. Struggling families often supported elderly parents, sometimes at the expense of feeding children. Like Dr. Townsend, most Americans did not want to live in a society that forced old people to eat from garbage cans. Townsend Clubs had gained half a million members across the country by 1935. As with Long's Share Our Wealth Plan, however, Townsend's numbers did not stand up to scrutiny. The plan would cost $20 billion a year—or half the national income—to support 9 percent of the population. Nonetheless FDR asked the Committee on Economic Security, which Frances Perkins chaired, to draft legislation for an alternative old-age pension plan.

The gold standard found its most ferocious foe in Father Charles Coughlin, who broadcast a radio program—*The Golden Hour of the Shrine of the Little Flower*—from Detroit every Sunday at three p.m. Coughlin began as a simple priest who went on the radio to raise money for his parish building fund, and he became a populist economist preaching bimetallism to the nation. His beautiful radio voice, his gentle homilies, and his broadcast reach earned him the nation's largest radio audience. Coughlin sympathized with Detroit's unemployed autoworkers and drew on a long-standing anti-Communist social justice movement within the Catholic Church.

Coughlin originally argued that "the New Deal is Christ's Deal" and hoped for political influence within the administration. But New Dealers grew increasingly wary of him as he pretended to speak for FDR. "The President is about to remonetize silver," the radio priest announced, when Roosevelt had no intention of doing so.[52] Coughlin began to criticize the New Deal in 1934. He advocated more inflation and became vocally anti-Semitic. Toward the end of the year, he denounced both the Republican and the Democratic Parties and founded the National Union for Social Justice, which became known as the National Union Party.

These New Deal critics promised Americans more than Roosevelt could deliver, even as they tried to address the Great Depression's core issues. Long and Coughlin presented political challenges in 1934 and 1935, while Townsend's followers hounded their elected representatives to provide for the elderly. None of the three had a workable program, but many people believed that the New Deal didn't work either. Both Republicans and Democrats feared the popular fervor that the three men generated, which reminded some of the passion stirred by Hitler and Mussolini's speeches. Nonetheless FDR realized that they popularized solutions for problems that his administration would have to address.

THE NEW DEAL STATE

By 1935, FDR's third year in office, he moved from economic triage to economic rehabilitation. The Works Progress Administration aggressively attacked unemployment by providing government work to the unemployed. Congress passed the National Labor Relations Act to codify union rights in the workplace and arbitrate labor disputes to avoid costly strikes and layoffs. Frances Perkins drafted the Social Security Act to provide a social safety net for the elderly poor and for impoverished children. Black New Dealers worked to address African Americans' economic plight along with their civil rights, even as white southern Democrats fought to limit both. Stabilizing the spending power of these segments of the population would smooth the business cycle and give the federal government more direct involvement in the economy.

Stimulating the economy through government spending suggested that FDR had embraced the theories of the British economist John Maynard Keynes. The son of a Cambridge economist, Keynes had tried to prevent the incorporation of punitive economic measures against Germany into the Treaty of Versailles, on the grounds that reduced German spending would lead to international economic instability. Proven right by the onset of the Great Depression, Keynes then argued against Great Britain's budget cuts in response to the downturn. Keynes argued that in depressions governments should spend, not cut, even if spending created budget deficits. A brilliant mathematician, Keynes demonstrated that every dollar that government spent stimulated consumer spending by two or three times. Increased purchasing power stimulated industry and boosted tax revenues, balancing the budget in the long run.

At Frances Perkins's suggestion, Roosevelt had met with Keynes in 1933. FDR complained to her that Keynes had "left a whole rigmarole of figures." In turn, Keynes complained to Perkins that he had "supposed the

President to be more literate, economically speaking."[53] However complicated Keynes made his theory seem when he explained it, the point was simple: the government could either save or spend, and spending generated economic recovery. FDR did not embrace Keynesian economics as a philosophy; instead, he assessed his own experience in the past two years and factored in labor's demands for a higher standard of living. He had tried both spending and saving, yet the Depression remained intractable. In 1935 he began spending.[54] He soon faced an exceptional challenge in expanding the federal government's economic role as the Supreme Court began ruling legislative programs from the First Hundred Days unconstitutional.

Spending to Save: The Works Progress Administration

In April 1935, Congress approved the Emergency Relief Appropriation Act that gave FDR $5 billion to spend through executive orders. He used it to create the Works Progress Administration (WPA). Unlike the Public Works Administration, in which private industry employed people in government-funded projects, the WPA enabled the government to hire people directly. Ultimately, the WPA employed one out of every three unemployed people—eight million—and spent $11 billion in eight years. WPA workers constructed bridges, dams, high school gyms, and schools, and they built or improved 650,000 miles of road. In San Francisco, they built the Cow Palace, and in Connecticut, they built bridges over the Merritt Parkway.

The WPA sponsored the Federal Art Project, the Federal Theater Project, and the Federal Writers Project, which together saved a generation of creative people and brought art, drama, and history to the public. Working on commission for the WPA, the artist Grant Wood, who had painted *American Gothic* in 1930, designed murals for the library at the University of Iowa. The novelist Richard Wright began writing *Native Son* while employed by the Writers Project. The novelist John Steinbeck used WPA-funded state travel guides to research *The Grapes of Wrath*.

Many Republicans deplored the WPA as a "boondoggle" that wasted tax money on lazy workers. Some quipped that WPA stood for "We Poke Around." A Nashville woman wrote to the president to point out a flaw:

> To the Govner Mr. Roosevelt,
>   . . . Lisen half the men you have Put to work taken there maney When they get paid an spends it for whiskey some don't

Com home with a Peny as have a wife an 4 an 5 Children and not
a Bite to eat. . . . my husban does the same way an I am tired of
it. . Coudent you have there checks mailed to there home. . Can
help us wimen in that way . . . .
                              Just a friend
p.s. if my husban new this he would Kill me[55]

Certainly some WPA workers didn't work, but the WPA itself did work.
Unemployment figures dropped from around 18 percent to 14 percent in
two years. The program renewed the nation's infrastructure and invigorated
its cultural apparatus.

The Limits of the Possible:
Southern Democrats and New Deal Inequities

Inequalities abounded in New Deal programs, many of them enshrined in
the legislation itself, the passage of which depended upon powerful white
southern Democrats in Congress. Because of voting restrictions in the one-
party South, the white Democrats served more consecutive terms in office
and represented fewer people than senators elsewhere in the nation. For
example, Georgia senator William Julius Harris served from 1919 until his
death in 1932. Richard Russell, who replaced him, took office in 1933 and
formed an anti-New Deal coalition in 1937; he served until 1971. These
powerful representatives gained the seniority necessary to control congressional committees. The Senate Committee on Armed Services is a case in
point. During the period 1933 until 2001, with the exception of six years,
southerners chaired the committee or its predecessor, the Committee on
Military Affairs.

Often a New Deal measure had to exclude African Americans to get
out of committee or to gain white southern support on the floor. For example, the NRA exempted certain occupations from its oversight, such as the
fertilizer industry, farm labor, and domestic work, all of which employed
large numbers of African Americans. Southern congressmen initially
objected to the NRA's minimum wages, which paid the same rates to whites
and blacks, but they lost that battle and settled on a geographical differen-
tial that allowed southerners to be paid less than northerners. By planning
production, employers were able to eliminate casual and part-time jobs.
Since African Americans held those jobs in disproportionate numbers, they

nicknamed the NRA the Negro Removal Act and dubbed the Blue Eagle "that Jim Crow bird."[56]

The Agricultural Adjustment Act's payments to landowners to curtail planting put sharecroppers out of jobs. The AAA required that the landowner pass some of the government payment on to his sharecroppers, but that happened only in some bureaucrat's dreams. Pauli Murray, a young North Carolina black woman who worked as a sharecroppers' advocate, explained that white landowners had no intention of handing over AAA money to their tenants: "It's easy for white men to string colored folk along. Promises made are lightly broken; like promises to children or to animals, there's little honor in them."[57] Despite the migration of many black southern sharecroppers to northern cities, the institution continued. Nonetheless, sharecropping continued in certain agricultural regimes and places. In the mid-1930s sharecroppers made up 60 percent of those who raised cotton. In Oklahoma, 180,929 farmed, but 110,700 of them did not own land.

Roosevelt believed that sharecropping retarded agricultural progress, and aid to black and white southern sharecroppers came with strings. In April 1935 he founded the Resettlement Administration (RA) by executive order to dispense 400,000 loans to improve small farms and move farmers into new federal communities. Some of the loans went to sharecroppers to acquire a mule for plowing or to buy canning equipment. RA director Rexford Tugwell opposed programs to end sharecropping quickly because he believed that many sharecroppers were not ready for land ownership. He set up a grandiose bureaucracy to supervise loan recipients' personal and occupational habits. If farmers failed to learn his lessons, Tugwell could relocate them. The RA built several new farm communities, but Tugwell's heart lay with the three towns that the RA built: Greenbelt, Maryland; Greenhills, Ohio; and Greendale, Wisconsin. Critics saw the RA as a symbol of New Deal overreach. It employed 19,700 people and spent $450 million in two years on programs with mixed success.

Constitutional Challenges to the New Deal

In early May 1935 *A.L.A. Schechter Poultry Corp. v. United States*, Schechter's challenge to its forced compliance with NRA rules on wages, hours, and food safety, reached the Supreme Court. Many New Deal programs rested on a broad construction of the constitutional power to regulate interstate commerce. Schechter's attorneys argued that all the company's business was transacted within New York State; hence it was not subject to federal regulation. The plaintiffs also argued that the NRA took up lawmaking authority that the Constitution reserved for Congress. The Supreme Court agreed unanimously on both counts. It found NRA regulation of Schechter's firm to be outside the scope of the interstate commerce clause. Moreover, it agreed that Congress had handed over legislative power to an administrative agency.

FDR realized the ruling's gravity. "We have been relegated to the horse-and-buggy definition of interstate commerce," he complained. The finding that an administrative agency had usurped congressional authority "jeopardized the very concept of rulemaking independent regulatory agencies."[58] The only way forward would be to litigate the constitutionality of every piece of New Deal legislation. The court's ruling hung over Congress as it passed two important bills, the National Labor Relations Act and the Social Security Act. New Dealers suspected that the Supreme Court would overturn both.

The Wagner Act

The Supreme Court's decision in *Schechter* was a setback for labor, since it had depended on Section 7(a) of the NIRA to organize. Anticipating the ruling, Senator Robert Wagner (D-NY) sponsored the National Labor Relations Act (NLRA) to guarantee labor the right to organize. The Wagner Act, as the NLRA was called, required employers to refrain from interfering with union election campaigns and to negotiate fairly with unions. Wagner described it this way: "It seeks merely to make the worker a free man in the economic as well as in the political field."[59] The NLRA legalized collective action, such as strikes, and outlawed the blacklist. It also outlawed the company union, an employee organization within one firm, which many employers had founded in response to Section 7(a). It legalized the majority rule of the closed shop: if a union won the majority of workers' votes, all workers at that location had to allow the union to speak for them. Most important, the Wagner Act created an enforcement arm, the National Labor Relations Board (NLRB). It could force companies to the bargaining table, fine them for breaking the rules, arbitrate a settlement, and order them to rehire workers unfairly fired.

Frances Perkins had known Wagner since the two had joined in investigating the Triangle Shirtwaist Factory fire. She found him self-aggrandizing, resented the fact that he called her Frances instead of Secretary Perkins, and thought he had squandered opportunities as head of the NRA's Labor Committee. But she generally agreed with his politics. Despite their shared goals, she thought the law impossible to enforce. She and Roosevelt feared the power of the proposed NLRB, which would serve as prosecutor, judge, and jury. At first, Perkins quietly tried to sink the bill; FDR declared his support only when its passage seemed certain.

Congress weighed business opposition before it approved the bill in July 1935. The National Association of Manufacturers opposed it strenuously, and the *Commercial and Financial Chronicle* called it "objectionable . . . [and] revolutionary."[60] But the NRA's failure ensured the NLRA's success. Many congressmen wanted to prevent labor unrest like that in 1934, when the unenforceable Section 7(a) had raised workers' expectations without offering them protection. Some supported the NLRB enforcement arm because the NRA had none and had been unable to protect workers in 1934. Others voted for the bill because laws in their home state had already adopted many of the act's features.

After the act passed, it presented a much bigger target for its detractors. Within two weeks, fifty-eight lawyers signed a petition arguing that it was unconstitutional. Employers across the country sought and won injunctions against it, pending court challenges. Within the administration, its management faced hurdles. Wagner had blocked a move that would have made the NLRB part of Perkins's Labor Department, but FDR told the board to report regularly to Perkins. After a few weeks, the board quit consulting her. Nobody was happy, and the NLRB struggled for its first few years.

The Social Security Act

Perkins had a great deal more success with the Social Security Act, which became arguably the New Deal's single most important legacy. She led a committee charged to draw up plans to protect individuals' economic security, and it met for months to draft legislation on old-age pensions, unemployment compensation, and support for needy families. Perkins originally wanted to include health insurance so that an illness would not bankrupt a worker, but she dropped that proposal after the American Medical Association attacked it as "socialized medicine."[61]

The committee tried to design the bill to meet the inevitable Supreme Court test. When Perkins attended an afternoon tea at Justice Harlan

Stone's home, she worried aloud about where to find constitutional authority for social security. Justice Stone leaned over and whispered into her ear: "The taxing power, my dear, the taxing power."[62] Social security funds could be generated by taxing employers and workers, then distributing those taxes as old age pensions. To fund unemployment compensation, one of Perkins's committee members consulted with his father-in-law, Supreme Court justice Louis Brandeis. The justice pointed his son-in-law toward a Supreme Court case on the estate tax that allowed individuals to deduct inheritance taxes paid to their state from their federal taxes. Constitutionally, the federal government did not usurp a state's taxing power if it gave credit for state taxes paid. Practically, this meant that if a state taxed to pay unemployment benefits, then those taxes offset federal taxes and stayed in the state. This enabled states to run unemployment insurance independently, set the amount and duration of payments according to local conditions, and get federal tax credits as an incentive. It was not a perfect plan but it was probably a constitutional one.

Perkins built the Social Security Act on the life cycle of the industrial worker to include unemployment compensation and old-age pensions. Backed by Eleanor Roosevelt, progressive women who had established Mothers' Aid in their states and worked in the federal Children's Bureau lobbied to include Aid to Dependent Children to assist families without a male wage earner. The old and the young were particularly vulnerable to an industrial capitalist economy that demanded that wage laborers save in ways that farmers, who owned land, did not. The employer's reward from the bargain—a flexible labor force at its disposal—required that it make a contribution to the workers' long-term welfare. The Social Security Act recognized that the transition from an agricultural to an industrial nation mandated a role for the government to ensure the smooth running of the capitalist system.

The Social Security Act accomplished far-reaching results using conservative methods. It cost the government nothing, since taxes funded it. The worker and the employer paid up front, and it took a higher percentage of income from low-wage workers. It boosted the overall economy by fulfilling FDR's wish to purge the workforce of those over sixty-five, over half of whom were on relief in 1934. Perkins presented the completed bill as a Christmas present to FDR on December 24, 1934. It would take years to make much of a difference to most people, but when it did, that difference would be enormous. As a policy shift, it institutionalized the federal government's responsibility for the economic well-being of its citizens.

Criticism of the act did not follow typical left or right political divisions. On the right, the National Association of Manufacturers called it socialism, but the president of the national Chamber of Commerce supported it. On the left, African Americans bitterly complained about the exclusion of all domestic workers—maids, cooks, servants—jobs held disproportionately by black men and women. It excluded farmworkers and low-wage church employees. Others complained that it would not start until 1940. One critic pointed out that it was ridiculous to withhold old-age benefits until the age of sixty-five, since the average man lived to be sixty. The Social Security Act became law on August 14, 1935, and *The Washington Post* immediately dubbed it "the New Deal's Most Important Act," noting that "this legislation eventually will affect the lives of every man, woman and child in the country."[63]

United Against Fascism: A Popular Front

Senator Huey Long (D-LA) smoldered as the New Deal ignited. He opposed the Social Security Act because the government bore no part of its expense. He also opposed FDR's Revenue Act of 1935, which imposed a 75 percent tax on incomes over $5 million. Its critics called it the "Soak the Rich" tax, but Long argued that the Revenue Act would give little to the poor compared to his own Share Our Wealth Plan. With the 1936 election in mind, Long complained that Roosevelt and Hoover had been "twin bed mates of disaster" and predicted: "If the Democrats nominate Roosevelt and the Republicans nominate Hoover, Huey Long will be your next president."[64] But a local enemy ended Long's national threat in early September 1935. As the Kingfish walked down the hall in the Baton Rouge statehouse, the son-in-law of a political adversary jumped out from behind a pillar and shot and killed him.

Just two days before that bullet stopped Long's drive to power, the Nazi Party's annual convention in Nuremberg passed "The Law for the Protection of German Blood and German Honor." The Nuremberg Laws mirrored Virginia's 1924 Racial Integrity Act. The Germans defined a Jew as someone with as many as three Jewish grandparents, a provision less strict than Virginia's definition of an African American or a Native American as someone with one great-grandparent of that heritage. Virginia and Germany prohibited marriage between such designated persons and "whites." Germany explicitly banned extramarital sex between Jews and non-Jews and prohibited Jews from employing German domestic workers and displaying the national flag.

The Germans used southern lynchings to characterize their policies as mild methods to prevent violence. Just a few weeks before the Nuremberg convention, Julius Streicher, publisher of *Der Stürmer*, told twenty-five thousand Nazis: "We do not kill Jews in Germany. . . . The treatment of Negroes in America [is] far worse than that accorded Jews by the Nazis."[65] Virginia's racial purity law did not lead to genocide, but it survived Nuremberg's by twenty-two years, until 1967, when the Supreme Court ruled it unconstitutional in *Loving v. Virginia*.

Hitler repudiated the Versailles Treaty by discontinuing reparations payments in May 1933 and initiating conscription in the armed forces in March 1935. Thinking of the *Lusitania*, Congress passed the Neutrality Act of 1935, which forbade U.S. citizens to travel on ships of hostile nations. With the 1917 arms lobby in mind, the act also forbade selling arms to belligerent nations. In October 1935, Mussolini's invasion of Ethiopia confirmed African Americans' fears that fascist racism would spread, and African Americans demonstrated against it in New York.

In response to the rise of fascism, in late 1935 the Seventh Comintern Congress reversed the Soviet line and announced a Popular Front to unite liberals, socialists, and Communists to fight fascism. After the Popular Front, CPUSA membership grew from 26,000 in 1934 to 85,000 by 1939. Most important, it allowed Americans on the far left to work with moderate social reformers.

Civil rights activism burgeoned in the Popular Front as African Americans capitalized on the racial hatred that drove German fascism. In December 1935 some black leaders and athletes talked about boycotting the 1936 Olympics in Berlin in solidarity with the Jews. Talk of a boycott faded in favor of letting black athletes compete against the vaunted racial superiority of the Germans. The blazingly fast Ohioan Jessie Owens joined fourteen other black athletes in Berlin.

To avoid international criticism, Hitler ordered anti-Semitic graffiti removed from walls and temporarily banned press attacks on Jews. Nonetheless he reportedly complained, "Americans ought to be ashamed of themselves for letting their medals be won by Negroes."[66] Owens won four gold

No. 86251

ORIGINAL.

James R Miller

UNITED STATES OF AMERICA.

Certificate of Residence.

Issued to Chinese _Other than Labor_, under the Provisions of the Act of May 5, 1892.

This is to Certify THAT _Wong Fay_, a Chinese _Other than Labor_, now residing at _San Bernardino_ has made application No. _5512_ to me for a Certificate of Residence, under the provisions of the Act of Congress approved May 5, 1892, and I certify that it appears, from the affidavits of witnesses submitted with said application that said _Wong Fay_ was within the limits of the United States at the time of the passage of said Act, and was then residing at _San Bernardino_ and that he was at that time lawfully entitled to remain in the United States, and that the following is a descriptive list of said Chinese _Other than Labor_ viz.:

NAME: _Wong Fay_   AGE: _30 years._
LOCAL RESIDENCE: _San Bernardino_
OCCUPATION: _Doctor & Druggist_ HEIGHT: _5 ft. 4½ in_ COLOR OF EYES: _Brown_
COMPLEXION: _Medium_
PHYSICAL MARKS OR PECULIARITIES FOR
IDENTIFICATION: _Two large scars over right ear._

And as a further means of identification, I have affixed hereto a photographic likeness of said _Wong Fay._

GIVEN UNDER MY HAND AND SEAL this _9_ day of _April_, 1894 at _Redlands_ State of _Calif_

O. M. Welburn
Collector of Internal Revenue,
per James R Miller
District of _Calif_

Wong Fey's Certificate of Residence Wong Fey, an immigrant from China, was able to enter the United States after the passage of the 1892 Chinese Exclusion Act because he was "other than laborer," in fact, a doctor and druggist. This certificate of residence allowed him to live in San Bernardino, California, in 1894.

William F. Fonvielle Fonvielle's yearbook photograph at Livingston College, Salisbury, North Carolina, shows him around 1893, near the time that the college newspaper editor set off on his southern trip to report on the spread of segregation. African American college students like Fonvielle saw themselves as representatives of "the Race" and were careful to conform to Victorian middle-class standards of gentlemanly dress and deportment.

***First to Fall in the Spanish-American
War*** (clockwise from top left) When the *USS
Winslow* came under attack on May 11, 1898,
officer Worth Bagley of North Carolina, cook
Elijah B. Tunnel of Virginia, and sailor George
Meek of Ohio became the first men to die in
the Spanish-American War. The ensuing conflict brought northerners, southerners, and the
sons of slaves together as they fought the short
war that forged a new national identity as a
global power.

Woodrow Wilson and Alice Paul Thomas Woodrow Wilson, shown here before winning the 1912 presidential election, met his match in Alice Paul. The radical woman suffragist, shown here on board a ship in 1914, led protests at the White House throughout World War I. Both proved to be uncompromising advocates for their ideals—but Paul alone prevailed.

Leading the Suffrage Parade Labor lawyer Inez Milholland, dubbed by the *New York Times* "one of the most beautiful women in the United States," mounted on Grey Dawn to lead the National American Woman Suffrage Association parade on March 3, 1913, the day before President Woodrow Wilson's inauguration. Milholland subsequently left NAWSA for Alice Paul's National Woman's Party. Her death in 1916 inspired NWP leaders in their suffrage fight during WWI.

Harry T. Burn   This twenty-four-year-old legislator's deciding vote in the Tennessee legislature completed the ratification of the Nineteenth Amendment in 1920. Burn switched his vote to approve woman suffrage in accordance with his mother's wishes.

Oscar de Priest   Representing Chicago as the first black congressman in the twentieth century, De Priest points to the "For Members Only" sign on the House of Representatives restaurant following an attempt by Howard University students to eat there in 1934.

Frances Perkins   Secretary of Labor Frances Perkins in 1945 wearing one of her customary hats. She inspired, crafted, and helped pass the most significant social welfare legislation of the New Deal.

Mary McLeod Bethune   Pictured here in front of the U.S. Capitol building around 1950, Bethune was a formidable founder of the Black Cabinet during the New Deal.

Huey Long   Charismatic Senator Huey Long of Louisiana, speaking with his customary flourish on the campaign trail for Senator Hattie Caraway in Arkansas in 1932. At first a New Deal supporter, Long turned to more radical economic measures in his Share Our Wealth Plan and announced his candidacy for the presidency weeks before he was assassinated in 1935.

Salaria Kea Facing employment discrimination at home, African American nurse Salaria Kea joined the Republican Medical Services in the Spanish Civil War. In Spain, she married an Irish volunteer and was detained for six weeks by German troops. Americans such as Kea who fought in the Spanish Civil War felt desperate to stop fascism as the United States remained neutral.

Charles Lindbergh Lucky Lindy (right), America's favorite aviator, inspects German aircraft in Munich in 1938 on a U.S. government-sponsored trip to appraise the air power of European nations. He returned to the U.S. greatly impressed with the German *Luftwaffe*.

Seasoned Politician and First Lady   Eleanor Roosevelt speaking in favor of FDR's nomination for a third term at the Democratic National Convention in Chicago on July 18, 1940.

Pearl Harbor Heroes   First Lieutenant Lewis M. Sanders (far right) and Second Lt. Philip M. Rasmussen (second from left) after receiving the Distinguished Service Cross for their actions on December 7, 1941.

Interned at Heart Mountain   Stanley Igawa's basketball team, the Whippets, at Heart Mountain Relocation Camp. The labeling is unclear, but Igawa seems to be the first player on the right in the first row.

Hiroshima   Misled about the dangers of radiation, war correspondents from around the world, such as the man pictured here, reported from Hiroshima in the days and weeks after the atomic bomb destroyed the city, killed 140,000, and sickened hundreds of thousands more.

medals and tied two world records, and African Americans used the Olympics to claim full citizenship. W. E. B. Du Bois attended the Olympics and predicted (after he was safely out of Germany) that Hitler would declare "world war on Jews."[67]

CEMENTING THE DEMOCRATIC ASCENDANCY

The presidential election of 1936 would be a referendum on the New Deal. It marked the beginning of the New Deal coalition, cementing a national Democratic ascendency that would last for decades. Northern African Americans abandoned the Republican Party for the Democrats, entering into an alliance with northern industrial workers and white southern Democrats. The new Congress of Industrial Organizations revived labor and supported the coalition by moving more workers into the Democratic Party.

The New Deal coalition often overlooked a widening split between liberal and conservative Democrats at the local and state levels but hung together to elect Democrats to Congress and the presidency. FDR would take his sweeping victory as a mandate for the government's role in the economy and in individual lives. Remedies born in crisis proved the basis for a liberal state.

Labor's Rise

The July passage of the Wagner Act presented organized labor an unprecedented chance to rebuild, but many in the AFL thought that the organization was not up to the task. Union membership had grown from 7 percent of workers in 1930 to 16.6 percent in 1935, but it failed to represent most female and black workers. The exclusions sprang in part from the AFL's composition as a craft union, bringing together skilled workers across industries, and in part from discrimination. Only 45 of the AFL's 111 unions admitted African Americans at all. Those that did generally segregated them in Jim Crow locals. Asa Philip Randolph, president of the Brotherhood of Sleeping Car Porters, had been trying for a decade to get the AFL to recognize his black union. Empowered by the Wagner Act, Randolph finally won AFL recognition for the Brotherhood in 1935.

At the AFL's October 1935 convention, United Mine Workers president John L. Lewis staged a revolt. Lewis grew up in the company town of Cleveland, Iowa, and went to work in its coal mine at seventeen. At the convention, he argued against craft unionism in favor of industrial union-ism: organizing entire industries and representing all workers in them. The United Automobile Workers had already organized along these lines. The Wagner Act, with its emphasis on *workplace* negotiations, supported Lewis's vision. As John Lewis got up to address the AFL, Bill Hutcheson, president of the Carpenters Union, called him a bastard. Lewis punched him in the jaw, lit his cigar, and walked down the aisle to take the podium. The follow-ing month, Lewis launched the Congress of Industrial Organizations (CIO). He faced two challenges: to bring AFL members into the CIO and to orga-nize nonunion workers. CIO unions soon discovered that in most work-places they would have to wage war to implement the Wagner Act.

Workers began organizing and striking with renewed vigor in 1936. Four factors contributed to labor's gathering strength. First, signs began to point faintly toward a recovery. New building permits rose, unemployment dropped by almost 5 percent in a year, and the percentage of business fail-ures continued to decline. Personal income rose for the third straight year. Second, the Wagner Act offered a sort of organizing handbook, scripting the role of the employer, the employee, and the government. Third, John L. Lewis began to organize workplaces across craft lines and job categories into CIO unions. He took this vertical organizing to the steel plant that Andrew Carnegie had built through vertical trusts. Thus, it was both symbolic and strategic when, in June 1936, Lewis announced the Steel Workers Organiz-ing Committee, invited the governor of Pennsylvania to a picnic, and called upon him to enforce the Wagner Act at the Homestead Steel Mill. The governor promised to do so. The CIO organized the plant from bottom to top and in March 1937 won a contract with Homestead. Despite numerous setbacks in organizing other "little steel" companies, such as Republic and Bethlehem, by 1941 the union had organized the entire industry.

The fourth factor behind labor's rise in the late 1930s was the most controversial: the sit-down strike, which began on January 29, 1936, at the Firestone Tire Company in Akron, Ohio, and spread around the world. It started on a night shift when Clay Dicks, an ardent union man, got into a fistfight with a nonunion man on the shop floor. The bosses fired Dicks, and an eerie silence fell over the line as the men built tires. At two a.m. the workers cut off their machines and fell back a step. They sang "John Brown's Body," then "Glory, Glory, Hallelujah!" and sat down to stay for a while.

Without the line's production, the rest of the factory sat idle. After Firestone workers had been sitting inside the factory for three days, workers at Goodyear Tire across town sat down too. Sit-down strikes spread to other industries and across the Atlantic to France.

As a tactic, the sit-down strike gave workers extraordinary power. Instead of being relegated to a picket line outside factory property, they held the power of production. Sit-down strikes paralyzed factories and minimized violent retribution because the owner's property lay in the strikers' hands. Finally, sit-down strikes attracted great news coverage. The story became "what are they doing in there and when are they coming out?" as opposed to "picketing continued." By the time the United Auto Workers (UAW) went on strike in Flint, Michigan, in November 1936, the strikers knew how to maximize the theater of the sit-down. Union membership doubled from 1930 to 1940, reaching nine million that year.

The CIO organized black workers along with whites, a departure from the AFL practice. It made sense to organize all workers in a single workplace, and it deterred nonunion African Americans accepting jobs as strikebreakers. In the South, the integrated unions such as the Food, Tobacco, Agricultural and Allied Workers of America–CIO brought black southerners into an industrial democracy. Many of those who voted in union elections voted for the first time in their lives, and black men and women took leadership positions in unions. The participation of black southerners in unionism contributed to broader efforts for civil rights by protecting workers' rights to speak out and training leaders.

The 1936 Election and Modern Liberalism

Despite the ominous developments overseas, the administration remained focused on domestic challenges. In his January 1936 State of the Union speech, FDR considered the New Deal's cumulative effects. Unemployment had dropped by 33 percent, and personal income had risen 50 percent. Farm income had increased by almost 60 percent, and corporations celebrated a $6 billion profit increase over the dismal losses of 1933. The WPA and the CCC had put 70 percent of the unemployed to work.

The Supreme Court continued to limit Roosevelt's policy choices. In January the court found the Agricultural Adjustment Act unconstitutional in *United States v. Butler*. With the New Deal's prime programs—the NRA and the AAA—deemed unconstitutional, FDR argued that the Supreme Court "virtually prohibits the President and Congress . . . to intervene reasonably in the regulation of nation-wide commerce and nation-wide agriculture."[68]

An unapologetic Roosevelt ran on his record in 1936 and defended an activist federal government. In June the Republican Party nominated for president Alfred Mossman Landon, who had won the governor's seat in traditionally Democratic Kansas. Down-to-earth Landon—much was made of his habit of borrowing pipe tobacco—was unconnected to wealthy Republicans in urban areas. Roosevelt pretended to be the common man, but Landon actually was. FDR warned voters that a Republican victory would reinstate elite economic rule.[69] Father Coughlin's creation, the National Union Party, nominated William Lemke for the presidency. Coughlin accused Roosevelt of being a Communist and hinted at armed resistance if FDR won. He began openly to praise Hitler and Mussolini. Finally, the Catholic Church called him to account, and Lemke ended up with less than 2 percent of the vote.

The election's outcome was never in doubt. Landon won only Vermont and Maine, for a total of eight electoral votes. Roosevelt won the largest popular majority ever, 60.8 percent, and the largest Electoral College margin since 1820, 523 of the total 531. With Roosevelt's victory, voters affirmed the New Deal.

The 1936 election is most notable for the electoral realignment that it initiated. Large numbers of voters abandoned the Republican Party for the Democrats, who would go on to win five of the following seven presidential elections. The Democrats represented the nation's working class, urban dwellers, immigrants, African Americans, Catholics, and midwestern farmers, even as they maintained support among white southerners. More than 80 percent of African Americans—the many who voted in the North and the few who voted in the South—voted for Roosevelt in 1936 and would continue to do so for the remainder of the century and beyond.

This New Deal coalition formed a majority Democratic Party that would hold the balance of power for three decades. The Republicans increasingly became the party of big business and ideological conservatives such as those in the Liberty League. White southern Democrats always disagreed with the growing Democratic support for civil rights and civil liberties, and in the 1960s and 1970s their discontent would fragment the party.

The consensus of the New Deal coalition was that the federal government should play a vital economic role and exercise responsibility for the basic welfare of the American people. Government had grown dramatically to police the financial markets and actively regulate the currency. It eased unemployment, encouraged unions, and took an active role in the employer-employee relationship. Through planning and direct intervention, the government took control of agricultural policy from land use to marketing. Two acts, the Federal Emergency Relief Act and the Social Security Act, redefined the government's relationship with the individual. The federal government took responsibility for public welfare.

Modern liberalism, emphasizing government economic activism and a social welfare system, began in FDR's first term. The overwhelming victory in the 1936 election ratified it, and it became the cornerstone of American life.

CHAPTER 6

A RENDEZVOUS WITH DESTINY, 1936–1941

NOTHING MUCH EVER HAPPENED to Ada Margaret Olsson, whom everyone called Peggy. Born in Junction City, Kansas, in 1916, she had lived ever since in the same white frame house with the big front porch on the wide street under the vast prairie sky. Her dad directed the high school band, so they survived the Depression better than many of their neighbors. Her father's parents had immigrated to the Midwest from Sweden, and her mother's parents came from England, but Peggy's world was small. She was twenty years old when Franklin Delano Roosevelt accepted the Democratic nomination for a second term on June 27, 1936.

Boy Scout Gordon Sterling had experienced hard times in 1932, when his dad lost his job in a typewriter factory in New York, but by 1934 his father had found work in Hartford, Connecticut. A junior in high school in 1936, Gordon started hanging out at the local airstrip and talked the pilots into teaching him how to fly.

His contemporary, eighteen-year-old Phil Rasmussen, listened to the president from his family's home in Boston. His father, a Danish immigrant, had hung on to the house through the Depression working as a painting contractor. Rasmussen set his sights on entering Pennsylvania's Gettysburg College in the fall.

Lew Sanders worked at the radio store in Elkhart, Indiana, where his wife Madge was the payroll clerk. But his weekend life as a barnstorming pilot seemed much more exciting than selling radios. When FDR's voice came across the airwaves into his shop, Lew was twenty-nine years old, and he wondered what he had to show for it. He dreamed of joining the U.S. Army Air Corps so that he could fly full time.[1]

Roosevelt used his nomination acceptance speech to reach Peggy, Gordon, Phil, and Lew. The president recalled his first term: "In those days we feared fear. . . . We have conquered fear." But he warned, "I cannot, with candor, tell you that all is well with the world. Clouds of suspicion, tides of ill-will and intolerance gather darkly in many places." To those who had come of age during the Depression, he said, "To some generations much is given. Of other generations much is expected. . . . This generation of Americans has a rendezvous with destiny." During his first term, Americans had waged a war against "want and destitution." But this, he added, "is more than that; it is a war for the survival of democracy. . . . I am enlisted for the duration of the war."[2] It would be up to Peggy and Gordon and Phil and Lew to fulfill that destiny—to ensure freedom's survival—even though on that warm summer evening in 1936, they could not imagine it.

During Roosevelt's second term, tension arose over the growth of the liberal state, the best methods by which to fight the Depression, whether to rebuild the country's weak military, and the contours of U.S. neutrality as fascist aggression grew in Europe and the Pacific. In 1937 and 1938 FDR's priorities remained ending the Depression and institutionalizing the New Deal's social welfare agenda. In 1937 the economy unexpectedly dipped, just as FDR tried to add justices to the Supreme Court. Court-packing, as Roosevelt's initiative became known, cost him public support and energized anti–New Dealers, now united in a coalition of Republicans, midwestern Democrats, and white Southerners. The coalition opposed governmental spending, which it said slowed the rate of the country's military preparedness.

In 1937 an overwhelming majority of Americans opposed sending U.S. troops to fight fascism, even though Roosevelt thought that eventuality likely. When war broke out in Europe in 1939, the debate's parameters shifted to whether the United States should use defense dollars to aid Britain, and if so, in what ways. FDR spent valuable time appeasing those who wanted to cut government spending, and military allocations suffered as a result. These domestic and foreign events, from the summer of 1936 until December 7, 1941, show the connections between the Depression's end and the war's beginning. Military spending did more to end the Depression than any single New Deal program. The growth of the federal government during the economic war of the mid-1930s gave the United States the structure, personnel, and planning expertise that it needed to prepare the nation to wage a military war.

THE NEW DEAL AT HIGH TIDE

In his 1937 inaugural address, the first to occur in January, Roosevelt pledged to help the "one-third of a nation [that was] ill-housed, ill-clad, ill-nourished," but privately he complained that the Supreme Court prevented him from doing his job.[3] When it ruled the NRA and the AAA unconstitutional, the court had limited the scope of interstate commerce and Congress's ability to delegate rule making to administrative agencies. In mid-1936, in *Morehead v. New York ex rel. Tipaldo*, the court had found unconstitutional the New York state minimum wage law for women and children on the grounds that it violated liberty of contract—the right of individuals to bargain freely with employers. FDR exploded that the court made the workplace a "no man's land where no Government—State or Federal—can function."[4] Unless something changed, the court would overturn the Wagner Act, the Social Security Act, and every other piece of New Deal legislation. The First New Deal might have rankled the Supreme Court, but it had saved people's lives. The fight against the highest court in the land was on in the court of public opinion.

Court-packing: FDR's Plan

The Constitution does not set the number of Supreme Court justices. Before 1937 there had been numbers greater and lesser than nine sitting justices. Roosevelt suggested to his cabinet that he increase that number. As Secretary of the Interior Harold Ickes remembered, Frances Perkins stood alone in her opposition, "but I suppose that was to be expected of a woman. Apparently she thinks we ought to pussyfoot on the Supreme Court issue."[5] Perkins was right, but this time Roosevelt chose not to listen to her.

In early February 1937, FDR submitted the Judiciary Reorganization Bill to Congress. It increased the number of justices on the Supreme Court and in the lower federal courts by providing that if a justice or federal judge reached his seventieth birthday and failed to retire within six months, the president could nominate another to work beside him. The bill would allow FDR immediately to appoint six new justices, since six of the nine sitting on the Supreme Court were over seventy years old. With a backlog of cases clogging the courts, Roosevelt argued for the bill as an efficiency measure.

The court-packing bill, as it became known, marked the end of Roosevelt's long honeymoon with the American people. He told Americans in a fireside chat on March 9, 1937, that the Supreme Court deserved much of the blame for the continuing Depression. The people must "save the Constitution from the Court." He asserted his right to appoint justices, just as his predecessors had. If the current members would not retire, he had a responsibility to act. He pointed out that since the court's opinions generally fell five to four against New Deal programs, one person had the power to overturn legislative will.[6]

Roosevelt overplayed his hand. Listeners heard in the speech rumblings of a Huey Long, echoes of authoritarian European dictators, and a little bit of unbecoming whining. Adding six New Dealers to the nine sitting justices looked like a presidential power grab. Disguising it as an efficiency measure disturbed even apolitical people who remembered their grade school lessons on the separation of powers. Moreover, as the economic news improved in late 1936 and early 1937, many thought the president should divest, rather than increase, executive power. Princeton University's president suggested that the "time has come for a healthy skepticism of an emergency justifying revolutionary proposals."[7] Groups as diverse as the Grange, the Daughters of the American Revolution, and liberal attorneys condemned the bill. The united opposition to it across ideological, political, class, and regional lines stunned FDR.

With Democratic majorities in both the Senate and the House, the Judiciary Reorganization Bill marked the first sign of considerable legislative resistance to FDR's initiatives. To salt Roosevelt's wound, several New Deal Democrats led the Senate opposition. Senator Burton Wheeler (D-MT), who served on the Judiciary Committee, was "flabbergasted" when he heard of the court-packing scheme. Wheeler had built his legal reputation as a young federal prosecutor when he refused to file ungrounded cases for the Justice Department during the 1919 Red Scare and exposed the 1922 Teapot Dome bribery scandal. A novel based on his life became the film *Mr. Smith Goes to Washington*, with the beloved Jimmy Stewart playing Wheeler.[8]

Senator Wheeler, who had been the first member of the Senate to endorse FDR in 1932, now called the Judiciary Reorganization Bill "fundamentally unsound, undemocratic, and reactionary in principle." Changing the composition of the Supreme Court, he asserted, could be done only by constitutional amendment. He reminded Americans that in Germany there was "one who sits in the driver's seat and makes the subservient branches of the government bow to his will. And he does it in the name of modern democracy."[9] Wheeler built a coalition of midwestern and western Democrats to oppose the bill. This faction would combine with southern Democrats to thwart Roosevelt.

Some southern Democrats had long opposed New Deal programs that treated African Americans as full citizens; now they worried that a more liberal court might rule against Jim Crow laws. The court-packing bill brought them allies from other regions. In 1936 they were also dismayed that northern, urban black voters had so strongly supported FDR's reelection and worried that he might undertake to represent African Americans more vigorously. Southern white Democrats like Senator Carter Glass of Virginia owed much to the existing power structure, including the congressional seniority system and the ability of the Supreme Court to curb New Deal programs. Glass called the court-packing bill "a repugnant scheme to disrupt representative government."[10]

Court-packing: From Defeat to Victory

In a damning report on the bill in May 1937, the Senate Judiciary Committee disparaged it as "devious," an astonishing insult to the president. The report pointed out that, with authoritarian governments on the rise elsewhere, an independent judiciary mattered more than ever. One commentator equated the report with a secession manifesto for conservative Democrats. Despite this slap in the face, Roosevelt's first-class temperament rose to the occasion, and he invited all 407 congressional Democrats to a rural retreat the next weekend. The only item on the agenda was to relax and have fun, while FDR sat in a chair under a tree and "radiated geniality," especially to the seven Democrats who had contributed to the report.[11]

During the hottest July in memory, senators itched to leave Washington as the Senate majority leader from Arkansas, the FDR loyalist Joseph Robinson, pushed the Judiciary Reorganization Bill along, buoyed by enough senatorial promises to pass it. But after days of debate in the muggy Senate chambers, Robinson died of a heart attack. Burton Wheeler turned the death into political capital: "Had it not been for the Court Bill [Robinson] would be alive today. I beseech the President to drop the fight lest he appear to fight against God." The Senate ultimately voted 70 to 20 against court-packing. *The New York Times* reported that "many Senators" considered it "the worst defeat suffered by a president since the Senate rejected President Wilson's League of Nations."[12]

Nonetheless, because of events that unfolded concurrently with the Judiciary Reorganization Bill's failure, the Supreme Court began to uphold New Deal programs. Just after the bill's introduction in March, the Supreme Court had surprised everyone by upholding a Washington state minimum wage for women in the case *West Coast Hotel Co. v. Parrish.* Few knew that the decision predated the court-packing bill, so it appeared to defer to the impending legislation. Justice Owen Roberts, who usually voted with the four or five conservative justices, had switched his vote and upheld the minimum wage. Pundits called it "the switch in time that saved nine." Roberts changed his mind about liberty of contract not because of the court-packing bill but because he had begun to question the court's dismantling of New Deal legislation in general. Law reviews had condemned the court's decisions over the past two years, and citizens had hanged effigies of the justices. Roberts understood that lower courts had begun to limit liberty of contract and expand the definition of interstate commerce, and those cases would soon clog the Supreme Court's calendar. Moreover, Roberts considered FDR's popularity, as evidenced by his recent landslide victory.

When Frances Perkins heard the decision in *West Coast Hotel,* she hugged Roberts, who was married to her best friend, and said, "Owen, I am so proud of you! . . . A man of your social standing and intelligence who is not afraid to change his mind!" Roberts looked sheepish and protested that a technicality made *West Coast Hotel* more constitutional than *Tipaldo.*[13] Nonetheless, Roberts remained on the liberal side. In August, Roosevelt appointed Senator Hugo Black of Alabama to the court. Black was the exceptional southern Democrat who had supported all of Roosevelt's New Deal legislation. Liberals now outnumbered conservatives six to four.

Roosevelt won the court and lost the Congress. Anti–New Deal Democrats began openly to oppose FDR's leadership and New Deal principles. The loss of support left him weakened just when an unexpected economic collapse waited in the wings, and it undermined his confidence in his ability to lead American public opinion. Formerly, he had felt public approval like the wind at his back; now he feared the cross-currents of disapproval.

The "Roosevelt Recession"

Mauled by the court-packing fight and worried about fascist aggression, at least Franklin Roosevelt could take some cheer from his partial victory over the Great Depression. In a speech in August 1937, he implied to Americans that the worst was over. Economic news from the first and second quarter of 1937 bolstered his confidence. Unemployment had fallen from roughly 25 percent of the workforce to just over 14 percent, leaving seven million people still seeking work, the lowest number since 1930. Manufacturing output exceeded 1934 figures by 40 percent, and national income rose from $42 billion in1932 to $72 billion. The stock market appeared robust.

With such promising news, Roosevelt moved to fulfill his 1936 campaign promise to balance the budget. He lacked the political capital to continue huge deficit spending, even if he had wanted to. In 1937 he asked Congress for a public works budget 66 percent smaller than that of 1935, cutting much of the WPA and PWA funding. Congress tried to reduce that appropriation even further but failed. Still, eliminating $2 billion from public works programs resulted in layoffs and directly reduced consumer spending.

The Social Security taxes withheld from paychecks for the first time in 1936 and 1937 took another $2 billion out of circulation; the first payouts to retired workers would not start until 1940. Wage gains, long overdue and often won by the CIO, increased some unionized workers' purchasing power, but at the same time they reduced the capital available for business investment. Since the summer of 1936, the Federal Reserve had worried that excess reserves—money sitting in deposit in member banks—would prompt unwise lending. It twice raised gold requirements so that regional branches had to maintain gold at 50 percent of their currency reserves. Thus, with unemployment still relatively high and production levels still recovering, the Fed tightened the money supply and credit.[14] Finally, businesses lacked the will to invest in increased production or new ventures. The Great Depression had taught management the lesson of preserving equity for hard times, so companies sat on cash. Some speculated that business colluded to withhold investments in a capital strike to restrain Roosevelt.

The prosperous summer of 1937 turned back to the future to relive the devastating fall of 1929. The stock market crested in August and proceeded to lose over one-third of its value by December. The index of industrial activity fell from an August high of 117 to 76 nine months later, back to 1934 levels. Four million newly unemployed workers joined the seven million already without jobs, pushing the percentage back up to 20 percent. The stock market bottomed out at a 43 percent loss. Some estimated that two-thirds of the progress made from January 1933 to August 1937 had been lost in thirteen months.

Herbert Hoover's shadow loomed over the White House. The Republicans and anti–New Deal Democrats sneeringly named the downturn the "Roosevelt Recession," as the administration fell into disarray. A Roosevelt staffer observed, "All the courage has oozed out of the President."[15] Roosevelt's confidence had hitherto put others at ease, inspired hope, and allowed him to charm opponents without acceding to their requests. It had enabled him to act when Hoover had remained frozen. It had restored consumer faith in banking, persuaded people of different political ideologies to work together, and encouraged experimentation.

Faced with a recession, like Hoover in the dark days of 1932, Roosevelt urged no action. In October 1937 he told the cabinet, "Everything will work out if we just sit tight and keep quiet."[16] But with the president quiet, the conflicting opinions that underlay the New Deal's experimentation deepened into ideological trenches from which administrators sniped at one another. Their arguments were not just about the future, they were about the past: which programs had actually worked and why?

Advisers offered conflicting remedies to stanch the downturn. Secretary of the Treasury Henry Morgenthau, a close friend and Hyde Park neighbor of the Roosevelts, promoted a balanced budget to restore business confidence. Others argued for increased government spending. Antimonopolists wanted to break up big business and more closely regulate finance. Ivy League economists and lawyers saw big business and big labor as facts of life and advocated centralized government planning to manage them. Roosevelt's advisers fell into factions as the Roosevelt Recession worsened. In November, tired of sitting tight, Roosevelt called a special session of Congress and introduced legislation to bolster the economy. But Congress figured that it could blame this recession on FDR and defeated all but one of his proposals.

Roosevelt realized that he had to start spending to stimulate the economy. In the next annual budget, which he submitted in April 1938, he asked for $5 billion for public works and relief. He gave up balancing the budget and talked Morgenthau out of resigning in protest. Congress approved loosening gold requirements, knowing that if it rejected the Fed's request, the Roosevelt Recession might be renamed the Congressional Recession. By June the stock market rallied, and commodity prices rose. Government spending had rallied the economy. Henceforth Roosevelt believed in the power of spending, even if he still failed to grasp John Maynard Keynes's "rigmarole of figures." This time, however, spending did not lower unemployment.

Implementing a National Economic Policy

Despite Roosevelt's congressional troubles, two crucial pieces of New Deal legislation passed in 1938: the Fair Labor Standards Act and a revised Agricultural Adjustment Act. Together with the Social Security Act, they set federal policy for the remainder of the century and became the New Deal's major legacies. The new AAA reprised the legislation on agriculture but removed a tax that the Supreme Court had found unconstitutional. It established federal commodity supports as the cornerstone of agricultural policy.

The Fair Labor Standards Act (FLSA) of 1938 established the wage and hour policies that henceforth served as the foundations of governmental labor regulation. Frances Perkins had spent months writing the bill before FDR brought it to Congress in May 1937. Arguments abounded over the specific features, such as whether the minimum wage should be a set rate nationally or vary by region. Perkins carefully compromised on details but not on principles. In the final law, states had to adopt a minimum wage, but each state could determine the amount, provided it was above twenty-five cents an hour. Some 200,000 people made less than that. If a state chose to put the minimum wage at twenty-five cents, it had to raise it annually by five cents for five years. The maximum workweek began at forty-four hours and then dropped to forty in three years. The white southern congressional bloc succeeded in excluding domestic and farm workers, effectively depriving most black southerners of the law's benefits. However, the bill's principles—no child labor, a minimum wage, a standard workweek, and overtime pay—became rights to which workers felt entitled.

Roosevelt then tried to bring the southern economy in line with the rest of the nation's. He formed the Advisory Committee on Economic Conditions in the South in 1938, staffed by twenty-two southern white liberals outside government who submitted their report to Roosevelt in the summer. The president acknowledged publicly, "The South presents right now the nation's No. 1 economic problem—the Nation's problem, not merely the South's." He named exhausted land, low farm income, sharecropping, and "absentee ownership" of southern industry as problems that resulted in deficiencies in education, housing, and health.[17] The report did not separate economic data by race, so the South could no longer hide behind its Jim Crow system. Roosevelt quoted the report on the stump through the South, where he supported New Deal candidates in the Democratic primaries, trying to unseat those southern congressmen who had bedeviled him over the court-packing bill, the Roosevelt Recession, and the Fair Labor Standards Act.

But Roosevelt wasted the summer and his strength on the South. Every one of the Roosevelt-endorsed candidates lost to anti–New Deal Democrats. To make matters worse, New Deal congressmen lost their seats elsewhere in the country as well. The Republicans gained eighty seats in the House and eight in the Senate in November 1938.

FASCIST AMBITIONS, AMERICAN NEUTRALITY

As the economy improved in 1938, the debate over U.S. policy toward fascist aggression heated up. Most Americans wanted their country to stay neutral in the face of the growing threat. From 1934 through 1936, the Special Committee on the Munitions Industry, led by Senator Gerald Nye (R-MD), convinced the public that the munitions industry had colluded with bankers to push the United States into the Great War. A best-selling 1935 book, *Merchants of Death*, and a Great War memoir, *War Is a Racket*, by the distinguished Marine Corps General Smedley Butler, exposed deals among munitions manufacturers, financiers, and the government. Nye admired the pacifist senator Robert La Follette (R-WI), who had opposed World War I, and Republicans in the upper Midwest harbored considerable resistance to intervention that echoed William Jennings Bryan's populist idea that war precludes domestic reform.

The Nye Committee set the stage for Congress to pass a series of Neutrality Acts. Senator William Borah (R-ID), who had been an irreconcilable against the Treaty of Versailles back in 1919, was the force behind the 1935 and 1936 Neutrality Acts. Senator Burton Wheeler (D-MT), who had attacked court-packing, staunchly supported the Neutrality Acts. These conservative midwesterners joined with a group of southern anti–New Deal

Democrats, most of them representing agrarian districts steeped in populist politics. Thus the congressional anti-interventionists of the late 1930s resembled the irreconcilables who had opposed the Treaty of Versailles, but with wider representation.

When Hitler began to rearm Germany in 1935, Great Britain and France had not followed suit and therefore sought to buy equipment from the United States. The Neutrality Act of 1935 prohibited U.S. companies from trading in war materials with nations at war and warned that any American traveled at his own risk on the ship of a belligerent nation. Congress renewed the act in 1936 and 1937. Since no European nation had declared war, the acts had little tangible effect. They did have considerable propaganda value within the United States, since they focused public attention on the advantages of neutrality. Roosevelt feared that they would prevent a quick U.S. response if war did break out.

Japanese Aggression

By late 1938 it became clear to Roosevelt that Japanese ambitions in the Pacific and the spread of fascism in Europe mandated that the United States prepare to defend itself. Japan had held resource-rich Manchuria since 1931, aided by an army that used aeronautical and automobile technology under license in the 1920s from British and American manufacturers.[18] Some 80 percent of Japan's oil supply came from the United States. In July 1937 Japanese troops in Manchuria engaged Chinese soldiers in local border skirmishes. The attacks followed a tumultuous six months in which the Japanese economy plunged. Japan had weathered the early global depression by devaluing its yen and capitalizing on the worldwide drop in the price of raw materials. Japanese manufacturing imported cheap raw materials, employed cheap labor paid with devalued yen, and established a robust export market for its cheap goods in China, the United States, and Europe. But as the Depression ebbed, the yen rose and the cost of raw materials went up. America (which had made up 20 percent of Japan's export market) and Europe (which had represented a 12 percent share) turned elsewhere to buy better-quality goods. With costs rising and sales falling, the Japanese trade deficit reached $31 million in the first six months of 1937. The royal family, the military, and businessmen wanted Japan to develop its own supplies of raw materials and a larger captive consumer audience. The country's traditional political parties imploded.

In June, *The New York Times* reported, "Big Fascist Party Forming in Japan."[19] The Japanese army and navy took over politics and began to eliminate opposition, citing the Soviet Union, Germany, and Italy as examples of good government. Japanese forces attacked Shanghai in mid-August and captured Nanjing by the end of 1937. The Japanese sought raw materials, especially oil, and captive markets.

The American people overwhelmingly favored the Chinese and deplored Japanese aggression. As the Japanese attacked Shanghai, the film *The Good Earth* appeared in the United States. Derived from Pearl Buck's sympathetic portrait of a poor Chinese farming couple making it against the odds, the "Chinese couple" in the movie were westerners—Paul Muni and Luise Rainer—surrounded by Chinese extras. It won two Oscars that year and cemented Americans' good feelings toward China. Simultaneously, Americans read about thousands of Chinese "wolf children," orphaned by the Japanese, dying of starvation on the streets of Shanghai. Parents admonished their own children to clean their plates and "think of the poor starving children in China."[20] Women began to boycott silk stockings, made from Japanese raw silk imports. Spurred by such mottos as "Did your stockings kill babies?" consumers pressured dime stores such as F. W. Woolworth's to discontinue the purchase of other cheap Japanese goods.[21]

In part, racism fueled the fiery reaction to Japanese aggression. U.S. newspapers painted the Japanese as unnatural people whose airplanes "mow[ed] down women and babies" and whose children grew up "weak and crippled." American missionaries in China reported the carnage when the bombs hit their schools and hospitals. It seemed more dastardly than the Great War example of German submarines bombing civilian ships. Only a depraved nation could bomb cities from the air, Americans thought. Newspapers routinely called the Japanese "Japs."

Japanese atrocities escalated, and the world recoiled. From Shanghai, Japanese troops marched to Nanjing, as Japanese newspapers reported avidly on the contest between two officers to see which of them could kill one hundred people by sword on their way there. When they reached Nanjing, the Japanese murdered 300,000 people, most of them civilians, looted, and raped 20,000 women. They beheaded, disemboweled, and buried alive civilians, including babies. Foreigners who had stayed behind filmed it all and released the news to an outraged world.

As the Japanese ran riot over China, Lew Sanders, the Indiana radio salesman and weekend barnstormer, itched to fight them in the air. At the time, the entire U.S. military had only 855 airplanes. Within the services, generals had neglected aviation, and the Depression and congressional reluctance to authorize military spending stalled the delivery of the B-17 and B-15 heavy bombers that the air corps requested in 1936. The B-15 existed as a slow-moving prototype, but the four-engine B-17 showed real promise when the army finally received twelve in the summer of 1937. The army air corps played a difficult catch-up game from 1937 to 1939. When the Japanese bombed cities, pilots like Lew Sanders wondered if the time would come when his country might ask him to do something similar.

European Fascism, U.S. Neutrality

Some Americans and Europeans saw fascist power as a counterweight to European Communist movements in Spain, France, and Germany. Since 1931 the Spanish Republicans had been in the majority and formed the Second Spanish Republic, which had Communist support. Spanish nationalist and antisocialist General Francisco Franco raised a military force to depose the duly elected government in July 1936. Hitler and Mussolini sent arms and air support, and Franco's Nationalists fought the Republicans for three years. Increasingly fascist, the well-armed Nationalists annihilated Republican troops and civilians in the brutal civil war. The Neutrality Act of 1936 did not prevent U.S. trade in arms with the combatants, because the conflict there did not involve two nations.

The Spanish Civil War captured the imagination of democrats, socialists, and Communists worldwide. Some 35,000 foreign volunteers joined the Republicans, and more than 2,800 Americans formed the Abraham Lincoln Brigade and fought in Spain. Ernest Hemingway wrote *For Whom the Bell Tolls* about it, black actor and singer Paul Robeson cheered volunteers in it, and more than eight hundred Americans died in it. Salaria Kea, a black woman from Akron, Ohio, the only woman in the brigade, served as a nurse. Franco triumphed on April 1, 1939. Spain remained officially neutral when war broke out in Europe, but Franco's fascist state cooperated with the Axis Powers and persecuted Jews who fled through France and across its borders.

With concerns about Japan and fascist Europe rising, the 1937 Neutrality Act incorporated the language of the 1935 and 1936 acts, but included a cash and carry policy for nonmilitary-related materials that Roosevelt had requested. The federal government could sell U.S. arms and materials to warring nations if they paid cash and arranged for transportation. All this was hypothetical since no nations, not even Japan and China, had actually declared war. In 1937 the United States started selling arms to the Chinese, carried on British transport. Private American companies continued to sell arms to the Japanese. But the significance of cash and carry lay in the future. If Germany attacked France or Britain, it could provision itself from American stocks.

Despite the predominant isolationist spirit, a growing minority in America realized that the Nazi persecution of the Jews and Hitler's unbounded ambition for land—for *Lebensraum*, or elbow room—made war in Europe inevitable and presaged U.S. intervention. The number of German Jews trying to flee their homeland rose in 1937. Some applied for emigration to the United States at consular services within Germany, and others fled to other European countries from which they applied to emigrate to the United States. The Immigration Act of 1924 allowed Germany the highest number of immigrants annually: more than 51,000. In 1937 only 27 percent of that quota was used, despite the rising number of Jews applying to emigrate from Germany. The State Department forbade the immigration of those who were unable to prove that they could support themselves, keeping immigrant numbers low. Roughly 4,500 Jews immigrated each year from 1934 through 1937. That year Roosevelt quietly ordered European consulates to include poor emigrants, and in 1938, 40 percent of the German quota was filled. From 1938 until Pearl Harbor in 1941, the number of Jewish refugees accepted by the United States increased to an average of 20,000 annually.

In March 1938, after Germany annexed Austria with the collaboration of the Austrian Nazi Party, the State Department combined the Austrian and German immigration quotas to aid the 180,000 Austrian Jews. Fifty thousand Jewish refugees made it out of Germany and Austria. But the United States refused visas for tens of thousands of others. In the summer of 1938 Roosevelt supported a conference to publicize their plight, but he refused to raise the quotas or to entertain schemes to increase the numbers, for example, by mortgaging future years' quotas. When dealing with Jewish immigration, Roosevelt remained mindful of domestic politics and Americans' diffuse anti-Semitism. Privately, he became convinced in 1938 that the

United States would have to fight Hitler, and he wanted slowly to win over the American public to that eventuality.

Aggression and Appeasement

Hitler believed that the United States would never intervene, even as his aggression eroded Americans' isolationist proclivities from 1938 to 1941. He considered the United States weak militarily, riven by the Depression, and unwilling to participate in international affairs. He declared, "Because of its neutrality laws, America is not dangerous to us."[22] The United States had done nothing about Italy's invasion of Ethiopia or Japan's aggression in China. Focused on America's supposed weaknesses, Hitler overestimated U.S. sympathy for the Nazis. He admired the South's Jim Crow institutions and understood that white southern politicians checked New Deal liberalism. He believed that the strength of the United States resided in its racially discriminatory state laws, and he commissioned a survey of ethnic groups' rights around the United States.[23]

In 1938 Hitler began to agitate for control of the ethnically German part of Czechoslovakia, an area that Germans called the Sudetenland. Nazi propaganda spun stories of Czech abuse of Germans and argued that the Treaty of Versailles denied the three million ethnic Germans their "self-determination." Hitler would come to their rescue. British prime minister Neville Chamberlain conferred with him in Munich in late September 1938. Hitler told Chamberlain that he would occupy the Sudetenland, but that if Great Britain allowed that, he would stop there. Chamberlain believed Hitler, and Britain and France were eager to avoid war. With the prologue to the Great War in mind, Chamberlain agreed, signed the Munich Pact, and returned to London to proclaim "peace in our time." Some accused him of appeasing Hitler.

That fall, the U.S. Army Air Corps commander, General Henry "Hap" Arnold, sent American hero Charles Lindbergh to assess Great Britain, France, and Germany's air power. In 1927 "Lucky Lindy, the lone eagle," had become the first transatlantic solo pilot. When kidnappers took and killed his firstborn son, nicknamed "the eaglet," in a bungled ransom attempt in 1932, it became the crime of the century. During the three-year ordeal leading to the execution of the kidnapper, Americans embraced shy Charles and his warm wife Anne. Their personal ordeal seemed even worse than the public ordeal of the Great Depression, and they bore it with dignity.

Once in Europe, Lindbergh found the British and French air forces woefully inept, but the German Luftwaffe impressed him. He praised the quality and number of the German planes and lauded their crews. Two weeks after Germany occupied the Sudetenland, Lindbergh accepted a medal honoring his 1927 transatlantic flight from Hermann Göring, commander in chief of the Luftwaffe. The most admired man in America, Charles Lindbergh, admired the German military buildup.[24]

As Charles Lindbergh met with Göring, Lew Sanders, the weekend barnstormer and weekday radio salesman from Indiana, enlisted in the army air corps. Perhaps he saw Chamberlain's actions as appeasement. If there was a war, Sanders wanted to be in on it, but he was in the distinct minority. A Gallup poll taken in September 1938 found 73 percent of Americans in favor of the Neutrality Act's arms embargo. Sanders joined an air corps that was ranked twentieth in the world, with fewer than nineteen thousand personnel to fly and maintain its four thousand planes.

Hitler paused barely six weeks after the Munich Pact before he moved against the Jews. On November 9 and 10, after a young Polish Jew shot a German diplomat in Paris, party-sanctioned Nazi youth gangs attacked Jews in Germany, burned synagogues in Berlin and Westphalia, and looted Jewish businesses. Although storm troopers turned up on the streets *before* the rioting started and watched without intervening, Nazi authorities called the violence a "spontaneous demonstration" and pretended to have calmed the crowds. The hoodlums broke so much glass that the riot became known as Kristallnacht (Crystal Night). The Nazis blamed the violence on the Paris murder's "monstrous provocation" and fined Jews to clean up the damage. The regime ordered all Jewish shops to close and, shortly afterward, confiscated all Jewish property.[25]

Kristallnacht and the Nazis' contorted excuses startled many Americans who had simply wished the problem away. U.S. Jews and many African Americans called it a pogrom, a massacre designed to eliminate an entire ethnic group. After Kristallnacht, Roosevelt recalled the German ambassador, Hugh Wilson. Prominent people, including Eleanor Roosevelt, called for a revision of the immigration quota system. Americans began to use the broad term *racism* to encompass discrimination against Jews abroad and minorities at home. That year the American Anthropological Association unanimously passed a resolution condemning racism.

The Outbreak of War in Europe

Alarmed by fascist aggression and appalled by the condition of the U.S. military, in mid-November 1938 Roosevelt called for the construction of "airplanes and lots of them."[26] He planned to build 20,000 new planes in the next two years, many of them bombers, and another 24,000 by 1941. He hoped to sell some to Britain and France, while General Hap Arnold wanted to keep as many as possible for the army air corps.[27]

On March 15, 1939, Hitler invaded the remainder of Czechoslovakia. Astonishingly, Chamberlain immediately defended the Munich Pact in the House of Commons as the correct decision at the time. Members expressed outrage at his continuing self-defense; one argued that the prime minister had sold the Czech people into slavery. German newspapers retorted, "Germany does not shrink from assuming responsibilities for non-German peoples."[28] A House of Commons debate urged a coordinated plan among nations to stop Hitler's aggression.

On the morning of August 23, 1939, the world awakened to discover that Germany and the Soviet Union had signed a Nonaggression Pact, despite the USSR's strong antifascist stance. Poland, sandwiched between the two countries, saw the pact as the latest move in a war of nerves as Germany threatened it. On August 24, Britain announced its determination to stand by Poland, which called up troops. Roosevelt proposed a truce and arbitration between Poland and Germany, but Hitler now claimed openly that he should have free rein in eastern Europe. The British retained their confidence as their statesmanship floundered, arguing that "the German assumption that Poland could be overrun in a week or two is regarded in military circles as a hallucination."[29] The Nazis pretended to negotiate with Poland by demanding that it simply cede to them some of its territory.

At dawn on September 1, 1939, Germany invaded Poland from the west, north, and south, its tanks rolling over the flat Polish plains. As Lindbergh might have predicted, the well-equipped Luftwaffe bombed civilians and destroyed Polish towns from the air. Britain and France declared war on Germany on September 3. In the House of Commons, Chamberlain's voice broke as he remonstrated that "all I have worked for is in ruins." As he took his seat, the member for Epping rose. Winston Churchill's words banished Chamberlain's lamentations, calling for "a war to establish on impregnable rocks, the rights of the individual, . . . a war to establish and revive the stature of man."[30]

On September 17 the Red Army moved into eastern Poland to seize territory that the Nonaggression Pact had secretly promised to the Soviet Union. On September 27 Hitler and Stalin signed a Friendship Pact. By October 2 the occupation was complete, and Hitler's ambition unbounded.

Roosevelt responded to these events with the promise that the nation would remain neutral, but he added, "Even a neutral cannot be asked to close his mind or his conscience."[31] Anti-interventionists such as Borah, Nye, and Wheeler recharged their campaign to keep the country out of war. Robert A. Taft, the son of William Howard, was elected as a Republican senator from Ohio in 1938 and quickly became the public face of anti-interventionism. In mid-September 1939, Roosevelt called Congress into a special session to revise the Neutrality Act of 1937. FDR sighed, "I regret that the Congress passed the [Neutrality] act. I regret equally that I signed it."[32] The anti-interventionists remained firm, despite the now present danger, and even fought Roosevelt's request that the cash and carry provision allow selling war matériel to Britain and France. Charles Lindbergh went on the air on September 15 to warn that U.S. entry into the European war would sacrifice a generation of young men to remedy "a quarrel arising from the errors of the last war." He cautioned that Americans should fear Asians, not Germans. Europe and the United States should band together to "defend the white race."[33] Americans did not want to fight, but a poll in the fall of 1939 showed that 85 percent of them wanted Britain and France to win. Another poll reported that only 24 percent were in favor of supplying aid to the Allies.

In November 1939, Congress authorized the cash and carry provision to make war matériel available to Britain and France, and anti-interventionists made peace with it, hoping that selling arms and equipment would prevent sending troops. Roosevelt asked for only a modest military spending increase in the next budget, but on April 3, 1940, the House Appropriations Committee reduced his request by $10 million. The anti-interventionist Republicans and anti–New Deal Democrats let their antipathy for FDR cloud their judgment. Opposed to intervention abroad, they nonetheless talked about building a strong defense, but they sabotaged Roosevelt's efforts to do so. U.S. military forces were substandard, with a weak Pacific navy and some obsolete planes. The anti-interventionist William Borah died in January 1940, but Nye, Taft, and their allies carried on the obstructionist politics. Their opposition slowed the U.S. buildup of forces until the second half of 1940.

The Conundrum of Preparedness

Six days after Congress cut FDR's military budget, 135 divisions of German troops moved west and north and, by mid-May 1940, took over Denmark, Norway, Holland, Belgium, and Luxembourg. Then by the coast in northeastern France, near the Belgian border, German troops cut off British and French troops, pushing them toward the sea at Dunkirk. The French tried to hold the line, but the Luftwaffe's 1,200 fighter planes and 1,600 bombers wreaked havoc. The British Royal Air Force and the French had only 898 fighters and 377 bombers, most of which were obsolete. They took heavy losses. As the Germans relentlessly drove the French and British onto the beaches, British naval forces and civilian fishing boats sped across the channel. They rescued 100,000 French and 238,000 British troops. The Dunkirk defeat cost Britain many of its planes and pilots, and most of its tanks and heavy weapons remained in German hands. The defeat reduced British military manpower to only 10 percent of Germany's. The British found themselves with only a few hundred thousand rifles and five hundred cannons, many of them recently commandeered from museums.

In early May 1939, following Chamberlain's resignation, the new prime minister, Winston Churchill, had remarked, "Never has a great nation been so naked before her foes." After Dunkirk the situation worsened, until the only thing left to the British was the will to win. Churchill exhorted, "We shall defend our island, whatever the cost may be. We shall fight on the beaches, we shall fight on the landing grounds, we shall fight in the fields and in the streets, we shall fight in the hills. We shall *never* surrender." [34]

Privately, he told FDR that Britain's fall was likely, and that if the United States did not enter the war soon, it would be too late. He also warned Roosevelt that he was counting on him to "keep that Japanese dog quiet in the Pacific."[35] The ignominy of Dunkirk reversed U.S. public opinion on sending aid to Britain, which 70 percent of the nation's newspapers supported in the late spring of 1940.

In May 1940, Roosevelt asked for over $1 billion in new military spending to support increased aircraft and naval production. Congress voted $500,000 more than he asked. FDR returned to ask for additional appropriations in late May and June; over a few weeks, Congress gave him $17.6 billion for preparedness. But the highly influential isolationist Charles Lindbergh took to the radio again, characterizing the U.S. reaction to German expansion as "hysterical." Roosevelt confided to his close friend Treasury Secretary Henry Morgenthau, "I am absolutely convinced that Lindbergh is a Nazi."[36]

The next week Italy joined Germany in the conflict, and on June 13 the French general defending Paris withdrew his troops to spare the city's destruction. The Germans marched in on June 14, 1940, pausing on the way to hang a swastika over Versailles. In less than two months, the Nazis had swept through Denmark, Norway, Holland, Belgium, and Luxembourg, defeated the British and French at Dunkirk, and marched into Paris. The debate over the U.S. response reached clamorous levels. *The New York Times* summarized U.S. obligations as threefold: saving the Allies by "material aid," keeping the United States out of the war, and quickly building U.S. defenses to "keep the totalitarian threat out of this hemisphere."[37]

The *Times*'s formulation, masquerading as a strong statement, actually testifies to the strength of anti-interventionism sentiment, particularly in Congress. In late June, less than 10 percent of the general public favored declaring war on Germany, but 70 percent supported aid to Britain. Deep divisions arose in the military over how to support Britain while building American defenses. Valuable time had been forever lost. For his part, FDR hoped that the Nazis could be defeated without the commitment of U.S. ground troops. It was an iffy foreign policy: if Britain could hold out, if Japan stayed out, if a strict blockade could be imposed on Germany, and if the U.S. could send naval and air support.[38] But Roosevelt knew that the Nazis were not the country's only enemies. In the fall of 1940, he sent U.S. naval forces to Hawaii to deter the Japanese from following Hitler's example and taking Pacific islands.

PREPARING A NEUTRAL NATION

The horrific events of the spring and summer unfolded in tandem with the Democratic and Republican nominating conventions for the 1940 presidential election. Franklin Roosevelt had expected to retire after two terms, but at some point in the spring of 1940, he decided that the war in Europe mandated that he run for an unprecedented, but not unconstitutional, third term. Five days before the Democratic Convention on July 10, waves of German planes began bombing the British coastal defenses in what became known as the Battle of Britain. Without naval defenses, the British could do little but shoot at German aircraft from the ground and engage them in aerial dogfights that resulted in high casualties. British intelligence had cracked the German military communications code, and by mid-July they intercepted information that Hitler planned to invade England by sea as soon as German bombing broke the British resolve.

A Third Term

At the Republicans' convention in late June, the catastrophic events in Europe influenced them toward nominating Wendell Willkie, a little-known but exceptionally charismatic former businessman from Indiana. Interventionist Republicans in the media promoted Willkie, who ultimately gained the nomination after a brutal convention fight against the anti-interventionists who favored Senator Robert Taft. Willkie agreed with the administration's policy of arming the Allies, and when talk of a peacetime draft surfaced in July, Willkie supported that as well.

The Democratic Convention in Chicago in mid-July proved a desultory affair. FDR did not attend, and the delegates drafted him without much drama—or much overt enthusiasm. Roosevelt chose his very progressive agriculture secretary, Henry Wallace, as his running mate, a pick that almost caused mutiny in the ranks. A Republican until 1936, Wallace dwelt on esoteric aspects of corn genetics in conversation, alienated southern Democrats who believed that he was an integrationist, and embraced spiritualism. Nonetheless, his intense loyalty appealed to Roosevelt. The anti–New Deal Democrats considered him a turncoat former Republican who went along with Roosevelt's most authoritarian plans.

Despite their support for FDR, the delegates almost rioted in the aisles at the Wallace announcement. Eleanor Roosevelt, dispatched to speak in favor of Wallace, recalled, "The noise in the room was deafening." It was an inauspicious time for the first-ever speech at a party convention by a first lady, but when ER rose and walked to the stage, the delegates became silent. She justified Roosevelt's third-term aspirations and Wallace's nomination as necessary to confront the crisis at hand: "You cannot treat it as you would treat an ordinary nomination in an ordinary time. We people in the United States have got to realize today that we face a grave and serious situation." The president, Eleanor said, "must be on his job" and would not be able to campaign as he had in the past. She concluded, "We cannot tell from day to day what may come. This is no ordinary time."[39]

After the conventions came silence. Willkie squandered his buzz by retreating for five weeks with his staff to plan the campaign and oddly decided to delay his acceptance speech until mid-August. The only possible advantage of that strategy was to avoid letting Roosevelt know his platform. Without a platform to attack, Roosevelt, the consummate campaigner, faltered. He seemed dispirited by the lack of enthusiasm for him at the Democratic Convention and was slowed by a serious bout with the flu. He also felt weakened by the divisions within his administration and by disputes among military leaders over material aid to Britain, which some now saw as a futile gesture that drained U.S. resources.

Just before the Democratic Convention, Roosevelt had appointed two Republican interventionists to his cabinet. William Franklin (Frank) Knox, who had been Alf Landon's vice-presidential running mate in 1936, became secretary of the navy. Henry Stimson, a highly respected Wall Street lawyer who had served as Herbert Hoover's secretary of state, was one of the few American leaders who stated bluntly that it might be necessary for the United States to fight to save Britain and France. FDR appointed him secretary of war. Both men would prove vital to America's preparedness, but in the late summer and fall of 1940, that time had not yet arrived. FDR had a minor heart attack in 1940, and his subsequent months-long bout with "flu" may have reflected his slow recovery from it. The public, indeed most of those close to him, had no inkling that his doctors must have told him to take it easy, the usual prescription for heart trouble at the time.

But Roosevelt also suffered from what he saw as a lack of popular support. He had believed for some time that Britain would fall if the United States did not intervene, but he simply could not act in defiance of American opinion. Some of those closest to him despaired at his inertia. They urged him to lead and to let the public follow. He privately engaged the pollster George Gallup to measure public opinion on specific issues, but that immediate feedback seemed to confound him even more. Uncharacteristically, he allowed events to force him to act, rather than acting ahead of them.

Strengthening the Military

After Congress's May-June appropriation of an additional $17.6 billion for defense spending, two accomplishments in September allowed Roosevelt to harness the anti-interventionists' own strong defense rhetoric to move forward. First, he knew that Britain simply would not be able to defend itself if the Germans breached the Channel, as its decrypted cables promised. On September 2, by executive order, he transferred surplus destroyers to Britain in exchange for two bases, one in Bermuda and the other in Newfoundland. FDR's inclination to please everyone paid off in the transaction, since Britain got its destroyers (but found them to be outdated tin cans), and the isolationists gained offshore bases for defense.

The Selective Training and Service Act, passed in September 1940, represented the same sort of compromise. A group of elite New Yorkers, who as young men had helped organize civilian preparedness before World War I, began a movement for a peacetime draft in June 1940. FDR withheld support because he feared the idea would fail and result in a costly congressional setback for preparedness. With the help of Stimson and Knox, the Selective Service Bill's canny civilian supporters won over the reluctant army chief of staff, George Marshall, who often seemed to have difficulty supporting defense measures inclined toward intervention. FDR did not endorse the bill until August. He began to push it two weeks later, when Wendell Willkie acknowledged that "some form of selective service" was the "only democratic way to secure the trained and competent manpower we need for a national defense."[40]

The nation's first peacetime draft finally passed because the current armed forces were inadequate even to defend America, and the short-time enlistment requirement—a one-year stint—would not prove a major sacrifice. Every man between twenty-one and thirty-five had to register for the draft. By the time the bill passed, 75 percent of the population supported it. The administration used part of the congressional military appropriation to build forty-six military bases across the country.

As FDR sent destroyers to England and Congress approved the Selective Service Act, a group of idealistic college students tried to forge an anti-intervention position that they believed addressed difficult facts and protected the United States. The America First Committee (AFC) argued that the United States should discontinue its fruitless aid to Britain, since when the British went down in defeat, they reasoned, the Germans would hold the United States accountable for trying to help. Better to build U.S. forces to protect its own citizens against totalitarianism after Britain fell. Seen from this perspective, moves such as selling destroyers to Britain endangered the United States.

Those who organized and joined the America First Committee in the fall of 1940 believed that they practiced a sort of realpolitik, while their parents and grandparents followed a foreign policy forged by outdated traditions that tied America to a feudal Europe. Yale University students organized the committee when they returned to school after the eventful summer 1940. It grew to be the largest U.S. peace movement in history and claimed 800,000 members in 450 chapters. Its charismatic and brilliant undergraduate leader was junior Kingman Brewster, who would later become president of Yale. Future president Gerald Ford joined, Jack Kennedy sent a contribution, and his brother Joe founded the America First chapter at Harvard. In the beginning, the AFC represented a new generation's rejection of its parents' mistakes during and after World War I. The United States had already fought a war to save Britain—in 1917—and its leaders had squandered the peace by bringing on a Great Depression.

Kingman Brewster went to see Charles and Anne Lindbergh at their Long Island home and persuaded Charles to give a speech at Yale. In October 1940, as three thousand students marched into Woolsey Hall to hear him, they passed through the rotunda with its carved marble plaques bearing the name of every single Yale student ever killed in military service— even the Confederates. Lindbergh told them, "We must either keep out of European wars entirely, or participate in European politics permanently. Personally, I believe that if democracy is to be saved, it will not be by the forceful imposition of our ideals abroad, but by the example of their successful operation at home."[41] Elsewhere in the Ivy League, appalled faculty made their displeasure with the America Firsters clear to their students. Harvard students responded by picketing an interventionist meeting, carrying signs that read, "Let's send 50 over-age professors to Britain."[42]

Despite this youthful energy, Brewster worried that old-guard midwestern anti-interventionists would come to control the organization, and they did. They lacked the idealism for protecting American rights that inspired their younger colleagues, arguing that it was virtually impossible to invade the United States. Nonetheless they granted that the country should build some defenses to enhance its natural protection. FDR's old nemesis Senator Burton Wheeler joined the AFC and argued that aid to Britain allowed the United States to wage an undeclared war in Europe, which weakened defenses at home. The older, conservative AFC members hated Roosevelt because they thought that his ambition drove him toward war and that his hypocritical British aid schemes simply disguised his motives.

On the evening of September 7, 1940, the German Luftwaffe again bombed the people of London and continued to do so for fifty-seven straight nights. German Air Marshal Hermann Göring assured Hitler that recent missions over Royal Air Force (RAF) bases in southern England had eliminated the British air defense and that bombing London would break the British will. The Blitz destroyed a million homes and killed forty thousand people. The resolve of the British people to "keep calm and carry on" in the face of the Blitz ultimately convinced Hitler that they would not abandon London, and the bombing stopped in May 1941. Meanwhile the RAF regrouped in the countryside. The resolve of Londoners and the rejuvenated RAF caused Hitler to postpone his plans for an invasion by sea. That decision may have cost him the war.

Some of the America First Committee's arguments were probably right: Britain might never defeat the Germans without American military involvement, and arming the British would drain American resources at a time when the U.S. military was in shambles. Nonetheless, they overestimated the idea of Fortress America. They only had to look to occupied France, known as Vichy France, to see the real danger to the United States from a German takeover of the British Commonwealth. The Germans had taken over administration of France's colonies—what was to stop a Nazi occupation of Bermuda if Britain fell?

Who Will Fight?

Another group of young Americans studied the facts and came to a different conclusion. The young people who enlisted in the armed forces in mid-1940 agreed with the America Firsters on one thing: the country was moving toward war. Ada Margaret Olsson—Peggy—had graduated from nursing school and then served as a civilian nurse at the Fort Riley, Kansas, army base. Unlike Charles Lindbergh, Olsson realized that the United States would have to enter the war. The Army Nurse Corps had only eight hundred nurses, and most army camps relied on civilian staff. But a rumor circulated that nurses would be drafted when war came, and she wanted to sign up before that happened. She joined the army nurse corps on June 4, 1940, and became a second lieutenant, the rank at which all graduate nurses entered. At twenty-four, the young woman from Junction City, Kansas, accepted Roosevelt's invitation to a rendezvous with destiny.

Phil Rasmussen joined on September 9, after the Germans had bombed London for two nights. He had just graduated from Gettysburg College, and his father had taught him his own house painting trade. Rasmussen arrived at the Air Corps Tactical School at Maxwell Field in Montgomery, Alabama, in the fall of 1940. Squadron Commander Lew Sanders, the former barnstorming Indiana radio salesman, taught him to fly already-obsolete Curtiss P-36 Hawk fighters. The P-36s had no armor, even though they were pursuit planes designed to engage enemy aircraft. Two machine guns, a .50 caliber and a .30 caliber, were mounted on the front and mechanically set to fire *through* the propeller's rotation. They "fired at about the same speed as a funeral march cadence," Rasmussen recalled.[43] The Germans would have laughed at such planes. The aviation cadets joined the Forty-sixth Pursuit Squadron of the Fifteenth Fighter/Pursuit Group.

In January 1941 the Forty-sixth Pursuit Squadron left the mainland in its P-36s aboard the aircraft carrier *USS Enterprise.* When they got close enough to Hawaii, the pilots flew the planes off the ship to Wheeler Army Airfield on Oahu. The Hawaiian Department constituted the largest American overseas command, with a total of 35,000 people in the Pineapple Army and Navy. Around 37 percent of Hawaii's 423,000 people were of Japanese descent, some of whom were second- and third-generation agricultural workers.

At Wheeler, the pilots' training began in earnest. Lieutenant Sanders told them, "Learn something every time you fly. There's a war coming on. I don't know just when, but knowing what you're doing is your life insurance."[44] Gordon Sterling, the Hartford Boy Scout who began hanging out at the airstrip in high school in 1936, graduated from the Advanced Flying School at Maxwell in May 1941 and joined the Forty-sixth Pursuit Squadron in Hawaii in June. The next month the army air corps became the army air force.

The military did not extend these opportunities to African Americans. When a black teacher in Charlotte, North Carolina, sought information about enlisting in September 1940, recruiting officials beat him up. African

American leaders had fruitlessly lobbied Congress to be sure that the Selective Service Act prohibited racial discrimination. The situation recalled for African Americans the lesson of World War I, when they were relegated to the worst military jobs, promised better treatment as a reward for fighting, and returned home to racial massacres. As young white people across the country began to enlist in the latter half of 1940, young black people strategized.

For the past five years, African Americans had been drawing parallels between the German treatment of Jews and U.S. racial politics. Now they walked a fine line between expressing patriotism and demanding civil rights. In September 1940, Eleanor Roosevelt addressed the annual convention of the Brotherhood of Sleeping Car Porters at the request of its president, Asa Philip Randolph, whose newspaper the federal government had banned during World War I. "That war," Randolph observed, "neither won democracy abroad or at home."[45] This time Randolph was determined to fight for equal treatment in the armed forces and in defense industry jobs and to use the emergency to gain civil rights for black Americans.

THE MARCH TO WAR

The 1940 November presidential election revolved around the candidates' tortured explanations of their positions on intervention. Willkie and Roosevelt agreed on the larger contours of aid to Britain, but they became mired in discussions of the hypothetical scenarios that might prompt U.S. entry into the war. Toward the end of the campaign, Willkie tried to distance his position from Roosevelt's by arguing that FDR would certainly send in troops. On the stump nationally in October, FDR repeatedly promised, "Your boys are not going to be sent into any foreign wars, except in case of attack." A few days before the election, speaking in Boston, FDR dropped the last phrase, "except in case of attack," suggesting that he would not send troops in any circumstances. When Willkie heard FDR over the radio, he exclaimed, "The hypocritical son of a bitch! This is going to beat me."[46] If FDR's new formulation sounded different, the meaning of "your boys are not going to be sent into any foreign wars" hinged on the word *foreign*. If Americans were attacked on American soil, on the mainland or in its territories, it was no longer a foreign war. Roosevelt won all but ten states, and Democrats gained congressional seats and comfortably held their majority. But FDR seemed exhausted and muddled after his victory.

The Arsenal of Democracy

In Roosevelt's fireside chat in late December 1940, he spoke not of war but of national security. The British fleet stood between the United States and the Germans, and if it met defeat, the Nazis would be on U.S. beaches. "We must be the great arsenal of democracy," FDR argued.[47] But Britain was broke, rendering the cash and carry program useless.

Roosevelt had accomplished the destroyer-bases deal through an executive order, but in January 1941 he turned to Congress to approve a Lend-Lease Bill to supply war matériel to Britain. Roosevelt explained that if your neighbor's house was on fire, you would not charge him rent before you let him borrow your hose. You simply expected him to give it back to you after he put out the fire. That was what we would do with the British: lend them materials and expect them to return them later.

Opponents of the plan argued that Lend-Lease amounted to financing Britain's war effort, making the United States a target for Germany. Delivering the arms would be risky: the British could not afford to divert ships to pick up the arms, and sending U.S. ships to Britain risked an incident with the Germans that would bring the country into the war. Congress added an amendment stating that the act did not authorize U.S. convoys to Britain, and FDR denied having ambitions to send them.

Senator Burton Wheeler argued that Lend-Lease squandered U.S. resources and compared it to the 1933 Agricultural Adjustment Act. Instead of killing every fourth newborn pig, now FDR would "plow under every fourth American boy," Wheeler alleged. Roosevelt called that statement "the most dastardly, unpatriotic thing that has ever been said." The president spoke frankly: "If Great Britain goes down, the Axis Powers will control the continents of Europe, Asia, Africa, Australasia, and the high seas. . . . It is no exaggeration to say that all of us, in all of the Americas, would be living at the point of a gun."[48]

Congress appropriated $7 billion, and FDR signed the Lend-Lease Bill on March 11, 1941, with a 66 percent public approval rate. It enraged the Germans, who had maintained a policy of avoiding criticism of the United States. With Lend-Lease in place, any vestige of American neutrality fell away, and it seemed a foregone conclusion that the United States would fight if Britain fell to the Germans. Although America Firster Kingman Brewster had testified against the bill, it was now the law. As a loyal

American, Brewster knew that he had to support it. He resigned from the America First Committee.

Human Rights and the March on Washington Movement

Three months earlier, on January 6, 1941, Roosevelt had used his State of the Union address to articulate the American values under siege. He underscored the "unprecedented" nature of the European war. Unlike other foreign wars, it threatened the United States because it threatened democracy itself. If we waited until Britain fell, it would be too late. Only "slackers or trouble makers" could argue that "an unprepared America, single-handed, and with one hand tied behind its back, can hold off the whole world." Then he reminded Americans of the four freedoms that they were defending. "The first is freedom of speech and expression—everywhere in the world. The second is freedom of every person to worship God in his own way—everywhere in the world. The third is freedom from want . . . everywhere in the world. The fourth is freedom from fear . . . anywhere in the world."[49] The Four Freedoms depended on global economic stability and a reduction in arms. The United States could not defend them here if it waited too long to defend them abroad.

African Americans applauded the Four Freedoms speech and tried to join their white peers in the country's defense. In May 1941, 100,000 people packed Chicago's Soldier Field for an "I Am an American Day" that brought together Ethel Waters, Pat O'Brien, Don Ameche, and Catholic, Jewish, and Protestant religious leaders. The audience was greeted by black demonstrators carrying signs reading, "We Are Americans, Too, But We Are Denied Jobs in Defense Industries; We are Jim-Crowed In or Excluded From the Armed Forces. We Object." The police arrested them.[50]

That month A. Philip Randolph organized the March on Washington Movement to demand defense jobs and equal treatment in the armed forces for African Americans. He was pro-intervention and supported Lend-Lease. Randolph and others negotiated with FDR, often with Eleanor's help, but failed to persuade the president to desegregate the armed forces. The campaign for nondiscrimination in defense jobs met with more sympathy, since the administration had advised contractors to desegregate, but had little success amid industry opposition. The March on Washington's slogan would be "We loyal Negro-American Citizens demand the right to work and fight for our country."[51]

Concerned that 100,000 African Americans would arrive in midsummer in Washington, FDR met with NAACP secretary Walter White and A. Philip Randolph on June 18. He offered to phone the heads of defense plants and tell them to give African Americans equal opportunities. But Randolph insisted on an executive order to prohibit discrimination in defense industries and the federal government. FDR finally agreed, and Randolph edited the final version. Executive Order 8802, issued June 25, 1941, banned discrimination in defense industries or government, and it formed the Committee on Fair Employment Practices to review complaints. Randolph canceled the march.

Order 8802 was a groundbreaking declaration by the federal government that job discrimination was un-American. It opened up thousands of defense and government jobs to African Americans, and the Fair Employment Practices Committee rocked white supremacy in the South by attempting to enforce it. Twenty-two years later A. Philip Randolph would embody the continuity of the long civil rights movement when he planned the 1963 March on Washington for Jobs and Freedom.

The German Invasion of the USSR

At three-thirty a.m. on the morning of June 22, 1941, General Georgy Zhukov woke Joseph Stalin with the news that the Germans were bombing towns in Belorussia. Stalin was stunned. He had squandered the months since the Nonaggression Pact, when he should have been arming the USSR. For his part, Hitler had grown frustrated at British resistance to the Blitz. He dared not risk an invasion of Britain at that moment, since it might bring the United States into the war, but his well-supplied troops stood ready to fight. Moreover, the Nazis hated the Communists, and Germany's alliance with the USSR had simply been a convenient way to take Poland. Sending in some 153 divisions and 3.6 million troops, Hitler believed he could prevail over the USSR quickly, in the three and a half months before winter began. He would then divide the fertile Ukraine among German farmers, tap the Baku oil reserves on the Caspian Sea, and seize eastern Russia's industrial might. With that new strength, he could turn again to Britain. If that invasion brought the United States into the war, Germany would have all the resources that it needed to win. That afternoon Churchill came on the airwaves to affirm that Britain would support the Soviet Union.

Most Americans hated Stalin as much as they hated Hitler. When

Senator Harry S. Truman (D-MO) heard of the invasion—Operation Barbarossa, as Hitler dubbed it—he declared it a godsend: "If we see that Germany is winning, we ought to help Russia, and if Russia is winning, we ought to help Germany, and that way let them kill as many as possible."[52] Two days after the invasion, FDR announced that the United States would support the USSR with war matériel.

Neutrality and disarmament—the lessons of World War I—had produced an inertia that hampered U.S. preparedness and bitterly divided the American public. In the summer of 1941, arguments for preparedness and anti-intervention converged on the issue of Lend-Lease. The United States should have begun to build its military earlier—in 1937—if only to establish an adequate defense, but the anti-interventionists had argued that mobilizing would lead to involvement in foreign wars. Now staying out of war depended on arming the Allies with weapons that the United States might need for defense in the immediate future. Army Chief of Staff George Marshall opposed sending 50 percent of the country's brand-new B-17 bombers to Stalin, as FDR suggested, at the expense of training U.S. pilots. Anti-interventionists thundered against arming "Bloody Joe."

Moreover, delivering armaments to Britain and the USSR brought the United States into the war zone. FDR sent half the U.S. fleet to the North Atlantic and declared a longitudinal security zone for the United States that extended east to Iceland. He sent four thousand marines to Atlantic rim bases, and the navy shadowed British Lend-Lease supply convoys, sometimes engaging German submarines. In the next six months, the ships would experience four German attacks, including the October 23 sinking of the *Reuben James* at a loss of 115 U.S. sailors.

Increased defense budgets finally banished the Great Depression in late 1941. The unemployment rate, which had been almost 20 percent in 1938, fell steadily each year, to 10 percent in 1941. The gross domestic product rose in the same period from $86 billion to almost $127 billion. To manage mobilization, FDR organized wartime production under a new Supply Priorities and Allocation Board and gave it the authority to put industry on a war footing by planning and, if necessary, rationing.

In late August, Roosevelt and Churchill met in Newfoundland and issued a communiqué that became known as the Atlantic Charter. It promised to pursue self-determination for nations, free trade, nonaggression, and freedom of the seas. Joseph Stalin did not endorse the Atlantic Charter. By

May 1941, 55 percent of Americans supported the Atlantic convoys, despite the fact that 75 percent thought they would lead to war.

Mobilizing in Peacetime

Second Lieutenant Gordon Sterling arrived in Oahu in the summer of 1941; a month later so did Second Lieutenant Peggy Olsson. She would nurse the Pineapple Army—soldiers, sailors, and their dependents—at the beautiful Schofield Barracks Hospital close by Wheeler Field. Hawaii was a paradise for young officers, with formal dances at the officers' club three nights a week. Olsson worked from seven to nine each morning, boarded a military bus to the beach for a swim, then returned to work after lunch. The only army gear issued them were gas masks and "old World War One little tin . . . helmets." Regulations demanded that they wear formal, floor-length gowns when off-duty after six p.m. Olsson fell in love with Gordon Sterling. He asked her to marry him, and she accepted his ring. Sterling told Olsson that he was convinced that war would come soon.[53]

Shortly after Olsson had arrived in Honolulu, on July 16, Roosevelt signed an executive order requiring governmental approval on oil shipments from American companies to the Japanese. With American sales accounting for 80 percent of Japan's oil consumption, the order effectively embargoed Japan's oil. On July 26, FDR froze the Japanese government's U.S. assets in retaliation for its takeover of French Indochina. Ominously, Japan had signed a treaty with Germany and Italy the previous year pledging mutual defense in case of an attack.

As America Firsters, congressional anti-interventionists, and Gordon Sterling faced the probability of attack, Charles Lindbergh seriously misread the public mood in a speech in Des Moines on September 11, 1941. He named the "major war agitators" who he thought were misleading their fellow citizens. He characterized those who believed war to be imminent as "a small minority of our own people; . . . we must know exactly who they are. The three most important groups who have been pressing this country toward war are the British, the Jews, and the Roosevelt administration." He continued, "Behind these groups, . . . are a number of capitalists, Anglophiles, and intellectuals who believe that the future of mankind depends upon the domination of the British empire. Add to these the Communistic groups who were opposed to intervention until a few weeks ago." He virtually accused the Roosevelt administration of treason for diverting U.S.

resources to Britain, complaining that the "American army has a few hundred thoroughly modern bombers and fighters—less in fact, than Germany is able to produce in a month."[54] Lindbergh was right about the country's lack of preparedness but wrong about its mood.

THE SHOCK OF ATTACK IN THE AIR

The Japanese attack on Pearl Harbor damaged U.S. Pacific forces and deeply frightened the American people. The Japanese used the advantage of surprise to fan out quickly over the Pacific and secure sorely needed rubber and oil resources. As devastating as the attack was to Pearl Harbor, the U.S. armed services regrouped quickly and deployed to fight the war on two fronts. The dramatic opening of World War II put aside isolationist/interventionist arguments and galvanized Americans' determination to win the war.

Peggy Olsson and Gordon Sterling spent Friday evening, December 5, together, but on Saturday she had to work late, so could not see him. They planned to join several of the Forty-sixth Pursuit Squadron pilots at a beach party on Sunday afternoon after her morning shift. That Sunday morning she heard two terrible explosions, and the nurses ran outside. A corpsman yelled to them to go inside and "stay away from the windows. The Japs are bombing!" Olsson recalled that the Japanese pilots came in so low that she could see the "scarves around their necks and the bands around their foreheads" as they strafed the hospital.[55]

The day before, Saturday, Gordon Sterling and Phil Rasmussen had lined up their new P-40s wingtip to wingtip for a ten a.m. inspection. They were living in temporary officers' quarters at Wheeler Field and had just completed a weeklong exercise simulating air defense of Hawaii. After the inspection, an officer ordered the newer planes—P-40s—dispersed to embankments around Wheeler Field for protection, but the commanding general revoked the order. The generals were worried about sabotage, not attack, and they lacked the manpower to protect separate clusters of planes. The general ordered the planes parked in tight rows so that the guards could see them.[56]

On Saturday night Phil Rasmussen went to Trader Vic's, where he had "several" of their trademark "one to a customer Zombies" into the wee hours of Sunday morning. As he drove his new convertible back to Wheeler, he noticed the battleships decorated stem to stern with lights. They reminded him of an amusement park. His pilot buddy, riding shotgun, murmured, "What a wonderful target they would make."

Early on Sunday, Rasmussen recalled, "I was standing in the latrine looking out at this very peaceful scene of the hangar line where the aircraft were lined up wingtip to wingtip: our good P-40s, our best line aircraft . . . [but the obsolete] few P-36s were scattered not in that lineup. . . . Suddenly this airplane dove out of the sky over the hangar line, dropped an object which exploded into a huge orange blossom and then pulled up sharply. I saw these two 'meatballs' on this plane, the insignia a solid red circle of the rising sun." He ran for his shoes and his .45, which he strapped on over his pajamas. When he reached the flight line, the P-40s were exploding "like a chain of Chinese firecrackers."

Phil Rasmussen, Squadron Commander Lew Sanders, and two other pilots ran out to four unarmored and unarmed P-36s scattered on the periphery. They jumped in and taxied them over to the embankments to arm them. One pilot realized that his parachute was too large for him and ran back to get another. When he did, Gordon Sterling sprinted out and jumped into the plane. He threw his watch to one of the armorers on the ground with the words, "Give this to my mother, I won't be coming back." The four planes took off toward Bellows Field, trying to get above the clouds.[57]

At nine thousand feet, Rasmussen recalled, "we met a bunch of Zeros, which was the worst thing that could happen to us in the airplanes we were flying." Sanders said, "They saw us. . . . We dived on them and started firing." The mechanism on Rasmussen's P-36 that enabled the guns to fire through the propellers failed: one gun jammed and the other one began rapidly firing on its own. He had to hold it back manually with one hand while he flew the plane with the other. A Zero tracked Sterling and sent a barrage into his P-36. Rasmussen kept firing at it as his own plane burst into flames. Nearby, sailors at Kaneohe Naval Air Station saw Gordon Sterling's plane plunge into the ocean.[58]

Another Zero began strafing Rasmussen's burning plane. He "let that .50 caliber slide back in again and it started firing by itself . . . and I saw him smoking." Then Rasmussen strafed a Zero piloted by Iyozo Fujita. "A P-36 [Rasmussen's] started attacking my plane," Fujita recalled. "It was so close I couldn't get away. We were dog-fighting. So I decided to die. . . . I approached the P-36 to crash my plane into it, but then suddenly it turned and flew away from me."[59] Actually, Rasmussen's plane did not fly away; it fell to six thousand feet. It had no hydraulics, no canopy, and no landing gear. Following Rasmussen's descent, Lew Sanders motioned to him to turn back to Wheeler Field.[60]

Fujita believed that he had killed Rasmussen: "I thought maybe I had hit it and it had gone down, but much later I heard the pilot of that plane is still alive." Rasmussen skidded onto the soft grass runway. All was devastation: "The P-40s were all lined up, their backs broken and their noses pointing toward the sky. As I looked down towards Pearl Harbor, I saw this huge cloud of smoke covering the whole horizon, and amidst this huge black smoke were these huge orange blossoms exploding."[61] Rasmussen's unarmored P-36 had 450 bullet holes in it; Sanders's had 500.[62] The bullet-ridden, obsolete, malfunctioning P-36s flown by pilots in their pajamas amounted to a fitting memorial to the preparedness debate of the past three years.

In the Harbor

The Japanese attack on the nine battleships at Pearl Harbor depended on taking out the airplanes at Wheeler Field quickly and completely. With this accomplished, the Japanese planes rolled over the battleships, which rode two by two at the docks. Sailor Richard Fiske recalled that when the first airplanes came in about twenty-five feet above the water, "we thought this was going to be a drill." Three bombs hit the *West Virginia*, and five more, aimed at the *West Virginia*, hit the *Oklahoma*. "Devastation was going on over in battleship row," said one man who fought all day in his skivvies.[63]

Zenji Abe, a Japanese pilot, recalled, "My target that day was supposed to be an aircraft carrier in the harbor, either the *Enterprise* or the *Lexington*. But neither was there at the time of the attack. I was very disappointed by this, and we had to turn to attacking a battleship. Later, I found out the ship I attacked was the *U.S.S. Arizona*."[64] The *Lexington* had left port a day earlier, just as the battleship *Nevada* arrived to find the *Arizona* docked in its place. The *Nevada* berthed beside it. Ray Johnson, a navigator's assistant on the *Nevada*, saw the results of Zenji Abe's bomb: "The *Arizona* blew up 50 feet ahead of us. It was the biggest, blackest, loudest noise I've heard in my life." The ship split in two amid raging fires and explosions. On the *Arizona*, seaman Clyde Combs survived Abe's bomb: "This thing went off, probably on the fourth deck. It tore things up something terrible with all the doors open. All the lights went out. You couldn't breathe. There was smoke. . . . You couldn't see, you couldn't hear, you were gasping, and you were grasping around there trying to figure out where you were."[65]

Six brothers from Iowa, the Pattens, who made up the navy's largest family, worked in the *Nevada*'s boiler room. The Patten boys woke up planning to listen to Oregon play Duke in the Rose Bowl that day, but shortly after eight a.m., the *Nevada* "started shaking like a three or four scale earthquake" when the *Arizona* blew up. The Japanese planes came in over the *Nevada*, but gunners fended off several before one blew a hole in the ship's hull. The commander ordered the crew to steam out of the harbor, and the *Nevada* was headed for open sea by 8:18. When a wave of Japanese planes hit the ship with three large bombs, the commander ran the ship aground outside the harbor and saved the crew.[66] One thousand, one hundred seventy-seven men died on the *Arizona*.

It was 7:57 a.m. when Dorris Miller, a seaman and cook on the *West Virginia*, finished the breakfast cleanup and heard an explosion. Eight more bombs followed. Miller, son of a black tenant farmer, had attended a segregated school in Waco, Texas. His family had been in Texas for three generations, his dad could not read or write, and they had never really got ahead, even before the Depression. In 1936 Dorris gave up on school and applied to the Civilian Conversation Corps, but his timing was bad—Congress had just cut appropriations for jobs programs, bringing on the Roosevelt Recession of 1937. He helped his father around the farm, worked with his mother in the kitchen, and roamed around the scrubland shooting squirrels for the family's dinner pot. He had only two marketable skills: cooking and shooting. If he had been a white man, he could have joined the army to shoot. But he was a black man, so he joined the navy to cook.[67]

Cooks have battle stations, and Miller arrived at his to find it destroyed. His lieutenant commander ordered him to carry the ship's fatally wounded captain off deck, which he did. Another lieutenant ordered Miller to load an antiaircraft machine gun. Miller had never fired one, but there was a second one on deck. After Miller loaded the white man's gun, he loaded the other one and began firing it himself. They shot at Japanese airplanes until they ran out of ammunition.

At the hospital, Peggy Olsson began mixing morphine. Wounded sailors lay on litters outside the hospital. Olsson remembered, "They were all young, good looking kids—and I noticed most of them had beautiful teeth. That's what I noticed most—young kids." Nurse Mary Louise Laager remembered, "As far as I could see [there] were litters with patients dying, some already dead. . . . One young man said, 'I just graduated from high school.' I think he knew he wasn't going to make it, because he was bleeding from everyplace. . . . He said to me, 'Nurse, will you take my graduation ring off and see to it my family gets it?' This is the only time that day I cried."

"In the afternoon they told me Sterling was lost," Olsson recalled. "They never got his body or anything." Then she said, "Your insides quiver when you're scared, and you have to go to the bathroom all the time. . . . It was all just like a big dream, really—a terrible dream." In the days that followed, she "worked, just worked." After the attack, in addition to her gas mask and tin helmet, the army gave her a pocketknife to slit her wrists with if the Japanese captured her. She did not use it. Nor did she ever marry during her lifelong career in the army nursing corps.[68]

Declaring War, Uniting America

Japan's attack on Pearl Harbor had been a stunning blow but a strategic failure. The Japanese destroyed the eight battleships tied up in the harbor, along with ten other vessels and almost two hundred new planes; they had killed 2,403 men. Nonetheless the three aircraft carriers out of port escaped damage, and the Japanese failed to destroy the island's repair facilities or its oil reserves. The attack united the American public. After Pearl Harbor there were no more "war agitators," to use Charles Lindbergh's phrase, only aggrieved citizens forced to fight to protect themselves and their children.

At noon on Monday, December 8, President Roosevelt addressed Congress as 60 million Americans listened in by radio. In a grave and angry tone, he said, "Yesterday, December 7, 1941—a date which will live in infamy— the United States of America was suddenly and deliberately attacked by naval and air forces of the Empire of Japan." He emphasized that the Japanese had planned the attack while negotiations were going on in Washington. They had "deliberately sought to deceive the United States by false statements and expressions of hope for continued peace." A state of war with Japan had existed since eight a.m. December 7, and now FDR asked Congress officially to declare war. Roosevelt concluded his address by asserting that "always will our whole nation remember the character of the onslaught against us."[69] His implication resonated with Americans broadly—the surprise attack was a sign that the Japanese lacked honor.

Senator Thomas Connally (D-TX) asked FDR, "How did it happen that our warships were caught like tame ducks in Pearl Harbor? How did they catch us with our pants down?"[70] Congress was embarrassed that army and naval commanders seemed to have been unaware of any danger to Pearl Harbor. In the next four years, Republicans began a whisper campaign implying that Roosevelt had known of the impending attack: he had not. U.S. intelligence had been intercepting Japanese transmissions but had only partially broken the Japanese code. Early on December 7, Army Chief of Staff General George Marshall had learned that a decoded message suggested there would be a strike somewhere in the Pacific at 1:00 Eastern Standard Time, or 8:00 a.m. Hawaiian time. The message reached Pearl Harbor at 7:33, but the Japanese attacked before the warning reached the command. Virtually no one imagined Hawaii would be a target. It was out of range of aircraft based in Japan, and there was no precedent for a massive attack from aircraft carriers. In fact, Japan had sailed its carriers to the limit at which they might remain undetected and launched aircraft whose round trips almost exhausted their fuel.

On December 11 Germany and Italy declared war on the United States and named themselves the Axis Powers. The German-controlled government of Vichy France joined them, as did Japan, Hungary, Romania, Bulgaria, and Yugoslavia, among others. The United States, Great Britain, and the USSR headed the Allies, with the help of smaller countries scattered around the world.

In the days following Pearl Harbor, the Japanese conducted a pan-Pacific sweep. They sank two British ships off Malaya and attacked the Philippines, a U.S. commonwealth. They took British Hong Kong and Burma and captured the U.S. territories of Guam and Wake Island. They bombed the Philippines on December 7 and landed there on December 20 to engage U.S. ground troops under General Douglas MacArthur, who had retired in 1937 to serve as a consultant to the Philippines and reactivated his commission in July 1941. In less than a week, the Japanese had gained access to oil supplies and secured military bases across the Pacific.

The Japanese government's attack on Pearl Harbor allowed Americans to enter the war as a unified nation, leaving behind the isolationist and anti-interventionist arguments that had impeded mobilization. If the Japanese had not attacked, the United States might have declared war on Germany in the spring of 1942, pulling a riven nation into war. But Japan did attack, and those December events softened the acrimony between isolationists like Charles Lindbergh and interventionists like fighter pilot Phil Rasmussen. After December 7, 1941, the domestic security of the United States would be a global pursuit.

CHAPTER 7

THE WATERSHED
OF WAR:

AT HOME AND ABROAD, 1942–1945

S TAN IGAWA WAS fifteen years old on December 7, 1941. In 1935 his
single mother, Kimiko, had moved the family from Kona, on the
main island of Hawaii, to California. Neither Kimiko nor Stan had
ever been to Japan. She was a nisei—the U.S.-born child of Japanese immigrants—and hence an American citizen. Stan's grandparents were
issei: they had been born in Japan and immigrated to Hawaii in the nineteenth century as laborers on a coffee farm. Stan was a second-generation
U.S. citizen, a sansei. He was an all-American boy who loved basketball and
his Los Angeles high school. He too had a rendezvous with destiny.[1]

Immediately after Pearl Harbor, military leaders feared a Japanese
invasion of the Pacific Coast. John Lesesne DeWitt, the commanding general of the army's Western Defense Command for the Pacific States, mistakenly believed that Japanese planes were flying reconnaissance missions over
California. On December 8, Eleanor Roosevelt bravely sped to the West
Coast to set up emergency defense measures. She had been working for
months in Washington's Office of Civil Defense. From San Francisco, she
argued that Japanese Americans "must not feel they have suddenly ceased
to be Americans."[2] But General DeWitt disagreed.

World War II changed the American people at the time and forever
after. It sparked unprecedented mobility. Black southerners left for European battlefields and California defense jobs. Millions of women relocated
for work, and married women left their homes for employment. In the war's
four years, the percentage of women in the workforce rose from 27 percent

to 37 percent. Women in the armed services became a permanent part of the country's defense.

Class mobility often began when a service member donned a uniform and sent part of his pay home. From 1941 through 1945, steady incomes for working people distributed wealth more evenly, strengthening the nation's middle class. The war brought dramatic changes in the racial caste systems as well. Through canny strategies—sit-ins, protests, and lawsuits—African Americans highlighted their importance to the war effort and condemned Germany's racist persecution of the Jews. The Double V campaign—victory against fascism abroad and against racism at home—laid the foundations of the civil rights movement of the 1950s by recasting racial tolerance as a democratic imperative.

Wartime employment ended the Depression, which had waned since defense industry jobs began to proliferate in 1940. Government spending incurred an enormous war debt.

A partnership between government and industry forged a military-industrial complex that continued after the war. The federal government grew as New Deal agencies became models for wartime administration, and previously anti–New Deal corporations converted willingly to defense production. Fighting a two-ocean war enabled the United States to develop strategic strongholds that would bolster postwar national interests. As a third- and fourth-term president in wartime, Roosevelt vastly expanded the powers of the presidency.

ENTER THE UNITED STATES

When Winston Churchill heard about the Pearl Harbor attack, he was elated that the United States would enter the war. He arrived in Washington on December 22, 1941, to strategize with FDR. Churchill lived in the White House for three weeks, ordering a sherry before breakfast, two scotch and sodas for brunch, and a ninety-year-old brandy at bedtime. He enjoyed himself immensely, and he and FDR talked at length about how to share intelligence, plan strategy, and deploy troops and supplies.[3]

World War II took place in a series of distinct theaters that simultaneously vied for planning, manpower, and resources. The naval war in the North Atlantic had begun with Lend-Lease. The war against the Japanese in the Pacific absorbed enormous energy—this was the war that Pearl Harbor survivors Phil Rasmussen, Lew Sanders, and Dorris Miller would fight. U.S. Army Air Force pilots based in England bombed strategic sites in Germany, resulting in enormous destruction and civilian casualties. A North African campaign established a launching platform that began with the invasion of Italy through Sicily. Finally, the Allies landed in Normandy, France, on D-Day and fought their way to Berlin. Through it all, the Soviets fought the majority of German divisions on the Eastern Front.

Forging Allied Strategy

Winston Churchill was not the United States' only ally: Joseph Stalin, whom Roosevelt had never met, proved a problematic third partner. Tensions within the alliance ran deep. Fighting on the same side as the Communists in a war to save democracy was difficult for Churchill and Roosevelt, who always kept in mind Communist containment after the war. Stalin's central aim was to defeat Germany and then to gain control of eastern Europe to provide a shield in future conflicts.

Roosevelt and Churchill understood Stalin's goals but needed the Soviet Union to continue fighting the Germans. Churchill's anti-Communism and his personal dislike of Stalin challenged Roosevelt to referee long-distance communications between the two. Even if Stalin had agreed to some mutual postwar goals, FDR would have doubted his sincerity. Roosevelt simply avoided talking with Stalin about the postwar world, which was easy enough since they could not meet face to face. Roosevelt focused on winning the war at the smallest cost in American lives. He thought he could handle Stalin afterward, perhaps through a new League of Nations.

The British and Americans wanted to delay a massive troop landing in Europe to increase its chance of success, but Stalin wanted a cross-Channel invasion as soon as possible to draw German forces away from the Eastern Front. Roosevelt promised Stalin that U.S. ground troops would cross the Channel before 1942 was over, but Churchill argued that an invasion would be impossible in that time. The United States and Britain had to build landing craft and transport vessels; they did not accomplish that task until 1944. They also needed time to plan a massive operation in secrecy, and they lacked the personnel and equipment to vanquish the Germans once they were on the continent. The American and British lives saved by delaying the European invasion came at the cost of Soviet ones. Late in 1942 the Allies invaded northern Africa but did not cross the Channel to draw German troops from the Russian front. That year Hitler threw 80 percent of his troops against the USSR. If Roosevelt had reason not to trust Stalin, Stalin had reason not to trust Roosevelt.

The Pacific Response

In Pearl Harbor's aftermath, no one wanted to chase the Japanese across the Pacific more than Lew Sanders, Phil Rasmussen, and Dorris Miller did. The Pacific War would be a new kind of war, coordinating air, sea, and land forces across the separate services. Coordination among the Allies—mainly the Republic of China and the British Commonwealth countries of India and Australia—would be important as well. The ultimate target was Japan.

On February 19 more than two hundred Japanese planes bombed Darwin, Australia, to destroy Torres Strait naval defenses between New Guinea and Australia and eliminate a staging point for Allied Pacific resistance. A week later, on February 27, a combined Allied naval force suffered a defeat in the Dutch East Indies (Indonesia) that killed over two thousand sailors. Japan gained a virtually unlimited rubber supply.

General Douglas MacArthur's forces had been losing to Japanese ground troops since they landed on the Philippines in late December 1941. By March 1942 his commanding officers ordered him to evacuate to nearby Corregidor. He left behind his army to hold the Bataan peninsula, to the west of Manila Harbor. In early April 72,000 Americans and Filipinos fighting there surrendered. In what became known as the Bataan Death March, Japanese marched their prisoners eighty miles north to concentration camps, killing up to ten thousand along the way. Subsequently MacArthur and his command evacuated to Australia. By April the Japanese held Burma, the Dutch East Indies, Thailand, Malaya, Wake Island, Guam, Hong Kong, Sumatra, Singapore, the Philippines, and parts of New Guinea and the Solomon Islands.

Most Japanese Pacific holdings had neither large populations nor useful infrastructures. Some were simply specks in the vast ocean. Some had oil; others' utility lay in their strategic locations. From these toeholds, the Japanese controlled the Pacific seaways by the summer of 1942. Dislodging Japanese troops from rugged islands with dense jungles and underground defenses would come at an enormous loss of life. The Japanese hoped to destroy the U.S. fleet early in the war and then negotiate a peace that left them with their South Pacific territories. If they did not accomplish that, the United States and Britain would win in the long term.

In China, Japanese land troops continued to fight Chiang Kai-shek's nationalist forces, which had retreated to the interior. The United States and the USSR sent aid but not troops, hoping to keep the Japanese occupied in a ground war that would drain their resources. It was a counterpart to the European strategy, where Britain and the United States delayed opening a second front while Germany fought the Russians. But the strategy left China in chaos.

As the Japanese bombed Darwin through May and June 1942, their submarines entered Sydney harbor. Their immediate goal was not the occupation of Australia. Instead, the Japanese occupied New Guinea and aimed to take the Australian territory of Papua in the island's southeastern region, where the Allies had a base at Port Moresby. If they prevailed, they could cut the Allies' supply lines and control the Torres Strait. However, the Allies' cryptology project, called Magic, had finally mastered the Japanese code and forewarned them of the plan.

Over May 3–8, 1942, in the Battle of the Coral Sea, the U.S. and Australian naval and air forces turned back a Japanese amphibious fleet at Port Moresby. The Japanese exploded the *Lexington*, the aircraft carrier that had eluded them at Pearl Harbor, and heavily damaged the *Yorktown*. The battle resulted in a draw, but it marked the first time the Allies had stopped the Japanese. *The New York Times* did not exaggerate when it called the battle "the opening engagement in the decisive phase of the Battle for the World."[4] With the sea route foreclosed, the Japanese decided to deploy overland from their northeast position in New Guinea to capture Port Moresby to the south. Australian troops and some American marines walked in single file northward through the mountainous jungle on an old sixty-mile mining trail called the Kokoda Track to engage the Japanese. Australian forces fought all summer and fall before they drove the Japanese back to the northern coast.

The Battle of the Coral Sea and the Kokoda Track victory set the boundaries of engagement in the South Pacific. The Allies had thwarted Japanese ambition at a crucial moment. The Japanese would not control the seaways around Australia, and the conflicts drew a line from west to east across the South Pacific from which the Allies could move toward Japan.

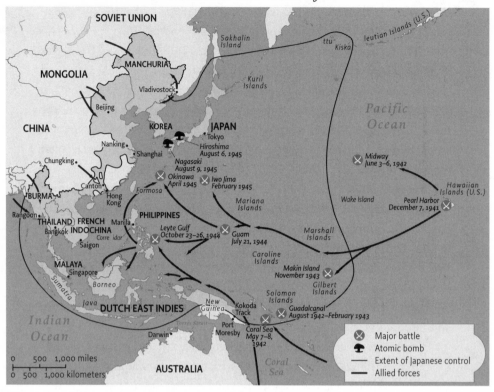

Island Hopping

A month later the Battle of Midway drew a second line from north to south in the Central Pacific. Tiny Midway Island lies about 2,500 miles southeast of Tokyo and 1,300 miles northwest of Honolulu. As a strategic post, it loomed large. Japanese occupation of Midway, where the United States had an airfield, would provide them control of the eastern Pacific and a platform to attack Hawaii. The Japanese strung out their fleet as they planned a surprise attack. Having destroyed the *Lexington* and heavily damaged the *Yorktown* in the Coral Sea, they aimed to obliterate the remaining two U.S. aircraft carriers, the *Hornet* and the *Enterprise*.

Alerted by Magic, the Americans made Midway the antithesis of Pearl Harbor. Admiral Chester W. Nimitz, commander of the Pacific Fleet, pulled the damaged *Yorktown* from the Coral Sea back to Hawaii, ordered it patched up in seventy-two hours, and sent it to Midway. Instead of the two aircraft carriers the Japanese expected, there would be three.

Japanese planes attacked the Midway airfield on June 4 but inflicted only moderate damage because U.S. planes were on the three aircraft carriers. Pilots from the *Yorktown*, *Enterprise*, and *Hornet* bombed the four Japanese carriers as their planes refueled on deck and destroyed all four. The Japanese lost over 200 planes and 3,000 men. Captain Takahisa Amagi, of the aircraft carrier *Kaga*, estimated that 80 percent of the men on his ship died, including 50 percent of the pilots.[5] The loss began a precipitous decline in the number of skilled Japanese pilots, even as U.S. pilot training geared up. U.S. war industries vastly improved the caliber of U.S. aircraft and produced 47,000 planes in 1942.

General MacArthur moved north from Australia as Admiral Nimitz pushed west from Midway. In August 1942 the Americans took the offensive in the Solomon Islands. Strung about the Coral Sea, the Solomons formed a protective barrier for the Australian seaways. On Guadalcanal, one of the Solomons, the Allies threw sixty thousand men against a dug-in Japanese force half that size. The Battle of Guadalcanal lasted for almost six months and demonstrated how difficult it would be to win island by island. Yet that was the strategy that U.S. forces had to follow—island hopping to Japan—with Australian naval support, while the British fought in Burma.

During 1942 Phil Rasmussen and Lew Sanders remained in Hawaii training new pilots. By year's end, the Army Air Force dispatched seasoned fliers to aircraft carriers and Pacific bases, and Sanders took command of the 318th Fighter Group of the Seventh Air Force, charged with protecting Hawaii. With each battle in the Central Pacific over the course of the war, his group inched closer to Japan. It provided the air support for the invasion of the Marianas: Saipan, Guam, and Tinian. Once there Sanders's pilots pioneered using a congealed gasoline—napalm—in combat. He recalled, "We tried Jap motor gas and oil, with the napalm powder, and it was quite successful."[6] Unlike the U.S. forces, the Japanese did not have usable radar on their ships and aircraft. From Midway onward, the Allies used this deficit to their advantage.

Just before the Battle of Midway, Admiral Nimitz had awarded the Navy Cross to Mess Attendant First Class Dorris Miller, the black cook who machine-gunned Zeros during the Pearl Harbor attack. The navy sent him stateside on a war bond tour, where he spoke to black audiences in late 1942 and early 1943. That spring he became a petty officer, ship's cook third class on the escort carrier the *Liscome Bay*. The *Liscome Bay* deployed to the Central Pacific around Makin Island. As Phil Rasmussen engaged the Japanese from a nearby carrier, a Japanese torpedo struck the *Liscome Bay*'s stern and detonated its bomb magazine. The ship sank with nine hundred sailors aboard, Miller among them.

After the Battle of Makin Island, the Forty-sixth Fighter Squadron and Phil Rasmussen returned to Hawaii, where they began training on new very long-range (VLR) fighter planes called P-51 D Mustangs. The P-51 was a single-seat, one-propeller plane fitted with auxiliary external gas tanks nicknamed Tokyo Tanks. It had a bomber's range—1,650 miles—which meant that a single pilot, strapped into the cockpit, flew the plane for eight hours to protect the larger B-29 Superfortress bombers. Only the most experienced and coolest pilots could attempt such a trip. Rasmussen hoped that soon he would be able to fly one all the way to Japan.

The Politics of Internment

On February 19, 1941, President Roosevelt issued Executive Order 9066 to authorize Secretary of War Stimson to "prescribe military areas . . . from which any or all persons may be excluded."[7] The government would provide transportation, food, and accommodation for those relocated. On its face, the order might apply to anyone. In fact, it applied to citizens and resident aliens of Japanese, Italian, and German heritage. In practice, it removed 110,000 Japanese, 300 Italians, and 5,000 Germans from their homes and sent them to inland internment camps.

On March 2, 1942, General DeWitt, commander of the Western Defense Command, declared the coasts of California, Washington, and Oregon to be military areas and ordered residents of Japanese descent sent to internment camps. Elsewhere, Italians and Germans were arrested and screened for loyalty, and a few domestic fascists among them were interned. But DeWitt argued that all people of Japanese descent—even second-generation sensei—who lived on the coast were naturally "subversive," members of "an enemy race," whose "racial strains are undiluted." DeWitt called them "over 112,000 potential enemies at large." After May 9, 1942, they would be interned.[8] Roosevelt created the War Relocation Authority (WRA) to manage the task. The WRA made up a card on everyone sent to internment camps, including Stan Igawa. His WRA card noted that he spoke, wrote, and read both Japanese and English, had never been to Japan, and had completed two years of high school in Los Angeles.[9]

The WRA created ten isolated concentration camps: in California,

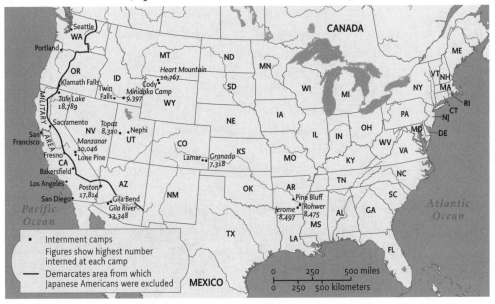

Manzanar and Tule Lake in Death Valley; in Idaho, Minidoka Camp; in Utah, Topaz; in Colorado, Granada; in Wyoming, Heart Mountain; in Arizona, Poston and Gila River. Two camps in Arkansas on the Mississippi River brought Japanese Americans into the Deep South, confusing Jim Crow laws and customs. Stan Igawa's family went to Heart Mountain. Despite the wrenching blow of losing his home, Igawa joined fellow internees in cooperative life, eating communally and going to school. As he would do with everything in life, he made the best of it.

On May 11 Eleanor Roosevelt's article "Race, Religion, and Prejudice" appeared in *The New Republic*. She steeled herself to the Japanese internment, but she drew the line there. The United States was "fighting for freedom, and one of the freedoms we must establish is freedom from discrimination . . . either because of race, or of color, or of religion," she argued. She urged Americans to work for equality—legal, economic, educational, and political—for Jews and African Americans during the war.[10] After the war, she predicted an end to immigration discrimination against the Chinese and Japanese. For now, Japanese Americans would have to wait.

At the Manzanar Internment Camp in July 1942, twenty-seven-year-old Chiye Mori wore her hair in a tight bun, chain-smoked Lucky Strikes, and wore men's shirts with the tails out over men's khaki pants. A decade earlier, at Long Beach Polytechnic High School, she was the only person of Japanese ancestry in the high school writers' club. Back then she dressed in feminine white blouses and modest black skirts and won a National Scholastic Prize for her poetry. One of her poems, "Japanese American," described the nisei predicament.

> Clay pigeons traveling swiftly and aimlessly
> On the electric wire of international hate.
> Helpless targets in the shooting gallery of political discord.[11]

On December 7, 1941, she was the assistant editor of *Rafu Shimpo*, the Japanese-English newspaper published in Los Angeles's Little Tokyo.

In late March 1942 Mori put the last issue of *Rafu Shimpo* to bed, packed her bags, and boarded a bus to Manzanar Relocation Camp. There the dust blew all day, and it was either too hot or too cold. Some 2,032 internees lived in wooden barracks and ate in mess halls. With the camp commander's blessing, she and her former colleagues started the *Manzanar Free Press*. She knew that the reports officer censored every word in the paper, yet she became editor in July, when her colleagues quit in protest of censorship.

A UPI reporter—the first to report from an internment camp—wrote from Manzanar that the internees "have quickly fallen into a normal pattern of living." He asked Mori her opinion on internment. She responded, "If Japan wins this war we have the most to lose. We hope America wins and quickly. We voluntarily evacuated . . . [to] demonstrate our loyalty."[12] What Mori said to the press was one thing, but what she said around the newspaper office was another. A younger nisei colleague recalled, "I had never come across anyone who could talk about politics and who damned the leaders of our country like she did."[13]

Others resisted internment altogether. Fred Korematsu was four years younger than Mori, also a native Californian, and living in San Francisco. He refused to report to his designated assembly relocation center and had plastic surgery on his eyelids so that he might pass for Chinese. But he was arrested on a street corner, accused of spying, and convicted of violating the law. After September 1942 his appeal slowly wound its way to the Supreme Court.

On the eve of the first Pearl Harbor anniversary, a riot broke out at Manzanar. The FBI had been recruiting informants among the internees at the camps, and several men savagely beat a suspected informer. The victim claimed to recognize his attackers' eyes through ski masks, and three men were arrested. Hundreds of internees demonstrated against the arrests, and two were released. A crowd gathered, sang the Japanese national anthem, and threatened to kill informers. Enraged by the anthem, military police turned a Thompson submachine gun on the crowd, killing two and injuring sixteen others. The camp administration smuggled out the terrified informants.

Mori wrote a scathing story about the assault on the crowd, which she published without running it by the camp censors. The authorities condemned her to the Tule Lake Segregation Center, an internment camp with a restricted compound for divisive internees. Chiye Mori found herself exiled from exile.

The Manzanar riot provoked the War Relocation Authority to force interned Japanese into a new program known as Loyalty Registration in February 1943. Some administrators hoped that if Japanese internees signed the Loyalty Registration questionnaire, they could leave the camps and contribute to the war effort. Others hoped to identify radicals. Registration revealed deep discontent. Asked whether the respondent would be willing to fight for the United States, one-half either answered no or refused to do so until they regained their civil rights. Asked if they would swear allegiance to the United States and renounce their allegiance to Japan and to the emperor, a substantial number, mostly people who had lived in Japan at some point, demurred.

A year later, in January 1944, the armed forces began drafting nisei young men among the internees. Some complied, others resisted. Several hundred internees were convicted of violating the Selective Security Act and sent to prison. Stan Igawa was seventeen when he read about the nisei draft resisters in the Heart Mountain internment camp paper. The paper called them "slow-witted" and said they "lacked physical and moral courage."[14] Throughout 1943 and 1944, Igawa attended high school in the camp and played on the Whippets, his basketball team. He promised himself that when he graduated, he would prove his courage and enlist in the army. In late 1944 the Supreme Court ruled in *Korematsu v. United States* that internment camps were constitutional and upheld Fred Korematsu's arrest for defying internment.

North Africa and the Casablanca Conference

Throughout the spring and summer of 1942, Churchill hesitated to launch any large-scale invasion, hoping to strengthen Allied forces and weaken Germany on the Eastern Front. The Germans had set up a puppet government run by French collaborators in Vichy, France, which managed the country and its colonies under German supervision. The French leader Charles de Gaulle had escaped to Britain, where he headed up the Free French Forces, whose troops consisted primarily of French colonial Africans. Within France, an underground resistance tried to subvert German occupation at every turn. French resistance fighters, many of them adolescents, created an intelligence network that sent information to Britain.

Roosevelt believed that an Allied invasion of Vichy French Algeria and Morocco might be greeted by its residents as liberation. Once there, American troops could head west across North Africa to join the British, bogged down in Egypt. That country was key to the Suez Canal and the gateway to the Middle East. The British had succeeded against the Italians there until February 1941, when German General Erwin Rommel's Afrika Korps landed two divisions. A joint British-American movement across North Africa could secure the canal and provide a base for an Italian invasion.

As the British Eighth Army engaged Rommel in northern Egypt in November 1942, British and U.S. troops, under General Dwight David Eisenhower's command, landed along the coast from Safi, Morocco, to Algiers in Operation Torch. In an amazing feat, Royal Air Force bombers flew from England to Genoa, an historic city on the Italian Mediterranean. They bombed the port and war industries that supplied the German troops in North Africa and flew home, a fourteen-hundred-mile round trip. When Roosevelt heard that Operation Torch had gone off with low casualties, he exclaimed, "We are striking back!"[15] Within weeks of the invasion, the North African Vichy governments crumbled, their troops joined the Allies, and all turned east toward Egypt.

In January 1943, Roosevelt met Churchill in Casablanca, Morocco, to discuss a cross-Channel European invasion, code-named Operation Overlord. Army Chief of Staff Marshall, who supported an immediate invasion across the English Channel, accompanied him. But World War I trench warfare made Churchill imagine another lost generation's blood lapping up on the cliffs of Dover. He hoped that targeted invasions could divert the Germans in the Mediterranean, while the Soviets defeated them in the east.

The delaying strategy depended on a Soviet victory in the ongoing titanic Battle of Stalingrad. The previous July, Hitler had ordered General Friedrich Paulus and his Sixth Army to capture the city before winter. Stalingrad would give the Germans a transportation hub on the Volga River.

From that perch between the Black and Caspian Seas, German forces could move south into the oil-rich Caucasus and reach Rommel in Africa.

At Casablanca, Churchill persuaded FDR to delay a cross-Channel invasion in favor of invading Italy, which he called the "soft underbelly of the Axis."[16] The two leaders agreed to move through Sicily, only ninety-six miles from Africa, defeat the Italian and German troops there, and continue to mainland Italy. Churchill and FDR also devised a strategy for the U.S. Army Air Force and the Royal Air Force to bomb German industrial facilities from England so that an invasion across the Channel would be less costly. Upon leaving Casablanca, Roosevelt blurted out before the press that the Allies would accept nothing short of German unconditional surrender. A shocked Churchill publicly supported FDR's proposal but privately believed that it would prolong the war. Roosevelt maintained that calling for unconditional surrender had been a slip of the tongue, but it was a slip that might reassure Stalin.

The Russian Front

Stalin felt betrayed by the cross-Channel invasion delay. He suspected that the United States and Britain might invade Italy, win back France and the Low Countries, and make peace with Germany, leaving the USSR to fight on alone. Conversely, Roosevelt and Churchill did not trust Stalin to keep fighting the Germans once he repelled them from Soviet soil. Roosevelt broke one promise to Stalin—to mount a full-fledged invasion across the Channel—and made another. Americans would keep fighting until Germany's unconditional surrender eliminated any threat to the Soviet Union.

German forces had slashed through eastern Europe to occupy Stalingrad. Fourteen-year-old Shifre Zamkov, a Russian Jew from Belarus, witnessed the cruelty of the German push. "The Germans took the Russians in captivity as prisoners of war," she recalled. "And we saw the treatment. It was inhumane." Then "they started the executions with the Jewish population, . . . shooting them against the wall." Her family fled into the forest in the summer of 1942, just as German troops reached Stalingrad. Russian soldiers hiding there led the Zamkovs and other Jewish families eastward—toward the front, their only hope. They wandered for weeks in German-held territory.

By the end of October 1942, a quarter-million Germans occupied 90 percent of Stalingrad. Stalin sent one million troops into the city, many of whom died within days. Germans fought Soviets hand to hand in the few buildings left standing. The street-fighting Soviets ate rats and dead German horses. Stalin ordered General Georgy Zhukov to mass troops to the north and south, and by late November, the Soviets secured a united western perimeter, trapping German troops in the city to the east. Hitler forbade Paulus to break out through the western line and promised to supply the troops by air. In December 28,000 Germans died of starvation.

German troops to the west of Zhukov's line fled toward Shifre Zamkov's wandering band. When the Luftwaffe bombed a nearby railroad station, she feared the worst, but the attack heralded her rescue. The Germans were bombing Russian troops advancing from the east. "Russian new soldiers and new weapons . . . came from deep in Russia," she recalled. [17] Paulus surrendered the Sixth German Army on February 2, 1943.

More than half a million Axis troops had died in the battle of Stalingrad. The Soviets captured 100,000 Germans, of whom 75,000 died within three months. The USSR suffered incredible losses: 478,741 dead, 650,878 wounded, and 40,000 dead civilians. The battle claimed almost two million people. The Soviets sentenced their prisoners as war criminals, and only 6,000 Germans ever returned home: in 1955. By then Shifre Zamkov had been living in New Haven, Connecticut, for six years.

In the spring of 1943, Joseph Stalin flexed his muscles with his allies. The Soviets had stopped 80 percent of Germany's forces and were now headed to Berlin. Stalin needed western arms, but he told FDR and Churchill that the Allies' delayed second front strained their alliance. In May and June 1943, Stalin withdrew his ambassadors from London and Washington. In August about 60 percent of German troop strength still fought on the Eastern Front. Postponing the cross-Channel invasion had saved British and American soldiers from the carnage that befell the Soviets, but it strengthened Stalin's bargaining power with the Allies. When Roosevelt and Churchill met in Quebec in August 1943, Churchill finally green-lighted Operation Overlord.[18] The Soviets moved westward so quickly that Roosevelt and Churchill made contingency plans in case the Soviets conquered Germany before D-Day.

MOBILIZING THE HOME FRONT

Home front mobilization in 1942 benefited from the defense buildup of the previous two years and the passage of the Selective Service Act in 1940.

Moreover, during the New Deal, Washington had accumulated the structural and managerial experience to deploy resources swiftly. While many had criticized the centralization of power in Washington in 1939, by 1942 most Americans were relieved to have a robust federal government fighting the Axis Powers.

To manage America's war effort successfully, civilian government, military command, and private industry came together to mount four initiatives, all of which required departures from free market operations. First, the government seized control of war matériel and production. Second, it apportioned resources to win the war and manage home front shortages. Third, defense industries recruited a new kind of civilian workforce. Fourth, the government tightly controlled the wartime economy, from setting wages and prices to taxation and borrowing.

War Production and Consumption

In January 1942, Roosevelt gave the War Production Board (WPB) vast powers to manage raw materials and production. To head the WPB, he tapped Sears, Roebuck CEO Donald Nelson, who asked one question: "what method will most quickly give us the greatest volume of war production in this particular industry?"[19]

Nelson shut down the auto industry's production of civilian cars and temporarily halted used car sales. The 1941 production of four million new passenger cars dropped to 200,000 in 1942, and the WPB rationed the half-million unsold cars that had already been sent to dealerships. The steel and rubber that had been used for automobiles on Chrysler shop floors became instead M-3 tanks, which infantrymen nicknamed "General Grants" or "General Lees." A thirty-five-mile-per-hour national speed limit conserved gas and tire rubber.

Equipping the armed services demanded inventing substitutes for commodities that the nation lacked. For example, by 1944 domestically produced synthetic rubber replaced 90 percent of the natural rubber that previously came from Japanese-held Indonesia. Silk had to be diverted to parachutes from silk stockings, so women went bare-legged while scientists developed nylon.

Government contracts went to large corporations—those that could find their way through the bidding process, lobby Congress, and produce goods quickly at unprecedented volume. These companies were compensated on a cost-plus basis that guaranteed a profit, and the government paid for plant modernization. A government contract was not only patriotic, it was a moneymaker. Fewer than fifty corporations won half of all federal contracts.

WPB freeze orders ended the production of consumer goods such as bicycles and diverted raw materials to war production. Smaller companies risked bankruptcy if they could not find substitutions. A factory that made animal traps converted to bullet cores. Those that continued to produce goods for civilian consumption, such as vinyl records, often recycled their own materials. Some retailers sold used goods alongside new ones.

Rationing boards issued the coupons required to limit the purchase of certain goods. At first, oil, gas, and tires headed the list. When the Office of Price Administration announced on Halloween 1942 that people would be limited to one cup of coffee a day, Americans went into caffeine withdrawal. Planes and ships could not be spared to import coffee beans. People quit driving and took crowded public transportation. Cigarettes, sugar, and silk fell under rationing, followed by ketchup, butter, and cheese.

By 1943, 40 percent of the gross national product went to war production. For the first time in history, the United States used all of its industrial capacity.

Labor on the Move

War mobilization sparked unprecedented labor mobility. People who had never worked as wage earners found jobs. Entire job categories that had been reserved for white men now hired women and minorities, previously considered unequal to the task. Many workers relocated for higher pay, and by war's end, one in five Americans had made a significant change of residence. These opportunities meant that the worst jobs—for example, sharecropping and domestic work—permanently lost many workers.

Defense production centered in California, where 1.5 million people migrated, and the population increased by 14 percent in 1942. Some 300,000 people moved to Michigan, where auto factories were retooled to produce tanks and airplanes. At the Ford-built Willow Run Bomber Factory, between Detroit and Ann Arbor, employees braved the Michigan winter in "tiny store box shacks with tarpaper nailed on the outside and a hole punched through the roof."[20] Willow Run workers produced one B-24

Liberator bomber almost every hour around the clock, every day. As California and Michigan grew, Oklahoma and Arkansas shrank. A half million people left the two states, following the 400,000 who had left during the Depression. Newcomers crowded into northern industrial cities, military bases, and shipyards. More than 17 percent of defense spending went to build and improve southern military bases at places like Norfolk, Virginia, and Mobile, Alabama, signifying the power of congressional southern Democrats.

At first, black southerners moved to southern cities for jobs, but by 1943 many abandoned the South for the North and West. African Americans in West Coast cities doubled, tripled, and in some cases quadrupled by 1945. The Fair Employment Practices Committee opened up defense industry jobs theoretically without regard to race, but black workers often found the best opportunities foreclosed. Buoyed by the wages that servicemen sent home and by the available defense jobs, one-third of sharecroppers quit. In the Mississippi Delta, planters used German prisoners of war to pick cotton.[21]

Landowners and agribusiness sought farmworkers who would not demand decent wages or go on strike. The United States had forced noncitizen Mexicans out of the country during the Depression, but FDR invited them back to work in 1942 through the Bracero Program. Braceros, Spanish for "manual laborers" (those who use their arms), signed short-term labor contracts in California and twenty-five other states. The contract workers were men, but some brought their families, who also worked in the fields.

Some 167,925 workers signed contracts from 1942 through 1945. Crispin Espinosa, a teenage orphan, signed on when he saw program fliers posted in his Mexican village. Espinosa picked grapes in Monterey County, California, where he ate bologna on maggot-infested bread and craved a drink of water. The bracero system exploited the workers, who lacked U.S. wage and hour protection and were far from home. But the program lasted for twenty years, and many Mexicans returned repeatedly to the United States. Babies born in the United States were U.S. citizens, and those children grew up on both sides of the border. Some workers put together contracts and stayed, and some married U.S. citizens. Between 1942 and 1965, some 4.5 million braceros worked in the United States. Espinosa came of age as a bracero, married, and brought up eight children in California. He became a U.S. citizen at eighty-two.[22]

Women's Work and Working Women

World War II accelerated and cemented profound changes for women in the labor force. At first, some feared that women would shirk their duty, but Secretary of Labor Frances Perkins confidently predicted that they would respond to job recruitment and the lure of fair wages. In 1940 about one in four women worked, the same percentage as in 1910. Some six million women entered the workforce for the first time during the war, for a total of 18 million by 1945. Seven million women worked directly in defense industries. College women harvested crops in the women's land army during the summers.

Women's war work changed the workforce in ways that varied according to race, class, and generation. Wartime women's employment continued the Depression uptick of white married women working outside the home. Black married women had always had high labor force participation rates, difficult to measure but probably over 50 percent. In the population at large, 15.2 percent of all married women worked in 1940, but by 1945, 24 percent did, many of them over forty.

New gender norms emerged as the war reshaped American society. Young adult men were scarce in civilian life. In 1940 fifty million men aged 18 to 45 registered for the draft; in 1943 nine million men served in the armed forces; by 1945 three million more had joined them. Overcrowded cities seemed to be cities of women. In Detroit, working women's numbers doubled from 182,000 to 387,000, and seven other cities experienced the same percentage increase. Women enjoyed unprecedented freedom of movement, both to relocate and to use public space. They earned their own money and often controlled their husband's military checks. The chaos of crowded cities filled with war workers meant that women squeezed onto city buses with men, went to dance halls with other women, and walked into restaurants alone.

Moreover, women abandoned low-paying, domestic, temporary, or seasonal jobs for full-time, well-paid, permanent jobs with more responsibility. Instead of sewing at home to augment their husband's income, women sewed parachutes to support themselves. Black women fled white women's kitchens. Some southern white women found this so astonishing that they believed that Eleanor Roosevelt had recruited their maids to join "Eleanor Clubs." Before the war, a woman performing skilled factory tasks would have been a curiosity. When Labor Department officials visited defense plants in 1943, they found women in professional and technical positions in 60 percent of the plants. Women worked in almost every job that men did—from lumberjack to stevedore. The War Department declared, "A woman is a substitute, like plastic instead of metal."[23] There were far fewer Rosie the Riveters than clerical workers microfilming service records, but the public perception of women's capabilities changed.

Some 350,000 women, including 6,500 black women, joined the armed forces. Combat was closed to women, but they could work in war zones. Army Chief of Staff George Marshall supported women's military service and recognized the myriad noncombat jobs waiting to be filled. Congress authorized the Women's Army Auxiliary Corps in May 1942; in September 1943 it became the Women's Army Corps (WAC). The navy established the WAVES—Women Accepted for Volunteer Emergency Service—in July 1942, but did not accept black women until December 1944. Some 86,000 women served in the WAVES, remaining stateside until late in the war.

The public worried simultaneously that military service would masculinize women and that hypersexual servicewomen would seduce soldiers. WAC leaders steered a vigilant course between policing—and denying—lesbianism and enforcing strict behavior codes. Servicewomen repaired tanks, planes, and ships, expedited paperwork, gathered intelligence, worked as air traffic controllers, and provided health care to the troops.

At war's end, labor unions and heavy industries combined to reclaim for men the industrial jobs that women had performed. By January 1946 one million women had left or lost their jobs in factories, but there were still one million more female factory workers than in 1940. Women entered clerical, sales, and service positions in unprecedented numbers by 1947. One economist predicted that "the wartime opportunities afforded women to earn an independent living will not be surrendered lightly. . . . Women will contend with men for employment in whatever jobs are available."[24] The WACs and the WAVES, with the support of the top brass, won permanent status after the war.

Selling the War at Home

With domestic full employment and money flowing home from service members, the entire home front enjoyed unprecedented prosperity. In 1941 the richest 5 percent of Americans owned 26 percent of the nation's wealth, but by 1945 their share decreased to 16 percent. Farm income doubled during the war, and corporate profits rose by 70 percent. Industrial wages rose by 47 percent from 1939. Perhaps the most stunning figure was the increase in personal savings: from $6 billion in 1939 to $38.9 billion in 1945.[25]

With more money chasing fewer goods, inflation accompanied prosperity. When prices rose 10.9 percent in 1942, the Office of Price Administration instituted price caps and invited the public to report any overcharging. Inflation peaked in 1943 at 6.1 percent and fell the following year to 1.7 percent. Taxes pinched the consumer as well. The 1942 Tax Revenue Act raised income taxes and lowered the minimum income that could be taxed. The vast majority of those employed paid some income tax by 1945. In addition, a 5 percent "victory tax" was imposed on purchases for the war's duration. Taxes had never been higher, but neither had wages.

Nonetheless, taxes could not pay for the war. The government borrowed enormous sums. In 1944 and 1945 defense spending reached $775 billion, almost 40 percent of the gross national product, the highest proportion before or since. It consumed 89.5 percent of the federal budget. The government avidly promoted war bonds, helped by a team of popular superheroes. Superman joined Batman and Robin to encourage Americans to "Sink the Japanazis with Bonds & Stamps."[26] Americans bought over $185 billion in bonds.

Since most industries produced war goods that consumers could not buy, they used advertising budgets to promote war bonds, admonish people to save scarce resources, and shore up their brand names. Even purely domestic products carried a war message. Kleenex warned, "Don't be a public enemy! Be patriotic and smother sneezes with a Kleenex. . . . America needs every man—full time."[27]

The Hollywood Writers Mobilization for Defense argued that "wartime function of the movies is to build morale," and directors asked themselves, "Will this picture help win the war?"[28] Male actors rushed to enlist—Academy Award–winning Best Actor Jimmy Stewart had to gain ten pounds to make the weight requirement to become a combat pilot— and female actors circled the globe to entertain the troops. Ronald Reagan, an army air corps reserve officer, became active in 1942 and made training films.

Extremely conscious of the movies' effect at home, on bases, on America's allies, and on its enemies, the censors forbade movies that depicted gangsters, racial discrimination, wasteful living, or Allied imperialistic motives, or that discounted other Allied nations' contributions. Another rule prohibited portraying Americans as superior or nationalistically smug. The National Association of Broadcasters forged a code that forbade upsetting listeners. The nation heard no weather reports during 1942 for fear they would aid an aerial invasion.

The Office of War Information (OWI) oversaw all printed material, including comic strips. DC Comics star Superman became a private who failed inspections because he kept bursting out of his khakis to reveal his skintight Superman outfit. Eventually his commanding officer gave up on keeping him up to spec. When ordered to "take that hill," Private Superman went to the front line, lifted the hill up on his shoulders, and brought it back to his captain: "Taking the hill, Sir, as you ordered."[29]

A great propaganda machine turned against the Germans, Italians, and especially the Japanese. Hollywood director Frank Capra made seven films collectively entitled *Why We Fight* that became required viewing for millions of servicemen and packed civilian theaters. In *Know Your Enemy—Japan* he portrayed the Japanese soldier as the product of centuries of Japanese bloodlust, obedience, and fanaticism. "We're Gonna Have to Slap the Dirty Little Jap (And Uncle Sam's the Guy Who Can Do It)" was the title of a popular song. The Marine Corps magazine, *Leatherneck*, reported on a marine who had collected as "souvenirs—eleven ears from dead Japs. It was not disgusting, as it would be from the civilian point of view. None of us could get emotional over it."[30]

HUMAN RIGHTS AT HOME AND ABROAD

The war against fascism was a war for democracy, and for African Americans it fired dreams of full citizenship. The media's portrait of a tolerant United States provided them an opportunity to push for actual racial tolerance. Most Americans knew that the Nazis had sent the Jews to concentration camps to work and starve; however, they did not know that the SS began in 1942 to build extermination camps. Sympathy for Jewish refugees grew as the war progressed, and the State Department finally eased some restrictions in 1944—too late. By linking foreign and domestic racism, African Americans portrayed racial intolerance as un-American.

The Double V Campaign

In World War I black leaders had struck a bargain to fight first and be rewarded later, but in World War II they fought for democracy and their rights simultaneously. Defense industries and the armed forces needed African Americans, and the government worried about "Negro morale." A. Philip Randolph and the NAACP's Walter White had hoped to force the president to desegregate the armed services, but he did not, even though he desegregated defense industries. An order in 1940 had reversed each service's right to set separate black enlistment quotas and established a 10 percent service-wide cap, roughly the percentage of black Americans in the population. Previously, the army had had the highest percentage of black troops at around 8.0 percent. Secretary of the Navy Frank Knox, who believed African Americans incapable of fighting, argued for a lower cap.

Although he avoided desegregation of the services, FDR opened up more opportunities within them, including combat, for African Americans in segregated units and allowed more black officers to command black troops. In the army and navy, African Americans rose from menial jobs. The U.S. Army Air Force and the Marine Corps had previously excluded African Americans; now the air force established a black flight school at Tuskegee College in Alabama, and the Marine Corps accepted them. The first black pilots began flying in 1943 and distinguished themselves in the Italian campaign. After Eleanor Roosevelt returned from a base tour, where she saw black soldiers turned away from films and excluded from gyms, she complained to Army Chief of Staff Marshall. In March 1943 the War Department desegregated all base recreational facilities.

A leading black newspaper, *The Pittsburgh Courier*, promoted Double Victory: victory abroad over fascism and victory at home over racism. The *Courier* had been the first to identify Dorris Miller, whom the navy had reported to be "an unnamed Negro messman."[31] After Randolph called off the march on Washington in 1941, he continued the movement behind it, teaching its participants nonviolent direct action based on Mahatma Gandhi's philosophy. When Pauli Murray, a Randolph supporter and Howard University law student, organized African Americans to sit in at segregated Washington restaurants and picket outside in 1943, Eleanor Roosevelt invited her to tea at the White House.

Black soldiers, some for the first time with disposable incomes, joined the NAACP in large numbers. Langston Hughes's 1943 poem "Jim Crow's Last Stand" exudes their optimism.

> *Pearl Harbor put Jim Crow on the Run.*
> *That Crow can't fight for Democracy*
> *And be the same old Crow he used to be . . .*
> *When Dorie Miller took gun in hand*
> *Jim Crow started his last stand.*[32]

As African Americans exercised their rights at home, wartime pressures in urban areas produced civil unrest. In 1942 a riot in Detroit against black newcomers to a white neighborhood prompted the headline "Hitler Invades America."[33] In 1943 there were 240 racial incidents in forty-seven cities, with white attacks on African Americans in Detroit, Los Angeles, and Mobile, Alabama. In Beaumont, Texas, several hundred whites burned and looted the black neighborhood and killed two men in what a black newspaper called a "week end of terror, worse than anything visited upon the Jews by Nazi fanatics at the height of their pogroms."[34] They were unaware of the wholesale murder of Jews that was beginning in German concentration camps. In January 1944 the Swedish sociologist Gunnar Myrdal published a massive study of U.S. racial discrimination, commissioned by the Carnegie Corporation in the 1930s. *An American Dilemma* argued that democracy's survival depended on extending full civil rights to all Americans.

The sympathies of Japanese Americans and African Americans were occasionally joined by their experiences of discrimination. When Suji Kimura rode from Colorado in 1943 to Tule Lake Segregated Camp, she sat beside a young black woman from Memphis traveling to Utah to visit her husband, who had been injured on board ship off Australia. Kimura purchased sandwiches for the black woman, whom bus station restaurants would not serve. "I thought of her traveling all the way from Memphis alone," Kimura reflected later. "I thought of her husband wounded in action. Our 'Democracy' has a long ways to go yet." Nisei Japanese troops stationed near Birmingham, Alabama, refused to abide by the black-white color line on buses. When a nisei soldier saw a white bus driver kick a black serviceman as he stepped off the bus, the Japanese soldier punched the bus driver.[35] In 1946 the U.S. Supreme Court in *Morgan v. Virginia* finally outlawed segregation in interstate travel.

The Holocaust in the Making

In the summer of 1942, British cryptologists intercepted information on Hitler's plan to exterminate the Jews in special camps. By December of that year, more than six death camps were in operation, and Eleanor Roosevelt learned that Germany had already executed two million Polish Jews. "The figure of executions in my area now exceeds 30,000," one German commander in Poland bragged to Berlin that year.[36] The British and the U.S. State Department tried to deflect attention from reports of the concentration camps, and Jewish groups protested the Allies' failure to act. Romania's offer to ransom seventy thousand trapped Jews for fifty dollars apiece drove New York Jews to run a display ad in *The New York Times* on February 16, 1943, headlined "For Sale to Humanity, 70,000 Jews."[37] The U.S. State Department and the British disallowed the ransom's payment.

The U.S. failure to aid the Romanian Jews proved the last straw for thirty-one-year-old lawyer Josiah E. Du Bois, Jr. He worked in Henry Morgenthau's Treasury Department, which practiced wartime financial diplomacy. Knowing it would have been possible to ransom the Romanian Jews, Du Bois wrote an outraged memo to his boss: "One of the greatest crimes in history, the slaughter of the Jewish people in Europe, is continuing unabated." He accused State Department officials of covering up "Hitler's plans to exterminate the Jews." Morgenthau presented Du Bois's "Report to the Secretary on the Acquiescence of This Government in the Murder of the Jews" to FDR on January 16, 1944. Six days later Roosevelt created the War Refugee Board (WRB). Working around the State Department, the WRB evacuated and resettled 200,000 Jews in the next fourteen months.[38]

THE WAR IN EUROPE

By the summer of 1943, the European war turned to favor the Allies—or the United Nations, as FDR preferred to call them. The British cryptologists at Bletchley Park created a system nicknamed Ultra to decipher German messages. Using radar and Ultra, the Allies could follow German submarines. By the summer of 1943, U.S. ships supplying Britain and the USSR through the North Atlantic and Artic Ocean traveled in relative safety.

Soviet troops continued to chase the Germans west, as the British Eastern Task Force, advancing from Egypt, met the Allies in Tunisia and defeated Rommel in May 1943. As Churchill and FDR had agreed at Casablanca, British and U.S. troops landed in Sicily in July, and by mid-August they held the island. Sicilians greeted the British and Americans enthusiastically, chanting, "Down with Mussolini." But the Allies failed to capture 100,000 Axis troops who escaped to mainland Italy.

The Italian Invasion

Faced with a threat from General Eisenhower to send five hundred planes to bomb Rome, Italy signed an armistice with the Allies on September 3, 1943. The Italian king imprisoned Mussolini, but German commandos freed him, and he fled to his northern Italian home. There he founded the Italian Socialist Republic, propped up by the Germans.

On the day of the armistice, Allied forces landed in Salerno, on Italy's east coast, and in Taranto on the west. German troops, bolstered by reinforcements, still held Italy, and they sometimes took Italian troops prisoner rather than allow them to surrender. Over the next year, Americans battered Germans in Italian cities and across the countryside. Donald Spencer and Fred Lee's Ninety-second Infantry Division went to Tuscany, where it fought furiously on Lucca's ancient walls, and then to Italy's northwestern Ligurian coast. The Ninety-second comprised the historic Buffalo Soldiers, a division of African American troops nicknamed for its exploits in the nineteenth-century West. The Ninety-second fought alongside British and nisei soldiers; Lee recalled the nisei soldiers as "exceptionally tough, disciplined, and brave." When Lee married his Italian sweetheart, his best man was one of his nisei comrades. Donald Spencer won five Bronze Stars, learned Italian, and also married an Italian woman.[39]

Some 200,000 Italian partisans fought the Germans and provided intelligence to the Allies. German troops proved surprisingly difficult to dislodge, and 60,000 Allies died trying. Estimates of Italian partisan deaths vary widely, but most small northern Italian towns mark their sacrifice on street corners and in public squares. Pushed into northern Italy, German troops held ground there until the surrender in May 1945.

Bombing Germany

Prior to a cross-Channel invasion, the Allies hoped to disable Germany's industrial war machine through strategic bombing. In the winter of 1942, the U.S. Army's Eighth Air Force joined the Royal Air Force at bases scattered around southern England. Later that summer it joined the RAF in bombing German targets in France. At first the RAF bombing had been wildly inaccurate; only one in five bombs landed within five miles of its target. By the spring of 1943, Americans in Flying Fortress B-17s used the Norden bombsight to successfully target bases, transportation facilities, and industrial sites from 36,000 feet by day, while the RAF bombed them by night. The unheated planes flew at high altitudes in temperatures to fifty degrees below. One of the B-17's five gunners fired a Browning M2 machine gun through a turret above the cockpit; two waist gunners fired through a hole in the fuselage; and a gunner on folded knees fired from the turret on the tail. The ball turret gunner rode in a small Plexiglas bump on the aircraft's bottom. A navigator and bombardier crouched in the Plexiglas nose under the pilot's seat—"like animals at bay," as Eleanor Roosevelt put it when she climbed into one in England.[40] A radio operator, pilot, and copilot completed the crew. The B-17 could carry up to eight thousand pounds of bombs, depending on altitude and range. About one-third of the Eighth Air Force's planes were B-24 Liberators, smaller planes that flew farther but tended to catch fire more easily.

In March 1943 the Allies bombed Berlin as part of an overall strategic campaign to undermine German morale and cut transportation lines. An Iranian visitor described it: "All the major railroad stations in Berlin have been completely demolished . . . not a wall is standing at the airport." The "population of Berlin is living underground," the eyewitness inadvertently told Roosevelt and Churchill, to whom Ultra provided the account.[41]

On the Eighth Air Force's worst day, Black Thursday, October 14, 1943, it lost 60 planes out of a total force of 291, and 639 men died. The army air force suspended daylight operations temporarily but resumed in January when Very Long Range (VLR) P-51 Mustang fighter planes began to escort the B-17s and engage German fighter planes. The brave pilots and crews who flew these missions—day after day, night after night—knew that their bombs killed German civilians, but they believed they were winning the war.

The strategic bombing destroyed 33 percent of Berlin and 80 percent of Mainz, along with 50 percent of twenty-three other German cities. The Nazis rebuilt rapidly until March 1943, when the Allies obliterated their heavy industrial capacity in the Battle of the Ruhr. The bombing cut off electrical power and burned up oil supplies. In all, the Allies dropped more than 914,637 tons of bombs, killed over 300,000 German civilians, and wounded 800,000. By the time the Allies invaded northern France, they faced a much-diminished enemy, but one that fought for its life.

The Tehran Conference and Operation Overlord

In late November 1943 Roosevelt met Stalin for the first time at a gathering of the Big Three in Tehran, Iran. Satisfied that the Allies had the strength to defeat the crippled German forces in Europe, Churchill and Roosevelt set the date for Operation Overlord for May 1944, and Stalin confidentially promised to fight Japan after the German surrender. Poland's fate proved a sticking point. A Polish government-in-exile in London wanted independence and prewar borders. The USSR sponsored the Union of Polish Patriots, who vied to form the new government. Since Poland had been the pathway through which Russia was invaded, Stalin wanted to use it as a buffer state. Churchill and FDR agreed to cede to the USSR the one-third of Polish territory that the USSR had annexed in 1939.

The Allies differed among themselves on postwar Germany's fate. Churchill feared a weak Germany, based on the lessons of World War I. When stripped of wealth and territory, Germany became more hostile and the European economy had suffered. Roosevelt toyed with schemes to prevent German reindustrialization. Stalin wanted friendly Communist governments in the eastern European buffer zone between Germany and the USSR. On the way home from Tehran, Roosevelt stopped in Tunis to ask General Eisenhower to command Operation Overlord. The crafty and congenial "Ike" could manage the joint British-American enterprise on the ground, in the air, on the water, and in political circles.

The English Channel is twenty-one miles wide at its narrowest point. On a clear night from Dover Beach, one can see the glimmering lights of the French coast at Calais. This spot, the Dover Strait, was the likeliest site of a cross-Channel invasion. Early in 1944 the Germans learned that Operation Overlord was the code name for an invasion that might occur anywhere from the Balkans to Portugal. Meanwhile in England, General George Patton pretended to be commanding two huge forces, one massing near Dover to invade at Calais and the other near Edinburgh to invade Norway. Operation Bodyguard deployed the fake Operation Fortitude forces deliberately to mislead Hitler so that the Allies could stage the most massive invasion in history elsewhere.

Hitler believed that he could stop an Allied invasion since he had sixty-two divisions in the Low Countries and France. He confided to the Japanese ambassador, whose wartime correspondence was being transmitted to FDR and Churchill: "all they can do is establish a bridgehead." He believed that the bold and decisive German character lent itself to launching massive invasions, while the meeker British and Americans conducted little pinprick landings. He cited Italy, where the Allies had sent in a relatively small force to chip away at the enemy. In late May, Hitler told the Japanese ambassador that he expected action in Norway, Denmark, and all along the French coast.

Under Eisenhower's command, U.S. General Omar Bradley's First Army and British Field Marshal Bernard Montgomery's Twenty-first Army planned to invade two hundred miles southwest of Calais, on the Cotentin Peninsula in Normandy. Stretched like a fat index finger pointing toward England, the peninsula had flat, wide beaches on its eastern side and an excellent port at its tip in Cherbourg. There were no other large cities, a condition important to the Allies, who dreaded the inevitable French loss of life in the invasion's aftermath. If the Allies could clear the Germans from the peninsula, they could maintain naval and air links to England and bring in a steady supply of fresh troops.

Success depended on surprise. The invaders would be sitting ducks if the Germans attacked them in the Channel. They needed the French Resistance's help to determine German locations and get local support, but FDR and Churchill were reluctant to share specifics with their leader in exile in England, General Charles de Gaulle, whom Churchill found pompous. Instead of specifics, they told the Resistance that the invasion would follow within fifteen days after the BBC Free French radio station broadcast the poet Paul Verlaine's words, "Les sanglots longs des violons de l'automne" (the long sobs of the violins of autumn). Another poetic line, "Blessent mon coeur d'une langueur monotone" (wounding my heart with a monotonous languor), signaled a forty-eight-hour countdown.[42] Unfortunately, the Germans learned of the verses through torturing a French Resistance leader, but still Hitler discounted a massive invasion.

The Channel was too rough and the weather too foggy to fly in May, the Tehran deadline. The naval vessels, which would have to leave England at midnight under the cover of darkness, needed a full moon to navigate. Clear conditions were also needed for planes to cover the troops and drop paratroopers inland up and down the coast. Around six-thirty a.m. the tides had to be at midrange: not too high, or the landing craft risked running aground on German defenses, and not too low, or the troops would be killed more easily on the wider beach. On June 2, 1944, Allied bombers destroyed much of the French transportation system, which should have put the Germans on alert. The tides would be right on June 5.

D-Day

On England's south coast, 57,500 American and 75,215 British soldiers waited. Six battleships floated amid 6,500 other vessels. Ten thousand planes stood ready. British and American officers told their generals that 90

World War II in Europe and North Africa

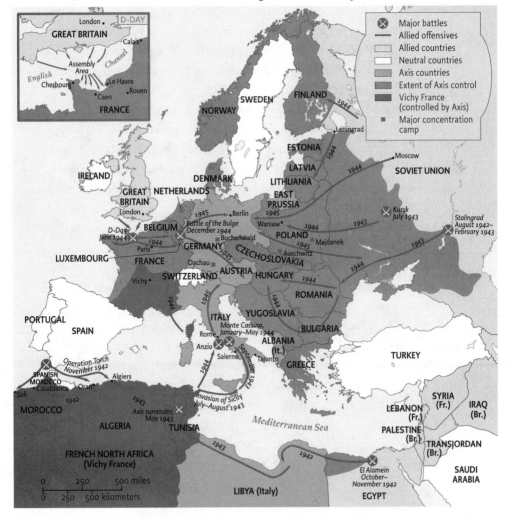

percent of their men expected to die in the landing. The Allied command secretly planned for more than 70,000 troops to be killed, wounded, or missing: not the 90 percent that the troops themselves projected, but still a horrific loss of over 50 percent of the landing force. The British also projected between 20,000 and 60,000 dead and wounded French civilians.

June 5, the first designated D-Day, was stormy. June 7 promised bad weather as well, and after that it would be another month before the tides and the moon were right. On June 6 a small window of relatively good weather was predicted from the early morning hours into the afternoon. Eisenhower made the decision to go. When Germans in northern France heard "Blessent mon coeur d'une langueur monotone" on the evening of June 5, they warned their commands from Norway to Spain. But the unfavorable weather, Hitler's underestimation of the Allies, and the fictive stories that Operation Bodyguard had created meant that German forces expected minor assaults along the coast or perhaps a large landing at Calais, certainly not one massive invasion on the Cotentin Peninsula.

The one-hundred-mile-wide flotilla left England at midnight. The Allies' ten thousand planes took off for France before daybreak. The troops themselves had not seen any landing maps: ship cartographers prepared them overnight to avoid leaks to the Germans. In three-dimensional rubber, the maps revealed what lay ahead: broad and sandy beaches, moderately high dunes, one-lane roads, pastures, villages, and German tanks. They named the landing beaches. Nearest to Cherbourg, troops hit Utah and Omaha Beaches at six-thirty a.m. Paratroopers dropped at Utah. Then farther to the east and down the peninsula came landings at Juno, Gold, and Sword Beaches, with paratroopers at Sword. Planes also dropped dummies in parachutes to confuse the Germans.

But at Omaha, sand-covered cliffs gave Germans a forty-five-degree angle down to the beach. The new Allied "swimming" tanks sank, drowning their passengers and leaving the disembarking forces to maneuver around them without cover. War correspondent Ernie Pyle reported disabled boats drifting a mile out. As landing craft approached the beaches, heads, legs, arms, and torsos floated by. Terrified men had to run into the firing guns rather than take cover in the sand. Approximately 60,000 men waded onto Omaha Beach, 2,000 to die, the rest to crawl ashore over their fellow soldiers.

Toward Berlin

Three days after the landings, Hitler retained his forces at Calais, awaiting an invasion there. The Luftwaffe mounted a feeble response to the invasion. Hitler's underestimation of the Allied fighting forces led him to forbid his troops to withdraw from the Cotentin Peninsula. The Allies fought them hedgerow after hedgerow and pushed them south, establishing an unbroken Allied line at the peninsula's base. On July 10, Montgomery's forces took Caen, and on July 18 Americans liberated Saint-Lô. On August 6, to the west, Saint-Malo fell. Meanwhile reinforcements, including General Patton's Third Army, poured into Cherbourg's port. Almost 4,500 Allied forces died in the invasion, a horrible toll but an astonishingly low one: not 90 percent as the troops expected, not 50 percent as the commanders expected, but 3 percent. Up to ten thousand French died, many in the weeks-long bombing operations that followed D-Day.

By mid-August, German forces in Paris, undermined by the Resistance and facing attack by Free French forces with U.S. support, retreated from the capital. The departing German commander ignored Hitler's orders to destroy the city. When Allied troops landed on beaches in southern France, the Germans simply melted away.

A month after D-Day, John W. Pehle, the executive director of the War Refugee Board, begged the War Department to bomb the industrial facilities at Auschwitz and Birkenau, the transportation lines into them, and their "elaborate murder installations" to prevent the killing of more Jews. The War Department turned him down, arguing that the sites could not be bombed with precision from high altitudes, lay beyond the medium bombers' range, and would divert aircraft needed to push through France.[43]

By mid-September, supply problems held back the Allies. Patton's Third Army had turned southeast toward Germany but exhausted its fuel. The British took the port of Antwerp, but did not have the resources to restore its operations. All supplies came through Cherbourg, even though the armies had moved hundreds of miles east. Instead of supplying Patton, Eisenhower allocated fuel to Field Marshal Montgomery to move southeast across the Rhine and into Germany. Montgomery came close to, but failed to cross, the German border, thwarted in Operation Market Garden in late September. In October, Patton's Third Army headed east across France to

Metz, a city thirty miles from the German border, where it fought German troops until late November. The Allies now held a line facing the German border from Patton's Third Army in the south to the Netherlands, where Montgomery's forces and the United States' Ninth and Third Armies camped.

Meanwhile Marshal Zhukov led Soviet forces toward Berlin. Setting a blistering pace, the Soviets took Belarus in July, Romania in August, Bulgaria and the Baltic States in September, East Prussia in October, and Hungary and Czechoslovakia in December. They now controlled eastern Europe. German armies evacuated Greece in October, and British troops entered Athens.

VICTORY AND REALPOLITIK

Germany's defeat seemed probable when Franklin Roosevelt won a fourth term in November 1944, but those close to the president worried that he would not live to see it. At sixty-two, FDR had high blood pressure, heart failure, and hardening of the arteries. He appeared ashen, except for lips that turned purple from lack of circulation. He experienced dizzy spells and lost his train of thought as oxygen failed to reach his brain. His strong upper body, which had masked his paralysis for over two decades, shriveled. His daughter Anna knew he was gravely ill. His physician assigned a full-time cardiologist to shadow him.

Democratic Party leaders had pressed FDR to drop the unpopular vice president Henry Wallace from the 1944 ticket. Roosevelt acquiesced and chose as his running mate Senator Harry S. Truman (D-MO). Truman, who had served in France in World War I, was a failed haberdasher and county judge with modest political ambitions. Plainspoken and approachable, Truman was elected to the U.S. Senate in 1934 and chaired the committee on defense contracts. He had no foreign policy experience but was an avid anti-Communist. In the 1944 election, Roosevelt and Truman faced Thomas E. Dewey, Republican governor of New York, who blamed Roosevelt for personally hoarding federal power and increasing the deficit. Dewey failed to appeal to the electorate, who thought that winning the war depended on a strong, well-funded government and an experienced president. Dewey won only twelve states; nonetheless it was FDR's closest race.

The Politics of War

In mid-December 1944 German troops pushed west on the Allied line that was shadowing the German border. The Allies retreated a bit before they stopped the Germans in the Ardennes Forest in eastern Belgium, creating a semicircle that bent west. Through a snowy Christmas and bitter January, they fought the Battle of the Bulge. Germans pounded Montgomery's forces and the U.S. First and Ninth Armies. Twenty thousand Americans died, but by February the Allies pushed the Germans back, and the Allied line straightened. Then they crossed the Rhine and fought their way across Germany, while U.S. and British pilots firebombed Dresden, killing 25,000 German civilians. The Soviet troops were within striking distance of Berlin.

The victories of war become the realpolitik of peace. In February 1945, when Roosevelt and Churchill met Stalin at Yalta, a war-damaged Russian resort on the Black Sea, the president looked deathly ill. With Soviet forces occupying eastern Europe and nearing Berlin, Stalin was in an excellent bargaining position. Churchill and Roosevelt acknowledged that the USSR had a claim to war reparations but were reluctant to impose crippling debt on devastated Germany. The USSR would control the part of eastern Poland it had annexed in 1939, as well as Latvia, Lithuania, and Estonia. The Communist-dominated Union of Polish Patriots had already set up a provisional government, to the dismay of the Polish government-in-exile in London. Since the Soviets occupied Poland, the British and Americans had no recourse—short of war—to dislodge the Red Army.

To counter Soviet power, Churchill insisted that France have an equal role in supervising Germany after the war. The Allied Control Commission split Germany into four parts among France, Britain, the United States, and the USSR and divided Berlin into four sectors. They agreed to establish a new League of Nations called by FDR's nickname for the Allies: the United Nations.

What the Big Three failed to agree on was just as significant. Churchill and FDR had earlier announced that Stalin would have no influence in Italy or Greece because Soviet troops had not fought there. Stalin countered that the USSR should control the rebuilding of Czechoslovakia, Romania, Bulgaria, and Hungary, since British and American troops had not fought in eastern Europe.

Roosevelt knew that an invasion of the Japanese home islands would consume all available U.S. troops, and he wanted Stalin to reaffirm his commitment to attack Japanese troops in China upon the German surrender. Stalin did so but demanded the concession of a warm-water Chinese port. Roosevelt proposed that Chiang Kai-shek be made an equal partner in postwar negotiations and the spokesman for the Chinese, but the Soviets refused, since the Chinese Communists, led by Mao Zedong, had begun a full-fledged civil war.

The decisions that the Allies had made about how to fight the war shaped each country's bargaining power at Yalta. Churchill feared that FDR had conceded too much to the Soviets in exchange for their commitment to fight the Japanese. Nonetheless, no one left Yalta thinking that they had crafted a permanent blueprint for peace.

Roosevelt's Death, German Surrender

At the end of March, Roosevelt and his daughter Anna went to Warm Springs, Georgia. For almost two weeks he rested, and Anna invited over Lucy Mercer Rutherfurd, the woman with whom FDR had fallen in love during World War I. Anna knew that her father was dying, and she knew that her mother was ill suited to provide consolation. When Henry Morgenthau came to dinner, his heart sank when he saw FDR: "He had aged terrifically and looked very haggard. His hands shook so that he started to knock the glasses over." The next day, April 12, as Lucy Mercer and Franklin sat together for a portrait, FDR said, "I have a terrible pain in the back of my head."[44] The stroke killed him two and a half hours later.

After she learned of FDR's death, Eleanor called Truman into the White House, put her hand on his shoulder, and said, "Harry, the President is dead." She had already telegraphed their four sons on duty: "He did his job to the end as he would want you to do."[45] She soon learned that Lucy Mercer had been with Franklin and relived the grief that she had felt as a young married woman. Years later she recalled that when FDR died, "I experienced an almost impersonal feeling." She realized that FDR "might have been happier with a wife who was completely uncritical. That I was never able to be, and he had to find it in other people." Ultimately, Eleanor Roosevelt said of her husband, "I was one of those who served his purposes."[46]

As the funeral train crept back from Georgia to Washington, people lined the route, many sobbing. A horse-drawn wagon carried the casket, flag-draped and secured with thick rope, from Union Station to the White House. Hundreds of thousands thronged the sidewalks. They buried Franklin Roosevelt in the garden at his Hyde Park home. A lone bugler blew taps. President Harry S. Truman recalled, "I felt like the moon, the stars, and all the planets had fallen on me."[47] On April 25, two weeks after Roosevelt's death, he learned the details of the Manhattan Project to produce an atomic bomb, which Roosevelt had hidden from him.

The war in Europe ended quickly after that. In April 1945, Italian partisans of the Garibaldi Brigade found Mussolini hiding in a railcar in a small village on Lake Como. They took him out and shot him. U.S. troops moved west through Germany, discovering horror after horror. Vincent Tubbs, correspondent for the Baltimore *Afro-American*, advanced with the U.S. Twelfth Armored Division on Dachau. Tubbs reported that he could smell Dachau before he saw it. "It was like burning brown sugar with a low, sour stench of unwashed bodies," he reported. The retreating Nazis had tied prisoners to logs and set them on fire. One smoldering man stirred and kissed Tubbs's hand. Tubbs put it simply: "The inmates, those dead and those surviving out of the 4,000 internees there, were Jews."[48] Homer Smith, another black reporter, approached from the east with the Soviet troops. When they arrived at Auschwitz on January 27, 1945, he saw towering bales of human hair.[49]

Hitler shot himself in his Berlin bunker on April 30, eighteen days after Roosevelt died at Warm Springs. The German Supreme Command signed a document of unconditional surrender on May 7, but the Soviets were not present. Germany surrendered a second time the following day in Berlin, repeating the humiliation so that the Soviets could witness it. All Allied resources must now go into defeating the Japanese.

WAR'S END

Throughout 1943 and 1944, the Allies continued to hop from island to island, facing only one challenge from the Japanese navy at the Marianas, which included Saipan, Tinian, and Guam. On every island, however, the landing forces fought their way across beaches and through jungles against fierce, dug-in Japanese troops. In 1944 the United States increased ground and air support in China to fight alongside General Chiang Kai-shek's nationalists. The main objective remained reaching the Japanese home islands and forcing unconditional surrender.

Advancing by Sea and Air

By the fall of 1944, U.S. naval forces flanked the Philippines as MacArthur returned to liberate the islands. The Allies bombed the Japanese facilities, and an extensive network of pro-U.S. Filipino guerrillas sabotaged Japanese efforts. On October 20, MacArthur landed on Leyte, a Philippine island.

The U.S. Navy and the Imperial Japanese Navy met three days later in the Battle of Leyte Gulf. For three days, twelve U.S. battleships fought nine Japanese battleships in four separate engagements. It ended disastrously for the Japanese, who lost three battleships and four aircraft carriers, along with twenty other vessels. More than 7,500 Japanese died, as did 1,500 Allied pilots and sailors. The epic battle destroyed the capability of the Japanese navy, and MacArthur retook the Philippines.

Only Japan itself—comprising almost seven thousand small and four large islands, Hokkaido, Shikoku, Kyushu, and Honshu—remained of strategic value. With Germany and the other Axis Powers having surrendered, no one believed Japan could win. But Japan fought with a zeal that defied surrender—especially unconditional surrender. Running out of oil, the Japanese pilots in the Philippines took off on kamikaze flights with only enough gas to reach the target.

With the Japanese navy rendered useless, some U.S. commanders hoped that heavy aerial bombardment of the home islands, coupled with a sea blockade, might force surrender. But Army Chief of Staff Marshall believed that the Allies would have to invade the four large Japanese islands. President Truman struggled to get up to speed quickly by studying the strategies and personalities involved. After the Battle of Leyte Gulf, the Allies began planning to invade Okinawa, an island 340 miles from Japan, from which they could more easily launch bombing runs over the home islands.

During that fall of 1944, Phil Rasmussen flew very long range P-51 Mustangs, escorting B-29 bombers from Saipan to Tokyo. Lew Sanders was stationed in Saipan as well. The B-29, successor to the B-17 Flying Fortress and nicknamed the Superfortress, could fly 5,600 miles at a high altitude at moderate speed, loaded with average bomb tonnage. It was 3,000 miles round trip from Saipan to Tokyo. To gain the additional 400 miles, General Curtis Le May ordered lower-altitude night bombing, stripped gunners and arms, and fuel-loaded planes. Their purpose was to "fire bomb," literally to ignite, Japanese cities. The bombing campaign continued into the spring of 1945 and killed over 100,000 people. The P-51 Mustang pilots flew the eight-hour round trip to Tokyo strapped into their solo cockpits. In a grisly battle in mid-February 1945, U.S. Marines took the island of Iwo Jima, seven hundred miles from Japan, with cover from Lew Sanders's 318th Fighter Group. In March, Phil Rasmussen and Lew Sanders moved to Iwo Jima's Central Field.

On April 1, 1945, Sanders's 318th Fighter Group provided air cover for the long-planned invasion of Okinawa, lying halfway between Iwo Jima and Japan. The Japanese knew it would be their last stand outside the home islands. Sanders flew through kamikaze pilots determined to use their planes as weapons and coffins. By the time the Allies took the island on June 22, almost 100,000 Japanese troops had died in the battle, along with 12,000 Allies. The Japanese convinced Okinawan civilians that the Americans would rape and murder them and handed out grenades for group suicides. Almost 100,000 people committed suicide or were the victims of "mercy killings" by family members. Moments after his mother strangled his sister to spare her torture, Takejiro Nakamura was astonished to confront an American soldier, who handed him candy and cigarettes. Other Okinawans' worst fears were confirmed as reports of U.S. soldiers raping Okinawan women became frequent, particularly after occupying troops arrived.[50]

Twelve days later Rasmussen and Sanders heard that Franklin Roosevelt had died. With Germany's surrender at the month's end, they believed their last mission would be to provide air cover for the home island invasion. If the Japanese fought there as they had on Okinawa, that invasion would cost hundreds of thousands of lives.

Eighteen-year-old Stan Igawa enlisted in the U.S. Army on June 22, 1945, the day Okinawa fell. Thanks to Eleanor Roosevelt's efforts to modify the internment orders, by the end of 1943, one-third of those interned had either returned to their homes or accepted war work away from the camps. From October to June 1944, Igawa worked at a civilian job. By the time he enlisted, he knew that the Americans had one task left: to invade Japan. He wanted to be one of those Americans.

The Manhattan Project

Truman was involved closely in the invasion plans, and every scenario painted a bloodbath. If the Japanese failed to surrender until the Allies reached the Tokyo Plain on Honshu, advisers predicted 220,000 Allied casualties, with 46,000 killed, 170,000 wounded, and 4,000 missing. Some predicted a cost of one million American lives to occupy the home islands. Emperor worship demanded that soldiers die to spare him humiliation; hence, unconditional surrender meant unconditional war. If the Japanese continued their kamikaze attacks, facilitated mass civilian suicides, and fought to the last man, Truman predicted "an Okinawa from one end of Japan to the other." He privately hoped that the July 16 test of the new atomic bomb would make the invasion unnecessary.[51]

Before the United States entered the war, Jewish refugees from Europe had raised the alarm that Germany was planning to develop a secret bomb. A Hungarian Jewish refugee, Leó Szilárd, thought it possible to produce a nuclear chain reaction as a war weapon, and he joined with physicist Albert Einstein, another Jewish refugee, to convince skeptical government authorities. When Germany began to hoard uranium in 1939, Roosevelt created the Advisory Committee on Uranium. By January 1942, FDR authorized development of the atomic bomb "to see that the Nazis don't blow us up." Unknown to the Allies, the Germans gave up on their atomic project that year.[52]

The Manhattan Project, based at Los Alamos, New Mexico, produced three atomic bombs by August 1945, a feat that most scientists had thought impossible only four years earlier. European refugees, U.S. physicists, and thirty British scientists joined the project and worked in secrecy. J. Robert Oppenheimer, a California physicist, directed the scientists, but all reported to General Leslie Groves, an engineer, who moved heaven and earth to produce the factories, parts, workers, and even cities required to build the bomb. Only Roosevelt, Churchill, Vice President Wallace, General Marshall, Secretary of War Stimson, and a few others knew of the project at first. By the time the scientists perfected a nuclear chain reaction late in 1942, a new town, Oak Ridge, Tennessee, had been built in a remote valley with abundant energy from a nearby TVA dam. Some 78,000 people eventually lived in Oak Ridge, working in factories to process uranium and assemble bomb parts. A similar facility of 17,000 grew in Hanford, Washington, on the Columbia River, where workers processed plutonium. All together about 125,000 people worked in "secret."

Roosevelt did not share the secret project with Stalin, but the Soviets knew about it and code-named it ENORMOZ. By the fall of 1944, Klaus Fuchs, a German-born British scientist on the Manhattan Project, was passing its secrets to the USSR. Word of the project spread haphazardly among high U.S. government and military officials. FDR spilled the beans to Omar Bradley when Bradley was a lieutenant colonel but did not tell his commanding officer, General Eisenhower. People in the Treasury Department wondered if government-confiscated silver was going into a weapon. An unbalanced scientist on the Manhattan Project visited Eleanor Roosevelt at her New York apartment and told her about it. She recklessly included the news in a letter to her favorite young soldier. Those who knew the truth were bound to secrecy, while others had only a vague understanding of what they had heard.

Evelyn Webb, a tall, gangly, redheaded teenager from the North Carolina mountains, worked at Oak Ridge. She thought it odd to spend months working on a production task when she could not be told what the product was. Oak Ridge workers had a vague idea that they were building a weapon. What that weapon would become, when they would finish it, and how it would be used were beyond their wildest imaginings.

Potsdam

The final wartime Allied conference took place from July 17 until August 2, 1945, outside Berlin in Potsdam. Truman arrived early to meet Churchill, who came with Clement Attlee, his opponent in the still-undecided British parliamentary elections. Churchill had loved Roosevelt; Truman seemed to resent that relationship. Roosevelt and Churchill had decided that they "might perhaps" use the bomb on Japan.[53] After FDR's death, Secretary of War Stimson appointed a committee to determine what to do with it. The committee never seriously entertained not using it, nor did Truman.

On July 16 in Potsdam, Truman learned of the first successful atomic bomb test in New Mexico. The next day Truman met Stalin, who did nothing to assuage Truman's anti-Communist predilections. When the British election results came in, Churchill had lost, and Attlee took his seat at the table. Stalin promised that the USSR would declare war on Japan by August 15, and a very tense Truman relaxed just a little. When Truman revealed to Stalin that the United States now possessed a "powerful new weapon," Stalin's deadpan reaction surprised him. "All he said was that he was glad to hear it, and that he hoped we would make 'good use of it against the Japanese,'" Truman recalled.[54] In fact, Stalin had known for a month about the scheduled test and thought Truman's disclosure was meant to threaten the USSR.[55]

The pressing business was what to do about Germany. The Allies agreed to prosecute war criminals and to demilitarize the country completely, including dismantling heavy industry and chemical facilities. The

Allies would divide Germany into zones, as agreed at Yalta. At Potsdam they redrew Germany's eastern border, reducing the country's size by 25 percent. The USSR could extract reparations from its East German territory in compensation for the horrific price it had paid in the war. The Soviets installed a Polish Communist government, which the other three Allies recognized.

On July 26 the Potsdam Ultimatum demanded Japan's immediate unconditional surrender to avoid "prompt and utter destruction." When the conference ended, *The New York Times* gushed that the president felt "elated over [the] reported Soviet concessions."[56] There had been only one significant concession: the Soviets had finally made public their promise, forged at Tehran and reiterated at Yalta, to fight Japan.

Nuclear War and Japanese Surrender

It was midmorning on August 7 when Evelyn Webb and her Oak Ridge co-workers heard the call to assemble in the cafeteria. A manager climbed up onto a table and announced that the United States had dropped an atomic bomb on Hiroshima, Japan. Then he told them that they had made that bomb. They cried, danced, and sang. "We thought we had ended the war," Webb recalled, "we just didn't think about anything else."[57]

That day at 10:45 EST, Truman told the American people about the bomb from the *USS Augusta*, on his way home from Potsdam. "We have spent more than two billion dollars on the greatest scientific gamble in history, and we have won," he said. A B-29 Superfortress had dropped "an atomic bomb, possessing more power than 20,000 tons of TNT," on the Japanese city of Hiroshima. The next day *The New York Times* revealed that the bomb had a "a destructive force equal to the load of 2,000 B-29s and more than 2,000 times the blast power of . . . the world's most devastating bomb."[58] Truman implied that the United States had several bombs ready; in truth, there was only one more immediately available. The Manhattan Project promised a third by mid-August and three more in September. The USSR entered the war against Japan two days after the Hiroshima bombing.

Truman never considered not using atomic bombs if Japan failed to surrender after the Potsdam Ultimatum; nor did he hesitate to use them on civilians. Japan insisted that bombing a city of 318,000 people violated international law against targeting civilian populations, but the United States pointed to Hiroshima's supply depot, port, and quartermaster station as military targets. At first, no one could tell what damage had been done, because an "impenetrable cloud of dust and smoke" covered Hiroshima. Then Tokyo radio announced that the dead were '"too numerous to be counted . . . practically all living things, human and animal, were literally seared to death." Most Americans believed that they were exaggerating, but many understood that the world had changed forever. Correspondent Hanson W. Baldwin noted, "Yesterday we clinched victory in the Pacific, but we sowed the whirlwind."[59] Over 150,000 people died in Hiroshima, most of them civilians.

A split in Japan pitted the hard-right military faction against the emperor, whose advisers advocated surrender. Three days later, on August 9, a B-29 dropped a second atomic bomb on Nagasaki, a port city and the site of Mitsubishi's shipbuilding and arms factories. Home to 253,000 people, 80,000 Nagasaki residents died. The second bomb contained plutonium from Hanford, Washington. Japan offered to surrender if the emperor could remain in place.

On August 15, 1945, three years and 250 days after Phil Rasmussen and Lew Sanders shot down the first Japanese Zeros at Pearl Harbor, Emperor Hirohito announced Japan's unconditional surrender. Miraculously, Rasmussen and Sanders had survived the war; they became career air force officers and retired as colonels.

Two days after the Hiroshima bombing, the Manhattan Project director Robert Oppenheimer vigorously denied a U.S. physicist's warning that the radiation from the atomic bomb would continue to kill people and devastate the landscape for seventy years. Although he must have known better, Oppenheimer said that "there was no reason to believe the bomb explosion over Hiroshima left any appreciable radioactivity on the ground."[60]

U.S. scientists covered up the radiation sickness that followed. A month later the Australian reporter Wilfred Burchett entered Hiroshima. He reported people "now dying from uncanny after-effects" that included purple spots, gangrene, spontaneous bleeding from every orifice; drowning from bleeding in the lungs; and hemorrhaging from the soft tissue in the mouth. He filed his story as "The Atomic Plague." W. H. Lawrence of *The New York Times*, who arrived a day after Burchett, wrote a different account: "I am convinced that, horrible as the bomb undoubtedly is, the Japanese are exaggerating its effects in an effort to win sympathy for themselves." Deputy Head of the Manhattan Project Brigadier General Thomas Farrell argued that the bomb had exploded so high, there would be no risk of "residual radiation."[61]

The Legacies of World War II

Democracy—as a form of government and as a way of life—survived because of the Allied victory over fascism. At their height, the totalitarian Axis Powers controlled Europe and the Pacific. Early in the war, things could have gone differently. The Nazis could have invaded Britain, and Rommel could have prevailed in North Africa. The Allies could have lost the Battle of the Coral Sea, consigning Australia to Japanese imperial rule. After that, even the western hemisphere's isolation might not have saved the United States. Instead of this grim outcome, and despite the imposition of Soviet totalitarianism onto eastern Europe at war's end, democracy was the winner in the war.

The USSR had never pretended to fight for freedom, and mutual suspicion between that totalitarian state and the United States turned into a hostile Cold War that lasted the next fifty years. Roosevelt and Churchill's military strategies saved Western lives but taxed the Soviets beyond measure on the Eastern Front. At war's end, 20 million Soviets were dead, and the USSR occupied eastern Europe. In China, where 4 million had fought for the Allies and 14 million had died, a Communist insurgency formed a new government in 1949.

In the United States, a military-industrial complex, fed by defense spending, survived the war, and the possibility of nuclear annihilation remains a tangible legacy of the conflict. The country did not repay its World War II debt until the 1970s. Military readiness became the war's strategic lesson. In 1959, when President Dwight Eisenhower condemned the military-industrial complex, he nonetheless acknowledged that the collaboration between government and industry had driven scientific developments beyond anything FDR could have imagined. In January 1938 the U.S. Army had had 855 airplanes; twenty-three years later, Alan Shepard became the first American in space.

In the domestic economy, the Servicemen's Readjustment Act of 1944, known as the GI Bill, provided returning veterans unemployment compensation, medical care, educational subsidies, and access to mortgage funds. The GI Bill sent a generation of men and some women back to school, made home ownership a possibility for the masses, and helped build a suburban middle class.

For some Americans, ethnic and racial tolerance was the lesson of

World War II. Not everyone learned it, and those who did, did not always practice it. It would have to be repeated incessantly: demonstrated on buses in Montgomery, Alabama, taught to a new generation of students in the nation's integrated public schools, memorialized in its Holocaust museums, and made tangible in reparations to interned Japanese Americans.

Stan Igawa always seemed to understand ethnic and racial tolerance. After enlisting in the army in 1945, he became a major in the Korean War and served in the army reserve in Vietnam. He ended his working life as a park ranger at the Pearl Harbor National Monument, where he introduced the documentary film on the attack. Igawa noted that many Japanese people came to Pearl Harbor "because it is part of their history, too." He recalled, "Once, in the theater, I had a man come right up to my face and say angrily, 'I think it's a real insult to have a Japanese guy introduce the film.' I don't get into any arguments with them." Stan Igawa did not need to argue with anyone. His country might have once doubted it, but he always knew that he was an American.[62]

CHAPTER 8

A RISING SUPERPOWER, 1944–1954

EVERY PRESIDENT HAS a few advisers who matter more than most. For Harry S. Truman, one of these was Dean Acheson, the leading architect of America's post–World War II foreign policy. Acheson started his career as a protégé of the brilliant legal scholar and future Supreme Court justice Felix Frankfurter and, like many bright and well-credentialed young men, was tapped by Franklin Roosevelt to serve in his administration. As an undersecretary of the treasury, Acheson oversaw the Lend-Lease program during World War II and, always a quick study, became expert on finance and international relations. In 1944 he stood in for the ailing secretary of state, Edward Stettinius, at the Bretton Woods conference. He spent the first half of the Truman years as undersecretary of state, better qualified for the position than his boss, James F. Byrnes, the former South Carolina senator and Supreme Court justice whose term in office was marred by hostility and rivalry with the president. Acheson then served as a key aide to George C. Marshall, the general turned statesman who relied on his blunt advice.

Born in Middletown, Connecticut, the son of an Episcopal bishop, Acheson grew up in the heart of the New England establishment. A man whose brilliance was nearly as great as his self-assurance, he sailed through Groton, Yale University, and Harvard Law School. He would spend most of his career within a few blocks of the White House, shuttling back and forth between the law and government service.

Acheson was a man of words, eloquent words, from his carefully crafted speeches all the way to his Pulitzer Prize–winning memoir, published less than two years before his death in 1972. The quintessential polymath, one of the "wise men"—a bipartisan group of highly regarded foreign policy experts who advised presidents, diplomats, and pundits from World War II through the 1960s—he was as comfortable on Wall Street as he was in the Oval Office, as happy to spar with his fellow Yale trustees as with truculent members in Congress.

TRUMAN AND THE POSTWAR WORLD ORDER

Acheson's rise coincided with the unlikely ascent of Harry S. Truman to the White House. The president responsible for wrapping up World War II had little foreign policy experience. Other than spending part of 1918 serving in the military in Europe and later taking a short trip to Latin America, Truman lacked the worldly disposition of his predecessor. The only twentieth-century U.S. president without a college degree, Truman was a self-taught intellectual. "Mr. Truman read, I sometimes think, more than any of the rest of us," recalled Acheson.[1]

It would be left to Truman and his aides to figure out what role America would play in a radically altered world order. Before the war, the United States had been second to Great Britain in manufacturing might. It lacked the far-flung imperial holdings that symbolized "great power" status in the nineteenth and early twentieth centuries. Americans became bitterly divided over what role their country should play in the postwar world. But the United States emerged in 1945 as the world's leading industrial and financial power, a position that was the result, in part, of the devastation that Europe had suffered through two wars. America's postwar rise was an act of will, the result of economic policies that elevated the dollar, expanded America's markets across the world, built a massive military, and justified it with an unstable mix of international humanitarianism, militant anti-Communism, and missionary capitalism.

Bretton Woods

Before Truman took the oath of office, Roosevelt had been laying the groundwork for a new postwar economic and political order, and he relied on his financial and foreign policy advisers to make the case. Acheson argued that achieving the goals of the New Deal required economic expansion overseas: "So far as I know, no group which has studied the problem . . . has ever believed that our domestic markets could absorb our entire production under our present system," he testified before Congress in 1944. ". . . We cannot have full employment and prosperity in the United States without the foreign markets."[2] Everyone feared a recurrence of the Great Depression.

In 1944 Acheson represented the State Department at the Bretton Woods conference, a gathering of delegates from forty-four nations charged with creating a stable postwar monetary system that would prevent the wild economic fluctuations that had destabilized Europe and the United States during the interwar years. The conference spanned nearly the entire month of July at a resort in New Hampshire's White Mountains. British economist John Maynard Keynes worried that "acute alcohol poisoning would set in before the end" of weeks of tedious deliberations.[3] But one of the bright spots was a new friendship between Keynes and Acheson. Together the two worked closely to build a system of global finance, which included the creation of the International Monetary Fund to regulate the flows of currency globally, pegging the dollar to gold.

The Bretton Woods conferees also launched the International Bank for Reconstruction and Development (the World Bank) with two purposes: to finance the rebuilding of war-torn nations and to support growth in underdeveloped economies around the world. The delegates differed on what sorts of projects to prioritize. Given that nearly half of the delegates came from Latin American countries—and their support was essential—Keynes and Acheson pushed for a balanced approach, blending postwar lending to rebuild Europe and Asia and financial support for industrialization and economic development elsewhere. The World Bank, Acheson and the American delegation hoped, would bring the New Deal to the world by investing in European reindustrialization and, at the same time, exporting its signature pro-growth programs, especially the TVA and rural electrification, to developing countries. Bretton Woods would create a fiscal internationalism that would enrich America by creating new markets for U.S. goods and uplift the world.

The United Nations

If Bretton Woods was to stabilize the world economy, achieving peace and security would depend on another new international organization: the United Nations. In August 1944, shortly after Bretton Woods, the Roosevelt administration convened representatives of the Soviet Union, Britain, and China at Dumbarton Oaks in Washington to lay the groundwork for the UN. The meeting was contentious. The Americans and the Soviets squabbled over whether to count sixteen Soviet republics as separate nations. The two superpowers also disagreed on a Soviet demand that the five most powerful nations on the proposed UN Security Council (United States, Soviet Union, Britain, France, and China) have individual veto power.

The follow-up meeting, to be held in San Francisco in April 1945, was nearly canceled when FDR died. Within an hour of taking the oath of office, President Truman pledged that the meeting would move forward. In his first major address as president, on April 16, he proclaimed that the "responsibility of the great states is to serve and not to dominate the world."[4] To the 282 delegates from around the globe who gathered in San Francisco, Truman (via radio) urged the UN to "build a new world—a far better world—one in which the eternal dignity of man is respected."[5]

Despite their many differences, the UN delegates agreed on a lofty set of goals. The UN charter promised to "save succeeding generations from the scourge of war," as well as "to reaffirm faith in fundamental human rights, in the dignity and worth of the human person, in the equal rights of men and women and of nations large and small." In addition, the new international organization would "promote social progress and better standards of life."[6] The charter gave voice to representatives of nations worldwide through a general assembly. But it also gave individual Security Council members veto power over substantive resolutions, thus often thwarting general-assembly consideration of controversial issues. It established a strong consultative role for nongovernmental organizations (NGOs). Among the diverse groups from the United States that attended the San Francisco meeting were the American Legion, the National Lawyers Guild, and the NAACP.

NGOs brought their expertise and passion to the UN but often found themselves on the sidelines. One of the biggest conflicts among the delegates concerned the UN's power over human rights violations. The very definition of human rights was in question: Should the UN enforce the right of workers to unionize? Should it support colonial struggles for self-determination? What did it mean that the new organization was to "protect minorities"? John Foster Dulles, who represented the State Department in negotiations, attempted to tread a narrow path between liberals who hoped that the UN would be a forceful ally of labor and civil rights and Southern segregationists who feared international interference in the system of Jim Crow. As a compromise—which, tellingly, the Soviets also accepted—Dulles supported language "guaranteeing freedom from discrimination on account of race, language, religion, or sex," but added that "nothing in the Charter shall authorize . . . intervention in matters which are essentially within the domestic jurisdiction of the State concerned."[7] Civil rights activists were outraged.

Over time NGOs would shape the UN's humanitarian mission, lobbying for the Universal Declaration of Human Rights and the Convention on the Prevention and Punishment of the Crime of Genocide, both enacted in 1948. But the major powers, especially Britain, the United States, and the Soviet Union, watered down the provisions. Britain and the other imperial powers opposed UN intervention on behalf of their rebellious colonies; the Soviets argued that the UN would threaten "national sovereignty" by interfering with its domestic programs; and the United States did not want international meddling in Jim Crow.

The genocide convention—seemingly unassailable after the Holocaust—met with particularly strong American resistance. Frank Holman, a well-respected attorney and former head of the American Bar Association, argued that the convention "changes and nullifies domestic law." The UN, he warned, had created "the machinery for extraditing Americans charged with genocide and for shipping them overseas to be tried for acts committed in their hometowns," perhaps "for as little as having been charged with inflicting 'mental harm' on a 'national, ethnical, racial, or religious group."[8] The U.S. Senate feared that the UN would investigate civil rights abuses, a justifiable concern, given America's long history of mistreating African Americans and Native Americans. It refused to ratify the genocide convention.

Redeploying the Military: Occupation

At the end of World War II, few envisioned that the United States would soon find itself once again on a war footing. The country never had much of a tradition of standing armies, at least not large ones. Although the Democrats and Republicans jostled for power in Congress, they shared a bipartisan conventional wisdom after the war ended that emphasized the necessity of huge troop reductions and drastic cuts in military spending. Budgetary constraints weighed heavily. The federal debt reached an all-time record, nearly $242 billion in 1945, greater than America's entire gross domestic product that year. Both parties demanded deficit reduction measures. The small but vocal band of isolationists in Congress called for a policy of non-interventionism. New Dealers hoped to trade guns for butter. And ordinary Americans were just plain exhausted.

In the two years following the end of World War II, the American defense budget plummeted from $81 billion to $13 billion. The army reduced its ranks by some seven million troops, the Navy by 2.5 million. Demobilization and budget cuts required shuttering hundreds of shipyards and selling, scrapping, or retiring about six thousand ships. The U.S. Army Air Force, with two hundred combat units on call at the end of the war, cut the number to fifty. The American military nevertheless remained a mighty force in late 1947, with a little more than a million and a half troops serving worldwide.

The main task of the remaining American troops overseas was the occupation and reconstruction of former enemy nations. Occupation was a process that began piecemeal, first in Italy. Immediately after the fall of Mussolini in July 1943 and the victory over the Axis in Sicily in August, the United States and its allies began rebuilding Italy. Newsreels conveyed images of a benign takeover: Italians mobbing and hugging American soldiers, who were depicted as liberators. In a frenzied three weeks of intense writing, author John Hersey captured the vision of America as the great liberator, penning *A Bell for Adano*, a novel published in 1944. Hersey portrayed the occupation of Sicily as a humanitarian venture, embodied in the protagonist, Major Victor Joppolo, a Bronx-bred, Italian-speaking officer. Joppolo takes over a fascist-led town, falls in love with an Italian girl, restores the local fishing industry, and in the novel's culmination replaces the church bell that had been melted down to arm Mussolini's troops. The book would soon be turned into a wildly popular film.[9]

The occupation of Nazi Germany and Austria was to take a more aggressive form than Joppolo's benign mayoralty. In 1945 the Joint Chiefs of Staff issued a directive that Germany was "not to be occupied for the purpose of liberation but as a defeated enemy nation."[10] The victorious allies—Britain, France, the Soviet Union, and the United States—each controlled a quadrant of Germany and also divided the capital, Berlin, which was in the Soviet quadrant, into four parts. Together the allies agreed on a strict agenda of "de-Nazification" that included war crimes trials for Nazi military and political leaders.

Japan's surrender was even more abject. Hiroshima and Nagasaki had been leveled by the atomic bomb, and sixty-six Japanese cities had been mostly reduced to rubble during sustained air raids. About 2.7 million Japanese, between 3 and 4 percent of the country's population, had died in the war, and millions more were injured. At war's end, only a handful of Japanese ships remained afloat; nearly the entire air force had been destroyed. On September 2, 1945, Japanese officials gathered on the USS Missouri to surrender officially, dwarfed by the boat's massive artillery. Less than two weeks later, General Douglas MacArthur, who oversaw the occupation, declared Japan to be a "fourth rate nation," a deliberate effort to humiliate the former empire.

The U.S. charge was to pacify the country, to create enduring democratic institutions, to decentralize Japan's *zaibatsu* system (an economy directed by large industrial conglomerates), and prevent the rise of another militant Japanese empire. To that end, the United States convened war crimes trials, forbade prominent military and political leaders to take positions of authority, drafted a new constitution that created a parliamentary democracy and reduced the emperor to a symbolic role, and instituted land reforms to diminish the power of wealthy rural landowners who had supported the war. To Americans who had spent the wartime years hearing the Japanese denounced as subhuman and vicious "monkey-men," the prospect of democratization required draconian measures.

In many respects, the United States was ill prepared to impose military rule in Germany and Japan. When the fleeting thrill of liberation wore off, the military needed to provide special incentives, including hardship pay and the promise of cars and well-appointed apartments, to encourage warweary soldiers to reenlist in the occupation forces. Wherever possible, the United States relied on native language speakers, whether wartime refugees who had volunteered to serve in the U.S. military, like the young Henry Kissinger, whose family had fled Nazi Germany in 1938, or the children of Americanized immigrants, who were often distant from their parents' language and culture. Likewise the military recruited Japanese Americans—many of them nisei or sansei, some of them held in internment camps during the war—to support the American occupation of Japan, assuming, quite dubiously in many cases, that they had the language skills and cultural competencies to understand postwar Japan. To prepare carefully selected officers to oversee the occupation, the military supported training programs on American college campuses, immersing future occupiers in the language, geography, and history of their countries.

The early days of occupation hardly resembled Joppolo's humanitarian ventures: they were chaotic and often exploitative. Troops used their access to goods and power, not to mention the desperate circumstances of widows, single women, and war orphans, to get sex. Prostitution was rife. To maintain morale and discourage illicit activity, occupation officials tried to create licit spaces—on-base dances and social clubs—where troops could meet local women, rather than procure their favors. By the late 1940s, the military allowed officers and then enlisted men to move their families overseas.

THE ORIGINS OF THE COLD WAR

The occupations of Japan and Germany, which lasted until 1952, entailed everything from finding housing for refugees and providing them basic food and supplies to rounding up suspected collaborators and war criminals. Occupying forces reorganized local and regional governments, ousting fascists. But escalating tensions between the Soviet Union and the United States changed the nature of occupation in Germany. For the United States, exporting the Four Freedoms receded in importance in favor of neutralizing Communism.

Although the United States and the Soviet Union had been allied in the struggle against Nazi Germany between 1941 and 1945, the relationship had been one of convenience that quickly frayed at war's end. On February 9, 1946, Stalin stunned the United States and its allies with a speech that seemed to signal a new Soviet belligerence. While Stalin praised the Allies for their collaboration in defeating fascism, he denounced both world wars as the consequence of capitalist greed, and in words that American observers found particularly threatening, he called for a five-year plan to rebuild the Soviet economy. *The New York Times* ran a banner headline that sounded the alarm: "STALIN SETS A HUGE OUTPUT NEAR OURS IN 5-YEAR PLAN: EXPECTS TO LEAD IN SCIENCE."[11] Supreme Court justice William Douglas hyperbolically called it "the declaration of World War III."[12]

For all of Stalin's grand promises, the Soviets were hardly a military or economic threat to the United States. Much of his rhetoric was meant for Russian ears, to restore morale in a country that had suffered more than others during the war. The Soviet Union had a weak air force and navy. Its army had been decimated on the Eastern Front. It lacked nuclear weapons and had no effective air defense system to repel a missile attack. With at least twenty million of its people dead, vast agricultural regions laid waste, and tens of thousands of factories destroyed, its economy was crippled.

World War III was a long way off. American intelligence experts believed that it would take a decade or two for the USSR to rebuild its industrial and military capacity. In 1946 the Joint Intelligence Staff in the War Department noted that "the offensive capabilities of the United States are manifestly superior to those of the U.S.S.R. and any war between the U.S. and the U.S.S.R. would be far more costly to the Soviet Union than to the United States."[13]

But to many American politicians and opinion leaders, Stalin's were fighting words. In the month following his speech, U.S.-Soviet relations chilled. President Truman lashed out at those who called for the "appeasement" of the Soviets, drawing a comparison with the British decision to allow Hitler to annex the Sudetenland in 1938. Truman's Republican opponents accused him of inaction. Anything short of an aggressive policy to thwart Stalin would lead to "another Munich." Influential columnist Walter Lippmann argued that the United States needed "to reinforce, rebuild and modernize the industrial power of Western Europe, and to take a leading part in the development of . . . Asia."[14] That effort would require more than just dollars and American know-how: the United States would need to muster the "moral energy" to face the Soviet threat.

Kennan and the Long Telegram

On February 22, less than two weeks after Stalin's speech, George Kennan, the U.S. *chargé d'affaires* in Moscow, dispatched a "long telegram," warning of the Soviet Union's imperial ambitions. Kennan, who had joined the Foreign Service after graduating from Princeton, learned Russian and joined the staff of the U.S. embassy to the Soviet Union when it opened in 1933. Profoundly pessimistic, Kennan found himself the resident contrarian in Moscow. At a moment when many Western politicians and intellectuals were enraptured with the Soviet experiment, Kennan was hardheaded and skeptical. "Will the pathos of the burly, over-alled worker, with his sleeves rolled up, brandishing a red flag and striding over the bodies of top-hatted capitalists, ever grasp the hearts of people as it did just after the war?" he asked in 1935. "I doubt it."[15]

Kennan and Acheson got along, despite their very different styles.

Acheson was always more of an empiricist, someone who gathered data to make his opinion. Kennan, by contrast, was more ideological, trusting his gut instincts, particularly when it came to facing down the Soviets. Kennan had opposed de-Nazification on the grounds that former German leaders could be mobilized in the anti-Communist cause. His telegram hammered home the anti-Soviet point, arguing that "we have here a political force committed fanatically to the belief that with US there can be no permanent *modus vivendi*, that it is desirable and necessary that the internal harmony of our society be disrupted, our traditional way of life be destroyed, the international authority of our state be broken, if Soviet power is to be secure." He concluded that "how to cope with this force is undoubtedly [the] greatest task our diplomacy has ever faced and probably [the] greatest it will ever have to face," but that "the problem is within our power to solve—and that without recourse to any general military conflict."[16] Putting a rhetorical exclamation point on the anti-Soviet message, British prime minister Winston Churchill used the occasion of a March 3 address at a small Missouri college to warn of an "iron curtain" separating the Soviet Union from Western Europe.

Great Power Politics

By 1946, hyperbolic rhetoric aside, it was clear that World War II had changed the international balance of power. For all its economic and military troubles, the Soviet Union had risen to second place, after the United States, as a world power, victorious against the Nazis and eager to expand its sphere of influence in Europe and Asia. Britain, France, and of course Germany and Japan were "great powers" mostly in the past tense, with decimated militaries, bombed-out cities, frail economies, and thin public support for military engagement.

Their far-flung empires, churning with anti-imperial insurgencies, were in various stages of resistance and rebellion. In the years following World War II, France faced rebellions in Madagascar, Tunisia, and Algeria, and it found its imperial hold in Indochina under siege by a growing revolutionary movement. India rose against Britain, and the empire's influence in Egypt, Palestine, and the eastern Mediterranean, particularly Turkey and Greece, was on the wane.

Truman faced three foreign policy challenges in 1946 and beyond. Should the United States turn its arsenal toward the Soviets? Should the

United States fill the gap left by the decimated great powers? Should the United States intervene in anticolonial struggles worldwide?

RECONVERSION: THE HOME FRONT

The question of how to wind down World War II was equally pressing on the home front. No one knew exactly what the postwar social order would look like. Pessimists feared that, without the stimulant of wartime spending, the United States would plunge back into a depression. No one was certain how the 16.4 million World War II veterans, many of them traumatized by their experiences overseas, would integrate back into American society.

The 1946 film *The Best Years of Our Lives*, which won eight Oscars, captured the pensive mood. Three GIs return home to fictional Boone City, where they find their lives spinning out of control. Homer, who had been a high school football hero, struggles to come to terms with the amputation of both of his hands. Al, a banker, struggles to readjust and turns to drink. Fred, who has won the Distinguished Flying Cross for service as a bomber captain, is emasculated by his job as a drugstore soda jerk (the only work he can get) and divorces his dissatisfied wife when she has an affair with a better-off man. In the film's bleakest scene, Fred, having fled his unfaithful wife and troubled life, finds himself in a sprawling lot of decommissioned military planes, a flyer and his aircraft now without purpose.

Economic Anxieties

The Best Years of Our Lives was the highest-grossing film of its time—and a close second in viewership to *Gone with the Wind*—in large part because it captured popular angst. Divorce was endemic in the United States, reaching a peak of 31 per 100 marriages in 1945.[17] Joblessness spiked. Many veterans, hoping to return to their prewar jobs, instead took unemployment pay. Former soldiers without work were eligible for twenty dollars a week in benefits for up to one year. Civilian workers—including millions of African Americans and women who had worked for defense contractors during the war—feared, with good reason, that they would lose their jobs during the postwar "reconversion."

Black defense workers faced a particularly insecure future. Many lost their jobs because of veterans' preferences in postwar hiring, which counted military service toward seniority. Black workers complained that because they had been the last hired during the war, they were the first to be fired afterward. Many women also found themselves unemployed, their jobs reassigned to returning veterans, many of whom had little experience in the civilian workforce.

Corporate profits had skyrocketed during the war and afterward, but after V-J Day (the day marking Japan's surrender and the war's end), when production slowed, wages stagnated. Workers, who had benefited from overtime pay during the war, found themselves with lighter paychecks as employers reinstated the forty-hour week. President Truman contended that profitable firms could afford to pay workers more. "Wage increases are . . . imperative," he argued in October 1945, "to cushion the shock to our workers, to sustain adequate purchasing power and to increase national income."[18] Business leaders reacted bitterly, arguing that Truman had capitulated to organized labor and that industry could not afford pay hikes. The National Association of Manufacturers warned of "a wage-price spiral" and blamed the "labor monopoly" for "rais[ing] the prices of the things you need."[19]

Even more troubling was the prospect of mass unemployment. Would the United States tumble back into another depression? Union leaders, like Walter Reuther, head of the powerful United Automobile Workers (UAW), demanded that the federal government enact a full employment policy, including public works programs to build housing and provide work for the jobless. "We have but to mobilize for peace the resourcefulness and technical know-how which put the B-29 into the skies over Tokyo and sent the atomic bomb crashing into Hiroshima," stated Reuther optimistically, "and we can wipe out the slums and sub-standard housing, both rural and urban."[20] At war's end, nearly four in five Americans surveyed believed that "it should be up to the government" to ensure employment "for everyone who wants to work." Congressional Democrats, with Truman's support, began drafting "full employment" legislation, taking up the motto "sixty million jobs."[21]

The Great Strike Wave

The postwar tension over wages and security sparked the most intensive wave of labor unrest in American history. As soon as the ticker tape parades ended, unionists took to the picket lines. In the year following the end of the war, 4,630 work stoppages involving over five million workers affected nearly every sector of the U.S. economy. In late 1945, 200,000 General Motors workers walked out and would not return to work for 113 days.[22] In early 1946, some 93,000 meatpackers and 750,000 steelworkers went on strike; 180,000 electrical workers shut down every Westinghouse and General Electric plant in the United States and Canada. "The picketing in the larger plants," lamented Charles E. Wilson, GE's chief executive, "was literally hundreds of people, actually joining hands and going around in an ellipse in front of the plant so that nobody could get through."[23] GE executives were particularly flummoxed by the fact that the public seemed to be on the workers' side. Veterans, still in uniform, joined picket lines. Police officers often showed more sympathy to the strikers than to their bosses. Ministers and priests blessed the protesting workers. Management seemed, at least for the moment, to be on the wrong side of history.

The strike wave continued through the spring, leaving few sectors of the economy untouched. In April, 400,000 coal miners in Pennsylvania, West Virginia, Kentucky, Alabama, Illinois, and Iowa stopped work for forty days. And in May, 300,000 railway workers struck, paralyzing the nation's vast transportation system.[24] Tens of thousands of other workers—among them truckers, printers, lumberjacks, and clerical workers, even professional baseball players—also walked out of their jobs, demanding better pay, benefits, and more security.

Few of the strikes were violent: federal labor laws prevented employers from brutally attacking striking workers as they had in the labor upheavals of the 1890s or the 1930s. Moreover, employers seldom had recourse to "scabs," the slang for replacement workers. During demobilization, despite fears of joblessness, no huge reserve army of the unemployed stood ready to replace striking workers. In addition, the 1935 National Labor Relations Act had enshrined the principle of collective bargaining in the law, and the Truman administration used its clout to bring employers and union leaders to the negotiating table.

Resolving labor unrest proved challenging. In November 1945, President Truman assembled a national labor-management conference to lay "a broad and permanent foundation for industrial peace and progress," but despite his best efforts, the negotiations failed.[25] In early 1946 he created a federal fact-finding board to gather statistics on company profits and wages, hoping that hard data would serve as the basis for compromise. But he also wielded the power of government to shut down the railway workers strike, blaming it on "men within our own country who place their private interests above the welfare of the nation." Truman temporarily nationalized the railroads.[26]

Even if unionists regretted Truman's response to the railroad strike, they had little reason to be unhappy with the overall results of the strike wave. In late March 1946 an agreement between the UAW and General Motors raised wages by 18.5 cents per hour, a substantial gain. The United Steelworkers and the United Electrical, Radio and Machine Workers (UE) quickly accepted the same wage hike. The following year General Motors and the UAW would agree to cost-of-living allowances (COLA) that pegged wages to inflation, ensuring stability. This set a pattern that would play out in many other industries over the next few years, culminating in the "Treaty of Detroit," a five-year contract that Reuther negotiated with General Motors and Ford in 1950. The treaty gave workers high wages, ongoing COLA increases, excellent health benefits, and a generous pension plan, in exchange for a promise of peace on the shop floor.

The Failure of Fair Employment Practices

Not all workers benefited equally from the rise in wages and benefits after the great strike wave. African American workers, though they had made inroads in defense industries during World War II, were concentrated in the most menial jobs. They faced widespread discrimination at work. Whole sectors of the economy—particularly skilled, clerical, retail, and professional employment—remained nearly completely closed to them. Even industries that accepted black workers, like automobile manufacturing, steelmaking, and meatpacking, stuck them in the most unpleasant or dangerous jobs, lifting engines and spraying paint in car plants, stoking red-hot furnaces in steel mills, or cutting open cow carcasses in meat processing factories.

Ever since A. Philip Randolph's threatened March on Washington in 1941, civil rights activists had put jobs and freedom at the center of their agenda. In 1944 a coalition of nearly one hundred unions, civil rights organizations, and religious groups created an umbrella organization to lobby for a permanent Fair Employment Practices Committee. Leading the group was Anna Arnold Hedgeman, a formidable intellectual and astute organizer who had begun her career in the early 1920s with hopes of becoming a schoolteacher in her hometown, St. Paul, Minnesota. Since the school district was overwhelmingly white with only a few thousand black residents, St. Paul's school board simply wouldn't allow an African American to teach white students.

Instead, she made a career in the segregated world of social services.

She got a job working at the "Negro" YWCA in Springfield, Ohio, and quickly moved up the ranks, taking executive positions at YWCAs in Jersey City, Harlem, and Brooklyn. Living in Harlem and Brooklyn during the Depression, she moved leftward politically investigating the poor working conditions of black laundresses and domestic servants, joining "Do not buy where you cannot work" boycotts of white-owned stores, supporting the March on Washington movement, and spearheading a campaign against segregated blood banks during the war.

Hedgeman and her group lobbied Congress, wrote op-eds, and sponsored mass rallies around the country, focusing on early 1946, when Franklin Delano Roosevelt's Fair Employment Practices Committee (FEPC), a temporary agency, would dissolve. They won the support of President Truman and former first lady Eleanor Roosevelt, but their battle was uphill nonetheless. Congress refused to create a permanent FEPC in February 1946. Facing a filibuster by southern Democratic senators, FEPC supporters mustered only forty-eight votes, well short of the two-thirds needed to bring the bill to the floor. In the House, a bill to make the FEPC permanent languished in committee. Senator Theodore Bilbo (D-MS), in one of his politer moments, lashed out at the FEPC as a "damnable" law, one that "forced" black and white "affiliation and association" based on "the craziest, wildest, most unreasonable illogical theory."[27]

Bilbo found allies who didn't share his fiery rhetoric but nonetheless ferociously opposed civil rights in the workplace. Pro-business Republicans saw the FEPC as unjust interference with employers' decisions to hire, promote, and fire at will. The Dixie-GOP coalition prevailed—and it would win a steady streak of victories for the next two decades. Between 1944 and 1963, FEPC proponents introduced 114 fair employment bills in the House and Senate. All of them were buried in committee hearings or filibustered to death.

Frustrated by the stalemate in Congress, civil rights activists pushed for state and local antidiscrimination laws. Between 1944—when New York State passed a law forbidding discrimination by race, ethnicity, and religion—and 1963, two dozen states, all of them in the North and West, passed their own Fair Employment Practices laws. Sometimes those laws were weak, the result of business opposition to regulation. But particularly in states with growing black populations, like New York and New Jersey, civil rights laws gained broad Democratic support and the votes of pluralities or majorities of Republicans.

The 1946 Midterm Elections

The global uncertainty, labor unrest, civil rights struggles, and economic instability of 1946 galvanized Truman's opponents on both left and right. The president's position on the railway strikes alienated many in his party's sizable labor wing. Several union leaders, among them the UAW's Reuther and the Steelworkers' head Philip Murray, considered organizing a separate labor party, like those in Western Europe. Drained after months of strikes, exhausted unionists had little inclination to spend their energy getting out the vote in the 1946 midterms. Civil rights groups complained that Truman was too weak to challenge the Dixie-GOP coalition. To the right, hawks argued that Truman was wobbly in the face of Stalin's aggression and all too willing to sacrifice business interests to a grasping labor movement.

The Republican Party, sensing opportunity, ran a strong slate of congressional candidates. Voters of all persuasions chortled at the pun, "to err is Truman." In the weeks leading up to the midterm elections, the Frost advertising company, a firm working for the Republicans, came up with a simple slogan that captured the anti-Truman mood: "Had enough?"[28] In a November landslide, Republicans gained control of both the Senate and the House for the first time since 1930. Of the seventy-seven most liberal members of the House up for reelection, only thirty-six won.

Congress and Truman faced off again and again over the next two years, threatening many of the New Deal's achievements. Liberals like T.R.B., the pseudonymous columnist for *The New Republic*, bemoaned the harsh political climate. "This Congress brought back an atmosphere you had forgotten or never thought possible," he wrote. "Victories fought and won years ago were suddenly in doubt."[29] In 1947 and 1948, Truman wielded the veto sixty-two times. But Congress, truculent, especially on domestic labor and economic policy, overrode him fifteen times, more than any president to date other than the woefully inept Andrew Johnson, who succeeded Abraham Lincoln in 1865.

Taft-Hartley, Operation Dixie, and the "Right to Work"

Truman's congressional opponents pushed an aggressive agenda to unravel the New Deal, beginning with legislation to weaken the 1935 National Labor Relations Act. The leader of the antiunion effort, Ohio senator Robert Taft, nicknamed "Mr. Republican," had been elected to the Senate in the anti-Roosevelt midterm election of 1938. Over his three terms in office, he accepted some New Deal programs, including Social Security and public housing, but he was a fierce critic of any legislation that might strengthen labor.

The Taft-Hartley Act, passed in June 1947, gave the president the authority to intervene in strikes to protect national security. It empowered states to pass "right to work" laws that allowed workers in unionized companies to opt out of membership. It required all union leaders to sign affidavits stating that they were not members of the Communist Party. It forbade "secondary strikes," walkouts by workers in one firm in support of striking workers in another. And most significantly, it limited unions' use of the "closed shop," a practice that required that all workers in a firm that had elected union representation be members of that union and pay dues. President Truman denounced the legislation as "vindictive," argued that it would "restrict the proper rights of the rank and file of labor," and vetoed it.[30] But the Dixie-GOP alliance stood united and overrode Truman's veto, 68–25 in the Senate and 331–83 in the House.

Antilabor campaigns played out with special intensity at the state and local levels, particularly in the South and Mountain West, where over the next two decades, nineteen states would pass right-to-work laws that thwarted unionization. In the 1940s in Phoenix, Arizona, Chamber of Commerce leaders successfully led campaigns to lower business taxes, fought to limit the bargaining power of the city's once powerful trade unions, and used the promise of a "favorable business climate" to attract companies fleeing the old industrial cities of the Northeast and Midwest.[31] The result was an extraordinary economic boom in sparsely populated Arizona, as companies seeking low-wage workers began relocating factories there in the 1950s.

Labor's biggest defeats came in the states of the Old Confederacy. Operation Dixie, a CIO organizing effort that began in 1946, brought more than two hundred organizers to textile, furniture, steel, and cotton-processing plants in Virginia, the Carolinas, Georgia, and Alabama. Many were committed to both racial equality and unionism—a double threat to Jim Crow. Operation Dixie organizers reached out to black and white workers alike, arguing that union efforts would bolster everyone's wages and benefits.

Southern business elites used Taft-Hartley as a powerful weapon to fight the CIO campaign: right-to-work laws, enacted in Alabama, Arkansas, Florida,

Georgia, Mississippi, North Carolina, South Carolina, Tennessee, Texas, and Virginia by the early 1950s, weakened organizing drives. Accusations of Communism, sometimes true, discredited union organizers. Southern antiunionists also resorted to time-tested appeals to white supremacy. David Clark, who edited the *Textile Bulletin*, an industry publication, compared Operation Dixie's organizers to the "carpetbaggers" of Reconstruction and argued that the CIO "seeks to place Negroes upon the basis of social equality with whites."[32] Evangelical pastors circulated leaflets at factory gates accusing unionists of being godless Communists. In many towns, vigilantes attacked organizers. Local police departments, often in the pocket of industrialists, arrested and jailed unionists, and local magistrates sentenced many to hard labor on chain gangs. Operation Dixie collapsed in the late 1940s. Union membership in most of the South remained low for decades afterward.

COLD WAR, FIRST MOVES

Truman faced big hurdles in Congress when it came to labor, but on foreign policy he was able to build a bipartisan coalition of support. In 1946 and 1947 the United States and the Soviet Union jostled for power, first in the eastern Mediterranean and the Middle East. Greece, devastated by German occupation, exploded into full civil war, its robust Communist party battling traditional monarchists and fascist sympathizers for control. The United States and its allies worried about Soviet pressure on Turkey to control the Dardanelles, a strategic maritime link between the Black Sea and the Mediterranean, a nexus between Russia, Europe, and the Middle East. Tensions spread eastward to Iran, where United States, British, and Soviet troops tensely occupied a country that was supposed to be moving toward independence. The Soviet Union supported a rebellion led by ethnic Azeris in northern Iran, an area bordering the USSR, and refused to withdraw its troops from the contested region, despite a 1943 agreement to do so. The fate of Iran mattered perhaps even more than Turkey and Greece because of its vast oil deposits.

The Truman Doctrine and the Origins of Containment

In early 1947 the Truman administration stepped in, with Dean Acheson, now undersecretary of state, playing a key role. Acheson made a forceful case for aggressive engagement in Greece and Turkey. The bishop's son

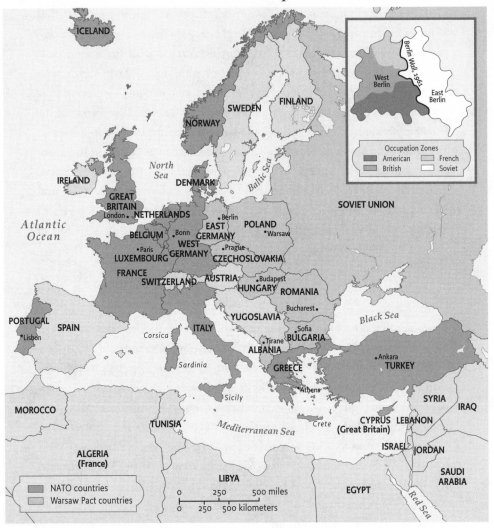

framed his foreign policy analysis in moral terms. "We are met at Armageddon," he argued. "Like apples in a barrel infected by one rotten one, the corruption of Greece would infect Iran and all to the East. It would also carry infection to spread through Asia Minor and Egypt, and to Europe through Italy and France."[33] It was neither the first nor the last time that Communism would be compared to a contagion that needed to be quarantined or contained. Both abroad and at home, policy makers justified anti-Communism as a necessary cure for a disease that could destroy the United States and the world.

Acheson provided the president with the blueprint for what would be called the Truman Doctrine. On March 12, 1947, in his first major foreign policy address since the disastrous midterm elections, Truman stood before Congress, requesting $400 million to shore up Greece and Turkey, on the grounds that "it must be the policy of the United States to support free peoples who are resisting attempted subjugation by armed minorities or by outside pressures."[34] Acheson wrote much of the speech because Truman was dissatisfied with early drafts. "I want no hedging in this speech," stated Truman. "This was America's answer to the surge of expansion of Communist tyranny. It had to be clear and free of hesitation or double talk."[35] Simple and strong, the address depicted the fate of two small countries as a matter of slavery and freedom, vital to the future of democracy. On May 15 the aid bill passed by overwhelming majorities in the House and Senate, Truman's first big bipartisan victory in the "do nothing Congress."

The principle behind the Truman Doctrine—that Communism was a contagion that needed to be quarantined wherever it sprang up—would guide American foreign policy for the next two decades. In the summer of 1947, George Kennan, writing anonymously as "Mr. X" in the pages of the journal *Foreign Affairs*, fleshed out what came to be called the strategy of "containment." A rising star in the State Department after his "long telegram," Kennan offered a simple, compelling rationale for the escalating Cold War, asserting that "the innate antagonism between capitalism and socialism" motivated the Soviet Union. The USSR, believed Kennan, would be relentless and creative. Soviet "political action is a fluid stream which moves constantly, wherever it is permitted to move, toward a given goal. Its main concern is to make sure that it has filled every nook and cranny available to it in the basin of world power." If Moscow was patient, opportunistic, and aggressive, argued Mr. X, the key to defeating the Soviets would be the "adroit and vigilant application of counterforce at a series of constantly shifting geographical and political points, corresponding to the shifts and maneuvers of Soviet policy."[36] Kennan thus defined containment.

The National Security Act

In July 1947, Congress enacted the National Security Act, a sweeping reorganization of American military and intelligence services. The law established a new cabinet position, the secretary of defense, who directed a new agency, the National Military Establishment (renamed the Department of

Defense in 1949). It created a new military branch—the U.S. Air Force—and empowered the Joint Chiefs of Staff (the top officers of the army, navy, and air force) to coordinate military operations. The law also established the National Security Council (NSC), to advise the president on foreign policy, and the Central Intelligence Agency (CIA), to direct espionage overseas. In 1948 the NSC gave the CIA the power to engage in clandestine operations abroad, targeting governments and organizations that threatened American political or economic interests. Truman and Congress had created a vast, centralized American security state unprecedented in American history.

The Marshall Plan

In 1947 the Truman administration—under a new secretary of state, General George C. Marshall—elaborated on the Truman Doctrine, with an eye toward strengthening Western Europe. Marshall was Truman's first strong secretary of state, a man of supreme self-confidence. He had first seen military action in the Philippines in 1902, served again in France during World War I, and rose quickly up the ranks. In 1939, Roosevelt named him army chief of staff. A master of both logistics and strategy, Marshall rose in prestige because of his leadership during World War II.

Marshall worked closely with Acheson and Kennan, whom he named to direct the Department of State's new Policy Planning Staff. Together they laid the groundwork for the next phase of the Cold War: an unprecedented infusion of economic aid to Western Europe. The European Recovery Program, quickly dubbed the Marshall Plan at President Truman's insistence, promised $16 billion in aid to the war-torn Western European countries. When Marshall announced the plan in June 1947, at Harvard's commencement, he described it as necessary to prevent "economic, social, and political deterioration of a very grave character." He emphasized the plan's humanitarian side. "Our policy is not directed against any country or doctrine but against hunger, poverty, desperation, and chaos." Still it built firmly on the Truman Doctrine. The president called the aid to Greece and Turkey and the Marshall Plan "two halves of the same walnut," which linked capitalism and democracy. The purpose of aid to Europe, Marshall went on, "should be the revival of a working economy in the world so as to permit the emergence of political and social conditions in which free institutions can exist."[37] He did not have to mention the Soviet Union, and he did not.

The Marshall Plan, however, faced an uphill battle in Congress. Senator Robert Taft led the opposition. Over his three terms in office, he had controversially opposed American intervention in World War II, denounced Japanese internment, and argued that fears of Soviet domination were overblown. Reaching beyond his shrinking isolationist circle, Taft led a chorus of Republicans who denounced the Marshall Plan as "a bold socialist blueprint" and a costly boondoggle.[38] Why should Americans channel billions into what Taft denounced as a European T.V.A.?

Despite the opposition, Marshall, a celebrated military man, retained public goodwill. He rallied pro-business Republicans, internationalists, anti-Communists, and liberals, all of whom found something to like in the plan. For corporations, it could expand the market for American exports. So long as the funds were not used for state-run enterprises, Europe could become fertile ground for American investment. For internationalists, the plan would reinforce the historic ties between the United States and Europe. For anti-Communists, it would stabilize European economies, weakening the influence of Communist parties and thwarting Soviet plans to extend their reach westward. For liberals, the plan was a humanitarian effort of the highest order, building infrastructure, creating jobs, and spurring consumerism throughout Europe.

By early 1948 the Marshall Plan had stalled in Congress, a victim of bitter partisan division. The Republican majority in the House and Senate did not want to hand the unpopular president a victory in an election year. But events in Central Europe in February shifted the debate. In early 1946, Czechoslovakia, free from German control, had created a multiparty government after a closely contested election—the prime minister was a Communist since his party had won a plurality of votes, but the president and foreign minister were not. In February 1948 the fragile government split. Within days the Soviets stepped in, toppled the president, and installed a pro-Moscow regime. Two weeks later the foreign minister was murdered. General Lucius Clay, who oversaw the occupation of Germany, warned that the events in Prague signaled "a subtle change in the Soviet attitude," at once "faintly contemptuous, slightly arrogant, and certainly assured."[39] Secretary of State Marshall warned of the gravity of the situation in Central Europe. In that context, advocates of the Marshall Plan pushed successfully for its enactment.

A blend of humanitarian and social democratic rhetoric, fearmongering, and strategic anti-Communism shaped Truman's Cold War foreign policy. He and his advisers were New Dealers enough to describe American foreign policy in the soaring rhetoric of Roosevelt's Four Freedoms. They were Cold Warriors enough to shift their aims to one version of freedom—free enterprise—at the expense of a more inclusive social democratic politics. And they were astute enough politically to capitalize on a sense of anxiety to build political will. For a few critical years in the second half of the 1940s, the ideal of expanding the New Deal worldwide collided with the imperatives of making a world safe for capitalism, in a climate of escalating fear. Ultimately security and enterprise would trump social democracy.

THE ELECTION OF 1948

The struggles over labor, civil rights, and Communism shaped the election of 1948, a four-way race against incumbent Harry Truman. It was the first presidential election since 1932 without Franklin Roosevelt on the ticket. Two of Truman's opponents had defected from the ranks of the Democratic Party, a reminder of the instability of Roosevelt's governing coalition.

Henry Wallace and the Progressive Insurgency

On the left stood former vice president Henry Wallace. A quixotic figure, he had gained the support of the New Deal's left flank during his time as vice president. "Some have spoken of the 'American Century,'" Wallace proclaimed in 1942. "I say that the century on which we are entering—the century which will come out of the war—can be and must be the century of the common man."[40] He was arguing with Henry Luce, the influential publisher of *Time* and *Life* magazines, who had envisioned an "American Century," when the United States would "exert upon the world the full impact of our influence, for such purposes as we see fit and by such means as we see fit."[41]

Wallace was the administration's strongest advocate of full employment, federal health insurance, and guaranteed annual wages, all programs that conservative Democrats and the GOP saw as dangerously socialistic. In 1944 FDR, facing pressure from party insiders who feared that Wallace could assume the presidency in the likely event that the ailing FDR died in office, named Truman his vice-presidential nominee, demoting Wallace, as the embittered vice president saw it, to secretary of commerce.

Wallace, a restless seeker (he had flirted with various religions, from

Catholicism to Theosophy), wandered further leftward, never veering from his agenda as an internationalist, advocate of human rights, and friend of labor. Rather naïvely, he found much to commend in Soviet Union, even if his critics unfairly charged that he was a Communist or a Communist dupe. Wallace used his position at Commerce to challenge Truman's foreign policy, denouncing the new president as a militarist. Finally, in September 1946, he publicly criticized British prime minister Winston Churchill for his belligerent stance toward the Soviet Union. Truman, furious, insisted on Wallace's resignation.

Unchained from the administration and using his new position as editor of *The New Republic* as a bully pulpit, Wallace railed against Truman, accusing him of capitulating to business interests, of unnecessary belligerence toward the Soviets, and of failure on civil rights and labor. After traveling the country in 1946 and 1947, giving speeches to rapturous audiences, he decided to mount a third-party effort for the presidency. As the Progressive Party candidate, he surrounded himself with left-liberal New Dealers and, to his later chagrin, with members of the Communist Party, who saw in his foreign policy and staunch New Dealism an opportunity to revive the Popular Front. A candidate, Wallace fearlessly defended civil rights on a tour through the South. He was frequently pelted with tomatoes and eggs but refused to relent on his position that "the poll tax must go."

Wallace ran an uphill battle. Most CIO unions had made their peace with Truman after he vetoed the Taft-Hartley Act. They put their formidable resources behind his reelection. While civil rights activists admired Wallace's courage in the South, Truman had won the fealty of black voters; hardly any black newspapers endorsed Wallace. But Truman's civil rights position spurred another revolt, this one from the right. Southern Democrats found little to like in the president's pro-civil-rights program.

The Dixiecrat Rebellion

White Southerners found themselves dismayed at Truman and increasingly uneasy with the Democratic Party itself. FDR had kept peace within party ranks by deferring to powerful southern Democrats. New Deal legislation had mostly frozen out African Americans, in exchange for southern votes. Social Security had excluded farm laborers and domestics, the two occupations that employed most African Americans. The administration of welfare, unemployment insurance, and old age assistance was left in the hands of state and local officials who blatantly discriminated against blacks. The Federal Housing Administration refused to underwrite home mortgages in racially mixed neighborhoods. The Agricultural Adjustment Administration's farm subsidies went to property owners, not to renters, sharecroppers, or debt peons, all disproportionally black. FDR even refused to back anti-lynching legislation for fear of alienating southern Democrats.

One of the bitterest pills was the 1944 Servicemen's Readjustment Act, popularly called the GI Bill. It provided returning veterans with unemployment compensation, medical care, educational subsidies, and access to mortgage funds. The GI Bill sent a generation of men and some women back to school, made home ownership a possibility for the masses, and built a suburban middle class. It helped prevent a postwar depression. But most of its benefits did not reach black veterans. Many colleges and universities refused to admit blacks, or they let in a token number. And few blacks could use GI Bill housing benefits, because banks, real estate brokers, and housing developers openly discriminated against them.

Some northern Democrats pushed their party to support civil rights for African Americans. At the 1948 convention, Minneapolis mayor Hubert H. Humphrey roused liberals with his argument that "the time has arrived in America for the Democratic Party to get out of the shadow of states' rights and walk forthrightly into the bright sunshine of human rights."[42] Southern delegations were outraged. When the convention supported Humphrey's position, many walked out, while others led an unsuccessful effort to replace Truman with Georgia senator Richard Russell, a congressional powerhouse and staunch segregationist. After the convention, many southern Democrats rallied behind South Carolina's governor, Strom Thurmond, the insurgent candidate of the new States' Rights Democratic Party, nicknamed the Dixiecrats.

Thurmond had begun his career as a staunch New Dealer, supporting Social Security, jobs programs, and a federal minimum wage but never wavering from his commitment to white supremacy. At twenty-two, Thurmond had fathered a daughter, Essie Mae, with Carrie Butler, a sixteen-year-old black girl who worked for his family, though it would be decades, after Thurmond's death in 2003, before the story became public. Running against Truman, he declared that not even the U.S. Army "could admit the nigger race into our theaters, into our swimming pools, into our homes, and into our churches."[43] But increasingly Thurmond cast his lot with pro-business opponents of civil rights, adopting their argument that anti-discrimination laws threatened economic liberty. It was a position that would lead Thurmond, over his later career, to seal the Dixie-GOP marriage and eventually to defect to the Republican Party himself in 1964.

Truman's Electoral Coalition

The odds seemed long against Truman's reelection. Not only did he face mutiny in his own party; his Republican opponent was the well-regarded governor of New York, Thomas Dewey, who had run against Roosevelt in 1944 and won 46 percent of the vote nationwide. Dewey represented the moderate wing of his party. A strong supporter of civil rights, he had signed a strong state antidiscrimination law in 1944. An internationalist, he strongly supported the United Nations and opposed Robert Taft and the Republican isolationists. Dewey also supported liberal programs such as public housing, generous unemployment insurance, government-funded highways, and Social Security. As he argued, "anybody who thinks that an attack on the fundamental idea of security and welfare is appealing to people generally is living in the Middle Ages."[44]

How could Truman beat Dewey if the Democratic electorate split? Truman's advisers boldly gambled that enough southern Democrats would remain loyal to the party to neutralize Thurmond's challenge. They poached key constituents from Wallace's shaky coalition, including organized labor. Some left-led unions supported Wallace, but radical unionists were weak in 1948, hobbled by factionalism and anti-Communism. Mainstream union leaders, who had been lukewarm to Truman in 1946, now backed him loyally because he took their side in the debate over Taft-Hartley. Many unions used their money and troops to get out the vote for Truman.

The president needed more votes, both among progressive whites who might lean toward Wallace and especially among black voters who, because of their mass migration northward, were increasingly powerful, particularly in closely contested northern states. In 1948 journalist Henry Lee Moon published an influential book called *Balance of Power: The Negro Vote*. Moon, a brilliant young writer, one of first black graduates of Ohio State's prestigious journalism program, was just the man for the job. He had covered racial politics for various papers, including *The New York*

Times, since the mid-1930s. During World War II he had worked as a writer for the CIO, traveling to the South to publicize its union organizing campaigns. In 1947 he became the NAACP's chief publicist. Moon's argument was simple: black voters, who had long supported the party of Lincoln but had recently defected to the Democrats, might switch back. Their votes could decide the fate of mayoral, congressional, and statewide elections, even the presidency.

Truman used his executive power to move forward on civil rights. He cared about winning black votes but also worried about America's international reputation. In October 1947 the President's Committee on Civil Rights, which Truman had created a year earlier, issued a report, *To Secure These Rights*. The committee argued that "domestic civil rights shortcomings are a serious obstacle" to America's influence in the postwar world.[45]

In July 1948, Truman boldly circumvented Congress and issued Executive Orders 9980, which banned discrimination in the federal workforce (in effect creating a permanent FEPC), and 9981, which desegregated the U.S. military. Echoing the language of the Double Victory campaign, Truman insisted that the armed forces maintain "the highest standards of democracy, with equality of treatment and opportunity."[46] Behind the scenes, many top military leaders quietly supported the move: it was costly to maintain separate barracks, separate dining halls, and even separate blood banks for black and white soldiers. In the fall—mostly off the radar of the white-owned news media but covered at length by the black press, Truman became the first major Democratic candidate to campaign in black neighborhoods, in both Harlem and North Philadelphia, hoping to appeal to black voters in closely contested states.

Neither Wallace nor Thurmond did particularly well. Both won about 2.5 percent of the vote. Wallace did badly even among the groups he saw as his base—organized labor and blacks. Thurmond won a majority of voters in Alabama, Louisiana, Mississippi, and South Carolina, but Truman swept the rest of the South. Republican Thomas Dewey scarcely benefited from the split ticket. He had run a lackluster campaign. In a low-turnout election, Truman lost some closely contested states, including Dewey's New York, Michigan, and Pennsylvania, but he eked out a victory in others, among them Ohio, Illinois, and California. Whether black votes put him over the top is uncertain, but it is clear that Truman moved fast on civil rights because he believed they mattered.

Few pundits believed that the Dixiecrat defection would be lasting. For the moment, the South remained solidly Democratic. The Dixie-GOP alliance would continue to weaken labor and thwart civil rights legislation, leaving the president little room to maneuver on domestic issues. For the next four years, international conflicts would take priority in Washington. Truman and Congress would find common cause in the aggressive pursuit of the Cold War at home and abroad.

ANTI-COMMUNISM AT HOME

For President Truman, the crusades against Communism abroad and at home were inseparable. Well before his 1948 campaign, he had laid the groundwork for an aggressive campaign against the "red menace." In March 1947, just after he announced the Truman Doctrine, the president signed Executive Order 9835, creating loyalty review boards to ferret out federal employees who were "disloyal to the Government of the United States." This category included the vanishingly small number who called for violent revolution or engaged in espionage against the United States. But the order also covered many more—those affiliated with any group "designated by the Attorney General as totalitarian, fascistic, communistic, or subversive."[47] Over the next several years, such investigations would extend to government contractors and, at the state and local level, to public employees of all stripes, from teachers to traffic engineers. About twelve hundred federal government workers lost their jobs during the Truman administration because of suspected disloyalty and, though precise figures are hard to assemble, thousands more at the state and local levels.

Roots of Anti-Communism

The anti-Communist crusade had deep roots, extending back to the battles in the 1880s and 1890s against anarchists and radicals who organized among immigrants in big cities like New York and Chicago. It was fueled by the systematic crackdown on dissent and the imposition of strict censorship laws during World War I. It intensified in fears of Bolshevism after the 1917 Russian Revolution and in crackdowns on suspected Bolshevik sympathizers in the immediate postwar years. During the 1920s, the Red Scare targeted labor activists, suspected anarchists, and socialists. It took new form during the New Deal. By the 1936 election, right-wing critics of Roosevelt regularly denounced the recognition of labor's bargaining rights, government job-creation and housing programs, Social Security, unemployment insurance, and aid to dependent children as Communist-inspired, ignoring their roots in homegrown, American reform politics dating back to the Progressives.

As the world hurtled toward World War II, the U.S. government had hunted suspected radicals. In 1938, Representative Martin Dies (D-TX) drafted legislation creating a special House Committee on Un-American Activities to investigate radical insurgencies. Dies and his committee targeted pro-Nazi groups but singled out the larger network of Socialist and Communist activists, during a period when the left had unprecedented influence on mainstream politics, intellectual life, and labor unionism. The 1940 Smith Act criminalized any activities or publications "advocating, advising, or teaching the duty, necessity, desirability, or propriety of overthrowing or destroying any government in the United States by force or violence," a law that brought members of pro-Nazi organizations as well as leftists to federal courts for trial.[48] After the war, as the American alliance with the Soviet Union quickly frayed, Smith Act prosecutions almost exclusively targeted members of Socialist and Communist organizations.

The key player in investigating suspected subversives was the Federal Bureau of Investigation. Founded in 1908, the FBI expanded substantially under J. Edgar Hoover, the secretive director who took over the agency in 1924 and would go on to lead it for forty-eight years. Beginning in 1939, Hoover ordered the agency to compile a secret "Security Index" of individuals perceived to be dangerous to the United States. That list grew to 26,000 names by 1954. By 1960 the FBI had compiled a total of 430,000 dossiers on organizations and individuals suspected of subversion. Using new technologies of surveillance, the FBI cultivated informants—more than 109,000 in 1953 alone—who monitored radical organizations and dissidents and watched over defense plants and other sites deemed to be vital to national security. The FBI sometimes eavesdropped on meetings and sent undercover agents to infiltrate left-leaning groups.

The Communist Party and Its Critics

The FBI paid special attention to members of the Communist Party (CP) and a number of affiliated organizations. Small in number and shrinking,

CP membership had peaked at around 100,000 during the Depression. The party had enjoyed a revival during World War II, when the United States and the Soviet Union were allies. But it shrank after the war, in part because of the party's strict rules, its expectation that members would devote their lives to the movement ("every evening to Party work"), and the rigid partisan discipline imposed by Moscow as the Cold War intensified.

About 40 percent of the party's membership lived in New York. Some were "fellow travelers," who were sympathetic to Communist goals, like Congressman Vito Marcantonio, a fiery Italian American who represented mostly Italian and Puerto Rican East Harlem and won voters with his energetic commitment to civil rights, his support for organized labor, and in the late 1940s, his critique of the Cold War. Ben Davis, Jr., a lawyer and one of the few blacks to hold elective office in the country—he was elected to New York's city council in 1943—was also a Communist. But in most places outside New York, Communists had little success at the ballot box. Unlike in Europe, where Communist parties became major political players in the postwar years, America's CP remained on the electoral fringe.

Mostly frozen out of office, Communists embedded themselves in labor unions or volunteered for groups seeking social change, particularly in the struggle for civil rights. Many black activists and intellectuals, even those with little sympathy for Communists, could not help but admire their commitment to racial equality. Dorothy Height, a devout black churchwoman who would have a distinguished career in the YWCA and other black women's groups, rejected Communists' atheism but was attracted by their energetic efforts on behalf of racial equality. "I went to all kinds of Young Communists groups' meetings, I was in everything," she recalled, "but I knew I was not and never would be a Communist."[49]

The Varieties of Anti-Communism

Even though some liberals and leftists admired the CP, many could not stomach party members' secrecy and their uncritical support for Moscow's shifting party line. The CP lost many followers for good when, in 1939, it endorsed the Hitler-Stalin pact, opposing intervention against Nazism, then changed positions again a little more than a year later when Germany invaded the Soviet Union. The harsh realities of life under Stalin's rule alienated many on the left. Some of the most pronounced critics of Communism in the United States came from the small but vocal Socialist Party and various socialist sects that denounced the Soviet Union's lack of democracy, its bureaucracy, and its industrial policies.

An even larger contingent of anti-Communists was liberal. Americans for Democratic Action, founded in 1947 by longtime New Dealers on the Democratic Party's left, railed against Communism. Mainstream Democrats saw the New Deal as a compelling alternative to both laissez-faire economics and Communism, providing for social welfare and a well-regulated economy while upholding the primacy of individual rights and the sanctity of private property. "What we saw in the Russia of the thirties," wrote historian Arthur Schlesinger, Jr., in his spirited defense of liberalism, *The Vital Center*, a 1949 best seller, "was a land where industrialization was underwritten by mass starvation, where delusions of political infallibility led to the brutal extermination of dissent, and where the execution of heroes of the revolution testified to some deep inner contradiction in the system."[50]

Religious beliefs also fueled anti-Communism. The most vocal critics of the Soviets were Roman Catholics, who denounced Russia as a haven of atheism and who singled out the persecution of religious minorities and the state control of religious expression. In 1930 Fulton J. Sheen, America's most influential priest, a brilliant philosopher and theologian, launched a popular radio program, realizing that he could reach a bigger flock with new media than with arcane theological treatises. Over the air in 1948, he offered an eleven-part denunciation of Communism, which he turned into a popular four-book series. In 1951, the year he was named a bishop, he launched his most successful venture, a television show, *Life Is Worth Living*, eventually reaching about thirty million viewers a week. He warned his viewers of the evils of the Soviet Union but also of their own moral laxity. Communism, he argued, "is not to be feared just because it is anti-God, but because we are Godless; not because it is strong but because we are weak, for if we are under God, then who can conquer us?"[51] It was commonplace on Sundays for Catholics to pray for their coreligionists behind the iron curtain. In 1952, Pope Pius XII issued a proclamation consecrating Russia to the Virgin Mary, leading Catholics worldwide to pray for the "conversion of Russia."

HUAC and the Anti-Communist Crusade

Red-baiting worked well at the ballot box. In 1946, for example, an ambitious California politician, Richard Nixon, won election to the House by denouncing his Democratic opponent, Jerry Voorhis, as a Communist. When he ran for the U.S. Senate four years later, he trounced his opponent, Helen Gahagan Douglas, by labeling her the "pink lady"; compiling a "pink sheet" that compared her votes with those of Vito Marcantonio. According to Nixon, she had voted with Marcantonio 353 times, in his view evidence of her Communist sympathies. He called her "pink right down to her underwear."[52] For Nixon, conflating liberals and leftists was political gold.

Not surprisingly, Congressman Nixon found his way to the House Un-American Activities Committee (HUAC). In the spring of 1947, he joined HUAC's high-profile investigation of the United Electrical Workers, a left-dominated union. HUAC provided a forum for conservative southern Democrats and pro-business Republicans to lambaste unions and civil rights activists as pawns of Moscow, and to undermine left-leaning critics of the American economy.

HUAC also extended its hearings to Communism in Hollywood. In October 1947 the committee investigated forty-one prominent actors, actresses, screenwriters, and directors. The hearings began with friendly testimony from Walt Disney and from Screen Actors Guild head Ronald Reagan, a B-movie actor who had put more energy into union politics than into his onscreen career. Ten witnesses refused to testify and were cited for contempt. Over the next several years, HUAC investigated the directors of films such as *The Best Years of Our Lives*, *Gentleman's Agreement*, which criticized anti-Semitism and racism in housing, and *Salt of the Earth*, which chronicled the struggles of Mexican-born mine workers. HUAC targeted nearly every type of cultural producer—poets, artists, novelists, even comic book writers—based on the assumption that they used their art to indoctrinate the masses.

HUAC traveled around the country, holding hearings in major cities, with special interest in teachers and professors, government workers, and labor organizers. Sometimes those hearings backfired. In Detroit, for example, HUAC chair John Wood (D-GA) targeted left-leaning auto unionists and civil rights activists. But during HUAC's visit to Detroit in October 1953, four of the first six witnesses he subpoenaed were African American, infuriating black Detroiters and leading to a dramatic confrontation. Coleman Young, a black labor leader (and two decades later Detroit's first black mayor), took the stand and faced down Wood. Young had imbibed radical politics at a local barbershop in his childhood neighborhood on the city's west side, and in the 1940s he had lost jobs at Ford and the post office for his outspoken efforts in support of unionization. A talented organizer and speaker, Young moved into CIO leadership, supported Henry Wallace, and in 1951 was a founder of the leftist National Negro Labor Council, which pushed for workplace civil rights and challenged the expansion of the auto industry into the Jim Crow South. Young chided Wood for using the term "nigra." When Congressman Donald Jackson (D-CA) suggested that Young was downplaying the progress of blacks, Young snapped back: "You can't tell me that Jim Crow doesn't exist in California."[53] He became a folk hero.

AN ESCALATING COLD WAR

Many were the crimes and many the victims of America's domestic crusade against Communism, but the Cold War abroad took a greater toll. While the United States continued to send economic aid and military support to Europe, the struggle against Communism intensified elsewhere in the world, particularly East Asia. The collapse of Japanese imperial rule in Manchuria spurred a civil war in China between the Nationalists, led by the unpopular and corrupt Chiang Kai-shek, and insurgents led by Communist Mao Zedong. The Soviets, who shared a long border with China, had a complex and troubled relationship with the country, supporting both Mao and Chiang in their struggle against Japan during World War II. Stalin also kept a distance from Mao, uncertain that China was ready for Communism. Truman and his advisers saw China as a sidelight in the Cold War and calculated that the cost of intervention in the bitter civil war far outweighed any possible geopolitical gains.

That decision backfired. In 1949, Mao and the Communists won control of the mainland, leaving Chiang and his supporters to retreat to the island of Taiwan (also known as Formosa), where they would establish a government-in-exile. The Truman administration then faced the searing accusation that it had "lost" China. Dean Acheson, now serving as secretary of state, took the brunt of the criticism, with Republicans calling for his resignation. The charge would haunt the Democrats for decades to follow and would indelibly shape the next phase of the Cold War in Asia.

By 1950, hoping to deflect criticism, Acheson adopted a hard line on China. Although Mao had signaled that he would welcome a rapprochement with the United States to serve as a counterweight with the Soviets, even a hint of diplomacy with the new regime was impossible. Supporters of Chiang Kai-shek—the "China lobby"—pressured the United States to recognize the Nationalists in Formosa as the sole legitimate Chinese government. Rather than viewing Mao's People's Republic of China as a potential rival with the Soviet Union and pitting the two regimes against each other, Acheson and the Truman administration treated the new regime as a Soviet ally.

In the wake of the Chinese revolution, Truman and Acheson made two momentous decisions that would embroil the United States in two devastating wars. In May 1950, during a visit to Paris, Acheson pledged that the United States would support the French in their struggle to preserve their colony, Indochina, against Vietnamese revolutionaries led by Ho Chi Minh. Thus began a quarter century of American engagement in Vietnam. And in June, the United States, with the backing of the UN, launched a massive military operation in Korea that led to a devastating three-year war that would worsen U.S. relations with both the Soviet Union and China, ravage large parts of the Korean peninsula, and leave nearly two million combatants and civilians dead.

The Korean War

Few places seemed more remote and less central to the Cold War than the former Japanese colony of Korea. In 1945, after the Japanese defeat, the Americans and the Soviets divided the country in half, as Soviet troops occupied the area north of the thirty-eighth parallel and the United States controlled the region to the south. Like many postcolonial regimes, Koreans were bitterly divided over their political future: authoritarian but generally incompetent nationalists under Syngman Rhee gained power in the south and the brutal, pro-Soviet regime of Kim Il Sung controlled the north, both hoping to govern a unified Korea after the occupations ended.

On June 25, 1950, Kim Il Sung launched a surprise attack on the South. The North Koreans were well armed, disciplined, and ruthless. Kim had Stalin's backing and a formidable arsenal from his Soviet benefactors. Kim also believed, without warrant, that his invasion of the South would spur an anti-Rhee insurgency, bringing the civil war to a decisive close. Rhee's regime was indeed fragile. His party had been defeated in April elections, and the United States was, for a time, unwilling to do much to prop up his rule. Both Stalin and Kim had good reason to believe that the United States, which had been bolstering its military presence elsewhere in Asia, would not bother to interfere. In January, responding to criticism about the loss of China, Acheson delivered a major speech in which he announced the creation of a "defense perimeter" in East Asia, pledging that the United States would respond to any aggressive military action within its boundaries. Notably, he did not include Korea..

Within days after crossing the thirty-eighth parallel, North Korean troops rolled through Seoul, the capital and largest city in the south, and advanced to Pusan, on the southernmost tip of the peninsula. The Truman administration responded readily. Truman got the UN Security Council to issue a resolution denouncing North Korean aggression. It passed because the Soviets were, at the time, boycotting the UN for its refusal to seat the People's Republic of China on the Security Council. Truman then proceeded with military engagement that he called a "police action" in Korea without going to Congress for a declaration of war. The decision set a precedent of ignoring Article I, Section 8 of the Constitution, which gave Congress the authority to declare war. Thereafter most of America's wars, including Vietnam, would be the result of presidential action, without prior congressional declaration.

Truman argued that the "police action" was necessary given the possibility of Communist expansion in Asia. It was also expedient, defusing the political charge that he had "lost" China. "If this was allowed to go unchallenged," recalled the president of the North Korean invasion, "it would mean a third world war, just as similar incidents had brought on the second world war."[54]

Truman's decision proved, at first, tremendously popular. His approval rating, which had plummeted in the aftermath of the Chinese revolution, skyrocketed. The president's critics on both left and right joined the cause. For liberals—including Henry Wallace, who opposed the Truman Doctrine—the war was necessary to uphold the UN resolution and bring democracy to the Korean peninsula. For others across the political spectrum, war was necessary to prevent future Communist aggression. Even Taft and the embattled isolationists supported intervention in Korea.

Truman dispatched Pacific commander General Douglas MacArthur to devise a plan to push back the North Koreans and within days ordered the deployment of troops in South Korea. MacArthur was anything but cautious, and the administration gave him great license to conduct the war according to his own instincts. In the short run, that decision to give MacArthur a free hand seemed a brilliant move. But in the long term, it proved disastrous both militarily and diplomatically.

On September 15, 1950, MacArthur directed one of the riskiest invasions in modern military history, a landing at Inchon Bay. The sea at Inchon saw huge tidal fluctuations, at low tide and much of the bay was a mudflat. Ships could carry troops close to shore only a few times a month without the risk of being stranded. The troops needed to make landfall by scaling a huge seawall. The gamble, however, paid off. Inchon was poorly defended, and the landing allowed American troops to flank the North Korean troops. The American public hailed MacArthur for turning the fortunes of the war around.

From then on, the situation on the ground worsened rapidly. Mac-Arthur decided to launch air and ground attacks north of the thirty-eighth parallel and threatened to bring troops up to the Korean-Chinese border. In response, the new People's Republic of China began massing troops on the border and joined in aid of the North Koreans in early November. Although MacArthur boasted that the war would be over by Christmas, the next few months were devastating. The North Koreans and their Chinese allies drove the UN troops back south of the thirty-eighth parallel in some of the bloodiest battles in any modern war; nearly ten thousand American soldiers were injured or killed. In late November, in one of the biggest slip-ups in his presidency, President Truman offhandedly suggested that the United States was considering the use of nuclear weapons in Korea. This drew howls of protest from America's allies.

In January and February 1951, MacArthur and the American troops succeeded in pushing the Chinese and North Koreans back to the thirty-eighth parallel, opening up the possibility for a cease-fire, which Truman and Acheson were considering as a prelude to negotiations. But MacArthur wanted much more—nothing short of a complete victory in North Korea and the unconditional surrender of China. To make his case, MacArthur held unauthorized interviews with the news media, criticizing his own commander-in-chief. Hinting that he did not trust Truman, the vain Mac-Arthur suggested that he himself negotiate directly with the Chinese. At home, hawks on the president's right hailed MacArthur's aggressive stance and lambasted Truman for not heeding his advice. Truman and Acheson were furious at what they saw as the general's reckless posturing and insubordination and decided to relieve MacArthur of his command. On April 11, 1951, that decision went public. The general returned home a hero, while Truman's critics shredded the decision as capitulation to Communism.

Over the next two years, the war in Korea bogged down: it was not a limited engagement as Truman had promised; nor was it punctuated by many decisive victories for either side. The United States stepped up air attacks on North Korean troops and targets, eventually dropping some 635,000 tons of bombs on the peninsula, more than it had used in the whole Pacific theater during World War II. Nearly every urban center in North Korea was reduced to rubble. At least a million North and South Koreans died as the result of the war, and 33,629 American soldiers were killed; more than 100,000 were seriously injured; and hundreds of thousands more were sickened by dysentery, bacterial infections, and other water- and insect-borne diseases. The conflict ended with an armistice on July 27, 1953, a few months after Truman left office, leaving North and South Korea divided at the thirty-eighth parallel.

Eisenhower

Truman could have run for reelection in 1952, since he was the last president not to be bound by the twenty-second amendment to the Constitution, which was ratified in 1951 and limited presidents to two terms in office. But the Democrats were beleaguered. Although the president had unleashed a costly Cold War, overseen a massive military buildup, and fueled an anti-Communist crusade at home, he faced harsh criticism from the right. The Republican Party platform criticized Truman and Acheson's containment policy for leaving "countless human beings to a despotism and Godless terrorism." It predictably denounced the Truman administration for having lost China and fumbled the Korean War. It also sanctimoniously announced that "there are no Communists in the Republican Party," suggesting that Truman's party, for all of its zealous anti-Communism, was somehow teeming with leftists.[59]

The Republicans chose a candidate who seemed highly qualified to carry forth America's Cold War aggressively: retired general Dwight David Eisenhower. A career military man who had become the mostly ceremonial president of Columbia University in 1948, he neither had political experience nor obvious partisan inclinations. Both parties had courted him.

On the campaign trail, Ike took a bellicose position, pledging to fight for the "liberation" of those who lived under Communist tyranny. But Eisenhower swiftly ended the costly, unpopular Korean War. The United States agreed to an armistice on July 27, 1953, leaving North and South Korea divided at the thirty-eighth parallel. In practice, Eisenhower's foreign policy differed little from his predecessor's. Both Truman and Eisenhower were committed to the policy of containment and maintained a large standing military. Both supported the National Security Act, and both supported the expansion of the CIA and its power to operate in secrecy.

McCarthyism

Tensions with the Soviets, the Chinese revolution, and the Korean War all intensified the domestic crusade against the red menace. The anti-Communist movement got a new face and a new name with the activities of a formerly obscure first-term senator. After three undistinguished years in office, Joseph McCarthy (R-WI) discovered the political value of red-baiting. First elected to the Senate in the anti-Democratic wave of 1946, McCarthy was a devout Roman Catholic, a short-tempered alcoholic and gambler, and like many in the GOP, a strong pro-business voice. He supported Taft-Hartley, allied himself closely with the home building industry, and used his position to denounce public housing as a threat to free enterprise.

Not until 1950 did McCarthy blast himself onto the national stage, at an unlikely venue: a Lincoln Day address to a group of Republican women in Wheeling, West Virginia. "The State Department is infested with communists," he charged. "I have here in my hand a list of 205—a list of names that were made known to the Secretary of State as being members of the Communist Party and who nevertheless are still working and shaping policy in the State Department."[55] The charges stung because, at that moment, McCarthy's fellow Republicans were accusing Dean Acheson and the State Department's China hands—its experts on the region—of treason for aiding and abetting the Chinese revolution. Although McCarthy's numbers were slippery, his charges prompted the Senate to launch its own investigations of subversion in the federal government and even in the U.S. military.

McCarthy initially riveted the nation with his investigations of reds, but eventually he lost the support of the news media, a growing segment of the public, and president Dwight Eisenhower. Eisenhower had remained silent as McCarthy ascended to the national stage. But the president grew embarrassed by McCarthy's bombast. In March 1953, CBS news reporter Edward R. Murrow, a pioneering investigative journalist and hardly a Communist sympathizer, dispassionately unraveled McCarthy's techniques, demonstrating that many of the charges that he had hurled were based on unreliable testimony, secondhand evidence or rumor, and outdated information. But McCarthy, unstoppable, turned his attention to the military, accusing the army, navy, and air force of harboring Communists and other subversives.

McCarthy's inflammatory charges prompted the media to dig into the story for themselves. By the fall, Murrow was on the trail of Milo Radulovich, an air force lieutenant who fell afoul of a military regulation that found an individual a "security risk if he has close and continuing associations with communists or people believed to have communist sympathies."[56] Radulovich, who had no leftist affiliations, faced dismissal because he refused to cut ties with his father, who had once belonged to a Communist front organization, and his sister, who was thought to be subversive because of her support for liberal causes. Under pressure after Murrow's exposé, the air force reinstated Radulovich.

By early 1954, McCarthy was under siege both from the new Democratic majority in Congress and from fellow Republicans whose backing he had lost. Millions of Americans tuned into the thirty-six-day-long Army-McCarthy hearings, broadcast by the three major television networks between April and June 1954. Shabby, often unshaven, and embittered, McCarthy was a made-for-TV villain, harshly interrupting the proceedings with his shrill demand, repeated again and again, for "point of order."

Behind the scenes, Eisenhower unraveled McCarthy's plans by squashing his efforts to subpoena key military officials and withholding key information from the investigation. Finally, on June 9, McCarthy lashed out against the army's attorney, the whip-smart and poised Joseph Welch, accusing his law firm of employing a Communist. In words that would forever scar McCarthy, Welch snapped back, "I think I never really gauged your cruelty or your recklessness." When McCarthy continued his aggressive line of questioning, the exasperated Welch finally asked, "Have you no sense of decency, sir, at long last? Have you left no sense of decency?" McCarthy fought back, but Welch interrupted again, stating that he was finished. The audience burst into applause, leaving McCarthy stunned.[57]

Even with McCarthy discredited, the anti-Communist battle was far from over. HUAC continued to hold hearings, and suspected Communists faced ongoing interrogations. Investigators at the state and local level continued to ferret out suspected Communists. The Philadelphia board of education, for example, fired several teachers who pleaded their Fifth Amendment rights when HUAC held hearings on Communism in the public schools.

All together, about ten to twelve thousand suspected Communists lost their jobs, usually because they refused to cooperate with investigations or renounce the Communist Party. Those without U.S. citizenship were often deported. Two suspected Communists, Ethel and Julius Rosenberg, were executed after being convicted of conspiracy to commit espionage on behalf of the Soviet Union. The Rosenberg trial generated an intense controversy over whether two innocent Americans had been convicted. Later evidence suggested that Julius had indeed passed secrets to the Soviets, though it is less certain that the information jeopardized American security and warranted the death penalty.

More commonly, uncooperative witnesses or those convicted of membership in subversive organizations faced jail time. Folk singer Pete Seeger, who helped popularize the civil rights anthem "We Shall Overcome" and had been a Communist through 1950, paid the price for defying his interrogators. Called before HUAC in 1955, Seeger offered to talk about his music and even to sing, but he refused to answer questions about his political affiliations: "I think these are very improper questions for any American to be asked, especially under such compulsion as this."[58] Convicted of contempt of Congress, Seeger was sentenced to a year in prison, and though he only served a day, his successful career was derailed. For seventeen years, he was barred from appearing on television and was turned away from major concert venues. Many of his recordings disappeared from stores.

Although the anti-Communist crusade barely slowed, Eisenhower's presidency seemed tranquil. The United States had risen to economic prominence. Observers celebrated American prosperity and consumerism. But the Cold War did not abate. Beneath a thin veneer of consensus and self-congratulation, the unresolved tensions of the Truman years persisted, particularly the poisonous divisions of race and the realities of an economy and consumer society that had brought unprecedented wealth to the United States but relied on workers and citizens, at home and abroad, who seldom saw the direct benefits of their hard work.

CHAPTER 9

IN AT LEAST
MODEST COMFORT:
POSTWAR PROSPERITY AND
ITS DISCONTENTS

FIFTH AVENUE BETWEEN 42nd Street and Central Park South bustled with commerce in the fall of 1946, the sidewalks packed with fashionable shoppers like Betty Goldstein, a stylish journalist who often spent part of her lunch hour checking out the latest ready-to-wear fashions. Business had picked up fast when the war ended, in part because of pent-up demand and unprecedented savings rates during the war. Without many opportunities to spend their wages wartime workers had squirreled away their paychecks in savings bonds and bank accounts, totaling some $150 billion. Even though she was just a few years out of college, Betty had money to spend. One of her favorite places was the luxurious Bergdorf Goodman store just a few blocks from her office. She was not prone to extravagance, but she adored black cashmere sweaters and occasionally splurged on high-end items, like her favorite accessory, a pair of Gucci gloves.[1]

Betty's office, at 11 East 51st Street, occupied a once-grand townhouse. As she climbed the building's imposing granite steps, a Bergdorf bag in hand, it was possible, if you did not know her Jewish name, to imagine her as the great-granddaughter of John Pierce, the Granite King, the nineteenth-century magnate who had built the magnificent stone edifice as a monument to his wealth. Or perhaps she was an Astor, the old-money mercantile family who had had lived at 11 East 51st just a few decades earlier, before the rich moved farther uptown.

The Granite King or the Astors would have cringed if they had ever returned to their ancestral home. The obsequious servants were long gone, their hush supplanted by the click of typewriters and frequent outbursts of heated debate. Their house had suffered, at least from the viewpoint of Gilded Age America, a grim fate: it was now the headquarters of the United Electrical, Radio, and Machine Workers of America, known as the UE. Between 1946 and 1952, Betty worked as a reporter for the *UE News*, the union's muckraking newspaper. "She bubbled over with energy," one of her friends recalled of those days. Despite her fashion sense, she was no Astor. She "talked in spurts, rarely finishing a sentence, her mind racing so fast the words couldn't keep up with it."

Born in 1921 in Peoria, Illinois, Betty had grown up in comfort. Her father owned a successful jewelry business. Her mother, who had written for the local daily before having children, stayed at home to raise her and her two siblings. One of the smartest students in her class and one of the most ambitious—"I want success and fame," she told a classmate—she left Peoria behind for elite, all-female Smith College. Smith's atmosphere mixed New England propriety, intellectual rigor, and at the time, a zeal for social justice. Her professors, many of them liberal internationalists, some even Socialists and Communists, did not protect their students from the world. By her junior year, Betty was taking courses on social policy, learning about psychology, and studying economics. On the recommendation of one of her professors, she spent most of the summer of 1941 at the Highlander Folk School in rural East Tennessee, a sort of summer camp for radicals that trained generations of civil rights and labor activists, where students read the poetry of the Harlem Renaissance, learned about Indian nationalist Mohandas K. Gandhi, and debated the tactics of sit-down strikes and draft resistance.

By the mid-1940s, Betty had discovered her lifelong passions—labor, politics, and feminism. Her prose was sharp and invariably radical. She lauded the CIO for giving workers "a power of their own to match that of their bosses." She believed that union wages and job security would give women financial independence and access to the booming postwar consumer culture. But she also worried about the rightward turn in American politics. She watched with anger as the UE saw its membership plummet under the Taft-Hartley Act. She lambasted HUAC, which hounded suspected Communists in the labor movement, many of them her colleagues.

Nearly everything that she did the next fifty years would touch on these issues, beginning with her work as a labor journalist in the 1940s, as a political organizer in Queens in the 1950s, and—under her married name, Betty Friedan—as the best-selling author of *The Feminine Mystique* and founder of the National Organization for Women in the 1960s. In the aftermath of the postwar anti-Communist crusade, she downplayed her radical past, but it indelibly shaped her career.

POSTWAR PROSPERITY

Betty worked for the UE during one of the longest economic booms in American history. The gross domestic product had increased by 4.8 percent in Truman's last four years. The national unemployment rate fell before reaching an all-time low of 2.9 percent in January 1953. Globally, the United States enjoyed unchallenged industrial power. By the late 1940s, more than half of the world's manufactured goods were American-made, including four-fifths of all cars. Almost two-thirds of the world's oil bubbled up from American soil, and more than half of the world's steel was forged in American foundries.

Postwar prosperity lifted the wages of tens of millions of American workers, in large part because big companies and powerful unions had successfully bargained for generous employment contracts. At the peak, in 1953, over a third of all American workers belonged to unions, including most of those in defense production, auto assembly, electrical manufacturing, steelmaking, and meatpacking. In the industrial belt that extended from New England down the Eastern Seaboard, across the Appalachians through the coal mining towns of Pennsylvania and West Virginia, and along the southern Great Lakes, unionization rates topped 50 percent. Even nonunion workers benefited. To compete with unionized firms and attract the best workers, many nonunion employers raised pay and offered good benefits.

Left Behind: African Americans and Farmworkers

Not everyone benefited from the postwar boom equally. African Americans had made big advances in wartime defense industries but saw only incremental gains in the two decades afterward. In the South—which recruited northern manufacturers looking for low-wage workers—blacks were usually frozen out of industry altogether. Regardless of their skill and experience, blacks were stuck on the bottom rung of the corporate ladder, in dangerous, unpleasant jobs, hauling heavy equipment, doing janitorial work, and stoking furnaces. Beginning in the late 1940s, many of those entry-level jobs disappeared, as companies like General Motors replaced unskilled workers with new "automated" labor-saving technology. Unlike whites, blacks had few chances to move up the ladder. Only 67 out of 11,125 skilled workers at GM were black in 1960. Without discrimination, many would have qualified for those jobs.

As Americans grew wealthier during the postwar boom, they bought more food. Food producers scrambled to meet a nearly insatiable demand for flash-frozen, canned, and ready-to-eat processed foods. Meat consumption skyrocketed, leading to the consolidation of small farms into enormous enterprises that factory-farmed chickens and pigs and mass-produced beef and dairy products. Growing demand for fruit and vegetables also transformed farming. In places like California's Central Valley, with rich soil but an arid climate, irrigation transformed farms into places where lettuce, tomatoes, grapes, and a huge variety of fruits and vegetables could be grown most of the year. In the 1930s, writer Carey McWilliams described the region's farms as "factories in the fields." By 1945, California had 5,939 farms of more than one thousand acres each, covering nearly twenty-five million acres.[2] American growers also expanded their investments overseas. United Fruit and Dole purchased produce from a network of vast plantations in Latin America, the Caribbean, and the Pacific islands, eager to capitalize on Americans' growing demand for tropical fruits like bananas, grapefruits, and pineapples, formerly luxury items.

Agribusinesses at home and abroad depended on a ready supply of cheap labor. Southern farms still relied on methods of labor dating back to emancipation, trapping blacks as debt peons and sharecroppers in conditions of near bondage. California relied on migrant farm laborers, many Mexican, who lived in converted chicken coops, cabins, trailers, or poorly ventilated huts. In fields and orchards, they were exposed to harmful pesticides and chemical fertilizers. The bracero program peaked in the mid-1950s, with some 450,000 Mexican guest workers crossing the border per year to work on American farms. American agribusinesses also relied on an army of landless peasants who picked coffee beans and fruit in Guatemala, cut sugarcane in Cuba and Jamaica, toiled on pineapple plantations in Hawaii, and harvested cocoa and coffee beans in Colombia.

Unlike industrial workers, whose wages, hours, and working conditions were regulated under New Deal legislation and often protected by vigilant unions, American farmworkers were on their own. They did not have the right to collective bargaining. Growers punished those who complained about their working and living conditions, sent injured or ill workers back to their homelands rather than treating them, and turned over labor union organizers to the authorities for deportation. Farmworkers also did not have a minimum wage. They were not eligible for Social Security. Growers profited from large government agricultural subsidies but did not pass the benefits down to their workers.

The "Family Wage" and Women Workers

For all the travails of agricultural workers, most commentators could not help but notice that a large share of white, blue-collar workers—especially those in unionized industries—were better off than ever. By 1960, about 60 percent of American households, including most of those headed by unionized workers, belonged to the middle class, earning between $5,000 and $10,000 per year, depending on family size. Colonies of cottages and hunting cabins, owned by auto- and steelworkers, sprang up in the northern Great Lakes, in the Alleghenies and Poconos, and along the Jersey shore. Sociologists talked of the "embourgeoisement" of American workers, arguing that as they grew wealthier, America would become a classless society. They believed conflict between workers and bosses would soon become a thing of the past.

For the most part, blue-collar workers expected a "family wage," namely that a male breadwinner's single paycheck should be large enough to support his wife and family. During the immediate postwar years, many unions supported a suspension of seniority rules so that men who had fought in the war could move back into their former jobs, even if that meant laying off women workers. For their part, many women welcomed the opportunity to leave behind assembly lines, to return home and have children.

Over her long career, Betty Friedan wrote about a lot of topics, but she took special interest in women's issues, especially the situation of women workers. After a brief period of resettlement in 1946 and 1947, when factories laid off women and hired returning servicemen in their places, women's employment began to rise again. By 1953, 48 percent of single women worked, as did 26 percent of married women, comprising a larger part of the workforce than they had during World War II. Single women needed paychecks; if their husbands had died in the war or returned disabled, their families depended on women's work. The family wage was insufficient for a growing number of households, which could not subsist on one check alone.

Betty Friedan had a special vantage point on these changes. Her employer, the United Electrical Workers, represented more women than any other union in the country. No industry had been more feminized than electrical manufacturing. Sophisticated aircraft required elaborate electronics; so too did tanks and jeeps and cars. The military and the general public had an insatiable demand for radios. While manufacturers sometimes resisted hiring women workers until circumstances forced them to do so, electrical manufacturers valued female laborers.

Electrical workers were also among the best organized and best paid in the country. When Betty started working for the UE, it was the third-largest industrial union in the country and one of the twelve out of thirty-five CIO unions led by Communists. The UE represented more than 600,000 workers, including those employed by the industry's giants, General Electric, Westinghouse, and RCA. Few unions put more energy into helping advance women workers. UE organizers pushed for equal pay for equal work, demanded the protection of seniority for women workers, and negotiated for still-unheard-of maternity leave policies, so that women could resume working after they had children. For Betty, the UE was part of a "revolution" in women's work, one that could be a model for improving the lives of all Americans.

The generational legacy of women's workforce participation in World War II set the stage for the women's movement of the 1960s and 1970s. Older married women who had gone to work for the first time during the war saw their young daughters join them. Those daughters might have taken time out of the workforce in the late 1940s and early 1950s to marry and have their own daughters and sons, but after childbearing, their wartime skills and a booming economy brought them back to paid employment. In 1956 the average age of women workers was forty; it had been thirty-two in 1940. By the 1960s, the granddaughters of women who had gone to work in World War II could point to two generations of working women as role models. Betty Friedan celebrated those changes. "Men," she wrote in one of her first articles, published in 1943, "there's a revolution cooking in your own kitchens—revolutions of the forgotten female who is finally waking up to the fact that she can produce things besides babies."

THE BABY BOOM

The expansion of women's paid work came into collision with postwar norms about gender roles and the family. The period from the mid-1940s to the early 1960s saw a celebration of the male-headed nuclear family, one that belied the gradual change in the relationship of women and the workplace. At its core was a profound and still unresolved conflict: how should women negotiate paid labor outside the home with the demands of child-rearing? For all the shifts in labor, domestic life remained women's domain. The normative mother would watch over her children in new informal "family rooms" that replaced the formal parlors of houses built between the 1840s and the 1920s.

Magazines geared to housewives, such as *Family Circle*, *Good Housekeeping*, and *Better Homes and Gardens*, saw their circulation skyrocket. *Good Housekeeping*'s subscription base doubled between 1943 and 1962, reaching over five million. In those pages, women could discover new recipes, read helpful hints for cleaning and household organization, and peruse advertisements for detergents, appliances, and child care products. And if they fretted about relationships, whether with their boyfriends, husbands, or kids, they could turn to advice columnists, most notably the pseudonymous Ann Landers (launched in 1942) and Abigail Van Buren (launched in 1956), who were syndicated in papers nationwide and, from the mid-1950s to the end of the century, written separately by Esther Lederer and Pauline Phillips, twin sisters, originally from Iowa.

Young Newlyweds

The family-centered culture of the postwar years resulted from a profound demographic shift that remade American households and the nation's very landscape. In 1950 the age of marriage fell to a historic low: the average woman married at 20.3 years, and the average man at 22.8. Along with marriage came children: families grew larger between the mid-1940s and the early 1960s, reaching an average of four children per woman of childbearing age. Even with more women in the paid labor market, heterosexual marriage and stay-at-home motherhood remained the norm and the ideal.

For most of American history, marriage had often been primarily a legal matter, bringing two families and their property together. But in the twentieth century—especially after World War II—many Americans came to see marriage as a vehicle for emotional fulfillment. The days of arranged marriages or loveless partnerships for the sake of children and inheritance faded as the marital bond was affective and emotional. In the 1940s and 1950s, clergymen, psychologists, and journalists used a new term, *companionate marriage*, to describe the new normal. Men and women were bonded by love, even if marriage was still legally a contractual relationship. A happy marriage should produce children—that went without saying—but it should also be personally fulfilling for both husband and wife.

Betty joined that trend. At age twenty-six, rather late for a woman of her generation, she married Carl, a theatrical producer. For Betty, the reasons for marriage were simple. She described herself as having "a pathological fear of being alone," but even more than that, she saw marriage as a vehicle for emotional fulfillment. In a paper she had written at Smith, she made what was a bold statement for the time: "marriage means togetherness." Like many marriages, however, Betty's was not a model of togetherness. She and her husband frequently argued. Having a family also came at a cost to her professional career. When she lost her job at the UE in 1952, she attributed it to the fact that she was pregnant with her second child. She resented that, despite her commitment to feminism, she remained the primary caregiver. Still, as a young mother, she remained politically engaged in the semisuburban housing development in Queens where she lived between 1950 and 1956. There, while her children frolicked in the garden, she organized mothers to protest rent hikes, push for civil rights, and improve the local school's curriculum.

Spock

Many of the young parents who were Betty's neighbors had come of age during the austerity of the Depression and the shared sacrifice of war. During the ordeal, they had made do with hand-me-down clothes. During the war, they had often been left to fend for themselves with Daddy off to war and Mommy working in factories, growing the Victory Garden, or mobilizing civilian defense. After nearly two decades of scarcity, emotional and economic, postwar parents put more energy than ever into raising happy, comfortable children.

Millions looked for advice on how to bring up baby, and they turned to experts other than their parents or grandparents. The most influential was Dr. Benjamin Spock. The son of an elite Connecticut family, Spock had attended Yale, graduated at the top of his class at Columbia Medical School, and spent six years studying and undergoing psychoanalysis in the 1930s, while beginning his career as a pediatrician. In 1946, Spock exploded the conventional wisdom—the emphasis on discipline, structure, and denial in childrearing— in *The Common Sense Book of Baby and Child Care*. He assumed a gentle, reassuring tone: "Bringing up your child won't be a complicated job if you take it easy, trust your own instincts, and follow the directions that the doctor gives you."[3] Spock also reinforced the notion that young mothers should stay at home with their children, one that even Betty Friedan took to heart. No book, other than the Bible, sold more copies. By the best estimate, about one-fifth of all American households in the postwar years had Spock on their bookshelves. One journalist described the book as one that "many mothers clutch like a pacifier" because it so relieved their anxieties.[4]

A NATION OF HOMEOWNERS

Americans had long valued domesticity and home ownership, but for most Americans through World War II, owning a home had been an unattainable dream. From 1929 to 1945, private housing development in the United States had nearly halted. The banking collapse during the Depression—not to mention the decline in most Americans' wages and savings—crippled the housing industry. During World War II, the federal government had diverted construction materials to the defense industry. Skilled workers found jobs building aircraft or contributing to the military's rapid construction of barracks, airstrips, and temporary encampments on the ground in Europe and the Pacific.

The Federal Government, Home Ownership, and Race
Still, the federal government had laid the groundwork for the postwar housing boom in the depths of the Great Depression. In 1933 the Home Owners Loan Corporation made low-interest financing available to those who wanted

to buy or repair their homes. In 1934, Roosevelt signed a law creating the Federal Housing Administration (FHA), which brought the government into the mortgage market. The FHA guaranteed mortgages, allowing lenders to offer long-term (usually thirty-year) loans with low down payments (usually 10 percent of the asking price). As late as the 1920s, home buyers had had to put as much as 50 percent down on a home and pay off the remaining amount in a period of about five years. Finally, the 1944 GI Bill extended low-interest home loans to returning veterans. The impact of these programs was nothing short of spectacular. Home ownership rates skyrocketed, from about 40 percent of all Americans in 1930 to over 60 percent in 1960. Builders scrambled to meet Americans' almost insatiable demand for new homes.

The housing boom came with one big restriction: keep "undesirables" out. During the 1920s, as African Americans began to migrate into American cities, housing developers devised strategies to keep new developments all white. Racially restrictive covenants, part of the language in deeds to most houses built between the 1920s and the late 1940s, used blunt language: "This property cannot be occupied by Negroes" or "colored" or "Ethiopians" (all terms referring to people of African descent) or "Orientals" or "Malays" or "Hindus" (people of Asian descent). Many covenants specified that properties could be sold or rented to "Caucasians only" (a term that referred to the alleged origins of Europeans in the Caucasus Mountains of Russia). "Semites," people of Jewish descent, usually appeared on the list of undesirables as well.

Racial categories also shaped federal housing policy. Beginning in the mid-1930s, the Home Owners Loan Corporation prepared "security maps" that determined what neighborhoods were eligible for government-backed home loans. The maps used a four-color scheme, designating areas as green (A), blue (B), yellow (C), and red (D). Neighborhoods colored green were the "best," blue were "still desirable," yellow were "definitely declining," and red were "hazardous." The presence of even a handful of blacks ensured a D rating. Only whites could get loans in top-ranked neighborhoods, including almost all the new suburbs that sprang up after World War II. Blacks, on the other hand, found themselves frozen out.

With these guidelines in place, real estate brokers considered it unethical to support racial integration. From the 1930s through the 1960s, the National Association of Real Estate Boards stated that realtors "should never be instrumental in introducing to a neighborhood a character of property or occupancy, members of any race or nationality, or any individual whose presence will be clearly detrimental to property values in a neighborhood."[5] Lest there be any confusion, an industry brochure offered guidance:

> The prospective buyer might be a bootlegger who would cause considerable annoyance to his neighbors, a madam who had a number of call girls on her string, a gangster who wants a screen for his activities by living in a better neighborhood, a colored man of means who was giving his children a college education and thought they were entitled to live among whites. . . . No matter what the motive or character of the would-be purchaser, if the deal would institute a form of blight, then certainly the well-meaning broker must work against its consummation.[6]

The result was that the vast new suburbs that appeared almost overnight in places like Park Forest, Illinois, and Lakewood, California. The famous Levittowns, the first on former farmland on New York's Long Island, the second just outside Philadelphia, were all white. Their developer, William Levitt, used the newest mass-production technology, with standardized components, to build new houses quickly and inexpensively. Levittowns attracted GIs and other first-time home buyers eligible for FHA and VA loans. Levitt's brokers refused to show homes to prospective black homeowners, even though blacks were eager to move to new houses in the job-rich suburbs. In Pennsylvania, Levittown even turned away a group of black World War II veterans who showed up in uniform.

LIFE IN THE CONSUMERS' REPUBLIC

One value that suburbanites held as dearly as segregation was privacy. Urban apartments were cramped, especially during the housing shortages of the Depression and World War II. People jostled together on sidewalks, subways, and buses. Because green space was at a premium, urbanites crowded together, sometimes tens of thousands at a time, on beaches, in parks, and at amusement parks.

By contrast, huge swaths of lawn separated suburban houses. Children played in backyard sandboxes and on swing sets instead of public playgrounds. Over the course of the 1950s and into the 1960s, private backyard swimming pools and neighborhood swim clubs (which, of course, reflected racial segregation) replaced public pools. The only major public events that brought suburbanites together out of doors on a regular basis were youth sports leagues and high school sporting events, both of which proliferated in the child-centered culture after World War II.

Postwar suburban homes were small universes of children, appliances, toys, food, and fulfillment. Manufacturers scrambled to cater to the needs of suburban families. Advertisers attempted to create new desires. Stores offered a cornucopia of exciting new goods for every member of the family.

The center of activity was the eat-in kitchen, which often had large windows overlooking the backyard, where Mom could watch the children play while preparing meals. The kitchen showcased the latest consumer technologies, from electric toasters to power blenders, both introduced after World War II. Homeowners with enough money could install one of the newly invented electric dishwashers. New electric garbage disposal systems allowed Mom to scrape off the dishes and wash the waste down the drain. The most useful kitchen appliance of all was General Electric's 1947 combination refrigerator-freezer, substantially larger than earlier stand-alone refrigerators or older iceboxes, where blocks of ice, used for cooling, took up much of the space. As refrigerator-freezers dropped in price, innovative manufacturers produced frozen foods and packagers developed new storage systems, including Tupperware boxes and cellophane sandwich bags.

Tuning In: TV and Mass Culture

Usually adjoining the kitchen was the family room, an informal gathering place, new to postwar houses, where the family could relax. There children's board games filled the shelves and toys littered the carpet. Carefully arranged furniture gave everyone a view of the newest and most popular household appliance, the television.

For decades, inventors had experimented with the tubes and circuitry and broadcast technologies for what would become television, but as late as the 1930s, TVs were still a bizarre, futuristic novelty. In 1946, after more than four years of making radios and radar and other electronic equipment for the military, RCA, a leading electronics manufacturer, expanded its production of TVs, encouraged that year by the licensing of twenty-six new television stations by the Federal Communications Commission.

At first, TV was a luxury item, even as broadcasters began to build a communications infrastructure and manufacturers put vast resources into improving the technology. In 1948 the Democrats and Republicans welcomed the televised coverage of their conventions, but only about 3 percent of Americans, most of them wealthy, had televisions. Still, the innovations paid off: by 1960, about 44 million American households—nine in every ten—had a television.[7] TVs were affordable and ubiquitous.

Television had all sorts of unexpected impacts on American society. As TV watching took off, movie theaters began to close, although for a time, "drive-in" theaters, where viewers could watch movies in the privacy of their cars, flourished. Live theaters, music venues, and even sports arenas saw attendance drop. Radio listenership began to decline, although fears of radio's death were greatly exaggerated. Because more and more Americans spent more and more time in their cars, radio had a captive and growing audience. Listening to the radio and watching TV, with the family and maybe some close friends, changed how Americans interacted in public.

With only three networks broadcasting, there was a limited repertoire of shows for people to watch. Television created a sense of commonality among Americans. Whether you lived in Dubuque, Iowa, or Los Angeles, California, or Florence, Alabama, whether you were a stranger, a family member, or a co-worker, you could talk about what you watched last night. Americans led more private lives, but at coffee klatches and cocktail parties, at barbecues and in bars, at the grocery store and at the desk, everyone could talk about TV.

On January 19, 1953, the day before President Eisenhower's inauguration, more than two-thirds of America's television-watching households turned to NBC's slapstick comedy *I Love Lucy*, to watch a hapless husband pace around a hospital waiting room as he waited for his goofy wife to give birth. The show coincided, happily on the same night, with news announcements about the birth of the first son of costars Lucille Ball and Desi Arnaz.[8]

TV also gave a boost to consumer culture, especially for children. Mass TV was only a few years old when companies realized that children spent hours a day in front of the small screen. In 1951 toymaker Hasbro broke new ground with commercials for Mr. Potato Head, the first toy to be advertised on TV. Over the next few years, toy companies introduced new products during children's shows and began spinning off kids' clothing, memorabilia, and toys from popular movies and programs. The sales of coonskin caps skyrocketed after Disney's successful 1955 film *Davy Crockett*. And Disney launched a full line of Mickey Mouse hats, musical instruments, records, and posters from its popular variety show, *The Mickey Mouse Club*.

TV watching was the most visible manifestation of what many prominent social critics called "mass culture," one that crushed individualism and group identities. Elites fretted that American culture would become "lowbrow," a term popularized in the 1950s. (It had originated in the science of craniology, to describe the wide brows and low foreheads that nineteenth-century scientists believed characterized intellectually inferior people.) Norman Cousins, the editor of the *Saturday Review of Literature*, argued that TV was "such an assault against the human mind, such a mobilized attack on the imagination, such an invasion against good taste as no other communication medium has known."[9] Even riskier, worried other mass culture critics, if every American watched the same three commercial networks, listened to near-identical newscasts, and watched the same advertisements, they would be subject to manipulation and propaganda.

For all the fears of mass culture, television, especially in its early days, played a critical role in shaping Americans' understanding of their own society, politics, and the world. Early television programs offered lengthy news stories and detailed coverage of political events. In 1950, Senator Estes Kefauver (D-TN) invited cameras into Senate hearings that he led on crime, moving the issue to center stage in policy debates. Kefauver became a national figure and, in 1956, was the Democratic Party's vice-presidential candidate. TV also brought issues that were remote to many Americans right into their living rooms, from haunting film footage of nuclear explosions to images of civil rights protesters facing off club-wielding police. TV did provide mindless entertainment. It made the fortunes of advertisers. But for better or worse, it also became a political force. Politicians rose and fell on camera. Social movements could vault from obscurity to global prominence if the news cameras turned in their direction.

Air-conditioned America

TV was but one technology that kept people indoors. The window electric air conditioner, first sold in 1951, transformed everyday life, particularly in the South and Southwest. Tens of millions of Americans thereafter drew their windows shut on muggy evenings, relaxing in the artificially cool air. As one observer put it in 1959, "people have just decided that it's part of the American standard of living, something we're all entitled to, just as we're entitled to heat in the winter and food on the table."[10] By 1970 more than half of all houses in the South had air conditioners, as did nearly every store, movie theater, restaurant, hospital, and hotel. In new housing developments, front porches became shrunken appendages or disappeared altogether. Who needed to sit outside when relief came at the turn of a switch?

Climate control had its biggest effect on industry and commerce, where it had been in use, on a very limited scale, since the turn of the century. Firms could now safely locate factories in places where the heat would otherwise wilt workers, damage fragile equipment, or overheat motors. Phoenix, Arizona, where temperatures regularly rose to 110 degrees in the summer, had just 65,000 people in 1940. It grew sevenfold in the next two decades, the desert blooming with defense manufacturers lured by cool indoor air and, just as important, a "favorable business climate," made possible by loose regulation, low taxes, and, under Taft-Hartley, open shop laws.[11]

Automobility

Suburbanites depended on automobiles to navigate the sprawling, decentralized landscape. It was difficult to walk to shops, sports, and schools. Many new suburbs did not have sidewalks. Few had traditional pedestrian-oriented downtowns; even fewer had good public transit systems. Instead, stores clustered in privately owned shopping malls, surrounded by vast parking lots.

No industry prospered more in the postwar years than auto manufacturing, and no company more than General Motors, then the largest corporation in the United States. During the war, GM had become a massive defense contractor, turning its factories, almost overnight, over to the production of aircraft engines, tanks, armored vehicles, the amphibious "duck" transport vehicle, and ammunition and torpedoes. When the war ended, GM made the transition back to civilian production with extraordinary success. Within a few years, the company's five passenger car divisions, each marketed toward buyers of a different socioeconomic status—Chevrolet, Pontiac, Oldsmobile, Buick, and Cadillac—captured more than 40 percent of the domestic car market. The 1949 models, the first to be totally reengineered inside and out to reflect a new postwar aesthetic, were GM's proudest. Thousands gathered at New York's Waldorf Astoria hotel to view the "sleek and sybaritic specimens of automotive splendor," among them a $30,000 Cadillac, the most expensive car ever built. GM also introduced its newest innovation, the Dyna-Flow automatic transmission.

In the fifteen years following World War II, car ownership more than doubled, from 28.2 million in 1945 to 61.7 million in 1960. That year 77 percent of American households owned a car.[12] The rise of the car had enormous economic implications, particularly for the consumption of oil and gas. Between 1948 and 1972, American petroleum consumption tripled. And although the United States had produced most of its own oil in the first half of the twentieth century, it depended more and more on foreign oil beginning in the 1950s, when about 10 percent of American oil came from overseas. By the 1970s, 36 percent of American oil was imported.[13]

EISENHOWER'S MIDDLE GROUND

Who was responsible for postwar American prosperity? What policies would strengthen the national economy? Business and politics had coexisted in tension for most of the first half of the twentieth century. Progressives had railed against monopolies and the corruption of government by big business. New Dealers argued for a mixed economy, using the power of government to create jobs, construct infrastructure, and provide a favorable climate for organized labor. But since the great strike wave of 1946, the Dixie-GOP coalition had advocated trimming the sails of organized labor. Eisenhower took their side.

Eisenhower's cabinet, jibed *The New Republic*, the nation's most influential liberal periodical, consisted of "eight millionaires and a plumber."[14] Treasury Secretary George Humphrey was a corporate lawyer. Secretary of Commerce Sinclair Weeks, a wealthy manufacturer, pledged "to create a 'business climate' in the nation's economy."[15] Secretary of Agriculture Ezra Taft Benson, the first Mormon cabinet member, was closely allied to agribusiness, worked to roll back New Deal farm aid and sought to expand America's export markets to benefit large-scale corporate farms with the capacity to transport produce overseas. The plumber, Martin Durkin,

Eisenhower's only Democratic appointee, lasted less than eight months as secretary of labor, his sympathy for organized labor out of sync with the new administration's politics.

The most controversial of Eisenhower's nominees was Charles E. Wilson, also known as "Engine Charlie," the chief executive of General Motors. Wilson's experience overseeing a vast, multinational corporation struck Eisenhower as ideal for the job of secretary of defense. Despite Eisenhower's blessing, many senators doubted that Wilson could separate his financial interests from the demands of government service. He held some $2.5 million in GM stock, and after he was nominated, he made headlines when he stated that he would not divest himself from his company's holdings, despite the fact that GM was a major manufacturer of military vehicles.

Wilson was blunt and, for a CEO, not particularly well versed in public relations. When asked if he would be willing to make a decision with "extremely adverse" effects on his company, he replied brusquely, "Yes sir, I could. I cannot conceive of one." He elaborated on the point, stating that "for years I thought what was good for our country was good for General Motors and vice versa. The difference did not exist. Our company is too big. It goes with the welfare of the country."[16]

The Senate conducted Wilson's nomination hearings in secret, as was commonplace with sensitive military and foreign policy appointments. But word of his testimony leaked out. An unnamed senator attributed these words to Wilson: "Certainly. What's good for General Motors is good for the country," leading to a firestorm of controversy.[17] To many commentators, Engine Charlie gave voice to the untamed power of corporate America. Wilson and Eisenhower spent days attempting to correct the record, and under pressure, Wilson reluctantly agreed to sell his GM stock. After he was confirmed, the Senate released the transcript of his hearings, which included the correct quotation.

Over his two terms in office, Eisenhower attempted a high-wire political act: straddling the New Deal and business interests. Eisenhower believed in "limited government," balancing the federal budget and opposing federal aid to public education, which he saw as best left to the localities and states. Still, with the exception of two years, 1953 and 1954, he had to collaborate with a Democratic majority in both the House and the Senate.

The majority of both parties—Democratic and Republican—supported massive government expenditures to expand the national infrastructure and bolster the military. Large majorities of Americans also supported programs to provide a safety net for the elderly, workers, and poor. "Should any political party attempt to abolish Social Security, unemployment insurance, and eliminate labor laws and farm programs," Eisenhower pointedly argued, "you would not hear of that party again in our political history."[18] Eisenhower presided over Social Security's expansion in the mid-1950s and supported efforts to broaden a signature New Deal program, the minimum wage, to include more workers. He also signed legislation in 1954 to fund "urban renewal" programs, including new civic centers, hospitals, universities, and middle-income housing in cities.

The Military-Industrial Complex

From the beginning of his term in office, Eisenhower was ambivalent about America's enormous defense budget. His secretary of state, John Foster Dulles, directed his international strategy. A lawyer, the scion of an establishment family, and a fierce anti-Communist, Dulles shared Eisenhower's interest in cutting expenditures while maintaining American superiority over the Soviet Union. In an influential 1954 memo, he called for a reduction in costly American ground forces and instead preparation for "massive retaliation" against the Soviets. That would entail substantial funding for research and development and lucrative government contracts to electronics and aircraft firms to develop new missiles.

On November 1, 1952, the United States tested its first thermonuclear or hydrogen bomb, a weapon that was exponentially more powerful than the bombs dropped on Hiroshima and Nagasaki, creating a three-mile wide fire cloud. In 1953 the Soviets responded with their own H-bomb test, leading to a further acceleration of the arms race. When Eisenhower entered office, the United States had about fifteen hundred nuclear warheads; by the end of the 1950s, it had nearly six thousand nuclear weapons. To demonstrate American nuclear superiority, the United States detonated close to three hundred nuclear weapons in the 1950s in weapons tests. At the same time, Eisenhower reduced the number of standing troops by nearly 700,000, a considerable cost savings.

Defense spending during the Eisenhower years spurred development, mostly in suburban and rural areas. Grumman, a major aircraft manufacturer, located a huge plant on Long Island, the cutting edge of massive industrial and residential sprawl. A flood of federal military contracts enriched aircraft, electronics, and related firms that turned Orange County, California into a magnet for engineers, electrical workers, and assemblers from all over the United States. Southern senators and congressmen, using their seniority, were particularly adept at securing federal contracts for firms in their districts.

The Interstate Highway System

In the name of national defense, Eisenhower also launched the largest public works program in American history, the construction of the interstate highway system, which Congress authorized in 1956. The idea of interconnecting the United States with a vast web of superhighways dated back to the 1920s, when the federal government began providing states with funds to construct better roads. During the Cold War, planners called for the expansion of highways to encourage the decentralization of vital industries to prevent a single nuclear attack from crippling American defense capabilities. Everyone liked the idea. Members of Congress could channel the money to their districts. Real estate developers would profit immensely from developing land near interstates for shopping, fast food, and industry. Manufacturers—still reliant on the costly and aging railway system (even most automobiles were shipped by train)—could now use the more flexible and less expensive trucking industry to bring goods to market. The interstate highway system would eventually span nearly 48,000 miles and open vast areas to metropolitan sprawl.

Anti–New Dealers on the Rise

Opponents of the New Deal were encouraged by Eisenhower's pro-business rhetoric but demoralized by his support for liberal social programs and substantial federal spending. Cultivating members of the Dixie-GOP coalition, they continued their crusade against organized labor, fighting unionization efforts in the South and Southwest. They fashioned a double-edged campaign to elevate the reputation of big business while fomenting antigovernment sentiment, all in the name of an abstract principle, "free enterprise."

The pioneer in selling free enterprise, scarcely known to the American public, was a GE executive named Lemuel Ricketts Boulware. Born at the turn of the century in a small Kentucky town, Boulware graduated from the University of Wisconsin, where he was a baseball star, before seeing battle as an infantry captain in World War I. He was ideally suited for the corporate world of the 1920s: a team player who took the jobs he was assigned and excelled in them—accountant, purchasing agent, comptroller, factory and marketing manager, and corporate vice-president. During World War II, he served as vice-chairman of the War Production Board. It was the perfect résumé for his high-level position at General Electric, one of America's largest and most prestigious corporations, overseeing labor relations in the wake of the 1946 strike wave.

Boulware's real strength was marketing. *Fortune* magazine described him as "a jovial, fast-talking man, [who] combines the folksiness of a Kentucky farm background with the fervor of a washing machine salesman."[19] At GE, Boulware sold a good that he truly believed in. "Management is in a *sales* campaign to determine *who* will run business and the country, and to determine if business and the country will be run *right*," he wrote in 1946.[20] The stakes were high. If management didn't win, he argued, the country would slouch into socialism.

Boulware learned valuable lessons in marketing from business organizations' efforts to thwart Franklin Delano Roosevelt's pro-labor and regulatory policies. Depression-era groups like the Liberty League had foundered because they were too insular, too defensive, and too naïve politically to have much influence. Boulware came up with new tactics and a new script. At GE, he directed a campaign to win the hearts and minds of both the general public and the GE workforce.

GE popularized the concepts of then-radical right-wing economists through catchy brochures and articles. Boulware personally funded early conservative think tanks, including the Mont Pelerin Society, a group of business leaders and economists, well outside the mainstream, who promoted an ideology of free markets. Boulware supported libertarian economists and theorists, among them Friedrich von Hayek and Milton Friedman, who argued against economic regulation and federal spending. But those ideas would matter only if they made their way from the elite down to the masses. To get the job done, Boulware's team prepared pro–free-enterprise pamphlets that they distributed to workers. Other business groups, most prominently the National Association of Manufacturers, launched their own campaigns, with PR men drafting magazine articles, films, sermon guides, and even school curriculums.

Ever innovative, Boulware adapted quickly to the new medium of television and in 1954 hired Ronald Reagan, a minor but charming Hollywood celebrity, who found his calling as the smiling face of GE. Reagan genially hosted *The General Electric Theater*, a popular evening television program. He used his role to hawk GE products but also to promote Boulware's ideology of free enterprise. Reagan traveled to GE plants and addressed business groups around the country as an inspirational speaker, challenging Communism, criticizing unions, and celebrating capitalism.

GOD'S COUNTRY

Boulware, Reagan, and other defenders of free enterprise had prominent foes, particularly among religious leaders. Advocates of the Social Gospel, a prominent movement within mainstream Protestant denominations, supported workplace safety regulations, minimum hours and wages laws, and unionization. They worried about greed, materialism, and exploitation in industrial America. Likewise Roman Catholic leaders had, since the late nineteenth century, criticized big business for mistreating workers, paying them poorly, and threatening family security. Catholics were among the staunchest supporters of organized labor. Priests and bishops alike regularly attended labor rallies and blessed striking workers. But by the 1950s, a growing segment of religious Americans, many Protestants and a small but vocal minority of Catholics, began to cast their lot with free enterprise, largely because they saw it as a bulwark against Communism.

The postwar years marked a resurgence of godliness in the United States, which by midcentury had a greater percentage of religious believers and regular churchgoers than any other country in the industrialized West. Social scientists might have believed that the West marched inevitably toward rationality and secularism, but church membership figures did not bear that out. In 1940, 64 million Americans belonged to religious congregations; by 1960, 114 million, or about four in five Americans, did.

A growing number of Americans—many of them self-proclaimed fundamentalists (who believed in the literal interpretation of the Bible) or evangelicals (who attempted to bring new souls into a personal relationship with Jesus)—set out to remake American society. Although they were often depicted as old-fashioned or backward-looking, they were anything but traditional, especially in their use of technology. New organizations like Billy James Hargis's Christian Crusade and Carl McIntire's American

Council of Christian Churches used radio and television to call on Americans to repudiate immorality and reject any compromise with "the Devil" of Communism.

Many evangelicals joined forces with those who defended the principle of free enterprise. McIntire, who had split from the mainstream Presbyterian Church in the 1930s, railed against debauched film and music and Communism at home and abroad. He elevated free enterprise to a biblical principle, and he was not alone. "The blessings of capitalism come from God," wrote Reverend James Fifield, one of the most influential theological defenders of the free market. "A system that provides so much for the common good and happiness must flourish under the favor of the Almighty."[21] For Fifield and McIntire, government programs that restrained economic liberty violated God's law. By the early 1960s, McIntire broadcast his message over more than five hundred radio stations nationwide, and the words of ministers like Fifield filled the pages of church bulletins and sermon guides. They provided seemingly godly reinforcement to Boulware and Reagan.

In combination, the corporate and religious advocates of free enterprise were remarkably successful. The stock figure representing big business, with his top hat and monocle, gave way to benign corporate figures like the zippy, futuristic Reddy Kilowatt, a figure representing progress. The grouchy Scrooge had been supplanted by the cheerful Reagan, while the Jesus who proclaimed that "it is easier for a *camel* to go through the eye of a needle, than for a *rich man* to enter the kingdom of God" lost out to a gospel of prosperity that preached wealth as a sign of divine favor.

TEENS, SEX, ANXIETY

But for all the sunny optimism personified by Ronald Reagan, the Eisenhower years were riddled with anxiety, particularly concerning children and especially teens. Over the 1950s, journalists stoked fears of an epidemic of "juvenile delinquency." Newspapers ran lurid headlines about teen gangs, even though crime rates remained level between the early 1930s and the early 1960s, and murder rates had plummeted from their peak in the first years of the Great Depression. Still, reports of teen antics, whether schoolyard brawls or minor acts of vandalism, took on outsize importance as evidence of a generation run amok. By the mid-1950s, parents fretted that their children had disappeared into a youth subculture of comic books, tawdry movies, sexualized music, and raunchy dress. Those fears of teenage rebellion dovetailed with a deep-rooted panic about sexuality and morality.[22]

Teenage Rebels

Most unsettling to parents was that their children seemed to be rejecting traditional notions of propriety. Middle-class boys began wearing tight T-shirts and blue jeans, clothes that had been long associated with the working class. Girls' skirts hiked upward, and their bathing suits showed more skin. And increasingly, boys and girls danced together, rather too closely for their parents' liking, to new rock 'n' roll music, which seemed to overturn longtime racial norms, drawing from black rhythm and blues music and expressing sexual urges with a degree of candor that shocked an older generation.

Many parents had believed that the suburbs would protect their children from the temptations of the city, but the private, car-centered world of postwar suburbia and more disposable income than ever gave teens new freedoms. In particular the car allowed adolescents to escape parental supervision, listen to rock 'n' roll music, and engage in sexual experimentation without the risk that Mom or Dad would find out. To assuage parental fears, suburban police departments patrolled "lovers' lanes" where teenagers parked and kissed and wooded parks where kids gathered to smoke.

Teenage rebellion, however worrisome to parents, was good for Hollywood. Two 1955 films, *Rebel Without a Cause* and *Blackboard Jungle*, attracted teens and outraged their parents. The protagonist of *Rebel*, the jean-clad, rakish James Dean, became a teenage heartthrob, even if the film's message reinforced the familiar refrain of adolescents driven to ruin by overbearing moms and emasculated dads. *Blackboard Jungle* featured Hollywood's first rock 'n' roll soundtrack, headlined by Bill Haley and His Comets' hit "Rock around the Clock." Fifties youth saw themselves in a new way: as a generation defined in opposition to the stodgy culture of their parents'. For the next few decades, the script of youth rebelling against authority, of fighting for freedom against conformity, would shape nearly every aspect of American politics, consumer culture, and family life. It was the precondition for the youth rebellions that would explode in American cities and on American campuses throughout the 1960s.

Comic Books and the "Seduction of the Innocent"

The panic over rebellious youth played out in advice columns, in films, and especially in the corridors of the national capitol. In 1953, Senator Estes Kefauver (D-TN), who had become famous with his televised hearings on crime, launched a full-scale investigation of juvenile delinquency, joining forces with Senator Robert Hendrickson (R-NJ). In April 1954 the major networks halted regular programming to broadcast Hendrickson and Kefauver's lurid hearings on comic books and their impact on children.

The star witness at the comic book hearings, psychiatrist Fredric Wertham, took the stand to summarize his best-selling book, *Seduction of the Innocent*. Wertham warned that comic books lured children to commit violent acts and engage in deviant sexual practices. "It is my opinion," he testified, "without any reasonable doubt and without any reservation, that comic books are an important contributing factor in many cases of juvenile delinquency."[23] He even argued that Batman and Robin, the crime-fighting superhero and his boy sidekick, promoted homosexuality. Within a few years, more than a dozen states passed laws regulating comic books, religious groups led comic book burnings, and the hundred-million-dollar-a-year comic book industry imposed strict self-censorship. It seemed a victory for Hendrickson, Kefauver, and Wertham that comic book circulation steadily dropped thereafter. But the menaces facing America's youth abounded.

The Lavender Scare

Wertham's fears about Batman and Robin reflected a deeper concern over what seemed to be, at midcentury, rampant homosexuality. At the time, most gays and lesbians kept their sexual identities hidden. The risk of disclosure was too great: they would lose their jobs, be ostracized by family and neighbors, and sometimes be sent to mental hospitals. Mainstream medical doctors and psychiatrists classified same-sex attraction as a serious mental illness. Against the odds, gays and lesbians found companionship and community in gay-oriented taverns, coffeehouses, dance halls, and theaters in nearly every major city. For a time, peaking in the 1920s, authorities tolerated gay urban life, even if they seldom approved of it, so long as it remained confined to theater districts, working-class neighborhoods, and racially mixed areas.

But the growing public presence of gays in cities led to calls for the regulation of sexual "immorality." By the 1930s, many municipalities began to crack down on patrons of gay establishments for "disorderly conduct." In some cities, authorities shut down restaurants and bars that served patrons who appeared to be homosexual. Hollywood also censored homosexuality. Under the 1934 Hays Code, an agreement among major movie studios, films could not depict gay or lesbian characters or even discuss the topic.

Still, gay subcultures thrived, especially in single-sex environments, including the military. During World War II, the U.S. armed forces forbade same-sex relations but did not single out gay men or lesbians on the basis of their identities. Around military bases, gay soldiers could usually find bars or clubs where they could meet discreetly. Many, especially from rural areas and small towns, were thrilled to discover that they were not alone in their desires.

The growing visibility of homosexuals provoked a crackdown after the war, fueled by fears of subversion more generally. What came to be called the "lavender scare" (referring to a color that was popularly associated with gays and lesbians) played out side by side with the anti-Communist crusade. In 1950, prompted by Senator Joseph McCarthy, the U.S. Senate launched an investigation into homosexuality in the federal government. Gays and lesbians, his Senate committee contended, were susceptible to blackmail. They might give up military secrets to protect their secret sexual identities. The committee went further: "the presence of a sex pervert in a Government agency tends to have a corrosive influence on his fellow employees. These perverts will frequently attempt to entice normal individuals to engage in perverted practices."[24] In 1952, Congress passed a law that forbade homosexuals (classified as "psychopaths" in the legislation) from entering the United States. Even applicants for tourist visas had to attest that they were not homosexual.

In 1953, President Eisenhower issued an executive order requiring government agencies, the military, and private companies with government contracts to purge all suspected homosexuals. The FBI worked closely with local police forces to gather information about homosexuals and the businesses that catered to them. Military investigators often confiscated mail, followed soldiers home, or simply acted on rumors, using the information they gathered to justify discharging thousands of gays and lesbians. Homosexuals expelled from the armed forces paid a high price. They were usually ineligible for GI Bill benefits, and without honorable discharge papers, they often had trouble finding work.

Many thousands more suspected gays came under the supervision of state and law enforcement officials and prosecutors. Around the country, police raided gay bars and coffee shops, arresting thousands of people, mostly gay men, on vague charges of disorderly conduct. Undercover police officers also engaged in entrapment schemes, propositioning gay men and then charging them with public lewdness. In Washington, about a thousand suspected gays and lesbians were arrested each year on various charges. In Philadelphia, over the 1950s, police arrested nearly a hundred gays each month, most of them in bar raids. Antigay witch-hunts touched nearly every state in the country. In 1955 and 1956, for example, the police in Boise, Idaho, interviewed more than fourteen hundred people in efforts to hound out suspected homosexuals.[25]

The stigma of homosexuality, the risk of prosecution, and the danger of losing a job did not destroy gay culture, particularly in big cities. Lesbians could go to bookstores and magazine stands to find sensationalistic novels—called pulp fiction because they were printed on cheap paper—with titles like *Women's Barracks*, *Odd Girl*, and *The Third Sex*. The most popular books sold millions of copies. Gays and lesbians alike scouted out friendly bars and restaurants, whose proprietors often paid off the police to remain open. Certain remote parks and beaches that were hard for police to patrol also became informal gathering places, particularly for gay men.

The frustrations, indignities, and dangers of gay life led a small but growing number of activists to form what they called "homophile" organizations to change the negative perceptions of gays in medical textbooks and the media, and to reform antihomosexual laws. The two most prominent were the Mattachine Society, founded in 1951 (named after a masked figure in medieval theater), and the Daughters of Bilitis founded in 1955 (named after one of the companions of Greek poet Sappho). These groups mostly worked behind the scenes, providing gays and lesbians safe places to meet, engaging in educational efforts, and quietly laying the groundwork for what would become a mass movement a few decades later.

Even amid the repression of the postwar years, some noteworthy legal changes undermined censorship laws and created openings for gay and lesbian activists and writers. In 1953 postal officials in Los Angeles confiscated copies of the first issue of *ONE: The Homosexual Magazine*, a homophile publication. The headline that prompted the censorship was the cover story headline, a two-word question: "Homosexual Marriage?" A year later postal authorities impounded the magazine once again on grounds that its content was obscene. *ONE*'s publisher filed suit, challenging the federal government. In the meantime, in its landmark *Roth v. United States* decision (1957), the Supreme Court issued a broad ruling defining obscenity as material that violated "contemporary community standards," leaving the exact definition vague. The court applied that reasoning to *ONE* in a 1958 ruling, allowing the magazine, and by implication other gay periodicals, to circulate freely.

The most prominent obscenity case involved Allen Ginsberg's book-length poem, *Howl*, published in 1956. Ginsberg, a disillusioned Columbia University dropout and poet, joined New York's gay scene in Greenwich Village, a neighborhood where men could find companionship in unmarked speakeasies and immigrant bathhouses. Like many budding poets, he found his way to San Francisco, where the North Beach neighborhood, with its tawdry burlesque bars and its mix of sailors on furlough and young men on the make, provided a bit of a refuge for gays. The center of gravity in North Beach was City Lights, a bookstore and publisher, run by the poet Lawrence Ferlinghetti.

In 1956, City Lights released *Howl*, to some notoriety. In the poem, Ginsberg evoked the gritty city, with its casual mixing of the races, free sex (including an explicit line about homosexuality), and plentiful drugs. San Francisco's district attorney ordered copies of *Howl* confiscated, on the grounds that it was obscene, and arrested Ferlinghetti and the City Lights bookstore manager, leading to a lengthy criminal trial. In 1957 a California judge ruled that however offensive the poem was, it was of "redeeming social importance" and could not be censored.

When it came to policing juvenile delinquents or gays, or censoring lascivious comic books or homophile magazines, it was hard to enforce conformity. By the late 1950s, encouraged by the shift in obscenity laws, mainstream publishers began to capitalize on gay-and-lesbian–themed books. The demand was too big for them to ignore. Filmmakers began to push at the boundaries of sexuality, and musicians even more so. The market for rebellious books, music, and movies was vast, ever changing, and extraordinarily lucrative, one part of a seemingly insatiable consumer culture in the postwar years.

THE BLACK FREEDOM STRUGGLE

Of all of the rebellions that remade post–World War II America, none was more unsettling to the status quo than the African American insurgency against segregation and inequality. The civil rights movement, which peaked in the postwar years, touched on nearly every facet of American life. Investigative journalists, lawyers, and academics published books and articles chronicling America's past and present of racial injustice and discrimination. Activists demanded that black Americans have full access to postwar prosperity, well-paying jobs, high wages, and the consumer marketplace. They challenged one of the taken-for-granted aspects of modern American life: the nearly complete racial segregation of America's housing. They resisted racially separate and unequal education. They demanded the right to vote and the right to political representation. And they began, slowly, to win major victories.

Jim Crow Public Accommodations

From the late nineteenth through the mid-twentieth centuries, from coast to coast, north and south, restaurants and bars that served whites usually refused service to any dark-skinned customer. In the South, blacks were subjected to Jim Crow laws that forbade them from sitting at the same lunch counters or using the same bathrooms and drinking fountains. Blacks and whites could not ride in the same train cars. Blacks had to give up their seats to white passengers on trolleys and buses. Movie theaters throughout the country excluded blacks altogether or confined them to seats in the "crow's nest," the balcony, most distant from the big screen. Public swimming pools everywhere were closed to blacks or open to them only on special "colored" days, after which the pools would be drained and refilled. Along the Rio Grande River and in parts of southern California, Mexican Americans complained of "Juan Crow," local discriminatory practices that still kept them out of white establishments.

Even wealthy travelers of the wrong complexion could not buy their way out of Jim Crow. Robert Joseph Pershing Foster, a black doctor from Louisiana, had to carry his surgical tools and a portable operating table to his patients' houses because white-run hospitals would not admit him. Frustrated, on April 1, 1953, he headed west to Los Angeles in search of better work. But even with a full wallet, Foster drove the few-thousand-mile-long trip between

Monroe, Louisiana, and Los Angeles nonstop because he couldn't find motels that would put him up. Sometimes the rejections were polite. "Oh my goodness," proclaimed a motel clerk. "We forgot to turn on the no-vacancy sign." Sometimes he was greeted with a scowl. And once in L.A., though he was an experienced surgeon, he could only find a job working for an insurance company, going door to door to perform health exams on policyholders. It would take Foster years to find a job that matched his skills. [26]

Segregation Under Siege

Foster's struggles represented the everyday indignities that blacks faced. Those indignities—getting kicked out of a restaurant, having to ride at the back of the bus, not being able to swim in a public pool—seemed especially egregious when the United States presented itself as the world's arsenal of democracy. At the same time, assumptions about racial difference and inferiority came under siege. During the 1930s, leading scientists began challenging the very notion of race as unscientific. Anthropologist Franz Boas argued that race was a cultural construct rather than a biological reality. Sociologists, like St. Clair Drake and Horace Cayton, published highly regarded books and popular articles that chronicled the effects of segregation and discrimination. Nearly everyone was familiar with Gunnar Myrdal's best-selling *An American Dilemma* (1944), which argued that racial discrimination violated the "American creed," a tradition of egalitarianism that ran throughout American history from the founders to the present day.

Those books and articles helped shift elite opinion about race, but it would take a lot more to undermine centuries of racial segregation. It would take what the leader of the March on Washington, A. Philip Randolph, called "pressure, more pressure, and still more pressure."[27] Much of that pressure, when it came to public accommodations, was at first informal. Authorities in Birmingham, Alabama, for example, reported eighty-eight cases of blacks occupying "white" places on city buses during the year following September 1941. White transit riders in Baltimore, Detroit, and Atlanta, among other cities, complained about black passengers deliberately jostling whites. Uniformed soldiers returning from service in the Pacific or Europe often responded angrily when confronted with Jim Crow on buses and at lunch counters.

Organizing Against Jim Crow

The struggle against segregation did not remain unorganized for long. In 1946 the NAACP, the nation's leading civil rights group with nearly a half million members, published a "how to" list for those who wanted to challenge segregated restaurants in northern cities: "If refused service, ask to see the manager. . . . If you have no witnesses, call the police." And finally: "Be polite at all times. Avoid creating a disturbance either in the establishment refusing service or the police station."[28]

Beginning in the 1940s, small bands of activists launched organized challenges to segregation. Leading the way was the Congress of Racial Equality (CORE). Founded in Chicago in 1942 by a group of black and white theology students, CORE directed its first protests against restaurants in the Windy City that turned away blacks. Creative and fearless, CORE members staged sit-ins, occupying restaurants and, when they were denied service, refusing to leave. CORE was especially influenced by what was happening a world away in India, where the nationalist leader Mohandas K. Gandhi faced off British colonizers by marching and engaging in nonviolent civil disobedience—that is, refusing to obey laws they considered unjust, and refusing to use violence against the police and military who tried to stop them.

CORE had a string of victories throughout the North in the mid-1940s, sitting-in at restaurants and roller-skating rinks in Cleveland, wading-in at segregated pools in Philadelphia and Fort Lee, New Jersey, and joining protests against jobs and housing discrimination. One of CORE's key organizers in the postwar years, Bayard Rustin, graduated from traditionally black Lincoln University, worked as a labor organizer, and spent part of World War II in jail for refusing to serve in the military. After the war, he was a tireless organizer in the South. "I traveled all over the country creating all kinds of demonstrations, sit-ins in restaurants, theaters, hotels, barbershops, and the like," he recalled.[29] Rustin, who was gay, also knew another form of discrimination—in 1953, he was arrested and convicted for having sex with a man—though he would not join the struggle for gay rights until late in his life.

In 1947 sixteen CORE members, eight black and eight white men, including Rustin, embarked on what they called the Journey of Reconciliation, the most daring act of civil disobedience of the time. The sixteen riders boarded southbound buses from Washington, D.C., into Virginia and

North Carolina, refusing to obey Jim Crow rules. Several, including Rustin, were arrested in North Carolina and sentenced to work on a chain gang for their blatant violation of the law. The Journey of Reconciliation did not attract a lot of media attention, but Rustin and several other riders would shape the ongoing civil rights struggle.

The Montgomery Bus Boycott

The movement to challenge segregated transportation took a dramatic turn in 1955. Rosa Parks, a seamstress in Montgomery, Alabama, refused to give up her bus seat to a white passenger. Parks was not simply tired after a long day of work. She was a longtime civil rights activist, committed to undermining Jim Crow. Born in 1913 in Tuskegee, Alabama, her family was part of the Marcus Garvey movement. Most black women of her generation were destined to do manual labor, but Parks graduated from high school (rare for black women in her state), married, and moved to Montgomery. From young adulthood, she was involved in civil rights. In the early 1930s, she and her husband had supported the Scottsboro Boys, a group of young men falsely accused of raping a white woman. At age thirty, she joined the local branch of the NAACP, serving as its secretary. Within a year, she took leadership of what became a nationwide campaign to bring justice to six white Alabama men who admitted kidnapping and gang-raping Recy Taylor, a black Alabama woman, but who faced no charges for their crime.

Working for the NAACP brought Parks into contact with a nationwide movement. She learned of civil rights protests in the pages of the NAACP's magazine, The Crisis. And she made connections with local and national activists. In the summer of 1955, just a few months before she was arrested for refusing to give up her seat, Parks had attended the Highlander Folk School in rural Tennessee where Betty Friedan had spent part of the summer of 1941. Scores of black passengers had refused in the past to give up their seats, but Parks's case sparked a mass movement.

In the aftermath of Parks's arrest, Montgomery activists planned a boycott of the city's bus system. A young minister, only twenty-five years old, Martin Luther King, Jr., rose as spokesman for the boycotters. Montgomery's leaders gathered in his living room and used his church for meetings. King, the son of one of Atlanta's most prominent ministers and already a brilliant preacher, was the ideal public face for the boycott. E. D. Nixon, the head of Montgomery's NAACP and Parks's close colleague, used his organization's national network to publicize the case.

Parks, King, and Nixon did not act alone. Local women provided the backbone of the boycott. Seasoned northern activists, including Bayard Rustin, headed south to provide their own lessons from more than a decade of organizing. And perhaps even more important, the Montgomery struggle attracted the national news media. In the age of television in particular, it was difficult for Americans to ignore Jim Crow and the struggle against it. But even with the pressure of unfavorable media coverage, and with some of the most talented organizers in the country, Montgomery's bus company and its white elites did not capitulate easily. The boycott would last nearly a year before Rosa Parks could sit wherever she wanted on the bus without fear of arrest.

Separate and Unequal Education

The events in Montgomery occurred amid an even higher-stakes battle in the civil rights struggle: the struggle for racial equality in public education. Just a little over a year before Rosa Parks refused to give up her seat, the U.S. Supreme Court ruled, in *Brown v. Board of Education*, that racially segregated public schools were unconstitutional. The battle over separate, unequal schools was harder fought than the battle to desegregate lunch counters and buses, and the victory was far from complete.

Educational credentials mattered more than ever in postwar America. For most of the early twentieth century, overall school attendance and graduation rates had been low: only about 25 percent of Americans born in 1900 graduated from high school. But as the economy grew more complex, fewer Americans worked with their hands. More worked in jobs that required at least basic reading, mathematical, and writing skills. The high school diploma became an essential credential for many jobs. As a result, between 70 and 80 percent of baby-boom generation children born between 1945 and 1965 graduated from high school.[30] College attendance and graduation rates also rose steadily after World War II, largely because white, male veterans used GI Bill funds to pay for college.

But the benefits of education were unevenly distributed. Black and Hispanic children were far more likely to attend underfunded, segregated schools, and in rural areas where nonwhite students worked the fields, school districts did not even open high schools for them. And even though racial minorities were technically eligible for the GI Bill, the program was administered in a discriminatory fashion. Most institutions of higher education, particularly in the South, refused to admit African Americans. Instead, most blacks who made it to college attended historically black institutions, long the training ground for the small black elite of doctors, engineers, ministers, and professionals. The most elite white institutions admitted few if any blacks. Princeton's class of 1961, for example, had one black student.

Despite all the obstacles they faced, African Americans put a high value on education. Black educational attainment had risen steadily since the early twentieth century, in part driven by the vast migration of African Americans to cities. There black children could attend high school, even if most of them were stuck in vocational or industrial courses. For all these problems, they came, like most Americans in the mid-twentieth century, to demand more than a rudimentary education, fully aware that employers put a greater premium on well-educated workers.

But for minorities nearly everywhere in the United States, the reality of separate, unequal education dashed their expectations. Black and Hispanic schools were usually shabby and overcrowded, often lacking basic facilities like libraries, gymnasiums, and sometimes even indoor plumbing. This pattern had been ratified in the 1896 Supreme Court decision *Plessy v. Ferguson*, which permitted racial separation so long as the facilities serving blacks and whites were nominally equal, which was almost never the case.

Teachers in segregated schools worked hard managing overcrowded classrooms. In rural areas, it was not uncommon for classrooms to mix older and younger students together. The situation in big cities was grim in another way. In 1950s-era Chicago, for example, black students regularly attended schools with fifty to sixty students per class, and many schools held two-part or double-shift school days. African American teachers mentored the brightest students, often visited families at home, and sometimes used their meager paychecks to buy supplies. Other than ministers, they were often the most revered members of their communities. But white-led school boards almost always paid nonwhite teachers less than their white counterparts and until the 1950s, even in the most open parts of the country, refused to let them teach white students.

Anna Arnold Hedgeman   A longtime civil rights activist, Hedgeman led the effort to create a Permanent Fair Employment Practices Committee to prevent racial discrimination in the workplace.

Henry A. Wallace   A staunch New Dealer and former vice president, Wallace challenged President Truman from the left. Here, he presents the Progressive Party budget, pledging to cut military spending and expand social services.

Betty Goldstein (Friedan)   In 1942, Betty Friedan graduated from Smith College, where she honed her writing skills and gained a passion for social justice, laying the groundwork for her career as a labor journalist and feminist advocate.

Lemuel Ricketts Boulware
A brilliant marketer, Boulware helped shape General Electric's antilabor strategy in the postwar years. Under his direction, GE prepared pro–free enterprise advertisements and hired Hollywood actor Ronald Reagan as the firm's spokesman.

Levittown Protests   In August 1957, William and Daisy Myers and their three children moved into a house in Levittown, Pennsylvania. They were the first African American family in the sprawling new suburb. For several weeks, white neighbors picketed, vandalized the property, and clashed with the police.

Freedom Riders White supremacists brutally beat Freedom Riders John Lewis (left) and James Zwerg when their bus arrived at the terminal in Montgomery, Alabama, on May 20, 1961.

March on Washington for Jobs and Freedom About a quarter million Americans, black and white, gathered in Washington, DC, on August 28, 1963, to demand federal civil rights legislation. They called for antidiscrimination laws and the expansion of economic opportunities for African Americans.

Johnson and Fulbright   On July 28, 1965, the day that he announced the deployment of 125,000 troops to Vietnam, President Lyndon Johnson (right) confers with Senator J. William Fulbright, chair of the Senate Foreign Relations Committee and one of the staunchest critics of his foreign policy.

The Battle of Hue   American troops, including an injured soldier, take cover in Hue on February 6, 1968, during the first week of a nearly month-long struggle for control over the ancient South Vietnamese city.

Carmen Roberts An opponent of school integration and an antifeminist organizer, Carmen Roberts (center wearing sunglasses) leads an antibusing protest in Detroit in the early 1970s.

Richard Nixon Eager to reach alienated white voters, Richard Nixon aggressively campaigned in suburban areas during the 1968 presidential campaign.

Urban Crisis   In the 1970s, New York and other major cities faced intense racial conflict and rising crime rates. In response to calls for law and order, in 1979, New York increased the police presence on its subways.

The AIDS Crisis   Protesters gathered in Washington, DC, on June 1, 1987, to challenge the Reagan administration's inaction on the AIDS epidemic.

Betty Dukes Wal-Mart emerged as the largest private employer in the United States in the late twentieth century, paying low wages to its heavily female workforce. Betty Dukes, pictured here outside its Pittsburg, California, store, launched a class-action lawsuit contesting Wal-Mart's discriminatory practices.

Patricia Thompson A public housing resident from New Orleans, Patricia Thompson (center) joined other Hurricane Katrina survivors testifying before Congress about their ordeal, December 6, 2005.

Rumsfeld at Abu Ghraib   Secretary of Defense Donald Rumsfeld meets with soldiers at the Abu Ghraib prison near Baghdad, May 13, 2004, shortly after revelations that U.S. soldiers had abused and tortured prisoners there.

The 2008 Election   Barack Obama often attracted large, racially diverse, and youthful crowds at his campaign rallies, such as this one in Oakland, California, March 17, 2007.

The NAACP's March on the Courts

Civil rights activists had challenged segregated schools in a piecemeal way beginning in the 1890s, but the protests escalated in the North during World War II and afterward. During the 1940s, black parents agitated against racially separate schools in Hillburn, Hempstead, and New Rochelle, New York; Trenton, Montclair, and Princeton, New Jersey; and Dayton and Hillsborough, Ohio. Taking the lead in most of these cases were black mothers who coordinated school boycotts. The NAACP, which had begun a legal attack on segregated schools in the 1930s, provided the parents with legal assistance and used its newspaper, *The Crisis*, to spread word of the protests.

Some of the riskiest cases—given the intransigent white opposition to integration—played out in the Old Confederacy. In Clarendon County, South Carolina, for example, local activists stepped up their protest against separate schools between 1947 and 1949, first demanding access to bus transportation, then filing petitions challenging separate schools. The protesting parents faced reprisals, in some cases losing their jobs. The Reverend Joseph DeLaine, who coordinated the campaign, lost his job, lost his house to arsonists, and fled the state.

Thurgood Marshall led the NAACP's march through the courts. A native of Baltimore and the grandson of slaves, Marshall had attended Howard University Law School before setting up a private practice in his hometown. In 1940, Marshall, only thirty-two, began a distinguished career as a civil rights attorney with the NAACP. Immensely talented, he immediately took on some of the organization's most prominent cases. Also on the team was the talented Robert L. Carter, a graduate of two historically black universities, Lincoln in Pennsylvania and Howard Law School in Washington. Carter traveled to out-of-the-way places like Cairo, Illinois, to challenge school segregation. He also worked closely with expert witnesses, including the black psychologist Kenneth Clark, who testified in the Clarendon County case about the damaging psychological impact of segregation on black students.

The NAACP fought segregated education on many fronts in the late 1940s and won early victories in three cases involving universities. In *Sipuel v. Regents of the University of Oklahoma* (1948), Marshall and the NAACP persuaded the U.S. Supreme Court to overturn a state law that made it a misdemeanor to educate black and white students together. The NAACP brought another case, on behalf of George McLaurin, a black student who had been admitted to Oklahoma's graduate school of education. The school's administrators cordoned off a special section of the library and cafeteria for McLaurin, where he would not come into contact with white students. They assigned him to desks placed just outside the doors to his classrooms, where he could listen to lectures without mingling with his classmates. In *McLaurin v. Oklahoma State Regents* (1950), the Supreme Court found that McLaurin could not get an equal education if he remained physically separated from his fellow students. The same day, in *Sweatt v. Painter*, the court ordered the University of Texas to admit Heman Sweatt, a black applicant, to the flagship University of Texas law school.

These victories whittled away at the "separate but equal" principle that had been in place since the *Plessy* decision. The NAACP now had some good precedents for taking on the biggest challenge of all, the widespread practice of officially segregating primary and secondary schools south of the Mason-Dixon Line. Working closely with local parents in Clarendon, South Carolina; Wilmington, Delaware; Prince Edward County, Virginia; Washington, D.C.; and Topeka, Kansas; the NAACP began to file suit in federal courts, laying siege to the entire system of separate education.

In 1953 the Supreme Court heard arguments in these five cases, bundled together, with Oliver Brown of Topeka as the first-named plaintiff. Brown's daughter, Linda, had been denied admission to the all-white school just a few blocks from her home. Kansas was one of five states outside the South with laws on the books that permitted racially separate schools.

Taking on the entire system of segregated education was risky, even if the courts were more open to civil rights than they had ever been. Civil rights advocates worried that the high court would be reluctant to overturn *Plessy*, on the grounds of judicial restraint, and would instead issue a compromise decision. They also lacked confidence that Chief Justice Fred Vinson would be able to bridge the court's divisions. But in September 1953, while the court deliberated, Vinson died.

The fate of *Brown* fell into the hands of the man whom President Eisenhower nominated to fill Vinson's spot: California governor Earl Warren. A moderate Republican, Warren had been an effective governor. Despite his party affiliation, he supported many New Deal programs, including welfare, economic regulation, and federal infrastructure spending, which greatly benefited his rapidly growing home state. Warren's red flag, for those who knew his past, was his support for the internment of Japanese Americans during the Second World War, a decision that he later came to regret.

Warren came to the bench with no judicial experience. His political background, however, proved to be his greatest asset. A skilled politician, he had an instinct for building coalitions and a willingness to forge compromises. Unlike many of his fellow justices past and present, he was not steeped in any legal theory. A pragmatist, he believed in deciding what was right and developing his legal rationale from there. On May 17, 1954, he announced a unanimous ruling that "in the field of public education, the doctrine of 'separate but equal' has no place. Separate educational facilities are inherently unequal."[31] Warren acknowledged Kenneth Clark's argument that segregation created "a feeling of inferiority" among black students, an argument important for bringing social science to bear on what, in the hands of another chief justice, could have been a narrower, strictly legal ruling.

Warren's politics, however, led him to proceed cautiously when it came time for the court to rule on how *Brown* would be implemented. Fearful of backlash, the court ruled in 1955 that segregated school districts had to comply with the *Brown* decision "with all deliberate speed." Those four vague words became a license for southern school districts to move forward at their own pace. In the border states, many districts acted quickly to abolish segregated schools. In northern districts, beginning in New York City in 1957, activists began to challenge the existence of segregated "neighborhood schools," where black students were segregated because of where they lived, not because of laws that required segregation. By the early 1960s, protesters and litigators in more than two hundred northern districts were using *Brown*'s language to demand rapid desegregation.

In the South, change happened slowly if at all. Some districts, like Greensboro, North Carolina, implemented token desegregation programs, admitting a handful of black students to formerly all-white schools but leaving racial patterns otherwise unchanged. Many more Southerners openly resisted *Brown*. In 1956, 101 members of Congress issued the "Southern Manifesto," declaring the *Brown* decision "a clear abuse of judicial power."[32] Southern state legislatures passed laws intended to thwart integration. Several allowed for the closing of integrated schools; others refused to commit state education funds for desegregation efforts. A common subterfuge was the introduction of "freedom of choice" laws that formally ended segregation, but made it difficult for African Americans to attend white schools. Many conservative activists outside the South endorsed such plans. In 1959, Prince Edward County, Virginia, simply disbanded its public schools, turning white schools into private academies and leaving black children locked out.

President Eisenhower expressed his misgivings about civil rights. Earl Warren later recounted a strange after-dinner conversation he had had with the president during the *Brown* deliberations. "These are not bad people," Eisenhower told Warren, commenting on southern whites. "All they are concerned about is to see that their sweet little girls are not required to sit alongside some big overgrown Negroes."[33] Privately, Ike called his nomination of Warren "the biggest damn fool mistake I have ever made."[34] For Ike, civil rights would only come gradually, through change of hearts and minds. The very idea of imposing civil rights orders rubbed against his belief in limited government.

But events at the beginning of the 1957 school year forced Eisenhower to act. The school district in Little Rock, Arkansas, admitted nine black students to the city's Central High School, a token effort to demonstrate compliance with the *Brown* ruling. But for many Arkansas residents and their grandstanding governor, Orval Faubus, nine students was nine too many. Faubus ordered the Arkansas National Guard to cordon off the high school. When the students attempted to enter the school building, guardsmen turned them away. Crowds of angry whites taunted the students. And the television cameras caught it all, projecting the images of angry whites screaming at well-dressed black schoolchildren to a worldwide audience.

Eisenhower summoned Faubus to a personal meeting and insisted that the governor relent and open Central High School. Under court order, Faubus withdrew the National Guard troops. But the situation worsened. Three weeks later, when the black students entered the school through a service entrance, an angry mob surrounded the school. In response to the chaos, Eisenhower federalized the Arkansas National Guard, taking it out of Faubus's control, and dispatched one thousand members of the elite 101st Airborne unit to Little Rock to restore order.[35] The president was furious at Faubus's insubordination but even more worried about the impact of Little Rock on America's image abroad. Secretary of State John Foster Dulles warned Eisenhower that the events at Central High were "ruining our foreign policy."[36] In his memoirs, Eisenhower wrote that the disorder in Little Rock "could continue to feed the mill of Soviet propagandists who by word and picture were telling the world of the 'racial terror' in the United States."[37]

Under federal supervision, the nine students enrolled and Little Rock quieted, but resistance to *Brown* did not slow down. Whether by tokenism or by violent resistance, by closing down schools and opening private, whites-only academies, or simply by ignoring the Supreme Court's orders, southern public officials flouted the law. By 1964 only 2 percent of black children in the South attended racially integrated schools.[38] It would take more than a decade of protest and violence to lay the groundwork for the sweeping federal civil rights and education reforms enacted in 1964 and 1965, which pried open the doors of Jim Crow schools.

Open Housing

Breaking open America's housing market represented an even bigger challenge than desegregating its schools. Defenders of the "American way of life" celebrated consumer choice and America's high rates of home ownership, but for African Americans, the housing market remained largely closed. Beginning in the early 1940s, civil rights activists in Chicago, Detroit, St. Louis, Los Angeles, and elsewhere launched a battle in the courts against racially restrictive covenants. Finally, in 1948, a unanimous U.S. Supreme Court ruled in *Shelley v. Kraemer* that the clauses that forbade the use or occupancy of a property by race, religion, or ethnicity were unenforceable in court.

Fair housing activists did not rest content after *Shelley*. Armed with optimism, they tried to break down segregated suburbia. No target was more inviting than the famous Levittowns. African Americans had tried to buy and rent houses from developer William Levitt since the late 1940s, but his company turned them away, even evicting whites who had invited black friends to their homes in Long Island's Levittown. The NAACP unsuccessfully pushed the Eisenhower administration to back integration in Levitt's developments. Eisenhower and his aides believed that government should not interfere with business decisions. A renter or seller should have the freedom to choose renters or buyers.

Once again, "freedom of association" provided whites with a powerful rationale for their opposition to civil rights. Beginning in the 1950s, realtors around the country led the charge against efforts to desegregate housing. Their argument tapped the pro-business rhetoric of the era. The government was attempting to "force" private individuals and real estate companies to sell to minorities, violating "homeowner's rights" and businesses' "freedom of contract." Advocates of fair housing, in their view, were Communists, attempting to undermine free enterprise. Cold War concerns prompted Eisenhower to act on Little Rock, but Cold War rhetoric also became a powerful tool to discredit the civil rights struggle.

In the late summer and early fall of 1957, just as Little Rock exploded, racial violence shattered the quiet of Levittown, Pennsylvania. On August 13, 1957, William and Daisy Myers and their three children settled into a little house at the corner of Daffodil and Deepgreen Lanes. Within hours, hundreds of angry whites gathered outside their home, breaking its windows and clashing with the police. The skirmishes continued for several weeks, but the Myerses did not budge. Bill Myers, a World War II veteran, took to weeding his lawn with the bayonet on his military-issued rifle, asserting his dignity in the face of violence. Finally the protests abated. But white Levittowners had sent a chilling message: moving to their neighborhood would come at a high price. In most of suburban America, African Americans were unwilling to subject themselves to harassment, and whites were unwilling to sell.

THE COVERT COLD WAR

For Eisenhower, foreign policy took priority over domestic concerns like civil rights. Elected as a Cold Warrior, he surrounded himself with hawks. For his part, Engine Charlie proved a disappointing choice for secretary of defense. He was so gaffe-prone that his critics joked that he had introduced automatic transmissions at General Motors so he could drive with his foot in his mouth. While the president increased military spending, particularly to enhance America's nuclear capacity, his administration also entangled the United States in a series of proxy conflicts with the Soviets, mostly on the small stages of developing countries and former European colonies throughout the world.

Iran

Just as Eisenhower wound down the Korean War, he increased the power of the CIA. With thousands of operatives worldwide, the agency infiltrated foreign governments, spying on the nation's enemies. But the CIA became much more than a well-funded intelligence operation. Its operatives infiltrated revolutionary organizations and took sides in civil wars and domestic power struggles, particularly in former European colonies. It collaborated with authoritarian regimes, provided training and financial assistance to the police in pro-American countries, and engaged in covert operations against America's enemies.

In the summer of 1953, the CIA staged one of its most audacious covert operations, leading a coup in Iran, a major oil producer, vital to American economic interests. Iran's prime minister, Mohammad Mosaddeq, nationalized foreign-controlled petroleum operations in 1951 and collaborated closely with Iran's near neighbor, the Soviet Union. The CIA coup replaced Mosaddeq with Mohammad Reza Shah Pahlavi, who was both pro-American and ruthlessly authoritarian. The unpopular shah gave the Americans and the British a cut of oil revenues, accepted hundreds of millions in American aid for development, and made Iran, for the time, an anti-Soviet bulwark. The Iran coup became a blueprint for similar CIA-supported insurgencies elsewhere in the world, most prominently Indonesia in the late 1950s and the Congo in the early 1960s.

Guatemala

The Cold War had made its way to the western hemisphere in the postwar years, but fighting leftism in Latin America was not at the top of the Truman administration's priorities. Indeed, those on the left side of the New Deal coalition found the new direction of Latin American politics was appealing. A burst of political reform between 1944 and 1946 brought the region from autocracy to democracy with real speed. Insurgent political movements, led by democratic leftists, inspired by the New Deal, Popular Front politics, and worldwide antifascism, toppled dictators, expanded voting rights, pushed for labor reforms, and demanded the redistribution of lands long held by wealthy planters. Reformers took power throughout Central and South America. By 1946, all but five countries in the region had democratically elected governments, mostly on the left.

Guatemala, a country of only about three million people, embodied not only the promise of democracy in Latin America and for the United States, the threat of leftism in the western hemisphere. In mostly rural Guatemala, a small, corrupt, wealthy planter elite, enriched by global demand for coffee and bananas, controlled the government in the early twentieth century. The majority of Guatemalans, many of Indian descent, lived in near-feudal conditions, dispossessed of their lands and forced into labor.

In 1944, Guatemalans toppled the autocratic regime of Jorge Ubico and a military successor. In the country's first-ever democratic election, they elected Juan José Arévalo, who promoted a version of social democracy, building a base in the countryside among landless and brutally exploited rural workers. Arévalo's successor Jacobo Arbenz, elected in 1951, instituted a sweeping land reform program, redistributing land long held by the planters and international investors. Arbenz authorized the appropriation of some 225,000 acres of land belonging to United Fruit, an American-based firm.[39]

In 1954, a CIA-backed coup toppled Arbenz, denounced as a Communist and loathed by the planter elite and the U.S.-based companies in Guatemala. Post–Arbenz Guatemala became a case study in American Cold War policy in the developing world. Despite its rhetoric of democracy, the United States propped up authoritarian, anti-Communist regimes in the name of stability and security. To Eisenhower and his successors a dictatorial, pro–United States regime was more useful than a democratically elected government that threatened American economic or geopolitical interests.

On the ground in Guatemala oppression and instability flourished. The brutal regimes that succeeded Arbenz used the power of state to silence dissent, crush labor and land reform movements, and bolster the small elite that benefited from international investment. The United States did not merely tolerate such excesses under Eisenhower and his successors: it encouraged them in the name of freedom. In 1966, again with CIA support, Guatemala used advanced technology to gather information about dissenters. The regime created death squads and systematically began to "disappear" its opponents, using the tactics of kidnapping, torture, and assassination to silence dissent. This brutality provided a blueprint for the "dirty wars" conducted by American-backed dictatorships in Chile and Argentina in the 1970s and 1980s.

The Guatemalan coup and repression—like so many American Cold War ventures—had unintended consequences. While the United States hoped that Guatemala would modernize, serving as a model for other countries, many Latin American leftists took home a different lesson. If the results of democratic elections could be overturned by American intervention, then it would take other means to accomplish social and economic changes. For many on the left, that meant leaving New Deal–type programs to the side, rejecting elections, and instead seizing power outside the electoral process. Che Guevara, who led a Communist insurgency in Cuba, for example, promised that "Cuba will not be Guatemala."[40] On that island, revolutionaries overthrew the corrupt Batista dictatorship in 1959 and instituted reforms much like those in postwar Guatemala but without democratic institutions.

Cuba

Cuba, the former Spanish colony, just ninety miles off the U.S. coast, had long been, in most respects, a dependency of the United States. In the mid-twentieth century, American investors dominated its economy and controlled its utilities, its extractive industries, and a sizable segment of its lucrative sugar production. American dollars flew thick in the sultry bars and luxury hotels along Havana's beaches. Three times since Cuba achieved its independence from Spain in 1898, the United States had sent troops to the island to protect American interests. In 1950, Cuba was in the hands of Fulgencio Batista, a former insurgent turned dictator. Batista had made his peace (and considerable profit) with outside economic interests, called off Guatemalan-style land reforms, and enjoyed little support outside the island's elite and the military.

In January 1959, less than two years from the end of Eisenhower's term in office, revolutionary insurgents led by Fidel Castro toppled Batista. At first, many Americans looked hopefully to Castro. He visited the United States in April 1959, met for three hours with Vice President Nixon, and stayed in a hotel in Harlem. But by the fall, relations with Castro began to sour when his regime embarked on an aggressive land reform policy. In the following months, Cuba confiscated nearly $1 billion in American holdings, signed a trade agreement with the Soviet Union, and recognized the People's Republic of China.

Eisenhower did not see anything to be gained by restoring Batista's unpopular regime to power, but he retaliated against Castro by imposing a trade embargo (including restricting the importation of Cuba's only lucrative cash crop, sugar) and freezing American aid. In the spring of 1960, he authorized the CIA to provide support and training for anti-Castro insurgents who hoped to assassinate Castro and stage a coup. By allying with the Soviets and Chinese and standing up aggressively to the United States, Castro made clear that he had learned from Guatemala: his regime would use military force, coercion at home, and aid from the Soviet bloc to ensure that he would not go the way of Arbenz. For the next several decades, Cuba would be the flashpoint of Cold War tensions in the western hemisphere.

SECURITY AND INSECURITY

Eisenhower's America was a paradoxical place, prosperous yet insecure. America at midcentury underwent transformations that few fully understood but whose ramifications many felt. A new, youth-oriented culture threatened an older generation. Women working and gays gathering surreptitiously threatened the normative family, just as it seemed more invincible then ever. Business leaders and conservative elites promoted a doctrine of free enterprise out of fear that, even under a Republican president, big government was unstoppable. A mass insurgency, led by the country's long-oppressed African Americans, threatened to undermine one of the deepest American traditions, that of racial inequality. American global might was unsurpassed, yet the threat of nuclear war loomed over the world, and insurgencies in faraway places like Guatemala and Iran seemed to pose an existential threat to the United States. The postwar years marked the beginning of a struggle that shaped the politics of the next few decades, between dissent and conformity, between social welfare and free enterprise, between racial and sexual equality and tradition.

CHAPTER 10

A SEASON OF CHANGE:

LIBERALS AND THE LIMITS
OF REFORM, 1960–1966

JOHN LEWIS SPENT his twenty-first birthday, Sunday, February 21, 1961, in a Nashville jail. He didn't exactly plan it that way. That day Lewis, a student at American Baptist Theological Seminary in Nashville, was scheduled to give his senior sermon, a meditation on the tenth chapter of the Gospel of Matthew, in which Jesus proclaims, "Think not that I come to send peace on earth. I came to send not peace but a sword."[1] It was an apt passage for an earnest young man who pledged nonviolence but whose actions as a protester provoked violence.

The previous evening Lewis and twenty-five other civil rights activists, most of them students, had been arrested for blockading the entrance to Nashville's glittering Loew's Theater, where hundreds lined up to watch Cecil B. DeMille's epic film *The Ten Commandments*. It did not take years of theological education to see the hypocrisy of white theatergoers cheering at the liberation of Pharaoh's slaves and admiring Moses as he led his people to the Promised Land. Nashville's theaters—if they let in black patrons at all—forced them to sit in the "crow's nest," high in the balcony, far from the screen. Loews made black patrons enter via the outdoor fire stairs, "out in the cold and rain, past garbage cans and up rickety metal steps."[2]

The son of sharecroppers who worked the rich soil of Alabama's Black Belt but barely earned enough to survive, John Lewis was a precocious student on the path to one of black America's most prestigious occupations: the ministry. There weren't many black lawyers or doctors, engineers or accountants. Even bright young men like Lewis—if they were lucky enough to go to college—often found themselves working as shop clerks or railroad porters, jobs that were beneath their education. The pulpit, by contrast, offered prestige and, for those as talented as Lewis, the promise of a life of more than modest comfort.

The budding minister, however, did not follow a straight path through his studies. On February 27, 1960, just a year before he was arrested for blockading the Loew's ticket booth, he had spent his first night in jail, hauled away from a Woolworth's lunch counter and charged with disorderly conduct simply for asking to be served a meal. Lewis helped convene the fledgling Nashville Student Movement, inspired by the lunch counter sit-ins in Greensboro, North Carolina, earlier that month. After weeks of careful planning and training in nonviolent tactics by seasoned movement strategists, they launched a nearly month-long peaceful assault on Nashville's dime-store lunch counters. The 1960s sit-ins reprised tactics that civil rights activists had been deploying since CORE's protests at segregated Chicago diners during World War II.

In the years following the Montgomery Bus Boycott, Lewis and his fellow students had watched the battles against Jim Crow in the South wax and wane. They chafed at many of their elders' calls for patience. Many of Nashville's leading black ministers counseled the students against direct action. Lewis's own parents, still hopeful that their son would rise to respectability and leadership, were "shocked and ashamed" when they learned that he had broken the law and been hauled off to jail. "You went to school to get an education," wrote Amie Lewis to her son. "You should get out of this movement, just get out of that mess."[3]

The real mess in Nashville resulted from white retaliation against Lewis and his fellow activists. Angry whites dumped food and put their cigarettes out on the backs of the nonviolent students as they patiently waited to be served. During one sit-in, they beat some of Lewis's friends as the police watched. But the violence in Nashville did not discourage the sit-in movement. Northern activists targeted chain stores, including Woolworth, Kress, and Kresge, with operations in Nashville and other southern cities. By March, Nashville's business leaders had reached a compromise with the movement: halt the protests and the lunch counters would be open to anyone who could pay. By the end of 1960, thousands of activists had joined sit-ins throughout the South. In October, Martin Luther King, Jr., was arrested after refusing to give up his seat at an Atlanta lunch counter.

KENNEDY AND THE LIBERAL REVIVAL

Many observers sensed change everywhere in 1960, not just at lunch counters. News reporters noted an awakening among both black and white youth, often expressed as a search for "authenticity" in a culture of conformity. In his best-selling 1956 book, sociologist C. Wright Mills criticized the "power elite," an interlocking system of military, business, and political leaders who shaped America's economy and politics. Mills believed that the challenge to established authority would come from a "new class" of well-educated youth in a prosperous America. "The Age of Complacency is ending," wrote Mills in 1960. "We are beginning to move again."[4]

The fundamental question was in what direction the United States would move. The answer remained far from clear. The protesters and counterprotesters in Nashville clashed over competing visions of what America should be. The struggle for civil rights was already reconfiguring party politics and raising fundamental questions about economics and political power. Should the New Deal, more than a quarter century old, be revivified or expanded? Was Eisenhower's pro-business vision right for the United States? For all their differences, members of both parties believed in aggressive engagement with Communism internationally. They fought mainly over who would wage the Cold War more effectively.

Democrats and Republicans Adrift

At the beginning of the 1960 campaign season, liberals were despondent, having lost the last two presidential elections. The New Deal had been tempered by more than a decade of stasis. Organized labor—still the Democrats' most powerful constituency—had seen its membership decline beginning in 1954. The party's southern wing had found common cause with the GOP over laws restricting labor, and the most rapid economic growth happened in the Sunbelt, especially in states with major defense contractors and attractive "right to work" laws that inhibited union organizing. Key Democratic constituencies also began to drift rightward. A majority of Catholics, who had reliably voted Democratic for decades, found Eisenhower attractive and rallied around conservative anti-Communists. White urbanites worried about growing black political and economic power, white suburbanites feared integration, and whites southerners opposed the civil rights insurgency.

The GOP, despite eight years in the White House, faced its own troubles. The Eisenhower administration presided over a deep recession that began in 1959. It seemed paralyzed by the Communist takeover of Cuba. The outgoing president fretted about a bloated "military-industrial complex" that jeopardized the federal budget. Vice President Richard Nixon, the Republican frontrunner to succeed Ike, had spent eight years overshadowed by Eisenhower, who did not particularly like him. Rather than giving him much responsibility to shape policy, Ike sent Nixon around the country to events he couldn't be bothered to attend.

The Democrats cast about for a new presidential candidate, someone who could bridge the party's growing north-south divide and credibly challenge Nixon. That would not be Senate majority leader Lyndon Johnson, a Texan whom the party's reform wing reviled, even as it grudgingly admired him for his legislative prowess. It would not be two-time loser Adlai Stevenson. Southerners would not rally for Minnesota senator Hubert Humphrey because of his early and outspoken support for civil rights in 1948.

The Rise of John F. Kennedy

Finally, Democrats rallied behind Massachusetts senator John F. Kennedy. At forty-three, he was one of the youngest contenders for the White House ever. His youthful good looks, and his comfort with the new medium of television, seemed to his admirers to embody change, even if liberals grumbled when he picked LBJ as his running mate. Still, Kennedy was a blank slate as the race for the presidency began. The scion of a wealthy Massachusetts family (his father had been FDR's ambassador to Britain), he had served with valor during World War II. With his family's financial backing, he had successfully run for Congress, winning the support of Boston's Irish Catholic–dominated political machine. In 1952 he won the first of two terms in the U.S. Senate, though he did not establish much of a record as a legislator. But influence in Washington came not just through writing laws or cutting deals. As a senator, Kennedy cultivated the Washington elite, published a Pulitzer Prize–winning series of vignettes of courageous political leaders, which had been ghostwritten by a family adviser, and appeared regularly on television news programs to opine on the political issues of the day.

Perhaps the most novel aspect of Kennedy's candidacy was that for all his Washington connections, he was a religious outsider, at least when it came to presidential politics. As one of the nation's most prominent Roman

Catholics, Kennedy came to be revered among his coreligionists as he moved onto the national stage. Though Catholics made up more than one-fifth of America's population—and formed a powerful voting bloc in key, closely divided states like Illinois, Pennsylvania, and New York—they were underrepresented in higher office.[5] Like the last Catholic contender for the presidency, Al Smith in 1928, Kennedy faced deep-rooted suspicion, especially among conservative Protestants, that he would be a tool of the papacy. But much had changed in the intervening three decades: prominent Catholic clerics like Fulton Sheen appeared on national television, Catholic immigrants and their children had served valiantly in World War II and Korea, and the American Catholic bishops zealously fought Communism.

Still, Kennedy had to reassure voters who had qualms about his religion. During the campaign, he used a speech to the Greater Houston Ministerial Association to pledge his commitment to an America "where no religious body seeks to impose its will directly or indirectly upon the general populace or the public acts of its officials."[6] He and most religious leaders, for the moment, agreed that religious belief belonged in the private sphere, not in the public square.

Kennedy campaigned on the vague promise to "get America moving again." Though Eisenhower, Nixon, and Kennedy differed little on foreign policy, Kennedy chastised his Republican opponent for standing still while the United States "lost" Cuba. He accused Ike and Nixon of allowing a "missile gap" with the Soviets to widen, and promised to pursue the Cold War more aggressively.

On the campaign trail, Kennedy called for a renewal of public service. He was cautious. He called for a reduction in taxes, gradualism on civil rights, and business-friendly, pro-growth policies to pull the country out of the economic slump. Telegenic and composed, he swept the 1960 presidential debates, the first time candidates in a presidential election had sparred face-to-face. His message about the power of government as a force for positive change captured the imagination of many Americans. In one of the closest presidential races in American history, Kennedy beat Nixon by just a little more than 100,000 votes out of more than 68 million cast nationwide. Some scholars suggest that Kennedy's close victory in both Texas and Illinois was the result of ballot-box-stuffing by Lyndon Johnson's well-oiled political operation in Texas and Chicago's infamous Democratic machine.

The Kennedy Technocracy

"The torch has been passed to a new generation of Americans," proclaimed Kennedy in his inaugural address. In soaring prose, he pledged that "we shall pay any price, bear any burden, meet any hardship, support any friend, oppose any foe to assure the survival and the success of liberty." Winning the Cold War would not simply be a matter of might. It would require uplifting the oppressed both at home and abroad. Kennedy called for sacrifice in a "struggle against the common enemies of man: tyranny, poverty, disease and war itself."[7]

Once in office, Kennedy established himself as the heir to Progressive reformers and New Dealers for his belief that the most effective government grew from a marriage of detached experts and government officials. In one of his most important addresses, in 1962, he summed up his philosophy of governance: "The fact of the matter is that most of the problems, or at least many of them that we now face, are technical problems, are administrative problems. They are very sophisticated judgments which do not lend themselves to the great sort of 'passionate movements,' which have stirred this country so often in the past."[8] He distanced his administration not only from the most passionate of movements, the struggle for civil rights, but also from the messiness of the legislative process. Instead, he sought the advice of the nation's most prominent economists, social scientists, and executives, particularly graduates and faculty of the most elite universities, including his alma mater, Harvard, his own version of Franklin Roosevelt's "brains trust."

When Kennedy asked James Tobin, a Nobel Prize–winning economist at Yale, to join his economic team, Tobin modestly demurred: "Mr. President, I am what you might call an *ivory tower economist*." Kennedy rejoined, "That's the best kind! Professor, I am what you might call an *ivory tower President*."[9] Kennedy believed that experts like Tobin, detached from the messy process of campaigning and lawmaking, would act in the national interest, not in their own self-interest.

Mostly uninterested in the details of domestic policy, Kennedy relied on his staff to set his agenda. His economic advisers persuaded him to adopt economic policies based on John Maynard Keynes's argument that government spending would stimulate economic growth. Like many political centrists, Kennedy at first prioritized government solvency through a balanced budget. But Tobin and Minnesota economist Walter Heller persuaded him that deficit spending would stimulate demand. Following their advice, he supported increased federal spending on the construction of schools, highways, and military bases. He also singled out "distressed areas" for federal aid, although critics complained that the administration just sent federal "pork" into districts to reward Democratic loyalists or to buy off critics.

Kennedy's tax policy was also Keynesian. His aides overhauled the federal tax code, creating a standard deduction, reducing tax-withholding rates, eliminating loopholes, and lowering the rate for the top tax bracket from 91 to 70 percent of individual income. Kennedy's economic team argued that lower taxes and a streamlined tax-collection system would stimulate consumer demand and spur growth. Getting tax reform through Congress was challenging. Many Republicans worried that tax cuts would unbalance the federal budget. Congress would not pass the new tax code until 1964.

CIVIL RIGHTS

For all Kennedy's faith in the judgment of cool, detached experts, he could not ignore the intensifying African American struggle for civil rights. He himself had been lukewarm toward the civil rights insurgents of the 1950s. He only tepidly supported the Civil Rights Act of 1957. The first such law enacted in more than eight decades, it was mostly a symbolic gesture. The act called for voting rights for African Americans but contained no enforcement mechanisms. It also created a federal Civil Rights Commission to investigate discrimination and recommend reforms. Kennedy refused to join liberals who wanted the law to be stronger. During his 1960 campaign, to attract black voters, he gestured toward civil rights. He pledged to end discrimination in housing with "the stroke of a pen" and prepared campaign materials to be distributed to black churches that touted his successful effort to persuade Atlanta officials to release Martin Luther King, Jr., from jail after his sit-in arrest.

Civil rights was not, however, a priority for the new president. That was largely a matter of political calculation. Kennedy had long been mindful of the restive southern wing of his party. In 1948, as a first-term member of Congress, Kennedy had witnessed Dixiecrat Strom Thurmond's rebellion. As Kennedy set his sights on higher office, he distanced himself from civil rights legislation and assiduously cultivated southern Democrats, just as FDR had during the New Deal. His choice of Lyndon Johnson, a prominent southerner, as his vice-presidential nominee discomfited northern liberals.

"A Great Sense of Hope"

Even though civil rights advocates had good reason to worry about Kennedy and more so about Johnson, they still hoped that the Democrats would be more responsive than Eisenhower and Nixon to their demands. Kennedy had given the Democrats' liberal wing nearly full control over the 1960 party platform, which they used to push for aggressive civil rights enforcement. But behind the scenes, Kennedy reassured his party's southern lions that he did not consider the platform to be binding.

John Lewis was one of the many young people who believed that, despite his record, Kennedy would be an agent of change. "I watched Kennedy's inaugural address that January with a great sense of hope," recalled Lewis. "Here was this young, vibrant man who seemed to represent the future just by his energy and age. He didn't mention race or civil rights in his speech, but I assumed that was simply a matter of political expediency. I believed that *he* believed in what we all believed in—The Beloved Community."[10]

Kennedy could not have cared less about Lewis's vision of an interracial society. For him, civil rights was a political obstacle that bitterly divided the Democratic Party. Rather than taking a principled position in favor of racial equality, he awkwardly tried to appease southern segregationists, especially when it came to nominations to the federal bench. About a third of Kennedy's appointees to the Fifth Circuit—which included Alabama, Florida, Georgia, Louisiana, Mississippi, and Texas—had records upholding Jim Crow laws. But nodding to his party's liberal wing, Kennedy also nominated prominent blacks to district and appellate court posts in the North, including longtime NAACP attorney Thurgood Marshall, Philadelphia civil rights lawyer A. Leon Higginbotham, and Wade H. McCree, a reform Democrat from Detroit. Kennedy hoped, at least, that he could paste together a coalition big enough to stave off a Republican challenge in 1964 by giving a little bit to everyone.

In trying to lower the temperature of the civil rights debate, Kennedy devised and implemented many of his most significant initiatives outside the public eye. In April 1961, for example, he created the President's Committee on Equal Employment Opportunity, which worked mostly behind the scenes to draft federal regulations to address the problem of discrimination by federal contractors. In 1962, Kennedy signed a little-noticed executive order calling for vaguely defined "affirmative action" in hiring by government contractors. Kennedy hoped that given small victories, labor and civil rights groups would cool their demands for a full-blown antidiscrimination law and that perhaps the party's southern constituents would pay little heed to bureaucratic directives.

The Freedom Rides

John Lewis was not satisfied with Kennedy's baby steps forward. Within months of the inauguration, it became clear to him that the White House would not take the lead on civil rights. Pressure had to come from below. Lewis and other activists made sure that it did. During Kennedy's first year in office, members of CORE, including several veterans of the 1947 Journey of Reconciliation, planned an assault on segregated interstate transportation. Beginning in April 1961, carefully trained interracial teams launched the Freedom Rides, traveling by bus across Virginia and the Carolinas, down to Georgia, Alabama, and Mississippi, refusing to give up their seats to whites and disregarding the ubiquitous "whites only" signs in bus terminals. The Freedom Rides attracted many youthful activists, including Lewis.

One of the key training exercises for the Freedom Riders was "role playing," in which potential riders tried out nonviolent responses to mock attacks. For Lewis—who had already been arrested five times—these were nothing new. But on May 4, in Rock Hill, South Carolina, Lewis and his fellow Freedom Riders found their skills tested when white thugs beat them in the bus terminal before the police dispersed the crowd. Lewis stumbled back onto the bus, his chest badly bruised and his head bloody.

The Freedom Riders (minus Lewis, who left for a few days for a fellowship interview) made headlines worldwide on May 14, when, just outside Anniston, Alabama, a group of white supremacists drove the bus off the road, lit it afire, and brutally beat the black and white passengers as they escaped. The photograph of the burning bus—on the front pages of newspapers worldwide—became an icon of southern intransigence. It accomplished the Freedom Riders' goal of putting the spotlight on white supremacy.

Battered and stunned, the Freedom Riders proceeded from Anniston to Alabama's largest city, Birmingham, in another bus, this time under police escort. But as the bus arrived at the city's main terminal, the police disappeared. Hundreds of whites converged on the Freedom Riders as they disembarked, beating them with bats, chains, and bricks. Some of Alabama's leading public officials had encouraged the mob violence, including the Birmingham police commissioner, Eugene "Bull" Connor, who had given the police orders to withdraw from the station just minutes before the Freedom Riders arrived.

Lewis and another group of Freedom Riders arrived in Birmingham on May 17, where they were arrested, imprisoned, and eventually shuttled to the Tennessee border in two unmarked cars. Lewis sat in the lead car, driven by none other than Bull Connor himself. Not intimidated, Lewis and his comrades sneaked back to Birmingham, intending to continue on their Freedom Ride. They didn't know that, embarrassed by the news coverage of the Rides, the Kennedy administration had quietly reached an agreement with Alabama governor John Patterson that the riders would be protected from further violence.

But the Alabama state police did not cooperate. On May 21, in a grim reprise of the Birmingham bloodbath, the police once again left the Riders unguarded. As the bus arrived in Montgomery, they once again faced mob violence. White vigilantes pummeled Lewis and his fellow Riders, beat several reporters, and left John Seigenthaler, a high-ranking Kennedy administration official sent to monitor the protests, bloody and unconscious. Stationed just blocks from the bus terminal, the police deliberately ignored the rampage.

Kennedy was furious at Patterson but just as angry at the Freedom Riders. "Can't you get your god-damned friends off those buses?" Kennedy asked domestic policy aide Harris Wofford, a supporter of the civil rights movement.[11] Many commentators, north and south, accused the Freedom Riders of stirring up violence. But the Freedom Rides continued unabated through the fall, as hundreds of nonviolent protesters went to jail, especially in Mississippi.

Cold War Civil Rights

The president worried that, in the midst of the Cold War, the grisly images of beaten protesters and reports of Freedom Riders sentenced to hard labor in southern prisons would damage America's carefully manufactured international image. In the struggle to win the hearts and minds of the third world, the Soviets used images of beaten protesters and burning buses as proof that America was a sham democracy. The Freedom Rides threatened to unravel more than a decade's worth of American cultural diplomacy, which included black diplomats appointed to American embassies in Scandinavia, government-sponsored tours by black celebrities like jazz trumpeter Louis Armstrong, and black-themed programming on the Voice of America.

Another well-publicized racial incident in the fall of 1961 embarrassed Kennedy. Chad's ambassador to the United States, Malik Sow, was driving from New York to Washington, D.C., along Maryland's Route 40, when a roadside restaurant refused to serve him. "He looked just like an ordinary run of the mill nigger to me," stated the waitress who rebuffed him. "I couldn't tell he was an ambassador."[12] Mainstream publications, including *Life* magazine, made it "story of the week" in early December—another blow to America's reputation. The State Department intervened, reaching an agreement with dozens of Maryland restaurants that they would not discriminate.

COLD WAR CRISES

The Route 40 incident starkly reminded Kennedy that Jim Crow and civil rights protests had international implications: they threatened the new administration's foreign policy. The Cold War intensified during Kennedy's first months in office. Despite Kennedy's rhetoric of change, he inherited a well-developed anti-Communist policy from his predecessors. He built on Truman's policy of containment, increased military spending, and continued Eisenhower's policy of fighting the Cold War in the developing world. However, Kennedy faced a series of escalating international crises on every front of the Cold War: Latin America, Europe, and Asia.

The Bay of Pigs

Less than three months after inauguration day, Kennedy authorized an attempted coup in Cuba. The plan was not his—Eisenhower's CIA had hatched it. On April 17, 1961, fourteen hundred anti-Castro insurgents, trained and armed by the United States, made landfall at the Bay of Pigs. The CIA had mistakenly assumed that tens of thousands of Cubans would hail the liberators and join them in overthrowing the Castro regime. Establishing a beachhead in the marshy bay proved to be a strategic error. A popular uprising did not ensue, and Castro, fully aware of the plot, deployed the Cuban military and put down the insurrection within hours. The debacle deeply embarrassed Kennedy.

Germany, the Soviets, and East-West Hostility

In the meantime, the Soviets and the East Germans, emboldened by their perception of Kennedy's weakness, challenged the United States in Berlin. By the fall of 1961, they completed construction of the Berlin Wall, which separated Communist East Berlin from the American-controlled West. The wall became a symbol of East-West hostility. A humanitarian disaster, it prevented the movement of political refugees into West Berlin. In the meantime, the Soviet Union stepped up support for insurgencies in Southeast Asia, Latin America, and central Africa.

Kennedy, who did not share Eisenhower's end-of-term misgivings about the military-industrial complex, greatly accelerated the production and deployment of nuclear weapons. In the summer of 1961 he expanded the military draft, stationed additional troops in Europe and Asia, pressed Congress to increase defense spending, and even urged ordinary Americans to build fallout shelters in case of an all-out war.

Despite his public warnings about the "missile gap," Kennedy was in an advantageous position vis-à-vis the Soviet Union. American airpower and weaponry were unsurpassed. The United States still had a substantially larger nuclear arsenal than the Soviets. Most Soviet nuclear weapons could not reach the United States. But the threat of nuclear war never seemed closer than during the weeks following October 14, 1962, when an American U2 spy plane discovered that the Soviet Union was installing intermediate-range ballistic missiles in Cuba, just ninety miles off the U.S. coast.

The Cuban Missile Crisis

The Cuban Missile Crisis had its origins earlier in the Kennedy administration. In early 1961, JFK had authorized the military to place nuclear missiles in Turkey and Italy, within range of Moscow and St. Petersburg. Khrushchev considered U.S. missiles near its border an "intolerable provocation." Kennedy also provoked the Soviets by stepping up the Cold War in Latin America, supporting efforts to assassinate Castro, and channeling aid to

Castro's enemies elsewhere in Latin America. Finally, he authorized military exercises over the Caribbean to unsettle the Cubans and demonstrate American strength.

On October 16, Kennedy responded to the discovery of Soviet missiles in Cuba by pulling together ExComm, a group of key military and foreign policy advisers, and close aides, who held intensive secret meetings to plan a response to the crisis. Some Pentagon officials promoted the invasion of Cuba, arguing that the missile crisis offered the perfect opportunity to topple Castro, a position that Attorney General Robert F. Kennedy, the president's brother, also urged. Others made the case for a targeted strike against the missile sites. A third group called for negotiations.

ExComm members debated the strategic significance of the deployment of the missiles. In a memo to the president, aide Ted Sorensen wrote that the Cuban missiles, "even when fully operational, do not significantly alter the balance of power—i.e., they do not significantly increase the potential megatonnage capable of being unleashed on American soil, even after a surprise American nuclear strike."[13] But other advisers feared the deployment was the first step in expanding Soviet capacity for a retaliatory strike in the event of war.

On October 22, in a televised speech, Kennedy made the startling public announcement about the missiles. He issued an ultimatum, finding a middle ground in ExComm's deliberations. If Khrushchev didn't withdraw the missiles, the United States would enforce a blockade of Soviet shipments to the island. Nodding to the hawks, Kennedy also promised that the use of any Cuban missiles against any target in the Americas would be regarded "as an attack by the Soviet Union on the United States, requiring a full retaliatory response upon the Soviet Union."[14] Two days later, with the blockade in place, Soviet ships turned back.

Khrushchev reacted with fury, denouncing Kennedy. Privately, however, both sides were open to negotiation. In a letter to Kennedy on October 26, Khrushchev proposed to withdraw the Soviet missiles if the United States pledged not to invade Cuba. On the twenty-seventh he publicly demanded that the United States withdraw its own missile installations in Turkey. The administration accepted Khrushchev's terms to dismantle the Cuban installation under UN inspection and agreed not to take military action against Cuba. Neither Khrushchev nor Kennedy mentioned the secret agreement at the heart of the deal: the United States promised to later remove its missiles from Turkey. On October 28 the Soviet government announced that it would disassemble and remove the Cuban missiles.

The truce with Khrushchev was at best uneasy. The successful negotiations had prevented war and begun the process of gradually slowing the arms race. Over the next year, Kennedy and Khrushchev agreed to a partial test ban treaty, entered into negotiations over an arms reduction treaty, and set up the White House–Kremlin hotline, so the two leaders could talk directly in case of another crisis.

But the Kennedy administration continued to fight the Cold War on many fronts. Using "soft diplomacy," the United States funded large-scale economic development projects in South America and Southeast Asia. In 1961, just weeks after the inauguration, Kennedy announced the creation of the Peace Corps, a popular program that would send idealistic young Americans to work on education, disease eradication, and agricultural and engineering projects throughout the world.

But the Cold War intensified. The United States and the Soviet Union continued their proxy battles through direct military support and clandestine activities in places as diverse as Vietnam, the Dominican Republic, and the Congo. Most consequential was Vietnam, where the Kennedy administration simultaneously channeled substantial economic aid, provided military support to anti-Communist forces, and supported CIA covert action. Kennedy increased the number of American military advisers there from about 900 in 1961 to 16,000 in late 1963, but did not commit the United States to an all-out war. At the same time, the propaganda war between the United States and the USSR intensified and, increasingly, affected the struggle for civil rights on the home front.

"WHERE'S THE PEN, MR. PRESIDENT?"

As the president directed his energies abroad, and moved slowly on civil rights, John Lewis expressed his growing frustration: "Where's the PEN, Mr. President?"[15] Throughout Kennedy's first and much of his second year in office, activists mailed thousands of pens to the White House to urge him to ban housing discrimination. Kennedy's staff warehoused the pens, and Kennedy did nothing, fearing the wrath of white voters who associated integrated housing with intermarriage and crime. But the pressure kept mounting. Kennedy could not dismiss hundreds of petitions from churches and celebrity endorsements of open housing. Members of CORE picketed new housing developments in Cleveland, New York, and Los Angeles. On the weekend before Thanksgiving, just after the 1962 midterm elections, timed to minimize controversy, Kennedy issued an executive order banning discrimination in all new housing constructed with federal funds. As Kennedy hoped, the order attracted little media attention.

Housing was one battleground in the multifront struggle for civil rights; public education was another. *Brown* continued to be a dead letter in the South, where public officials mostly ignored the ruling. In the North and West, however, civil rights activists used *Brown* to challenge segregated schools. In 1961 local officials in New Rochelle, New York—dubbed the "Little Rock of the North"—lost a court battle to maintain the town's segregated Lincoln primary school. Fired up by the victory in New Rochelle, activists took on segregated schools throughout the region. In 1962 the Englewood Movement, a diverse coalition of former Freedom Riders, activist lawyers, and black radicals, challenged segregated schools in a New Jersey suburb. By year's end, the NAACP was battling segregation in sixty-nine northern and western school districts. Over the next two years, hundreds of thousands of students in Chicago, Boston, Cleveland, and New York boycotted classes in segregated schools.

The Kennedy administration kept its distance from the northern school protests. But it could not ignore the media coverage of the University of Mississippi in September 1962, when James Meredith attempted to enroll. With legal support from the NAACP, Meredith won a Supreme Court ruling that struck down the university's discriminatory admissions policy. When he attempted to register for classes, however, Mississippi governor Ross Barnett encouraged defiance and, when violence erupted on the campus, refused to intervene. Angry mobs of white students, alumni, and area residents went on a rampage, injuring dozens of armed officials and killing two bystanders. The Kennedy administration deployed five hundred U.S. marshals, nationalized the Mississippi National Guard, and sent troops to quell the riot, before Meredith, under armed guard, enrolled.

Birmingham and the "Negro Revolt" of 1963

January 1, 1963, marked the centennial of the Emancipation Proclamation. Rather than celebrating, black America seemed to be in open rebellion. That spring Martin Luther King, Jr., and the Southern Christian Leadership

Conference (SCLC) chose Birmingham, Alabama, as a target of protest. On May 3 thousands of black protesters, many of them schoolchildren, took to Birmingham's streets. King and his co-organizers anticipated that local law enforcement officials, led by Bull Connor, would react with violence, a prophecy that turned out to be grimly true. Connor ordered policemen to sic their dogs and firefighters to blast their hoses on protesters. The photos of the violence appeared on the front pages of newspapers worldwide.

From his Birmingham jail cell, where he languished after being arrested for demonstrating without a permit, King defended his strategy: "We know through painful experience that freedom is never voluntarily given by the oppressor; it must be demanded by the oppressed." In especially pointed words, he lambasted moderates, perhaps even the president himself. "I have almost reached the regrettable conclusion," wrote King, "that the Negro's great stumbling block in his stride toward freedom is not the White Citizens Councilor or the Ku Klux Klanner, but the white moderate, who is more devoted to 'order' than to justice."[16]

The demands of the oppressed intensified in the following months. In late spring and early summer, 758 demonstrations broke out throughout the country. In seventy-five southern cities, 13,786 protesters were arrested.[17] Not all the demonstrations followed the nonviolent course that King advocated. In Birmingham, shortly after the police attacks, angry blacks took to the streets, breaking windows and looting stores. Mass protests, many of them violent, broke out in northern cities beginning in May and continued through the summer. In Philadelphia, dozens of activists were arrested for occupying city hall and blockading construction sites that had no black workers. Militants, including members of a fledgling black power organization called the Revolutionary Action Movement, joined the demonstrations. Many young protesters could barely contain their anger. Mocking the misuse of police dogs, young men in Philadelphia marched with mastiffs and turned a famous civil rights anthem into a military style chant: "We . . . Shall . . . Over . . . Come."[18]

White supremacists reacted aggressively. In June 1963, Alabama governor George Wallace, who earlier that year used his inauguration address to call for "segregation today, segregation tomorrow, segregation forever," defiantly stood at the entrance of the University of Alabama's main building to oppose the enrollment of two black students. After high-level negotiations with the Kennedy administration, which wanted to avoid a Mississippi-style bloodbath, Wallace let them in.[19] In Mississippi, on June 12, 1963, white supremacists assassinated NAACP leader Medgar Evers in his driveway.

The Kennedy administration entered a state of crisis. The passionate movements that the president had neglected seemed unstoppable. When Kennedy dispatched staffers to visit northern cities that had erupted in protest, they returned with a warning. The situation there was explosive. The administration had come to realize that the domestic crisis was every bit as grave as its troubles abroad. In a nationally televised address on June 22, 1963, Kennedy announced that his administration would draft civil rights legislation, though he was light on the specifics.

If Kennedy expected that his announcement would put a lid on protests, he was wrong. The next day Martin Luther King, Jr., headlined the hundred-thousand-person Walk for Freedom in Detroit. Rather than celebrating Kennedy's shift on civil rights, King encouraged protesters to push harder, saving especially harsh words for those who demanded blacks to be patient. "Gradualism," King argued, "is little more than escapism and do-nothingism, which ends up in stand-stillism."[20]

The March on Washington

Few took the argument against gradualism more seriously than John Lewis. While King was marching in Detroit, Lewis worked with a coalition of longtime labor and civil rights activists, convened by A. Philip Randolph, to plan a massive civil rights demonstration in the nation's capital. The March on Washington for Jobs and Freedom, held on August 28, 1963, packed the Mall with 250,000 people. In a rousing speech, King delivered his famous line, "I have a dream," using soaring language to unify America in pursuit of a common goal, a society where everyone would be "judged by the content of their character, not the color of their skin."[21]

The message of the March on Washington could not be boiled down to King's dream. The participants demanded well-paying, secure jobs and an end to workplace discrimination. A few weeks before the march, Randolph pulled together more than eight hundred union and civil rights leaders and gained the support of dozens of interracial unions. Tens of thousands of blue-collar workers—including meatpackers, department store stock handlers, auto assemblers, and steelworkers—packed buses rented by their unions. Thousands of unemployed men and women, their trips to Washington subsidized by unions and churches, joined them.

SNCC

John Lewis prepared one of the march's most radical speeches. Only twenty-three, he was one of the founding members of the Student Non-Violent Coordinating Committee. SNCC members were impatient with the carefully choreographed, media-oriented events staged by King and the Southern Christian Leadership Conference. They were skeptical of the SCLC's top-down organizing style and its ministerial leadership. Ella Baker, who had begun her career organizing among domestic servants in Harlem during the Depression, counseled SNCC activists and reminded them that leadership was not solely a male prerogative. At their most acerbic, SNCC members derided King as "de Lawd" and called for a more democratic movement.

SNCC members settled in the most troubled parts of the Mississippi Delta and the Alabama Black Belt. They mostly worked off-camera, uninterested in staging media events. Instead, they went door to door, winning the trust of sharecroppers and domestics, establishing "freedom schools" to bring them literacy and local history and civics education, and encouraging them to vote. SNCC organizers faced everyday violence. Local authorities cracked down on them with impunity, forcing many to go underground. The Kennedy administration, though it supported voting rights in principle, turned a blind eye toward the everyday harassment of black would-be voters.

By 1963, Lewis and fellow SNCC members harbored no illusions about the president. In the speech he prepared for the March on Washington, Lewis minced no words: "American politics is dominated by politicians who build their career on immoral compromising." In his view, Kennedy's proposed civil rights legislation was too little and too late, a weak attempt to mollify protesters while thwarting more systemic change. He concluded with even stronger language, comparing the civil rights movement to General Sherman's march through Georgia during the Civil War.[22] At the last minute, Randolph and other march organizers persuaded Lewis to tone down his speech, for fear of alienating the president. "I've waited my entire life for this opportunity," Randolph told Lewis. "Please don't ruin it."[23]

Quivering with anger, Lewis delivered a somewhat tempered version of his speech, cutting a key sentence: "We will not wait for the President, the Justice Department, nor the Congress, but will take matters into our own hands and create a source of power, outside of any national structure, that could and would assure us of victory." After the march Randolph and

King went to a White House meeting, and gained the president's assurance that he would push hard for civil rights legislation.

Unrest in the Streets

Over the fall of 1963, the movement followed the course that Lewis outlined, while the administration's efforts to push civil rights legislation moved forward haltingly. In Harlem the situation was so tense that a number of "near riots" broke out, usually sparked by arrests. Many northern police departments invested in military gear, preparing for what they believed was an inevitable race war. Blacks also reacted angrily in September, when four black schoolgirls died in a church bombing in Birmingham. Journalists called 1963 the year of the "Negro Revolt."

In October, John Lewis joined a protest at Rochdale Gardens, a massive apartment complex under construction in Queens, New York, where protesters formed blockades and chained themselves to cranes to protest the lack of black workers on the site. Lewis took the occasion to argue that "the Negro must revolt against not only the white power structure but also against the Negro leadership that would slow the Negro march to a slow shuffle."[24] Although Lewis remained committed to nonviolence and to integration, his words echoed those of Nation of Islam leader Malcolm X, who also joined the picket line at Rochdale Gardens that fall.

The Nation of Islam, a small African American religious sect founded in the early 1930s, had about 100,000 members at its peak. But its influence was greater because of Malcolm X's charisma and his unsettling and newsworthy message. Malcolm Little, raised in Michigan, had converted to the Nation while in jail for petty theft. He took the surname X, the single letter replacing the name of the family of slaveholders who had held his ancestors as chattel. Striking for his crisp dress and formidable oratorical skills, Malcolm argued that the white man was the devil, that blacks needed to take power into their own hands, and that integration was an impossible dream.

By late 1963, Malcolm X had more invitations to speak at public events than he could accept. He also wrote regularly for the black press and aired his views on national news programs; he disseminated one of his most important speeches, his November 1963 "Message to the Grassroots," through the new record label, Motown, produced by Detroit impresario Berry Gordy. The recording popularized Malcolm X's celebration of African and Asian revolutionaries. He lambasted the civil rights establishment as

"House Negroes" and "Uncle Toms" who "keep us passive and peaceful and non-violent."[25] He was particularly skeptical of King's version of civil rights. "There's no such thing as a nonviolent revolution. The only kind of revolution that is nonviolent is the Negro revolution. The only revolution in which the goal is loving your enemy is the Negro revolution. It's the only revolution in which the goal is a desegregated lunch counter, a desegregated theater, a desegregated park, and a desegregated public toilet; you can sit down next to white folks—on the toilet. That's no revolution."[26] Malcolm X did not reflect the majority opinion among African Americans, but he gave voice to the passion, anger, militancy, and race pride that many civil rights activists, even advocates of nonviolence like John Lewis, felt from Nashville to Birmingham to Queens.

PRESIDENT JOHNSON

Whether President Kennedy would have succeeded in calming the growing racial unrest and passing civil rights legislation are open questions, but there weren't many good reasons to be optimistic in late 1963. He was heading into what many expected would be a bruising reelection campaign and needed the support of southern Democrats. Many party leaders, including Lyndon Johnson, doubted that Kennedy had the skill to push any antidiscrimination law through Congress. Civil rights leaders feared that yet another empty, symbolic gesture would be coming from the White House.

Kennedy's Assassination

Those questions would remain forever unanswered. On November 22, 1963, the president who had hoped that technocracy would trump passion was undone in one of the darkest moments of passion in American history when he was felled by an assassin's bullet. Riding in an open-top convertible through the streets of Dallas, Texas, Kennedy was targeted by a mentally ill drifter, twenty-four-year-old Lee Harvey Oswald.

The assassin's troubled past, including stints in the Soviet Union and Cuba, fueled all sorts of conspiracy theories, as did the fact that Oswald was shot dead on November 24, before he could be interrogated. While there is no evidence that anyone other than Oswald was involved in the assassination, some pointed their fingers at the Cubans, others at the Soviets, and still others at a shadowy criminal underworld of Mafia bosses angry because the president's brother, Robert, the attorney general, was investigating them. Some harbored the far-fetched belief that a cabal of Texans who wanted to plant Lyndon Johnson in the White House was responsible.

However plausible or ridiculous the assassination theories were, none would ever be proven or disproven. Each was a symptom of the trauma surrounding the death of a young, telegenic leader, in office less than three years. Kennedy's death took on near mythic status in post–1963 America, in part because Americans projected their hopes and fears for the country onto the body of the slain president. What if? What if Kennedy had not died that November day?

Johnson's Rise

Lyndon Baines Johnson took the oath of office aboard *Air Force One* with Kennedy's widow, still wearing her bloodstained dress, at his side. He immediately promised to use his legislative skills to push through Kennedy's tax-reduction bill and free the civil rights bill from the quicksand of southern-dominated congressional committees and the steel trap of the filibuster. He also pledged much more: to expand voting rights to disenfranchised African Americans, to provide affordable higher education for "every boy and girl in this country, no matter how poor, or the color of their skin, or the region they come from," and to pass a national health insurance bill that Democrats since Roosevelt had advocated.[27]

Few liberals expected that President Johnson would be such a forceful advocate for the poor and disenfranchised. He had grown up in the Texas Hill Country, a poor area, home to mostly white hardscrabble farmers. For most of his childhood, rural Texas—like large parts of the South and Southwest—had been an economic backwater. The state's cotton production was declining. Most homes lacked electricity. Public schools, including the one near the border where Johnson had started his career as a teacher of mostly Mexican American students, were run-down and barely provided an education, particularly during planting and harvest season, when classrooms emptied.

The fortunes of Texas took a turn for the better during the New Deal, as powerful Democrats, including Johnson, channeled federal dollars to the Hill Country. When Johnson entered Congress in 1937, he badgered New Deal officials to extend power lines into the area. Rural electrification, along with federal funds for roads, hospitals, post offices, and schools, taught

Johnson a lesson that he carried with him for the rest of his career: government could transform the lives of "forgotten" Americans, like his constituents and neighbors.

Johnson won election to the U.S. Senate in 1948, after a bruising and corrupt primary. A ruthless campaigner, he portrayed his opponent as soft on Communism and civil rights. In San Antonio and along the Rio Grande, Johnson's supporters stuffed the ballot box to give him an edge—only eighty-seven votes statewide.[28] But once he was in office, Johnson's popularity soared as he masterfully channeled federal aid to his home state. Joining his fellow senators Strom Thurmond of South Carolina, William Fulbright of Arkansas, and Richard Russell of Georgia, he ensured that the Sunbelt became a major recipient of defense spending, highway construction funds, and tax breaks to buttress its growing oil industry. Without massive public works, Texas and most of the South would have remained underdeveloped economically.

Early in his career, Johnson also positioned himself against even modest civil rights reforms. He voted against antilynching legislation and denounced legislation to create a permanent federal Fair Employment Practices Committee as the first step toward the creation of a "police state." But as he moved into the Senate leadership and set his sights on higher office, he began to shift his position on racial issues. If he wanted a chance at the White House, he needed to put some distance between himself and white supremacy. Unlike many southerners, Johnson supported the 1957 Civil Rights Act, even if he had made sure that the final law was weak.

The Civil Rights Act of 1964

Under Kennedy, LBJ had strengthened his civil rights portfolio, but most liberals did not expect much from him. They were proven wrong. Johnson's crowning achievement was the enactment of sweeping civil rights reforms. During his first six months in office, he forged a bipartisan coalition of northern and western Democrats and key Republicans to bypass his own party's southern wing. He used the blunt tools of deal making that he had learned in his time as the Senate majority leader. He threatened those who were lukewarm on the bill and cut deals with key Republicans, including Minority Leader Everett Dirksen, who brought along enough GOP votes to break the Democratic filibuster. The Civil Rights Act of 1964, enacted on

July 2, forbade discrimination in commercial establishments and in both public and private schools. The act's lengthiest and most controversial section was Title VII, which forbade employers from hiring, promoting, and firing workers on the basis of "race, color, religion, sex, or national origin." It also created the Equal Employment Opportunity Commission (EEOC) to investigate claims of workplace discrimination.[29]

The Civil Rights Act was full of qualifications and hedges, the result of compromises to win the support of enough pro-business Republicans to overcome a filibuster, which under Senate rules at the time required sixty-seven votes. As a result, it left housing segregation untouched. The EEOC had the power to engage in "conciliation" with employers but could not bring lawsuits or file criminal charges against those who discriminated. If it detected a "pattern and practice" of workplace discrimination, it could refer cases to the Department of Justice for litigation.

Civil rights groups pushed aggressively for the act's enforcement. The NAACP and local attorneys began taking employers to court to force them to open jobs to black workers. Grassroots activists around the country used it to challenge trade unions that excluded blacks. Although the drafters of the Civil Rights Act had not spent much time discussing the prohibition against sex discrimination, women's groups began pushing for its enforcement. In 1966 the new National Organization for Women, whose founders included Betty Friedan, argued against the notion that a man should "carry the sole burden of supporting himself, his wife and family." It demanded "equal pay for equal work" and the rigorous enforcement of Title VII.[30]

Over the next few years, the Johnson administration expanded the reach of Title VII. In 1965, Johnson issued Executive Order 11246, which gave the newly created Office of Contract Compliance the power to terminate government contracts to firms that did not practice "affirmative action" in employment. What "affirmative action" meant would be defined in 1966 and 1967 in a series of policy experiments in four metropolitan areas that had been rocked by protests over workplace discrimination. In St. Louis, where civil rights protesters chained themselves to the Gateway Arch, then under construction, federal officials fashioned a "St. Louis Plan" that demanded that contractors provide evidence of their efforts to hire minorities. Similar plans were put in place in San Francisco, Cleveland, and Philadelphia after massive protests at construction sites there.

Northern White Resistance

Johnson had signed the Civil Rights Act just four months before that year's presidential election. He worried mightily about his prospects, with good reason. "We have lost the South for a generation," he told his aide Bill Moyers.[31] White voters in his home region called him a turncoat. There were also ominous signs for Johnson outside the states of the Old Confederacy. During the 1964 Democratic primaries, Alabama governor George Wallace, making his first run for the Democratic presidential nomination, swept predominantly white, blue-collar precincts in Gary, Milwaukee, and Baltimore, surprising many observers. He picked up 30 percent of the Democratic vote in Indiana, 34 percent in Wisconsin, and 45 percent in Maryland.

Whites all over the country were uneasy about civil rights. The crowd at Boston's 1964 St. Patrick's Day parade pelted NAACP officials with stones. Later that year, in a statewide referendum, California voters rolled back a civil rights law that forbade discrimination in the sale of housing by a two-to-one ratio. White parents in Brooklyn and Queens boycotted schools targeted for integration.

The negative reaction to civil rights built on a long history. Since the 1920s the movement of even a single black family into a white neighborhood in most northern cities had generated mob violence. In the twenty years following World War II, whites in Detroit had attacked hundreds of black home owners. Hundreds of thousands of whites fled to the segregated suburbs rather than accept black neighbors. In Chicago in the 1940s and 1950s, huge white mobs protested integrated housing and regularly attacked black youths using city parks, beaches, and pools.

Northern politicians had long catered to the racial fears of their white constituents. Throughout the 1950s and early 1960s, elected officials in Illinois, Michigan, California, Connecticut, and New York had led a campaign against "welfare chiselers," just as the ranks of blacks receiving public assistance was rising. Big-city mayors like Chicago's Martin Kennelly and Richard J. Daley and Detroit's Albert Cobo defended segregation in public housing projects. And even the mildest efforts to desegregate public education met with fierce resistance by politicians and parents who supported "neighborhood schools," even though in the sprawling postwar metropolis, fewer and fewer white students lived within walking distance of schools, and by 1960 a majority already rode buses each day.

Opposition to civil rights ran deeper than local battles over turf and schools. Right-wing activists criticized civil rights and racial integration, arguing that antidiscrimination laws interfered with management's right to hire and fire at will. They denounced laws forbidding discrimination in housing as "socialistic" or "communistic" incursions on individual freedoms to sell or rent to anyone they pleased. In 1962 the National Association of Realtors released the "Home Owners' Bill of Rights," proclaiming that "the individual property owner, regardless of race, color, or creed, must be allowed under law to retain the right to determine acceptability of any prospective buyer or tenant of his property."[32] Civil rights legislation, they believed, interfered with the free market and violated the constitutional right to freedom of association.

THE NEW RIGHT

The reaction to civil rights was the most prominent part of a right-wing insurgency against liberalism that had been gaining strength since the 1950s. On a beautiful fall weekend in September 1960, a group of well-dressed young white people, mostly men, gathered for a photograph on the manicured lawn of Great Elm, the Sharon, Connecticut, estate of William F. Buckley, Jr., the editor of a New Right-wing periodical, the *National Review*. Although they had come of age when America was at its peak of global economic and political power, they were anything but self-congratulatory. For them, postwar America was facing grave "moral and political crises." Both Democrats and Republicans, they argued, were complacent about the international Communist threat. The United States was afflicted by spiritual decadence, aided and abetted by leaders of both parties who expanded the power of government and thus restricted individual freedom.

To address that crisis—and to harness the energy of their generation—the Sharon conferees issued a brief manifesto. "The Sharon Statement" listed a series of "eternal truths," with "the individual's use of his God-given free will" the foremost. Freedom depended above all on a market untrammeled by regulations. The statement warned that "when government interferes with the work of the market economy, it tends to reduce the moral and physical strength of the nation; that when it takes from one man to bestow on another, it diminishes the incentive of the first, the integrity of the second, and the moral autonomy of both."[33] The statement fused religious individualism and economic libertarianism, echoing Lemuel Boulware and Reverend James Fifield, the postwar popularizers of the gospel of free enterprise.

The activists whom Buckley gathered at Sharon formed an organization called Young Americans for Freedom (YAF), which grew steadily in the early 1960s, establishing beachheads on campuses from Notre Dame to Arizona State, from Yale to UCLA. YAF's members mobilized against Kennedy and, even more so, against Johnson's expansive domestic agenda. By the end of Johnson's presidency, YAF had at least seventy thousand members nationwide.

Barry Goldwater

The New Right-wing insurgency found an intellectual and political leader in Barry Goldwater, an Arizona businessman turned Republican U.S. senator. A self-proclaimed frontiersman, he flew his own plane and belonged to an elite men's club whose members sometimes dressed in Native American garb. Goldwater romanticized frontier individualism, even though the development of the Sunbelt had been made possible by massive federal expenditures, especially for dams, electrification, airports, and highways. Most important, powerful Arizonans worked to attract several major military bases and dozens of defense contractors. In 1950, as federal dollars began to flow in, Phoenix was a dusty town of only fifty thousand on the edge of a vast, mostly empty desert; by the end of the century, it would be one of the nation's ten largest cities. Goldwater envisioned remaking America in the image of Phoenix, a place that put up few obstacles to business and protected a free market with a powerful military.

Goldwater's profile rose in the 1950s, as he traveled nationwide to address business groups about free enterprise and small government. In 1960, just months before the Sharon gathering, he turned a set of his speeches into what would become one of the most widely read political tracts of the twentieth century, *The Conscience of a Conservative*. Published by a right-wing vanity press, the book became a surprise best seller. By 1964, it had sold more than three million copies.

Goldwater offered a bracing view of post–World War II America. "Conservatives," he wrote, "are deeply persuaded that our society is ailing."[34] To him and his followers the United States was morally and spiritually bankrupt, its citizens seduced by the welfare state. Communism prevailed abroad because of America's effeminacy. Americans had lost the self-sufficiency and entrepreneurial energy that had made their country great. Politics and society needed wholesale renovation.

Goldwater was a radical individualist: "Every man for his individual good and for the good of his society is responsible for his *own* development."[35] He railed against the signature welfare programs of the New Deal, including Social Security, which he saw as soul-destroying. Welfare, he argued, "transforms the individual from a dignified, industrious, self-reliant spiritual being into a dependent animal creature without his knowing it."[36] The greatest hindrance to the fulfillment of human potential was nothing other than government itself: "Throughout history, government has proved to be the chief instrument for thwarting man's liberty."[37] Goldwater's moral critique of America and his staunch defense of free enterprise found him readers among evangelicals and Catholics, *National Review* subscribers, and members of the YAF and the Chamber of Commerce.

Goldwater and his supporters on the New Right were particularly upset by civil rights laws. The federal government, they argued, had unconstitutionally usurped the power of the states in service of experiments in "social engineering." Since the Supreme Court had decided *Brown v. Board of Education* in 1954, southern elected officials had couched their opposition to integration in terms of states' rights, a position that Buckley and the *National Review* endorsed. In 1958, Buckley's journal solicited subscriptions from the 68,000 members of the segregationist White Citizens' Councils— founded to resist the Montgomery Bus Boycott—on the grounds that "our position on states' rights is the same as your own."[38]

Goldwater himself professed support for the goal of racial integration: he claimed to believe in a color-blind America. But he vehemently opposed the *Brown* decision. Falling back on a narrow reading of the Constitution, he argued that education was a state and local prerogative and that any federal mandate that schools be desegregated was unconstitutional. As for the Civil Rights Act, he charged that it would hasten "the loss of our God-given liberties" and constituted "a special appeal for a special welfare."[39]

As civil rights leaders stepped up their demands, conservative writers reacted angrily. In 1963, the *National Review*'s Frank Meyer argued that the movement against segregation "was destroying the foundations of a free, Constitutional society."[40] Buckley called for the use of police repression to put down what he considered the lawless protests being led by Martin Luther King, Jr. The riots during the summer of 1964 only confirmed conservatives' belief that the civil rights movement had fostered a culture of lawlessness.

The Warren Court and Its Critics

Compounding the conservatives' sense of crisis was a string of Warren Court decisions on criminal rights. In *Gideon v. Wainwright* (1963), the court ruled that those charged with a crime had the right to legal counsel. Clarence Gideon, a Florida prisoner jailed for theft, had sent a handwritten petition to the court, arguing that he had been unfairly convicted because he could not afford a lawyer. After the ruling, the state retried Gideon and he won acquittal. Florida and many states instituted public defender programs to provide legal representation for the poor. In a follow-up case, *Escobedo v. Illinois* (1964), the court ruled that those charged with a crime had the right to counsel during police interrogations. The case foreshadowed the more famous 1966 *Miranda v. Arizona* decision, that those charged of a crime had to be read their rights, including the right to remain silent.

Critics of the court found more grist for their discontent in two cases involving prayer in schools. In *Engel v. Vitale* (1962) the court ruled that mandatory school prayer—still commonplace around the country—was unconstitutional. The case involved a complaint against the New Hyde Park, New York, public schools, where officials had replaced an explicitly Christian prayer with one that read simply "Almighty God, we acknowledge our dependence upon Thee, and we beg Thy blessings upon us, our parents, our teachers and our country. Amen."[41] A group of Jewish students objected to the words "Almighty God" and won their case on the grounds that such prayers violated the constitutional ban on the establishment of religion. A year later, in another controversial ruling, *Abington School District v. Schempp*, the court ruled on behalf of a group of Pennsylvania school students who challenged required Bible classes.

Conservatives denounced the court's civil rights, criminal justice, and religious freedom rulings. "They have put the Negroes in the schools," charged Alabama representative George W. Andrews. "And now they have taken God out."[42] Religious activists demanded a constitutional amendment to allow school prayer, which public opinion surveys showed that 77 percent of the American population supported. Barry Goldwater lamented that "our law enforcement officers have been demoralized and rendered inef-fective in their jobs."[43] The John Birch Society, an organization that believed that the federal government and the courts were agents of Communist sub-version and immorality, placed "Impeach Earl Warren" billboards on road-sides throughout the country.

From the Fringe to the Mainstream

The GOP, nominally the party of Lincoln, of Emancipation and Recon-struction, was long reviled in the South. But in 1964, Goldwater discovered the GOP's Promised Land: the Old Confederacy. Since 1960 the Republi-can National Committee had sent organizers to the South in what it called "Operation Dixie" (an ironic appropriation of the name of labor's postwar efforts to build unions in the South) appealing to southern whites disaf-fected by the civil rights movement. The defection of prominent Democrats, like South Carolina senator Strom Thurmond in 1964, only strengthened their position. Goldwater's support for states' rights and the freedom of association echoed southern white racists' growing use of color-blind rheto-ric to prop up racial segregation and racial privilege.

Goldwater and his supporters also sharply criticized Cold War foreign policy. Containment, they insisted, was capitulation to Communism. The Soviet Union and its allies must be defeated, not simply cordoned off. Ken-nedy's policy toward Cuba and Germany evidenced America's weakness. Brent Bozell, editor of the *National Review*, argued that Kennedy should have torn down the Berlin Wall and invaded Cuba. Overseas economic development programs were both ineffective and unconstitutional. The founders, argued Goldwater, had not envisioned providing economic aid to other countries. The United States was exporting New Deal "socialism" rather than fighting for an all-out victory against the red menace. "Ameri-can strategy must be primarily offensive," asserted Goldwater. "If we are to achieve victory," he continued, "we must achieve superiority in all of the weapons, military as well as political and economic."[44]

Goldwater summed up his arguments in his remarkable speech accept-ing the Republican nomination for the presidency at San Francisco in July 1964: "Extremism in the defense of liberty is no vice, moderation is no virtue."[45] The ideological purity of Goldwater's address fired up his support-ers, but it left much of the GOP establishment cold. Henry Cabot Lodge, who had been Nixon's vice-presidential nominee in 1960, felt wholly out of place among Goldwater's supporters. "What in God's name has happened to the Republican Party!" he fumed while looking through a roster of delegates. "I hardly know any of these people!"[46] When Goldwater delegates pushed through a resolution denouncing the Civil Rights Act of 1964, it proved too much for moderate Republicans. Many walked out of the convention in protest.

The Republican Party's implosion boosted Johnson's campaign. Republican voters in northeastern and midwestern swing states—those attracted to Eisenhower's temperate Republicanism—were likely to stay home or even to vote for Johnson. Goldwater's denunciation of Social Security to an audience of Florida retirees gave Johnson another line of attack. Johnson also warned that the self-proclaimed extremist would likely plunge the country into nuclear war, a theme that animated his speeches and made its way into ads, including the justifiably famous "Daisy" commercial (aired only once) that showed a little girl pulling petals from a flower before a nuclear bomb exploded overhead. Even Goldwater's campaign slogan became the butt of jokes. "In your heart you know he's right" became "in your guts you know he's nuts."[47]

Johnson won the 1964 election in one of the greatest landslides in American history, with 61 percent of the vote. Goldwater won his home state and broke the Democratic Party's stronghold in the South, picking up majorities in Alabama, Georgia, Louisiana, Mississippi, and South Carolina. But the Democrats picked up their largest majority in the House and Senate since 1936. Johnson would have a 155-seat margin in the House and 35 seats in the Senate.

The election results confirmed the views of those mainstream pundits who had denounced Goldwater and his supporters as far-right zealots. Social scientists, among them the influential Daniel Bell and Seymour Martin Lipset, saw Goldwaterites as the embodiment of a pathological "authoritarian personality," wholly out of touch with the liberalism that they believed defined the American political tradition. "When in our history has anyone with ideas so bizarre, so archaic, so self-confounding, so remote from the basic American consensus ever gotten so far?" asked eminent historian Richard Hofstadter after the election.[48]

But the political troops that Goldwater had mobilized, north, south, and west, remained optimistic after their crushing defeat. In the South, the Goldwater campaign had mobilized many whites to vote Republican for the first time ever. Goldwater volunteers, many of them women, held coffee klatches, fought to control school boards, and campaigned against rock and roll music. Methodically, they built a conservative movement at the grass-roots. On campuses, the YAF recruited ambitious conservative student leaders, many of whom would move into Republican leadership in the 1970s and 1980s, among them future vice president Dan Quayle. In the decades that followed, what seemed to most Republicans and Democrats to be the crackpot ideas of a few zealots would move into the mainstream.

THE WAR ON POVERTY

Johnson had every reason to celebrate his overwhelming victory. Just after the election, while lighting the White House Christmas tree, he crowed that "these are the most hopeful times since Christ was born in Bethlehem."[49] The election returns gave him a mandate for the ambitious legislative agenda he had been preparing since his first State of the Union address, in January 1964, when he announced: "The administration today, here and now, declares unconditional war on poverty in America."[50]

The "Discovery" of Poverty

Even amid the postwar prosperity, tens of millions of Americans found themselves left behind. In the early 1960s, journalists, intellectuals, and academics had "discovered" poverty in America. In 1962, Michael Harrington, a young socialist intellectual who had begun his career in the Catholic Worker movement helping the homeless on New York's Lower East Side, published a best-selling account, *The Other America*, that documented poverty and called for action.

Poverty affected every section of America: in 1960 nearly a quarter of the nation's population was poor. By the middle of the twentieth century, small farmers, once perceived as the backbone of the country, were an endangered species. The rise of government-subsidized agribusiness displaced independent farmers in the nation's most fertile regions. Many small towns in the Plains hollowed out, as farmers migrated to cities. Poverty was commonplace in rural America, particularly in the southern Black Belt, in Johnson's rural Texas, on the Great Plains, and in the rich farmlands of California, where migrant farmworkers struggled to get by. Just as hard hit were the nation's old mining towns. The anthracite coal region, extending from Pennsylvania south through the Virginias and west through Kentucky and Illinois, was ravaged by job losses as the mines closed. The spotlight of John F. Kennedy's fall 1960 campaign through West Virginia had made Appalachia's tumbledown shacks and shoeless residents the icons of poverty.

Between 1947 and 1963, Detroit—the epitome of American industrial power—lost almost 140,000 manufacturing jobs, as companies moved plants south and west to lower costs and replaced workers with labor-saving machinery.[51] The once-bustling ports of Brooklyn and Oakland grew quieter, as stevedores lost out to container shipping and cross-country trucking. The aging northeastern rail lines—owned by century-old companies like the Pennsylvania Railroad, which teetered on the brink of insolvency—passed the crumbling ruins of textile mills in Philadelphia, Baltimore, and Trenton. The patterns of poverty also reflected the enduring color line: in 1960 close to half of all African Americans were poor.

Poverty Warriors

In the early 1960s, major philanthropies, led by the Ford Foundation, began to channel funds to community programs that targeted the poor. Both Kennedy and Johnson recruited sociologists and economists who studied poverty and used their ideas to develop a major federal antipoverty initiative. In 1964, Johnson appointed Sargent Shriver, President Kennedy's brother-in-law, to direct his War on Poverty. "The sky's the limit," Johnson told Shriver. "You just make the thing work period. I don't give a damn about the details."[52]

But a full-fledged war would require massive expenditures, and Johnson was unwilling to provide the funds. In 1964 he had successfully shepherded Kennedy's tax reform legislation through Congress, but it came at the price of trimming costs elsewhere in his budget. So Shriver gravitated toward relatively inexpensive programs. One was the Job Corps, modeled after the New Deal's Works Progress Administration and Civilian Conservation Corps, but with only a fraction of the funding. Job Corps programs attracted only a small percentage of the unemployed and underemployed and plopped them down into isolated camps with poorly trained supervisors and inadequate facilities.

The most controversial of the War on Poverty programs, Community Action, targeted impoverished urban neighborhoods, rural counties, and

Indian reservations. Community Action Agencies (CAAs) were intended to give poor people a stake in the system by allowing them to oversee neighborhood organizations, preschools, health centers, and welfare offices. CAAs rested on the assumption that the "maximum feasible participation" of the poor would ultimately reduce poverty. Many CAAs, which operated with little government oversight, implemented controversial arts and theater programs; some engaged in political protests; and others created social service jobs for poor people. But CAAs did not receive enough funds or create enough jobs to make a dent in local poverty rates. And some of the programs, like Newark, New Jersey's, run by black power advocate and poet Amiri Baraka, became flashpoints of controversy.

The War on Poverty unleashed a political movement among the poor of a scale unseen since the Great Depression. In 1965 an interracial coalition of poor women challenged state laws that cut off families from receiving welfare. They worked with the support of attorneys who were funded under another Great Society program, Legal Aid, that provided legal assistance to the poor. In the South, local welfare administrators, eager to maintain the supply of inexpensive domestic workers, often denied black women benefits, even as they continued to support poor white women. Around the country, the National Welfare Rights Organization (NWRO), formed in 1965 and staffed predominantly by women, challenged intrusive home inspections to determine welfare eligibility. NWRO members demanded an increase in monthly payments so that they could afford better housing. Those efforts paid off. The Johnson administration streamlined welfare rules and increased stipends. The rolls of welfare recipients rose significantly in the mid- and late 1960s.

Public Education

As a former teacher, Johnson put a special priority on public education to pull people from poverty. The newly created Office of Economic Opportunity (OEO) channeled hundreds of millions of dollars to community organizations to implement the Head Start program, to provide preschool education to disadvantaged children. Johnson also dramatically expanded federal funding for public education, which had long been left to the states and localities. The 1965 Elementary and Secondary Education Act (ESEA)—which Johnson signed "in the one room school house near Stonewall, Texas," with his first teacher, "Miss Kate," sitting at his side—provided a billion dollars to fund schools that served poor children.[53] By 1968, 94 percent of American school districts had received ESEA funds to build new schools, improve curricula, and hire teachers.

In addition, Johnson signed into law programs that offered federally guaranteed student loans and direct grants to needy students, making college affordable to many for the first time. Great Society programs funded university libraries, created national arts and humanities programs, trained nurses, and supported research in mental health, heart disease, stroke, and disease prevention. College campuses, flush with federal support, expanded rapidly in the late 1960s.

Health Care

Also in 1965, Johnson succeeded where his predecessors had failed by creating federally subsidized health insurance programs for the elderly (Medicare) and the impoverished (Medicaid). President Franklin Roosevelt had used federal funds to build hospitals but had met with obstacles to providing universal government-funded health care. Harry S. Truman's efforts to create a national health insurance program had fallen to cries of socialism. Still, as a senator, Johnson worked mostly behind the scenes to increase federal spending on hospitals and medical research. But many liberals never gave up the hope of creating a broad national health system, and they pushed hard during the Kennedy and Johnson years.

Johnson was enough of a realist to make a case for something narrower than a national health plan. In 1964 he argued, "Every American will benefit by the extension of Social Security to cover the hospital costs of their aged parents."[54] Hospitalization costs had tripled since Johnson's first term in the Senate—from an average of $15 per day in 1950 to $45 a day in 1965. And as the United States grew wealthier, life expectancy had grown, leaving retirees to rely on a rickety system of charity or public hospitals or to raid their savings. Over half of elderly Americans had no health insurance at all in 1965. "We've just got to say that by God you can't treat grandma this way," Johnson put it in his inimitably folksy way.[55]

Johnson had higher ambitions than helping Grandma. He viewed federal health insurance as one of the greatest unfulfilled promises of the New Deal. If he passed it, he could outshine his Democratic predecessors. Drafted with Senator Wilbur Mills (D-OH), a master of taxation and budgeting, the final health care bill exceeded Johnson's expectations. In a "three layer cake," the program provided the elderly with hospital coverage, voluntary doctors' visits (which required an additional premium, with government subsidies if necessary), and insurance for the poor. Johnson signed the bill in Harry S. Truman's hometown, Independence, Missouri, on July 30, 1965.

Implementing Medicare and Medicaid proved to be a challenge. Many medical professionals, still concerned about "socialized medicine," threatened to boycott the program. Costs rose rapidly, outpacing inflation. But at least in terms of access, the programs met with immediate success. In 1965 one in five poor Americans had never been to the doctor; five years later, that figure had fallen to under 10 percent. Medicare proved especially popular among the elderly: all were covered by hospital insurance, and 93 percent chose the voluntary insurance for regular doctors' visits.[56] Within a few years of its enactment, Medicare became politically untouchable.

EXPANDING THE BOUNDARIES OF CITIZENSHIP: VOTING RIGHTS AND IMMIGRATION

Johnson's vision of a "great society" included more than alleviating poverty and providing economic opportunity. Since the end of Reconstruction, African Americans had lacked one of the fundamental rights of citizenship: the right to participate in the electoral process. And over the course of the late nineteenth and twentieth centuries, the United States had shut the nation's borders to people who were presumed to be inferior because of where they were born. One step to creating a more equal America was creating a more inclusive society.

"Massive Confrontation" in Mississippi

One of Johnson's most important tasks was to take care of some of the unfinished business of civil rights. During his first year in office, SNCC members stepped up their efforts for voting rights, recruiting hundreds of college students to run citizenship training programs, alternative "Freedom Schools," and voter registration campaigns in the South. In the Freedom Summer of 1964, thousands of black and white activists targeted the Mississippi Delta, one of the country's most isolated and impoverished regions. There Jim Crow took its most brutal form. A majority of Delta residents were black, but hardly any could exercise their basic citizenship rights: voting and serving on juries. Local landowners and public officials relied on violence to keep the population passive.

John Lewis, who had been elected SNCC chair, saw Mississippi as the last stand for voting rights. "Before the Negro people get the right to vote, there will have to be a massive confrontation," proclaimed Lewis, "and it will probably come this summer."[57] SNCC rejected the carefully staged, made-for-TV demonstrations that Martin Luther King and the SCLC had used to define the civil rights movement in the South. Their door-to-door, face-to-face efforts to build support for voting rights in the Delta lacked the drama that brought television cameras to places like Montgomery and Birmingham.

Key to SNCC's Mississippi campaign were activists like Robert Parris Moses, who adopted a self-effacing style, preferring to sit at the kitchen table in a shotgun shack instead of in a network news studio. Moses, educated at elite Hamilton College and Harvard, taught math and was one of the first black faculty members at the prestigious Horace Mann School in New York. In 1959, Moses had joined with Bayard Rustin in a demonstration for school integration, and in 1960, he headed to Atlanta to meet with Martin Luther King, Jr. There he found his calling: as a SNCC organizer in the Deep South. By 1961, he had planted himself in the Delta, where he coordinated SNCC's efforts and worked to build a statewide network of civil rights groups.

Working for years behind the scenes, SNCC members were well known and despised by whites in the Delta, especially when they began to bring would-be voters to local courthouses to register. Just as unsettling was the flood of northern-born student activists, many of them white, who arrived during the summer of 1964 to staff Freedom Schools and voting campaigns. These Freedom Summer volunteers—living with black activists, socializing with them in the open, and sometimes breaking the taboo of interracial dating—outraged white locals. Increasingly, SNCC activists and Mississippi voters faced violent reprisals. On June 21, 1964, three Freedom Summer participants—James Chaney, Andrew Goodman, and Michael Schwerner—were kidnapped and murdered by white supremacists just outside Philadelphia, Mississippi.

SNCC activists grew increasingly restive in the face of brutal reprisals and glacial change. Many resented Washington liberals for supporting the goal of voting rights in principle but not providing material support for those on the ground. Although President Johnson had signed the Civil

Rights Act, they still distrusted him profoundly. That distrust solidified during the 1964 Democratic National Convention, where the party refused to seat the Mississippi Freedom Democratic Party, an interracial delegation led by Fannie Lou Hamer. A sharecropper who stood up to the president and vice president, both of whom did not want to alienate Mississippi's all-white official delegation, Hamer made the evening news with her proclamation that "if the Freedom Democratic Party is not seated now, I question America."[58] For John Lewis, the convention debacle proved Johnson's treachery, "politics at its worst." Even as Johnson swept to office in November, Lewis viewed the convention as a "turning point," the beginning of a "loss of faith" in Johnson and in government.[59]

Selma and the Voting Rights Act

Voting rights activists stepped up the pressure. In March 1965 dozens of prominent civil rights, religious, and labor leaders joined members of SNCC in a well-publicized voting rights march from Montgomery to Selma, Alabama. One activist, Detroit-born Viola Liuzzo, who came south to support the enfranchisement campaign, was shot and killed by Klansmen. On March 7, John Lewis, who organized the march, took his most brutal beating, as protesters attempted to cross the Edmund Pettus Bridge into Selma. The police attacked several hundred marchers, injuring nearly seventy, many severely. Lewis suffered a fractured skull. Two days later the marchers again confronted the police, before turning back from the Pettus Bridge.

On March 15, Lyndon Johnson addressed the nation, calling on Congress to pass comprehensive voting rights legislation. As he had with the previous year's Civil Rights Act, he worked to forge a bipartisan coalition to thwart a southern filibuster. The day after Johnson's speech, under federal military protection, the marchers headed on to Montgomery. The tide had turned in favor of voting rights, though it took Johnson's legislative skill to bring it to a vote. The act, which Johnson signed on August 6, 1965, prohibited the use of such devices as literacy tests and poll taxes to disenfranchise voters. Under Section 5 of the act, the federal government had to approve "any voting qualification or prerequisite to voting, or standard, practice, or procedure with respect to voting" in districts with a history of past discrimination.[60]

Civil rights activists began to push for the implementation of the new law and to gain political office themselves in the South. Fannie Lou Hamer ran an unsuccessful campaign for Congress but finally won a seat at the Democratic National Convention in 1968. The year after the Voting Rights Act passed, John Lewis left SNCC to coordinate a large-scale voter registration campaign in the South. With the federal government forcing southern districts to enfranchise blacks, with the Department of Justice challenging illegal electoral practices, and with thousands of volunteers assisting new voters, the Voting Rights Act transformed the color of American politics in a very short period of time. In 1965 fewer than 200 blacks held elective office; by 1970 the figure had more than tripled to 764. By 1980 almost two thousand African Americans held elective office nationwide. One of the beneficiaries of the act was John Lewis himself, who won election to Atlanta's city council in 1981 and to Congress in 1986, as the U.S. representative from Georgia's fifth district.

Immigration Reform

Johnson and his congressional allies were also committed to another major shift from exclusion to inclusion. In October 1965, Congress passed the Hart-Cellar Act, the most sweeping immigration reform in decades. Since 1924, America had had a restrictive quota system in place that favored immigrants from northern and western Europe. In the intervening years, the nation modified its immigration laws somewhat. During World War II, the United States lifted the ban on Asian immigration but admitted only a token 100 immigrants per country each year. The 1952 Immigration and Nationalities Act lifted racial restrictions dating back to the nineteenth century but kept discriminatory national quotas in place, and it restricted suspected "subversives" and the "immoral," including homosexuals, from entering the United States. In 1964, Congress eliminated the bracero program, largely responding to critics of the harsh treatment of migrant farmworkers.

The Hart-Cellar Act lifted nation-specific quotas on immigration, made provisions for family reunification, set aside places for skilled workers, and gave special status to refugees fleeing Communist rule. The law changed the complexion of immigration to the United States. By the 1990s, 29 percent of immigrants would be Asian, a striking turnaround from the days of Chinese and Japanese exclusion. About 6 percent of immigrants came from

Africa, the first significant influx from that continent since slavery. Only 14 percent of immigrants originated in Europe.

Hart-Cellar, however, had unintended consequences for immigration from Latin America. It instituted the first numerical restriction on immigrants from the western hemisphere: a cap of 120,000 per year, not including spouses, parents, and children of U.S. citizens. Because that cap coincided with the end of the bracero program, it significantly reduced the ability of Mexicans legally to migrate to the United States. After 1965 the demand for Mexican labor in the United States did not abate, nor did Mexican workers' interest in crossing the border to work. But under the new caps, many Mexican workers would have to cross the border without documentation.

JOBS AND FREEDOM

For all the ambitions of Johnson's Great Society programs, they did not adequately address one of the root causes of inequality and poverty: the unequal economy. Despite an economic boom (unemployment fell below 4 percent between 1966 and 1969), millions of Americans remained trapped in poor-paying, insecure jobs. Labor and civil rights groups had long argued that remunerative work was a precondition for freedom. A just society required decent pay and humane working conditions.

Harvest of Shame

Farmworkers were near the bottom economically, trapped in insecure, dangerous jobs. The day after Thanksgiving in 1960, CBS had aired the documentary, *Harvest of Shame*, interviewing migrant workers and showing graphic images of their miserable housing, backbreaking labor, and bare cupboards. The film galvanized public support for efforts to improve conditions in the fields. In 1962, Cesar Chavez and Dolores Huerta founded the National Farmworkers Association (later the United Farm Workers, or UFW), to advocate for better wages and working conditions in California's Central Valley. Both had worked for the Community Service Organization, a grassroots group in California that challenged discrimination against Hispanics. Chavez had been a farmworker himself.

The UFW was not the first farmworkers' union, but it was the most visible and successful. UFW activists went from settlement to settlement, pressuring growers to provide decent housing to workers who often slept in converted chicken coops or in the open air. They demanded better wages. They improved conditions in many farm communities and, more than that, rallied thousands of farmworkers to demand even more systemic changes. In 1965, Chavez and Huerta led California grape pickers in a strike that would last nearly five years. They also built a broad base of support in college towns, churches, and big cities when they launched a well-publicized call to boycott grapes to put pressure on agribusinesses.

The Freedom Budget

Many labor and civil rights activists criticized what Bayard Rustin called Johnson's "skirmish on poverty." In late 1965, Rustin and A. Philip Randolph convened a group of prominent economists, labor unionists, and civil rights leaders who drafted the Freedom Budget, released in October 1966. The budget called for job creation programs to eliminate unemployment, a guaranteed annual income for poor families, and increased federal spending to eradicate slums, improve schools, and build public works.

Martin Luther King, Jr., sympathized with the Freedom Budget: he had called for a "bill of rights for the disadvantaged" that would expand opportunities for workers of all races. For King, the next stage in the movement was forging an interracial coalition committed to economic justice. He argued that "while Negroes form the vast majority of America's disadvantaged, there are millions of white poor who would also benefit from such a bill."[61] King also reached out—tentatively—to Chavez and the Farmworkers.

There was little political support for the Freedom Budget, but many activists, including King, turned their attention to improving pay and working conditions in the two sectors of the urban economy that grew in the 1960s: health care and public sector employment. In the manufacturing cities hemorrhaging industrial jobs and losing retail employment to the suburbs, hospitals and the government provided many of the new jobs. Orderlies, social workers, nurses, teachers, and sanitation workers—a growing number of them black and Puerto Rican—fought for better pay and benefits. King supported hospital workers' unions, including New York's 1199, which had helped bankroll the March on Washington. And he joined public employees, like Memphis's sanitation workers, in their fight for workplace dignity and better pay.

BLACK POWER, WHITE BACKLASH

Johnson had hoped that civil rights and antipoverty legislation would put a lid on protests in the streets. But in the mid-1960s, racial tensions escalated. Just weeks after Johnson signed the Civil Rights Act, riots broke out in three northern cities—Philadelphia, New York, and Rochester—sparked by clashes between blacks and the police. In August 1965 the mostly black Watts neighborhood of Los Angeles exploded after another police incident, just days after Johnson signed the Voting Rights Act. Thirty-four people died, most of them shot by law enforcement officials. Thousands of stores were looted and burned. When survey researchers interviewed Watts rioters, they discovered a deep well of frustration. Despite more than a decade of civil rights activism, they believed that their situation to be worse than ever. Johnson was unsympathetic. He directed the FBI to investigate the possibility that Communists were behind the riots. (They were not.) And he fumed that blacks were ungrateful for his legislative victories.

Black Nationalism

If Johnson had expected the black freedom struggle to wane after the passage of the Civil Rights and Voting Rights Acts, he was mistaken. By the mid-1960s, a growing cadre of black activists rejected civil rights laws as too little too late. White resistance had scarcely abated, blacks remained economically insecure, and schools and neighborhoods remained separate and unequal. SNCC, which had spent 1964 and 1965 agitating for voting rights and calling for inclusion in the political system, began to argue instead for black separation and self-determination.

Leading SNCC in its turn toward militancy and black nationalism was John Lewis's successor as SNCC's chair, Stokely Carmichael. A Trinidadian immigrant raised in New York, Carmichael had joined the Freedom Rides, attended the March on Washington, led voting rights efforts in Lowndes County, Alabama, and suffered beatings and jail several times. By 1965, Carmichael, like many members of SNCC, had given up hope that the Democratic Party would effectively represent black interests in the South or indeed nationwide.

In 1966, Carmichael helped found the Lowndes County Freedom Organization, with a crouching black panther as its symbol. A powerful orator who had learned the art at Harlem's speaker's corner and Howard

University, Carmichael roused a crowd at a June rally in Greenwood, Mississippi: "The only way we gonna stop them white men from whuppin' us is to take over. We been saying freedom for six years and we ain't got nothin'. What do you want?" The crowd chanted, "Black Power! Black Power! Black Power!"[62]

Carmichael popularized a concept with deep roots in black politics, north and south. His call for self-determination echoed the Garvey movement in the 1920s and also built on the rhetoric of anticolonial movements in Africa and Asia. His demand for a black-run movement echoed A. Philip Randolph's call for an all-black March on Washington in 1941. But the two words *black power* were electric in 1966. They gave voice to growing dissatisfaction with liberalism, pessimism about the seeming permanence of white racism, and a sense that armed self-defense was necessary for black advancement.

The same year that Carmichael spoke of black power, CORE adopted a platform calling for black separatism. SNCC repudiated its signature strategy and called for the violent overthrow of white supremacy. That cry for self-determination echoed in the streets of many big cities in the summer of 1966, among them Chicago and Cleveland, which exploded in days-long uprisings, marked by clashes between young black men and mostly white police forces. In the next two years, inspired by the Lowndes County symbol of black political power, activists in Oakland, Harlem, Philadelphia, Des Moines, and many other cities, created their own Black Panther Parties.

The Resonance of the Right

By early 1966, political strategists began warning Johnson that a growing "white backlash" against civil rights threatened to reduce his congressional majority. In the midterm elections, Republicans made gains in both the House and the Senate, picking up seats in Georgia, Tennessee, and Texas. Many northern and western Democrats, sensitive to their constituents' fears of racial integration, riots, and crime (which they often conflated), rallied around candidates who opposed school integration and called for stiffer antiriot measures.

In the West, Californians elected Goldwater supporter and conservative business spokesman Ronald Reagan as governor in 1966 on a ticket that emphasized law and order, small government, and school prayer. Civil rights legislation, black power, and rioting had confirmed the Right's fears of a breakdown in civility. Johnson's expansion of educational spending affirmed their view that the federal government unconstitutionally trammeled local rights. And the Great Society's health and antipoverty programs added another layer of soul-destroying, initiative-sapping programs to those launched during the New Deal, or so they thought. Still, through the mid-1960s, it appeared that groups like the Young Americans for Freedom and the Goldwater wing of the Republican Party would remain gadflies, not become major political actors.

But even if a majority of Americans remained skeptical of the New Right's demands for individual freedom, states' rights, and small government, its message began to resonate more widely. Over the next ten years, the angry Republican delegates who supported Barry Goldwater's quixotic bid for the White House would find a more receptive climate for their political vision, as discontent on America's streets intensified and, especially, as the United States waded into the deep turmoil of Vietnam. An increasingly vocal minority of blacks found a receptive message for their calls for group power. Within a few years of Lyndon Johnson's triumphs, one of the most common questions in the United States was "which side are you on?" That question would take on yet another dimension as Johnson fought a war abroad, one that came to be every bit as divisive as the wars that he fought on the home front.

CHAPTER 11

MAY DAY:

VIETNAM AND THE CRISIS
OF THE 1960S

O N MAY 1, 1968, Private First Class Lawrence James Merschel joined a "rat patrol" just outside Hue, the largest city in
the narrow sliver of South Vietnam where the coastal lowlands meet the mountainous jungle that extends for hundreds
of miles westward into Laos. Hue was a major center of Buddhist religious
practice and an old imperial city with grand palaces and pagodas. Its imposing stone citadel stood watch over the city and offered vistas over the Per-
fumed River to the mountains in the west and the hazy lowlands along the
China Sea to the east. By the spring of 1968, two-thirds of Hue lay in
rubble, the smoke of burning jungles polluting its air. The din of helicopters
and explosions of mortar fire penetrated the once-peaceful Buddhist tem-
ples. Hue and surrounding Thua Thien province became one of the bloodiest battlegrounds in the war for the future of Vietnam.[1]

The third of eight children, Larry Merschel grew up in the shadow
of war. His parents, Peggy and Jack, met during World War II and married just before Jack shipped off to France. By the time Larry was born in
1948, the United States engaged in a multifront battle against Communism. For young Larry, the Cold War was no abstraction. Throughout
elementary and high school in Wayne, Pennsylvania, a comfortable Philadelphia suburb, he and his classmates learned—through slide shows and
drills—how to protect themselves if the Russians launched an airstrike
on their hometown. They formed single-file lines and marched into the
school's basement fallout shelter, marked by distinctive yellow and black
signs. There they practiced taking cover among the barrels of crackers

and water, intended to nourish them as they waited out a storm of radio-active cinders.

In Larry's world, the Cold War was a matter not just of physical survival but of morality. At his home parish, St. Catherine of Siena, parishioners prayed for the "conversion of Russia." Young Catholics learned about the persecution of clerics like Joseph Cardinal Mindszenty in Communist-controlled Hungary. They celebrated the heroism of Tom Dooley, a Catholic medic who worked with refugees in Indochina, led the construction of hospitals in Vietnam, and worked with orphans in Laos, fighting what he considered to be the twin evils of disease and Communism. To Catholics, the Cold War pitted atheism and materialism against democracy and spirituality. It also mattered to Catholics that Vietnam's longtime postindependence leader, Ngo Dinh Diem, who had ruled from 1954 to 1963, was himself Catholic.

Larry was exactly the sort of young man whom the military hoped would enlist—morally serious and disciplined, with a strong sense of duty to his country. As a high school student, he was, as his sister Lisa described him, a "quiet, introspective young man." Like his father, a Sun Oil executive, Larry was tall, good-looking, and athletic, and although a bit taciturn, he exuded leadership. During his senior year at Radnor High School, he became cocaptain of the varsity basketball team and won his school's prize for "outstanding spirit and sportsmanship, ability and teamwork." In the fall of 1966, Larry started his freshman year at Villanova University, on a Navy ROTC scholarship. But the prospect of joining another team, for a cause far greater than that of glory on the basketball court, led Larry to enlist in the military. In April 1967, just before the end of his freshman year, he dropped his classes and headed off to basic training. "He felt that he was doing what had to be done," recalled his father, "and he felt he had to do this instead of attending college."

After basic training, Larry headed to Fort Campbell, Kentucky to join one of the army's most celebrated units, the 101st Airborne. Renowned for their valor in World War II, deployed to put down unrest in the streets of Little Rock in 1957 and in Detroit ten years later, the men of the Screaming Eagles underwent especially rigorous training, including in the unit's signature skill, paratrooping. By the time of the Vietnam War, however, hardly any Airborne members actually dropped to battlefields by parachute. Most were deployed in infantry and cavalry units that fought side by side with regular troops on the ground or, by 1968, in airmobile units, delivering troops to battlefields by helicopter and leading search and destroy missions that targeted suspected havens of insurgents on the ground in South Vietnam. Larry trained as an infantryman, part of the 101st Airborne's Second Squadron, 17th Calvary. On February 20, 1968, he deployed in the Thua Thien province about one hundred miles south of the demilitarized zone that separated North and South Vietnam.

THE ORIGINS OF THE VIETNAM WAR

The events that led to PFC Merschel's service in Vietnam had played out for more than a quarter of a century in the rice paddies and mountain jungles of Southeast Asia. During the 1940s, Ho Chi Minh, a charismatic Vietnamese revolutionary with close ties to the French Communist Party, launched an independence movement, challenged the Japanese occupation during World War II and fought the restoration of French colonial rule afterward. Ho gained strong support in rural Vietnam, especially among peasants who resisted the huge landowners who had expropriated their land and forced them into conditions of near-servitude as tenant farmers and sharecroppers.

Ho appealed to President Truman for American support, but the president ignored his pleas. The United States resolutely supported its French ally's efforts to hang on to its Southeast Asian colony. As Ho's insurgency led to a widespread rebellion, the United States stepped up its involvement. Beginning in 1950, the Truman administration provided substantial economic and military support for the French. Depleted by two world wars, France simply could not mount a counterrevolution in Southeast Asia without aid. By 1954, U.S. funds covered about 80 percent of the French military efforts in Indochina.

Dien Bien Phu and the Geneva Accords

Millions of dollars in foreign aid and hundreds of thousands of French troops proved no match for Ho's disciplined forces. The French military was unprepared for the guerrilla-style tactics of the Vietnamese revolutionaries. The war brought terrible casualties to both sides. Between 1946 and 1954, about 200,000 Vietminh and 70,000 French troops died. As casualties mounted, popular support in France for the counterrevolutionary struggle waned. The French nicknamed it "the dirty war." Finally, in April 1954, the French garrison at Dien Bien Phu fell to the rebels.

After months of negotiations in Geneva, an agreement temporarily partitioned Vietnam into the north, controlled by Ho Chi Minh and the Communist Party, and the south, led by Ngo Dinh Diem, a staunch anti-Communist and American puppet. The Geneva Accords called for a nationwide election in 1956 to create a unified government. Most of the major powers, including Britain, the Soviet Union, and China, signed the treaty, but the United States did not, for fear that, if the Vietnamese held elections, Ho Chi Minh would win.

Ngo Dinh Diem and Civil War in Vietnam

The Diem regime was corrupt and unstable. Vietnam was the second-largest recipient of American international aid for most of the 1950s. Diem and his supporters enriched themselves with American largesse. To shore up his legitimacy, Diem jailed his political opponents and staged a sham 1955 referendum in which he supposedly won the support of 96 percent of the South Vietnamese electorate. In 1956, he refused to hold the Vietnam-wide reunification election that had been required under the Geneva Accords. North and South Vietnam remained separate, with Ho establishing a capital in Hanoi, and Diem one in Saigon.

Perpetually insecure in his rule, Diem suppressed dissent and grew increasingly brutal. Still, the Eisenhower administration continued to support him. The United States provided training to the South Vietnamese police and military and dispatched a small force of military advisers to the country. Diem channeled U.S. economic development aid to cities, favoring his regime's cronies. He also empowered large landowners to consolidate their holdings and thus further impoverish the peasantry. Unpopular and autocratic, Diem's regime jailed, tortured, and murdered dissenters and censored opposition newspapers.

Diem's brutality drove growing numbers of Vietnamese, especially in rural areas, into the opposition. The Catholic Diem angered Buddhists— the majority religion—by marginalizing them in his regime. And even more consequentially, the Vietcong—a coalition of revolutionaries, nationalists, and opponents of Diem—gained control of villages throughout the countryside, winning over the peasantry by advocating land reform and opposing corruption. They used their growing strength to mount an insurgency against Diem's regime. In 1958 and 1959, rebels assassinated hundreds of Diem supporters, especially local government officials. The Diem regime stepped up its attacks on the opposition, and by 1960 a full-blown civil war had erupted in South Vietnam. The Vietcong and Buddhist dissenters, gathering under the banner of the National Liberation Front, deposed local officials who supported Diem, attacked rural landlords, appropriated land for the peasantry, and established bases throughout the countryside.

Kennedy and Vietnam

By early 1961, when John F. Kennedy took office, there were about nine hundred U.S. military advisers on the ground in Vietnam, providing tactical support to the South Vietnamese military and police. The Kennedy administration continued its predecessors' strategy of supporting the Diem regime but also began to lay the groundwork for greater American involvement in Vietnam. In the fall of 1961 the administration dispatched one of its most respected advisers, Walt Whitman Rostow, along with a key military adviser, General Maxwell Taylor, to assess the situation in South Vietnam.

Rostow, a Rhodes scholar and MIT economist, had a knack for distilling ideas down to simple formulations. He was said to have coined the phrase "New Frontier" to describe Kennedy's domestic agenda. Rostow had made his reputation as the most prominent advocate of "modernization theory," through his studies of comparative industrialization and the stages of economic growth. One of the key lessons he drew from economic history was that underdeveloped countries like Vietnam needed "benevolent authoritarianism"—dictatorships propped up by the United States—to build the institutions necessary for political stability and economic growth.[2]

What Rostow and Taylor found on their fact-finding trip was unsettling: they noted a "deep and pervasive crisis of confidence and a serious loss of national morale" in South Vietnam.[3] They argued for stepping up the deployment of American engineers, medics, and infantry to provide additional support for Diem's regime. Secretary of Defense Robert McNamara—who would serve both Kennedy and Johnson—concurred, arguing that "the United States should commit itself to the clear objective of preventing the fall of South Vietnam to Communism."[4]

McNamara, who joined the Kennedy administration after serving as Ford Motor Company's chief executive, encouraged the application of the latest thinking in planning, finance, and statistics to military strategy. He did not have much specific knowledge about Vietnam, but the numbers convinced him that the United States could easily handle the situation there. "It seems on the face of it," McNamara told Kennedy in November 1961, "absurd to think that a nation of 20 million people can be subverted by 15-20 thousand active guerrillas if the government and people of the country do not wish to be subverted."[5] McNamara believed that continued American economic aid would win the hearts and minds of the Vietnamese people, and that American military support would help Diem thwart the insurgents. In 1962 he returned optimistic from his first visit to Saigon, stating that "every quantitative measure we have shows that we are winning the war."[6]

Vietnam was not as central to Kennedy's Cold War aims as Cuba, Germany, and the Soviet Union, but the administration escalated spending and sent a growing number of military advisers to assist Saigon. The number of American troops in Vietnam rose to more than sixteen thousand at the end of 1963. In November 1963 the CIA cooperated with a military-backed coup against Diem. After the assassination of Diem and his brother Nhu, a dozen governments rose and fell in South Vietnam through 1965, all of them unpopular. The civil war intensified.

Covert Operations and the Gulf of Tonkin

When Lyndon Johnson assumed the presidency in late 1963, he inherited the mess in Southeast Asia. He kept Kennedy's foreign policy team mostly intact, and he agreed with those who argued that a victory in Vietnam was essential to American foreign policy goals. After two months in office, he authorized the military to engage in covert operations against the North Vietnamese. Over the summer of 1964, the White House began secret preparations to escalate the war in Vietnam, including planning for massive airstrikes on North Vietnamese supply lines.

The opportunity for that escalation came on August 2, after North Vietnamese patrol boats fired on two American destroyers in the Gulf of Tonkin. The ships were clandestinely supporting South Vietnamese operations along the coast. Johnson pledged harsh retaliation in the event of another attack. On August 4, after navy radar operators erroneously detected what they thought were torpedoes aimed at the American ships, the navy bombed North Vietnamese military targets. Johnson and his advisers hid their skepticism about the August 4 events—the president confidentially told aides that "those stupid, dumb sailors were just shooting at flying fish." But he used the event to get congressional authorization for "all necessary measures" to protect U.S. interests in Vietnam.[7]

Congress barely debated the Gulf of Tonkin resolution, which gave Johnson the authority to use military force in Vietnam. It passed on August 7, unanimously in the House and with only two no votes in the Senate, from Alaska Republican Ernest Gruening and Oregon Democrat Wayne Morse. Gruening was the earliest national critic of the war, on the grounds that given the corruption of the South Vietnamese government, "the allegation that we are supporting freedom in South Vietnam has a hollow sound," and that "all Vietnam is not worth the life of a single American boy."[8] Morse believed that Congress was abrogating its responsibility, under Article I of the Constitution, to declare war. As he feared, the Gulf of Tonkin resolution became a blank check to the president to escalate an undeclared war. Johnson colorfully concurred that "it was like grandma's nightshirt, it covered everything."[9]

LYNDON JOHNSON'S WAR

Johnson had a number of reasons for dramatically escalating the war. He cringed as Republicans excoriated the Democratic Party for being soft on Communism, and he desperately hoped to avoid a reprise of the GOP's damning critique of President Truman for "losing China" during the 1949 Communist-led revolution. Vietnam was, in the conventional Cold War view, an essential bulwark against the spread of Communism throughout Southeast Asia.

But Johnson's Vietnam strategy also grew from other, deeper motives that dated back to early-twentieth-century liberal internationalism, when leaders like Woodrow Wilson had justified foreign military engagements as necessary to bring civilization or democracy to the world. By the end of World War II, advocates of international economic development believed that bringing investment to the "backward" countries of Africa, Asia, and Latin America would simultaneously thwart Communism, expand the global market for American goods, and serve the humanitarian goal of eradicating global poverty.

In Johnson's most effusive moments, he described Vietnam as one front in the global war on poverty. He envisioned a Great Society in Vietnam. Building on one of the New Deal's signature accomplishments, he proposed a Tennessee Valley Authority to control flooding and generate electricity in the Mekong Delta. Rostow's vision of modernization spoke to Johnson's aspirations. Indeed, Johnson called Rostow "my intellectual" and promoted him to head the National Security Council in 1966. Like Rostow, Johnson believed that victory against the Vietcong was necessary to the larger strategy of containing Communism in Southeast Asia. And he saw it as an essential precondition for Vietnam's entry into the ranks of the developed world.

Public Support for the War

The first months of the war witnessed an outpouring of goodwill toward Johnson. The president's approval rating soared in the aftermath of the Gulf of Tonkin incident, and a sizable majority of Americans strongly supported the undeclared Vietnam War. How could the American public not support a war clearly rooted in Cold War imperatives, prompted by an apparently unjustified act of aggression against American troops, and defined as part of a plan to bring the benefits of economic development to an impoverished population?

Initially, support for the war was high across all demographic groups, particularly among younger Americans like Larry Merschel, who had reached adulthood during the 1950s and 1960s. In August 1965, a year after the Gulf of Tonkin resolution, Gallup found that 76 percent of Americans under 30 supported the war, compared to 64 percent of those 30 to 49, and only 51 percent of those over 49.[10] The oldest had lived through the horrors of both world wars; they acutely remembered World War II's more than 400,000 American casualties and 700,000 war-related injuries, and they recognized, in its aftermath, the long-term effects, of postwar traumatic stress.

Contrary to clichés about youthful opposition to the war, the age gap in public opinion would hold fast for the remainder of the war, as support for the war declined among every demographic group. The number-one song on the pop charts in 1966, Barry Sadler's patriotic "Ballad of the Green Berets," celebrated one of the military's most famous units, those "fearless men who jump and die" in service of their nation.

The Americanization of the War

Johnson and his key military advisers initially gained public support because they promised that the war would be quick and decisive. No one was more optimistic than General William C. Westmoreland, who commanded U.S. troops in Vietnam between 1964 and 1968. Westy, as he was nicknamed, oversaw military operations with brusque efficiency. A top graduate of West Point and a World War II veteran, he had also studied at Harvard Business School. "Westy was a corporation executive in uniform," argued historian Stanley Karnow. He evaluated military performance in quantitative terms, relying on detailed data to assess the threat of the North Vietnamese and Vietcong, and he used a grim metric of military success, the "favorable kill ratio."[11]

At the outset, Westmoreland believed that the United States could crush the Vietnamese rebellion through airpower and use "advanced technology to spare the troops an onerous offensive task."[12] Since World War II, American military planners had shared a nearly utopian faith in airpower as the key to American military might. The systematic application of American technology to war would reduce the number of American casualties while swiftly paralyzing North Vietnamese military production and halting enemy troop movements. American airpower had been crucial to victory in World War II against the technologically advanced Germans and Japanese, so it surely would allow the United States to prevail in a place that Johnson, off the cuff, called a "raggedy-ass, fourth rate nation."[13]

In February 1965 the North Vietnamese attacked the American air base at Pleiku, a city in the central highlands. The assault killed nine U.S. soldiers, injured many more, and destroyed a few dozen U.S. aircraft. The president responded angrily. "We have kept our gun over the mantel and our shells in the cupboard for a long time now," he stated. "And what was the result? They are killing our men while they sleep at night."[14] He pulled more than a gun from the mantel and authorized Operation Rolling Thunder, a massive airstrike on North Vietnamese military installations and industrial sites that also resulted in hundreds of thousands of civilian deaths. Rolling Thunder began the longest and most devastating aerial campaign in American military history. By 1968, the United States had dropped more than 3.2 million tons of explosives on Vietnam, more than the entirety of American bombing in both the Second World War and the Korean War.

But it soon became clear to Westmoreland that airpower would not be sufficient, especially in the large parts of rural South Vietnam that were under the control of the Vietcong, which embedded its troops in villages and hamlets. Just a few months after the United States launched Operation Rolling Thunder, Westmoreland requested a significant increase in ground troops. By late 1965 there were 185,000 American troops stationed in Vietnam, more than ten times the number in the last days of the Kennedy presidency. The Johnson administration also broadened the military draft, conscripting about 300,000 men per year from 1966 through 1968. All men between eighteen and twenty-five were eligible for the draft, but under a policy put in place after the Korean War called "manpower channeling," college and graduate students could get deferments while studying in a field considered to be vital to the national interest, such as physics. Those deferments extended to include the vast majority of college and graduate students. By January 1966, more than two million college students were able to defer military service.[15]

Pacification

In past colonial wars, including in the Philippines, the United States sought to pacify the civilian population, namely weakening popular support for insurgent troops. In Vietnam, pacification took different forms at different points during the war. It consisted of American efforts to flush out the enemy combatants from Vietnamese settlements, displace rural populations to reduce the influence of the National Liberation Front, and restructure Vietnamese society through programs of economic development. The first phase of pacification began in the Diem years, with the advice of the Kennedy administration. South Vietnamese government officials created "strategic hamlets," forcibly relocating Vietnamese peasants there and fortifying them to keep out NLF forces. The program was costly and ineffective. Many peasants, who wanted nothing to do with the war, became active enemies of the Diem regime. They allowed the Vietcong to move surreptitiously in and out of villages. Even those unsympathetic with the rebels often refused to support the South Vietnamese regime because of their anger at the process of being uprooted, often more than once.

By 1966, the United States, now directly involved in Vietnam, launched its own version of pacification. Building on Johnson's lofty Great Society rhetoric about "civic action," American aid officials worked with the South Vietnamese government to launch a program of democratization and economic development in villages that had been ostensibly purged of the Vietcong. Americans encouraged local elections and pledged to win over local populations by sponsoring agriculture, rural electrification, and public health initiatives.

But the instability of the population—particularly the high mobility of refugees and villagers' continued suspicion of the Saigon government and its American backers—greatly hampered rural development efforts. The massive depopulation of rural provinces and the environmental devastation wrought by massive airstrikes and the use of toxic herbicides to clear forests hampered agricultural reform. Corrupt local officials pocketed American dollars, and the military had little interest in supporting development efforts. By 1968, the rural pacification program was a shambles.

The lion's share of the remaining development funds went to managing the rapidly growing refugee population. All together, about 3.5 million Vietnamese people were displaced during the war. Some had moved voluntarily to the periphery of American military bases, where black market economies boomed. Residents there provided cheap labor and goods and services, from foodstuffs to prostitution, to the soldiers on American bases. One Vietnamese woman recalled the "gold rush" mentality that drew many rural residents to military encampments. But far more Vietnamese were forced out of their villages. In NLF controlled areas, residents who supported Diem fled persecution and assassination.

Many more fled the destruction wrought by ground war and especially by massive airstrikes and flamethrower attacks, using napalm, a gelatinous form of gasoline. Chemical defoliants, including Agent Orange, devastated some 20 percent of the land in South Vietnam—about the size of the state of Massachusetts—between 1965 and 1971. The roads of rural Vietnam teemed with haggard, hungry refugees, overwhelmingly women and children, often carrying little more than their clothes. With the agricultural economy destroyed, the dense, overcrowded refugee camps that housed many of the displaced could barely meet their needs. One study estimated that over half of all working-age refugees were unemployed.

Attrition

Despite Johnson and Rostow's dream of a modernized Vietnam, economic development became a sidebar to the most important objective: eliminating the Vietcong and destroying North Vietnam's military and industrial capacity. The key to victory was attrition by weakening the enemy through sustained air attacks and relentless ground operations. At every step of the way, Johnson acceded to Westmoreland's requests to expand American ground forces in Vietnam and steadily escalated the bombing raids.

Together, the U.S. and South Vietnamese troops greatly outnumbered the North Vietnamese and Vietcong. Coupled with their technological capabilities, the superiority of the American forces was clear in the casualty rates. Westmoreland, for whom demography was destiny, offered a grim statistical tally of the number of dead and captured. Ten to twenty Vietcong and North Vietnamese soldiers died for every American. After comparing notes on six of Westmoreland's press briefings that he attended, war correspondent Ward Just found that the "sessions had a striking similarity. The recurring message—'The Americans were on the offensive, the North Vietnamese and the Vietcong were on the defensive. But there was no sign of a break. Any questions?'"[16]

Skeptics from Within

President Lyndon Johnson trusted Westmoreland's data, even as the war dragged on. For Johnson and his most steadfast advisers, statistics and faith in technology overrode more impressionistic assessments of what was happening on the ground in Southeast Asia. The skeptics were few and isolated at first. George W. Ball, an experienced foreign policy hand, played devil's advocate in Johnson's inner circle. An attorney who shared his colleagues' faith in expertise, Ball had worked for the federal government on and off since the New Deal. He joined the Kennedy administration in 1961 and a year later was promoted to undersecretary of state. During the Kennedy years, Ball had warned Taylor and Rostow that "the Vietcong were mean and tough, as the French learned to their sorrow."[17] But few were interested in Ball's analogy with France's anticolonial debacle. Surely the U.S. military could do better.

Ball posed hard questions about Johnson's decision to Americanize the war in 1964 and early 1965. At each moment when Johnson planned to escalate American engagement, Ball wrote a memorandum taking the contrary position. He proved to be remarkably prescient. The affairs of Vietnam, he argued, were not central to America's Cold War goals. Ball explicitly rejected the "domino" theory of Communism, namely that Communism spread by toppling regimes one by one. "The great captains of history," he wrote, "drew their lessons from complex chess, not simple dominoes."[18] He echoed arguments that were gaining currency among other foreign policy experts in the mid-1960s. Growing tension between the two dominant Communist powers—the Soviet Union and China—led to a reappraisal of some of the fundamental tenets of the Cold War. There was no single monolithic Communist threat but rather multiple centers of Communist power that could be played off against one another. Vietnam was a minor stage in a large geopolitical struggle.

Ball also argued that the costs of military engagement in Vietnam greatly outweighed any possible benefits. Ultimately, he believed, the Vietcong would prevail against the South Vietnamese and their American allies, even if conventional measures currently suggested that the revolutionaries were losing. The South Vietnamese, he argued, lacked the solidarity necessary to establish an enduring, stable government and prevail against a well-organized revolutionary insurgency.

In a crucial memo to President Johnson on July 1, 1965, just as the administration dramatically escalated the ground war, Ball put his position most bluntly: "The decision you face now, therefore, is crucial. Once large numbers of U.S. troops are committed to direct combat, they will begin to take heavy casualties in a war that they are ill-equipped to fight in a non-cooperative if not downright hostile countryside." He continued: "Once we suffer large casualties, we will have started a well-nigh irreversible process. Our involvement will be so great that we cannot—without national humiliation—stop short of achieving our complete objectives." Clinching his point in italics, Ball warned: *"Of the two possibilities, I think humiliation would be more likely than the achievement of our objectives—even after we have paid terrible costs."*[19]

President Johnson shared some of these concerns. Behind the scenes, in private conversations with Defense Secretary McNamara, he worried "that it is going to be difficult for us to very long prosecute effectively a war that far away from home."[20] But he ultimately rejected Ball's arguments. McNamara, Rostow, and most of Johnson's inner circle clung to a simpler Cold War orthodoxy. They took as a matter of faith that the South Vietnamese regime was legitimate and, if restructured slightly, could be popular. And they believed that American firepower and know-how made victory inevitable.

In October 1966, Ball finally resigned from the Johnson administration, the most prominent official to leave to date because of disagreements about the conduct of the war. James Thomson and Bill Moyers, both Johnson loyalists who broke with the president on Vietnam, had preceded him. The departure of dissenting voices left Johnson increasingly isolated, surrounded by a group, among them Rostow, that political scientist Larry Berman called a "closed circle of decision making." But even that circle shrank, as other high-level officials resigned, including McNamara in 1967 and UN ambassador Arthur Goldberg in 1968.

Johnson's stubborn insistence that the Vietnam War was justified, necessary, and winnable generated greater skepticism outside the executive branch, even among some of his erstwhile political allies. As early as the summer of 1965, some key Democratic members of Congress began expressing concern about the escalation of American troop commitments, among them Senators Mike Mansfield (D-MT) and Richard Russell (D-GA). Those divisions came to light in January 1966, when Senator William Fulbright (D-AR) opened up hearings on the Vietnam War, giving a prominent pulpit to the war's critics.

Fulbright had been one of Johnson's closest allies and, at the president's bidding, had whisked the Gulf of Tonkin resolution through the Senate. But over the course of 1965, he had grown increasingly critical of the value of American intervention in regional wars overseas, including in the Dominican Republic, where Johnson had sent 23,000 American troops to put down a leftist insurgency in 1965, and Vietnam. Fulbright's Foreign Relations Committee hearings, which were covered extensively on national television, gave credence to the growing chorus of voices critical of the war. In 1966 and 1967 more members of Congress, many with impeccable anti-Communist credentials, argued against Johnson's war. In early 1967, Senator Robert F. Kennedy (D-NY) called for negotiations to end the war, earning the moniker "Ho Chi Kennedy" from the hawkish *Chicago Tribune*, whose editors, like many on the right, would settle for nothing less than total victory.[21]

THE ANTIWAR MOVEMENT

Fulbright, Kennedy, and Ball—despite their disagreements with the president—did not reject the larger aims of the war. They believed that the United States needed to prevail against Communism, and they argued that the war in Vietnam could, unintentionally, impede America's larger foreign policy aims. But growing numbers of Americans rejected both the war, and, in the process, America's Cold War foreign policy.

In March 1965, several months before Democratic congressmen raised concerns about the war, University of Michigan faculty and students held a teach-in on the Vietnam War, the first of thousands of such events held nationwide over the next several years. In April a broad coalition of religious and secular activists led a 25,000-strong march in Washington to oppose the war. One of the largest antiwar demonstrations to that date, it was a polite affair that attracted "more babies than beatniks," according to *The New York Times*.[22]

Opponents of the war represented different generations, acted on divergent motives, and disagreed on goals and tactics. Almost all the war's early critics came from the religious and political lefts. Since World War II, a dedicated band of activists, working through pacifist groups like the Fellowship of Reconciliation (FOR) and the War Resisters League, had argued for a militant, nonviolent resistance to war. They had mobilized quickly after Johnson announced Operation Rolling Thunder. "In the name of God, STOP IT!" pleaded FOR members to the president in April 1965.[23] Some were socialists who saw American military power as a tool of oppression. Others believed in the fundamental immorality of state-sanctioned violence. Still others, like Women Strike for Peace, offered a maternalist critique of the war, arguing that as mothers, they had their sons' and the nation's best interests at heart. But whatever their ideological differences, these groups collaborated in the struggle against the war, signing petitions and staging local and national protests.

Religion Against the War

Essential to the antiwar effort were members of traditional peace churches, especially the Quakers, the Mennonites, and the Brethren. Their more radical members joined protests, but most of them worked quietly behind the scenes, gathering medical supplies to assist Vietnamese refugees, printing antiwar pamphlets, and setting up centers to counsel young men on conscientious objection to the draft. Mainstream Protestants, Reform Jews, and a growing number of Catholics added their voices to the chorus of opposition. As early as November 1965, the Union of American Hebrew Congregations, speaking for Reform Jews, called for a cease-fire and a negotiated settlement.

In 1966 an ecumenical group of leading clerics, including Reinhold Niebuhr, Martin Luther King, Jr., Rabbi Abraham Heschel, Yale chaplain William Sloane Coffin, Jr., and Catholic priests Philip and Daniel Berrigan, joined forces to create Clergy and Laity Concerned About Vietnam, a group that would broaden the antiwar mobilization even further.

Especially prominent in the movement were Catholic antiwar activists, many of them priests and nuns who had been radicalized in the postwar years by the Catholic Worker movement, which embraced both pacifism and a commitment to help the poor. Part of a left-wing theological insurgency in the church, they challenged Catholics' reflexive anti-Communism. Priests like the Berrigans envisioned themselves as prophets against war and organized some of the most dramatic protests of the period. In October 1967, Philip Berrigan led the first of what would be at least one hundred protests at Selective Service centers in the next several years, pouring blood on draft cards in "a sacrificial and constructive act" to protest "the pitiful waste of American and Vietnamese blood, 10,000 miles away."[24]

The Rise of the Student Movement

The most visible opposition to the war arose on American college campuses. In the mid-twentieth century, war had remade American higher education. After World War II, military veterans, who had benefited from the GI Bill, flooded American universities. Most were older than the average college student, had families, and finished their coursework quickly. The Reserve Officer Training Corps (ROTC), a program to prepare college men for military leadership that had been created in 1916, expanded rapidly during the early years of the Cold War. By 1955, it had chapters on 313 American campuses.[25]

Many university faculties had grown somewhat more conservative after the war. McCarthyism had suppressed campus radicals. Scholars in the new field of American civilization emphasized the consensual nature of American politics and society; political scientists resuscitated the theory of American exceptionalism; business schools expanded rapidly; and physicists and chemists conducted secret research for the military and for firms that were contracted to improve weapons, radar, and other military technologies. By the time that the Vietnam War escalated, professors at Columbia, Penn, Michigan, Wisconsin, Chicago, and Berkeley engaged in high-level, classified research on chemical and atomic weaponry or military electronics systems. American universities proved central to the Cold War.

But it would be on campus that the Cold War consensus began to crack. Colleges were havens for political dissenters, reformers, the offbeat, and the eccentric. In the 1940s and 1950s, socialist students held earnest discussion groups at the City College of New York. Social Gospel Christians ran many campus ministries and sponsored events at the campus YMCA and YWCA at the University of Texas. Students frequented bars featuring folk music and coffee houses where they earnestly discussed existential philosophy and beat poetry.

The New Left

For the battered American left, campuses held potential, particularly in the early 1960s, when students began to organize around issues such as civil rights and the nuclear arms race. Students at Michigan, CUNY, Madison, and Berkeley had joined CORE's protests against segregated restaurants and lunch counters; and campus chapters of the National Committee for a Sane Nuclear Policy (SANE) proliferated. In 1962 a small band of socialists, closely allied with the labor movement, held a retreat in Port Huron, Michigan, and formed Students for a Democratic Society (SDS), with hopes of expanding their ranks by recruiting a younger generation of activists, especially those who had come of age in the postwar years.

It seemed an uphill battle. Since the 1930s, various socialist groups had aligned against the Communist Party over its allegiance to Moscow. But other than their disdain for Stalin and the Soviet Union, postwar socialists were a fractious lot, quibbling over minute differences in their interpretations of Marx, Lenin, Trotsky, and their latter-day heirs. A culture of disputation, however, created a vital intellectual infrastructure that nurtured leftist writers, even as their ranks dwindled. Radical theorists appeared in lively little journals like *Partisan Review* (founded in 1934), *Dissent* (1954) and *New America* (1960). Even if the American left was minuscule, its influence could be felt on campuses, in union halls (Oakland, Chicago, and Detroit had very active socialist groups), and in countercultural neighborhoods in big cities and college towns, including Greenwich Village, Austin, Ann Arbor, and San Francisco. The mainstream media took leftist intellectuals seriously. Many left-leaning writers, including Irving Howe, Dwight Macdonald, Michael Harrington, Betty Friedan, and Langston Hughes, their skills honed in the leftist press, penned articles for periodicals as diverse as *The New Republic, The New Yorker, Christian Century,* and even *Fortune.*

The Port Huron Statement, SDS's founding manifesto, articulated a broad set of principles in sweeping moral language that fused together elements of socialism, liberalism, and religious perfectionism, while eschewing the old partisan rhetoric of the left. Rather than advocating class struggle or denouncing state socialism, it called for "a democracy of individual participation" that would undermine the "depersonalization" of a modern bureaucratic society: "We would replace power rooted in possession, privilege, or circumstance by power and uniqueness rooted in love, reflectiveness, reason, and creativity." The statement's authors railed against what they considered the "crust of apathy" and the "inner alienation that remain the defining characteristics of American college life"; they blamed the "cumbersome academic bureaucracy" and those scholars whose work directly benefited corporations and the military.[26]

Some SDS activists formed the Economic Research and Action Project (ERAP), which sent students to work with white Appalachian migrants in Chicago and poor blacks in Newark. Organizing among the poor was difficult and frustrating and attracted only a small cadre of organizers. Most stayed on campus, hopeful that students would become the vanguard of revolutionary change.

Nothing fueled the rise of SDS more than the Vietnam War. In 1965 SDS chapters began to proliferate on campuses. At Swarthmore College, for example, SDS mobilized a third of the student body in February to protest Operation Rolling Thunder. In April, about 15,000 SDS members marched on Washington, demanding a cessation of the war. By 1966 and 1967, student radicals led campus protests against defense industries that recruited on campus, professors who conducted secret military research in their campus labs, and ROTC programs. At SUNY Buffalo and Wisconsin, protesters targeted Dow Chemical, which manufactured Agent Orange, a chemical defoliant used in Vietnam. Nearly everywhere that SDS had more than a handful of members, it coordinated teach-ins and protests against the war. The group's membership reached a peak of about 100,000 nationwide by early 1968, with more than three hundred chapters and perhaps another million or so loosely affiliated followers.

SDS was a decentralized organization that put as much value on process as outcomes. An anonymous SDS member quipped, "Freedom is an endless meeting," leading another to offer the hopeful embellishment that "talk helps people consider the possibilities open for social change."[27] SDS members did a lot of talking, but spoke without a single voice. On some campuses doctrinaire Maoists were able to commandeer chapters. And many anti-Communist "old leftists" fretted that student radicals were naïve in their support of revolutionaries like Che Guevara and Ho Chi Minh, whose portraits graced the walls of many dorm rooms and communal houses. But most SDS members were motivated less by revolutionary romance than by a sense that the "establishment" or "the system" needed to be challenged, be it in the form of university regulations of student behavior like parietals (rules that forbade members of the same sex from staying in each other's rooms overnight and that set curfews for female students) or the ability of the military to recruit on campus.

Hippies and Yippies

"Make love, not war." The popular slogan denoted the blurry boundaries between the antiwar movement and a loosely organized counterculture, one that celebrated personal liberation and fulfillment through sex or psychedelic drugs or music. Todd Gitlin, an early SDS leader and later a prominent sociologist, viewed the counterculture as a "less risky, more pleasurable" diversion from politics, "the Sixties' version of the fraternity-sorority culture of the Fifties."[28] For many young people, politics became a fashion statement: wearing long hair, loose clothes or none at all, beads, and sandals seemed a rebuke to businessmen in their wool suits and housewives in their A-line dresses.

There was a frivolity to the "hippie" culture that emerged in big cities in the mid-1960s, but to worried parents, it made the "juvenile delinquents" of the 1950s seem tame. Hippies took over San Francisco's Golden Gate Park for a "love-in" during the summer of 1967, stripping off their clothes, dancing, and shocking observers by doing what was usually done behind closed doors. In March 1968 thousands of young people, many of them disinhibited by smoking marijuana or dropping acid (the nickname for the hallucinogenic lysergic acid diethylamide), gathered for a "Yip-In" at New York's Grand Central Station, coordinated by members of the Youth International Party. Known as the Yippies, the colorful group, more theater troupe than political party, was led by Abbie Hoffman. The Yip-In, which the Yippies described as "a spring mating service celebrating the equinox," ended badly when some rowdy members of a collective called Up Against the Wall Motherfuckers climbed up to the station's trademark wall clock and pulled off its hands, announcing that they wanted to "fuck time"—the perfect excuse for hundreds of New York police to surge through the station in a bloody rampage that left hundreds injured and dozens arrested.[29]

The Yippies' founder, Abbot Howard (Abbie) Hoffman, famous for his bushy hair and flamboyant hats, was a jester with a serious mission: to mock the venality of power and celebrate its Dionysian alternative. A bit older than most of his followers, he had imbibed the "hep" culture of the beats as a college student in the late 1950s and, by the mid-1960s, proffered a gleefully subversive variant of youthful protest. "The goal now," he wrote in *The Realist*, one of hundreds of underground radical and countercultural newspapers that circulated in the late 1960s, "is to disrupt an insane society." He and his comrades practiced that disruption again and again. In one of the Yippies' most celebrated "happenings," Hoffman and his comrades tossed dollar bills from a balcony onto the floor of the New York Stock Exchange, bringing the whole operation to a halt as stock traders scrambled to scoop up the money.

The streets became stages in a theater of protest. Hoffman's comrade Paul Krassner described one antiwar demonstration with glee: "Throwing cow's blood. A costumed mock wedding of Military and Big Business. Overturning garbage cans. Painting a Rolls Royce in Day-Glo while the chauffeur cowers at the wheel in disbelief. Blocking traffic. Turning in false fire alarms. This was the Vietnam equivalent of Watts."[30]

For student radicals and hippies alike, the Vietnam War represented the ultimate perversion of the system. Out-of-touch, power-hungry liberals like Lyndon Johnson and the foreign policy establishment misled the public. War enriched major military contractors who funded defense research at leading universities, with the collusion of corrupt professors, deans, provosts, and presidents. Vietnam was a racist war, fought against people of color who were struggling for their own self-determination. And the war machine fed on the bodies of young men—American and Vietnamese— who sacrificed their lives for the establishment.

Draft Resistance

By 1967, many young men, some persuaded by the arguments of antiwar politicians and activists, others simply self-interested, found ways to keep from being drafted. Most of those who avoided service were well-to-do, well educated, or well connected. Young men from privileged families found all sorts of ways to avoid being shipped to Southeast Asia, from using their families' political clout to join the National Guard (whose units were seldom deployed abroad) to finding sympathetic doctors to document health problems that would render a draftee unfit for service. In 1968, when the Selective Service narrowed the criteria for graduate school deferment to men in training in medicine, dentistry, or divinity, applications to medical schools and seminaries skyrocketed.

Some half-million draftees petitioned to be recognized as conscientious objectors, claiming that they had moral reasons for opposing military service. In past wars, most COs had been members of traditional peace churches such as the Quakers. But by the mid-1960s, Reform Jews, Roman Catholics, and even agnostics claimed that they had moral reasons for opposing the war, if only they could convince a Selective Service board, an easier task in many cosmopolitan cities and college towns than in much of middle America. All together, 170,000 draftees, more than 100,000 more than in World War II, won conscientious objector status. Between 30,000 and 50,000 young men resisted the draft by leaving the country, most taking refuge in Canada and Scandinavia.

A WORKING-CLASS WAR

As a result of widespread draft avoidance, those at the bottom of the socio-economic ladder fought the war: the sons of America's fading industrial cities, its marginal farms, and its impoverished backcountry. About 80 percent of the 2.5 million who served in the military during the war came from working-class and poor families.[31] Many volunteers, especially those from places that had been left behind in the changing economy, saw service as a steady paycheck and an alternative to underemployment. This was a sharp contrast with World War I, when many college students joined the "preparedness" movement and zealously signed up to join the military. At that time many working-class men were deemed too unhealthy or too unintelligent to serve in the military. It contrasted sharply with World War II, in which widespread mobilization included the wealthy, the middle class, and the working class. Vietnam was a young man's war, fought disproportionately by high school dropouts and young men with diplomas but with few hopes of attending college. The average age of an infantryman in Vietnam was only nineteen, compared to twenty-six during World War II. Young men could be drafted at age eighteen but—until the Constitution was amended in 1971—only those twenty-one or older could vote.

The disproportionate number of soldiers and war dead who came from working-class families gave resentment a class tinge. "I'm bitter," recalled a firefighter who lost his son in Vietnam. "You bet your goddamn dollar I'm bitter. It's people like us who gave up our sons for the country."[32] Not surprisingly, support for the war strongly correlated with education: despite the prominent antiwar movement on campuses, those who had attended college were consistently more likely to support the war than their counterparts with a high school degree or less.

African Americans and the War

If students became the most visible opponents of the war, African Americans, whether on campus or off, were the war's earliest and most steadfast critics. In the 1960s, many blacks had looked hopefully to the military, the only substantially integrated institution in the United States. For black men in particular, enlisting offered an escape hatch from the grim urban economy or from the dying world of southern farm labor. Military service promised training, long-term health and pension benefits, and respect. In 1966 the Johnson administration launched Project 100,000, an antipoverty program that lowered military entrance requirements to provide opportunities to underemployed men. Of the 350,000 men who entered the program (it exceeded its numerical target), 41 percent were black, and about 40 percent of them were deployed to combat. Many black commentators viewed Project 100,000 in conspiratorial terms, and statistics from the first two years of the war did nothing to alleviate their concerns. Between 1964 and early 1967, African Americans suffered over 20 percent of U.S. casualties in Vietnam, although they made up only about 11 percent of the population. That imbalance was only temporary. Over the course of the entire war, blacks were not grossly overrepresented among the troops or the war dead. All together, blacks made up 12.5 percent of American casualties in Vietnam.

Racial tensions among the troops ran high, even though the military had been officially integrated since 1948. Black soldiers found it hard to advance through the ranks. They regularly complained of harassment by drill sergeants and officers. Petty arguments between black and white soldiers often exploded into brawls. Black soldiers were more likely to face courts-martial and were overrepresented in the ranks of those with less-than-honorable discharges. In the military's top ranks, African Americans comprised only 2 percent of officers. Many career white officers had come of age while the military was officially segregated and now adjusted only slowly to the change. Not surprisingly, blacks on the front lines in Vietnam began to embrace the rhetoric of the black power movement. Some painted black panthers and clenched fists on their helmets. Others joined Black Brothers United, one of many underground groups that gave soldiers a vehicle for dissenting from the war.

Civil Rights and the War

For their part, civil rights activists were, initially, badly split over the war, but for tactical more than ideological reasons. Many leaders of the SCLC, including Martin Luther King, Jr., shared misgivings about the war but feared that if they publicly opposed President Johnson, they would jeopardize civil rights legislation. One of the movement's key strategists, Bayard Rustin, who had been jailed for resisting the draft during World War II, took an equivocal stance on Vietnam. He criticized the war but counseled King and other civil rights activists to keep their antiwar sentiments quiet, for fear of alienating Johnson and other Democrats. CORE took a similar stance. By a narrow margin at its 1965 annual meeting, it passed a resolution denouncing the war, but at the urging of its leader, James Farmer (who like Rustin had been a war resister during World War II), tabled it for fear of alienating the civil rights movement's liberal allies.

Rustin and Farmer were increasingly out of touch with the rank and file in their organizations, who saw Vietnam as the latest example of a people's struggle for self-determination. As early as 1954, the singer and prominent leftist Paul Robeson had compared Ho Chi Minh's rebellion to slave uprisings, calling him the "Toussaint L'Ouverture of Indochina." Robeson worried that "Negro sharecroppers from Mississippi" would be dispatched "to shoot down brown-skinned peasants in Vietnam—to serve the interests of those who oppose Negro liberation at home and colonial freedom abroad."[33] If Robeson was a lonely voice in the 1950s, by the following decade black activists commonly made similar arguments. They depicted the war as one that served the interests of whites, threatened people of color, and relied on black Americans to do the dirty work.

As the war ground on, some prominent black public figures took a stand against Johnson's war. Among them was the heavyweight boxing champion Muhammad Ali, who declared himself a conscientious objector in early 1966, memorably stating that "I ain't got no quarrel with them Viet Cong." Antiwar activists embellished the quote, adding the phrase, "No Viet Cong ever called me nigger."[34] Ali was convicted of draft evasion in 1967, stripped of his heavyweight title, and banned from professional boxing, though he appealed the charges successfully and, in 1970, returned to the ring.

In a highly publicized April 4, 1967, sermon at New York's venerable Riverside Church, the Reverend Martin Luther King, Jr., urged an end to hostilities in Vietnam. "Surely this madness must cease. We must stop now. I speak as a child of God and brother to the suffering poor of Vietnam. I speak for those whose land is being laid waste, whose homes are being destroyed, whose culture is being subverted. I speak for the poor of America who are paying the double price of smashed hopes at home, and dealt death and corruption in Vietnam."[35]

Critics denounced Ali as un-American and railed against King for confusing his message. *The Washington Post* editorialized that King "has diminished his usefulness to his cause, his country, and his people."[36] But black celebrities like comedian Dick Gregory, singer Eartha Kitt, and actor Harry Belafonte, as well as black power activists including Stokely Carmichael and Angela Davis, joined King and Ali in their outspoken opposition to the war.

WAR AT HOME: THE URBAN REBELLIONS

The pronouncements of popular figures like Ali and King no doubt shaped black public opinion, but so too did events on the home front. The Americanization of the Vietnam War coincided with one of the most sustained periods of violence in American domestic history, what many called the "war at home." Between 1964 and 1967, hundreds of American cities exploded in riots. In the worst of the "long hot summers"—1967—uprisings occurred in 163 American cities and towns, ranging from Detroit in July, where 43 people were killed, 17,000 arrested, and tens of thousands of buildings destroyed, to small towns like Plainfield, New Jersey, Nyack, New York, and Wadesboro, North Carolina.

"Occupying Forces"

For those participating in the riots, Vietnam represented a touchstone. The Detroit riots broke out when police raided an illegal after-hours bar that was hosting a party for two black servicemen returning from the war. In Plainfield, undercover investigators reported that rioters praised Muhammad Ali and talked of self-determination against "occupying forces." National Guard units put down disturbances in Cincinnati and Tampa. Troops from the 101st Airborne, Larry Merschel's unit, joined the Michigan National Guard and the local and state police to put down the rebellion on Detroit's streets. Altogether 17,000 armed officials deployed in the Motor City. It was impossible not to compare the sight of jeeps and tanks in the streets and choppers hovering over America's burning cities to images from the war in Vietnam.

Many black critics of the war made explicit comparisons between Vietnam and American inner cities. Echoing decades-old critiques of American foreign policy by Marcus Garvey and W. E. B. Du Bois, Stokely Carmichael, the leading voice of the black power movement, argued that "we must recognize that Detroit and New York are also Vietnam."[37] One of the most outspoken critics of the war, Carmichael called the president a "buffoon" and Defense Secretary McNamara "a racist."[38]

By 1967 Carmichael and many black radicals viewed Vietnam as a potential ally in a global war of liberation. Blacks must "align ourselves with people of color around the world who are also oppressed," he argued. "The enemy around the world is the same." Carmichael saw both American inner cities and Vietnam as "occupied territories" whose residents mobilized for self-determination.[39] In Vietnam, peasants struggled against western colonialism, and in the United States, blacks struggled against "internal colonialism." Overseas possessions and inner cities alike were, in this view, places where whites enriched themselves by extracting resources and exploiting labor. For black radicals, the urban riots were nothing less than rebellions against white America's occupying forces: shopkeepers who got rich by charging high prices for inferior products and the police who brutalized blacks and suppressed dissent.

Law and Order Politics

The confluence of campus unrest and urban rioting fueled the alarm that the United States was out of control, plagued by disorder, and in need of policies to reinstate law and order. In 1964, Republican presidential candidate Barry Goldwater had argued that liberals aided and abetted disorder in the streets, and he called for a stronger police presence to restore safety and security, especially in America's cities. By 1966, the upsurge of campus protests and urban riots fueled calls for crackdowns on public dissent. That year California voters overwhelmingly elected to the governorship Ronald Reagan, who had run a campaign criticizing the ongoing campus rebellion at the University of California, Berkeley, the insurgency on the streets of Watts, and the growing black power movement. "Will we allow a great university to be brought to its knees by a noisy, dissident minority?" asked Reagan as he announced his campaign in January. "Will we meet their neurotic vulgarities with vacillation and weakness?"[40] His own answer was a clear no.

Johnson did not take the criticism lightly. In 1965, a month after Watts burned, he signed the Law Enforcement Assistance Act (LEAA), which provided unprecedented grants to local police forces. In its first two years, most of LEAA's $300 million went to riot preparation. With federal funds, local police departments purchased armored vehicles, tear gas, and high-powered rifles, preparing themselves to put down possible rebellions. The administration also provided training in antiriot techniques modeled after military counterinsurgency campaigns in Korea, Guatemala, and Vietnam. Around the country, police departments created paramilitary special weapons and tactics (SWAT) teams to control city streets. LEAA funding expanded exponentially in the next decade and a half. By 1981, the federal government had channeled more than $8 billion into a growing, federally-backed law enforcement system.

Behind the scenes, the Johnson administration also authorized the enhanced surveillance of antiwar and black radical organizations. J. Edgar Hoover, the FBI director, had spent decades investigating suspected Communists and gays; it was a small step from the Kennedy administration's approval of Hoover's wiretap of Martin Luther King, Jr. Cooperating with local police forces, FBI informants infiltrated student, antiwar, and black power organizations.

Many infiltrators were agents provocateurs, who goaded radicals into plotting acts of violence. One black power group, the Revolutionary Action Movement, was brought down in the summer of 1967 after revelations that its members plotted the assassination of black moderate leaders—a hare-brained scheme devised by an infiltrator. And in 1968 a group of Philadelphia SDS members were arrested in a plot to blow up the Liberty Bell after the police "discovered" incriminating evidence that they themselves had planted. Johnson authorized the CIA to launch Operation Chaos, an extensive program of spying against domestic opponents of the war, surreptitiously gathering information on hundreds of thousands of American citizens.

THE COLLAPSE IN PUBLIC SUPPORT FOR THE WAR

Efforts to curb dissent did little to change public opinion on the Vietnam War. Between 1965 and 1968, public approval fell sharply. Nothing played a greater role in fueling skepticism than the powerful, uncensored images of bloodshed that appeared in newspapers and, especially, on the televised evening news. One journalist called Vietnam "the living room war," for the ubiquity of images of dead and maimed bodies that shaped the public consciousness of the war. Every week beginning in 1967, *Life* magazine published the high school yearbook pictures of young American men killed in Vietnam. Gruesome photographs from the legion of photojournalists who accompanied the troops in Vietnam appeared in daily newspapers and on the evening news—soldiers burning thatched cottages with Zippo lighters; a young, naked girl screaming after being hit with napalm; a Vietcong rebel being executed at point-blank range on the streets of Saigon; a bloodied American soldier carrying a critically injured comrade over his shoulders. Previous wars had been equally horrible, but the tragedies of Vietnam were unfiltered, and to audiences accustomed to World War II–era newsreels or to the sanitized heroism of popular war films, they were shocking.

The Rise of the Antiwar Majority

Opinions about the Vietnam War varied by sex, race, class, and region. Men were more likely to be hawks; women, doves. Residents of the Southwest—

the part of the country that had been remade by the postwar military-industrial complex—supported the war more strongly than their counterparts elsewhere. Southerners, who sent disproportionately more young men to war than the rest of the country, were more likely to support de-escalation.

But by early 1968, a majority of Americans—men and women, from all regions—opposed the Vietnam War, and most wanted it to end quickly, though they had different explanations as to why. Some had come to believe that it was unwinnable; others that it was morally wrong. Some opposed the war because they thought it was being fought with inadequate resources; in their view, the United States was too soft. Those who opposed the war also diverged greatly on the means to ending it. A minority called for an immediate withdrawal from Vietnam, but just as many believed that the United States should dramatically escalate its airstrikes to accomplish a swift and decisive victory. On the extreme, some, including General Curtis Le May, who would be tapped by the independent George Wallace as his vice-presidential candidate in 1968, called for the use of nuclear weapons.

Opposition to the war did not, however, entail sympathy with the antiwar movement. Antiwar protesters proved even less popular than Johnson and the war. One of the most popular bumper stickers in 1968 was "America love it or leave it." Those who chanted "Ho, Ho, Ho Chi Minh, the Viet Cong are gonna win," or who defaced the American flag with peace signs, were considered a threat to society. The "do-goodniks" and "long-hairs" who led antiwar demonstrations seemed "un-American." Many who opposed the war also opposed what they saw as the erosion of respect for authority.

Dump Lyndon

The combination of urban unrest, escalating campus protest, and a seemingly unwinnable war all hurt the presidency of Lyndon Johnson. But the most consequential opposition came from within the ranks of his own party. Though he had been elected in 1964 by one of the most substantial margins in American history, his prospects had greatly dimmed a few years later. By 1967, Democratic opposition to Vietnam had coalesced into a "Dump Lyndon" insurgency on the party's left, though it seemed unlikely that any major Democrat would jeopardize his career by challenging the incumbent.

That changed on November 30, when Senator Eugene McCarthy

(D-MN) announced that he would be the anti-Johnson standard-bearer: "I am concerned that the Administration seems to have set no limit to the price it is willing to pay for a military victory."[41] McCarthy was an unlikely candidate. An unusually cerebral politician, he read Latin, wrote poetry, and steeped himself in Roman Catholic social teaching. Virtually unknown outside his home state of Minnesota, he had not been a major player in the Senate; nor had he been prominent among the president's critics. McCarthy's campaign slogan, "He stands alone," suggested a man of conscience, which he was, but also a politician without the ability to make the alliances necessary for success on the partisan battlefield.

McCarthy's campaign to unseat Johnson, as improbable as it was, galvanized liberal opponents of the war. Thousands of students went "clean for Gene," shaving their beards, cutting their hair, and replacing their countercultural garb with starched shirts, ties, or dresses, as they joined his New Hampshire primary campaign. On March 12, 1968, when McCarthy picked up 42 percent of the Granite State's Democratic primary vote and won a majority of the state's delegates, the Johnson campaign reeled.

TET AND BLOODY 1968

As Johnson weighed his political future, PFC Larry Merschel prepared for his deployment to Vietnam. Merschel supported the war and volunteered for the army out of a sense of duty. But he had the misfortune of being deployed to Vietnam in early 1968, during the worst few months of the war's worst year. American troop deployment reached its peak that May, at 535,000. That year 16,543 Americans died in action, comprising more than a quarter of all American casualties in the entire war. More than 27,000 South Vietnamese troops died in battle in 1968, as did an estimated 200,000 North Vietnamese and Vietcong fighters. It was also the costliest year of the war, with U.S. military expenditures in Vietnam topping $77 billion.

On January 1, 1968, as Merschel and his fellow troops at Fort Campbell, Kentucky, celebrated the New Year, the president offered a cautiously optimistic prognostication from his ranch in Johnson City, Texas. "We are very hopeful that we can make advances toward peace. We are pursuing every possible objective. We feel that the enemy knows that he can no longer win a military victory in South Vietnam. But when he will reach the point where he is willing to give us evidence that would justify my predicting peace this year—I am unable to do so—that is largely up to him."[42] The very same day Ho Chi Minh rallied his own people, offering his own resolution. Hanoi Radio broadcast his poem:

> *This Springtime certainly will be more joyous than all such previous seasons,*
> *For news of victories will come from all parts of the country.*
> *North and South (our people and our soldiers) will compete*
> *in the anti-American struggle.*
> *Forward we go,*
> *And total victory will be ours.*[43]

Both Johnson and Ho were wrong. The New Year would bring only the most tenuous advances toward peace, and total victory for no one.

The Tet Offensive

The Vietnam War took an abrupt turn in early 1968. The National Liberation Front had been planning a massive surge for months. At three in the morning on January 31, the first day of Tet, the Vietnamese holiday that marked the lunar New Year, a commando squad of nineteen National Liberation Front insurgents attacked the American embassy in Saigon, killing two military police officers, blasting the embassy door with antitank shells, and battling American soldiers and a helicopter force. Saigon was the most prominent of more than a hundred cities and towns that the North Vietnamese Army and the Vietcong targeted, among them five of the six largest cities in the South and 36 out of 44 provincial capitals. They caught American military leaders off guard.

The goal of the Vietnamese revolutionaries at Saigon and elsewhere in the Tet Offensive was not to achieve total victory, despite Ho Chi Minh's rhetoric. The insurgents were vastly outnumbered and weakened by years of heavy losses. Instead they hoped to humiliate and demoralize the South Vietnamese government and its American allies, and force a de-escalation of the war by bringing the United States back to the negotiating table.

The Tet Offensive was audacious but short-lived. At the U.S. Embassy, American troops killed all the attackers and secured the facility within hours of the raid, though not without drama. The military police protecting the grounds were unprepared, and two died. The fighting was chaotic. An American soldier threw a pistol up to an unarmed embassy official through a second-floor window, who used it to repel one of the attackers as he ran up the stairs. By midday, rubble and corpses littered the embassy gardens. In a stiff public statement after the embassy siege had ended, General Westmoreland declared victory, claiming that the Communists' "well laid plans

The Vietnam War, 1964–1975

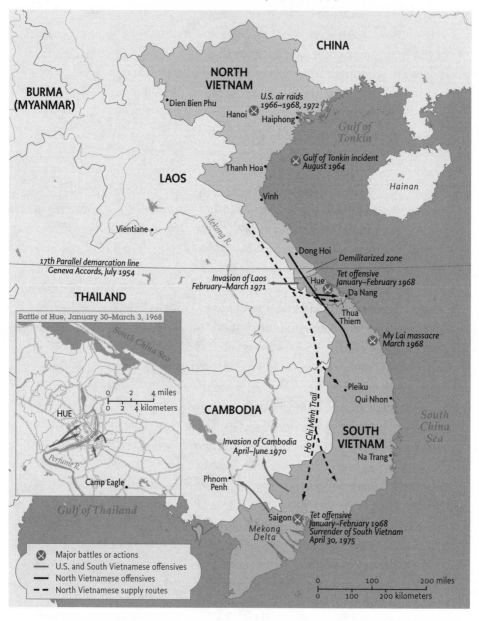

went afoul." But the televised coverage of the attack and its aftermath undermined Westmoreland's credibility.

The Tet Offensive lasted for only a morning in Saigon, and in many cities and towns, the rebels lost within hours or days. But in some parts of the country, fighting extended for weeks. Among the most bitterly contested places was Hue, a city of 140,000. Despite its strategic location, Hue fell astonishingly quickly to the rebels on January 31. More than three weeks of horror followed. After hoisting the yellow and red Vietcong flag aloft at the citadel in the heart of the city, the occupying forces engaged in a bloodbath, eventually shooting, clubbing to death, or burying alive supporters of the South Vietnamese regime. The death toll from the massacre was, from the outset, contested. Those sympathetic to the Vietcong claimed that 300 or 400 traitors died; the U.S. military estimated that rebels slaughtered somewhere between 2,800 and 5,700 public officials, military leaders, clergy members, merchants, and intellectuals.

Retaking Hue proved to be more difficult than repelling the attack on the American embassy in Saigon. For most of February, the United States bombed Hue and strafed it with gunfire. U.S. and South Vietnamese troops fought insurgent forces block by block. More than 13,000 of the city's 17,000 dwellings were destroyed or seriously damaged, and thousands of civilians died, maimed by shrapnel, crushed by rubble, or felled by gunfire. About 116,000 Hue residents fled to makeshift refugee camps in the nearby countryside. The South Vietnamese and U.S. troops would not recapture the city until February 25.

By Westmoreland's grim metric, the Americans and the South Vietnamese won a clear victory at Hue. Several thousand enemy troops died, and only a few hundred Americans. But images of the battle for the citadel in Hue—broadcast on the evening news for weeks in the United States— told a different story. The reports of television journalists accompanying U.S. troops in the streets of Hue added to the sense of a brutal and unwinnable war. From February 1968 onward, a dwindling minority of Americans supported it.

On February 27 the respected CBS news anchor Walter Cronkite, who had just returned from Saigon and Hue, declared that "the bloody experience of Vietnam is to end in a stalemate."[44] The same day General Earle Wheeler, chairman of the Joint Chiefs of Staff, requested the deployment of as many as 206,000 more American troops to Vietnam. Behind the scenes, top foreign policy advisers and military leaders—and even Westmoreland himself—began to question their assessment of the war's progress. Almost since the start of Tet, they had privately acknowledged that the offensive had weakened the South Vietnamese and served as a political and psychological boon for the Vietcong. Wheeler's request for a massive surge of troops generated an intense debate at the highest levels of government and in foreign policy circles. The call for negotiation and cease-fire, only a year ago a position held by a minority of liberals, gained traction.

On March 26, 1968, Johnson convened a private White House meeting with the "Wise Men," a blue-chip group of foreign policy advisers who had served various presidents since Franklin Roosevelt. Among them were former secretary of state Dean Acheson; former ambassador both to the UN and to South Vietnam, Henry Cabot Lodge; and former undersecretary of state George Ball. Acheson argued that the United States needed to disengage from Vietnam, and those assembled concurred. Almost a year and a half after he had resigned, Ball felt vindicated. "I share Acheson's view. I have felt that way since 1961—that our objectives are not attainable. In the U.S., there is a sharp division of opinion. In the world, we look very badly because of the bombing. That is the central defect in our position."[45]

On March 31, two months after the Tet Offensive began, Johnson gave a nationally televised speech that shocked the nation. "We are prepared to move immediately toward peace through negotiation. So tonight, in the hopes that this action will lead to early talks, I am taking the first step to de-escalate the conflict. We are reducing—substantially reducing—the present level of hostilities. And we are doing so unilaterally, and at once." As the speech wound to a close, Johnson announced, "I shall not seek, and will not accept, the nomination of my party for another term as President."[46]

Ground War in Thua Thien

Larry Merschel deployed to Vietnam on February 20, 1968, a little over a month before Johnson's stunning announcement. He joined his 101st Airborne comrades near Hue in Thua Thien province. Hue's hinterlands remained among the bloodiest battlegrounds of the war. During the early 1950s, Thua Thien had been a base of resistance to French colonialism, and in the late 1950s and early 1960s a center of Buddhist-led dissent against the corrupt and brutal South Vietnamese governments. As the civil war in Vietnam escalated, Thua Thien had provided some of the strongest support for the National Liberation Front. Even the village of My Thuy Phuong, where the 101st Airborne established Camp Eagle, its major base of operations in the region, was a hotbed of Vietcong support during the Tet Offensive.

General Westmoreland identified the region from Thua Thien northward to the Demilitarized Zone as key to post-Tet American strategy. Nearly half of all American troops deployed in Vietnam in 1968 were stationed there. After Tet, North Vietnamese and Vietcong troops took refuge in the jungles and hamlets outside Hue. American military planners, fearful of another attack on the city, worked to flush out the rebels. A month after Larry Merschel arrived, the 101st Airborne engaged in efforts to cordon off Vietcong troops, digging trenches around suspected havens, using flares to light up suspected enemy "nests," and attacking those who attempted to sneak through the lines.

Merschel's unit, the Second Division, 17th Calvary, went on "rat patrols" in the lowlands between Hue and the coast, seeking out insurgents by jeep and by foot in the marshes and jungles along the "Street Without Joy," the bleak, refugee-laden Highway 1 that connected Hue with points northward. Along with these search-and-destroy missions to capture or kill suspected insurgents, American and South Vietnamese officials recruited locals to create pro-Saigon local governments, police the communities, and lay the groundwork for economic redevelopment. The battle for Thua Thien became one of the longest ground operations of the war.

Disillusionment Among the Troops

Nearly every soldier had his horror stories from the forests and hamlets of South Vietnam, and most of them did not make the news. Instead, soldiers recounted their experiences in letters home and, using their own cameras and tape recorders, documented the war themselves. What they experienced and reported gave the lie to optimistic prognostications about favorable kill ratios and American invincibility. If many Americans on the home front felt a "credibility gap" between Johnson's statements and news coverage of the war, soldiers in the Indochinese jungles and swamps experienced it directly.

The troops on the ground in Vietnam also voraciously consumed the American print media. Although the military's own publications echoed official pronouncements on the war, most soldiers had access to American periodicals and, through them, learned of the raging home front protests and debates. In the spring of 1968, they knew that most Americans opposed the war, that antiwar protests proliferated, and that even mainstream politicians questioned the war. With Johnson and his close advisers shifting the administration's own position, confusion and tensions on the battlefields grew. What did Johnson's March 31 speech mean? Would the war end? What would the next president do?

Johnson's March 31 speech reverberated in Thua Thien. In letters home, twenty-year-old Larry, too young to vote, conveyed some of his own discomfort, though he did so in a light tone. "I can't have any say in who runs our government. I can't vote. I'd get arrested and heavily fined if I was caught drinking beer," he wrote. "But here I am—somebody is always getting unfairly treated, so I'll bear the burden with a smile."

THE SPIRIT OF REBELLION

In April 1968, as Larry and the 101st Airborne dodged bullets and shells in Thua Thien, disturbing news came from home. On April 4, in Memphis, Tennessee, Martin Luther King, Jr., was assassinated. More than one hundred American cities exploded in the most intense days of rioting in American history. The most extensive looting and burning happened in Washington, D.C., only a mile from the White House. A pall of smoke from burning buildings darkened the skies over the nation's capital. In Baltimore, riots lasted for four nights, and six people died. And in Chicago, which had already been ravaged by an uprising in 1966, eleven died in several days of discontent.

Campus protests exploded. In the semester that began the month of the Tet Offensive, major protests (involving at least a thousand people) erupted on more than two hundred campuses throughout the United States. On fifty-nine of those, students took over campus buildings. Students on at least another thousand campuses held smaller demonstrations or teach-ins, most directed toward the Vietnam War.

The antiwar movement also intensified on campuses with large populations of first-generation college students. They were the working- and lower-middle-class cousins, the brothers and sisters and classmates of the men fighting in Vietnam. Students marched at Wayne State University in Detroit and at Temple in Philadelphia, at historically black Jackson State University in Mississippi, and at Catholic Fordham and St. Louis Universities. Even at conservative Villanova, where Larry Merschel had matriculated, students began to raise their voices in opposition to the war and invited antiwar priest Daniel Berrigan to campus.

Revolt at Columbia

No campus got more press in the spring of 1968 than Columbia University, where students shut down the campus for eight days beginning on April 23. Since late March, members of Columbia's SDS had staged confrontational protests there, led by a charismatic junior, Mark Rudd. Born to a middle-class Jewish family in suburban New Jersey, Rudd had been a hardworking, disciplined high school student with a proclivity for math. But as an undergraduate, the confluence of the civil rights struggle and the anti-Vietnam insurgency radicalized him. In the winter of 1968, he visited Cuba and returned further resolved to be an agent of revolutionary change.

Over the spring semester, Rudd and his comrades in SDS, named the "Action Faction," stepped up protests. Rudd sent a letter to Columbia president Grayson Kirk, listing student demands, including the cessation of defense research on campus. Rudd memorably signed off, "Up Against the Wall Motherfucker," a salutation that outraged the staid President Kirk.[47]

On April 23, SDS members took a further step toward revolution. They marched against what they saw as faculty complicity with the war (a defense research center on campus) and racism (a gymnasium under construction in Morningside Park, bordering Harlem, that would be closed to community members). Over the next eight days, students occupied several campus buildings, briefly held the dean of the college hostage, and raided and pilfered the president's office. On April 24 a faction of black students ousted white protesters from the main classroom building and renamed it Malcolm X Hall. University officials, fearful that Harlem residents would riot, closed off the campus to outsiders.

On campus, the occupation generated an intense debate and counterprotests. Nearly two thousand students signed a petition denouncing the occupation, calling themselves the Majority Coalition; antiprotest students blockaded the main administration building, with hopes of starving out the student protesters. Sympathizers delivered takeout food—Mark Rudd's mother even dropped off a freshly cooked dinner for her son. Faculty members, some sympathetic with SDS, others fearful of violence, unsuccessfully attempted to broker a compromise between the protesters and the administration.

At two a.m. on April 30, more than eighteen hundred police officers raided the Columbia campus under the cover of darkness and arrested hundreds of students. They were particularly sensitive to the black students: an all-black unit of the police force peacefully led protesters out of Malcolm X Hall. But the late-night raids quickly turned bloody. Many police officers, resentful of what they saw as privileged students who lacked respect for authority, put black tape over their badges and took the license of anonymity to beat the protesters indiscriminately, even as they lay limp on the ground. About 150 students were injured. Dozens of faculty attempted to serve as peacekeepers; some of them were beaten and arrested too. That day Columbia SDS called for a general strike, and on May 1 the university suspended classes. For most of May and early June, at the paralyzed campus students skipped classes and many boycotted graduation ceremonies.

"Many Vietnams"

Cuban revolutionary Che Guevara was a hero to Rudd and to student protesters worldwide. His familiar face graced countless pamphlets and posters. But nothing solidified Che's reputation more than his 1967 critique of the Vietnam War. "How close and bright would the future appear if two, three, many Vietnams flowered on the face of the globe," argued Che, "with their quota of death and their immense tragedies, with their daily heroism, with their repeated blows against imperialism, forcing it to disperse its forces under the lash of the growing hatred of the peoples of the world!"[48]

Students worldwide saw their universities and cities as some of Che's "many Vietnams." At the beginning of the 1967–68 academic year, British students had engaged in a general strike at many major universities; and in the spring of 1968, demonstrations rocked campuses from Tokyo to Mexico City, from Berlin to Bombay. Youthful protesters in Prague challenged the Soviet occupation of Czechoslovakia. Media coverage of the protests worldwide brought the student protesters together virtually, as they challenged governments, denounced the war in Vietnam, and for a time felt a part of something that transcended their local concerns.

The biggest day for worldwide protests was May Day, the traditional occasion for leftist and pro-labor parades. That day students in Paris barricaded the streets of the Left Bank and began a monthlong battle with the police. Unlike students at Columbia, Jackson State, or Swarthmore, French students had a broad base of support, as hundreds of thousands of workers joined in solidarity, holding a nationwide general strike.

Rebellion in the Ranks

The spirit of rebellion made its way into the ranks of soldiers in Vietnam in countless ways, even among those who had little in common with protesters at Columbia or in Paris. Soldiers founded underground newspapers and magazines that viciously criticized officers and the war itself. Black power pamphlets circulated widely. Closeted gay soldiers circulated their own newsletter. Many soldiers adorned their helmets with peace signs or black panthers, signaling their sympathy for dissenters at home. And still others held late-night rap sessions on the morality of war. The letters column of *Playboy* became a public forum for anonymous GIs to report on their experiences, denounce their officers, and argue about military strategy,

For its part, the military did everything in its power to keep up the morale of GIs. The United States bankrolled dozens of large clubs on or near South Vietnamese bases, with booze, beer, and slot machines. (Gambling generated an estimated $23 million in revenue per year.) American and Filipino rock bands, well-known American actors, actresses, and comedians, and dancers and strippers entertained soldiers on bases and at off-base clubs. The army slapped together gymnasiums and movie theaters, installed pizza ovens and soda and popcorn machines, and even subsidized ice cream factories. Soldiers received their pay in "military payment certificates," a form of scrip that quickly became currency in Vietnam's rapidly expanding black market, to which military officials mostly turned a blind eye. Prostitution proliferated—in plain sight—in the settlements surrounding military bases.

But the military's efforts to boost morale fell short. The grim conditions in South Vietnam greatly demoralized troops, and many turned inward to express their frustration. Many soldiers began to escape by using marijuana, which was cheap and readily available in Saigon and in the hastily built trading centers that sprang up around American bases. Although there are no good estimates, internal military studies suggest that by the end of 1968, probably between a third and half of soldiers frequently smoked pot. About 1.5 million soldiers went AWOL (absent without leave) during the war, and some 450,000 left the military with a less-than-honorable discharge, many for insubordination, drug use, and petty crimes.

Tensions flared between the frontline troops and the GIs "in the rear," in support units on bases that seldom saw direct combat. Racially charged brawls erupted in mess halls and bars, echoing the struggles in the streets on the home front. At the extreme, the post-1968 years witnessed a significant increase in "fragging," anonymous attempts to injure or kill officers, often through the use of fragmentation grenades. By the military's conservative estimate, at least a few hundred fraggings occurred during the war.

The My Lai Massacre

Other soldiers turned their wrath on the South Vietnamese. Brutal attacks on civilians and rapes became alarmingly commonplace. Officers regularly covered up wartime atrocities, even if they were often common knowledge among the troops. One happened shortly after the end of the Tet Offensive, in a small hamlet called My Lai, in the Quang Ngai province, about 150 miles southeast of Hue, where the Vietcong had a strong base of indigenous support. The countryside was especially dangerous, and dozens of U.S. soldiers had been killed or maimed by landmines surrounding rebel bases. On March 16, 1968, an army unit, led by Lieutenant William Calley, raided a hamlet called My Lai, a suspected Vietcong haven. The military's intelligence was wrong: there were no rebel troops or caches of weapons to be found, just hundreds of terrified civilians.

Ordered to cordon off My Lai and capture combatants, Calley and his troops went on a rampage, killing somewhere between 347 and 504 villagers, most of them women and children. Calley himself herded about fifty villagers into a trench and killed them with automatic rifle fire at close range. Several elderly men died by bayonet, and troops shot women praying for their lives in the back. U.S. soldiers mutilated bodies, and raped some of the women and a child. The event would not be reported until 1969. After a lengthy investigation and court-martial, Calley was convicted of murder, though he only served a short sentence and went free on appeal.

The blood and gore, the terror of stumbling upon a landmine or walking into a snipers' nest, the horror of killing and watching civilians and comrades die, the anxiety and distrust among the troops themselves, the dehumanization of Vietnamese civilians as "gooks"—strained even the most disciplined soldiers. And for what? Putting one's body on the line for a war that fewer and fewer Americans on the home front supported seemed senseless.

At the end of 1968, someone prominently posted an antiwar petition that read simply, "Fuck War" at the 101st Airborne's Camp Eagle. Among others, Steve Sherlock, a Screaming Eagles officer who had enlisted as a "super war supporter," signed it.[49] Maybe, after months of slogging through the "Big Muddy," Larry Merschel would have agreed with the petition's sentiment too, though he probably would not have cared much for its language.

But he would not have the chance to sign. On May 1, 1968, while part of a search-and-destroy mission four kilometers northwest of Hue, Larry died when fragments from an exploding antitank mortar mutilated his body. He was buried in a closed casket. His parents begged to see their son one last time. The army would not let them.

CHAPTER 12

WHICH SIDE ARE YOU ON?:

THE BATTLE FOR MIDDLE AMERICA, 1968–1974

ARMEN ROBERTS, a thirty-one-year-old mother of two, became a political activist for the first time in the spring of 1970. She lived in a quiet lower-middle-class neighborhood in northeastern Detroit, about as close to the suburbs as you could get without crossing the city line. Married young to a truck driver, she was a stay-at-home mom who took pride in her impeccably neat living room and her lush front lawn. Stylish in a late-1950s sort of way, and though some of her friends wore miniskirts and bell-bottoms, the latest fashions did not tempt her. She liked her world just so.[1]

As hard as she tried, Roberts couldn't cocoon her family from social and political change. The neighbors' older children grew their hair long. She found their insouciant style and loud music upsetting. Even more ominous was the racial unrest that seemed to move closer and closer every year. Detroit had been a racial battleground for decades. Whites resisted integration by attacking black newcomers to their neighborhoods more than two hundred times in the period since World War II. Many more fled the "Negro invasion" and headed to the suburbs. By 1970, Detroit was on the brink of becoming a majority black city. Roberts and her neighbors hunkered down on their patch of segregated turf.

Whites had long dominated Detroit politics, but African Americans fought to be heard. In the late 1950s, blacks began to win elections to the city council and school board and used their positions to fight for civil rights. Other insurgents worked outside the system. Young black activists had taken over the campus newspaper at Wayne State, the city's major public institution, and turned it into a voice of black militancy. During Detroit's 1967 riot, someone had sprayed the words *Black Power* on a street, catching the attention of news helicopters. Someone else painted black a statue of Jesus at the local Catholic seminary. Tellingly, the local archbishop decided to leave the altered statue intact.

The black insurgency intensified after the riot. Local activists Milton and Richard Henry took African names, Gaidi and Imari Obadele, and formed the Republic of New Afrika, demanding that the U.S. government turn over land for the new country. In 1968 and 1969 a group called the League of Revolutionary Black Workers staged wildcat strikes at the city's Dodge and Chrysler plants, protesting systematic racial exploitation in the workplace.

Black and white students fought for power in Detroit's schools. At Mackenzie High School, black students walked out in October 1968, demanding an Afrocentric curriculum. At Cooley High School, which had been nearly all white through the mid-1960s, white students fought integration. At the beginning of the 1969–70 school year, they hurled bricks, beer cans, and bottles at their black classmates, shouting "get out of our school, Nigger!"[2]

Detroit's school board scrambled to deal with the unrest. On April 7, 1970, it announced a modest plan to integrate the city's schools. Carmen Roberts was furious that her son, who had just started at Denby High School, and her daughter, who walked to nearby Columbus Elementary, might have to transfer, all for the sake of what she believed was a dangerous effort in social engineering. Roberts and about 750 other white parents gathered to protest at the public school headquarters when the plan was announced. She called it "the day my life was to be altered from that of a complacent housewife to an active alert housewife."[3]

THE ELECTION OF 1968: DEMOCRATIC FRACTURE

Carmen Roberts represented the sort of voter whom the various candidates for the White House fought to win beginning in 1968—and even more so in the midterm elections of 1970 and the presidential election of 1972. White, working class, and urban, they had been the bedrock of the Democratic Party, but they had grown increasingly disaffected with civil rights, urban unrest, student rebellion, and the Vietnam War. Although working-class voters remained in the Democratic Party camp in 1968, they began shifting rightward with momentous consequences for national politics.

For over three decades, the Democratic Party had held together a fractious coalition across region and race. Blue-collar whites and African Americans in the North supported the party of the New Deal and turned out in large numbers for Kennedy and Johnson. Roman Catholics mostly remained on the Democratic side, attracted by the party's pro-labor policies and its support for the family wage. Republicans enjoyed their deepest support among suburban and rural Protestants in the Northeast, the Great Plains, and the West. The GOP's pro-business politics ensured a loyal following among small business owners and corporate executives alike.

Domestic strife, and the unpopular war, threatened to upend the political order. Southern whites, still overwhelmingly Democratic, rebelled against Johnson and their party's northern wing. Union members in the North, among the most reliable Democrats, grew uneasy with student rebellion and black unrest. The Democrats could count only on African American voters to turn out huge majorities for their candidates. On the right side of the aisle, Republicans sensed a real opportunity to break up the Democratic coalition for good.

The Democratic Challengers

Lyndon Johnson's announcement in March 1968 that he would not run for reelection left his fellow Democrats scrambling. Their first challenge, an impossibly difficult one, was to manage the party's deep divisions over Vietnam. Eugene McCarthy had captured the antiwar vote in the early primaries, but his constituency of young, well-educated voters was small, and he did not have the political skill to expand it. The Minnesota senator appeared elitist to many blue-collar voters, and he would not gain the support of many unions, especially those whose members continued to support the war. Southern whites saw him as just another meddling northern liberal. McCarthy did support civil rights legislation, but it was never his priority, and as a result, he did not have much appeal for black voters. He had succeeded in persuading Johnson of the political costs of the Vietnam War, but that single issue would not be enough to sustain a winning candidacy.

McCarthy paved the way for Robert F. Kennedy, a candidate with an impressive résumé and a compelling story of personal transformation. In the 1950s, Kennedy had established his "law and order" credentials as a Democratic staff attorney working with anti-Communist Wisconsin senator Joseph McCarthy, then as chief counsel to the Senate's investigation of the corrupt Teamsters Union leader, Jimmy Hoffa. Serving as attorney general in his brother's administration, RFK played a part in nearly every major presidential decision, including the Cuban Missile Crisis, the drafting of civil rights legislation, and the wiretapping of Martin Luther King, Jr. After his brother's death, RFK moved leftward, first as a critic of the Vietnam War, then as a passionate defender of the downtrodden, whether Hispanic farm workers or American Indians, whose reservations he insisted on visiting during the 1968 primaries despite the advice of his staff who saw nothing to be gained by targeting their votes.

Beginning in late 1967, Democratic activists led a "Draft Kennedy" movement, but RFK was reluctant to stand against the incumbent in what would probably have been a losing effort. But after McCarthy's impressive showing in the New Hampshire primary, Kennedy stepped in. McCarthy's supporters were outraged at what they saw as Kennedy's opportunism. Kennedy proved to be a formidable campaigner. He attracted enormous crowds at his rallies, sometimes emerging from the fray with his shirt ripped and hands bloodied by enthusiastic supporters.

Kennedy tried to hold together the fraying Democratic coalition of working-class whites and African Americans. To whites, he promised to crack down on urban crime; to blacks, he pledged his unwavering commitment to civil rights and federal job creation programs. He also pledged to use federal funds to rebuild decaying neighborhoods, like New York's Bedford-Stuyvesant, where he had spearheaded a community redevelopment effort with substantial foundation funds. And over time, by campaigning against the war, he won the trust of many left-liberal Democrats who agreed with McCarthy but saw him as unelectable.

On April 4, 1968, Kennedy's most impressive campaign moment came in downtown Indianapolis, where just before a rally, he got news of Martin Luther King, Jr.'s, assassination. He climbed to the roof of a car and, speaking without notes, offered a poignant, personal reflection on King's death. "We can do well in this country. We will have difficult times; we've had difficult times in the past; we will have difficult times in the future. It is not the end of violence; it is not the end of lawlessness; it is not the end of disorder. But the vast majority of white people and the vast majority of black people in this country want to live together, want to improve the quality of our life, and want justice for all human beings who abide in our land." He continued, "Let us dedicate ourselves to what the Greeks wrote so many years ago: to tame the savageness of man and make gentle the life of this world."[4] When Indianapolis proved to be one of the biggest major cities that did not riot that week, many credited Kennedy.

Few party insiders believed that Kennedy could carry the convention despite his name and charisma. Only fourteen states held Democratic primaries in 1968. The majority of delegate slots went to party regulars. Still Kennedy campaigned with intensity, hoping that if he won some of the biggest primaries, he might sway a closely contested convention. In May he headed to California, a must-win state. There he met with striking farmworkers, greeted voters in riot-torn Watts, and campaigned among working-class whites. At the Ambassador Hotel in Los Angeles on June 4, he celebrated his victory with a call for an end to "the divisions, the violence, the disenchantment" that plagued the United States during the election year.[5]

Early on the morning after her victory, as Kennedy greeted workers in the hotel kitchen, a mentally ill man, Sirhan Sirhan, who had been stalking him for weeks, shot and killed him. Sirhan, a Palestinian, was bitter about Kennedy's support for the State of Israel. The assassination of a second Kennedy, coming less than two months after Martin Luther King's death, seemed to many an apocalyptic portent, a sign of a country gone mad.

Hubert Humphrey

The frontrunner all along was Vice President Hubert Humphrey. Revered by members of the Democratic Party's liberal wing during the 1940s and 1950s, Humphrey had begun his career in Minneapolis. Elected mayor in 1945, he drafted the city's antidiscrimination ordinance, one of the nation's first. At the 1948 Democratic National Convention, he electrified liberals and outraged the Dixiecrats with his bold criticism of states' rights. Humphrey pushed for full employment policies, which would use government funds to create jobs for the unemployed. He built especially close ties with industrial unions.

By 1968, however, Humphrey had lost his luster. Despite his own misgivings about the Vietnam War, which he kept private, he loyally stood by Lyndon Johnson, alienating antiwar Democrats. As the stand-in for the incumbent, he won support from the party establishment, including big-city mayors like Richard Daley in Chicago, the heads of major unions, and southern power brokers, who could not bear the thought of Kennedy or McCarthy in the White House. Humphrey had not bothered to run in the Democratic primaries, instead gaining support through surrogate "favorite son" candidates like Florida senator George Smathers and Indiana governor Roger Branigin. After RFK's death, it was a foregone conclusion that he would be the Democratic standard-bearer in the fall.

The Siege of Chicago

For all of his confidence that he would be the party's nominee, Humphrey faced insurgencies from both left and right. On the left, tens of thousands of protesters—Yippies, Black Panthers, and antiwar activists—descended on the Democratic National Convention in Chicago. Spearheading the protests was Tom Hayden, a restless young activist who had grown up in Royal Oak, Michigan, a conservative middle-class suburb of Detroit, where the most prominent landmark was the Shrine of the Little Flower, anti–New Dealer Father Charles Coughlin's home parish.

As a student at the University of Michigan, Hayden had embarked on a search for authenticity. In June 1960 he decided to hitchhike across the country, "trying to mimic the life of James Dean."[6] He recalled that he was "interested in the bohemians, the beatniks, the coffeehouse set, the inter-racial crowd but I wasn't really part of them." He found himself and his political calling in Berkeley, where he fell in with a group of radical students and joined Martin Luther King, Jr., in a protest at the 1960 Democratic convention in Los Angeles. That fall he returned to Michigan, committed to building a student movement for social change.

Like so many white students on the left, Hayden gravitated toward the civil rights struggle. In 1961 he joined SNCC, and later that year he was arrested with seven other Freedom Riders in Albany, Georgia. Fired up by his experience, he helped found Students for a Democratic Society and drafted large parts of the Port Huron Statement in the spring of 1962. Two years later he led the group of SDS members who launched the Economic Research and Action Project, its antipoverty campaign, in Newark, New Jersey.

By 1965, Hayden turned away from antipoverty to antiwar organizing and visited Hanoi to express his support for negotiations to end the war. He helped the National Mobilization Committee to End the Vietnam War (known as Mobe, a coalition of about one hundred antiwar groups) to plan its October 1967 March on the Pentagon. In the months following the Pentagon protest, Mobe began planning for a massive demonstration at the Democratic convention in Chicago, intended once and for all to discredit the party of Lyndon Johnson. Hayden and Rennie Davis, another SDS veteran, led the organizing effort.

The other dramatis persona in the events unfolding in Chicago was Mayor Richard J. Daley, a formidable politician who controlled the city's Democratic machine. The product of Chicago's rough, Irish Catholic Bridgeport neighborhood, he had spent his childhood with street toughs who fiercely protected their turf, particularly from blacks who lived in nearby neighborhoods. Daley represented a brand of Democratic urban politics that had mostly disappeared: he used his office to reward his followers with patronage jobs and city contracts, while punishing his opponents by depriving their neighborhoods of prompt trash pickup and snowplowing.

For all his rough edges, Daley was an astute businessman who channeled federal urban renewal funds to massive, modern downtown and lakefront developments, pleasing the city's corporate leaders while creating more blue-collar jobs for his supporters. To showcase Chicago, he ordered the construction of huge redwood fences to shield journalists and delegates from the sight of the blighted neighborhoods that they would pass on their way to the convention.

For Daley, the convention protests affronted his street-brawling side and threatened his plans to market Chicago. For months before the convention, the Chicago Police Department's Red Squad infiltrated antiwar groups as far away as New York. The Yippies facetiously threatened to dump LSD into the city's water supply (public works officials estimated that it would take five tons to have any effect); Daley stationed police officers at the city's water treatment plants. The week before the convention federal judge William J. Lynch, Daley's former law partner, denied protesters permits to march in the streets or sleep over in the city parks. To control media coverage of demonstrations, Daley refused to provide electrical service to power cameras outside the convention hall.

On August 28, anticipating an all-out clash with the ten thousand protesters who had gathered in Grant Park, along Chicago's lakefront, Daley dispatched about eleven thousand police officers to the streets around the convention hotel, with thousands of National Guardsmen on standby. Under the glare of television cameras, over the hum of power generators, Hayden and his fellow protesters chanted, "The whole world is watching, the whole world is watching." A phalanx of police officers in full riot gear, most of whom had removed their badges so they couldn't be identified, charged into the crowd, shouting, "Kill! Kill! Kill!" They tear-gassed, beat, and arrested hundreds. Hayden and six fellow organizers (nicknamed the "Chicago Eight") were charged with conspiracy in a case that would wend its way through the courts for five years, before they won acquittal.[7]

Coming after summers of rioting, months of campus sit-ins and protests, and the chaos after King's assassination, the events in Chicago seemed irrefutable proof that the country was at the brink of collapse. If the Democrats could not maintain order at their own convention, how could they be trusted to govern the country? The protests inadvertently spurred demands for law and order. A majority of Americans—and huge majorities of whites—believed that the Chicago police had responded appropriately to the provocations of Hayden, Mobe, and the Yippies.

Insurgency on the Right: George Wallace

The cry for law and order galvanized Humphrey's opposition on the right. In February, Alabama governor George C. Wallace announced that he would run for the presidency as an independent, denouncing government violations of "states' rights," railing against campus protests, and calling for a more aggressive use of American airpower in Vietnam. "We're gonna have a police state for folks who burn the cities down," pledged Wallace.[8] After the debacle in Chicago, Wallace polled favorably with more than 20 percent of voters. By late September, he polled so well among northern, urban, working-class whites—the sorts of folks who cheered on Daley—that major unions, led by the United Automobile Workers, ran advertisements reminding voters that Wallace had a long antiunion record. Wallace's ratings fell in October, in part because his vice-presidential nominee, General Curtis LeMay—nicknamed "Bombs Away LeMay" by his detractors—had called for the use of nuclear weapons in North Vietnam. Still, in the November election Wallace picked up six southern states, including the four that Goldwater had won in 1964, the best showing for an independent presidential candidate since Theodore Roosevelt's Bull Moose candidacy in 1912.

NIXON AND THE "SILENT MAJORITY"

The beneficiary of the tumult in 1968 turned out to be the eventual Republican nominee, Richard Nixon, who accepted his nomination at the Republican convention in Miami, held just a week after the clashes in Chicago but almost eerily peaceful by contrast. There, to the roar of delegates, Nixon pledged to speak for "the great majority of Americans, the forgotten Americans, the non-shouters, the non-demonstrators. They are not racists or sick; they are not guilty of the crime that plagues the land. They are black and they are white—they're native born and foreign born—they're young and they're old. They work in America's factories. They run America's businesses. They serve in government. They provide most of the soldiers who die to keep us free. They give drive to the spirit of America. They give lift to the American Dream. They give steel to the backbone of America."[9] This sort of populist language offered a respectable gloss on Wallace's vitriolic denunciations of crime, riots, and student protest.

Nixon's nomination marked a remarkable turn in his political fortunes. Just four years earlier he had decided not to seek the presidency, but during the 1964 election, he had begun resuscitating his career. He refused to take sides in the bitter feud between the party's moderate establishment and its Goldwater-led insurgents. Although he was associated with the party's Eisenhower wing, he had a track record as a vehement anti-Communist, going back to his days in HUAC. The Goldwaterites admired his staunch anti-Communism. They especially appreciated that he stumped for Goldwater, rather than remaining on the sidelines, as did many moderate Republicans. Still, in 1968, Nixon was not the top choice of either the GOP's moderates or its right wing.

Romney, Rockefeller, and Reagan

In 1968, Nixon survived a bruising Republican primary season that was a battle for the future of the Republican Party. He had staked out the middle ground between the favored moderates, Michigan governor George Romney and New York governor Nelson Rockefeller, and the heartthrob of the right, California governor Ronald Reagan. Romney had made his name as an auto executive. He cared about balanced budgets most of all, but he also took positions that put him toward his party's left. He had no love for organized labor, but supported collective bargaining rights and, as governor, signed a law that recognized Michigan's public employee unions. Although he was a member of the Mormon Church, which relegated black congregants to second-class status (until 1977, blacks could not serve as bishops, one of the most important church offices), Romney strongly supported civil rights. But he proved to be an inept candidate, doomed by his shifting position on the Vietnam War. First he supported it; then he questioned it; then he told reporters that on a visit to Southeast Asia, he had been "brainwashed" by military officials. In late February, he dropped out, leaving Rockefeller to make a half-hearted run for the White House as the moderate standard-bearer.

Reagan, two years into his first term as California's governor, emerged as Nixon's most serious challenger. In 1964 he had enthusiastically campaigned for Goldwater, denouncing "the schemes of the do-gooders" and "those who would trade our freedom for the soup kitchen of the welfare state."[10] In 1966, riding a national antiliberal wave, he had handily defeated incumbent governor Edmund "Pat" Brown, a close ally of Presidents Kennedy and Johnson. Reagan blamed Brown for the uprisings in Watts and on the campus of the University of California, Berkeley, where "the ringleaders should have been taken by the scruff of the neck and thrown off campus permanently."[11]

Reagan railed against student radicals, visibly cringing as he described the lurid scene at a Berkeley dance: "The hall was entirely dark except for the light from two movie screens. On these screens the nude torsos of men and women were portrayed from time to time in suggestive positions and movements. Three rock and roll bands played simultaneously. The smell of marijuana was thick throughout the hall. There were signs that some of those present had taken dope. There were indications of other happenings that cannot be mentioned here." And he offered a damning critique of the collapse of moral authority. "How could this happen on the campus of a great university? It happened because those responsible abdicated their responsibilities."[12]

Reagan captured the imagination of the right, but even those uneasy with uppity students and gyrating torsos feared that he did not stand a chance of election. He was inexperienced and too closely associated with Goldwater's disastrous campaign. Reagan entered the convention with only a small percentage of votes. Party regulars—including Goldwater—lined up behind Nixon, who won the nomination on the first ballot.

Nixon's Victory

In Nixon, Humphrey faced a shrewd opponent. Determined to avoid the mistakes of his losing presidential bid in 1960, Nixon hired a team of brilliant ad men and strategists. The most talented among them was Roger Ailes. Only twenty-six, Ailes had made his name by transforming the image of Mike Douglas, a square Philadelphia television host, into a national celebrity. Nixon—edgy, sweaty, seldom photogenic—was an even more challenging client. To burnish Nixon's image as a man of the people, Ailes carefully staged "town meetings." The local media seldom learned that the events were packed with rank-and-file Republicans whose questions were screened in advance to put Nixon in the best light.

Nixon's team produced brilliant campaign spots, with ominous music and shots of angry protesters and rubble-strewn streets that captured Americans' anxieties about civil disorder. One ad, alluding to fears of sexual predation, showed the nude torso of a mannequin. Another showed a Vietnam battlefield strewn with dead bodies. The GOP spent almost twice as much as the Democrats on commercials.

Humphrey had one major advantage. In 1968, buoyed by government spending on the war and social programs, the economy was booming. Unemployment stood at only 3.6 percent, the lowest since 1953. Humphrey and his campaign team played on themes familiar to Democratic voters since the New Deal, depicting the Republicans as out-of-touch elitists. The vice president highlighted his party's long support for Social Security, the minimum wage, and pro-labor policies. He promised that he would keep America prosperous.

The election would not be decided on bread-and-butter issues, however. Humphrey got only 41.7 percent of the popular vote. Nixon eked out a victory with 42.3 percent. Wallace picked up most of those remaining. Nixon did not win a mandate, although more than 58 percent of the voters had repudiated Humphrey. Still, the Democrats held on to solid majorities in both the House and Senate. Liberalism was far from dead. Despite the strong economy, voters rejected the status quo.

NIXON IN POWER

Nixon's election did not immediately signal a rightward lurch. The new president had to work with a solidly Democratic House and Senate. He also had to balance his own party's competing interests carefully. To do that, he put together a political team that defied easy political characterization. Some of his most trusted advisers and high-profile appointments came from the GOP's moderate Rockefeller-Eisenhower wing. He also reached out to prominent Democrats, most notably tapping Daniel Patrick Moynihan, who had worked for Johnson, as his chief domestic policy adviser. Still others came from the New Right.

The Last Hurrah of the Moderate Republicans

Nixon's closest campaign aide and one of his few intimate friends, Robert Finch, was the most prominent of the new administration's moderates. Finch had been elected lieutenant governor of California in 1966, outpolling Ronald Reagan at the top of the ticket. During the convention, he made Nixon's short list of possible vice-presidential nominees, and Nixon rewarded him with a cabinet position of his choice. Finch chose to become secretary of Health, Education, and Welfare, a position that many Goldwaterites reviled after Eisenhower had created it in 1953. Many on the right viewed government-provided health insurance as socialistic, federal intervention in local education as unconstitutional, and welfare a reward for indolence, but Finch represented a bipartisan mainstream in support of each. He used his position to push for stricter health regulations and, for a time, was the administration's advocate for the swift desegregation of public schools in the South.

Finch was critical of welfare, but in conjunction with Moynihan, he supported a generous alternative, the Family Assistance Plan (FAP), which would have provided a guaranteed annual income for poor families, totaling about $1,600 per year for a household of four.[13] The plan had the advantage of simplicity. It would allow the administration to standardize welfare payments nationwide and reduce the bureaucracy of social workers who administered Aid to Families with Dependent Children. But it faced serious political headwinds. On the left, the National Welfare Rights Organization considered FAP payments insufficient and denounced its requirement that aid recipients find work. Critics on the right argued that it was a handout to the undeserving. Congress failed to pass FAP.

Other moderates joined Finch in the administration. For secretary of transportation, Nixon named liberal Massachusetts Republican John Volpe, who would go on to oversee significant increases in federal spending on public transit and the creation of the federal rail system, Amtrak. Nixon even appointed his former rival, Michigan governor George Romney, as secretary of housing and urban development, a cabinet post that Johnson had created as part of his Great Society reforms. Nixon, in the words of *The New York Times*, had appointed "a team of moderates."[14]

Nixon's Right Flank

Nixon also rewarded his party's right-wing insurgents. Their biggest prize was Vice President Spiro T. Agnew, who had begun his career as a moderate but then shifted sharply to the right while serving as Maryland governor. By the time Baltimore exploded in a riot after Martin Luther King, Jr.'s, assassination, Agnew had become a staunch advocate of law and order politics and a bitter critic of the student left, civil rights, and black power. Speaking just after the riot, Agnew lambasted the "circuit-riding, Hanoi-visiting . . . caterwauling, riot-inciting, burn-America-down type of leader," claiming that "some hard things needed to be said."[15] As vice president, he fired up the right wing with florid speeches denouncing the "thieves and traitors" who led campus uprisings and the "nattering nabobs of negativism" who denounced American foreign policy.[16]

Nixon also reserved places for right-wing activists in his speechwriting and policy staffs. The most notable was Patrick Buchanan, the scion of a Catholic, New Deal family, who vehemently repudiated liberalism and became one of the administration's loudest voices on the right. Nixon's special counsel was Harry Dent, a steely South Carolinian and former aide to Senator Strom Thurmond, the erstwhile Dixiecrat. Dent would be a key figure in helping the administration orchestrate its "southern strategy" to win over whites who were angry about civil rights.

REBELLION AND REPRESSION

Nixon had promised to restore order, but America during his first term was far from peaceful. Cadres of activists—many convinced that the United States was on the brink of revolution—turned their energies toward mobilizing the people. Some put their hopes in the Black Panthers, who called for a global struggle against capitalism and imperialism. Still others celebrated the Weather Underground, a minuscule but tightly disciplined band of revolutionaries who plotted spectacular acts of violence to destabilize the United States, in hopes of spurring a mass uprising. In March 1970 the Weather Underground accidentally blew up a Greenwich Village townhouse where they were constructing a bomb. Later that spring Weathermen took credit for bombing the New York City police headquarters. In July, as Weather activists dispersed and went into hiding, spokesperson Bernardine Dohrn issued a "Declaration of War," arguing that "revolutionary violence is the only way" to overcome "the frustration and impotence that comes from trying to reform this system."[17]

COINTELPRO

The escalating revolutionary rhetoric fueled growing repression against dissenting groups of all varieties at all levels of government. Nixon authorized the secret infiltration of antiwar, black power, and student organizations, expanding the Counter Intelligence Program (COINTELPRO) that dated to the Eisenhower presidency. Local police forces created their own special squads to spy on activists and wreak havoc. Undercover law enforcement infiltrators, posing as militants, hatched violent schemes to frame dissidents, including assassination plots—fueling the revolutionary fervor of activists while providing evidence of their danger to society. Police exploited intergroup rivalries, often goading militants to attack members of competing organizations for their ideological deviations. The presence of informants tore apart radical organizations. Paranoid for good reason, some radical groups brutally interrogated and occasionally murdered suspected "snitches."

Law enforcement officials made extra efforts to pursue black radicals, with bloody results. In 1969 alone, 27 Black Panthers were murdered and 749 arrested. In an incident that generated international outrage, Chicago police, working with an FBI informant, targeted Black Panther leader Fred Hampton. In a police raid early in the morning of December 4, 1969, police shot Hampton, asleep and possibly drugged to keep him from waking, three times, twice in the head at point-blank range.

The year 1970 brought little peace, as activists again stepped up protests around the country, and law enforcement officials responded with violence. The two most brutal incidents happened at the end of the spring semester, during a wave of campus protests against the war in Southeast

Asia. On May 4, Ohio National Guardsmen, patrolling the Kent State campus, shot and killed four unarmed students and injured nine others during a campus protest. Eleven days later, just after midnight on May 15, local and state police swept through Mississippi's Jackson State University campus, attempting to disperse an angry crowd of students, shooting into a crowd and shattering all the windows in a woman's dormitory. Two died, one shot by the police, the other trampled in the chaos that ensued. Twelve others were injured.

Construction Protests and the Rise of Affirmative Action

If Nixon hoped to silence the most radical dissenters, he also looked to calm less disruptive forms of dissent. In May 1969, in response to nonviolent civil rights protests at construction sites in Pittsburgh, Philadelphia, and Oakland, Nixon administration officials issued orders calling for "affirmative action" in government contracting that mandated "goals and timetables" for the hiring of minority workers as a condition of winning federal contracts.[18] Overnight, federal officials monitored hiring at construction sites and soon would do so in defense plants and in thousands of firms that produced everything from paper to cars to missile components.

Behind the affirmative action plan were two of Nixon's moderate appointees, Arthur Fletcher, one of the administration's several high profile black officials, and Labor Secretary George Shultz, a well-respected University of Chicago economist. For his part, Shultz was concerned that skilled workers kept wages high by excluding black workers. He hoped that affirmative action would ultimately drive down wages, especially on costly government construction projects. Nixon saw affirmative action as a cost-free form of "crisis management," hoping it would prevent urban unrest. Some of Nixon's political advisers believed inaccurately that they could win black votes. Nixon oversaw the expansion of the Office of Minority Business Enterprise and appointed several former civil rights activists, including CORE's James Farmer, to administration positions. He also reached out to black celebrities like Jackie Robinson in an unsuccessful effort to create a "black silent majority."[19] Nixon's seasoned campaign operatives had less principled motives, arguing that affirmative action could be a wedge to divide two key Democratic Party constituencies, white unionists and African Americans.

White Voters

The partisan allegiance of white voters, already up for grabs in 1968, became an obsessive concern with Nixon's aides. How could they win over people like Carmen Roberts? Pundits and pollsters provided contradictory advice, sometimes shoring up the moderates, sometimes the New Right. On one side were the respected analysts Richard Scammon and Ben Wattenberg, who argued in their influential 1970 book, *The Real Majority*, that American politics "shows signs of splitting into two battlefields: the old economic one and the new social one that deals with crime, drugs, racial pressure, and disruption." They argued that political success for the Republicans depended on winning the "unyoung, unpoor and unblack." Candidates needed to "listen to the center" and be *"responsive* to the real majority of voters—without being repressive to minorities."[20]

On the other side was Kevin Phillips, an impatient young campaign strategist who had worked for Nixon in 1968. In an influential *Washington Post* article and subsequent book, Philips identified a "New Republican majority," comprising whites in the South, in the West, and in suburbs everywhere. That majority was increasingly conservative on welfare, crime, and civil rights. Phillips's advice was to veer rightward, capturing the anger represented by George Wallace, and to look southward to capture disaffected white Democrats.

In the White House, Nixon aides diverged considerably on what strategy to pursue. Moderates like William Safire, Nixon's lead speechwriter, argued against the Phillips strategy, making a case that the Republicans needed a national rather than a sectional strategy. But many of Nixon's other political operatives, among them Harry Dent and political whiz kid John Ehrlichman, made a forceful case to the contrary: Nixon would seal a victory in 1972 if he repudiated school desegregation, open housing, and affirmative action. Dent pushed Nixon to win the support of the right by appointing "strict constructionist" judges. Nixon ultimately sided with the latter, bolstered by journalists' discovery of "white backlash."

The Revolt of the Middle Americans

In January 1970, *Time* magazine named white "middle Americans" its "Men and Women of the Year," hailing their "silent but newly felt presence" and their battle for "a system of values that they see assaulted and mocked everywhere."[21] In New York, journalist Pete Hamill, hanging out in bars, had documented the "revolt" of the white lower middle class in an article that circulated widely among Nixon's advisers. And a slew of reporters inspired by Hamill documented "middle-class rage" and "backlash" among angry "white ethnics," a new umbrella category to describe Catholic, working-class residents in hard-luck neighborhoods in Boston, Brooklyn, Philadelphia, Chicago, and Detroit. [22]

In each of these places, the story seemed to be racial resentment pure and simple. Residents pointed their fingers toward African Americans who were moving into their neighborhoods and, as a result of the newly instituted affirmative action programs, competing for their jobs. For them, civil rights laws were special favors to help blacks at their expense. "If I hear the four hundred years of slavery bit one more time," one of Hamill's informants griped, "I'll go outta my mind."[23] Just as ethnics had established themselves in American society as a result of perseverance, hard work, and discipline, so too should blacks lift themselves up, without the aid of special pleading or special preferences, they thought.

The Hardhat Protests

In the late 1960s and early 1970s, America seemed to be a nation of binaries: white or black, right or left, patriot or protester, housewife or hippie. These combustible resentments exploded dramatically on May 8, 1970, on Wall Street. There a group of youthful protesters gathered to mourn the recent Kent State shootings. During their lunch break, a few hundred "hardhats"—construction workers—charged toward the protesters, shouting "All the way, USA," and "Love it or leave it." Wall Street office workers cheered from the sidelines as the construction workers singled out "longhairs"—those who, more than their comrades, bent gender categories—beating and kicking them, while police officers stood aside. Only six construction workers were arrested after the melee that they had started. "These hippies are getting what they deserve," said hardhat John Halloran in the midst of the fracas.[24]

For the next few weeks, hardhats took to the streets in Pittsburgh, Buffalo, and San Diego, culminating in a massive protest on May 20, coordinated by Peter Brennan, the head of the Building Trades Council of Greater New York, whom Nixon would later appoint as secretary of labor. One hundred thousand white workers took to the streets, waving banners that read "God bless the Establishment" and "We support Nixon and Agnew." The president crowed, "Thank God for the hard hats."[25] He made political hay out of the protests, presenting construction workers as true conservatives, even if most trade unionists opposed Nixon's economic programs and many hated the war.

UNDERMINING INTEGRATION

How could Nixon's efforts to reach disaffected whites succeed with the administration's moderates pushing for programs like affirmative action for racial minorities, school integration, and open housing? The first test came in the spring and summer of 1970, when residents of Warren, Michigan, a blue-collar suburb of Detroit where only 28 residents out of 180,000 were minorities, rebelled against George Romney and the Department of Housing and Urban Development (HUD). The face-off began with HUD's decision to withhold a housing grant of almost $3 million until Warren implemented a plan to fight housing discrimination. Warren, the mayor pledged, would not be "a guinea pig for integration experiments."[26] When Romney visited Warren to explain the policy in July, a jeering crowd greeted him and he left under police escort. That fall Warren residents voted to refuse to accept any federal housing funds that required integration.

Nixon was furious at Romney, but throughout the fall and winter the housing secretary continued to promote residential integration. Romney, warned presidential aide John Ehrlichman, "keeps loudly talking about it in spite of our efforts to shut him up." Nixon replied tersely, "Stop this one."[27] But Romney did not shut up and would not resign, even when Nixon offered him the ambassadorship to Mexico. By 1971, Nixon's conservative aides fumed about HUD. Pat Buchanan recommended that the administration "tie the hands of HUD," lest Nixon become "the last worshipper in the Church of Integration before it closes down for good."[28] Nixon refused to fire Romney but instead weakened HUD's suburban housing programs and pledged that his administration opposed "forced integration."

School Integration

Even more vexing to the administration was the problem of racially segregated education. Under the 1964 Civil Rights Act and the 1965 Elementary and Secondary Education Act, the federal government required school districts, mostly in the South, to dismantle racially separate schools. In January 1969, Robert Finch pledged that there would be "no erosion of the guidelines."[29] The Department of Health, Education, and Welfare would withhold funds from school districts that practiced segregation. Using more than a billion dollars in federal funds, Finch created local desegregation councils, bringing together prominent white politicians, black ministers, and other civic leaders to make plans to dismantle Jim Crow schools.

Many southern school districts complied quickly—forced to do so by the threat of losing federal aid. At the same time, many whites opted out by withdrawing their children from newly integrated schools. In Mississippi, private school enrollments tripled between 1968 and 1970, especially in small towns in the Delta with large black populations. In Indianola, for example, nine hundred students applied for admission to the "seg academy" in 1969, to avoid desegregation.[30] To make the school affordable, local elites raised money for scholarships to help needy white students attend. Ten years later only 10 percent of Indianola's public high school students were white.

For opponents of integration, however, private education was no panacea. Only about 15 percent of white students across the South attended private academies. Most couldn't afford to do so. As districts came under orders to shut their all-black schools—and shuttle black students to formerly all white buildings—southern opposition to desegregation began to take new forms. Even as they told survey researchers that they were "colorblind" and did not mind sending their children to racially mixed schools, many southerners simply picked up and moved across city lines when court-ordered desegregation plans were implemented, a tried-and-true tactic borrowed from the North.

But in some of the region's largest school districts, whites could not flee. In Nashville, Tennessee; Jacksonville, Florida; and Charlotte, North Carolina, to name three, school districts extended across entire metropolitan areas. In the 1971 *Swann v. Charlotte-Mecklenburg Board of Education* decision, the Supreme Court upheld a school desegregation plan in Charlotte—a school district that included the central city, the suburbs, and outlying rural areas. Finding a school that was not under the court order essentially meant leaving the county altogether. So Charlotte residents put forth another argument: they advocated sending children to their "neighborhood schools" rather than busing them to other sections of town to accomplish integration. Because neighborhoods were deeply segregated by race, a neighborhood school was usually a single-race school. Charlotte adopted a plan that minimized travel but maximized integration, and the resistance died down quickly. By the mid-1970s, Charlotte became one of the few racially diverse large school districts.

Busing

Quickly and fairly peacefully integrated, Charlotte proved exceptional. In 1971 a Gallup poll found that 76 percent of respondents nationwide opposed the "busing of Negro and white school children from one school district to another."[31] It did not matter that by 1970, nearly half of all American public school students rode buses to school (only about 2 to 4 percent as part of desegregation plans). Antibusers defended the invented "tradition" of children walking or riding their bicycles to school, avoiding the charge that they were motivated by race. Black activist Julian Bond acerbically rebutted, "It's not the bus, it's us."[32]

The staunchest opposition to busing was north of the Mason-Dixon line, where women like Carmen Roberts rallied to protect their own segregated schools. In most northern metropolitan areas, black students were clustered in a handful of school districts. Since the early 1960s, the NAACP had significantly stepped up its legal challenge to northern school desegregation, although the law remained unsettled. Robert Carter, a longtime attorney for the NAACP, pushed the courts to move past *Brown* and its emphasis on "intentional" segregation. After *Brown*, federal judges had regularly ordered desegregation when it could be proved that districts had intentionally fostered racial segregation. But if there was no smoking gun that a district had deliberately excluded blacks—even if it was all white— the courts were reluctant to intervene. The existence of racially segregated schools, under Carter's theory, justified state action, regardless of whether school district boundaries had been drawn with discriminatory intent.

Finally, in the late 1960s and early 1970s, several court cases gained national attention. The two most important involved public schools in Denver and Detroit; both would make their way to the Supreme Court. In their argument on behalf of desegregation in the Denver public schools (*Keyes v. School District no. 1, Denver, Colorado*, 1973), NAACP attorneys succeeded in getting the Supreme Court to accept the "Keyes presumption," that if a district had engaged in segregation in one part of town, it would be presumed to have engaged in systematic racial discrimination, unless it could prove otherwise. Denver consequently had to institute a district-wide integration plan.

In Detroit, the NAACP decided to address the issue of metropolitan school segregation head-on. In an important 1971 federal district court case, *Milliken v. Bradley*, NAACP attorneys challenged racial segregation in Detroit and fifty-three surrounding school districts. They argued that federal and state policies were responsible for the "containment" of black students in urban schools and, at the same time, for maintaining a ring of all-white districts around the city. Federal district judge Stephen Roth agreed with the plaintiffs, concluding that state action was responsible for ending educational segregation, and that only a metropolitan-wide school desegregation plan could remedy the persistence of separate and unequal education for black and white students. Roth's decision would be appealed all the way up to the Supreme Court, which would hear arguments on the case in 1974.

The Antibusing Movement

Roth's decision unleashed a firestorm of protest. Now, it seemed, entire metropolitan areas would be subjected to court-ordered busing. Prominent elected officials denounced the ruling. Senator Robert Griffin (R-MI) proposed an antibusing amendment to the U.S. Constitution, drawing support from both Democrats and Republicans. Nixon, sensitive to the issue, denounced "forced busing" and told Finch's successor, Elliot Richardson, "to do what the law requires and not one bit more."[33] In March 1972, Nixon supported a national moratorium on school busing. Not to be outdone, Alabama governor George Wallace, mounting a campaign for the Democratic presidential nomination, railed against busing as the "most asinine and cruel thing I've ever heard of."[34] Amid the busing dispute, Wallace won the Michigan Democratic primary, sweeping all the majority-white precincts in Detroit, including Carmen Roberts's neighborhood.

On the ground, Roberts and her comrades around the country organized a grassroots antibusing campaign. The very acronyms that the antibusers chose for their organizations—Mothers Action Detroit (MAD), the National Action Group (NAG), and the National Association for Neighborhood Schools (NANS)—sybolized righteous, angry motherhood. Antibusing activists spoke not just as voters or taxpayers or citizens or homeowners but as moms. Who could be opposed to women who were, in the words of one of Roberts's comrades-in-arms, "just looking out for the good of their children"? One popular bumper sticker, targeting the judge who decided the *Milliken* case, read, "Roth is a Child Molester."[35]

Nixon and the Courts

Roberts and her colleagues were guardedly optimistic as *Milliken* made its way to the U.S. Supreme Court. The Nixon administration slowly shifted the balance of power on the court rightward, especially on civil rights. In June 1969, Nixon nominated Warren Burger, a well-known conservative and a strict constructionist, to succeed the retiring Earl Warren as chief justice. Nixon made special efforts to win the loyalty of southerners. When another Supreme Court seat opened in the fall of 1969, Nixon nominated Clement Haynsworth, a South Carolina judge whose segregationist record was so egregious that seventeen Republicans and the majority of Democrats voted him down. Nixon rejoined by putting up G. Harrold Carswell, who had a long history supporting racial segregation, including turning a public golf course in Florida private so that blacks could not tee up alongside whites. When Carswell's nomination failed as well, Nixon thundered that both judges had been "falsely charged with being racists" and rejected because of "the accident of their birth, the fact that they were born in the South."[36] Seeking to avoid controversy, Nixon nominated Harry Blackmun, a well-respected lawyer and close friend of Warren Burger, to the court. His confirmation generated little debate.

In 1971, Nixon nominated two more conservatives to the bench. The first, Virginia lawyer Lewis Powell, had a strong case. He had headed both the Chamber of Commerce and the American Bar Association. His impeccable conservative credentials as a defender of "free enterprise" earned him the suspicion of labor groups but scarcely enough to derail his nomination. Powell's civil rights record was also troubling. From 1953 to 1961, he had chaired the Richmond, Virginia, board of education. He had distanced himself from those who called for "massive resistance" to *Brown* but did nothing to comply with the Supreme Court decision. When he left office, only two of about 23,000 black children in Richmond attended school with whites. But unlike Carswell and Haynsworth, Powell had not spoken out in defense of segregation. He had criticized Martin Luther King, Jr., not over his goals but rather because he disagreed with the tactic of civil disobedience, which he linked to "organized lawlessness and even rebellion."[37] Powell did not have much respect for the black freedom struggle, but his defense of law and order provided no smoking gun. He won the Senate's approval with only one dissenting vote.

William Rehnquist, an Arizonan with close ties to Barry Goldwater, was far more controversial. His nomination hearing focused on a memo that he had written as a clerk for Justice Robert Jackson during the deliberations over *Brown v. Board.* "I realize that it is an unpopular and unhumanitarian position, for which I have been excoriated by 'liberal' colleagues," wrote Rehnquist, "but I think *Plessy v. Ferguson* was right and should be re-affirmed."[38] Rehnquist claimed that he was speaking for Jackson, but the justice was long dead. Rehnquist's critics pointed to his later, public criticism of the Warren Court for disregarding precedent. Some witnesses also testified that during the late 1950s and early 1960s, Rehnquist had harassed black and Hispanic voters at polling places. He successfully dodged the criticisms and won nomination, though with twenty-six no votes, including those of three moderate Republicans.

The shifting composition of the court bolstered Roberts and the anti-busing movement. In its 5–4 1974 *Milliken v. Bradley* decision, the Supreme Court struck down Roth's plan for cross-district busing, leaving local school district boundaries and administrative fragmentation wholly unchallenged. Four of the five in the majority were Nixon appointees: Chief Justice Burger and Associate Justices Blackmun, Rehnquist, and Powell. Associate Justice Thurgood Marshall issued a blistering dissent: "It may seem the easier course to allow our great metropolitan areas to be divided up into two cities—one white, the other black—but it is a course, I predict, our people will ultimately regret."[39]

THE PERSONAL IS POLITICAL

The mothers' crusade against busing touched on deep, primal fears of a society transformed not just by race but by new gender roles. For the conservative and the conventional, busing represented just one threat to parental control and the traditional family. It was bad enough, as Ronald Reagan had memorably put it, that hippies "dress like Tarzan, have hair like Jane, and smell like Cheetah."[40] But it was not just hippies who were subverting traditional notions of masculinity and femininity. In the second half of the 1960s, many high school students began to challenge school dress codes. In

Oak Lawn, a Chicago suburb, girls walked out of class in early 1967 to demand the right to wear miniskirts. Boys began to grow their hair long, in a style that had been viewed as feminine since the mid-nineteenth century. In small towns and conservative suburbs, schools expelled young women for wearing blue jeans instead of demure dresses. Wearing pants was inherently mannish, wearing revealing clothing was too sexual, and both were in their own ways subversive. Civil liberties groups took up the cause of these students, and by 1970, in the face of lawsuits and bad publicity, school districts began grudgingly to accept a range of dress styles in the classroom.

Radical Feminism

Radical feminism offered an even more subversive challenge to gender norms. In September 1968 a group of self-described radical feminists burst onto the scene in a theatrical protest during the Miss America pageant in Atlantic City. There protesters tossed the symbols of female oppression, including girdles, false eyelashes, and high-heeled shoes, into a "Freedom Trash Can" as news cameras recorded the scene. Contrary to subsequent myth, the protesters did not burn any brassieres. The event culminated in the coronation of a sheep as Miss America.

Robin Morgan, a young activist, had pulled together the Atlantic City event, along with members of her new protest group, the Women's International Terrorist Conspiracy from Hell, or WITCH. The group—like the Yippies, which Morgan had briefly joined—was deliberately, humorously subversive. Morgan, who had begun her career as a popular child actress (she appeared in a 1950s-era family show, *I Remember Mama*), was the perfect spark for the Atlantic City protest. She was an experienced—if jaded— new left activist, who had protested the Vietnam War, written for underground newspapers, and embraced the counterculture.

Morgan came to reject what she called the "counterfeit male-dominated left."[41] She had good reason. The left-wing social movements of the 1960s were riddled with sexism. In 1965, when Mary King and Casey Hayden drafted a manifesto calling for the equal participation of women in SDS activities, men at the meeting laughed and shouted them down: "She just needs a good screw."[42] In 1966 women in Students for a Democratic Society rebelled when they were left to cook and clean at the annual meeting, while men drafted resolutions and prepared speeches. The popular antiwar slogan "Girls say yes to boys who say no" offered a one-sided view of sexual freedom: women could either reward the rebellious with sexual favors or be denounced as "bourgeois" or "uptight."[43] Stokely Carmichael's infamous edict that the "only position for women in SNCC is prone," and Eldridge Cleaver's celebration of "pussy power" in the Black Panthers, seemed to condone a culture of sexual predation.[44]

In 1970, Morgan edited a best-selling collection of essays by leading feminists, *Sisterhood Is Powerful*, and with a group of feminists took over an underground magazine called *Rat*, where she issued an angry manifesto, "Goodbye to All That." Morgan lambasted those men who "degrade and destroy women by almost everything they say and do." For her, men on the left were just as culpable as those in power. "White males are most responsible for the destruction of human life and environment on the planet today. Yet who is controlling the supposed revolution to change all that? White males." Change would come only through a revolution "led by, *made* by those who have been most oppressed: black, brown, yellow, red, and white *women*—with men relating to that the best they can."[45]

The phrase that seemed to best encapsulate radical feminism's distinctive ideology was "the personal is political." It had been popularized by Carol Hanisch, another Atlantic City protester, who grew disaffected with flamboyant, media-focused protests. In a 1970 article, Hanisch captured one of radical feminism's key messages: what happened in the kitchen, in the bedroom, and in personal relationships reflected larger power dynamics in society. "One of the first things we discover," wrote Hanisch, "is that personal problems are political problems. There are no personal solutions at this time. There is only collective action for a collective solution."[46]

Off camera, that collective action took concrete form, in hundreds of women's medical clinics and bookstores, mostly in big cities and college towns. Feminists did their real work circulating mimeographed pamphlets and articles like "The Myth of the Vaginal Orgasm" or leading "consciousness raising groups," where women could meet and share their stories of oppression, sexual violence, and repressed longing. "Herstory" groups began rewriting the past with women at the center, recounting the histories of abolitionists like the Grimké sisters, the workers killed in the Triangle Shirtwaist Fire, and suffragists like Alice Paul.

Nothing was more personal and more political than the body. Radical feminists, for all their differences over strategy, found common ground by focusing on women's sexuality, reproduction, and health. In

1970 twelve feminists, calling themselves the Boston Women's Health Book Collective, compiled a short book, *Women and Their Bodies*. Nancy Miriam Hawley, one of the original authors, had organized a women's health class in Boston, taught by women for women. Traditional male doctors did not listen; women had no voice in managing their own health. "We weren't encouraged to ask questions, but to depend on the so-called experts. Not having a say in our own health care frustrated and angered us. We didn't have the information we needed, so we decided to find it on our own."[47] There was such a hunger for woman-centered health advice, on topics like pregnancy, menstruation, and abortion, that the book, despite its bland title, sold 250,000 copies. It was repackaged in 1973 as *Our Bodies, Ourselves*, eventually going through nine editions and reaching tens of millions of readers.

Gay Liberation

One of the controversial topics covered by the Boston Women's Health Book Collective was lesbianism. Same-sex attraction, with all the taboos surrounding it, had been an undercurrent in American popular culture and national politics throughout the postwar years. Gay and lesbian protesters, like those who regularly gathered at Independence Hall in Philadelphia in the mid-sixties, dressed conservatively, seldom talked in public about their sexual desires, and made their demands politely.

Homophile activists, like their counterparts in the black freedom struggle, also looked to the courts for recognition of their rights. Franklin Kameny, a leader in the Mattachine Society, recommended that "discriminatory laws and regulations be tested in the courts" and noted that "the Negro went to the courts and Southerners still don't like him. He nevertheless now has his basic rights."[48] Over the 1960s, encouraged by the expansion of minority rights in federal courts, homophile groups joined in suits defending gay publications from obscenity prosecutions.

One of the key attorneys who developed the strategy was David Carliner, a civil libertarian who had been expelled from the University of Virginia law school in the 1940s after he was arrested for distributing Communist literature. In the 1960s, Carliner challenged "moral turpitude" arrests, fought in the courts for gays who were fired because of "immoral conduct" off the job, and took on the important case—eventually decided by the Supreme Court—of a gay man, Clive Boutilier, who had been deported from the United States because of his sexuality. Carliner, hardened by years of fighting uphill battles, argued that change would come slowly: "Brick by brick, and stone by stone, the law is built. The homosexual is consigned to slow and piecemeal progress."[49]

By the late 1960s, however, many gays and lesbians were less patient than Carliner. Gay districts in big cities expanded over the decade, and although homosexuality was still frowned upon by many activists on the left, gays took inspiration from the tactics of the new left and began to protest. On June 27, 1969, several days of unrest broke out in Greenwich Village, after New York police raided the Stonewall, a gay speakeasy. The raid took a dark turn when one patron, fearful of being arrested and exposed, leaped from a window and impaled himself on a fence below. In the aftermath of the raid, thousands gathered on the street in front of the bar. *The Village Voice* wrote, "The gay brigade emerged from the bars, back rooms, and bedrooms of the Village." The protests lasted for three nights, as angry gays hurled bricks and bottles at the police, chanting, "I'm a faggot and I'm proud of it!" "Gay Power!"[50]

Gay power—like radical feminism and black power—was decentralized and local. In 1973 there were about eight hundred gay and lesbian organizations around the country, most in big cities and college towns. Gay enclaves, like Greenwich Village or the Castro in San Francisco, Boystown in Chicago, and Washington Square West in Philadelphia, quickly became oases of gay life. Their bookstores, dance clubs, bars, movie theaters, and bathhouses catered to gay newcomers and many out-of-towners who fled the still-closeted suburbs and small towns, even if just for a night or weekend.

With homophobia still rife in their ranks, civil rights and black power groups gave a mixed reaction to gay liberation. Many traditional feminists like Betty Friedan warned that lesbianism would erode popular support for feminism. But some prominent figures shifted their positions. In jail in 1970, Huey Newton of the Black Panthers listened to an audiotape in which French writer Jean Genet—who was sympathetic to black power—lamented the homophobic slurs that Newton's comrades regularly hurled. "How would you feel being called a 'nigger'?" Genet asked. "How do you think I feel hearing these words?"[51] Newton, shaken by Genet's heartfelt criticism, reappraised his stance and called for an alliance with the Gay Liberation Movement. "The terms 'faggot' and 'punk' should be deleted from our vocabulary," he instructed.[52]

Liberal Feminism and the ERA

Radical feminists and gays were the most visible faces of sexual liberation, and because of that they were a lightning rod for criticism. Newscasts took a mocking tone when it came to women's liberation activists. Eric Sevareid of CBS called feminism a "disease." One of the most influential news anchors, Howard K. Smith of ABC, began a story on feminism with a quote from Spiro Agnew: "Three things have been difficult to tame: the oceans, fools, and women."[53] Feminism was a complicated movement, but in the eyes of the news media and many gullible viewers, it boiled down to "bra burning," man hating, and lesbianism. But radicals, however newsworthy, were always a small minority of feminists.

Many feminists rejected the tactics and ideology of the women's liberation movement and kept their distance from sexual liberation of any variety. Betty Friedan, for one, viewed radical feminism and lesbianism as a distraction from NOW's agenda of formal equality, preferring the tactics of litigation and lobbying to theatrical protests. Mostly behind the scenes, on presidential commissions, and in reform organizations, liberal feminists fought for the full participation of women as equals to men in American politics and the economy. And by the late 1960s, they put their energy into fighting for the Equal Rights Amendment to the Constitution, a demand of feminists since the 1920s, when suffragist Alice Paul had launched the ERA movement.

Advocates of parity between the sexes had long found their staunchest allies in the Republican Party. From 1940 through 1972, the GOP platform endorsed the ERA. The amendment's staunchest opponents at that time came not from the political right but from trade unionists who feared that it would undermine special laws that protected women workers from long hours and dangerous labor. Indifference and outright opposition had kept the ERA trapped in congressional committees for almost a half century after Paul drafted it: only twice between the 1920s and 1960s did the bill make it to a full vote of the House or Senate, only to be quickly torpedoed. Still, there had been some bright moments for ERA advocates, including President Eisenhower's public endorsement in 1958.

For working-class women, equality in the workplace was especially remote. Women trade union activists strenuously fought for civil rights and, just as important, for dignity on the job. Myra Wolfgang, who had organized women workers in the auto industry, was one of the more creative tacticians. She fought to open all-male jobs in the Big Three car companies to women. She engaged in a sit-down at Michigan's state capitol to demand an increase in the minimum wage. In 1967 she decided to go after one of the most visible targets of all—Hugh Hefner's Playboy Clubs—as her seventeen-year-old daughter Martha went undercover as a "Bunny" to investigate working conditions. Feminists like Wolfgang found the very premise of Hefner's operations humiliating (Hefner, she argued, wanted women to be "obscene but not heard"), but she was especially outraged that Playboy's "bunnies," all "bare but not hare," worked long hours and had to subsist on their tips alone.[54] In 1969 she succeeded in winning union representation for Playboy Club workers in Detroit.

But Wolfgang, like many labor feminists, remained skeptical of the ERA until its passage in 1972, not because she believed in the inferiority of women but because she feared that employers would use equal rights as a pretext to speed up women's work and assign them to dangerous jobs. Women, she argued, were protected by special woman-only laws that limited overtime and put restrictions on physically demanding work. "It would be desirable for some of these laws to be extended to men," she testified, "but the practical fact is that an Equal Rights Amendment is likely to destroy the laws altogether rather than bring about coverage for both sexes."[55]

Still, by the early 1970s, the ERA had overwhelming bipartisan support. The language of the amendment, scarcely changed since Alice Paul had drafted it, seemed uncontroversial: "Equality of rights under the law shall not be denied or abridged by the United States or by any State on account of sex." President Nixon and most Republicans backed it. Labor groups hoped it would improve working conditions and wages, and Democrats, some stalwarts like Wolfgang excepted, unified around it. On March 22, 1972, eighty-four senators voted for the ERA.[56]

Antifeminism

Whether radical or liberal, feminism came under fire in the early 1970s. Antifeminist activists organized against the ERA, rallied against sexual liberation, fought the legalization of abortion, and denounced feminists and their supporters as out-of-touch radicals who hated men and subverted womanhood. They tied all these threads together with a call for traditional femininity and a celebration of motherhood.

The most visible antifeminist, Phyllis Schlafly, had been raised in a large, wealthy, and devout Roman Catholic family in St. Louis. She was a bright student, earning her bachelor's degree at Washington University and her master's at Harvard. Armed with a sharp pen, she became a leading right-wing activist. During the 1960 election, she denounced Nixon for his liberal position on civil rights. She made her name with her 1964 pro-Goldwater best seller, *A Choice Not an Echo*, a conspiratorial book that targeted the Eisenhower/Rockefeller wing of the Republican Party. Written with real flair, it argued that "secret kingmakers" had taken over the GOP nominating process, favoring candidates who capitulated to liberals. Her own party had become a shadow of the New Deal, accepting massive government expenditures, profiting from the welfare state, and pursuing an "America Last foreign policy" that let Communists seize power and rule unchecked.[57] Heavy on paranoia and short on evidence, the book excited right-wing insurgents. More than nine in ten delegates at the 1964 Republican convention claimed to have read the book, which sold more than three million copies.

Schlafly had little patience for the Nixon administration and even less for the bipartisan coalition in the Senate that had overwhelmingly voted to support the Equal Rights Amendment. She had already expressed her skepticism on the latter in a February 1972 essay, "What's Wrong with 'Equal Rights' for Women." She described equal rights as antithetical to the family, "the basic unit of society, which is ingrained in the laws and customs of our Judeo-Christian civilization." The family "assures a woman the most precious and important right of all—the right to keep her own baby and to be supported and protected in the enjoyment of watching her baby grow and develop."[58] The ERA, she argued, would destroy the two-parent family by undermining traditional gender roles, and most of all, it would deprive women of the favored position that they deserved. Women would lose the protection of men and would be forced to use disgusting men's bathrooms and to put their lives on the line in American wars. It was an argument that bore some resemblance to Wolfgang's insistence on protective legislation, except that it valorized motherhood and housework over paid labor, and traditional masculinity over equality of pay.

In September 1972, Schlafly launched the STOP (Stop Taking Our Privileges) ERA campaign, taking the battle against feminism to the states. It seemed at first, like most of Schlafly's efforts, more than a little quixotic.

The ERA seemed unstoppable. By mid-1973, twenty-eight states had already ratified the amendment. But behind the scenes, Schlafly inspired grassroots organizers. Her group trained activists to testify before state legislators and provided them with compelling talking points. She argued that advocates of the ERA were elitists, out of touch with everyday women, with those who worked hard, struggled to survive, and needed all the protection they could get. To religious women—an increasingly key constituency—Schlafly and her allies warned that the ERA spearheaded a radical agenda to withhold protection from the innocent, especially the unborn, and to promote homosexuality. That many ERA supporters had also advocated reproductive rights and sexual freedom only confirmed the link that Schlafly made.

The STOP ERA movement found support among Catholics, evangelicals, and small women's organizations that emerged to challenge feminism and the sexual revolution. One such group was Happiness of Womanhood (HOW), founded in Kingman, Arizona, in 1970 as a counterpart to the National Organization for Women. HOW founder Jacquie Davison, a mother of six, argued that "housewives have been called leeches, parasites and even legal prostitutes by some in the liberation movement. It's time for housewives who object to such insults to pull on the combat books and battle those dragging the word 'housewife' through the mud."[59] In 1972, HOW members led the charge against the ERA, testifying before Congress and sometimes engaging in less polite forms of protest. During California's contentious debate over the ERA, HOW sent boxes of live mice to legislators who supported the amendment, with a simple cover letter: "Do you want to be a man or a mouse?"[60]

Carmen Roberts was a fan of Schlafly and a member of HOW. In a 1974 interview, using language that echoed Schlafly's, she criticized "libbers" for being disconnected from "the majority of women in the United States." Photographed in her impeccable living room, standing behind a vacuum cleaner, Roberts celebrated the joys of childrearing and housekeeping. She warned of the dangers of women's liberation. "What happens to a man and his masculinity when you are now his equal?" she asked. Women were already powerful, she believed, precisely because they were superior to men. "Women have always been placed on a pedestal in this country," she argued. "To make her equal is to make her stoop to equality as far as I am concerned."[61]

Roberts saw "forced busing" as one in a series of interrelated issues that threatened "family unity and togetherness," including the ERA, taxation, and crime. In 1973, Northeast Mothers Alert (NEMA), Roberts's antibusing group, joined a legal challenge to a Michigan law that mandated sex education in the public schools. Providing support to NEMA was the Center for the Public Interest, a conservative legal advocacy organization. It had been created, along with the right-wing think tank the Heritage Foundation, in 1973, with funds from a group of Goldwater supporters, among them Joseph Coors, a Colorado brewer, and Richard Mellon Scaife, a wealthy Pittsburgh businessman.

Roberts feared that a conspiracy of government officials, educators, and feminists sought to undermine parental control of their children. "Parents must and do have a right to guide the moral development of their children without interference from the state, from the schools, or from militant women's liberationists," she argued.[62] The battle against sex education and reproductive rights, like that against busing, was an attempt to protect the family from a multifront attack.

However forceful her arguments on behalf of the "traditional family," Roberts pursued a political career that belied her stay-at-home rhetoric. She traveled nationwide giving speeches, leaving her children in the care of her husband. After she was elected to the city school board, she earned her high school degree and went on to nursing school, all while her daughter was still at home. Like so many conservative women who made a career denouncing feminism, she was an unacknowledged beneficiary of a movement that had made it acceptable for mothers to pursue an independent career outside the home.

Nixon's Response

President Nixon found the shifts in gender and sexuality bewildering. Although he seldom raised the issues publicly, he felt freer behind the scenes to express his opinion that "homosexuality, dope, immorality are the enemies of strong societies." In his view, "homosexuality destroyed" the Greeks and contributed to the fall of Rome, because "the last six Roman emperors were fags."[63] But even if Nixon's views were intemperate, there was little support for gays in the political mainstream. In the 1970s only a few politicians—mostly from big cities, many of them minorities, like New

York's Bella Abzug, Shirley Chisholm, and Ed Koch; Philadelphia's Robert Nix; and Oakland's Ronald Dellums—supported legislation that forbade discrimination against gays. Their legislative efforts went nowhere.

If Nixon mostly ignored the sexual revolution, he could not so easily pass over calls for the ERA, which enjoyed deep support in his own party. Even First Lady Pat Nixon endorsed it. But Nixon found himself buffeted by competing advice on the amendment—just as he had been on civil rights. Ever since his first run for office, he had been on the record as a supporter of the ERA, but a lukewarm one at best. As the proposed ERA wended its way through Congress, he sidestepped the issue neither endorsing the amendment again nor repudiating his past position. The executive branch was split. Some political advisers saw support for the ERA as a way to win wavering women voters; the most moderate welcomed it as the culmination of decades of Republican efforts; and still others were skeptical or outright critical. Nixon's congressional liaison viewed the ERA as "insane," and conservative speechwriter Pat Buchanan wrote, "One prays the silly amendment would perish."[64] For the moment, Buchanan did not speak for his party's majority, but women like Carmen Roberts and Phyllis Schlafly, organizing at the grassroots, would fight the ERA for a decade—and in the process remake the Republican Party.

Roe v. Wade

For activists on Nixon's right, the Supreme Court remained a fickle ally. In 1970, in *Goldberg v. Kelly*, the Burger Court held that states could not cut individuals' welfare and disability payments without a hearing, and in a close decision in 1971, it liberalized capital punishment laws. For many, the Burger Court's defining case was *Roe v. Wade*. Roe was the pseudonym of plaintiff Norma McCorvey, a thirty-five-year-old Dallas woman who challenged the Texas state law that forbade abortions. She had lived a hard life. Married at sixteen to an older man, McCorvey ran away from her abusive marriage, lost custody of her first child to her mother, and gave up her second to adoption. In 1969 she found herself pregnant again, and without much support other than a string of lousy jobs, she decided to procure an abortion. She was unable to make a claim of rape (one of the few grounds for legally ending a pregnancy in Texas) and found no clinics to provide the service. A young, inexperienced, but ambitious lawyer, Sarah Weddington, took on McCorvey's case, which wended its way, over a three-year period, to the U.S. Supreme Court.

In the years leading up to *Roe*, feminists had moved the issue of reproductive rights to the center of their agenda. In the early 1960s, after a spate of gruesome birth defects caused by thalidomide, an antinausea drug that many women took during pregnancy, a group of doctors and medical reformers pushed for less restrictive abortion laws. They found sympathetic legislatures in fourteen states that passed laws between 1967 and 1972 permitting therapeutic abortions in the case of fetal deformities or risks to the mother's health. Radical feminists—building on their demand for women's bodily autonomy—pushed further.

In 1969 members of the New York chapter of the moderate National Organization for Women and the radical collective Redstockings demanded the legalization of abortion on feminist grounds, arguing that, as in the case of sexual relations, women should be able to control their own bodies. Making the personal political, they led demonstrations and held public events in which women spoke out about their experiences with coerced sex and unwanted pregnancies. Others, like the National Association for the Repeal of Abortion Laws (later the National Abortion Rights Action League, or NARAL), founded in 1969, appealed to deep American traditions of individual liberty, defining abortion as a right. But its legislative efforts were halting. Only New York, Hawaii, Alaska, and the District of Columbia loosened abortion laws. So NARAL and affiliated groups took to the courts. By 1971 about seventy abortion cases were at some stage of litigation in state and federal courts.

In 1972 the Supreme Court heard two sets of oral arguments on *Roe*, and in 1973 it upheld the right to abortion during the first twelve weeks of pregnancy by a 7–2 vote. The court found that while the Constitution "does not explicitly mention any right to privacy," the court had recognized "a right of personal privacy" in previous cases, including *Griswold v. Connecticut*. In his concurring opinion, Justice Potter Stewart stated even more forcefully that "we recognize the right of the individual, married or single, to be free from unwanted governmental intrusion into matters so fundamentally affecting a person as the right of a woman to decide whether or not to terminate her pregnancy." Among Nixon's appointees, only Rehnquist voted no, a harsh blow to the GOP's right wing.[65]

After the *Roe* decision, the abortion rate rose steadily, reaching an all-time peak in 1980 of 359 abortions for every thousand live births. The debate over abortion also intensified, swirling around two competing sets of rights: the "right to choose" and the "right to life." This dichotomy continued to define the debate, even if the majority of Americans in the aftermath of *Roe* saw abortion in far more complicated terms: as a tragedy that was sometimes necessary, as something to be avoided but not banned outright. Both sides in the abortion debate borrowed language and strategies from the civil rights movement. They demanded that the government protect the rights of an oppressed group (women) or a voiceless minority (fetuses), engaged in lobbying and legislative efforts to transform state law, used religious rhetoric to win supporters, and especially in the case of antiabortion activists, deployed the tactics of civil disobedience and, sometimes, disruption and violence. Nixon sided with advocates of the "right to life," arguing for "the sanctity of human life, including the life of the yet unborn."[66]

THE ELECTION OF 1972 AND WATERGATE

Abortion was but one of a series of contentious issues that swirled around the election of 1972, along with feminism, school desegregation, and backlash politics. Vying to obstruct Nixon's path to reelection was a Democratic Party in flux. The party's left pushed for a rewriting of party rules to prevent debacles like the failure to seat the Mississippi Freedom Democratic Party in 1964 and the triumph of pro-Humphrey party bosses in 1968. The reformers made the nominating process more democratic than ever before. They required the party to expand the representation of blacks, women, and youth, and to choose convention delegates from the grassroots rather than at the statewide level. This time around the party's primaries and caucuses would have real significance: party regulars would have control of nothing close to a majority of the delegates. The results were stunning: the diverse Illinois delegation to the 1972 convention included civil rights firebrand Jesse Jackson but not dealmaker Mayor Richard Daley. One stalwart Democrat complained, "There is too much hair and not enough cigars at this convention."[67]

The primary season was raucous for the Democrats. Hubert Humphrey, still tainted from his 1968 loss, ran a lackluster campaign as the establishment candidate, garnering the support of organized labor but little enthusiasm otherwise. Two senators faced off: Edmund Muskie from Maine, a well-respected moderate who was initially viewed as the frontrunner, and George McGovern from South Dakota, a former history professor and longtime critic of the Vietnam War. Alabama governor George Wallace made his most credible run for office yet, winning Democratic primaries in Florida, Tennessee, and North Carolina, and finishing second in Indiana, Wisconsin, and Pennsylvania, before he was shot in Laurel, Maryland on May 15. Paralyzed from the waist down, Wallace dropped out of the race but not before achieving sweeping victories in Maryland and Michigan, where he won every predominantly white precinct in Detroit, including Carmen Roberts's.

Nixon's advisers were not, however, satisfied to watch the Democrats bloody themselves politically or to benefit from the fissures between the party's youthful reformers and its old guard. Rather, they did their best to rig the outcome, building on a set of strategies they had developed during Nixon's first months in office.

Dirty Tricks

The linchpin of Nixon's efforts to undermine his political foes was the wonderfully named Committee to Re-Elect the President, or CREEP, which included key White House aides and party operatives. CREEP was ruthless. In July 1969, Massachusetts senator Edward M. Kennedy drove his car off a bridge in Chappaquiddick on Martha's Vineyard, resulting in the death of the young woman in the car with him; thereafter CREEP began its own investigation, hoping to doom Kennedy's chances of ever running for the presidency. Beginning in 1970, it launched surreptitious efforts to raise funds from major corporations in $100,000 increments, raking in about $20 million. It put pressure on donors to pay up before April 7, 1972 when a law requiring the disclosure of campaign contributors would come into effect. A Wall Street broker, under indictment, delivered his contribution, $200,000, wholly in cash, in a briefcase to CREEP's treasurer. Much of CREEP's money ended up in a Mexican bank account where it could not easily be traced.

CREEP also set up a "dirty tricks" operation, using funds to support elaborate espionage efforts against major Democratic Party figures. Its operatives went undercover into Democratic campaigns, stealing campaign documents and planting false rumors about candidates. A CREEP operative obtained press credentials so that he could fly in Democratic candidate George McGovern's plane and eavesdrop. CREEP held fake rallies for Nixon's opponents and letting the real campaigns pay the bills, and distributed incendiary, false campaign literature. To discredit Muskie, whom Nixon's advisers saw as the most serious threat, CREEP operatives fabricated a letter attributed to Muskie that used the ethnic slur "Canucks" to refer to French Canadians, and it spread rumors that Muskie's wife was a loose-tongued alcoholic. Muskie shed tears at a press conference responding to the accusations, making him appear weak and "unpresidential." After that his candidacy struggled. During the Florida primary, where Muskie faced George Wallace, CREEP circulated a flyer asking voters to "Help Muskie in Busing More Children Now."[68]

One of the CREEP's dirtiest tricks occurred in May, just after George Wallace was shot. Nixon hatched a scheme involving his aides H. R. Haldeman and John Ehrlichman to plant a story "that a McGovern/Kennedy person did this. Know what I mean? Rumors are going to flow all over the place. Put it on the left right away."[69] Nixon's henchmen broke into the apartment of Arthur Bremer, Wallace's would-be assassin, planting McGovern brochures and, in the process, disrupting a criminal investigation.

The secret White House Special Investigations Unit, created in the summer of 1971, worked hand in glove with CREEP. The unit ran under the supervision of Nixon policy advisers John Ehrlichman, Charles Colson, and E. Howard Hunt, all of whom had been architects of Nixon's strategy to capitalize on white backlash. Nixon ordered his aides to compile an "Opponents List" of people never to be invited to the White House and, more ominously, an "Enemies List" of prominent celebrities, journalists, political analysts, and politicians to be thwarted by any means necessary.

G. Gordon Liddy, a shadowy espionage expert, led many of the unit's efforts to discredit Nixon's enemies. Dressed as workmen (their nickname was "the plumbers"), they broke into the office of the psychiatrist of Daniel Ellsberg, a defense analyst who had released classified documents about the Vietnam War, and attempted to break in to the Brookings Institution, a liberal think tank. Nixon's critics were also subjected to one of the stealthiest and most troubling dirty tricks: the White House ordered the IRS to investigate the tax returns of think tanks, including Brookings, as well as liberal lobbyists, journalists, professors, and other political foes.

The Downfall of a President

Those crimes might never have come to light had it not been for a bungled break-in on the evening of June 17, 1972, at Democratic National Committee (DNC) headquarters in Washington's posh Watergate Hotel. Five well-dressed men, carrying surveillance equipment, were caught just outside the office of DNC chairman Lawrence O'Brien. Two of them had address books with E. Howard Hunt's name in them. The following day a pair of young, ambitious journalists at *The Washington Post*, Bob Woodward and Carl Bernstein, got wind of the arrests and began their own investigation. But in the meantime, Nixon denied any knowledge of the break-in, fired his aides associated with the event, and behind the scenes—and also illegally—ordered the CIA to pressure the FBI to stop investigating the break-in. It seemed, for the moment, that the botched burglary would be soon forgotten.

Nixon's opponent in 1972 was widely perceived as the most left leaning of the Democratic candidates, South Dakota senator George McGovern. A decorated World War II veteran, former history professor, and longtime critic of the Vietnam War, McGovern had the support of the Democratic Party's reformers and also benefited from Edmund Muskie's tumbling campaign. McGovern was, however, no radical. "I can present liberal values in a conservative, restrained way," he asserted. "I see myself as a politician of reconciliation."[70] He pledged to govern from the middle.

Many pundits and politicians worried that McGovern would not appeal to the Democratic Party's blue-collar base. "The people don't know McGovern is for amnesty, abortion, and legalization of pot," stated Missouri senator Thomas Eagleton, in a widely quoted statement that was unattributed to him, just after McGovern won the Massachusetts primary. Once "middle America—Catholic middle America, in particular," learned of it, "he's dead."[71] Middle America proved not to be very tolerant of McGovern or of Eagleton, who would later be McGovern's vice-presidential nominee, until he withdrew after press reports that he had undergone shock therapy for depression.

Eagleton's quip took on a life of its own, turned alliterative by Nixon's surrogates, who accused McGovern of being in favor of "acid, amnesty, and abortion." McGovern did support amnesty for those who fled overseas to avoid the draft, but he never endorsed LSD or even the legalization of marijuana, and he was opposed to the Supreme Court decision on abortion, which he thought was a matter best left to the states. But McGovern's actual positions did not matter once Nixon ran him through the thresher. The Yippies' endorsement of McGovern and the demand by Democratic delegates, despite McGovern's pleading for "moderation," for floor votes on then-controversial issues like gay liberation, allowed Nixon's campaign to brand McGovern as hopelessly out of touch with the American mainstream.

Nixon won the 1972 election in one of the greatest landslides in American political history, taking all but Massachusetts and the District of Columbia. But the Watergate break-in, mostly ignored during the election, moved back to the front pages afterward. Woodward and Bernstein, the *Washington Post* reporters, had been following CREEP's paper trail, filing reports about its shadowy bank accounts, and getting inside information from an informant nicknamed "Deep Throat," whose identity—Mark Felt, the associate director of the FBI—would not be revealed until 2005. Felt, whom Woodward and Bernstein had first met after the attempted assassination of Wallace, proved an invaluable source, confirming many of their stories and pointing them to the very heart of the Nixon administration. Woodward and Felt's meetings were right out of the pages of a thriller. When Woodward wanted to meet his informant, he placed a flowerpot on his balcony. To avoid surveillance, the journalist walked, took taxis, and traced circuitous routes through the city. Felt, fearful of wiretaps, met with him late at night in Washington parking garages. "They are underhanded and unknowable," Felt described Nixon and his team.[72]

In early 1973, the Watergate cover-up began to unravel. In January the Watergate burglars were tried before federal judge John J. Sirica, a Republican, a Nixon supporter, and a tough jurist nicknamed "Maximum John" for his willingness to dole out long sentences. During the Watergate trials, he asked pointed questions, sometimes maddening the defendants' attorneys. "I had no intention of sitting on the bench like a nincompoop and watching the parade go by," he later recalled.[73] The jury found the five burglars guilty.

At the same time, Senator Mike Mansfield, the Senate majority leader, launched a bipartisan investigation of the Watergate affair, with a respected southern conservative, North Carolina senator Sam Ervin, as the chair of the hearings. Behind the scenes, Solicitor General John Dean and CREEP member Jeb Magruder testified before a grand jury, pulling investigators closer to the Oval Office. In March a fearful Nixon invoked executive privilege, stating that no one in his administration would testify before the hearings, but he was on dubious legal grounds. In April, just after forcing his aides Haldeman and Ehrlichman to resign, and firing his counsel, John Dean, Nixon urged Colson to refuse to answer questions about the burglaries: "You say we were protecting the security of this country."[74]

In the summer of 1973, testimony before Ervin's committee—especially by Dean—was damning to Nixon, revealing CREEP's nefarious activities, including the plumbers' break-ins and wiretapping. The other startling revelation was that since 1970, President Nixon had recorded some 3,700 hours of conversations in the White House. In October, under pressure, Nixon turned over some of the tapes to Judge Sirica, including one that had been recorded just three days after the Watergate break-in; it included an eighteen-and-a-half-minute deletion. In October Nixon agreed to the appointment of a special prosecutor, Harvard Law professor Archibald Cox; but on October 20, 1973, in what came to be called the Saturday Night Massacre, he fired Cox from the position. Further undermining the administration's credibility, Vice President Spiro Agnew had resigned just ten days earlier, on non-Watergate-related charges: he had accepted bribes while governor of Maryland and evaded taxes.

Watergate dominated the news nearly every day, weakening Nixon and, more important, further undermining public trust in government. Little else that occurred in late 1973 and the first half of 1974 restored any of it. On April 30, Nixon released redacted transcripts of the tapes but still held back from a full release, continuing to invoke executive privilege. That claim went before the U.S. Supreme Court, which unanimously ruled on July 24, 1974, that the president's assertion of "privilege depends solely on the broad, undifferentiated claim of public interest in the confidentiality of such conversations." A narrow assertion of privilege, based on the "need to protect military, diplomatic, or sensitive national security secrets," would have been acceptable as well, but in this case, the administration made no such claim.[75] The court ordered the tapes released, and Nixon complied. Facing charges of impeachment from the House of Representatives, he resigned the presidency on August 8, 1974.

Watergate proved a landmark in domestic politics. Public faith in government at all levels had been plummeting ever since Lyndon Johnson's "credibility gap" on the Vietnam War. Nixon's malfeasance solidified public sentiment that politicians were inherently corrupt and that government could not be trusted. Nixon also unwittingly reinforced a broader sensibility—forged in the polarized domestic politics of the late 1960s and early 1970s—that whatever side you were on, government was on the other. For the right, government had sided with the hippies and pornographers, the busers, rioters, and abortionists. For the left, it had abused police power in order to silence dissent, whether by the Panthers or by the Yippies.

That corrosion of the public trust made it more difficult for government, under Nixon and beyond, to respond to the most sweeping and consequential changes of the 1970s: the collapse of postwar economic growth, the restructuring of the American economy, the rise of increasingly autonomous global corporations, the steady rise in economic inequality, and the erosion of American power in the world.

CHAPTER 13

"A SEASON OF DARKNESS":

THE TROUBLED 1970S

J OHN "BOOK" KSIONSKA left the bleak anthracite-coal-mining town of Shenandoah, Pennsylvania, in the early 1950s. The old mines, mostly tapped out, were closing, and many of those who stayed behind were too elderly or sick to work, stooped from crawling through the mine shafts or ravaged by black lung disease. Book didn't have to travel far to find a new opportunity. At twenty-nine, he was one of the first workers in the new U.S. Steel Fairless Works plant, a massive complex that sprawled over 3,900 acres along the Delaware River in the rapidly growing suburbs between Philadelphia and Trenton, New Jersey. Book started in the furnace, a young man's job, hot and grueling, but still a step up from the mining job he had held for a few years after serving in World War II. Book was a proud union man who moved up the ranks to become an officer in the United Steel Workers of America (USWA) Local 4889, and he benefited from the good wages, seniority, health insurance, and a generous pension plan that the USWA had negotiated. Eventually he advanced to running a crane at the plant's dock.[1]

With his paycheck, he could easily afford one of the new houses that had appeared virtually overnight in the suburbs surrounding the plant. U.S. Steel built some of its own workers' housing, modest single-family detached homes just beyond the factory gates. And William Levitt had just planted one of his massive Levittowns nearby, with a wide variety of houses priced for the broad middle class: steelworkers and schoolteachers, accountants and engineers. "It was like a future city being born," Book recalled. "There were no layoffs, just new plants and businesses opening up." Book bought a brand-new house in 1952 for about $12,000. After paying it off for thirty years at just $69 per month, he owned it outright.

"I came along at a time when you could still buy something for a dollar," Ksionska, in his late fifties, told a reporter for *The Philadelphia Inquirer* in 1983. He lived comfortably, taking up golf and spending his time off fishing and hunting. With thirty years seniority by then, his job was safe, and his pension was guaranteed. Still, he couldn't hold back his gloom: despite his hard work, his children lived in a world that was a lot less secure than his. Fairless Works shed workers by the thousands, one of whom was his son Jim. "But someone like my son, where can he go? The times have turned around. It reminds me of the days before I came here, when I was a miner."

Jim Ksionska followed in his father's footsteps. A blue-collar child of suburbia, he took his first full-time job at the Fairless Works in 1974, right after graduating from high school. The pay and benefits were too good to resist—and with a recommendation from Book, the job was his for the asking. Still, the next nine years were rough, as the steel industry faltered and the economy fluctuated wildly. In 1975, U.S. Steel laid off 2,300 workers at the plant; in 1982, it laid off another 3,500. "I've been in and out of there so often, I feel like a yo-yo," Jim lamented. During one layoff, he found temporary work in the kitchen at a local country club, learning to cook. The holidays in 1982 were grim: a local charity gave away about five hundred turkeys to laid-off steelworkers, and as the economic slump dragged on, many relied on a local food bank to provide for their families. It was especially tough for Jim, who had a toddler at home and a monthly mortgage payment ten times his father's. Many of his neighbors had a hard time keeping up payments on their homes. Between 1974 and 1982, interest rates for thirty-year mortgages had steadily risen from about 9 percent to nearly 15 percent. Desperate for a paycheck, some of his friends drove to Atlantic City to work in the casinos; others left their families and headed to the Sunbelt in search of work. But they were often disappointed. The economy was in a deep recession, and if they were lucky enough to find work, their paychecks were usually slimmer than those they had brought home from U.S. Steel.

THE WAR'S END

The one thing that Jim Ksionska did not have to worry about was being sent overseas. His father had served in the navy in World War II, and many of his older friends had done their time in the Big Muddy. But by the time he graduated from high school, in 1974, the war in Vietnam was winding down, and the draft was over. The war's long end had begun in 1968, with the collapse of public support for military intervention in Southeast Asia. During the presidential election that year, the question was not whether the war would end, but which candidate would end it sooner. During his first campaign for the White House, Richard Nixon had suggested that he might take a different course of action than Hubert Humphrey and Lyndon Johnson, hinting at a "secret plan" to end the Vietnam War and, much to the surprise of many observers, calling for the abolition of the draft and the creation of an all-volunteer military. "A system of compulsory service that arbitrarily selects some but not others," he argued in October 1968, "simply cannot be squared with our whole concept of liberty, justice, and equality under the law."[2]

Nixon did not, however, have a secret plan, and the war would grind on for nearly seven more years. He and his advisers did not share Johnson's fatal optimism that the war was winnable, but they were in a bind, caught between a skeptical public, a demoralized military, and a vocal contingent of hawks, many in the GOP, who could not tolerate a unilateral American withdrawal. How could the United States emerge from the debacle without appearing to capitulate to the North Vietnamese? In Nixon's first year of office, ten thousand American troops died, more casualties than in any year but 1968. As the war intensified, opposition mounted. October and November 1969 witnessed the largest antiwar protests to date. Nearly a million people took to the streets in major cities calling for a moratorium on bombing and an end to the war.

Vietnamization

The Nixon administration viewed the protesters as a nuisance. But whatever Nixon thought of the antiwar movement, he was sensitive to public opinion. In November 1969 he announced plans to "Vietnamize" the war, which would entail a steady reduction of American ground troops while channeling even more military aid to the South Vietnamese army. "The defense of freedom," stated Nixon, ". . . is particularly the responsibility of the people whose freedom is threatened. In the previous administration, we Americanized the war in Vietnam. In this administration, we are Vietnamizing the search for peace."[3] In late 1971, as the United States continued to draw down troops, Nixon suspended the draft, defusing one of the major sources of domestic discontent. By the spring of 1972, about 74,000 American troops remained in Vietnam—about an eighth of the number stationed there in 1968.

Vietnamization did not, however, bring an end to hostilities. As ground troops headed home, Nixon ordered the escalation of air raids on suspected Vietcong supply lines, including the secret bombing of targets in neighboring Laos and Cambodia. These military operations were unauthorized by Congress and hidden from the public and even from many of the president's close aides for four years. In early 1970 the United States launched a massive airstrike on northern Laos, bordering Vietnam. Although Cambodia was neutral, the United States began bombing there in March 1969 and over the first year dropped 110,000 tons of bombs on the country.

While the bombing continued, the North Vietnamese and United States engaged in secret negotiations to end the war that met with frustration again and again, for more than three years. Nixon and his advisers believed that the stepped-up air attacks would weaken North Vietnamese resolve to allow the United States to negotiate from strength. That proved to be a serious miscalculation. "The [North] Vietnamese were very tough— true believers in Communism," recalled General Vernon Walters, a state department adviser involved in the negotiations.[4]

"Peace with Honor"

Guiding Nixon's foreign policy was the former Harvard professor Henry Kissinger, a German Jew who fled Nazi persecution in 1938, served with U.S. forces in World War II, and earned three degrees at Harvard, including a Ph.D. in government. Charming and, by the accounts of most of his admirers and critics, opportunistic, Kissinger had a steel-trap memory, an unsurpassed mastery of diplomatic history (he knew what Metternich whispered to Castlereagh), and a wealth of connections in both political parties. He had advised the Kennedy and Johnson administrations, even though he was known as a conservative. In the mid-1960s he gravitated to the power center of the GOP, allying first with presidential aspirant Nelson Rockefeller, then shifting his allegiance to Nixon. In 1969, Nixon named him his national security adviser and four years later, promoted him to secretary of state.

Kissinger's Vietnamese counterpart was the Communist Party official Le Duc Tho. A steely negotiator, he won Kissinger's grudging admiration for his "subtlety, his acumen, his iron self-discipline."[5] In late 1969, Kissinger proposed an armistice in exchange for the release of American prisoners of war, and a concession that allowed Hanoi to retain control over large parts of rural South Vietnam. But South Vietnamese leader Nguyen Van Thieu refused to allow Communists to control parts of his countryside. Le Duc Tho had little incentive to cede ground to the weak and unpopular South Vietnamese government.

In 1972, after Hanoi launched a ferocious attack just across the demilitarized zone separating North and South Vietnam, the Nixon administration again stepped up its air war, hopeful that the United States would finally demoralize the North Vietnamese and bring them back to the table. Over the summer, Le Duc Tho and Henry Kissinger resumed negotiations, and in October, just weeks before the U.S. presidential election, they reached a tentative agreement: the North would cease fire in South Vietnam, while the United States would halt the bombings and promptly withdraw its remaining troops. North and South would be reunified, and elections would be held. Kissinger even held out the promise of American funding for the reconstruction of Hanoi. At an October 26 news conference, Kissinger crowed, "Peace is at hand."[6]

But weeks later the agreement dissolved. The South Vietnamese government balked, in part because Thieu feared that the Communists would prevail in post-reunification elections. To satisfy him, Nixon and Kissinger offered new terms: as a condition for the U.S. withdrawal, Thieu would remain in power. Le Duc Tho refused, and negotiations halted. In December the air force launched a Christmas campaign against Hanoi, dropping 36,000 tons of bombs on the North Vietnamese capital over a twelve-day period, the most intense air attack of the entire war. Once again Kissinger and Tho negotiated and finally, on January 23, 1973, reached an agreement that differed little from what had been on the table in the summer and early fall.

On January 27, the parties announced a cease-fire, but the war did not end. The United States continued bombing Cambodia. Thieu and the South Vietnamese army, still propped up by American military aid, resisted North Vietnamese control in rural areas, and skirmishes continued to break out.

Nixon had promised "peace with honor," but the situation for the next twenty-seven months was bloody, and the resolution disastrous. In April 1975 the Khmer Rouge, led by the genocidal dictator Pol Pot, took control of bomb-ravaged Cambodia; later that month Thieu fled Saigon after a North Vietnamese offensive. On May Day, more than a decade after Lyndon Johnson had Americanized the war, seven years to the day after Larry Merschel's death, and five years after Nixon had begun Vietnamization, the United States evacuated the American embassy by helicopter, and Saigon became Ho Chi Minh City.

NEW DIRECTIONS IN THE COLD WAR

While the war in Southeast Asia dragged on, Nixon and Kissinger turned their attention to Moscow and Beijing. Nixon was a Cold Warrior but in many respects an unorthodox one. Since the 1960s, foreign policy experts had challenged the conventional view of the Cold War as a bipolar struggle, pointing to deep tensions within the ostensibly monolithic Communist bloc, particularly the Sino-Soviet conflict. This more nuanced view of Communism came from the think tanks, leading international relations scholars, and even a growing cadre of Republicans who had long accused the Democrats of losing China and being soft on Communism. In 1966 the Ripon Society, an influential group of GOP moderates, released a report calling for a "searching re-examination" of policy toward Beijing, including reconsidering the position that Taiwan was "the only 'legitimate' government of all China."[7] It was a message that neither mainstream Republicans nor President Johnson heeded for the moment, but it reflected new thinking among analysts in both parties who had begun to see Communism as polycentric, and who began to argue that the United States should jettison the simplistic Cold War binaries of the previous quarter century.

The evidence of a fractured Communist world was abundant. The Russians and Chinese coexisted uneasily. In 1962, Sino-Soviet relations had worsened when the USSR sided with India in a border dispute with the Chinese. Most ominously, China and the USSR periodically struggled over questions of territory and sovereignty, particularly along the jagged border that separated northwestern China from the Soviet territories along the Ussuri River. In March 1969 the Red Army and the Chinese People's Liberation Army skirmished along the Ussuri, with hundreds of casualties. The

Soviets threatened to attack Chinese nuclear facilities in the region. As fears of a Sino-Soviet war spread, the Chinese and Soviets managed to resolve the conflict, but mutual mistrust and hostility remained deep.

The Opening to China

The Nixon administration decided to exploit the situation. In July 1971, Kissinger made a bold gambit. While on a diplomatic visit to Pakistan, he secretly flew to Beijing to meet with Chinese premier Zhou Enlai. The outreach to China was risky because the United States still recognized Taiwan as the sole legitimate Chinese government, and at the very time of Kissinger's trip, it had taken a vocal position against the admission of the People's Republic of China to the UN Security Council.

Kissinger found Zhou to be "one of the two or three most impressive men I have ever met," and the two talked for almost twenty hours.[8] The wide-ranging conversation was remarkable for its candor: Zhou demanded that the United States grant self-determination to Asian countries and leave the fate of Taiwan to the People's Republic of China. He bluntly told Kissinger that "American friends always like to stress the dignity, the honor, and the face of the U.S. . . . the best thing for you would be to withdraw all your armed forces lock, stock, and barrel and withdraw all other foreign forces and do so on your own initiative. That would be the greatest honor." Kissinger listened but argued for a go-slow approach to U.S.-Chinese relations: "We should not destroy what is possible by forcing events beyond what the circumstances will allow."[9] But the two leaders found common ground in Zhou's description of the Soviets as "greedy and menacing to the world."[10] They agreed on an extraordinary next step: President Nixon would visit China, meet with Mao Zedong and Zhou, and begin redefining U.S.-Chinese relations.

Nixon's visit to China in February 1972 was a made-for-television event, complete with carefully staged footage of the president shaking hands with Mao Zedong and walking along the Great Wall. All three major networks spent four hours covering the historic banquet that brought together the leaders of both countries. Nixon toasted Zhou and Mao: "This is the day, this is the hour for our two peoples to rise to the heights of greatness which can build a new and better world."[11] Zhou offered a more poetic description, praising the two powers for bridging "the vastest ocean in the world, 25 years of no communication" between the United States and

China.[12] Later China donated two rare giant pandas to the National Zoo in Washington. Two quite different critics, however, found nothing great about the opening to China. The right-wing commentator Clarence Manion called Nixon's China policy "madness" and called the president "an anti-communist 'also ran.'"[13] And the Soviets considered Nixon's "shock" nothing short of "collusion" with the Chinese, with "grave consequence for the Soviet people."[14]

SALT

In May, with the triumphant tour to Beijing just behind him, Nixon traveled to Moscow for a summit with the Soviet leader Leonid Brezhnev, the culmination of nearly three years of behind-the-scenes negotiations. From 1969 to 1972, the two superpowers had engaged in Strategic Arms Limitation Talks (SALT). In 1970 the rivals settled a dispute over a Soviet naval base in Cuba. And in 1971 they reached an accord over the governance of Berlin, lowering some barriers to travel between East and West. The China trip had given Kissinger and Nixon more clout with the Soviets. A deal with the United States would be a counterweight to the Washington-Beijing thaw. Nixon's summit with Brezhnev resulted in the first Anti-Ballistic Missile (ABM) treaty. Optimistic observers hailed the summit as the beginning of "détente," a warming of relations between the two rivals.

The Cold War in Latin America: Chile

Détente did not, however, bring a halt to the brushfire wars against Communism, particularly in the developing world. There the Cold War had devastating consequences. Nixon stepped up his predecessors' policy of providing military aid and support to anti-Communist regimes, often through covert operations directed by the CIA. Latin America was of particular concern. In 1970 the Chilean people elected Salvador Allende, a leftist and staunch critic of the United States. That year the CIA backed a failed coup, providing money, weapons, and other support to rightist military leaders. Kissinger was particularly worried about what would happen if Allende remained in power. Chile "could end up being the worst failure of the administration—'our Cuba'—by 1972," he warned, suggesting that he would be blamed for losing another American ally to the Communists.[15]

Once in office, Allende nationalized about five hundred firms, some of the largest owned by the United States, expanded the Chilean welfare state, and allied with Cuba. Nixon responded by imposing economic sanctions on Chile in 1971. Behind the scenes, the United States worked to destabilize Allende's regime, providing support to authoritarian forces and encouraging a military coup on September 11, 1973, in which Allende was killed and replaced by the dictator Augusto Pinochet. Pinochet's regime was brutal: the army assassinated a few thousand Allende supporters, arrested and tortured an estimated thirty thousand more, harassed antigovernment journalists (killing one American reporter), and silenced many labor and community organizations critical of the regime.

Pinochet turned the country into a petri dish for a new, harsh economic experiment promoted by the "Chicago boys," a group of neoliberal economists, most of them trained at the University of Chicago. The Chicago boys called for strict austerity measures, the privatization of welfare programs, the lifting of tariffs, and efforts to curb the influence of trade unions. Chile's economy expanded significantly in the second half of the 1970s and early 1980s, but so did poverty and inequality, particularly in the sprawling, squalid slums outside Santiago. In ways that no one, except perhaps the Chicago boys themselves, anticipated, the Chilean economic experiment would shape economic policies in the United States just a few years later.

ECONOMIC SHIFTS

America's rise to global power in the twentieth century was military but even more so economic. Since World War II, the United States had dominated the production of cars, steel, electronics, and oil, exported its consumer goods worldwide, and attempted to impose American-style development in Latin America, Asia, and Africa. But by the 1970s, American economic power was fading. Unemployment rose steadily, as did inflation. American investments flowed overseas, and consumers depended more than ever on imports. Few understood the scope of the momentous economic shifts that were remaking the domestic economy and reshaping America's place in the world. Even fewer understood their causes.

For the most part, Nixon and his administration accepted the pro-growth economic consensus that had prevailed since the 1940s. They began as Keynesians, in practice, if not in name. Government spending and tax policy together, they believed, were tools that, if used carefully, would perpetuate steady economic growth. "Let's build some dams," stated Nixon in 1969, to stimulate the economy.[16] After some deliberation, and facing congressional pressure, Nixon ended his first year by reducing taxes, mostly by increasing the personal exemption and cutting rates for the poorest Americans. At the same time, the administration bolstered spending. Fiscal conservatives, those who called for reducing taxes and government spending at the same time, were for the moment on the sidelines.

Stagflation

A shaky and unpredictable economy began to erode the foundations of growth economics. Unemployment rose steadily from 3.4 percent during Johnson's last full year in office to 6.1 percent in December 1970.[17] The composition of the labor force also changed. The number of working-age Americans skyrocketed as the baby boomers graduated from high school and college. Women entered the workforce in rising numbers. And by the early 1970s, new immigrants, particularly from Latin America, entered the labor force in growing numbers, an unexpected consequence of the 1965 Hart-Celler Act. Between 1964 and 1970 alone, 10.1 million new workers entered the U.S. labor force, and they were younger, more racially and ethnically diverse, and more female than ever before. Those workers were, however, poorly paid. In 1970, Hispanic workers earned only 55 cents for every dollar earned by whites. The same year women workers earned only 59.4 cents for every dollar earned by men.

Inflation rates, which had held between 1 and 1.6 percent annually between 1959 and 1965, began to creep upward in the late 1960s, in part because of the expense of the Vietnam War. In 1970 annual inflation was close to 6 percent; the increase in consumer prices was even greater. It was not supposed to be this way: mainstream economists held that unemployment and inflation were inversely correlated—inflation up, unemployment down, and vice versa. Pundits deployed a new word in the early 1970s, "stagflation," to describe the stagnant economy, with rising inflation and falling employment.

The United States and the Global Economy

The position of the United States in the global economy eroded. After World War II, it had taken the Western European nations and Japan had taken two decades to recover from the demographic and economic devastation of war, even with massive financial aid, including funds from the Marshall Plan. The United States and its allies channeled money to the "developing world," in hopes of bolstering economies and creating markets for American-made goods, but those efforts were halting. And the Soviet bloc regimes had anemic industrial economies, held back by creaking industrial technologies. Russia's factories were mostly state-of-the-art for the 1920s and 1930s, when the country had undergone massive industrialization; Poland, East Germany, and Yugoslavia had rebuilt after World War II, but largely on the Soviet model rather than adopting the new, automated technologies that revolutionized Western manufacturing. And China was still overwhelmingly agricultural.

By the late 1960s, the economic balance of power had begun to shift. Germany and Japan saw huge growth in steel, auto, and home appliance manufacturing. Taiwan, the bulwark of Chinese resistance to Mao, benefited from a massive infusion of U.S. aid. Soon its electronics industry made inroads into Western markets. South Korea, a significant recipient of American economic support after the Korean War, invested in massive new steel mills and also began to compete with the United States.

American trade policy also spurred economic development overseas. In the early 1960s, President Kennedy signed legislation that rewarded American firms for opening new plants in Europe and eliminated import tariffs. American companies got tax breaks for importing parts produced abroad for domestic production. European and Asian manufacturers produced goods more cheaply; their industries were heavily subsidized by the state, and American firms ramped up their foreign investments, with long-term consequences for the domestic economy.

Gradually, the balance of trade—the difference between the value of the goods and services that the United States sold abroad versus what it imported—shifted. The U.S. trade surplus began to dwindle in the late 1950s, the result of economic recoveries abroad and currency policy. The 1944 Bretton Woods agreements had made the American dollar, pegged to gold, the bedrock of the global economy. In the world economy of the late 1950s and 1960s, the strong dollar, which made American exports more expensive, began to bite into the ability of American manufacturers to sell overseas. Conversely, U.S.-based firms and consumers took advantage of the strong dollar to import Asian- or European-made goods cheaply. American dollars flooded into Western Europe and East Asia, where industrial development, spurred by the rapid expansion of import markets in the United States, accelerated. The United States began to pay more for goods and services from overseas than it took in, and gradually America's global industrial dominance began to wane. In 1971 the United States had a negative balance of trade for the first time since 1893.[18]

Wage and Price Controls

Washington's economic, monetary, and trade policies had set the stage for the economic crisis of the 1970s, but Congress and the White House struggled to come to grips with these changes. Nixon knew that his political fate turned on the domestic economy, even if he preferred to put his energies into diplomacy. In his January 1971 State of the Union address, he promised "a new prosperity: more jobs, more income, more profits, without inflation and without war."[19] That year the administration made curbing inflation its top priority. When steel prices rose by 12 percent in January, Nixon threatened Bethlehem Steel, the industry's leader, by calling off talks to limit steel imports from Europe. Bethlehem cut its price increase by half. And to curb high construction costs in the unionized building trades where average wages and benefits had risen 18 percent over the previous year, Nixon suspended the 1931 Davis-Bacon Act, a law requiring that workers on government contracts be paid the "prevailing wage," usually the union-negotiated wage.

The secretary of labor crowed that the suspension of Davis-Bacon hit unions "the way a two-by-four gets the attention of a mule."[20] With his big stick, Nixon created a Construction Industry Stabilization Committee and restored Davis-Bacon on the condition that union carpenters, electricians, plumbers, and others working on government projects accept lower wages and benefits. In August 1971, Nixon froze wages and prices for ninety days, a move that angered the unions but was immensely popular with the public because inflation slowed considerably.

The Nixon administration also faced a currency crisis that threatened the economy. With inflation rising quickly, foreign investors dumped dollars for gold, destabilizing money markets. So in August 1971 the administration undid the Bretton Woods agreement, unhitching the U.S. dollar from gold and allowing the dollar to float on world currency markets. Bankers at the IMF circulated a mock obituary: "R.I.P. We regretfully announce the not unexpected passing away after a long illness of Bretton

Woods, at 9 P.M. last Sunday. Bretton was born in New Hampshire in 1944, and died a few days after his 27th birthday. . . . The fatal stroke occurred this month when parasites called speculators inflated his most important member, and caused a rupture of his vital element, dollar-gold convertibility."[21] The death of Bretton Woods dramatically reshaped international money markets. Within months, the value of the dollar fell on world markets by 13.5 percent against the West German mark and 16.9 percent against the Japanese yen. To strengthen America's balance of trade, the administration put a 10 percent surcharge on all imports.

THE OIL SHOCK

Nixon's greatest economic challenge involved the oil market. For the entire postwar period, the United States had been both the world's leading producer and consumer of petroleum. The American economy depended on cheap oil. The rise of suburban America was based on the family house and car. In 1970 more than four in five Americans owned at least one car. Most of them were gas-guzzlers. The average passenger car traveled only 13.6 miles per gallon. The expansion of industry to rural areas, especially the Sunbelt, was made possible by the rapid growth of the interstate highway system, unleashing a massive cross-country trucking industry that also depended on inexpensive fuel. Even the asphalt used as a cheap paving material was petroleum-based. Oil heated houses, powered factories, and generated electricity to keep American home appliances and lights glowing. Agribusiness depended on gasoline to fuel massive industrial tractors. Rural communities sprayed oil on unpaved roads to control the dust. Plastic toys, appliances, and bottles, made from petroleum derivatives, were ubiquitous.

OPEC and Israel

Gas hungry, the United States came to rely more and more on overseas oil sources. Domestic oil production peaked in 1970 at nine million barrels a day. With domestic production slowing, demand continued to rise. American oil imports doubled over the next three years alone. A growing share of that oil came from the vast deposits controlled by the member nations of the Organization of the Petroleum Exporting Countries (OPEC). Founded in 1959, OPEC brought together Kuwait, Iran, Iraq, Saudi Arabia, and Venezuela to control oil prices and regulate production. As a result, the fate of motorists in

Levittown, aircraft manufacturers in Los Angeles, and air-conditioning users in Arizona increasingly depended on events half a world away. By 1973, 42 percent of American oil imports came from the Middle East.[22]

Oil politics increasingly revolved around one tiny country, a nation without any petroleum fields of its own but one of America's most important allies: Israel. Ever since President Harry S. Truman recognized the new state of Israel in 1949, the country had taken on outsize significance in American foreign policy. Many liberals saw the new Jewish state as a humanitarian project, a necessary refuge for the millions of European Jews who had survived the Holocaust and then huddled in displaced persons camps for years after the war. Cold Warriors across the political spectrum saw Israel as a strategic ally, a pro-U.S. bastion in a region where the Soviets were making significant inroads. American Jews, about 2 percent of the population, were initially divided over the merits of Zionism, a movement for Jewish nationalism that dated to the nineteenth century. By the 1970s the prominent Jewish intellectual Norman Podhoretz, on an odyssey from leftist to neoconservative, noted an "extraordinary development—the complete Zionization, as it might be called, of the American Jewish community."[23] His measure of this was the overwhelming support of American Jews for the Israeli state. Some Christians, especially fundamentalists, also zealously promoted the state of Israel. They saw the Jews as the legitimate heirs to the biblical Promised Land, and their resettlement and the ensuing regional conflict as the unfolding of God's plan. This unlikely coalition propelled bipartisan support for Israel. By 1974, Israel was the largest recipient of American foreign aid.

Israel's Arab neighbors fiercely contested its boundaries and viewed the new state as illegitimate. The 1947–49 war for Israeli independence had led to the dispossession of millions of Palestinians, whose land and homes Israel appropriated for new settlements. Palestinians called the period *al-Naqba* or the Catastrophe. Border skirmishes, especially with Syria, were frequent in the 1950s and 1960s. Egypt and Israel disputed control over the Sinai Peninsula. Displaced Palestinians based in the West Bank (an area to the west of the Jordan River, controlled by the Kingdom of Jordan) challenged Israeli authority and demanded the right to return to their lands.

The struggles culminated in Israel's Six Day War with Egypt, Jordan, and Syria, in June 1967. Israel took control over most of the Sinai, East Jerusalem, including Jerusalem's Old City, the West Bank, and the Golan

Heights. In the aftermath of the war, hundreds of thousands of Palestinian refugees fled to Jordan. The Israeli occupation of the Sinai, which had been in Egyptian hands for millennia, fueled already-intense anti-Israeli sentiment throughout the region. Israel drew new boundaries, and the tensions in the region continued.

A little more than six years later, on October 6, 1973, on the Jewish holy day of Yom Kippur, Egyptian forces advanced across the Suez Canal into the Israeli-controlled Sinai Peninsula, and the Syrians raided the contested Golan Heights, catching the Israelis off guard. Nearly three weeks of fighting ensued; Israel pushed back the Syrians in just a few days, then advanced north into Syria and bombed Damascus. The struggle with Egypt was longer and bloodier: it took a few weeks and substantial American military support to push Egyptian troops back to the Suez. Many surrounding Arab countries sent troops to support the Egyptians and Syrians, and both the United States and the Soviet Union provided substantial military aid to their respective allies. Tensions between the Americans and the Soviets were greater than they had been since the Cuban Missile Crisis, threatening to unravel détente. The Pentagon put American troops on a worldwide alert. Over the next several years, the United States would substantially increase its military support of Israel.

The Oil Crisis

Although the war ended with a tenuous cease-fire in late October, Saudi Arabia used its power over oil production to punish the United States for its support for Israel. On October 16 the Arab oil states raised oil prices dramatically and the next day announced that they would curtail oil production by 5 percent per month, escalating future oil prices. On October 20, as the United States stepped up military support for Israel, OPEC announced an oil embargo, banning oil shipments to the United States and several of its allies. The embargo, which would last until March 1974, brought disastrous results.

In early November 1973, as the embargo began to take effect, President Richard Nixon addressed the nation in prime time, presenting "a very stark fact: We are heading toward the most acute shortages of energy since World War II."[24] He encouraged Americans to turn down their thermostats by six degrees to conserve energy. He asked airlines to reduce flights by 10 percent. Announcing "Project Independence," to free America from its reliance on foreign oil, Nixon called for reducing the speed limit on interstate highways to 55 miles per hour, and he halted a federal program to convert coal-fueled electrical generation plants to oil. The Senate nearly passed legislation calling for the coupon rationing of gasoline, just as the country had rationed consumer goods during World War II. To prepare, the White House ordered the Bureau of Printing and Engraving to print between ten and fifteen billion coupons.

The oil embargo hit home for Book and Jim Ksionska and their neighbors. Between Thanksgiving and the New Year, the subdivisions around Fairless Hills usually glowed with Christmas lights. Residents festooned their rooflines with brightly colored bulbs and their shrubbery with blinking white lights that looked like snowflakes. But "Christmas 1973," reported a local newspaper, "was a season of darkness."[25] Everyone switched off the lights to save energy.

December was a dark month in other respects as well. Every business that depended on oil—and that was nearly all of them—suffered. Crude oil prices had risen a stunning 470 percent since January 1973. The Big Three auto companies and major airlines announced layoffs just before the holidays; trucking companies reduced shipments during the peak holiday season; farmers halted plowing. School districts closed for winter break early, to save on fuel costs. And as gas prices rose, the cost of just about everything else did too.

Christmas 1973 was just the beginning of a bleak winter. The supply of gas dropped and prices skyrocketed. Customers, hundreds deep, waited for hours in line to fill up their cars. Gas station attendants came to work with pistols to protect themselves during the brawls that regularly broke out among impatient commuters cutting the lines. "These people are like animals foraging for food," stated a gas station attendant. "If you can't sell them gas, they'll threaten to beat you up, wreck your station, run you over with a car."[26] Gas siphons became popular items, the fuel tanks of cars parked overnight on city streets the targets. In one prominent heist, bandits "gas-jacked" an ARCO tanker at gunpoint, stealing all 8,500 gallons of fuel and abandoning the truck.[27]

The situation grew worse in the New Year. In February 1974 about 100,000 independent truckers, demanding a reduction in gas prices, went on strike, blockading the nation's highways for eleven days. Using their citizens' band (CB) radios to coordinate protest convoys—and to dodge law enforcement officials—the truckers were the most visible face of rebellion against the oil shock. With food deliveries cut off, grocery store shelves quickly emptied. Eventually several state governors deployed National Guard units to keep the roads open, prevent violence at roadside rest areas, and restore shipping.[28]

In the meantime, gas grew even scarcer: about one-fifth of all American service stations in February had none at all. To control the lines, the nation implemented a gas rationing system: gas stations would be open on alternate days to cars with license plates ending in even and odd numbers. The long lines were one symbol of changing times, but for many Americans the independent truckers become heroes of resistance. Over the next few years, CB radios exploded in popularity and songs like C. W. McCall's 1975 hit "Convoy" celebrated "a thousand screamin' trucks" who broke the speed limit and faced off "smokies" (police officers) "as thick as bugs on a bumper" as they barreled across country.[29]

RECESSION AND DISILLUSIONMENT

The oil shock plunged the domestic economy—already shaky—into what observers called the "great recession." Unemployment rose to 5.4 percent in January 1974, and even more unsettling, inflation skyrocketed, reaching 12 percent. The unprecedented combination weakened consumer confidence and led to sharp rises in joblessness. The stock market collapsed, losing 37 percent of its value between March and December 1974.

The instability of the markets coincided with instability in the U.S. government. When President Gerald Ford assumed office after Nixon's resignation on August 9, 1974, he sought, in vain, to restore confidence in both government and the economy. On September 8, Ford attempted to put the crimes of his predecessor behind him when he pardoned Richard Nixon, shielding the former president from any Watergate-related criminal charges. In awkward prose, Ford told Americans that "my conscience tells me clearly and certainly that I cannot prolong the bad dreams that continue to reopen a chapter that is closed."[30] The controversial decision doomed his long-term political prospects but allowed him to turn his attention to the other unfinished business that Nixon had left him: the cratering economy.

Whip Inflation Now

A little more than a month after he pardoned Nixon, Ford took the occasion of one of his first major policy speeches to rally the country around a campaign to "Whip Inflation Now," calling for a nationwide voluntary effort to conserve energy, eliminate waste, and support the administration's efforts to stimulate investment. "Through the courtesy of such volunteers from the communication and media fields," stated Ford, "a very simple enlistment form will appear in many of tomorrow's newspapers along with the symbol of this new mobilization, which I am wearing on my lapel. It bears the single word WIN. I think that tells it all. I will call upon every American to join in this massive mobilization and stick with it until we do win as a nation and as a people."[31] The branding effort was a success—but in ways that Ford had not intended. Hard-nosed critics, like Federal Reserve head Alan Greenspan, denounced WIN as a publicity stunt that "didn't reflect any practical, conceivable policy that could be implemented." He doubted that any voluntary efforts would curb inflation.[32] But still, the White House issued hundreds of thousands of red and white lapel buttons that read WIN. Chain stores promoted WIN in their ads. Inflation rates continued to rise.

"A Profound Sense of Disillusionment"

To pessimists, and there were many, the oil shock, raging inflation, and high unemployment symbolized a larger problem facing the country: the American century, a long period of unsurpassed economic and diplomatic power, seemed to be over. In June 1974 a Gallup poll had found a "profound sense of disillusionment, even despondency," among Americans. For the first time, survey researchers reported that a majority of Americans "considered their future bleaker than their past."[33] Americans were turning inward, expressing less concern about America's engagement in the world and more with domestic problems. That inward turn came at a moment when America's place in the world was in profound flux. The economy was shaped, more than it had been in decades, by shifts in the global economy. Kokomo was affected by Kuwait; Toledo by Toyota City; Levittown by London.

Jim Ksionska might not have taken the job at Fairless Works if he had known the troubles that were undermining the American steel industry. Given the state of the economy in 1974, when he graduated from high school, he considered himself lucky to get a union job, close to home. But steelmaking, one of America's most formidable industries since the nineteenth century, was a bellwether of the sweeping changes in the global economy. Steel, used in skyscrapers and bridges, car chassis and engines, forklifts and forks, toasters and turntables, had made the fortunes of some of America's wealthiest dynasties, including the Mellons, Carnegies, and Fricks. Steel manufacturing had also indelibly shaped America's landscape, from the iron mines in northern Minnesota and Montana to the coal seams in Pennsylvania, West Virginia, and Kentucky. Its impact could be seen in the vast shroud of soot that turned Pittsburgh's day into night. Steel's power showed in the vast mills, like Book and Jim Ksionska's Fairless Works, that extended in an industrial belt from Baltimore to Bethlehem to Pittsburgh to Youngstown, Cleveland, Detroit, Gary, and Chicago.

The rise of global competition—aided and abetted by American trade and currency policy—pushed domestic steel into crisis. European steel firms sometimes sold their product (already relatively cheap because of the strong dollar) at a loss in the United States to undercut their domestic competitors. American-based steel manufacturers lobbied unsuccessfully for trade protections and, in the meantime, introduced new labor-saving technologies and cut their workforces to remain profitable. Still, the market share of steel produced abroad rose steadily. By 1977 about one-fifth of American steel was imported, and many of the old cities with steel mills began to lose population and rot away.

One of the casualties—it died a slow death—was the Fairless Works plant. Built in 1951, it employed between 7,000 and 10,000 workers during its first two decades. But between 1975 and 1982, its managers fired a total of 5,800 of those workers; the remaining few thousand, including Book Ksionska, took wage cuts. In 1985, Fairless Works employees walked out, subsisting on the union strike fund at $60 per week and winning only token concessions. Book, protected by seniority, hung onto his job until retiring in 1988. Within a few years, the plant had almost completely shut down.

The Fairless Works story played out with grim regularity throughout industrial America. Shipbuilding moved overseas to the Baltic. Auto parts suppliers jumped to Canada, taking advantage of the weak Canadian dollar. The auto industry, trapped in its big car/big oil paradigm, began to lose market share to Japanese and European competitors who built small, fuel-efficient cars. "The man with a wife and four kids and a shaggy dog can't get into a Vega," remarked Mack Worden, GM's vice-president of marketing in

1974, explaining his company's reluctance to expand its line of compact cars.[34] He misunderstood both family structure (families were shrinking) and the demand for fuel efficiency in an era of economic trouble.

By the mid-1970s, as the auto industry continued to reel from competition, American Motors, the weakest of the industry's firms, put out the Gremlin and the Hornet, two small cars—one with special denim interiors—that failed miserably. In 1972, Ford pioneered its compact Pinto, which had a defect that sometimes caused the car to explode when hit from behind. General Motors began working on a successor to the Vega, the tinier and tinnier Chevette, introduced in 1979. But the interventions proved too timid. American Motors struggled for survival and eventually went defunct in 1987. Chrysler declared bankruptcy in 1979 and had to be bailed out by the federal government. General Motors and Ford steadily lost market share to Toyota, Datsun, and Volkswagen and in the process shed tens of thousands of jobs and closed dozens of plants to remain viable.

Economic Restructuring and Labor Unrest

American industries struggled mightily in the new global economy of the 1970s, haltingly adapting to price controls, new currency rules, and intensifying international competition. As profit margins diminished, companies began to speed up production and cut labor expenses. The goal was straightforward: to produce more goods at less expense. For decades, companies had been experimenting with new technologies to replace workers with machines. The advent of new computer technologies spurred the process. Assembly lines, once bustling with life, grew increasingly mechanized. And low-skill, entry-level jobs began to disappear. At the same time, managers worked the remaining workers harder. In many industries, companies pitted two plants against each other, a process called parallel production. The plant that achieved a higher output would get additional resources; the loser would face cutbacks and sometimes be closed.

Workers responded angrily. Between 1970 and 1974, America saw more labor strife than in any period since the Great Depression. Nearly nine million workers, including Book Ksionska, walked off their jobs in 1,670 separate strikes. In March 1970 about 180,000 postal workers nationwide struck for two weeks, leading to the deployment of National Guard units to deliver mail. The following month 40,000 coal miners stopped working, demanding better conditions and health care coverage. Many of them suffered work-related injuries and debilitating chronic diseases, like black lung, which came from breathing coal dust. That fall the United Automobile Workers led a massive, two-month-long strike against General Motors. The auto manufacturer lost $1 billion in profits, and the UAW nearly went bankrupt. But in the end, the union achieved many of its goals, including higher wages and a "thirty years and out" deal that allowed workers who had been with the company three decades or more to retire with full pensions.

The wave of labor unrest was not simply confined to heavy manufacturing. The United Farm Workers, which had spent years organizing the mostly Mexican field hands working the orchards and vineyards of California's Central Valley, stepped up its call for an international grape boycott, collaborating with churches and student groups and unions. In 1970 they succeeded in forcing California grape growers to offer better wages and working conditions.

None of those strikes seemed as much a sign of the times, however, as the March 1972 shutdown of the Chevrolet Vega plant in Lordstown, Ohio. Lordstown's workers were young—their average age was only twenty-four—and they lived in a culture infused with youthful rebellion. To a local journalist, they looked just like hippies: "Many wear their hair shoulder length, have grown mustaches or beards and come to work in hip-hugging, bell-bottomed trousers. They are probably better educated than any generation of workers in the history of American industry. They were taught to question traditional values and encouraged to stand up and be counted." Whereas many of the old auto plants were segregated by race, black and white workers mingled on the shop floor at Lordstown, and many would drink and smoke together after work.[35]

Journalists called Lordstown the "workers' Woodstock," but there was not a lot of love on the assembly line. The General Motors Assembly Division (GMAD), nicknamed "Get Mean and Destroy" by assembly workers, set production quotas at 100 Vegas an hour, compared to 55 cars an hour at most auto plants. With a partially assembled car passing by workers every thirty-five seconds, there was no time to pause. Facing pressure to move at almost superhuman speed for eight hours (or more with overtime), workers resisted, deliberately slowing down the assembly line, challenging the authority of supervisors, and sometimes sabotaging cars. Speedup was a failure: many Vegas came off the assembly line shoddily assembled or with missing parts. Workers "just want to be treated with dignity," stated Gary Bryner, the twenty-nine-year-old president of the Lordstown UAW local. "That's not asking a hell of a lot."[36]

Finally, in March 1972, after months of unrest, Lordstown workers walked out for three weeks in one of the most acrimonious strikes of the era. In the end, GMAD increased the size of the workforce and reinstated workers who had been fired for disciplinary reasons. Vega production, a little slower, went on. The work stoppage cost General Motors nearly $150 million and was, for most commentators, a sign of "blue-collar blues," the nagging insecurity and discontent of speedup in an age of growing international competition.[37]

Speedup was only one tool to reduce labor costs. Another tried and true method was to relocate factories to low-wage regions, places where workers were not unionized, taxes were low, and local governments were lax in their enforcement of workplace safety laws. Since 1950 capital had been fleeing the heartland of American industrialism, the old cities of the Northeast and the Midwest, for the low-tax, antiunion South, aided by a massive reorientation of federal defense and infrastructure spending toward the Sunbelt. Powerful southern Democrats had long used the power of their seniority in Congress to steer appropriations toward their districts. Places like Phoenix, Arizona, and Orange County, California, once economic backwaters, became major centers of defense production. Old defense centers like Detroit and Chicago were hobbled. Massive federal subsidies to the oil industry, which grew under Eisenhower, Kennedy, and Johnson, fueled economic growth in Texas and Louisiana, turning sleepy Houston into a boomtown. And new shipping technologies—particularly container shipping by truck, which required access to superhighways—led to the decline of the dense, crowded ports of Brooklyn, Philadelphia, Baltimore, New Orleans, and Oakland. A shipping boom remade the part of the swampy Meadowlands of northern New Jersey into the Port of Newark. Likewise, Newport News, Virginia, and the port of Los Angeles, took advantage of abundant land, rail lines, and access to interstate highways to expand. But these new megaports, heavily mechanized, did not create enough jobs to replace those that disappeared on the rotting old wharves.

By the early 1970s, many firms were looking even further afield to cut costs. Major textile firms set up new production facilities in the Dominican

Republic and Hong Kong. Electronics manufacturers, in search of cheap female labor and loose regulations, began to expand plants abroad. RCA, the major television, radio, and phonograph producer in the United States, had shifted production several times. During World War II, it had cut employment in its flagship Camden, New Jersey, plant and moved jobs to Bloomington, Indiana, lured by low taxes and a ready supply of women workers from the region's declining farm economy. In the mid-1960s, RCA opened a plant in Memphis, Tennessee, a state with few union workers and low wages. And in 1968 it opened a massive facility in Ciudad Juárez, Mexico, part of Mexico's free trade region, just across the Rio Grande from El Paso, Texas. Donald Baerresen, an economist who promoted the Mexican border to American firms, highlighted the "large supplies of relatively inexpensive, unskilled labor located close to the United States."[38] By 1973, 168 other American electronics firms had located just south of the border. Left behind were tens of thousands of American workers living in places with the shells of old, redbrick factory buildings where light bulbs, radios, and televisions had once been made.

THE ENVIRONMENTAL CRISIS

For a century and a half, the rise of cities and factories, industry and suburbs, railroads and personal cars had altered the American landscape. Each of these economic and population shifts had dramatic environmental consequences. Book Ksionska had left behind the declining anthracite region of Pennsylvania, with its huge slag heaps, for the brand-new Fairless Works, which had replaced thousands of acres of farms and wetlands with parking lots, furnaces, and warehouses. He traded up one environmental disaster for another. Lifeless ponds that held the steaming water discharges from the plant's cooling system now surrounded the site of the steel mill.

The nearby Fairless Hills and Levittown neighborhoods, like most American suburbs, were an environmental mess. Developers bulldozed forests and meadows to build new housing. Residents poured tons of fertilizer on their lawns, which ran into local streams, leading to massive algae blooms that sucked oxygen out of the water. They sprayed insecticides to kill off lawn-eating bugs and used DDT to exterminate the mosquitoes that made summers miserable. In a 1962 best seller, *Silent Spring*, Rachel Carson described an environmental disaster that was painfully close to home: right in the backyard. DDT was decimating suburban bird populations. And what about people? Carson issued a stark warning. "If we are going to live so intimately with these chemicals—eating and drinking them, taking them into the very marrow of our bones—we had better know something about their nature and their power."[39]

Over the postwar years, more and more Americans came into contact with wilderness, industrial, and postindustrial landscapes, usually through their car windows. What they saw ranged from the sublime to the degraded. The advent of the interstate highway brought more Americans than ever into remote forests, seashores, and mountains. Road trips also took them through some of the grim manufacturing zones in places like Cleveland, so polluted that the Cuyahoga River, filled with flammable chemicals, caught on fire in 1948, in 1952, and again in 1969. In Los Angeles, "acrid blue-gray air" would descend over the metropolitan area for weeks at a time, obscuring the beautiful mountain views and causing what doctors called "smog disease," with symptoms including burning throats and a shortness of breath.[40] In the suburbs, it was possible to see firsthand the transformations wrought by the bulldozer in the countryside. "They paved paradise to put up a parking lot," sang Joni Mitchell, in a popular hit.[41] Over the course of the 1960s and 1970s, the suburbs became the hotbed of "quality of life" politics, which included demands that open land be protected from sprawl.

From steel mills to fast-food restaurants, from burning rivers to mountains enshrouded in smog, it was impossible to ignore the human impact on the environment. By the 1960s, Americans began to pressure politicians to protect fragile landscapes from development and open them to tourism. President John F. Kennedy created the National Lakeshore and National Seashore system to protect coastlines and open them to recreational use. Johnson's Great Society expanded these commitments. In 1964, Johnson signed the Wilderness Act, protecting nine million acres, most of it already owned by the federal government. This was followed in 1965 by the Water Quality Act, which curbed industrial and agricultural discharge into lakes and rivers, and in 1968 by the Wild and Scenic Rivers Act, to protect pristine waterways. None of these laws was particularly effective, but they signaled a new federal commitment to environmentalism and led activists to push for more.

The Environmental Movement

By the late 1960s, longtime preservation and conservation groups like the Sierra Club, founded in California in 1892, competed for influence with more militant organizations, influenced by the tactics of other activist groups. The Environmental Defense Fund (founded in 1967), for example, used the courts—imitating the strategies of civil rights litigations—to challenge polluters, mounting lawsuits against DDT manufacturers and other industrial polluters. Friends of the Earth (founded in 1969) took its cue from the counterculture and antiwar movements, mobilizing supporters with back-to-the-earth rhetoric and engaging in disruptive protest. The Natural Resources Defense Council (founded in 1970) lobbied for environmental regulations and deployed scientists to produce expert reports critical of pollution, overpopulation, wildlife loss, and nuclear power.

What was most striking about environmentalism was its broad appeal. At a moment when the nation seemed irreconcilably divided over war and peace, civil rights, and feminism, it gave bipartisan support to protecting the land, water, and air. Nothing made that clearer than Earth Day, April 22, 1970, when over 20 million Americans in places as diverse as Green Bay, Wisconsin, and Birmingham, Alabama, gathered to demand action on the environment. No single day of protest in American history brought together so many people: Earth Day dwarfed the March on Washington in 1963 and the massive march against the Vietnam War in October 1969.

Although counterculturists and student leftists dominated some Earth Day events and captured the headlines for their dramatic protests—for example, dumping gallons of oil into the fountain at Standard Oil's San Francisco headquarters—most Earth Day events were ecumenical affairs. Philadelphia's Earth Day, one of the country's largest, with thirty thousand participants, included suburban parents and schoolchildren, hippies, church leaders, college students, and members of the Chamber of Commerce, which underwrote the event. Politicians of both parties jostled for prominence, including Democratic presidential hopeful Edmund Muskie and Senate minority leader Hugh Scott. Nearly two-thirds of members of Congress gave speeches at Earth Day events around the country. Beat poet Allen Ginsberg led Philly's crowd with chants, environmental crusader Ralph Nader denounced corporations for polluting rivers, and Pete Seeger, Judy Collins, and the cast of *Hair* performed.

The major news media covered Earth Day more extensively than any event other than the moon landing and presidential funerals. The popular morning television program *Today* dedicated four shows to the environment, leading off with host Hugh Downs declaring, "Our Mother Earth is rotting with the residue of our good life. Our oceans are dying, our air is poisoned. This is not science fiction. And it is not the future; it is happening now and we have to make a decision now."[42]

Environmental Regulation

Behind the scenes, businesses complained to Nixon, who was an ambivalent environmentalist at best. "In a flat choice between jobs and smoke," he reassured corporate leaders who worried about the cost of implementing clean air measures, jobs would win. To auto executives Lee Iacocca and Henry Ford II, Nixon denounced environmentalists as not "really one damn bit interested in safety or clean air. What they're interested in is destroying the system."[43]

But business lobbyists could not stop the bipartisan well of support for environmental legislation. In the fall of 1969, Congress passed the National Environmental Policy Act, and in the summer of 1970, Nixon used an executive order to create the cabinet-level Environmental Protection Agency. That year, Nixon signed the Clean Air Act, restricting both industrial and automobile emissions. In 1972 the EPA banned DDT, and it would use its powers to enforce a panoply of new environmental regulations. That year Congress also passed several key laws, including the Clean Water Act and the Marine Protection, Research, and Sanctuaries Act, which brought places like the Santa Barbara Channel, San Francisco Bay, and Boston Harbor under federal jurisdiction. Capping the wave of legislation, in 1973 Congress passed the Endangered Species Act, bringing federal protection to hundreds of creatures, from tiny snail darter fish to giant elk. Many states—including Republican-controlled Massachusetts, New Jersey, California, and New York—passed their own environmental regulations, putting strict controls on land use, setting aside funds for the creation of state parks and wilderness areas, and in the case of California, capping auto and industrial emissions.

THE URBAN CRISIS

The shift in policy gave rise to a guarded optimism about the environment, but on the other "crisis" of the 1970s—the travails of American cities—the pessimism was crushing. The old Rust Belt cities hemorrhaged jobs and population and struggled to provide city services. On the West Coast, Oakland struggled to remain solvent, as companies decamped to "greenfields"— undeveloped sites—in the East Bay. Back east, Philadelphia raised local income taxes to deal with a growing budget deficit. In Detroit, the city's first black mayor, Coleman Young, elected in 1973, cut city employment and closed dozens of parks and recreation centers. In Baltimore, city efforts staved off a budget crisis by cutting funding to the police, leading to an outbreak of the "blue flu" in 1974. With most police calling in sick, looters took to the city's streets, cleaning out stores and vandalizing properties.

New York Is Burning

Worst hit of all was New York. The city lost 600,000 jobs between the mid-1960s and mid-1970s. The housing market collapsed as landlords in decrepit neighborhoods like Manhattan Valley, the Lower East Side, and Harlem simply walked away from their buildings, unable to pay for costly repairs. About ten thousand apartments per year in the early 1970s were left empty. Many property owners decided it was more lucrative to collect insurance than to rent at a loss, leading to an epidemic of arson. Large parts of the South Bronx burned to the ground.

Population loss and disinvestment gutted New York's tax base. The city had long provided excellent social services to its residents, including a network of city-run hospitals, a well-managed public housing authority, and one of the world's only twenty-four-hour public transit systems. But the infrastructure groaned with age, and the city teetered on the brink of insolvency.

The streets of big cities like New York, Philadelphia, and Los Angeles also filled with the mentally ill and homeless, many of whom had been released from psychiatric hospitals. Advocates of deinstitutionalization hoped that community-based health centers would deliver services more humanely, but budget cuts made that impossible. The bleak setting of abandoned apartment buildings, trash-strewn streets, and graffiti-covered trains served as the grim backdrop for Martin Scorsese's apocalyptic 1976 film,

Taxi Driver, whose protagonist, Travis Bickle, passes through seamy Times Square bitterly describing the scene: "All the animals come out at night—whores, skunk pussies, buggers, queens, fairies, dopers, junkies, sick, venal. Someday a real rain will come and wash all this scum off the streets."[44] Bickle's New York captured what many believed was the apocalyptic end of urban America.

One apocalypse was barely averted during the grim winter of 1974–75, as New York City's bond market collapsed. Crushed by debt, the city teetered on the brink of bankruptcy before state and federal officials offered billions in loans to pay the city's bills. The bailout, however, exacted a high price. The city drastically cut public services, deferred maintenance on the run-down subway system, let parkland revert to nature, cut welfare expenditures, laid off police officers, firefighters and teachers, and trimmed municipal workers' wages. Life in New York got harder.

The city's underfunded and demoralized police could not respond to rising crime, the city's hospital system struggled to serve hundreds of thousands of uninsured patients, and population and job flight continued unabated. New York hit bottom in August 1977 when, after a massive power outage, tens of thousands of city residents took to the streets, looting stores and setting more than a thousand fires. City officials estimated that $1 billion in property was destroyed.

The "War on Crime"

In 1975, *Time* magazine lamented that cities had become "canyons of fear."[45] Between 1965 and 1975, rates of violent crime soared. Scholars debated the extent and magnitude of lawlessness in the United States: Was the sharp increase in burglary or assault an artifact of better reporting or an actual measure of growing violence? Was the pervasive fear of crime the result of lurid news coverage by local television news programs competing for viewers with a strategy of "if it bleeds, it leads"?

One crime statistic could not be ignored. The number of murders in the United States doubled in just fifteen years, from 10,000 in 1965 to over 20,000 in 1980.[46] Horrible stories of grisly serial murders grabbed the headlines and became the subject of a burgeoning genre of "true crime" best sellers, fueled by the voyeuristic coverage of the California cultist Charles Manson, who ordered his followers to commit seven murders in 1969. The sadistic Houston killer Dean Corll kidnapped, tortured, and killed at least twenty-eight adolescent boys between 1970 and 1973. Ted Bundy went on a murderous spree in Washington State and Utah in 1974. Mass murders were far from normal, but they occupied an outsize place in the American imagination of the 1970s. America seemed to be in the grip of remorseless killers.

Calls for law and order had been on the rise since the mid-1950s, even before any measurable increase in crime rates occurred, stoked by fears of an epidemic of comic-book- and Hollywood-fueled juvenile delinquency. When the Warren Court expanded the rights of the accused in *Miranda* and other criminal procedure cases, conservatives argued that the courts coddled criminals rather than punishing them. The fear of lawlessness intensified with urban unrest and campus disorder, leading politicians across the political spectrum to capitalize on fears of crime. But how to respond to growing crime was a matter of debate. Liberals called for economic assistance to the poor, arguing that poverty caused crime. In 1968, Congress passed gun control legislation with a large bipartisan majority, hoping to curb the increase in firearm-related deaths. The 1968 Omnibus Crime Control and Safe Streets Act committed billions to the fight against crime, most of it to fund local police departments.

Still, crime, especially violent crime, rose. By the early 1970s, fear of criminality had turned into a full-fledged panic, with conservatives and liberals alike calling for "law and order" measures, including stricter law enforcement and stiffer sentences for convicted criminals. New York led the way. New York governor Nelson Rockefeller, who had long emphasized rehabilitation and antipoverty efforts to curb crime, changed his position: "Once the orderly structure of society is breached, where does it end?"[47] Politicians and police departments turned their attention to illicit drugs, especially marijuana, heroin, and cocaine. In 1973, Rockefeller supported the nation's strictest antidrug laws.

Also in the 1970s, Congress and the states began introducing mandatory minimum sentencing laws, particularly for drug offenses. By 1980 seventeen states had introduced laws limiting parole, resulting in longer jail stays. The result was a staggering increase in the number of prison inmates, many serving longer sentences than ever. In 1970 about 322,300 Americans were arrested on drug-related charges, compared to more than 1,375,600 in 2000. Young black men were disproportionately represented among those arrested and incarcerated.

Calls for law and order also resuscitated demands for the death penalty. During the postwar period, public support for capital punishment had fallen in the United States, as it did in most Western countries. No American was executed between 1966 and 1976. In 1972 the Supreme Court narrowed the legal basis for capital punishment, ruling that in practice, the death penalty was arbitrary and that methods of execution violated the constitutional ban on cruel and unusual punishment. But in 1976 the Supreme Court, with several conservative members appointed by President Nixon, opened a window for the reinstitution of the death penalty. Utah put the murderer Gary Gilmore to death by firing squad in 1977, and within a few years, thirty-seven states had modified their laws and resumed capital punishment.

One of the few growth industries during the 1970s and early 1980s was incarceration. In most respects, the prison system in the United States was a mess. Jails were old and run-down and, by the early 1970s, hotbeds of rebellion. In 1967 there were five prison riots in the United States, a figure that rose each year, peaking at forty-eight in 1972. The biggest was the uprising at upstate New York's Attica Prison in 1971, which left thirty-nine dead. Attica and the prisoners' movement put a harsh spotlight on the conditions in America's jails, leading to growing litigation to improve prison conditions. This, combined with court-ordered caps on the number of prisoners per facility, the dramatic increase in arrests and convictions, and the panic over crime, fueled a steady increase in prison construction over the next thirty years. While the federal government dealt with stagflation, and while cities and states imposed austerity budgets, spending on prisons grew exponentially.

Support for tough crime measures was truly bipartisan. Massachusetts senator Edward M. Kennedy, who was on the Democratic Party's left, was an early and staunch supporter of mandatory sentencing laws. Governor Jerry Brown in California, a well-known liberal, joined conservatives in the state legislature in instituting tough sentencing requirements and supporting the construction of dozens of new jails. California's debt for prison construction rose from $763 million to $4.9 billion between the mid-1970s and the late 1980s.[48] Massive barbed-wire-enclosed prison complexes sprang up all over the country, mostly outside big cities, often built at the behest of legislators from dying small towns and agricultural communities who were eager to create jobs in their districts.

POLITICAL REFORM

The fear of decline loomed over the United States by the mid-1970s, even if it remained one of the wealthiest countries in the world. The signs of collapse were everywhere: a president had resigned in disgrace, and the country had lost the war in Vietnam, run out of gas because of OPEC, and lost market share to Toyota. Inflation and unemployment hit record highs. The environment was poisoned, the cities were dying, and predators lurked everywhere. And government—from corrupt Nixon to bankrupt New York—seemed to be failing.

For some politicians, the crisis presented opportunity. In the wake of the Watergate scandals—and general disaffection with the presidency—Congress passed a series of reforms intended to curb presidential power. The War Powers Resolution (1973) reinforced Congress's power to authorize military intervention; the Budget Impoundment and Control Act (1974) created the Congressional Budget Office and limited the president's power to overrun congressionally approved budgets; and the Privacy Act (1974) restricted the government's ability to collect and disseminate personal information. In the months after Nixon's resignation, in an attempt to curb political corruption, Congress instituted strict campaign finance reforms, put limits on individual spending on elections, established a system of public funding for presidential campaigns that would remain in place for the next thirty-four years, and created the Federal Election Commission to monitor campaign spending.

The Watergate Babies

The so-called Watergate babies, most of them moderate Democrats, swept into office in the midterm elections of 1974. In the House and Senate they promised to sweep the halls clean with the brooms of reform. One of the major reforms they enacted was limiting the filibuster, reducing the number of votes required to bring a debate to cloture in the Senate from 67 to 60; another was the abolition of the House Un-American Activities Committee. They also reorganized the seniority rules in the House and Senate that had allowed long-serving members, mostly from the South, to dominate congressional committee chairmanships.

The Watergate babies did more than restructure Congress; they also worked to create a third way between New Deal and Great Society liberalism, of which they were skeptical, and pro-business Republicanism, which they embraced. In Colorado, Gary Hart (who had been a key campaign operative for George McGovern) made a successful run for the U.S. Senate in 1974, appealing to voters as a moderate who would work on "quality of life" issues, most notably environmental protection. Hart, like many of these "new Democrats," as they came to be called, argued for shrinking government, stepping back from controversial and expensive social programs, and unleashing an entrepreneurial spirit. "We're locked into these '60s definitions of liberal-conservative which don't work anymore," he argued. "The issues of the '70s are not liberal or conservative, they are not left-right issues . . . and they will not yield to 'New Deal thinking.'"[49] Hart decisively beat the incumbent Republican, picking up a wide swath of self-proclaimed moderates from both parties.

The "new Democrats" (who would sometimes be called "Atari Democrats" in the 1980s, named after a popular first-generation video game manufacturer) argued that their party's future lay in empowering a high-tech economy rather than in continuing to shore up a decaying manufacturing sector. They saw trade unions—still one of the Democratic Party's most powerful groups—as an obstacle to pro-business policies. And they believed that Democrats needed to distance themselves from "special interest" groups, including labor but also racial minorities, if they wanted to succeed nationally. Many older northeastern and midwestern Democrats remained skeptical, but around the country, "new Democrats" began winning office at the state and local levels.

The Rise of Jimmy Carter

The post-Watergate reform impulse—and the widespread sense of political, economic, and international crisis—opened the way to a most unlikely presidency. In 1976, Jimmy Carter, an engineer, peanut farmer, and Southern Baptist lay preacher. He often returned to his hometown, Plains, Georgia, to lead Sunday school classes while he was both Georgia's governor and the U.S. president. Carter emerged from a crowded pack of candidates to win his party's nomination and victory against the unpopular incumbent, Gerald Ford. Carter was the first president to declare that he was "born again," reaffirming his Baptist faith as an adult. He represented a growing segment of Americans, many in the Sunbelt, who practiced evangelical Christianity and proudly proclaimed their faith publicly.

Carter's overt religiosity stood in sharp contrast with nearly every president of the twentieth century, all of whom practiced their Christianity quietly, occasionally appearing at Sunday services, but seldom arguing that their faith informed their politics. John F. Kennedy had to pledge that he would not be a tool of the Catholic Church; Carter, by contrast, reminded voters that his politics were guided by his religion. Carter's morality came to the limelight in, of all places, the pages of *Playboy*, where he told readers that he was a sinner who had committed "adultery in my heart" by looking lustfully at women other than his wife. In the White House, Carter called for family values, arguing that "we need a stable family life to make us better servants of the people" and even suggesting that Department of Housing and Urban Development staffers who "are living in sin" get married.[50] Carter's cultural conservatism allowed him to pick up southern voters and religious whites who had begun to defect to the GOP in the late 1960s.

THE CARTER PRESIDENCY

For all the novelty of being a born-again Christian in the White House, Carter faced economic and global crises for which his religion did not offer many answers. The problem of stagflation persisted throughout the late 1970s, and increasingly, Carter adopted a politics of austerity: reduce government expenditures to curb inflationary impulses. In his inaugural address, he set a somber tone. "We have learned that 'more' is not necessarily better," he stated, "that even our great Nation has its recognized limits."[51] His presidency unfolded in the shadow of Vietnam and the disillusionment of Watergate. Carter was no wheeling-and-dealing, grandiose politician like Lyndon Johnson. As he taught Bible lessons, he seemed to inhabit a moral world far, far away from Nixon's. With his background as a farmer and a nuclear engineer, he exuded a technical competency that the bumbling Gerald Ford had lacked.

A Technocrat in the White House

It was that last quality, his penchant for technocracy, that seemed to distinguish Carter the most. Kennedy had admired scientists and economists and delegated policy making to them. Johnson had disdained "the Harvards" who dominated Kennedy's administration, preferring the arm-twisting and cajoling of congressional deal making. Nixon was a mix of the two. He had professors like Kissinger and Shultz in his cabinet and took a strong hand in foreign policy, but he was happy to leave most of the details of domestic policy to his staff, checking in only when it affected his political prospects. Carter, by contrast, was obsessively concerned with detail. He micromanaged every aspect of his administration's social, economic, and foreign policy. That proclivity showed up in the pages of the 178-page report of Carter's Urban Policy Research Group, a turgid document that focused on an issue that was not very high on the president's list of priorities. The president read every page, underscoring key passages with a ruler and jotting down comments in his neat handwriting in the margins.

Carter also employed a rhetoric of postpartisanship. During his campaign, he had distanced himself from the "Washington mess," emphasizing the need for "limits" to government reach, echoing Republican criticism of the Great Society. Likewise, Carter rejected "selfish special interests" that were a "menace to our system of government," echoing Republican criticism of civil rights activists, labor unions, and liberal reform groups that had supposedly captured policy making. He and his advisers also echoed the GOP's silent majority strategy, appealing directly to disaffected white middle-class voters, the "average, hard-working American" who struggled to make ends meet by working hard in "homes, factory shift lines, beauty parlors, barber shops, livestock sales barns, and shopping centers."[52]

At first, it seemed that Carter would focus on unemployment, which remained doggedly high—over 7 percent—when he entered office.[53] Early in his term, Carter called for stimulus spending, most notably through a modest tax rebate (it would average about fifty dollars per household) and federal efforts to curb unemployment, including full employment legislation that labor and liberals had been demanding since World War II. Carter also supported government-funded job training to bolster the fortunes of those displaced by collapsing industry. Under pressure from big-city mayors and civil rights leaders to do something about the urban crisis, he pledged support for comprehensive urban reform.

Carter's job-creation record was mixed at best. He expanded the 1973 Comprehensive Employment and Training Act, which created about 725,000 federal jobs at its peak in 1978. But he dropped the tax rebate within months of introducing it, on the grounds that it was expensive and unnecessary as unemployment rates temporarily fell. He found political support for the full-employment law (sponsored by two liberal lions, former vice president Hubert Humphrey and Congressman Augustus Hawkins [D-CA], one of the few African Americans in the House and a staunch ally of organized labor) but at the cost of compromise on its provisions. By the time it made its way through the House and Senate, it was little more than symbolic. Carter's comprehensive but underfunded urban reform provided only about $600 million of new urban spending. His urban policy was a warmed-over version of Nixon's: fund small-scale community development organizations that had the will but not the capacity to address the mass of urban problems that they faced.

Inflation and Austerity

All these programs ultimately fell to Carter's budgetary ax. A little more than a year into office, the administration turned its attention from the unemployment side of stagflation to the inflation side. The annual inflation rate skyrocketed, rising from 6.5 percent in 1977 to 11.3 percent in 1979. Carter's political response to inflation was confused. He attempted to curb wage and price increases, calling for controls on both, a failed reprise of Nixon's policy. By 1978 he called for austerity measures. He embraced arguments from the political right that blamed government deficits for the economy's troubles.

Leading the charge toward austerity was Carter's chief inflation adviser, the Cornell University economist Alfred Kahn, who advocated dramatic reduction in government spending. Carter proposed cuts to social programs, a reduction in the federal workforce (he promised to hire one government worker to replace two who quit or retired), and cost controls on government contracts. Kahn advocated free market reforms. Greater competition, he argued, would weaken trade unions, lower wages, and curb inflation. "I'd love the Teamsters to be worse off," he argued. "I'd love the automobile workers to be worse off."[54]

The economy worsened. When Carter took office, unemployment had been at 7.1 percent. It fell to 5.8 percent—still high—in 1979, before returning to 7.1 percent again in 1980.[55] The value of the dollar plummeted, increasing the cost of American imports, most notably oil, thus driving up the prices of many commodities. Inflation also skyrocketed, rising 14.8 percent between March 1979 and March 1980, the largest increase since the lifting of price controls after World War II.[56]

Deregulation

Like the Watergate babies, Carter offered a critique of bureaucracy that was a softer version of conservative critiques of the New Deal and Great Society. He pledged to institute "comprehensive" government reform, including the streamlining of bureaucracy, the reduction of paperwork, and most consequentially, the rollback of government regulation. "One of my Administration's major goals," Carter stated, "is to free the American people from the burden of over-regulation."[57] To that end, he directed Kahn to oversee his deregulation efforts. "I have more faith in greed than in regulation," Kahn argued.[58] When it came to regulation, he believed that the costs often outweighed the benefits. Of environmental regulations, Kahn contended, "the cost per life—say per year of additional life expectancy—is just astronomical."[59]

With Kahn's guidance, the Carter administration put up hurdles to new regulations, including a regulatory review council that would conduct cost-benefit analyses of any proposed regulations and give businesses a strong voice in future regulations. Carter also pushed for legislation to lift controls on airlines, deregulate the trucking industry, and weaken communications regulations, allowing for the proliferation of competing telephone companies rather than large regional monopolies. Most significant, he called for a rollback of Depression-era banking regulations. Without exaggeration, he called deregulation "the greatest change in the relationship between Government and business since the New Deal."[60]

Many would later associate deregulation with a right-wing political agenda. Carter's call for free markets and Kahn's paeans to greed warmed the hearts of conservatives like Barry Goldwater, who enthusiastically supported deregulation as a necessary first step to dismantling big government. The National Association of Manufacturers, which had fought New Deal labor laws and Nixon-era environmental laws alike, lined up behind Carter's plans. But deregulation also had staunch supporters on the left. Consumer advocate Ralph Nader, who had crusaded for environmental regulations, joined Carter on the grounds that competition would lower prices and give consumers more choice in the marketplace. Senator Edward Kennedy (D-MA), to the left of Carter on most issues, led the Senate in pushing for deregulation in trucking to cut overhead and reduce prices. Even though many on the left would later regret deregulation, consumer advocates and key liberals were decisive players in the process.

Perhaps the most consequential shift was in banking. In 1978, Carter signed the International Banking Act, which allowed foreign-held banks to acquire American banks and compete for business in the United States. Even more important was the Depository Institutions Deregulation and Monetary Control Act, signed by Carter in 1980, which ushered in a new era of financialization by loosening credit, lifting interest-rate ceilings on bank deposits, and allowing financial institutions to create interest-bearing checking accounts and offer adjustable-rate mortgages. The act also allowed savings and loans to issue credit cards. With the lifting of interest-rate ceilings, lending institutions could expand the availability of credit to borrowers who had once been considered too risky.

Credit cards, once symbols of wealth because banks limited them to customers able to make their payments, proliferated in the 1980s and 1990s. By 1984 more than half of all American households had credit cards. Savings and loan institutions and consumer banks dramatically expanded lending to higher-risk customers, increasing their profits but also creating a spiral of indebtedness and a decline in individual and household savings. The decline in financial sector regulations played out with grim consequences in many households that got bogged down in debt. And it laid the groundwork for two future financial crises, the savings and loan crisis in 1987 and the collapse of major investment banks because of predatory mortgage lending in 2008.

The Energy Crisis

Of all of the economic problems that Carter inherited from his predecessors, the most difficult involved energy. He was inaugurated during one of the coldest winters in modern American history, a chill that coincided with a severe natural gas shortage. America grew increasingly dependent on foreign oil in the 1970s: by the time Carter entered office, more than half of American petroleum came from foreign sources. At first, Carter echoed Nixon's earlier calls for conservation. In his first televised address, in April 1977, he appeared in the White House library, seated casually, wearing a cardigan sweater. He called for a "comprehensive energy policy," arguing that solving America's energy problems was the "moral equivalent of war."[61]

A few months later Carter announced the National Energy Plan (NEP), which called for conservation, energy efficiency standards for appliances and cars, the development of alternatives to fossil fuels, taxes on firms that continued to use petroleum and natural gas, and the lifting of price ceilings on oil and gas. The NEP generated intense controversy. Republicans saw it as big government interference in a market best left to its own devices. They resisted any efforts to use the tax system to encourage conservation. Still, with bipartisan support, a weakened NEP passed in November 1978, with Carter's energy efficiency measures in place, and a plan gradually to lift the price ceiling on oil and gas, but without a tax to discourage consumption. But the NEP would face troubles from the get-go, mainly because its emphasis on conservation through the uncapping of gas prices collided directly with the administration's war on inflation.

The Iranian Revolution

Within weeks of Carter's signing of the NEP, the United States faced even bigger problems. In late 1978 oil production in Iran came to a virtual halt when Islamic fundamentalists challenged the regime of the shah, Mohammad Reza Pahlavi. The United States had propped up the shah since 1953. An autocrat, Pahlavi and his supporters had grown rich on petrodollars. He attempted to Westernize Iran while using his secret police to brutalize and censor his political foes. His chief opponent, the fundamentalist Ayatollah Ruhollah Khomeini, led a resistance from exile in nearby Iraq. In the mid-1970s the popular resistance to the shah intensified, culminating in massive demonstrations in Tehran in 1978. Huge student-led strikes and violent street protests shut down the capital for weeks at a time. The crisis in Iran caught the Carter administration—and nearly every American foreign policy expert—off guard. They had all embraced the view of the shah's regime as secular and modernizing, as symbolized by the luxury resorts along the Persian Gulf and the glittering, high-end shops in downtown Tehran.

In early 1979 the shah fled Iran, leaving huge construction projects unfinished and the country unstable. The Ayatollah Khomeini returned from exile and took leadership, drafting an Islamic constitution. Like the shah, he cracked down brutally on dissent, but unlike the shah, he denounced the United States as the root cause of his country's problems.

The crisis in Iran—and an OPEC decision to increase oil prices—precipitated an energy crisis every bit as severe as the one in 1973–74. Carter was never one to sugarcoat a grim scenario. In April 1979 he announced that the "nation's energy problem is serious—and it's getting worse."[62] His proposed solution—the immediate decontrol of oil prices, along with a windfall tax on oil company profits—satisfied no one. Gas prices shot up by over 50 percent in the first half of 1979, and Carter's anti-inflation policy met its limits.[63]

"No Gas, My Ass"

Six years after the first oil shock, history seemed to be repeating itself, but even more grimly: gas lines once again, angry drivers waiting for hours to pay $1.79 per gallon if there was any fuel left at the pumps. On June 23, 1979, a balmy Saturday afternoon, that anger flared up just a few miles from Book Ksionska's house. That afternoon Denny Riley, a twenty-one-year-old trucker, rounded up a group of his friends who pulled their rigs into the Levittown intersection known as Five Points, a major crossroads with four gas stations. Blaring their air horns and blasting music, they slowed to a halt. The disruption attracted a crowd. Within hours about five hundred people gathered, cheering and waving homemade banners. Bill Brown, a friend of Riley's, pulled up in his rig, and when the police asked him to move along, he defiantly leaped to the top of his cab and waved at the cheering crowd. By evening the crowd grew restive: the police arrested sixty-nine demonstrators.

On Sunday several trucks and a larger, angrier crowd, about two thousand strong, gathered again at Five Points, along with three hundred police officers. As the police attempted to disperse the crowd, hitting people and trucks with nightsticks and chasing protesters with police dogs, tempers flared. Protesters chanted "No gas, my ass!" and tossed firecrackers into the air, pelted the police with stones and bricks, broke service station windows, attacked gas pumps, and lit a car and van on fire.[64] One hundred seventy-nine people were arrested, including a trucker who was charged with running over a police officer's hand. "What happened to Levittown's tranquility?" worried *Newsweek*.[65]

Malaise

Just three weeks after the Levittown gas riot, President Carter gave his "malaise" speech, which would become a defining moment of his presidency. On the evening of July 15, he offered a somber portrayal of a national crisis that was, at core, existential rather than political or economic, though he never actually used the word *malaise*. "Why have we not been able to get together as a nation to resolve our serious energy problem?" he asked. To answer that question, he met with ordinary Americans, clerics, and community leaders, soliciting their advice. After weeks of listening, he concluded: "It is a crisis of confidence. It is a crisis that strikes at the very heart and soul and spirit of our national will. We can see this crisis in the growing doubt about the meaning of our own lives and in the loss of a unity of purpose for our Nation."[66] Though Carter hoped the speech would spur a call for national renewal—and for a moment it did bolster his popularity—it became an epitaph for postwar America.

The events that played out in late 1979 and early 1980 constituted a depressing coda. In November 1979, when Carter permitted the exiled shah to come to the United States for cancer treatment, a group of radical Islamic activists stormed the American embassy in Tehran and took fifty-two Americans hostage. The hostage crisis would play out for 444 days, gripping the American public and fueling a sense that the United States was indeed powerless worldwide. On April 24, 1980, the president authorized a rescue mission that failed spectacularly, with eight U.S. soldiers dead and no hostages freed. For Carter, the crisis—replayed nightly on the evening news—was at least as devastating as the Tet Offensive had been for Lyndon Johnson, a sign of presidential and, by implication, national impotence.

THE TURN TO THE RIGHT

That year Carter would face a political opponent who promised an easy answer to America's crises. He was Ronald Reagan, the longtime right-leaning Republican candidate who promised a new, assertive style of leadership: "I will not stand by and watch this great country destroy itself under mediocre leadership that drifts from one crisis to the next, eroding our national will and purpose."[67] Counter to Carter's ruminations about America's malaise, Reagan exuded confidence. Facing the crisis in Iran, he promised swift military action. Reagan swept the election, winning 50.8 percent of the popular vote to Carter's 41 percent. Independent, former moderate Republican John Anderson picked up 6.6 percent. But the 1980 election was less a moment of resolution than the opening of a new period of political turmoil.

The United States had lurched rightward in the sixteen years since

Barry Goldwater challenged Lyndon Johnson. That rightward turn resulted in part from grassroots organizing by Republican insurgents, but it was also the consequence of long-brewing suspicions of government rooted in the debacles of Vietnam and Watergate. For all their differences, Carter and Reagan shared a bipartisan consensus that government was too big and regulation too burdensome. They shared a belief that austerity measures could restore the nation's economy. And they both advocated market-friendly policies that would encourage competition. That bipartisan consensus—as much as the unresolved struggles over family, race, and culture—would reshape American politics for the next three decades.

Just a few years before Reagan won election, the writer Michael Harrington argued that "America is moving vigorously left, right, and center all at once."[68] Even if 1980 marked a rightward turn in national politics, the political climate was still muddled. In Book and Jim Ksionska's suburban Philadelphia district, voters had backed Carter by a narrow margin in 1976 and joined the Reagan sweep in 1980 and again in 1984. But presidential politics offered only one glimpse into the fluid political world of the time. In 1978 voters in the Ksionskas' district elected a moderate Democratic Watergate baby and staunch environmentalist. In 1980 they voted him out of office. But two years later, amid the troubles at Fairless Works and a deep recession, they reelected the Democrat, who ran ads featuring closed factories.

For the next several years, Harrington's dictum held true: Congress switched control from Democratic to Republican and back again. The new Republican president pushed domestic and foreign policy rightward but faced more limits than his fervent supporters had expected. Centrist Democrats gained influence and refashioned their party, rejecting Carter's gloomy rhetoric but embracing many of his administration's ideas about austerity, bureaucracy, and regulation. And in the meantime, more and more Americans lived like the Ksionskas, stuck in the political middle, uncertain of their economic futures or their political identities. In its 1985 hit, the band Camper van Beethoven captured the ambiguity of the age: "Everything seems to be up in the air at this time."[69]

CHAPTER 14

THE NEW GILDED AGE,
1980–2000

I N **1994** BETTY DUKES took a five-dollar-per-hour part-time job as a cashier at Wal-Mart. The national chain targeted places like her hometown, Pittsburg, California, an industrial city on the Sacramento River Delta that had reached its economic peak in the mid-twentieth century. The town's racially diverse, mostly blue-collar residents liked Wal-Mart for its friendly employees, its long opening hours, and most of all, its rock-bottom prices. It was expensive living in northern California, even in a gritty working-class town. Buying their food, clothing, electronics, and household supplies at Wal-Mart helped many families, barely getting by after they paid their rent or mortgage, make ends meet at the end of the month.[1]

Betty's job didn't pay much, but the retail sector was one of the few options open to women like her, without a lot of skills and education. And for a devoutly Christian woman, Wal-Mart seemed like an ideal employer. She admired what she called the "visionary spirit" of the company's founder, Sam Walton. Wal-Mart promoted an ideology of family and faith and prided itself on being a big company with the heart of small-town America.

Betty worked hard at Wal-Mart, and after her first year, she earned a promotion to a full-time position and a modest raise. In 1997, having compiled a sterling record, she became a customer service manager. Still she grew frustrated with her position in the company. She was a manager in name only. She still got paid by the hour, just a little above minimum wage, despite her experience. She was particularly upset to watch as the company provided special training for male employees and promoted them to salaried positions. She wanted to move up to a better job, but her boss refused. Adding to her growing bitterness, she discovered that she earned fifty cents an hour less than another customer service manager, a man, who had less experience than she did.

Betty complained, first to the store manager and then, when he brushed her off, to Wal-Mart's regional office. Things took a turn for the worse. Her supervisor started keeping close track of her comings and goings. The scrutiny was unusual. If she returned a minute or two late from a break, it went down on her record. One day when she called in sick (using one of the sick days allowed under company policy), she got an earful. Citing a detailed list of minor infractions, the company demoted her in 1999, putting her back to work at the cash register and cutting her hours. She took a pay cut too. In 2000 she filed a lawsuit against Wal-Mart, accusing the chain of discrimination. Her lawyers found other women workers with similar stories at Wal-Mart stores throughout the country. The suit was a class action, filed in federal court in California. Betty and the other plaintiffs eventually lost their suit in the U.S. Supreme Court in 2011 on technical grounds. But the story revealed much about the transformation of American politics and economics in the late twentieth century.

Pittsburg's Wal-Mart was store number 1615 of more than three thousand Wal-Marts worldwide. In 1962 an enterprising businessman, Sam Walton, had launched the first, Wal-Mart Discount City, in tiny Rogers, Arkansas. Walton, the son of a land appraiser, had grown up comfortably in Missouri. After college and military service, he started his career in retail, purchasing and running small variety stores in Arkansas, Kansas, and Missouri. By the early 1960s, he was ready to start his own chain. The timing was right. In 1962, when Walton opened his first Wal-Mart, three other discounters—Kmart, Target, and Woolco—opened their first stores as well. The last third of the twentieth century saw a proliferation of discount stores. Discounters like Wal-Mart made their money by keeping prices low but selling a high volume of goods.

Wal-Mart took advantage of shifts in the national economy. Walton could not have created his nationwide retail empire without the benefit of decades of federal programs. Rural electrification during the New Deal had opened the way for the expansion of business and manufacturing in places like Arkansas. Federally funded highways facilitated the quick and inexpensive shipping of clothes, food, and household items by truck from warehouses to stores. Federal labor laws, dating back to the 1947 Taft-Hartley Act, made it hard for retail workers to form unions, particularly in states like Arkansas.

Sam Walton opened his first stores in rural areas, where he found a ready source of low-wage workers, most of them women, victims of the collapsing agricultural economy. Having a low-wage workforce was key to his strategy to shave every penny he could from his company's overhead. His first stores—and the factories and warehouses that supplied them—were nearly all in areas with weak unions. His home base, Arkansas, was a deeply antiunion state. It had added a right-to-work amendment to its constitution in 1944, and immediately after the passage of Taft-Hartley in 1947, it had rushed through a right-to-work law. Throughout his career, Walton fiercely fought organized labor.

At the center of Wal-Mart's marketing was an idealized image of its small-town roots. Wal-Mart described its workers as "family," and in its early years, it often hired multiple generations of workers, from grandparents to grandchildren. Walton also promoted Christian values among the workforce. Beginning in the 1970s, he funded college courses in free enterprise, eventually at more than seven hundred state universities and Christian colleges, mostly in the South and lower Midwest. Walton also promoted an ethic of "service" among his company's mostly female workforce. "Mr. Sam calls this 'Servant Leadership,'" declared Sam's *Associate Handbook* in 1990, the manual distributed to all the firm's employees.

But for all his support for family values, Walton was no fan of the family wage. Over his career, he fought to keep the minimum wage low, and he cut costs by purchasing goods from suppliers that relied on poorly paid workers, increasingly overseas. He also fought to reduce corporate and individual taxes and to loosen international trade barriers. By the time he died in 1992, he had turned his firm into America's largest employer, with 371,000 employees at 1,928 stores. And the policies that he promoted enjoyed bipartisan support. The rise of Wal-Mart's America was the consequence of dramatic political shifts that had roots in the postwar years, but that accelerated beginning in the 1980s.

THE REAGAN REVOLUTION?

The economy was on everyone's mind in the early 1980s. With unemployment over 7 percent, interest rates pushing 20 percent, and inflation sky high, the prognosis was grim. In his final debate with President Jimmy Carter in late October, Ronald Reagan asked, "Are you better off than you were four years ago? Is it easier for you to go and buy things in the stores than it was four years ago? Is there more or less unemployment in the country than there was four years ago? Is America as respected throughout the world as it was?"[2] It was a simple and powerful rebuke to Carter's presidency.

Sixteen years after Barry Goldwater had gone down to defeat and pundits had declared the New Right dead, the United States elected one of its most conservative presidents ever. Carter picked up 41 percent of the vote, winning only six states and Washington, D.C. Reagan took the returns as a mandate for sweeping change. Reprising arguments that he had made since he was a spokesman for General Electric in the 1950s, he stated in his inaugural, "In the present crisis, government is not the solution to our problem; government is the problem."[3]

Though Reagan had decisively defeated Carter, polls suggested that a sizable majority of Americans did not share his philosophy of government. He came to office with a Republican majority in the Senate, the first in nearly twenty-five years, but the House was still solidly Democratic. Despite talk of a "Reagan Revolution," the American electorate supported programs that Reagan had long denounced, including Social Security, assistance to the poor, federal funding for public schools, and Medicare and Medicaid.

Still Reagan moved forward aggressively on his agenda. Less than a month after he took office, he pledged "to put the nation on a fundamentally different course, a course leading to less inflation, more growth, and a brighter future for all of our citizens."[4] That course included a 30 percent cut in income and corporate taxes, significant cuts in federal social programs, and a tight monetary policy to reduce inflation.[5]

The Tax Revolt

Reagan subscribed to the theory that tax cuts would unleash corporate investment, which would then "trickle down" to ordinary citizens in the form of more jobs and higher wages. Taxpayers, he believed, would work harder if they could keep more of their paychecks, and as a result, the economy would grow. By this reasoning, it followed that even if tax rates were lower, more revenue would flow into federal coffers. In other words, tax cuts would pay for themselves.

Reagan was inspired by Representative Jack Kemp (R-NY) and Senator William Roth (R-DE), who had introduced legislation in 1977 to cut federal income tax rates by 30 percent. The tax-cutting agenda got a boost from Arthur Laffer, a young conservative economist at the University of Southern California who had worked in the Nixon and Ford administrations. In 1974, Laffer became famous on the right for the "Laffer curve," a graph that he drew on a napkin to illustrate his hypothesis that high taxes discouraged work. Tax cuts, he argued, would encourage productive activity and, in time, increase tax revenue. Few economists took the Laffer curve seriously, but right-wing politicians did. Jude Wanniski, a conservative editorialist at *The Wall Street Journal*, wrote that the Laffer curve "set off a symphony" in Reagan's mind; he believed "instantly that it was true and would never have a doubt thereafter."[6]

The first battleground of the tax revolt was Reagan's home state of California. There in 1978 voters overwhelmingly approved Proposition 13, a statewide referendum that cut state property taxes by 57 percent and required all municipalities to put property tax increases up for a vote. Prop 13 was the brainchild of wealthy businessman Howard Jarvis, a longtime anti–New Dealer and Goldwater supporter who had spent most of the 1960s and 1970s organizing against taxes. The Constitution, he argued, did not call for the protection of "life, liberty and welfare or life, liberty, and food stamps."[7] Jarvis inspired tax rebels in solidly Democratic Massachusetts, where in 1980 a majority voted for Proposition 2½, a ballot initiative that capped local property tax increases.

Whether the tax revolt would go viral remained an open question well into the 1980s. Many moderates and liberals worried that tax cuts would have unintended negative consequences. They could point to California's public schools, which received most of their funding from property taxes. In many communities, voters without school-aged children were often reluctant to support property tax increases, and school funding dropped. The pinch was especially sharp in those older industrial cities and suburbs, like Betty Dukes's Pittsburg, whose public schools struggled with budget cuts because of the steady decline of the town's fishing, canning, and steel industries. Over the 1980s and 1990s, California's public schools suffered— districts put off maintenance, cut teacher pay, and tolerated crowded classrooms to make ends meet. Around the country, many voters were not yet ready to join Jarvis's rebellion.

Reaganomics

On February 18, 1981, President Reagan announced a comprehensive economic plan, with four prongs: a cut in federal spending, a reduction in income taxes, economic deregulation—accelerating and expanding programs begun under Carter—and a tightening of the money supply. Cutting domestic programs would wean Americans from their "dependency" on government. Fiscal tightening would reduce inflation. Reagan promised that if his program was enacted, the federal budget would be balanced by 1984. Lifting "haphazard and inefficient regulation" would, in his view, spur corporate investment and job creation. He also called for creating a program of "tax incentives for investment," allowing investors larger and faster tax write-offs, on the untested assumption that companies would use tax savings to expand production and hire new workers. At the same time, however, he pledged to strengthen the national defense, a particularly costly priority.[8] "The whole thing is premised on faith," explained David Stockman, a former congressman from Michigan who directed Reagan's Office of Management and Budget. "On a belief about how the world works."[9]

Many did not share Reagan's faith. Fiscally conservative Republicans were skeptical of arguments for deep tax cuts. For decades, the GOP had staunchly supported balanced budgets, which meant increasing taxes if spending rose. Many worried that if tax revenue fell, Reagan would not be able to sustain his promise to bolster the nation's defense. During the Republican primaries, his leading opponent, George H. W. Bush, had denounced Reagan's ideas as "voodoo economics." Some economists warned that tax cuts would fuel inflation. Reagan faced an uphill battle in Congress.

On March 30, 1981, John Hinckley, a mentally ill, twenty-five-year-old from a wealthy Texan family, attempted to assassinate the president. Reagan, gravely injured but conscious, survived the assault, and did so with characteristic humor and grace. He bantered with doctors and told his wife, Nancy, "Honey, I forgot to duck." After an outpouring of public sympathy, Reagan's approval ratings skyrocketed. He and his advisers used the goodwill to build momentum for his economic plan.

Reagan's tax and budget passed in August 1981, with the support of most Republicans and a small number of Democrats, nearly all of them from the South. Even if most Americans did not share Reagan's optimism that tax cuts would pay for themselves, most liked the idea of paying a little less every April 15. Many middle-class American taxpayers had seen their tax rates rise during the 1970s, not because they were wealthier but because inflation had bumped them into higher tax brackets. Reagan's reform would, for a time, reduce the effect of "bracket creep."

Reagan's tax cuts, however, benefited the wealthy far more than the middle class. The top tax rate, for the top earners, fell from 71 percent of income to just 28 percent. The tax rate on capital gains fell from 28 to 20 percent, and corporate tax rates fell from 46 to 35 percent. The result was a staggering increase in the annual income of the wealthiest Americans. The top 1 percent of income earners saw their annual after-tax income rise 256 percent in real dollars between 1976 and 2006.[10] By contrast, over that same period, the poorest fifth of the population saw an income increase of only 11 percent. Over the long run, the benefits of tax cuts did not "trickle down" from the rich to middle- and working-class Americans.

Reagan's tax cuts did not pay for themselves. The president's faith in the Laffer curve proved misguided. Over the 1980s, federal deficits skyrocketed, exacerbated by dramatic increases in defense spending, which constituted nearly a quarter of the 1982 budget. Domestic spending also proved difficult to trim. A tenth of federal spending went to servicing the federal debt, and the government could not fail to meet its fiscal obligations without triggering an economic crisis. Forty-eight percent of the federal budget went to Social Security and Medicare, programs that enjoyed broad bipartisan support. Only about one-fifth of the federal budget consisted of discretionary programs, ranging from infrastructure projects like the expensive interstate highway system to education spending, and a panoply of mostly small antipoverty programs. Even drastic cuts to those programs would not substantially reduce the deficit. Between 1981 and 1989, federal debt tripled, reaching $2.8 trillion.

Deregulation also had unintended consequences. Reagan used the power of the presidency to weaken the enforcement of environmental regulations (many passed less than a decade before he entered office). Secretary of the Interior James Watt loosened regulations that limited commercial mining, cattle grazing, and oil and gas extraction on federal lands. Several regulatory agencies, including OSHA, the EPA, and the FDA, cut the number of inspectors to enforce regulations protecting worker safety, water supplies, and food. The loosening of SEC regulatory oversight of Wall Street encouraged insider trading scandals in the mid-1980s. Executives like Michael Milken and Ivan Boesky made fortunes by getting advance word of pending mergers and acquisitions and using that information to buy stocks before their prices shot upward.

Congress and the administration also rewrote regulations governing savings and loan (S&L) associations, allowing them to expand their pool of investments to include risky mortgages and loans, most notably lifting the cap on mortgage interest rates. For most of their history, S&Ls had been conservative with their investments and local in their orientation. In the new loosely regulated financial regime, S&Ls grew exponentially and gambled on tempting but often unwise investments, from remote vacation housing developments to hastily constructed strip malls. When many of those investments failed, S&Ls collapsed. Nearly sixteen hundred S&Ls failed between 1980 and 1994, most of them in 1987 and 1988. Eventually the costs of bailing out those institutions exceeded $150 billion.

THE SOCIAL SAFETY NET

Reagan's wing of the Republican Party had been fighting the New Deal for decades and mostly losing. But now that they were in power, they trained their sights on social welfare spending, beginning with Social Security. Since 1935, Social Security had become the costliest domestic program. Many Americans viewed its central provisions—old age and disability insurance—as inalienable rights. Social Security had support in both parties. President Eisenhower had enacted reforms that dramatically expanded its rolls. In 1972, President Nixon authorized the adjustment of Social Security payments to the cost-of-living index. As a result, during the inflationary 1970s, Social Security spending skyrocketed.

Social Security Reform

The Republican right had long despised Social Security as an expensive welfare program that bolstered big government and stifled the free market. In the 1950s and 1960s, Reagan denounced the Social Security payroll tax as coercive and instead backed a voluntary system of savings for retirement. It was a principled position but deeply unpopular. In 1976, Reagan had suffered a stinging defeat in the Florida Republican primary because of his support for privatizing Social Security. Politically astute, he began shifting his position in the late 1970s, publicly stating his support for Social Security but calling for a radical overhaul of the program.

In May 1981, Reagan proposed raising the eligibility age for Social Security to 67. (Seniors at that time were eligible for partial payments at 62½ and full payments at 65.) He also argued for reducing Social Security checks by 25 percent for those who took early retirement. It was one of the biggest miscalculations of his presidency. Democrats howled in opposition. "It is a rotten thing to do, a despicable thing," stated Speaker of the House Thomas P. O'Neill, a Boston liberal whose mostly blue-collar constituents revered the New Deal.[11] By the 1980s, the elderly were living longer, voted at higher rates than younger people, and had an effective voice through Washington lobbyists, particularly the American Association of Retired People, which had millions of members and the resources to fight. In a crushing 96–0 vote on May 20, the Senate rejected Reagan's plan. It was an early reminder of the limits of the "Reagan Revolution."

Embarrassed by his defeat, Reagan appointed a commission to reform Social Security. In 1983 the president and Congress agreed to a payroll tax hike to bolster the funds available to pay beneficiaries. For the moment, the Social Security system was solvent (though rising life expectancies and the graying of the baby boom generation would put pressure on the system a few decades in the future). It would not be until the 2000s that the Republicans, this time with control over both the White House and Congress, would revive the idea of privatizing Social Security, and again they would fail decisively.

Aid to Families with Dependent Children

Reagan, however, had some success in chopping less popular social welfare programs. Since the 1950s, conservatives had criticized Aid to Families with Dependent Children (AFDC), the program commonly known as welfare, which mostly supported impoverished single mothers and their children. They argued that AFDC created a culture of "dependency," discouraging poor people from engaging in paid labor outside the home. Many blamed welfare for unleashing a culture of immorality that broke down families and destroyed the work ethic. The program's supporters countered that it had played a role in reducing overall poverty rates, which had fallen by half between 1959 and 1979. In fact, poverty rates remained below 10 percent through the economically troubled 1970s.[12]

There was no evidence of a causal relationship between welfare, joblessness, and family structure. Beginning in the early 1970s, AFDC payments steadily declined, and they would continue to fall in value for twenty-five years. Unlike Social Security, AFDC was not indexed to inflation. As a result, between 1973 and 1989, the value of an average monthly welfare check fell by 40 percent. Welfare payments seldom proved sufficient to support a family. By the 1980s, the vast majority of welfare recipients engaged in paid labor, often off the books, to make ends meet. Welfare also had little impact on family structure. It was true that fewer and fewer Americans married; those who did saw marriages dissolve into divorce more frequently; and a steadily growing percentage of children were born to single women. But these patterns held across all socioeconomic groups, whether or not they received welfare checks.

Many Americans saw welfare in racial terms. Though the majority of AFDC recipients throughout the period were white, media accounts of poverty focused on African Americans, in part because they were concentrated in cities, as were most news outlets. Surveys showed that many whites believed that blacks were ungrateful, happier to take "handouts" than to work hard, and inherently lazy. Black welfare mothers, the argument went, lived extravagant lives on the proceeds of their AFDC checks, while hardworking white Americans barely made ends meet.

Reagan offered his own version of the story, featuring a fictitious "welfare queen." "There is a woman in Chicago," he proclaimed during his 1976 campaign. "She has 80 names, 30 addresses, 12 Social Security cards, and is collecting veterans' benefits on four non-existing deceased husbands." Reagan's story brought audiences to their feet, but it was a fabrication, woven together from a country music song and news reports about a Chicago woman in the early 1970s who had used four aliases and earned about $8,000 fraudulently.[13]

The Limits of Welfare Reform

For all his antiwelfare rhetoric, Reagan found it difficult to cut many of the programs on his list. Medicare and Medicaid were popular among hospital administrators and doctors because they enabled poor and elderly patients to pay their bills. Food stamps, another War on Poverty initiative, had wide bipartisan support. Big-city Democrats knew that many of their working-class and poor constituents benefited from the program. Senators from agricultural states, many of whom were Republicans, supported food stamps because their use expanded the market for produce and meat.

To many Reagan critics, cutting support to the poor was heartless. When the Department of Agriculture issued a directive in the fall of 1981 that ketchup could be considered a vegetable—a response to Carter and Reagan administration cuts to the National School Lunch Act, a popular but costly Truman-era program that provided subsidies to schools to feed needy students—critics mocked the president. Welfare activists, many of them veterans of the civil rights and feminist movements of the 1960s, staged hunger strikes and marched on welfare offices, fighting against what they called Reagan's "war on the poor." For the moment, they had enough congressional allies to hold back Reagan's proposed cuts. Reagan did not eviscerate aid to the poor, but his antiwelfare rhetoric played a key role in further delegitimizing already unpopular welfare programs.

By the mid-1980s, conservative think tanks, encouraged by Reagan's policies, began to draft welfare reform programs that called for mandatory work requirements for AFDC recipients, time limits on welfare payments, and further funding cuts. In one of the most important—but largely unnoticed—social policy experiments of the 1980s, the Reagan administration issued waivers that allowed states to modify welfare laws and institute work requirements. Several states with Republican governors, most notably Pennsylvania, instituted punitive new welfare laws. Those experiments would lay the groundwork for nationwide welfare reform efforts in the 1990s.

Jobs and Urban Policy

The administration had only limited success in cutting welfare, but Reagan's budgetary ax fell on programs that helped poor people find work. The Comprehensive Employment and Training Act (CETA), signed by Nixon in 1973 and expanded by Carter, had provided job training for the unemployed, ex-convicts, and impoverished youth. The Reagan administration replaced CETA in 1982 with the underfunded Job Training Partnership Act, which provided incentives to private employers to train workers. All together, the administration cut federal labor market programs drastically, from $15.6 billion in 1980 to only $5 billion in 1985. If poor people were to escape welfare, they would have to fend for themselves.

But the administration did not do much to improve the fortunes of low-wage workers. In June 1981, Reagan and Congress set the minimum wage at $3.35 per hour. It would not increase again until April 1990. During that period, the value of the minimum wage fell by 44 percent. Workers in the economy's most rapidly growing sectors, including unskilled service work and retail employment, often had to take more than one job to make ends meet. Working-class families were particularly hard hit. By the end of the 1980s, a full-time minimum wage job was insufficient to lift a family of four out of poverty. For employers like Wal-Mart, the minimum wage was a boon. It allowed them to keep prices low and profits high.

Urban Spending

The conservative administration also cut urban spending. Many big cities were losing population, and with it congressional seats and clout in Washington. By 1980 a plurality of Americans lived in suburbs. And it was there that Reagan and the Republicans had made some of their biggest electoral gains. Urban spending, in their view, was a zero-sum game: unworthy urban residents benefited while hardworking suburbanites paid the bill. Federal urban spending fell from 12 percent of the budget in 1980 to only 3 percent in 1990. But those spending cuts came at a time when many urban problems were worsening. Urban infrastructure was crumbling. One of the most unsettling problems was the sharp increase in homelessness, the result of inadequate housing, the unstable economy, cuts in welfare spending (especially for single people), and the deinstitutionalization of the mentally ill. By best estimates, 500,000 to 600,000 people were without homes in 1987. Many blamed Reagan administration policies, but the president deflected criticism by arguing that "people who are sleeping on the grates . . . the homeless . . . are homeless, you might say, by choice."[14]

Reagan and Labor

One of the biggest economic shifts in the last quarter of the twentieth century was the disappearance of well-paying jobs—particularly union jobs with relatively good wages and benefits. Nearly as many union members had voted for Reagan as for Carter in 1980. Reagan was also the only president who had been a union member. From 1947 to 1952, and again in 1959–60, he had been president of the Screen Actors Guild, which negotiated wages, a generous pension plan, and health care benefits for its members.

But Reagan forever altered the trade union movement during his first year in office. In August 1981 the Professional Air Traffic Controllers Organization (PATCO), a union that had endorsed Reagan, voted to strike. Reagan threatened to fire PATCO members who did not return to their jobs within forty-eight hours. The strike was illegal, and Reagan used law and order rhetoric to call them back. "What lesser action can there be?" he responded when a journalist asked why he had taken such a strong position. "The law is very explicit. They are violating the law."[15] Nearly eleven thousand remained off the job and, much to their surprise, Reagan followed through. He fired them and called in military personnel to oversee the air traffic system. Conservatives hailed Reagan for showing his mettle and for striking a blow against organized labor.

Organized labor had been gradually declining since the 1950s, but Reagan's response to PATCO emboldened employers to stand up to striking workers. Between the end of World War II and 1980, there had been only three years with fewer than two hundred major strikes. Between 1981 and 2014, only two years (1981 and 1982) had more than one hundred strikes. In Reagan's last year in office, there were only forty.[16] Union membership declined steeply, from about a quarter to a sixth of the workforce. The private sector was hardest hit: in 1990 only about 8 percent of its workers were unionized.

One of the beneficiaries of the PATCO strike was Wal-Mart. Sam Walton's first wave of expansion had largely been in nonunion states in the South and lower Midwest. When workers organized to demand better pay, the firm fiercely resisted. In early 1982, when warehouse workers at the company's Searcy, Arkansas, facility petitioned for a union election, Sam Walton made a personal visit. One warehouse worker pointed out that the firm paid $1.50 an hour more in a Texas facility. Walton bluntly replied, "I can hire you for less in Arkansas." One worker recalled that Walton intimidated them. "He told us that if the union got in, the warehouse would be closed." The Searcy workers decided to keep their jobs and voted down the union. PATCO had taught them a harsh lesson: if they as much as supported a union, their livelihoods were in jeopardy.[17]

Sam Walton began to expand his retail empire well outside its base in the South and in the border states. Between 1980 and 1992, the chain added more than sixteen hundred stores, many in places like Pittsburg, California, that had once been hotbeds of union organizing. During the Truman and Eisenhower years, Pittsburg's steelworkers, chemical industry workers, and dockworkers, most of them men, had been among the best paid in the country. In 1991, when Wal-Mart opened there, workers like Betty Dukes, mostly women, had no one to bargain for better wages or to protect them from discriminatory employers. They were left to their own devices. They started at the minimum wage—only $4.25 per hour that year. They worked irregular hours, did not get overtime pay, had little vacation time, and received no health benefits. Many Wal-Mart workers were so poor that they qualified for food stamps.

RELIGIOUS REVIVALS

Ronald Reagan always put economic issues first. But over the course of his administration, he gave voice to the concerns of some of his staunchest supporters, members of the burgeoning religious right. Reagan was not particularly devout. He had come of age in Hollywood, a place that many conservative Christians saw as the fount of immorality. He had divorced and remarried and was never an attentive father. As governor of California, he had signed into law one of the most liberal abortion laws in the country.

But Reagan and his advisers were attuned to major changes in American religious practices and affiliations during the 1960s and 1970s. Mainstream Protestant denominations saw their membership drop, while evangelical churches exploded. Between 1970 and 1985, the Southern Baptists saw a membership increase of 23 percent. The Assemblies of God, a Pentecostal denomination whose members spoke in tongues, grew by 300 percent in the same period. By 1980 about 20 million viewers regularly tuned in to programs such as Jim and Tammy Faye Bakker's *PTL Club*, Pat Robertson's *700 Club*, and Jerry Falwell's *Old Time Gospel Hour*. In the 1980s more than 110,000 of America's estimated 400,000 churches were evangelical or fundamentalist.[18] "It was a wonderful time for Christianity," remembered Jan Lindsey, who evangelized on college campuses.[19]

Evangelical religion thrived in part because it responded to frustrations and uncertainties in the United States and the world. Jan Lindsey and her husband Hal discovered that their audiences responded with enthusiasm to the prophetic message that the world was entering its final days. Drawing parallels between apocalyptic biblical prophecies and current events, Hal Lindsey's 1970 book, *The Late Great Planet Earth*, sold 28 million copies within two decades. The calamities of global wars, the clash between the United States and the Soviets, and especially conflicts in the Middle East were all portents of the End Times, the moment when earth would be ruled by the Antichrist, Jesus would return, and the true believers would be raptured, leaving the troubled earth and joining the Lord. Lindsay's books were popular because they gave meaning to the incomprehensible.

The Religious Right

Those who opted to "choose Jesus Christ as their personal Lord and Savior" also began to make the personal political, denouncing liberalism, homosexuality, abortion, crime, and pornography, and blaming liberal politicians for enabling a culture of permissiveness. Many ministers wove political messages into their sermons: those who were saved by Jesus had a responsibility to save society from the temptations of sexual liberation and the collapse of the family.

It was but a small step from calls of personal responsibility and respect for authority to denunciations of "secular humanism," a term popularized by another best-selling evangelical author, Francis Schaeffer. Over the course of the 1970s and 1980s, many on the religious right began to step up their political involvement. Their rhetoric reprised themes from the postwar years—the dangers of godless Communism, juvenile delinquency, and homosexuality. But these themes took on a new urgency in the shadow of the struggle for civil rights, the rise of the counterculture, the feminist insurgency, and sexual liberation movements.

The new phase in the politicization of conservative churchgoers dated to court challenges to religiously affiliated segregated academies in the 1970s. In *Green v. Connally* (1971), the Supreme Court ruled that religious institutions that discriminated on racial grounds could not claim tax-exempt status under the Internal Revenue Code. For much of the 1970s, the ruling was only loosely enforced, leading to a proliferation of all-white Christian schools in the South. By the mid-1970s, however, civil rights groups demanded that the IRS enforce *Green*. When the IRS revoked the tax-exempt status of Bob Jones University, a fundamentalist institution in South Carolina that forbade racial mixing, conservative critics howled that the government was infringing on religious freedom. In 1978 the IRS tightened its rules and began to hold hearings to determine whether segregated Christian academies should be eligible for tax exemption.

Paul Weyrich, a conservative political activist, had been trying to mobilize evangelicals since 1964 with limited success. Weyrich, a Catholic, began his career as a congressional staffer, supported Goldwater, and worked closely with anti–New Deal business groups. In 1974, joining with Colorado brewing magnate Joseph Coors, Weyrich founded the Heritage Foundation, a conservative think tank. Heritage promoted free enterprise and rallied against the minimum wage, welfare programs, and labor unions. Still, it was difficult to rouse working- and middle-class Americans around a pro-business agenda. Weyrich had a hunch that he could do better by stirring up popular discontent around religious and cultural concerns.

At first, mobilizing evangelical Christians was an uphill battle. "I utterly failed," he recalled of his early efforts to create a conservative Christian political movement. But much to his surprise, the new IRS rules sparked a mass mobilization. "What changed their mind," recalled Weyrich, was "Jimmy Carter's intervention against the Christian schools, trying to deny them tax exemption on the basis of so-called de facto segregation."[20]

Religious and racial resentment proved a potent combination. Ministers denounced the IRS for enforcing "racial quotas." They argued that the IRS directive was proof that secularists were using government power to silence religious expression. In 1979, Weyrich met with the televangelist Jerry Falwell and launched the Moral Majority, which raised nearly $100 million in its first two years and claimed to have registered nearly ten million conservative voters. "If you would like to know where I am politically," stated Falwell, "I am to the right of wherever you are. I thought Goldwater was too liberal."[21]

The Reagan administration rewarded the Moral Majority. In 1982 it intervened in the Bob Jones University controversy, reversing the IRS decision to deny the school tax-exempt status. The Bob Jones battle ended up in the Supreme Court, which issued an 8–1 decision upholding the IRS. Bob Jones would not get a tax exemption. The ruling was a blow to Reagan, who faced charges that his administration endorsed racism.

Reagan also appointed prominent religious conservatives to his administration. James Watt, the secretary of the interior, used his bully pulpit to promote Christian ideas. In an address to Falwell's Liberty University, Watt called for a "Christian revolution."[22] But he was more concerned with curbing environmental regulations than with spreading the Gospel. Surgeon General C. Everett Koop, appointed in 1982, had joined the crusade against "secular humanism" and was a staunch opponent of abortion. In 1984 the conservative preacher James Robison opened the Republican convention, and Falwell called Reagan and his administration "God's instruments in rebuilding America."[23] But in practice, Reagan often disappointed the religious right.

Abortion Politics

Evangelicals stepped up their mobilization against abortion in the late 1970s and 1980s, moving it to the center of the conservative agenda. The antiabortion movement demanded the recognition of the personhood of the fetus. It denounced feminists and their emphasis on women's reproductive freedom. It depicted abortion as a selfish choice. And it called for a reassertion of traditional male authority.

Neither side in the debate captured the complicated attitudes of most Americans toward reproduction and abortion. Most Americans, including religious believers, were ambivalent about abortion, particularly late in pregnancy. They viewed it as a tragedy, best avoided but sometimes unavoidable. Public opinion surveys consistently showed that a majority of Americans believed that the decision to terminate a pregnancy should be a private choice, decided by a woman in consultation with a counselor, minister, or family member. In 1981 and 1982, polls showed that only about one-third of Americans wanted to ban abortion.[24] But abortion politics was intensely polarized. Both sides could point to one striking pattern: the rate of abortions in the United States had increased steadily—rising from about 20 per 1,000 in 1973 to a peak of 29 per 1,000 in 1980.[25] For religious opponents of abortion, this was incontrovertible evidence of moral decay. For supporters, it was a proof that legalized abortion met a demand. To turn back abortion, the pro-life movement would turn to the courts.

AIDS

Religious politics also shaped the Reagan administration's response to one of the gravest health crises of the twentieth century. In 1981 doctors began noticing that young men, many of them gay, appeared with unexplained symptoms, among them virulent pneumonia and a rare cancer called Kaposi's sarcoma. Within a few years, the disease, named acquired immunodeficiency syndrome (AIDS), would go from a medical oddity to an epidemic. One of its early victims was Stuart Garcia, a brilliant, charismatic Texan who entered Columbia University the fall that Reagan was elected. President of Columbia's student government, Stuart was, in the words of a classmate, "one of those people who seemed destined to do something important."[26] He also had a lively life off campus, joining gay dance parties at downtown nightclubs. But his health took a turn for the worse the year after he graduated. In 1985 he began coughing violently and was hospitalized, the first of many times. Less than a year later, after struggling with 106-degree fevers and excruciating pain, he died. He was twenty-three.[27]

Stuart was one of 11,932 Americans to die of AIDS in 1986. But federal support for AIDS research remained a low priority. In 1983 the administration rebuffed health officials from eleven cities who asked for support to manage the epidemic. The federal Public Health Service, whose director pledged that year to make AIDS a priority, suffered budget cuts for the next few years. In September 1985 the president mentioned AIDS publicly for the first time but again trimmed funds for AIDS research. In the spring of 1986, a few months before Stuart's death, Reagan asked Surgeon General Koop to issue a report on the disease. Koop's report called for abstinence, monogamy, and condom use. The last angered some religious conservatives. Secretary of Education William Bennett denounced "condom-mania" as "a species of self-delusion."[28]

AIDS remained near the bottom of the list of presidential priorities. Under pressure, the president created a committee to investigate AIDS in 1987, including several prominent conservative religious leaders. But his decision to name one gay doctor to the panel angered many of his conservative allies. The administration, argued Senator Gordon Humphrey (R-NH), "should strive at all costs to avoid sending the message to society—especially to impressionable youth—that homosexuality is simply an alternative lifestyle."[29]

In the meantime AIDS activists stepped up pressure on the president. In October 1987 a half million protesters marched in New York, convened by a new organization, the AIDS Coalition to Unleash Power (ACT UP). Over the next several years, AIDS activists would pressure Congress to substantially increase AIDS funding. In the next decade, they would embark on a massive AIDS education effort and would successfully advocate the loosening of pharmaceutical regulations to allow for early testing of promising medications on AIDS patients.

Turning the Courts Rightward

Reagan gave only symbolic support to religious conservatives' drive for a constitutional amendment to outlaw abortion. But the administration worked through the courts to push a conservative agenda that encompassed abortion and much more. That began with his court appointments. In 1981 he nominated the first woman justice to the Supreme Court, Sandra Day O'Connor. Many conservative advocates worried: although she was a favorite of Barry Goldwater, her positions on abortion and women's rights were suspect. Still, she won Senate approval with overwhelming bipartisan support. She would be one of Reagan's few moderate appointees. In the next few years, the Department of Justice implemented an unprecedented process to screen potential judges for their views on regulation, abortion, affirmative action, and criminal procedure. By 1989, Reagan had named 344 of 714 federal district and appeals court judges. His appointees were the youngest of any twentieth-century president, the average just under fifty years old. They were almost uniformly to the right of federal judges named by Reagan's predecessors.[30]

In the late 1970s and 1980s, many states and localities, under pressure from religious groups, passed laws to discourage abortions. Reagan directed the Department of Justice to support these laws. But the administration's intervention did not tip the scales. In *Akron v. Akron Center for Reproductive Health* (1983), the Supreme Court struck down a city ordinance that had required doctors to inform women that the fetus "is a human life from the moment of conception" and set a twenty-four-hour waiting period for women who planned to have an abortion.

The administration continued to challenge *Roe v. Wade*. In 1986, Solicitor General Kenneth Starr argued *Thornburgh v. American College of Obstetricians and Gynecologists* (1986), defending a Pennsylvania law that required doctors to inform women that abortion was risky, to file detailed reports, and to favor live births over abortion if the fetus was at a late stage of development. The court was bitterly divided. In a 5–4 decision, it struck down the restrictions. "The states are not free, under the guise of protecting maternal health or potential life, to intimidate women into continuing pregnancies," wrote Justice Harry Blackmun for the majority. In their dissent, Justices William Rehnquist and Byron White denounced *Roe v. Wade* as "fundamentally misguided." Advocates of reproductive freedom celebrated the narrow victory but worried that if the Court shifted rightward, *Roe* might be overturned.

Another 1986 decision, *Bowers v. Hardwick*, this one involving gay sex, cheered conservatives. The case involved two Georgia men who were arrested for engaging in consensual oral sex. The case gave the court another opportunity to consider the "right to privacy," which the court had found and protected in its contraception and abortion cases. Did that right extend to homosexuality? In a strongly worded majority opinion, the court ruled no. Justice Byron White, writing for the majority, argued that the Constitution did not protect "a fundamental right to engage in homosexual sodomy." Giving legal recognition to gay sex, concurred Chief Justice Warren Burger, would "cast aside millennia of moral teaching."[31]

Supreme Court Politics

In the wake of these contentious cases, Reagan got the opportunity to reshape the Supreme Court. Each nomination was more contested than the one before. In 1986 he elevated William Rehnquist, the court's most conservative member, to the position of chief justice. To fill Rehnquist's seat, Reagan nominated a crusading right-wing jurist, Antonin Scalia, who had made his name as a proponent of "textualism"—the notion that judicial interpretations should rely on a narrow reading of original legislative texts. Both won Senate approval but with significant Democratic defections.

A year after Scalia joined the high court, Reagan nominated Robert Bork to fill another vacancy. Bork, a controversial law professor and former solicitor general in the Nixon administration, argued that the Supreme Court had wrongly decided the landmark *Brown v. Board of Education* case because it relied on social science. He had opposed the Civil Rights Act of 1964. And he criticized *Roe v. Wade* for relying on a "right to privacy" that was not enumerated in the Constitution.

In the past, most Supreme Court nomination hearings had been brief and uncontroversial. Bork's was not. Feminists, civil rights leaders, and liberal law professors lined up to testify against him. Senator Edward Kennedy, brother of the slain president, offered one of the harshest critiques. "Robert Bork's America is a land in which women would be forced into back-alley abortions, blacks would sit at segregated lunch counters, rogue police could break down citizens' doors in midnight raids, children could not be taught about evolution."[32] Bork was feisty and often arrogant during his confirmation hearings. That hurt him. After weeks of bitter public debate, the Senate rejected his nomination, 58–42. Reagan then successfully nominated a soft-spoken conservative, Anthony Kennedy, to fill the seat, and since he lacked Bork's baggage, the Senate quickly confirmed him. Later federal judicial nominees learned from Bork's experience. Fearful that they would be "Borked," they dodged controversy, refusing to disclose their positions on hot-button issues like abortion and affirmative action.

"PEACE THROUGH STRENGTH"

For Reagan, no issue was as pressing as the battle against Communism. He had long argued that the United States would prevail in the Cold War only by flexing its military might. In the 1950s he had criticized the policy of containment. In the 1960s he supported Barry Goldwater's position that the United States should consider using nuclear weapons in Vietnam. In the 1970s he denounced Nixon's opening to China and détente with the Soviet Union. Arms reduction treaties, he contended, appeased the Soviets and jeopardized American security. During his first term, he drew his core foreign policy advisers from the most prominent critics of détente. Many—like Alexander Haig, the secretary of state, William Casey, the CIA director, and Caspar Weinberger, the secretary of defense—were proponents of "peace through strength," advocating militarization rather than negotiation with the Soviets.

Reagan had blamed his predecessors for a lack of resolve in confronting America's enemies abroad. A case in point was the Iranian hostage crisis, which entered its 444th day when Reagan was inaugurated on January 20, 1981. Just after he was sworn in, he learned that the Iranian government had released the American hostages. The resolution to the crisis was the result of Carter's behind-the-scenes diplomacy, but the timing benefited Reagan. It gave him a clean slate on his first day in office.

The Defense Buildup

Reagan began by significantly increasing defense spending, one of the priorities in his first budget. It rose from 5.3 to 6.4 percent of the gross domestic product between 1981 and 1989. The administration channeled funds into constructing expensive new bombers, including research for a high-tech "stealth" bomber that would evade conventional radar. Reagan also authorized the deployment of 572 new intermediate-range nuclear missiles in Western Europe, within easy striking distance of the Soviet Union.

Reagan's nuclear policy was particularly unpopular in Europe, where mass protests against Euromissiles erupted in 1982. On the home front, Americans were also concerned about the arms race. By the summer of 1982, nearly two-thirds of Americans supported a "nuclear freeze," calling for both superpowers to halt the construction and deployment of new weapons. In July one million Americans, many members of liberal religious organizations, marched in New York City in support of a freeze, the largest demonstration in American history.

In early 1983 the Reagan administration's relations with the Soviets were icier than ever, and the president escalated the war of words. He continued to assert that the USSR was on the brink of military supremacy, despite mounting evidence that the Soviet regime was weak and unpopular, its military technologies inferior, and its economy in crisis. In a speech before the National Association of Evangelicals in March, Reagan spoke of "sin and evil in the world" and pointed to the Soviet Union as an "evil empire." He denounced the nuclear freeze as "a very dangerous fraud."[33]

That same month, Reagan announced the Strategic Defense Initiative (SDI), calling for the creation of a space "shield" of X-rays and lasers to protect the United States from incoming nuclear missiles. He rejected the long-standing American doctrine of "deterrence of aggression through the prospect of retaliation." In the context of the "evil empire" speech, some commentators feared that SDI would be cover for the United States to build a first-strike capability against the Soviet Union. Few scientists believed that Reagan's program was feasible. Critics nicknamed SDI "Star Wars," suggesting that it was no more real than science fiction. Budget hawks argued that SDI would be an expensive boondoggle, costing as much as a trillion dollars. But Reagan did not let it go. The program would survive until the early 1990s, when the Bush administration and Congress dramatically cut funding for the program to balance the federal budget. The Clinton administration would dismantle it in 1993.

One of the unintended consequences of the arms buildup was that it stimulated a boom in research and development and military technology. Suburban Boston, Silicon Valley, and Los Angeles were flush with federal dollars, pulling them out of the economic slump sooner than most of the rest of the country. Federal spending also launched a high-tech economy. Universities introduced student-accessible computer centers in the early 1980s, the personal computer went from a novelty item to a mass-produced necessity in less than ten years, and microchips transformed everyday electronics. The number of jobs for electrical engineers and computer scientists skyrocketed. By the early 1990s, local area networks and the Internet began connecting computers into what would be later named the World Wide Web.

The rise and success of American high-tech industries did not result from tax cuts and deregulation. In fact, no American industries relied more on government spending than did computing, electrical engineering, and communications equipment. All had emerged as the result of Cold War–era federal spending on science and research, much of it defense-related. Federal research funding for Cold War–related research and development programs took off in the 1980s, after stagnating during the fiscally troubled Nixon and Carter years. Between 1982 and 1988, federal research and development spending nearly doubled. By the decade's end, 40 percent of all research and development in the computing industry was federally funded; nearly half of communications technology research—including the systems that were the basis of the Internet—came from the federal government. Government programs also bankrolled university laboratories, computer science, and electrical engineering. In 1985 alone, computer science programs received 83 percent of their funds from the federal government.[34] Members of Congress jostled for federal appropriations to their districts, hoping to become the "next Silicon Valley," the computing industry's hub outside San Francisco.[35] Those efforts paid off in the 1980s, when the influx of government spending to contractors and universities fueled the rise of the Route 128 corridor outside Boston, the Research Triangle in North Carolina, and the semiconductor center of Austin, Texas.

AMERICA IN THE WORLD

While the administration pushed to win the arms race, it put more resources into winning the Cold War around the world. The United States aggressively intervened in civil wars in the Middle East and Latin America. The administration hoped to overcome the "Vietnam syndrome" but faced widespread public and congressional skepticism about its counterinsurgency operations. To end-run around public opinion, the administration stepped up covert operations, with disastrous consequences.

The Volatile Middle East

Politics in the Middle East were especially volatile in the 1980s. The Reagan administration's foreign policy there did not help. In Afghanistan, Shi'ite Muslims, inspired by the Iranian revolution, rose against the Soviet-backed Communist regime in 1979, resisting efforts to secularize the country. The USSR responded by sending troops, embarking on what would be a ten-year war. About 25,000 Soviet troops died, most in brutal ground combat. Four hundred thousand Afghans died in Soviet airstrikes. Many considered the Afghan war to be the Soviet equivalent of Vietnam—costly, bloody, and unwinnable.

When the war broke out, the Carter administration had authorized modest CIA support for the anti-Soviet uprising, but the Reagan administration stepped up the effort. CIA operatives secretly provided weaponry to the mujahideen, a force controlled by Afghan warlords. The CIA also collaborated closely with Islamic groups in neighboring Pakistan, where the rebels established bases. While Reagan viewed the mujahideen as "freedom fighters," his administration ended up empowering Islamic radicals in both Pakistan and Afghanistan who would later turn against the United States, embroiling the country in its own long, inconclusive war in Afghanistan a little more than two decades after the Soviets launched theirs.

Nearby, the United States found itself entangled in the Iran-Iraq war, a brutal eight-year conflict that began in 1980 and ended in a stalemate, with over 400,000 dead. The Reagan administration allied itself with Iraq and its autocratic leader, Saddam Hussein. In 1982 the State Department removed Iraq from its list of terrorist nations and encouraged a robust market exchanging American arms for Iraqi oil. Reagan administration officials, concerned that the Iranian theocracy would get access to Iraq's vast oilfields, overlooked Hussein's use of illegal chemical weapons and his brutal repression of dissent. A 1983 memo captured America's view that "any major reversal of Iraq's fortunes" would be "a strategic loss for the West."[36] Reagan administration officials hoped, in vain, that with American aid, the Hussein regime would become less repressive.

Reagan faced equally daunting challenges in Lebanon. Since gaining its independence from France in 1943, the country had struggled to hold together a government that included its rivalrous Muslim minority, divided between Sunnis and Shi'ites, its substantial Christian population, and its minority Druze. In the 1970s and early 1980s, it was torn by civil war. Skirmishes between bordering Israel and Syria added to the tension, as did the presence of Palestinian Liberation Organization (PLO) forces near the Lebanese-Israeli border and in Beirut. In June 1982 the United States supported Israeli attacks on the PLO in Lebanon. In August, Reagan made the momentous decision to send U.S. Marines there as part of a peacekeeping force: "In no case will our troops stay longer than 30 days."[37] But they stayed longer, and the situation worsened. In October 1983 a suicide bomber attacked a U.S. barracks at the Beirut airport, killing 241 Americans. The United States did not retaliate. For three and a half months afterward, Reagan pledged to keep marines in Lebanon as long as they were needed. If American troops withdrew, he argued in early February, "we'll be sending one signal to terrorists everywhere: They can gain by waging war against innocent people."[38] But faced with congressional opposition and public skepticism, Reagan backtracked, and on February 7, 1984, the United States pulled out of Lebanon.

"Rollback" in Latin America and the Caribbean

The Reagan administration was particularly concerned with what it considered to be Soviet "expansionism" in Latin America and the Caribbean. Its primary targets were leftists in El Salvador and Nicaragua. El Salvador was embroiled in a bloody civil war, led by revolutionaries who challenged its corrupt military leadership and demanded reforms to redistribute agricultural land to the impoverished peasantry. El Salvador's authoritarian government, which Reagan supported, brutally silenced dissent. In 1980, El Salvadoran death squads had murdered the popular Roman Catholic archbishop Oscar Romero, a critic of the regime, and had raped and murdered four American-born nuns who worked with the country's impoverished peasants.

Throughout the 1980s, the United States provided funding and training for El Salvadoran counterinsurgency forces, often with bloody results. In December 1981, El Salvadoran troops massacred more than eight hundred people in El Mozote, executing men and boys and gang-raping women and girls before killing them and burning the village. The El Salvadoran government denied its involvement, and the Reagan administration maintained, despite abundant evidence to the contrary, that reports of the massacre were "not credible." Reagan administration officials saw El Salvador as an opportunity to avoid the "mistakes" made in Vietnam. "El Salvador represents an experiment," a military report stated, "an attempt to reverse the record of American failure in waging small wars, an effort to defeat an insurgency by providing training and material support without committing American troops to combat."[39]

Nicaragua

The administration was most concerned with Nicaragua where, in 1979, a left-wing insurgency, the Sandinistas (named for the early twentieth-century Nicaraguan revolutionary Augusto Sandino) had overthrown dictator Anastasio Somoza, whose family had ruled the country for over six decades. The Sandinistas had military and economic ties with Cuba but also deep support in the Catholic Church, particularly among proponents of liberation theology, a movement led by priests and nuns who argued that the church needed to side with the poor against exploitative landowners and autocratic governments.

In November 1981, Reagan authorized $19 million to train and arm the Nicaraguan Contras, the counterrevolutionary opponents of the new Sandinista government. Aid to the Contras, however, was unpopular, especially among Americans who feared that the small Latin American country might become another Vietnam. In December 1982, Congress approved the Boland Amendment (named for the Massachusetts congressman who sponsored it), which forbade the use of U.S. defense funds to overthrow the Nicaraguan government.

The Reagan administration exploited a loophole in the Boland Amendment: it did not forbid ongoing funding to CIA covert operations in Nicaragua. Those activities came to light in March 1983, when a Soviet ship struck a mine placed in a Nicaraguan harbor as part of a CIA plan that Reagan had authorized. In April the president attempted to rally Congress and the public to support military and economic aid to what he called Latin America's "freedom fighters." "El Salvador is nearer to Texas than Texas is to Massachusetts," argued Reagan. "Nicaragua is just as close to Miami, San Antonio, San Diego, and Tucson as those cities are to Washington."[40] The president attempted to calm fears that—as his critics put it, "El Salvador is Spanish for

Vietnam." He told "those who invoke the memory of Vietnam, there is no thought of sending American combat troops to Central America."[41]

Grenada

Still, Reagan hoped to overcome the "Vietnam syndrome," and he found an opportunity to do so in Grenada, a former British colony of about 100,000 residents in the Caribbean. In 1979 a Marxist regime had taken charge. Reagan warned about ties between Grenada, Cuba, and the Soviet Union and asserted that Grenada's construction of a nine-thousand-foot runway would allow Soviet bombers easy access to the western hemisphere. On October 25, 1983, just after a military coup destabilized the Grenadine government, Reagan authorized Operation Urgent Fury, dispatching about eight thousand military personnel to the island. Several dozen died in the brief war, including sixteen Americans. It was America's first international invasion since Vietnam, and it was popular at home. Nearly two-thirds of Americans supported Reagan's decision.

The Iran-Contra Crisis

With the memory of Vietnam still vivid, Congress and the public remained unwilling to support Reagan's efforts to destabilize Nicaragua. In December 1984, Congress enacted a revised Boland Amendment, forbidding the United States to provide any aid to the Contras. In an end run around the Boland Amendment, the National Security Council (NSC) launched new schemes to support the Contras. NSC head Robert McFarlane negotiated a deal with Saudi Arabia to provide funds to the Contras, about $2 million per month in 1985.

Later that year McFarlane (who resigned from the NSC in December 1985), his successor, retired Admiral John Poindexter, and an NSC aide, Marine Lieutenant Colonel Oliver North, launched an even more elaborate and bizarre plan to fund the Contras. The United States sold arms secretly to Iran, quixotically hoping to empower pro-Western Iranians while prolonging the bloody Iran-Iraq war. As a quid pro quo, the United States asked the Iranian regime to pressure Lebanon to release seven Americans being held hostage by militants there. The plot grew more twisted. The proceeds from the arms-for-hostages deal would be channeled through intermediaries in Israel to cover up the American connection and sent to the Contras.

The scheme began to unravel in October 1986, when a plane delivering arms to the Contras crashed in Nicaragua. Over the next month and a half, investigative journalists began to piece together the story. In mid-November, the president denied that the United States had been behind the Iran-Contra affair, stating that his administration "did not—repeat—did not trade arms or anything else for hostages."[42] But evidence mounted to the contrary. On November 25 the president and his attorney general, Edwin Meese, stunned the nation by reporting that the essence of the story was true, that Poindexter was resigning, and that the White House was setting up a special committee to investigate. In December, Reagan named Lawrence Walsh, a well-respected attorney, as an independent counsel to investigate the case. The House and Senate launched their own investigations. The president's popularity plummeted, although no evidence emerged that he had been aware of the plan.

Between 1987 and 1990, investigations proceeded. Eleven Reagan administration officials were ultimately convicted, but most received light sentences. Poindexter and North had their convictions overturned on an appeal. And the remaining six defendants, including McFarlane and former defense secretary Caspar Weinberger, were pardoned by Reagan's successor, George H. W. Bush in late December 1992, shortly before his term ended.

Gorbachev and Reagan

Between 1985 and 1991, events in Moscow fundamentally altered the direction of the Cold War. The Soviet regime had been dysfunctional for years. Its situation worsened in the early 1980s when the elderly and ill premier, Leonid Brezhnev, died. His successors, part of the Communist Party's entrenched, aging leadership, Yuri Andropov and Konstantin Chernenko, both died in office. Their passing marked a generational shift. In March 1985, Mikhail Gorbachev, only fifty-four, rose to power as secretary general. He vowed to institute reforms to deal with the sclerotic Soviet economy and the inept and unpopular bureaucracy that oversaw it.

Gorbachev inherited the costly Afghan war. He also faced growing insurgences in Eastern Europe, most notably in Poland, where Solidarity, led by labor leader Lech Walesa, had been challenging the Communist regime since the late 1970s. Solidarity drew strong support from the Catholic Church, including Cardinal Karol Wojtyla, who would be named Pope John Paul II in 1978. The Soviet economy could not meet the needs of the nation's population. Its farms were vast but so unproductive that the nation needed to import much of its grain. Its antiquated factories lumbered along with unmotivated workers manning aging machinery. The populace, especially in big cities, suffered crippling shortages of everything from green vegetables to shoes.

Gorbachev instituted a series of long-overdue reforms, intended to shore up the crumbling Soviet regime. He began by announcing a policy of *glasnost* or openness. His regime lifted strict censorship rules, allowing newspapers to report on Russia's dire social and economic problems. Soviet dissidents, who had long faced persecution, exile, or harsh sentences in work camps, suddenly found public outlets for their essays. At the same time, Gorbachev took modest steps toward democratization, allowing for contested elections in the Soviet Union's far-flung ethnic republics, unwittingly unleashing currents of nationalism.

For all Reagan's skepticism about the Soviet Union, he was more hopeful than many of his advisers about Gorbachev. In November 1985 the two leaders met in Geneva. The discussion was inconclusive, but both leaders came away from the meeting impressed with each other. They scheduled a second summit, to take place in Reykjavik, Iceland, the following October.

At that meeting, both sides discussed arms reduction proposals. Reagan started from a position of strength. He put on the table a several-year-old proposal known as the "zero option," which previous Soviet leaders had rejected. Under the zero option, the United States would not station intermediate-range nuclear missiles in Western Europe if the Soviets withdrew theirs from Eastern Europe. To Reagan's surprise, Gorbachev accepted the offer and pushed even further. The Soviet premier proposed that both countries reduce their stronghold of nuclear weapons by 50 percent. Reagan rejoined by proposing that both countries eliminate their strategic nuclear weapons, but only if the United States could maintain an arsenal for self-defense. Gorbachev countered by calling for an elimination of all nuclear weapons by 1996. The two leaders met privately—without their aides—to discuss the plan further, but they hit a wall. Gorbachev demanded that the United States give up its SDI system. Reagan refused. The talks ended in an impasse.

In the meantime, Gorbachev intensified his reforms. He pushed for *perestroika*, a program of economic restructuring that loosened central control over the economy. Gorbachev also allowed for the formation of privately-run businesses. And in a reform unimaginable just a few years earlier, Gorbachev allowed foreign investors to form partnerships with state-controlled firms.

Reagan's position on the Soviet Union was quickly shifting, in part because by 1987 he had replaced most of his hardline advisers (several of whom had resigned during the Iran-Contra scandal) with Nixon- and Ford-era supporters of détente. He remained open to further negotiations with Gorbachev, but he continued to criticize the Soviet Union publicly and offered support to Eastern European dissidents. In June 1987 he stood at the Brandenburg Gate separating East and West Berlin and issued one of his boldest challenges to date: "General Secretary Gorbachev, if you seek peace, if you seek prosperity for the Soviet Union and Eastern Europe, if you seek liberalization: Come here to this gate! Mr. Gorbachev open this gate! Mr. Gorbachev tear down this wall!"[43]

In December, Gorbachev and Reagan met again, this time in Washington. Gorbachev had begun winding down the costly Afghan war, was continuing to push for reforms, and hoped to reach an agreement with the United States, in part to reduce the heavy economic burden of militarization. He agreed to set aside, for the moment, his concerns about Star Wars, in part because the U.S. Congress, dominated by Democrats, had slashed SDI funding. Both sides agreed to substantial reductions of intermediate-range arms. Reagan's popularity soared, although not among right-wing Republicans who believed that he had betrayed his principles. Senator Jesse Helms (R-SC), a longtime Reagan supporter, told reporters, "The President doesn't need to discard the people who brought him to the dance." William F. Buckley, Jr., wrote that Reagan had "disappointed" him.[44]

G. H. W. BUSH AND THE CURRENTS OF REPUBLICANISM

Nineteen eighty-eight seemed at first a hopeful year for the Democrats. Reagan Republicans had never warmed to Vice President George H. W. Bush. The son of a patrician Connecticut senator, Bush had a long résumé when he moved into the White House. His career reflected the shifting currents of Republicanism in the last third of the twentieth century. He had unsuccessfully run for office in 1964, opposing the Civil Rights Act. Two years later he reinvented himself as a moderate, winning election to Congress from suburban Houston.

For the next fourteen years, Bush aligned himself with the Rockefeller-Nixon wing of the GOP, taking moderate positions on civil rights, the legalization of abortion, and the Equal Rights Amendment. Nixon rewarded him for his loyalty by naming him ambassador to the United Nations in 1970. During the 1970s, Bush built a foreign policy portfolio, supporting Nixon's policy of détente, serving as U.S. envoy to China and CIA director under President Ford. In 1980, as the favored candidate of Republican moderates, he lost to Reagan but accepted the vice presidency and served loyally, though he was overshadowed by his boss and distrusted by his party's right wing.

The GOP's conservatives never warmed to Bush, although he tried hard to win their support. To prove his right-wing bona fides during the 1988 primaries, he pledged—much to his later regret—that he would never raise taxes, a position far stronger than Reagan's. He strongly opposed abortion and gun control, repudiating his once moderate views. And he pledged to appoint strict conservatives to the federal bench.

Bush's Democratic opponent, Massachusetts governor Michael Dukakis, was a centrist who ran on the slogan "competence, not ideology," but Republicans branded him as out of the mainstream. Bush portrayed Dukakis as the anti-Reagan, someone who would be weak on national defense and raise taxes. In a controversial ad, with strong racial overtones, the GOP depicted Dukakis as soft on crime, blaming him for furloughing a convicted murderer, Willie Horton, who raped a woman when he was out of jail. Bush crushed Dukakis, winning in forty states.

FROM COLD WAR TO GULF WAR

Given his résumé, George Bush made foreign policy his top priority. But no one could have predicted the extraordinary events that played out in his first year in office. In April and May 1989, thousands of Chinese students gathered in Beijing's immense Tiananmen Square to call for democracy in China. On June 3–4 the Chinese regime brutally put down the protest, killing some three thousand demonstrators, injuring thousands more, and jailing leading dissenters. Bush, familiar with China from his time there in the 1970s and committed to maintaining good relations with the emerging economic superpower, resisted efforts to punish China's leaders. In 1990 he supported and Congress authorized legislation that renewed China's "most favored nation" trading status, ensuring the continued flow of cheap Chinese goods to the United States. American economic interests in China trumped the anti-Communist agenda.

The Revolutions of 1989

Events in Eastern Europe over the next few months were even more surprising. In August 1989, Polish dissidents toppled the Communist regime in Warsaw. Solidarity's Lech Walesa formed the country's first non-Communist government since the end of World War II. Nationalists in the Soviet Baltic republics of Estonia, Latvia, and Lithuania all declared independence from the Soviet Union. On November 9, after days of protests in Berlin, East German students swarmed the Berlin Wall, tearing down the most prominent symbol of the Cold War. Later that month hundreds of thousands of pro-democracy demonstrators gathered in Prague, demanding free elections, which lifted the dissident poet Václav Havel to the presidency. In December, Romanian rebels assassinated Communist leader Nicolae Ceauşescu and his wife. The following year, Communists lost control in Yugoslavia, in the process unleashing intense ethnoreligious conflicts that single-party rule had suppressed. In Moscow, Mikhail Gorbachev struggled against Communist Party regulars who hoped to restore order in the Soviet empire. In 1991 his government fell.

The abrupt end to the Cold War led congressional Democrats to demand a "peace dividend" in the form of dramatic defense budget cuts. But the Bush administration found itself in the position of dealing with the messes that the previous administration had left behind in Latin America and the Middle East. In Panama, General Manuel Noriega had been a useful conduit for aid to the Contras, but he ran a kleptocracy, enriching himself through arms and narcotics trafficking. In December 1989, Bush authorized Operation Just Cause, sending 28,000 American troops to depose Noriega. The invasion was quick: Noriega was captured and brought to the United States, where he was convicted on drug charges.

The Persian Gulf War

The Middle East was even messier. In the aftermath of the Iraq-Iran war, Saddam Hussein attempted to consolidate his power and fill his country's depleted coffers. Like Noriega, Hussein was no longer useful to the United States, but worse, he aggressively threatened American interests. He set his sights on neighboring Kuwait, a small, oil-rich nation on the Persian Gulf. In August 1990, Iraqi troops invaded and conquered the sheikhdom. The combined nations controlled one-fifth of the world's oil supplies.

The United Nations condemned the invasion of Kuwait. With hopes of forcing a nonmilitary solution, the UN also called for a global embargo on trade with Iraq. In August, Bush announced the deployment of 230,000 troops to the region and assembled a thirty-five-nation coalition to push back Iraq. The coalition included several Middle Eastern countries, among them Bahrain, Egypt, Saudi Arabia, Syria, and the United Arab Emirates. Eventually more than a half-million troops would serve in the Persian Gulf.

Iraq was isolated politically and crippled by the embargo, unable to sell its oil internationally. In November the UN pledged swift military action if Iraq did not vacate Kuwait by January 15. But Saddam Hussein was unrelenting. In Baghdad his military captured thousands of Western hostages, threatening to use them as "human shields" in the event of a war.

On the home front, Bush faced skepticism, especially among congressional Democrats. The memory of Vietnam still loomed over national politics. In December the House of Representatives passed a resolution that emphasized the need for the president to get congressional authorization before starting a war. In January 1991 the Bush administration—buoyed by polls showing growing public support for military action against Iraq—decided to go before Congress to ask for approval for "emergency powers." James Baker, the secretary of state, argued that the president would "be making a big mistake to undertake a war as big as this" without putting it to a vote. He also wanted to overcome the "debilitating post-Vietnam hangover."[45]

In early January the House and Senate held an intense two-day debate on a possible war. The House passed a resolution of support by a comfortable 250–183 margin, but the Senate vote was a razor-thin 52–47. Two Republicans opposed the intervention, but ten Democrats supported it. Nine of the ten Democrats were from the Sunbelt, and they included some of the party's moderate and conservative luminaries, among them future vice president Al Gore, future Senate majority leader Harry Reid, and future presidential candidate Joseph Lieberman.

On January 16, Bush authorized Operation Desert Storm, a massive airstrike on Iraq. The Bush administration carefully managed media coverage of the unfolding war. Echoing language from World War II, officials talked of the "liberation" of Kuwait. And remembering Vietnam, they put tight reins on journalists, requiring them to travel with military escorts and preventing them from photographing the wounded and dead. During the Vietnam War, television viewers had seen grisly photographs from the front lines, but during the Persian Gulf War, news broadcasts carried visuals of aerial bombing campaigns, showing the night sky of Baghdad flashing with explosions.

On February 24, American-led ground forces stormed Iraqi troops, who beat a hasty retreat. The ground war lasted a mere hundred hours. Only 148 Americans were killed in combat. By best estimates, about 25,000 Iraqi soldiers died. The swift, decisive victory against Iraq seemed to put the "Vietnam syndrome" finally to rest. Bush's popularity skyrocketed. American flag sales jumped, and Americans placed ribbons on their cars reading "I support our troops." But the administration withdrew troops from Iraq with Saddam Hussein's regime still in power. The Bush administration had decided against a prolonged military engagement in Iraq.

THE LOW-WAGE ECONOMY

The celebrations at the end of the Gulf War could not mask troubles in the domestic economy. Stagflation was a distant memory, but unemployment remained stubbornly high. It reached a postwar peak of 9.7 percent in 1982 and would not fall below 5 percent until the economic boom of 1997–2001. Even more troubling, most Americans suffered stagnating or falling incomes. Between 1979 and 2012, productivity (the amount of output per worker) increased by 74.5 percent in the United States, but the median worker saw only a 5 percent increase in wages. For the lowest fifth of workers, wages actually fell during the period. Gaps in household wealth widened significantly. Nearly all the gain in wealth went to the top 10 percent of the population, largely the consequence of Reagan's tax cuts. Much of that growth benefited the top 1 percent, largely because of the sharp drop in capital gains taxes. Throughout the 1980s, America grew poorer and less equal.

Cutting Costs

As Americans' incomes stagnated and fell, American businesses began to adapt to the needs of thrifty consumers. Discount retailers like Wal-Mart introduced innovative warehousing and marketing practices to cut costs.

Wal-Mart pioneered barcode technology, which allowed the company to keep track of every transaction and to trim overhead. As it grew, Wal-Mart also benefited from its massive purchasing power. To keep prices low, it pitted manufacturers against one another, forcing them to cut production costs or lose its business. The company wrapped itself in the mantle of patriotism but pushed for the deregulation of international trade laws so that it could procure even less expensive goods from overseas manufacturers.

By 1990 more than half the clothes sold in the United States were manufactured abroad, mostly in Latin American and Asian sweatshops where poor pay, long hours, and lax environmental and safety regulations drove down costs. American consumers benefited from the flood of low-priced goods onto the market. After 1978 clothing prices rose more slowly than the consumer price index. Beginning in the early 1990s, the price of women's clothes, the largest segment of the market, dropped sharply.[46]

Those manufacturers that remained in the United States—particularly food producers that operated on a low profit margin—also began a quest for cheap labor and loose regulation. Tyson Foods, which started as a family business in Springdale, Arkansas, and did not go public until 1963, emerged as a giant in chicken processing. A supermarket executive hailed Tyson as "light-years ahead of the industry in taking chicken and giving you another product out of it."[47] In the 1980s, Tyson sold twenty-six varieties of chicken patties and even attempted (unsuccessfully) to market a "giblet burger." Over the next decade, it had bought out dozens of competitors, taking advantage of newly deregulated financial markets.

Like many fast-growing firms in the last two decades of the twentieth century, Tyson combined two strategies. It took advantage of government subsidies to expand, lobbying for tax breaks for its new facilities. In its home state, Arkansas, it found an ally in Governor William Jefferson Clinton. Like many governors competing to attract investment and jobs, Clinton offered Tyson substantial tax incentives to keep its factories in state. In exchange, Tyson executives generously contributed to his campaign coffers. Between 1988 and 1990 alone, the Clinton administration provided Tyson with $7.8 million in tax breaks.

The second strategy was to ruthlessly cut labor costs. Tyson, like Wal-Mart and other major firms, expanded in places with weak unions. It successfully resisted unionization among chicken processors, truckers, and warehouse workers. By the mid-1990s, Tyson (and many other food-processing firms) began recruiting Mexican and Guatemalan immigrants, most of them undocumented, to work in their factories. To keep wages low, they openly violated immigration and labor laws.

IMMIGRATION

Immigration became one of the most contentious political issues in the United States in the late twentieth century. Since the 1965 immigration reform, the number of newcomers to the United States had skyrocketed. In 1970 only 5 percent of the American population consisted of immigrants. But the numbers of newcomers rose steadily: 4.5 million legal immigrants arrived in the 1970s, 7.4 million in the 1980s, and 9.1 million in the 1990s. For all of American history before 1970, the vast majority of immigrants had come from Europe. But by the end of the twentieth century, about half of newcomers were Latin American, most of them from Mexico, and about a quarter originated in Asia, about half from the Philippines, China, and India. Counting undocumented immigrants is difficult, but by best estimates they comprised about 28 percent of all immigrants in the United States in 2000. Most immigrants clustered in a handful of gateway states, especially California, New York, Texas, and Florida.

Debating Immigration

Support and opposition to immigration defied conventional political divisions. Blue-collar workers, including many Democrats, feared that immigrants would take their jobs. Environmental organizations, concerned with population growth, demanded immigration restriction. Cultural conservatives argued that new arrivals were un-American and unassimilable. Many reprised nativist arguments from the Progressive era, arguing that immigrants were disease-ridden and prone to crime, although data showed that they were actually less crime-prone than native-born Americans. And building on the antiwelfare rhetoric of the post-1960s years, anti-immigrant activists argued that newcomers cost taxpayers when they collected food stamps, disability benefits, and unemployment insurance. But economists showed that immigrants paid more in payroll taxes than they drew in public support.

Defenders of immigration celebrated America's growing diversity. Many churches—especially the Roman Catholic Church—took a strong pro-immigrant stand. Latin American immigrants were overwhelmingly Catholic, and they filled the pews when many native-born parishioners were leaving the church. By the end of the century, Hispanics comprised about one-third of all Catholics in the United States. Pentecostals and Mormons, both rapidly growing denominations, also proselytized in immigrant communities. Business leaders, many of them Republican, were among the most vocal advocates of immigration. Big firms like Tyson joined small businesses—builders, restaurateurs, nursing home owners, and landscapers—to oppose immigration restriction. They worried that native-born workers were unwilling to do menial jobs like skinning chickens, busing tables, washing dishes and floors, mowing lawns, and changing bedpans.

Immigration Reform

In 1986, Congress passed the Immigration Reform and Control Act (IRCA). IRCA contained a patchwork of provisions, giving a little to all sides in the immigration debate. It legalized about three million undocumented immigrants who had been in the United States since 1982, required employers to verify the immigration status of their employees, and tightened border controls, greatly expanding the U.S. border patrol. But Reagan and Bush administration officials only sporadically enforced verification laws. "We got here to get government off the backs of hard-working businessmen," noted one Reagan administration official, "not to add to their burdens."[48] Loose enforcement encouraged employers to seek out undocumented immigrants for low-wage labor. It also encouraged a black market in false identification papers. At one Tyson plant in Tennessee, ninety workers used the same California ID as proof of citizenship.[49]

IRCA's emphasis on tightening the border actually encouraged undocumented immigrants to stay in the United States. Most Latin American migration had been circular—many migrants were "birds of passage" who crossed the border when they needed work and returned home when they had earned enough. Tough border restrictions halted that circular migration, because migrants worried that if they returned home, they might not be able to reenter the United States.

The steady growth in undocumented workers, particularly in California, spurred an intense anti-immigrant backlash in the 1990s. In 1994, California voters approved Proposition 187, a law that excluded undocumented immigrants from health care, welfare, and public education.

Although a federal court ruled 187 unconstitutional, it inspired anti-immigrant legislation throughout the country. In 1996, Congress passed a law denying Social Security, disability, unemployment, Medicare, and welfare to immigrants during their first five years in the United States, regardless of their legal status. Many localities began enacting anti-immigrant ordinances, among them English-language-only laws. But the public remained deeply divided on immigration at the turn of the twenty-first century. The Democrats tended to be more open to immigrants, while the Republicans were split between pro-business advocates of immigration reform and cultural conservatives who feared that newcomers would dilute the American national character. The only policy that both parties supported was tightening border controls and reducing the number of undocumented immigrants. The number of immigrants removed from the United States rose sharply in the 1990s, reaching a peak of over 1.8 million people in 2000.

POLITICS AND THE SLUMPING ECONOMY

The legacy of Reaganomics came to haunt Bush in the early 1990s. Having inherited massive deficits and $2.8 trillion in federal debt, Bush faced a choice between two Republican doctrines: to balance the budget or to keep taxes low. He was inclined toward the first but beholden to the second. On the campaign trail, hoping to win over skeptical conservatives, he had impetuously promised: "Read my lips. No new taxes." Bush, however, had to abide by the terms of a 1981 law that required the sequestration of federal funds and a government shutdown beginning in October 1990 if a balanced budget could not be achieved by 1993. Reagan had signed the law when he was infatuated by the Laffer curve. Bush was stuck having to comply. It was mathematically impossible to reduce the deficit without increasing revenues.

Bush's 1990 budget called for various "users' fees," a euphemism for taxes. Conservative critics, led by House minority whip Newt Gingrich, howled. Through the summer and fall of 1990, Bush and the Democratic leadership hammered out a compromise that included spending cuts and a gas tax increase, but Congress refused to enact it. Democrats were happy to weaken Bush in a midterm election year, and the Republicans would not accept the tax increase. In October, with no agreement in sight, the federal government shut down for three days. Finally, in late October, Bush and congressional leaders brokered a deal, modestly increasing taxes on upper-income earners. The budget passed, just a few weeks before the midterms, with a majority of Democrats supporting Bush. Bitter Republicans complained that Bush had sold out the principles of Reaganism and held it against him for years to come.

The deficit was only one of the economic woes facing Bush. Beginning in the fall of 1990, the economy fell into recession. The stock market was volatile, interest rates were creeping upward, and unemployment rose steadily, reaching a peak of 8.2 percent in February 1992. For many Americans, already financially insecure, the recession hit hard.

The economy—and Bush's turnaround on taxes—dominated the 1992 election. Bush fended off a primary challenge from angry right-wing commentator Pat Buchanan, but he faced another threat during the general election. Many Republican voters gravitated toward an independent candidate, the Texas billionaire Ross Perot. A conservative on social policy and an advocate of less regulation and low taxes, Perot hearkened back to the mid-twentieth-century Republicans like Robert Taft in his call for economic protectionism. Bush had just negotiated the North American Free Trade Agreement (NAFTA) with Mexico and Canada, which Perot contended would create a "giant sucking sound" of American jobs lost to Latin America.[50]

Clinton and the Democratic Leadership Council

Bush also met a formidable opponent in the Democratic nominee, William Jefferson Clinton, the Arkansas governor. Clinton was the most prominent member of the Democratic Leadership Council (DLC), a group of insurgent Democrats founded in 1985 who argued that for the Democratic Party to survive, it needed to move rightward on civil rights, foreign policy, and especially economic policy. DLC members argued that liberals had lost touch with the majority of voters, particularly white working- and middle-class men. Their goal was to persuade centrists "to change the party rather than changing parties."[51]

In the late 1980s, the DLC fashioned a "third way" politics, embracing conservative arguments about the need for a robust anti-Communism. They supported aid to the Contras and bucked mainstream Democrats by backing Bush during the Gulf War. DLC members also echoed the Republican critique of welfare as corrosive of the work ethic. They distanced themselves from affirmative action and worried that white voters saw the party as captive to minority "special interest" groups.

The DLC was particularly attractive to younger Democrats from the Sunbelt. Its first six chairs were all from southern or border states, where Democrats felt particularly vulnerable to Republican challengers. Many other DLC members represented wealthy suburban districts, whose voters rejected Reagan's social conservatism while embracing his tax cuts and pro-business policies. The DLC's pro-business politics attracted substantial corporate support. By 1991–92, of its one hundred "sustaining members," fifty-seven were corporations and another twelve were professional and trade associations.[52]

In 1990, Clinton took the helm of the DLC, using it as a platform to launch his campaign for the presidency. He traveled the country, met with wealthy donors, and tapped the DLC's new think tank, the Progressive Policy Institute (PPI), to prepare position papers for his candidacy. The PPI's name was a nod to early twentieth-century reform politics, inspired by Theodore Roosevelt's Progressive Party, adapting "basic American political principles to changing circumstances."[53] The PPI and the DLC emphasized the need for "post-partisan" politics, calling for a third way between New Deal–Great Society liberalism and Reagan Republicanism.

At its 1990 conference, the DLC laid out its principles in the "New Orleans Declaration," a document that became a blueprint for Clinton's candidacy. The "Democratic Party's fundamental mission," it stated, "is to expand opportunity, not government." This meant embracing pro-business policies, including free trade, a streamlined, business-friendly tax code, and government subsidies for high-tech research and development. It criticized welfare for maintaining the poor "in dependence." Finally, the DLC echoed Republican calls for "individual responsibility," arguing for "preventing crime and punishing criminals, not in explaining away their behavior."[54]

On the campaign trail, Clinton pitched himself as a bipartisan defender of "middle-class" values and interests. "The change I seek and the change we must all seek isn't liberal or conservative. It's different and it's both."[55] That meant repackaging many Republican ideas. Clinton defended government's role in society but criticized "tax and spend" politics. He argued that welfare should be "a second chance, not a way of life." Playing to culturally conservative white voters, he made headlines for criticizing Sister Souljah, a black rapper, for allegedly endorsing black-on-white violence. And in a particularly melodramatic moment, he left the campaign trail to preside over the execution of a mentally retarded black man, Ricky Ray Rector, who had been convicted of murdering an Arkansas police officer.

It was far from clear whether the electorate shared Clinton's centrist vision. Independent candidate Ross Perot ran a lackluster campaign but still managed to pick up 19 percent of the vote, much of it from conservative voters angry at Bush's decision to raise taxes. Clinton benefited from the split vote and picked up 43 percent of the vote, most if it from traditional Democratic voters, including African Americans, union members, and a plurality of women. Despite his efforts to win whites, he picked up only 39 percent of their votes, although he did win five southern states, the best Democratic showing there since 1976.

CLINTON AND POLITICAL TRIANGULATION

In office, Clinton engaged in what commentators called the politics of "triangulation," appealing to cultural liberals, fiscal conservatives, and big business all at once. It proved to be a challenging task. Many on Clinton's left hoped he would deal with wage stagnation and joblessness. They looked to two appointees on Clinton's left, both professors: Harvard's Robert Reich (who had been a Rhodes scholar with Clinton) was secretary of labor; and the Berkeley economist Laura D'Andrea Tyson chaired the Council of Economic Advisers. Both highlighted growing inequality and called for federal funding for job training and stimulus spending to create public sector jobs.

"Budget Hawks"

Reich and Tyson were drowned out by Clinton's pro-business advisers, led by Robert Rubin, who left his job at investment bank Goldman Sachs to serve as head of Clinton's National Economic Council; Lloyd Bentsen, a DLC member and former Texas senator who was Clinton's secretary of the treasury; and budget director (and later chief of staff) Leon Panetta, a centrist who had begun his career as a Republican and Nixon staffer, then switched parties.

These "budget hawks" persuaded Clinton to prioritize deficit reduction. They argued that a balanced budget would bring confidence to bond markets and lower interest rates, thus loosening credit, allowing homeowners to refinance their homes, and jump-starting the economy. "We're all Eisenhower Republicans," Clinton told his advisers just three months after he was inaugurated. ". . . We stand for lower deficits and free trade and the bond market. Isn't that great?"[56]

Republicans had their own reasons for supporting deficit reduction. House Speaker Newt Gingrich, one of the most ambitious and conservative Republicans of his generation, represented a suburban district outside Atlanta. In 1983 he founded the Conservative Opportunity Society to promote free-market policies, pressuring Reagan from the right. In 1990 he was elected House minority leader. Gingrich believed that deficit reduction "changes the whole game . . . You cannot sustain the old welfare state inside a balanced budget."[57]

Clinton's first budget, in 1993, was a compromise between Democrats and Republicans, not unlike Bush's 1990 budget agreement. It called for modest tax increases, caps on discretionary spending, and a slowdown in the growth of Medicare, one of the costliest items in the budget. But the deficit hawks persuaded Clinton to jettison his middle-class tax cut and trim most of the stimulus spending that liberals had demanded. The bill squeaked through Congress.

NAFTA

In late 1993, Clinton pushed through NAFTA, lending his support to the trade treaty that President Bush had negotiated with Mexico and Canada. Free trade had been a top priority of the DLC. Many major corporations, including Wal-Mart (whose board members included Clinton's wife Hillary until she resigned before the 1992 campaign) and Tyson Foods (which had funded both Clinton and the DLC), wanted to lower trade barriers so they could import cheaply produced goods and expand their markets abroad. The Business Roundtable, a major lobbying group, mobilized 2,400 member corporations to lobby for NAFTA. Major manufacturers and retailers also joined the effort.

Most Republicans supported NAFTA, but it faced stiff opposition among Democrats, who argued that it would accelerate "runaway jobs" to Mexico, where companies would have easy access to cheap labor without the burdens of environmental and safety regulations. Clinton countered that NAFTA would encourage American "competitiveness" and, over time, expand American firms' market share. NAFTA passed with only 27 Democratic votes in the Senate and 102 in the House. As NAFTA's critics had feared, the treaty fueled the dramatic expansion of American firms south of the border.

Health Care Reform

Clinton was confident that he would win bipartisan support for another key policy, health insurance reform. Health care costs had skyrocketed to 12 percent of the gross domestic product in 1992. In the 1970s and 1980s, employer spending on wages had increased by only 1 percent, controlling for inflation. But employer health-benefit costs had risen by 163 percent. Almost 38 million Americans were uninsured, a stark contrast to every other Western democracy, all of which had enacted some form of national health insurance in the twentieth century.[58] Polls showed strong public support for systemic reform.

During his first week in office, Clinton put together a health reform team, led by his wife Hillary, a shrewd lawyer but an inexperienced politician. Over the next eight months, the group met secretly, arousing suspicion, and in September it issued a thirteen-hundred-page proposal. The plan reflected the market-oriented political shifts of the previous fifteen years. It left the responsibility for health insurance in the hands of private employers but called for a system of "managed competition" that would give government a role in negotiating lower premiums. Many big corporations supported the plan, especially one of its key features, an "employer mandate" that required all employers to provide insurance. They worried that, in the absence of a mandate, companies that opted out of providing health care would have an advantage over those that did provide it. Most small businesses, however, opposed Clinton's plan, because they kept costs low by not providing insurance to their employees.

Small business groups intensively lobbied Congress. So did the health insurance industry, fearful of cost controls. Republicans, hoping to deprive Clinton of a victory, put pressure on wavering members. They all capitalized on the health plan's complexity. As one health care reform supporter noted, "If you're explaining it, people's eyes glaze over. If you're attacking it, you only need that one rhetorical salvo." That one salvo was "government-run health care."[59] By early 1994 the tide had turned against Clinton's plan, which critics labeled as socialistic. Republicans painted a picture of a bloated government bureaucracy rationing health care and restricting access to doctors. The health care reform collapsed. Thereafter the number of uninsured Americans rose and medical costs continued to skyrocket. Most Americans remained unhappy with the health care system, but there was little incentive to reform it after Clinton's plan died.

THE CONTRACT WITH AMERICA AND WELFARE REFORM

Six weeks before the 1994 midterm elections, Republicans issued the Contract with America. The high point of postwar conservatism, it called for a constitutional amendment that would require a balanced budget and limit taxation. It promised to promote businesses by trimming regulations and passing a 50 percent cut in capital gains taxes. It reiterated law and order themes dating back to the 1960s, including expanding the use of the death penalty and providing more funds for law enforcement and prison construction. It built on Reagan's war on welfare, calling for "a tough two-years-and-out" limit on benefits and "work requirements to promote individual responsibility." It promoted "family reinforcement" through tax credits for children, adoption, and elder care. And, as a first step toward fulfilling Barry Goldwater's decades-old dream of the privatization of Social Security, it advocated tax-sheltered retirement accounts.[60]

Gingrich and Clinton

The Republicans swept the 1994 midterm elections, winning 54 seats in the House and 9 in the Senate. For the first time since 1954, Republicans controlled the entire legislative branch. Under the leadership of new Speaker Newt Gingrich, the House aggressively pushed the Contract with America. The Republicans united around an austerity budget that included significant cuts to federal education funding and Medicare, combined with tax cuts for the highest-income earners. Clinton fought back, calling the GOP proposals "anti-family" and focusing on Medicare, which was very popular among the elderly.

Congress set a deadline of November 14, 1995, for a budget agreement. If a budget was not passed, government offices would be unfunded, and the federal government would shut down. On November 13 negotiations between Republican leaders and the president broke down. The government shut down for five days in November and for twenty-two days in December and January. Gingrich and the Republicans—who had been uncompromising throughout the process—took a political hit. By sizable margins, the public blamed Gingrich and the GOP for the gridlock. Finally, in early January, under pressure, Republicans agreed to a compromise, accepting modest cuts in social programs and leaving their proposed tax cuts on the table.

In his 1996 State of the Union address, President Clinton made the Reaganesque proclamation, "The era of big government is over." During that election year, Clinton moved rightward on social issues, hoping to outrun the Republicans. He announced his support for the Defense of Marriage Act, a law that defined marriage as a union between a man and a woman. He stepped up his calls for personal responsibility. And most consequentially, he found common ground with the Republicans over one of the core issues in the Contract with America: welfare reform.

Ending Welfare as We Know It

Since his days in the DLC, Clinton had argued for "personal responsibility." He and conservatives alike argued that poverty was the result of dysfunctional families, parents who lacked the motivation to work, and teens who engaged in crime and promiscuous sex. Behind all these changes was an overgenerous welfare system. Poor people needed a dose of "traditional values" like thrift, deferred gratification, and work discipline.

This criticism of welfare focused mostly on urban African Americans, who lived in communities that had been the hardest hit by disinvestment and depopulation. Since the 1950s old industrial cities had been ravaged by the flight of jobs. Residential segregation by race remained stubbornly high: between 1940 and 1990, it had hardly changed. The sociologist Douglas Massey wrote an influential book in 1993 describing the pattern as "American apartheid," noting that in most major cities, blacks and whites lived almost completely separate lives. Real estate brokers refused to show houses to minorities in suburban communities, often places where the best-paying jobs were concentrated. African American children were trapped in racially segregated, crowded, underfunded schools. Many inner-city communities were also ravaged by mass incarceration. In the 1990s about a third of black men in their twenties were in jail or on probation or parole. Employers seldom hired men with a criminal record.

The conservative critics of welfare focused on culture. The influential political scientist Lawrence Mead argued that blacks have a "deep conviction that they have to 'get things from white people' if they are to live a decent life." He also claimed that blacks had abandoned the work ethic of their grandparents' generation. "In that era, working hard and going to church were much of what black culture meant. Today, tragically, it is more likely to mean rock music or the rapping of drug dealers on ghetto street corners." Welfare reform, he argued, would change all that.[61]

In 1996, President Clinton and Speaker Gingrich negotiated the Personal Responsibility and Work Opportunity Reconciliation Act. A triumph of bipartisanship, it abolished AFDC, replacing it with a new program called Temporary Assistance for Needy Families (TANF). Nodding to Clinton's emphasis on work, the act provided states with funds for job training. Nodding to Gingrich, it also provided grants to pro-marriage programs, many run by churches. It was telling that ending poverty was not even listed as one of the law's primary goals. As Representative E. Clay Shaw (R-FL), one of the bill's sponsors, argued, TANF was about discipline. "You're going to have some who are just not going to be able to make it," he stated. Welfare reform "presented a certain amount of pain for not being able to take control of your life."[62] The reform forced individuals to fend for themselves, whatever the consequences might be.

Welfare reform grew out of the failure of policy makers to grapple with the wrenching structural changes that had created persistent, concentrated urban poverty. The new, daunting eligibility rules discouraged many needy parents from applying for TANF, even though they were eligible for support. In the decade following the enactment of TANF, welfare rolls nationwide dropped by nearly 60 percent. By contrast, poverty rates fell modestly in the late 1990s, mostly because of economic growth, not because of welfare reform. But those modest gains came at the price of growing insecurity. A 1999 study of poor families in thirteen states reported finding "evidence of lives made harder by the loss of cash assistance." To make ends meet, families often missed rent and utility payments.[63] Many resorted to unregulated day care programs or left their children with grandparents so they could find work. When poverty began rising again in 2001, their situation would get worse.

THE BOOM AND INCOME INEQUALITY

Even if the poor struggled during Clinton's second term, the American economy was stronger than it had been in more than two decades. In 1997 unemployment fell below 5 percent, the first time since 1973. It would eventually fall to 3.9 percent in 2001. The boom of the 1990s proved the old adage that rising tides lift all boats. In 1999 median household income in the United States reached an all-time high (in 2000 real dollars) of $42,418. Every racial and ethnic group saw increases: black household income reached a peak of $33,447, and Hispanics $30,439. The increase, however impressive, proved to be temporary. During the recession of the early 2000s, household incomes stagnated and, in real dollars, fell again.[64]

The increase in income in the late 1990s did not overcome the longer-term trend of dramatically worsening inequality in the United States. Between 1979 and 2006, the poorest fifth saw only an 11 percent after-tax income increase; the second and middle fifths saw an 18 percent increase and 21 percent increase respectively, and the fourth fifth saw a 32 percent rise. At the top, the gains were much greater. Those with income in the eightieth to ninety-ninth percentiles saw a 55 percent income increase; and the top one percent saw a 256 percent rise.[65]

Tax Cuts

In the late 1990s, a bipartisan consensus emerged around policies that benefited the wealthiest Americans and particularly big businesses. Republicans targeted estate taxes, which Senator Trent Lott (R-MS) described as "a monster that must be exterminated."[66] Both Clinton and Republicans supported a reduction in capital gains taxes on stocks, home sales, and other investments. Clinton pushed for some modest benefits for middle-income taxpayers, including a tax credit for education expenses. In 1997 an overwhelming bipartisan majority passed the Taxpayer Relief Act, which cut taxes by about $400 billion. The law reduced capital gains taxes from 25 to 20 percent, a boon to wealthy Americans, for whom stocks, bonds, and real estate holdings comprised a greater share of household earnings than the majority of Americans. It also sheltered estates worth $1 million or less from the taxation, benefiting about 1 percent of the population.

The Dot-Com Boom

Stock prices skyrocketed in the 1990s, greatly surpassing corporate profit rates and increases in productivity. The end of the twentieth-century witnessed a wave of lucrative mergers and acquisitions. Some of the biggest growth came in new high-tech industries, particularly firms based in Silicon Valley that had long been nurtured by Cold War spending but now developed civilian applications, including high-definition screens and microchips. The biggest advance was the creation of the World Wide Web, building on decades of advances in networking and telecommunications technologies for the military.

Investors were particularly attracted to new "dot-com" firms that proliferated on the Internet, spurring massive speculation. In 1995, Jeff Bezos founded Amazon.com, the first large-scale online bookstore; in 1998, Sergey Brin and another Ph.D. student at Stanford launched the search engine Google.com. Investors, hoping to strike it rich, flooded new startups with funds. The value of high-tech stocks increased fivefold between 1995 and 2000. Recent college graduates flocked to high-tech centers in Silicon Valley, Austin, and Seattle. But in 2000 the dot-com economy collapsed, triggered by a bubble of investment in unstable startup companies. Some firms, like Google, Yahoo, and Amazon, would survive, but many smaller enterprises collapsed, and the tech economy remained volatile for several years afterward.

Financial Deregulation

The most sweeping transformations in the 1990s involved the deregulation of the financial sector. Here too Clinton found common cause with conservative Republicans. Beginning in 1995, the president's economic advisers pushed for a "financial services modernization," including repeal of one of the signature New Deal regulations, the Glass-Steagall Act, which forbade banks to speculate in stocks and real estate using individual depositors' money. Glass-Steagall also prohibited banks from owning firms that sold securities. Clinton's aides knew that "allowing banks to engage in riskier activities like securities or insurance could subject the deposit insurance fund to added risk."[67] It was a risk that they were willing to take.

In 1999, Clinton signed the Gramm-Leach-Bliley Act, which undid

Glass-Steagall's regulations. The financial services industry immediately took advantage of the new circumstances. New "megabanks," often organized into nominally separate legal entities, engaged not only in traditional activities such as lending, but also in brokerage, investment banking, insurance, asset management, and the creation of securities and derivatives markets. Over the next eight years, banks created all sorts of new high-risk financial products, without close regulatory scrutiny.

The riskiest involved home mortgage lending, one of the Clinton administration's top priorities. In 1995 the president launched National Homeownership Day, offering a new rationale about personal responsibility. "You want to reinforce family values in America, encourage two-parent households, get people to stay home?" Clinton answered his own question: "Make it easy for people to own their own homes and enjoy the rewards of family life and see their work rewarded. This is a big deal."[68] By the late 1990s, lenders, including Washington Mutual, New Century, and Countrywide, began targeting working-class and minority communities with high-interest loans, often with substantial up-front closing costs and hidden fees. The loans were immensely profitable but also incredibly risky.

Predatory loans were especially appealing to those working Americans whose wages had stagnated or fallen. To cover rising costs—a child's college tuition, a major home repair, or medical bills—a growing number of homeowners took out home equity loans, borrowing against the value of their house. In the meantime, loosely regulated financial institutions bundled mortgages together as securities and sold them on the secondary market, at great profits. So long as housing prices continued to rise and the profits to be made from securitized mortgages went up, lenders grew more and more lax in their standards. The market would begin collapsing in 2007, with devastating consequences for home buyers who suffered foreclosures, and for investors who were left holding nearly worthless assets.

IMPEACHMENT

For most of Clinton's second term, however, few worried about the future. The economy seemed unstoppable. But the news media and public were distracted by lurid scandals that engulfed the president and dominated the headlines. Early in his term, Clinton's conservative opponents spun out a number of charges against him, the most serious involving allegations of corruption around Whitewater, a complex Arkansas real estate deal in which Clinton had invested. In 1994, Chief Justice William Rehnquist named Kenneth Starr, a lawyer in the Reagan and Bush administrations, to investigate the charges as an independent counsel. He would find no wrongdoing involving Whitewater.

Complicating the situation, in 1994 an Arkansas woman named Paula Jones filed a civil suit against the president, charging him with sexual harassment. To conservative critics, who saw Clinton as a libertine (Gingrich had once called him a "counterculture McGovernik"), the Jones suit was grist for the mill. The president, hoping to quash Jones's suit, claimed executive immunity. In 1997 a federal court ruled against him, allowing the suit to proceed.

In late 1997, Jones's attorneys got word of something they hoped would help their case. Clinton and Monica Lewinsky, a presidential intern in her early twenties, had had oral sex in the White House. Clinton's liaison with Lewinsky began during the government shutdown in November 1995. Over the two years, the two met occasionally, with Lewinsky performing oral sex on the president nine times. They sometimes engaged in phone sex. Their clandestine meetings might have remained secret, except that Lewinsky began confiding the affair to Linda Tripp, a disgruntled former White House secretary, who secretly recorded the conversations,

In November 1997, Jones's attorneys deposed Clinton in the ongoing suit. When asked if he had had sex with Lewinsky, Clinton stated, "I have not had sex with that woman." Starr, having failed to prove the Whitewater allegations but eager to prove that the president was unethical, shifted gears. He accused the president of perjury, for lying in his deposition. To make his case, Starr called Lewinsky before a grand jury, where she confirmed that she had performed oral sex on the president. Starr entered into evidence Lewinsky's semen-stained blue dress.

On September 11, 1998, Starr produced a 453-page-long report on every aspect of Clinton's relationship with Lewinsky, replete with sexually explicit details. In the next three months, the House of Representatives investigated the charges against Clinton and, on December 19, voted to impeach him on grounds of perjury and obstruction of justice. Clinton went on trial in the Senate, which needed a two-thirds majority to remove him from office. For thirty-seven days, the Senate debated the charges against him. On February 12, 1999, the impeachment failed. Only 45 senators, all Republicans, voted to convict him of perjury, and only 50 of obstruction of justice. Most Americans thought Starr had overreached his authority, and while many disapproved of Clinton's conduct, his approval ratings remained high.

FOREIGN AFFAIRS

During the Clinton impeachment furor, few Americans paid much attention to international relations. A major survey conducted in late 1998 showed that only 2 to 3 percent of respondents ranked foreign policy as a primary concern. When asked to name the "two or three biggest foreign policy problems facing the United States today," the most popular response was "I don't know."[69] The lack of interest was in part the consequence of the end of the Cold War, in part a sharp decline in American media coverage of international relations in the 1990s. Many newspapers had closed or downsized their overseas bureaus.

Many of the foreign policy controversies of the Clinton years seemed distant to the American people. A civil war in Rwanda led to the genocidal killing of some 800,000 Tutsi by the Hutu majority in the spring and summer of 1994. The United States made no significant response. The administration also faced major humanitarian crises in the former Yugoslavia, which was torn apart by a brutal civil war. In 1994 and 1995, Serbian leader Slobodan Milošević ordered the massacre of thousands of Bosnian Muslims and displaced tens of thousands more. The United States supported the United Nations, which sent several thousand peacekeeping forces there. Some members of Congress called for more aggressive action, but there was little public support for a military engagement in the Balkans. In early September 1995, Clinton committed American troops to engage in airstrikes on targets around the Serbian capital, Sarajevo. In November the United States brokered the Dayton accords, imposing a cease-fire in the region.

In 1998 the United States faced a more ominous challenge from Al Qaeda, an extremist Muslim group led by Osama bin Laden, the wealthy son of a Saudi Arabian oil magnate. Bin Laden established a base of operations in Afghanistan and, from there, directed terrorist attacks on American targets. In August that year Al Qaeda took credit for the bombing of U.S. embassies in Kenya and Tanzania, which killed more than three hundred people. In retaliation, Clinton authorized airstrikes on an Al Qaeda base in Afghanistan and a factory in Sudan, suspected to be producing arms for Bin

Laden's organization. Neither involved any major military engagement—Clinton was wary of committing troops to fight the terrorist organization. But in the late 1990s, CIA operatives, who closely monitored suspected terrorist groups throughout the Middle East, began to warn that Al Qaeda was planning an attack on targets in the United States. In October 2000, Al Qaeda operatives bombed the *USS Cole*, a destroyer stationed in the Persian Gulf, killing seventeen American marines.

AT CENTURY'S END

American intelligence agencies were on high alert on December 31, 1999. Just two weeks earlier, border patrol agents at the Canadian border had stopped an Algerian national with a car full of explosives and timers. In Seattle, where protesters had taken to the streets to protest the World Trade Organization meeting in 1998, city officials were so fearful of violence that they canceled the city's New Year's fireworks display. Around the country, with the millennium looming, paranoid Americans girded themselves for the chaos that they expected would break out when the Y2K bug prevented computer systems from recognizing dates beginning with 20 rather that 19. Rumors had been spreading for months that a massive computer shutdown would freeze the nation's power grid, shut down banks and air traffic control centers, and crash the economy.[70] Those fears proved unfounded.

On New Year's Eve a quarter-million revelers crowded the Strip in Las Vegas, a place where gambling palaces had boomed during the economic upswing in the late 1990s. About a million gathered in New York's Times Square, despite a blizzard that struck the city the night before. The city, flush with money just a quarter century after it declared bankruptcy, dispatched thousands of workers on overtime to clear the sidewalks and streets. Limousines lined up at chic restaurants like Windows on the World, perched atop the World Trade Center, which had five thousand bottles of champagne—about two bottles per guest—ready for revelers.

On the New Year, which fell on a Saturday, many workers, hungover from the night before, stumbled to work. Many Wal-Mart associates did not get the day off. At the beginning of 2000, the world's single largest retailer now operated 1,821 discount stores, 650 SuperCenters, and 453 Sam's Clubs in the United States and 850 more overseas. Many of them were open twenty-four hours, 365 days a year. Wal-Mart also chose January 1, 2000, to launch a new online venture. Consumers could order more than 600,000 items online, a larger inventory than in its most brick-and-mortar stores.

President Bill Clinton welcomed in the millennium: "Seldom in our history and never in my lifetime has our Nation enjoyed such a combination of widespread economic success, social solidarity, and national self-confidence, without an internal crisis or an overarching external threat."[71] The days of stagflation were remote. The Cold War was over. The United States was not at war, despite lingering fears of a terror attack. But the moment was fleeting. In the next several years, the country would be entangled in two wars. The contradictions of the 1990s boom—extraordinary wealth but deepening inequality—would become untenable. Intense partisan divisions would erode social solidarity. Deregulation and financial speculation would culminate in the greatest economic crisis since the Great Depression. America was still freighted by the burdens of the long twentieth century, unable to resolve the tensions between its promise of opportunity and its pervasive economic insecurity, its optimism and its deep-seated fears, its unsurpassed military power and its unease with the devastation of war, its persistent divisions of race and ethnicity. Americans at the new millennium hoped to overcome the past. But the past would indelibly shape their future.

CHAPTER 15

UNITED WE STAND, DIVIDED WE FALL, SINCE 2000

PATRICIA THOMPSON LIVED a hard life in one of the poorest cities in America, New Orleans. Born in 1956, she lost her mother when she was four and grew up with her struggling grandmother. "I've seen the hungry days," she recalled. "I've seen the days with no lights and water in the house. . . . I wouldn't wish my childhood on a dog." When she was seventeen, she left her grandmother and moved into the St. Thomas public housing project, a place that embodied all the contradictions of the New Deal. St. Thomas had been built to provide modern, affordable homes to working-class residents, but it was completely segregated by race, cut off from the surrounding city.[1]

Inspired by civil rights activists, Patricia Thompson worked to make St. Thomas a better place to live—an uphill task in the 1980s and 1990s, when federal housing support was collapsing, buildings were crumbling, and life for poor people like her got harder. In the mid-1980s, as crime was rising, it took police more than twenty-five minutes to respond to emergency calls in the project. But Thompson strove to make life better for herself, her six children, and her community. She helped start a health clinic and got a job working on a foundation-sponsored project to reduce teen pregnancy. Then in 1996 the New Orleans Housing Authority got funds from a Clinton administration program called Hope VI to demolish St. Thomas and replace it with mixed-income private housing. By 2001, most of the project had been bulldozed, and its more than three thousand residents scattered throughout the city. A new Wal-Mart would be built just a few blocks away. Thompson moved to another project. In the early

2000s she worked for a church doing social services. She earned about $200 a month.

On August 27, 2005, Thompson and her neighbors got word that a major hurricane was headed right toward New Orleans. About 80 percent of the city's residents evacuated, but many, like Thompson, could not. "I had one dollar in my pocket," she told an interviewer. "I did not have a vehicle, so there was no way for us to get out." That year more than a quarter of New Orleans residents, most of them black, did not own a car. The city's public transit system had struggled for decades with cuts in federal and state funding, and like many states, Louisiana did not have an extensive intercity bus or rail system. For those left behind as the storm approached, the scene was chaotic: "People are trying to get water, people are trying to get food. People are trying to steal cars, whatever they can do to help themselves and get out of that city." Without a car, and without money, Thompson was stuck.

In one respect she was lucky: she lived in a sturdy brick building, perhaps the only advantage of living in a housing project in a city of mostly wood-frame houses. She weathered the 140 mph winds that buffeted the city, staying on the second floor above the raging floodwaters that covered about 80 percent of the city when the levees broke. But when the electricity and power went out, she couldn't stay. Her daughters joined a crowd that went into a Wal-Mart to scavenge for food. "At this point, it's not stealing," she stated, "it's survival." Finally Thompson and her family headed to the Crescent City bridge, hoping to cross to Jefferson Parish, a community where she had relatives and that had not been flooded as badly by the hurricane. There she and hundreds of others were turned back by the police at gunpoint. She joined a huge crowd of people who gathered outside the city's convention center, where the Federal Emergency Management Agency (FEMA) provided meager rations. There was not enough to eat, so she and her daughters went back to abandoned stores to find food. She recalled the grim scenario of sleeping on the city's streets: "People were dying all around us. We were sleeping next to human feces and urine. All around you watching people die, watching them scream for help." More than eighteen hundred people died during the hurricane, most of them in New Orleans.

Patricia Thompson bore the heavy burdens of history. Her life had been shaped indelibly by the politics and policies that remade the United States in the hundred years leading up to the fateful day when the hurricane struck. She lived in a city whose social geography had been shaped by a long history of segregation, one that had been only partially undone by the civil rights legislation that passed when she was just a child. She lived in buildings that had been constructed as part of an experiment in providing "decent housing" for millions of Americans during the Great Depression, World War II, and the postwar years. But as these projects suffered decades of disinvestment, her quality of life deteriorated. And she had lived through a free-market revolution that put faith in the private sector to revitalize communities like St. Thomas. She had found work and support through foundations and churches, the nonprofit organizations that stepped in, with few resources but a lot of goodwill, to address the needs of the most disadvantaged Americans at the turn of the twenty-first century. Hurricane Katrina was not only a personal disaster for Patricia Thompson and many other residents of America's Gulf Coast; it was also one of the most important domestic political crises in a crisis-torn period in American history. It was a natural disaster whose worst effects were almost entirely man-made.

THE ELECTION OF 2000

Katrina was a defining moment for the administration of President George W. Bush. Just five years earlier Bush had been the Republican nominee for the nation's highest office, but was by no means the frontrunner. Both he and the Democratic nominee, Albert Gore, Jr., hailed from states that bordered hurricane-ravaged Louisiana. Both candidates came from distinguished political families; both were sons of the 1960s, still shadowed by the Vietnam War; both had had elite educations; both were devout Christians; and both believed, to differing degrees, in reducing the size of government. One was the heir of Ronald Reagan and the son of a past president. The other was hoping to take over the reins of power from a popular incumbent.

Gore had graduated from Harvard in 1969 and volunteered to serve in the army, knowing he stood a strong chance of being dispatched to Vietnam. He worked as a military journalist but spent most of his enlistment stateside, eventually putting in just a few months in Southeast Asia. Five years later he won election to Congress from Tennessee, and in 1986, following in his father's footsteps, he won election to the U.S. Senate. Like many southern Democrats, Gore aligned himself with the Democratic Leadership Council, where he worked with Bill Clinton. In 1992, Clinton tapped him as his running mate. As vice president, Gore established a record on environmental issues and on science and technology. Well respected for his intelligence, he was a centrist and, like President Clinton, an advocate of streamlining government, cutting deficits, and using governmental power to help business.

Bush, the grandson of a Connecticut senator and son of President George H. W. Bush, had graduated from Yale in 1968. Eager to demonstrate his patriotism but reluctant to take the risk of being sent to Vietnam, he volunteered for the Air National Guard. At that time, few guard members were dispatched to the war. Bush remained a reservist for six years, earned an MBA at Harvard, and entered the oil business. In 1978 he tried—and failed—to follow his father's path by running for Congress. Unsuccessful as a politician, he was well connected among the Texas business elite and, by the early 1990s, quite wealthy. He invested in real estate and was part owner of the Texas Rangers baseball team. But his itch to follow his father's footsteps and win political office persisted. In 1994 he rode a well-funded campaign to win the governorship of Texas and, during the 1990s boom, laid the groundwork for his nomination as Republican candidate for the White House in 2000.

Gore and the DLC

Most pundits thought that Gore had a clear shot at the Oval Office. His boss, President Clinton, had survived the impeachment proceedings and remained a popular figure. The economy was stronger than it had been in decades. Since 1964 every winning Democratic candidate had hailed from the South. Key Democratic operatives did not expect Gore to sweep the Old Confederacy, but they hoped that he would appeal to enough southern voters to win his home state, Tennessee, and perhaps Arkansas and a few others.

Gore, a longtime advocate of a smaller and "smarter" government, chose as his running mate a fellow member of the Democratic Leadership Council, Joseph Lieberman. The Connecticut senator was known for his hawkish foreign policy, his willingness to break ranks and vote with the Republicans, and his deep support on Wall Street. On the campaign trail, Gore offered his own version of what had become conventional wisdom among centrist Democrats, namely that running on competence would be more effective than appealing to Democratic "special interests" or reviving New Deal and Great Society politics. Gore distanced himself from President Clinton, preferring to run his campaign without the incumbent's assistance. Still he followed Clinton's script closely, pledging to fight for "middle class families and working men and women."[2]

It was a sign of how much the Democratic Party had changed that rather than pushing for higher wages or stronger unions as New Deal Democrats had done, Gore echoed a familiar Republican refrain: cut taxes for the middle class. On the campaign trail, he pledged to enact business-friendly policies, although his call for stricter environmental regulations worried business leaders, particularly in the heavy industries dependent on oil and coal. Gore was also candid about his religion, using stump speeches to call for more government support to faith-based organizations. As a campaigner, however, he was stiff and came across as arrogant, particularly during the presidential debates, when he implausibly claimed that he had invented the Internet.

Bush's Christian Campaign

Bush—whose politics were considerably to the right of his father's—promised large tax cuts and pledged to reform Social Security. In this respect, he was Reaganesque. But unlike his father or Reagan, he foregrounded his evangelical Christianity on the campaign trail. "I feel like God wants me to run for president," he said to Reverend James Robison, a prominent televangelist.[3] When asked during a Republican primary debate who his favorite philosopher was, he immediately named Jesus Christ. Many on the religious right—who had felt marginalized since the Reagan years—rallied around Bush. He publicly stated his opposition to abortion, medical research on embryos, and gay marriage.

As he moved onto the national stage, Bush highlighted another side of his faith: "compassionate conservatism." Some critics, like Republican pundit David Frum, were skeptical of the concept, seeing it as a transparent effort to win over moderates. "Love conservatism but hate arguing about abortion? Try our new *compassionate conservatism*—great ideological taste now with less controversy." During his acceptance address to the Republican National Convention, Bush defined the term: "Government . . . can feed the body. But it cannot reach the soul." Rather than encouraging entitlement, government should empower the poor and the faith-based organizations that helped them: "My administration will give taxpayers new incentives to donate to charity, encourage after-school programs that build character, and support mentoring groups that shape and save young lives."[4]

Bush v. Gore

The choice between Bush and Gore was unappealing to many voters. Some gravitated toward Green Party candidate Ralph Nader, who was running for president for the third time. A longtime environmental activist who had made his reputation challenging unsafe cars and environmental degradation, Nader argued that both parties were beholden to "oligarchs" who "subordinate democracy to plutocracy." The Gore camp worried that in a close race, "Nader's Raiders" would attract disaffected liberals. In the last few days of the race, Gore stepped up his own populist rhetoric, charging that a Bush victory would result in "a massive redistribution of wealth from the middle class to the wealthiest few." Bush responded by charging Gore with engaging in "class warfare."[5]

Only about half of eligible voters turned out on Election Day. The election revealed deep fissures in the electorate. Bush swept the South, including Gore's home state. He also picked up nearly every state in the Mountain West, where his small government rhetoric was popular. Gore, for his part, won throughout the Northeast, particularly in racially diverse metropolitan areas. The most notable gap separated men and women: Gore picked up about 11 percent more of the female vote than did Bush. Nader picked up only 2.7 percent of the vote, but just enough to tip the balance away from Gore in one key state: Florida.

On the evening of November 7, 2000, presidential candidates George W. Bush and Albert Gore, Jr., huddled with their families and close political advisers, anxiously watching the election returns. As evening turned to morning, the results remained inconclusive. More than 100 million Americans had voted, yet the outcome was too close to call. Gore had eked out a tiny margin nationwide—about 540,000 votes over Bush—and had won 266 of the 270 Electoral College votes needed for victory, compared to Bush's 246. The election eventually hinged on the returns in Florida, which initially showed Bush ahead by about 500 votes. Both campaigns sent teams to Florida to attempt a full recount. The balloting process had been full of problems. In one Florida county, several thousand votes had been accidentally cast for conservative independent candidate Pat Buchanan because of a flawed ballot. Both sides debated whether to count ballots with "hanging chads," the result of problems with outdated punch card technology.

The election ended abruptly on December 12 when the Supreme Court called for an end to the Florida recount, leaving Bush with several hundred votes more than Gore in that state. The *Bush v. Gore* decision was without precedent. Writing for the court's 5–4 majority (all five yes votes were cast by Nixon and Reagan appointees), associate justice Antonin Scalia stated: "The counting of votes of questionable legality does in my view threaten irreparable harm to petitioner [George W. Bush], and to the country, by casting a cloud on what he claims to be the legitimacy of his election." The decision shocked legal observers across the political spectrum, but it brought the contested election to a close. Without Florida, Gore lost the Electoral College 271–266, the closest margin ever. He conceded to Bush.

BUSH IN OFFICE

During Bush's first few months in office, "compassionate conservatism" seemed to top his list of priorities. He devoted a lengthy section of his inaugural address to the theme. He pledged that his administration would reflect the diversity of America, and he appointed more women, Asian Americans, Hispanics, and African Americans to his cabinet than had any of his predecessors. But his cabinet choices reflected more than a symbolic commitment to diversity. His secretary of labor, Elaine Chao, was married to one of the most conservative senators, Mitch McConnell (R-KY). Unlike most past labor secretaries, she had no experience with organized labor, and her record was staunchly anti-union. Bush's secretary of the interior, Gale Norton, was a former mining industry lobbyist and a vehement critic of environmental regulation. Norton supported opening federal lands to oil extraction and mining. And Bush's foreign policy team, dominated by Vice President Richard Cheney and Secretary of Defense Donald Rumsfeld, called for rolling back the multilateral strategies of the first Bush and Clinton administrations. They argued that the United States should revive Reagan's Star Wars program and use American military force abroad to accomplish "regime change."

Education Reform

Bush prioritized domestic issues at first. Three days after his inauguration, he delivered a comprehensive education reform plan to Congress called No Child Left Behind (NCLB). For a conservative politician, it was a bold expansion of federal power over education, which had been almost completely the responsibility of states and localities until Lyndon Johnson's Great Society. NCLB required standardized testing to measure educational progress and imposed "accountability" on school districts for their students' academic achievement. The federal government would reward districts and states that saw an improvement in test scores with greater funding. If test scores failed to improve, the law allowed parents to send their children to better schools in their districts. And if test scores stagnated or declined, NCLB required school districts to reorganize or close "failing schools."

No Child Left Behind enjoyed broad bipartisan support. Republicans hailed it for making schools more competitive. Democrats supported it because it increased federal education spending, particularly in poor districts. But NCLB generated intense controversy in practice. Many teachers disliked having to "teach to the test." And many state and local education officials found it difficult to improve test scores. Cheating scandals—often instigated by principals fearful of losing funding—erupted in many districts, including Atlanta, where an investigation found that teachers had changed student answers to improve test scores. Over the next dozen years, Congress would amend but not end NCLB. Under pressure to show "metrics" of progress, school districts closed schools with low test scores. New education entrepreneurs—many with the backing of major investors and private foundations—developed special school curriculums to help students pass standardized tests. And advocates of the privatization of public education used NCLB's emphasis on test scores to argue (without much data to prove their point) that turning public schools over to the private sector would lead to better scores and greater student success.

Faith-Based Initiatives

Bush also expanded federal grants to religious groups. His first executive order created the White House Office of Faith-Based and Community Initiatives. He pledged that "when we see social needs in America, my administration will look first to faith-based programs and community groups, which have proven their power to save and change lives."[6] In another executive order, Bush exempted religious organizations that received federal funds from regulations that forbade discrimination.

Bush named a conservative Democrat, John DiIulio, to direct the faith-based initiatives, but he resigned after eight months. DiIulio had had in mind a program that would fund churches like Patricia Thompson's in New Orleans to work with the truly disadvantaged. But instead, the program became intensely politicized. "There is no precedent in any modern White House for what is going on in this one: complete lack of a policy apparatus," complained DiIulio. The administration's political team "talked and acted as if the height of political sophistication consisted in reducing every issue to its simplest black and white terms for public consumption, then steering legislative initiatives or policy proposals as far right as possible."[7]

No presidency had been as explicitly religious as Bush's. He brought leading evangelicals into his inner circle, among them speechwriter Michael Gerson and attorney general John Ashcroft (who swiftly ordered that the classical statues in the Department of Justice be draped because of their nudity). Bush began his cabinet meetings with a prayer. Speechwriter David Frum—who was Jewish—was discomfited when he discovered that for White House staffers, "attendance at Bible study was, if not compulsory, not quite uncompulsory either."[8]

President Reagan and the first President Bush had greatly disappointed religious conservatives, but George W. Bush did not. On his second day in office (which coincided with the twentieth-eighth anniversary of *Roe v. Wade*), he addressed a pro-life group and announced that he would institute a "gag rule" that forbade the use of government funds for any international organization that provided abortion services or lobbied on behalf of abortion rights. Later that year he issued an order banning federal funding for scientific research using embryonic stem cells derived from embryos that were left over from the process of in vitro fertilization. Scientists used these cells in their search for cures for Parkinson's disease and diabetes. "At its core," stated Bush, "this issue forces us to confront fundamental questions about the beginnings of life and the ends of science." For the president, the answer was clear: "human life is a sacred gift from our creator."[9] Bush also supported the teaching of "intelligent design" in classrooms, an alternative to evolution.

Bush's explicitly religious positions won the enthusiastic support of evangelical Christians. "This is the most receptive White House to our concerns and to our perspective of any White House that I've dealt with," stated Richard Land, the head of the Southern Baptist Convention. "In this administration, they call us, and they say, 'What is your take on this? How does your group feel about this?'"[10] Evangelicals, who had not turned out in high numbers during the 2000 election, would be Bush's most avid supporters for the next several years. Grateful that they had support at the highest levels of government, conservative Christians mobilized to reelect Bush in 2004 and to use that election to push statewide referenda on key conservative causes, most notably laws restricting same-sex marriage.

Tax Policy

Bush's most consequential domestic accomplishment was an overhaul of the tax system, one that was far more sweeping than Reagan's. After his father veered from his "no new taxes" pledge in 1990, it had become orthodoxy among Republicans that even a modest increase in taxes would be political suicide. Even though the Reagan tax cuts had had mixed results and the Clinton tax reforms preceded the most sustained economic boom since the 1960s, Republicans now argued that taxation was stalling economic growth. Bush promised "tax relief," reprising arguments from the 1970s and 1980s that cutting taxes would spur investment, create jobs, and improve the economy. The administration also echoed the supply-side economics that had been in vogue among Republicans since the 1980s: namely, that tax cuts would increase income and, as a result, boost government revenue over time.

In June 2001, the President signed the Economic Growth and Tax Relief Reconciliation Act. The law had sailed through the Republican-controlled House of Representatives and passed the closely divided Senate with the support of several Democrats, mostly conservatives from southern states. An immensely complicated law—the result of intense lobbying by business interests—it cut taxes by $1.35 trillion over a ten-year period. It reduced the top tax rate from 39.6 to 35 percent, expanded tax shelters for retirement plans, and gave a rebate of a few hundred dollars to everyone who had paid taxes in 2000. One of the law's most far-reaching measures was a planned reduction in the federal estate tax over a ten-year period, before its complete elimination in 2010. Bush's tax reforms would, however, expire in 2011, at which point the law would have to be reauthorized. Bush and the law's proponents hoped that, by then, the tax cuts would be politically impossible to repeal.

Bush's tax cuts had the same effects as Reagan's: they brought windfalls to the wealthiest taxpayers. About 45 percent of the total tax reductions went to the richest 1 percent of taxpayers; only 13 percent went to the bottom 60 percent. The result was that income inequality, which had been steadily growing since the 1970s, worsened. By 2005 one scholar found that "the richest three million people had as much income as the bottom 166,000,000."[11] The wealthy did very well, but incomes for most other Americans continued to stagnate or fall.

Bush's assumption that rich taxpayers would use their tax savings to create jobs and spur economic growth proved to be wrong. Instead, they fueled a speculative boom in real estate and in stocks and bonds. Many of the richest Americans invested in hedge funds and speculated on risky and exotic financial instruments like derivatives that only a handful of financial experts fully understood. Banks poured trillions into collateralized debt obligations, particularly home mortgages that had been bundled into securities and sold with the promise of high returns. Since 1999, investment banks and hedge funds had been poorly regulated. The Bush administration cut funds and weakened the enforcement power of the Securities and Exchange Commission and other regulatory agencies. The result was a wild west of speculation that made many wealthy investors phenomenally rich.

In a grim repetition of 1980s history, reality again disproved the Laffer curve hypothesis that tax cuts would pay for themselves by increasing income and federal revenue. Instead, federal revenue dropped. By 2002 the Clinton-era surplus had disappeared. In 2004 the federal deficit peaked at $375 billion, a record high. To his critics, Bush had become a "big government conservative," who cut taxes for the rich while escalating federal spending. Among his administration's biggest outlays would be military spending. During his first seven months in office Bush had focused on domestic concerns. No one expected that he would soon become a wartime president.

9/11

The skies along the eastern seaboard were crystal clear on Wednesday, September 11, 2001. Around eight a.m., nineteen hijackers took control of four passenger jets in a carefully calculated plan to terrorize the United States. They turned two aircraft, laden with jet fuel, into giant missiles, flying them into the upper stories of the twin towers of New York's World Trade Center. They flew a third into the Pentagon, the headquarters of the Department of Defense, just outside Washington. Passengers in the fourth plane got news of the previous attacks and struggled with its hijackers; the plane crashed in a field in rural western Pennsylvania. In New York, hundreds of firefighters and police officers rushed to the twin towers, tending to the injured and helping thousands of workers escape. Just before ten a.m., in a terrible roar, the first World Trade Center tower, weakened by fire, collapsed. The second fell about half an hour later. All together 2,977 people died on 9/11, most of them in New York.

Al Qaeda

The terrorist organization responsible for the 9/11 bombings, Al Qaeda, was well known to American intelligence officials. Its leader, Osama bin Laden, had grown up in one of Saudi Arabia's wealthiest oil families and had been drawn to Afghanistan in the 1980s, during the bloody war against the Soviet occupation. Al Qaeda based its operations in the rugged mountainous region along the Afghan-Pakistani border.

Al Qaeda's rise was one of the many perverse results of the Cold War. During the 1980s, the Central Intelligence Agency had funded Bin Laden's fighters against the Soviets. But when the Cold War thawed, Bin Laden's funding dried up. In the early 1990s, enraged by the Persian Gulf War, by the American use of his native Saudi Arabia as a military base, and by ongoing American support for Israel, Bin Laden declared war against the United States. Al Qaeda also recruited throughout the Islamic world, attracting small but fiercely dedicated followers, mostly young men, committed to holy war.

The 9/11 assault was the most brutal in a string of Al Qaeda attacks on American targets. In 1993 Al Qaeda had detonated a truck bomb at the World Trade Center, killing six people. In 1998 it took responsibility for attacking the American embassies in Nairobi, Kenya, and Arusha, Tanzania, which killed several hundred more. And in 2000 Al Qaeda operatives suicide-bombed the *USS Cole*, a destroyer docked in Yemen, killing seventeen American sailors.

Fighting Al Qaeda had not been one of the Bush administration's top priorities. When Bush took office, intelligence officials were less concerned with the risks that Al Qaeda posed on the home front than with its potential to inflame tensions and religious conflict in the volatile Islamic countries of the Middle East, Africa, and Indonesia. During the spring and summer of 2001, Bush's foreign policy team began to discuss a long-term plan to neutralize Bin Laden's organization, but they did not anticipate that Al Qaeda was planning a massive attack on American soil. The bipartisan federal commission that later investigated 9/11 noted that during the summer of 2001, American intelligence officials received "a stream of warnings" of an impending attack, perhaps "something very, very, very big."[12] But the Bush administration ignored them.

Homeland Security and the War on Terror

Within days of the attack, President Bush announced an aggressive response. "Our war on terror," he told Congress on September 20, "begins with Al Qaeda but it does not end there. It does not end until every terrorist group of global reach has been found, stopped, and defeated." He pledged to use "every means of diplomacy, every tool of intelligence, every instrument of law enforcement, every financial influence, and every necessary weapon of war" to thwart the threat of terrorism.[13] This was the strongest language that any president had used since the Cold War. Bush warned that the struggle would not result in any quick victories, but by suggesting that the United States would target "every" terrorist group and use "every" means at its disposal to defeat them, he set impossibly high expectations for victory. Unlike national armies, terrorist organizations were decentralized and elusive. They used the Internet to recruit members worldwide. They communicated using encrypted messages, often through decoy websites that were difficult to track. They went underground and reorganized when they were threatened. New groups sprang up, particularly in fractious countries like Afghanistan, Pakistan, and Syria, often evading detection until they acted.

Would Americans commit to an all-out struggle against such a hard-to-define enemy? At first, the answer seemed to be yes. Bush's popularity skyrocketed after 9/11. Sales of American flags took off, and surveys showed the public to be more hawkish then it had been in decades. Commentators suggested that, for the first time since the 1960s, Americans seemed united around a common cause.

The Bush administration and Congress moved quickly to mobilize public opinion. In October, Congress hastily drafted and passed the USA PATRIOT Act (an acronym for Uniting and Strengthening America by Providing Appropriate Tools Required to Intercept and Obstruct Terrorism). The sweeping piece of legislation expanded the power of intelligence agencies to gather information about suspected terrorists. It allowed national security officials to intercept the electronic communications of American citizens suspected to be supporting terrorist activities. And it created a special Foreign Intelligence Surveillance Court that operated in secret to authorize federal investigations. The administration also created a secret domestic surveillance program—one that would not be revealed to the public for four years. In the search for "sleeper cells" and potential terrorists, intelligence officials intercepted millions of telephone calls and Internet communications, installed spy software on computers and telecommunications devices, and demanded that Internet providers and telephone companies hand over records to the government.

More public security measures only added to the fear of imminent attack. The new Department of Homeland Security issued color-coded warnings of possible terrorist threats, signaling to the public that another 9/11 could happen at any moment. Airports instituted elaborate security screening procedures, under the supervision of the new federal Transportation Security Administration. The budget for homeland security skyrocketed, transforming local law enforcement. Flush with federal grants, police departments purchased expensive military equipment, including armored cars, tanks, and armor-piercing weapons.

In the name of fighting the war on terror, the Bush administration also empowered the CIA to detain suspected conspirators at secret centers. To give investigators as much leeway as possible, the Department of Justice issued a special memo in September 2002 that permitted the use of interrogation techniques that fell afoul of international treaties and domestic laws forbidding torture. John Yoo, a Harvard-educated attorney who worked at Justice, argued that suspected terrorists were not protected by due process provisions. Bush authorized the creation of "military tribunals"—outside the judicial system—to investigate terrorists. In early 2002 the government began constructing a secret prison, in Guantánamo Bay, Cuba, to hold suspected terrorists for indefinite periods. The U.S. held suspects at "black sites," unnamed prisons in Lithuania, Iraq, Thailand, Afghanistan, Poland, and Romania, where the CIA could interrogate and torture detainees without having to comply with American law.

Torture and Human Rights

The administration reinterpreted a federal law that banned torture by offering the narrowest possible definition: Torture consisted only of "the most extreme acts" that were "equivalent in intensity to the pain accompanying serious physical injury, such as organ failure, impairment of bodily function, or even death."[14] That loose definition put the United States at odds with international human rights laws that forbade the use of violence against prisoners. And it gave interrogators license to deploy new techniques such as waterboarding (simulating the act of drowning) to force prisoners to talk. CIA operatives waterboarded the key planner of the 9/11 attacks, Khalid Sheikh Muhammad, 183 times in a single month. In an effort to gain "total control" over detainees, they also used such tactics as sleep deprivation (forcing prisoners to stay awake for days at a time), mock executions, and forced rectal feeding. One prisoner was confined in a coffin-sized box for eleven days. Others were sodomized. In 2014, a congressional committee would issue a scathing report, presenting evidence that the "CIA's use of its 'enhanced interrogation techniques' was not an effective means of acquiring intelligence or gaining information from detainees."[15]

THE WARS IN AFGHANISTAN AND IRAQ

Afghanistan became the first international battleground in Bush's war on terror. The country was under the control of the Taliban, Islamic fundamentalists who had also provided a haven for Bin Laden and his Al Qaeda operation. Brutal and repressive, the Taliban imposed strict religious rule on the war-torn country, destroying non-Muslim religious sites, forbidding the formal education of girls, and suppressing what they considered to be godless Western culture. Less than a month after 9/11, the Bush administration deployed American troops in Afghanistan, ordered air attacks on Taliban bases, and provided assistance to the Northern Alliance, a loose confederation of anti-Taliban forces. By the end of 2001, the Taliban had been routed.

Hundreds of suspected terrorists were captured and shipped to America's military prison at Guantánamo Bay, where they would be held indefinitely, without access to lawyers or the right to communicate with the outside world, their lack of rights justified on grounds of a "national emergency." Bin Laden, however, remained at large, and the region remained unstable. During the 2002 fiscal year, the United States deployed 5,200 troops in Afghanistan. By 2008, nearly 31,000 troops were stationed there.

Regime change proved to be expensive. In early 2002 Bush announced a "Marshall Plan" for the reconstruction of Afghanistan that included funding for military training, public education, and public works. "We're working hard in Afghanistan," he declared. "We're clearing minefields. We're rebuilding roads. We're improving medical care." The rhetoric echoed a call by Lyndon Johnson for a TVA for Vietnam's Mekong Delta and met with a similar fate. The new Afghan regime, propped up by American aid, struggled with corruption and faced intense opposition in much of the countryside. Al Qaeda and other anti-American groups hid in the impenetrable mountains bordering Pakistan. The Taliban regrouped and continued to skirmish with Afghan troops and their American allies, gradually regaining control in many regions. Just as the Russians found themselves bogged down in a costly effort to take control of Afghanistan in the 1980s, so did the United States see few positive long-term results from its costly engagement there.

Iraq

Behind the scenes, the Bush administration set its sights on another major target, Saddam Hussein's Iraq. His oil-rich dictatorship had not been involved in the 9/11 attacks and opposed fundamentalists like the Taliban and Al Qaeda. But from Bush's first days in office, his foreign policy advisers had warned, even if they lacked evidence, that Saddam Hussein was working to build weapons of mass destruction (WMD) in a bid to extend his power in the region.

Many Bush administration officials saw the resolution of the 1991 Persian Gulf War, which had left the dictator in power, as a failure. After the Gulf War, the United Nations had instituted an economic embargo on Iraq and forbidden arms trades with Saddam Hussein's regime. In the late 1990s, a group of conservative foreign policy experts—several of whom would later assume top positions in the Bush administration—began arguing that the

United States should oust Saddam Hussein as a part of a larger post–Cold War project to depose anti-American regimes worldwide. Secretary of Defense Rumsfeld, his chief deputy, Paul Wolfowitz, and Vice President Dick Cheney, the hawkish former senator from Wyoming and former Nixon and Ford aide, put Iraq at the top of the Bush administration's foreign policy agenda well before 9/11.

The "Axis of Evil"

By late 2001, with the Taliban out of power in Afghanistan, Bush turned his attention toward "regime change" elsewhere in the world. In his 2002 State of the Union address, he singled out Iraq, Iran, and North Korea. "States like these and their terrorist allies," he argued, "constitute an axis of evil, arming to threaten the peace of the world. By seeking weapons of mass destruction, these regimes pose a grave and growing danger." His rhetoric echoed Ronald Reagan's "evil empire" statement by making a moral case for an aggressive foreign policy. In the wake of 9/11, Bush explicitly linked these regimes to the threat of violent attacks on the United States. "They could provide these arms to terrorists, giving them the means to match their hatred." Bush's strong language alarmed many of America's allies, who believed that it was a call for war.[16]

No place embodied the "axis of evil" for Bush more than Saddam Hussein's Iraq. That regime, argued Bush, "continues to flaunt its hostility toward America and to support terror."[17] The administration's hawks argued that Saddam Hussein destabilized the Middle East, continued to threaten American economic interests there, and jeopardized America's ally, Israel. They also believed that a post–Saddam Hussein Iraq would serve as a beacon for democracy throughout the Middle East. Bush also began to make a case for the necessity of preemptive warfare. "If we wait for threats to materialize, we will have waited too long," he told graduates of West Point in June 2002. "We must take the battle to the enemy, disrupt his plans, and confront the worst threats before they emerge. In the world we have entered, the only path to safety is the path of action, and this Nation will act."[18]

Selling the War

Over the summer and fall of 2002, Bush and his advisers began making the case for military engagement, on the grounds that Saddam Hussein was building weapons of mass destruction and supporting terrorism. Independent observers were skeptical that Iraq had developed WMD, or even had the capacity to do so, in large part because the country's economy had been hobbled by UN sanctions. But the president insisted otherwise. In a September 2002 address, Bush forcefully argued: "The Iraqi regime possesses biological and chemical weapons, is rebuilding the facilities to build more . . . [and] is seeking a nuclear bomb and with fissile material could build one within a year."[19] Administration officials deflected arguments that there was no evidence for these claims. "We don't want the smoking gun to be a mushroom cloud," warned national security adviser Condoleezza Rice in a statement that the president and other administration officials would repeat.[20]

Behind the scenes, some Bush administration officials were skeptical of war with Iraq. Secretary of State Colin Powell worried that it would require a massive commitment of American ground troops and lead to a costly, long-term engagement. As Powell had memorably told the president, "You are going to be the proud owner of 25 million people. You will own all their hopes, aspirations and problems. You'll own it all."[21] The cost of reconstructing Iraq would be high, and Powell doubted that the U.S. military had the capacity to oversee a transition to democracy in a regime that was bitterly divided by religious sectarianism and that lacked the institutions or history of democratic governance. Powell argued that continuing sanctions against Iraq would keep Saddam Hussein in check.

Some Republicans—including several veterans of the first Bush administration—made the case that going after Saddam Hussein would detract from efforts to target Al Qaeda. Liberal critics argued that a war in Iraq was a crude political ploy to mask the administration's failure to capture Bin Laden. Toppling the Iraqi dictator would provide more tangible evidence of victory against terror than the ongoing clandestine operations against Al Qaeda. Activists on the left resuscitated the Vietnam analogy and suggested that Bush, a former petroleum industry executive, was willing to spill "blood for oil" and that Vice President Cheney had financial interests in companies that would profit from the reconstruction of Iraq.

Throughout the second half of 2002 and early 2003, Bush and his foreign policy team took every occasion to reiterate their argument that Saddam Hussein possessed WMD. Most major newspapers and television news programs reported the administration's arguments uncritically, creating what diplomatic historian Fredrik Logevall called a "permissive context" for entering a war.[22] Both *The New York Times* and *The Washington Post* would later apologize for burying stories that presented evidence that contradicted the administration's position.

That permissive context set the tone for legislation authorizing the president to conduct military action against Iraq, which passed with large majorities in both the House and the Senate and was signed by President Bush on October 16, 2002. The public—still fearful of terrorism—rallied behind the call for war. Liberal internationalists, including many in the Democratic Party's mainstream like former president Clinton, echoed the Bush administration's position on Iraq. The "liberal hawks" used periodicals like *Slate*, *The New Republic*, and *The New York Times* to call for war.

Bush clinched his argument in his State of the Union address in January 2003. Although UN inspectors had found no evidence that Saddam Hussein's regime had WMD, Bush cited a British intelligence report that Iraq "had sought significant quantities of uranium from Africa" and had attempted to acquire aluminum tubes for the construction of nuclear weaponry. When Colin Powell addressed the United Nations in late January, he presented what he called incontrovertible evidence that Saddam Hussein had weapons facilities and was harboring key Al Qaeda leaders. Both claims proved false. A few years later Powell retracted his remarks, claiming that he had been fed misleading intelligence. But it was too late.

Powell, who was highly regarded, persuaded many Americans that the administration's case was valid. But most of America's allies remained skeptical of American claims about WMDs and concerned that a war in Iraq would destabilize the Middle East. Of the major powers, only Great Britain supported Bush. British prime minister Tony Blair shared Bush's moral argument in favor of toppling autocratic regimes and pledged to join the United States. The Americans and the British tried but failed to win United Nations support.

Operation Iraqi Freedom

With the backing of a hodge-podge "coalition of the willing" that included Britain, Australia, and about forty small countries that offered mostly symbolic support, Bush decided to buck the United Nations. On March 17, 2003, the president warned Saddam Hussein that if he did not step down, the United States would attack. Two days later the United States deployed about 140,000 troops in what the Pentagon called Operation Iraqi Freedom. The Iraqi army, badly trained, was caught by surprise by what Secretary

Rumsfeld called a strategy of "shock and awe." Massive airstrikes broke Iraqi lines, and U.S. troops marched into the heart of the country. Within five weeks, Baghdad had fallen, and Saddam Hussein had gone into hiding.

His swift collapse seemed to vindicate the strategy of "regime change." On May 1, 2003, dressed in a flight suit, President Bush appeared on the *USS Abraham Lincoln*, an aircraft carrier stationed off the coast of San Diego. Under a banner that read "Mission Accomplished," he announced the end of major combat operations and hailed the "liberation of Iraq" as "a crucial advance in the campaign against terror." America and its allies were the agents of liberty. "In the images of celebrating Iraqis," he continued, "we have also seen the ageless appeal of human freedom."[23]

"Mission Accomplished"

Bush's speech was ill timed. Within months it became clear that the war in Iraq was far from over. Saddam Hussein had brutally held together a country that was deeply divided by religion and ethnicity. The "liberation" of Baghdad was followed by intense sectarian violence. Sunni and Shi'ite Muslims struggled for power; rebels attacked both Iraqi government forces and American troops; and news of car bombings dominated the headlines. Bush and his aides, however, remained optimistic about the possibility of a democratic Iraq and increased the number of American troops in 2004 to maintain order until the country stabilized.

The rationale for the Iraq War quickly crumbled away. Investigators searched for evidence that Saddam Hussein had stockpiled WMD. Military and intelligence officials scoured factories, rifled through Iraqi government records, and interviewed former government officials, scientists, and military leaders, but they found no evidence of such weapons. They also looked long and hard for a smoking gun that Hussein had bankrolled Al Qaeda. They found nothing. In a particularly tasteless filmed skit at the 2004 White House Correspondents Association dinner, President Bush scuttled through the White House in a spoof search for WMD, even crawling under the Oval Office desk.

The situation in Iraq worsened over the next several years. The country plunged into civil war, and its weak, American-supported government could not contain the disorder. In mid-2005 the Department of Defense reported about 500 "weekly security incidents" occurred in Iraq, most of them bombings. The number increased to 1,000 in the summer of 2006 and peaked at

1,600 in June 2007. By 2008, after a "troop surge," about 250,000 American troops were committed to the Iraq War.[24] Because the military relied on reservists and volunteer forces (there was no draft during the Iraq War), many troops were ordered to extend their tours of duty, a move that was particularly unpopular among the ranks. The number of violent incidents declined for a time after the surge, but Iraqis lived in constant fear of car bombings, kidnappings, and shootings.

Abu Ghraib

In April 2004 grim photographs from Abu Ghraib, a notorious prison long operated by the Saddam Hussein regime, further discredited the American war effort. Nearly three-quarters of the prisoners held there by American forces had committed no crimes. For months reports had been filtering out through human rights organizations that the military and the CIA were systematically torturing Iraqi prisoners, administering brutal, sometimes fatal beatings, hanging them by their wrists and leaving them dangling, and raping them. The story exploded when *The New Yorker* magazine investigated the story and obtained photographs of soldiers, male and female, laughing as they abused inmates, sexually molested them, walked them naked on dog chains, and punched them. The most striking photograph showed a hooded Iraqi prisoner standing on a cardboard box, with wires attached to his fingers, toes, and penis. All together eleven U.S. soldiers were tried and convicted for their participation in the Abu Ghraib incident.

Some of those charged asserted they had acted with the approval of their superiors, and evidence mounted that higher military officials had condoned abuse and torture in Abu Ghraib, Guantánamo, and other secret U.S. prisons. Bush and other administration officials denounced the abuses and attributed them to a few "bad apples." But the prison abuses occurred in a permissive atmosphere resulting from administrative decisions dating back to 2001 that justified torture and held that the United States was not bound by human rights accords or the laws of war when dealing with suspected terrorists.

The situation in Iraq scarcely fit the ideal of "liberty" that Bush and his advisers had imagined. The country's infrastructure had collapsed. Its economy was a shambles. And the war exacted a huge price in lives. Between 2003 and 2011, about 4,500 Americans and, by conservative estimates, between 100,000 and 200,000 Iraqis (some estimates reached over 600,000) died because of war-related injuries. Instability in Iraq fueled the growth of terrorist and radical Islamic organizations. About half of all terrorist incidents worldwide in the 2000s occurred in post-invasion Iraq. Saddam Hussein himself was tried, convicted, and executed by the Iraqi government in 2006, but no one saw the new regime as a beacon of liberty or the source of stability in the Middle East. The invasion and occupation of Iraq proved a costly foreign policy failure.

THE LIMITS OF CONSERVATISM

The cost of pursuing the two wars was immense. Between 2001 and 2012, Congress appropriated $1.4 trillion for the wars in Afghanistan and Iraq, but as one analyst argued, "those figures vastly understate the total costs." By conservative estimates, the United States paid another $3.5 trillion for costs such as foreign aid to the war-torn countries, interest on money borrowed to pay for increased military expenses, and medical and disability expenses for veterans.[25]

During past wars, presidents had evoked the concept of shared sacrifice, rallying the population to buy war bonds, accept rationing, or pay for military expenditures through increased taxes. During the Iraq War as well, it became commonplace in political speeches, editorials, and in public discourse to call for supporting American troops. Uniformed armed service members got priority seating on airlines, cheers at sporting events, and countless rallies in high school gyms. But increasing taxes to pay for the massive military expenditures was out of the question in an era of "no new taxes." The federal budget deficit skyrocketed, and the Bush administration and Congress, already primed to cut domestic programs in the service of small government, axed spending in many areas, including scientific research, transportation infrastructure, and regulation.

"Political Capital" and Social Security Reform

The 2004 election was closely fought, as Bush faced off against Senator John Kerry (D-MA). A decorated Vietnam veteran, Kerry had initially supported the Iraq War, but by 2004, as the war dragged on, he expressed skepticism about its goals. Kerry, a moderate, also criticized the Bush administration's positions on abortion, stem cell research, and homosexuality. The campaign was ugly. A group of Vietnam veterans, funded by right-wing donors, claimed, without basis, that Kerry had lied about his service in Vietnam. Evangelical Christians mobilized around gay marriage and abortion. And a conservative Catholic bishop denied Kerry—a practicing Catholic—communion because of his position on reproductive rights.

Bush pledged, if reelected, to stay the course. The election would occur less than two years after he launched the war on Iraq. Although the war's critics grew more vocal, Bush did not face the systematic opposition that had hampered Lyndon Johnson. American taxpayers did not feel the pinch of wartime spending or domestic sacrifice. Young men had no fear that they would be drafted. By the standards of World War II, Korea, and Vietnam, the American body count was small.

After a decisive election victory, Bush crowed, "I earned capital in this campaign, political capital, and now I intend to spend it."[26] At the top of his list was the privatization of Social Security. For decades, Republicans had targeted the program, one of the last survivors of Franklin Delano Roosevelt's New Deal. Goldwater had argued for its dismantling, and Reagan had attempted and failed a radical restructuring of the program. In the 1990s Bush had told members of the Cato Institute, a libertarian think tank, that privatizing Social Security was "the most important policy issue facing the United States today."[27]

He made the case that Social Security was irreparably broken and would collapse because of the rapidly aging population. He proposed to privatize the program, calling for the creation of "personal accounts" that would allow individuals to divert funds from payroll taxes to the stock market. Supporting Bush were a series of corporate and conservative think-tank-sponsored "AstroTurf" (as compared to grassroots) organizations like "For Our Grandchildren" and "Alliance for Worker Retirement Security." But those organizations were no match for the broad opposition that Bush faced from Democrats, from mass membership organizations like the American Association of Retired People, and from the public more widely. Social Security, as it had been under Reagan, was still a "third rail," politically untouchable. Bush's plan went nowhere.

Katrina

When Hurricane Katrina hit the Gulf Coast in August 2005, the Bush administration was caught off guard. The president was on vacation at his ranch in Crawford, Texas, and remained there two days after the hurricane struck. Even though the evening news showed horrific photographs of people trapped on their rooftops in Pascagoula, Mississippi, and New Orleans, bloated bodies floating through debris-strewn canals, and chaos outside the New Orleans Superdome, where more than twenty thousand people crowded in a makeshift refugee camp with few provisions, Bush said nothing until the fourth day after the storm hit.

Bush's silence was a sign less of personal insensitivity (which many felt at the time) than of bureaucratic failure, a consequence of the administration's shifting priorities. The Federal Emergency Management Agency (FEMA), which was responsible for disaster relief, was ill prepared to respond to Katrina. Created by President Carter in 1979, FEMA had been folded into the Department of Homeland Security after 9/11. The agency became a second-tier organization in a huge national security bureaucracy, ill managed and politically marginal. Disaster relief took second place to counterterrorism efforts. No one knew exactly what power FEMA had or how it should respond. Two days after the hurricane struck, Marty Bahamonde, the only FEMA official on the ground in New Orleans, sent an urgent message to Michael Brown, the head of FEMA, reporting that the situation was "past critical" and noted that people were running "out of food and out of water at the dome." Brown sent a terse reply four minutes later. "Thanks for the update. Anything I need to do or tweak?"[28]

On Wednesday, August 31, *Air Force One* flew over the Gulf Coast on its track from the president's Texas ranch back to Washington. On Friday, September 2, Bush toured the Mississippi coast, infamously praising Brown for doing "a heckuva job." Only then did the federal government begin to send relief dollars and federal assistance to the devastated region. After a harrowing week struggling to survive on the streets of New Orleans, Patricia Thompson was finally evacuated on Saturday, September 3. She resettled in College Station, Texas, where she found work at an elementary school and financial assistance and housing through a local evangelical church.

Rebuilding after Katrina would be a gargantuan task. The hurricane had wiped out several towns on the Gulf Coast, killed more than 1,800 people, destroyed 160,000 houses and apartments, and left $108 billion of damage in its wake. In its aftermath, the Bush administration decided to turn New Orleans into a model of privatization. In September the president announced the creation of a "Gulf Coast Opportunity Zone" in which he waived federal air quality control and trucking safety regulations. He also waived a federal law that required contractors on government projects to be paid the local prevailing wage. Rather than putting federal money into the reconstruction of housing, the administration created Katrina trailer parks, leaving it to the private sector to provide, or not, affordable housing in the long term. Rebuilding New Orleans happened painfully slowly, especially in the neighborhoods that had been home to the city's poorest residents. The city grew wealthier and whiter after Katrina.

Post-Katrina relief efforts also relied heavily on faith-based community organizations. Hundreds of faith groups, with budgets ranging from a few hundred to a few million dollars, attempted to fill the gap left by the federal government. But Katrina tested their capacity. A detailed study of more than two hundred religious groups found that they "did not have sufficient trained staff, resources, or protocols to provide more than limited and short-term assistance."[29]

One of the most consequential post-Katrina experiments, which won the support of the Bush administration and both centrist Democrats and most Republicans, was a plan to privatize New Orleans's public schools. Scott Cowen, the president of Tulane University, argued that Katrina offered "a once in a lifetime opportunity" to transform public education.[30] Ten years after the hurricane, nine out of ten students in New Orleans attended charter schools, run by nonprofit organizations. Although educators intensely debated whether charter schools were more effective than public schools—the best evidence showed that there is little difference in educational outcomes—reformers saw the Crescent City as a laboratory for school reform that could be replicated nationwide.

Deregulation and the Financial Crisis

The economy of the early 2000s, more than in the past, rested on a volatile foundation: the housing market. Wages remained stagnant throughout the period, but housing prices skyrocketed, in large part because interest rates reached an all-time low. Federal Reserve chairman Alan Greenspan, who had directed central monetary policy since the 1980s, used the tool of interest rate cuts to curb inflation and stimulate economic growth. But in the early 2000s, as the economy slowed, he took an even more drastic measure. The Federal Reserve steadily cut the prime rate, the interest that banks charged for interbank loans. It bottomed out at 1 percent between 2002 and 2004, the lowest since the early 1950s. Greenspan's rationale was that lower interest rates would fuel a housing boom. Ready credit would lead to a rise in home values. Homeowners would benefit from the growing equity in their properties and spend more, bolstering the economy.

Greenspan's actions set off a mad scramble in the housing market. Lower interest rates attracted first-time homebuyers. Those who already owned homes rushed to refinance their mortgages. Many gambled that their houses would continue to appreciate and took home equity loans, which they used to make home improvements, pay for skyrocketing college tuition expenses, or cover extraordinary health care expenses. The home became a sort of ATM, a source of easily available cash, so long as home values continued to rise.

Thousands of new mortgage origination firms sprung up virtually overnight, taking advantage of the seemingly boundless market. "Lending standards," wrote one analyst, "became almost comical. Buyers could get a mortgage with no income and no assets. Paperwork was scant."[31] Predatory lenders often overcharged customers, relied on fraudulent home appraisals, and hid exorbitant fees. They offered adjustable-rate mortgages that lured borrowers with low interest rates that quickly escalated to several points above the prime rate. Many of those lenders targeted minorities who had long suffered from discrimination in home lending. A group of housing economists found that in 2006 more than a quarter of all loans nationwide charged unusually high interest rates, "including 49 percent and 39 percent of loans made to African Americans and Hispanics, respectively."[32]

Wall Street investors fueled the madness. They took advantage of loose regulations, particularly the Clinton administration's repeal of the Glass-Steagall Act in 1999. They basked in the antiregulatory fervor in the Bush administration. The federal agencies that regulated banking and financial firms turned a blind eye toward risky lending practices. Sheila Bair, a moderate Republican who chaired the Federal Deposit Insurance Corporation (set up during the New Deal to protect depositors from bank failures), called for a tightening of mortgage lending rules but faced fierce opposition from Wall Street and from within the Bush administration itself. "I frequently found myself isolated in advocating for stronger regulatory standards," she recalled. From the Federal Reserve to the boardrooms of major banks, everyone believed that "market forces" would lead firms to "self-regulate."[33] Major financial firms, among them Countrywide Financial, Citigroup, Wells Fargo, JPMorgan Chase, and Lehman Brothers, bundled together risky loans and sold them as securities to eager investors. As long as real estate prices continued to rise, everyone seemed to be a winner. Consumers bought more; investors earned high returns; investment banks made massive profits.

The mortgage market began to collapse in 2006, when lenders ratcheted the interest on adjustable-rate mortgages upward. For the first time in years, housing values began to drop. Places like Euclid, Ohio, a working-class suburb just east of Cleveland, were the canaries in the coal mine. Euclid was exactly the sort of community that predatory lenders targeted: its residents, hurt by the collapse of the region's industrial economy and the rise of the low-wage service sector, earned moderate incomes. Nearly a third of Euclid's residents were African Americans who hoped to own their own homes in a suburb that had long excluded them. In 2006 and 2007 alone, lenders initiated foreclosures on more than six hundred houses in Euclid as homeowners saw the monthly payments on their adjustable-rate mortgages rise 50 percent or more. The city of Euclid installed alarm systems in some vacant houses to keep out scavengers and squatters. It spent more than a million dollars maintaining the foreclosed properties and mowing lawns.

By 2008, what happened in Euclid was happening everywhere in the United States. Housing values plummeted, and more than a million homes were lost to foreclosure nationwide that year, as homeowners struggled to meet payments. The collapse in confidence in securitized, high-risk mortgages devastated some of the nation's largest banks and lenders. The home financing giant Fannie Mae alone held an estimated $230 billion in toxic assets. In September 2008 the giant investment banking firm Lehman Brothers collapsed, sparking panic across the economy. The entire banking system teetered on the brink. Lending came to a virtual halt, and consumer spending plummeted. Wall Street firms panicked, and the stock market plummeted. In November the Federal Reserve used $800 billion to buy up mortgage debt, to save major banking institutions.

THE ELECTION OF 2008

The economic crash and the disaster of Iraq weighed heavily on the presidential election in 2008. President Bush was deeply unpopular. Wall Street was reeling. Homeowners faced record foreclosure rates. Many commentators worried that Americans would make a run on banks in a grim repetition of the early years of the Great Depression. The political climate aided the Democratic Party. Two years earlier Democrats had swept the midterm elections, winning control of both the House and the Senate for the first time since 1994.

The Candidate of "Hope and Change"

The Democratic nominee, Barack Obama, had risen from political obscurity, launching a presidential campaign just two years after he had been elected to the U.S. Senate from Illinois. His background was unusual: he was born in 1960, when interracial marriage was taboo in much of the United States and forbidden in most of the South, to a white mother and an African father. Obama had grown up in Hawaii and graduated from Columbia University before working for almost three years as a community organizer on Chicago's South Side. He achieved his only significant victory when he persuaded the Chicago Housing Authority to remove asbestos from the Altgeld Homes, a low-income housing project. Frustrated at the limitations of organizing, Obama attended Harvard Law School and became the first black editor of the *Harvard Law Review*. There he succeeded in winning the support of liberal students who saw him as one of their own, black students who believed he would advance the goals of civil rights, and conservative students who trusted him because he took their ideas seriously and gave them voice on the law review's editorial board. It was a formula for bipartisanship—respect your opponents and use your skills of persuasion to win them over—that would be a model for his political career.

In 1991, with his law degree in hand, he moved back to Chicago, worked on a voting rights campaign, practiced law, and taught courses at the University of Chicago Law School. In 1996 he was elected to the Illinois State Senate, representing one of the most liberal districts in the country. In Springfield, Obama reached out and befriended some Republicans, even as he voted fairly consistently against them. By 2003, when he set his sights on the U.S. Senate, he had moved to the center of the Democratic Party. On most issues—welfare reform, regulation, and economic policy—his policy choices were fairly close to Bill Clinton's. Only on foreign policy issues did he veer toward his party's liberal wing, initially opposing the Iraq War and criticizing Bush's surveillance and detention policies.

In 2008 Obama ran for president as a fresh-faced alternative to the Washington status quo, pitching himself as a candidate who would bring the country together after a period of divisiveness. Since his national debut as a keynote speaker at the Democratic National Convention in 2004, he had pitched himself as a reconciler, drawing from his own interracial family history to make the point. The audience roared when he called out, "There's not a liberal America and a conservative America; there's the United States of America. There's not a black America and white America and Hispanic America and Asian America; there's the United States of America. The pundits, the pundits like to slice and dice our country into red states and blue states: red states for Republicans, blue states for Democrats. But I've got news for them, too. We worship an awesome God in the blue states, and we don't like federal agents poking around our libraries in the red states."[34]

Many Democrats in 2008 were skeptical that a majority white nation would elect a black president. During the primaries, Obama faced a formidable opponent, the New York senator and former first lady Hillary Rodham Clinton, who pledged to return the country to the economic prosperity and peace that it had enjoyed during her husband's presidency. But Obama electrified Democratic audiences with his call for "hope" and "change." Clinton denounced the concepts as gauzy, played on her experience as a policy maker and senator, and argued that she had the maturity and experience to win. In a closely fought season of primaries and caucuses, Obama edged out Clinton and won the nomination.

The Maverick

Obama faced a divided Republican Party and a weak Republican candidate. John McCain had occasionally bucked his party's right wing, and he had earned their skepticism as a result. He had been a prisoner of war in Vietnam, married into a wealthy Arizona family, and enjoyed a long career in the Senate. But he faced an uphill battle. He defined himself as a "maverick," attempting to create a little distance between himself and the Bush administration. McCain launched his campaign with an advertisement that evoked the 1960s, contrasting images of protest in the streets with his valiant service in the military. It was not a propitious beginning. In late August he made the electrifying announcement that he had chosen a virtually unknown Alaska politician, Sarah Palin, as his running mate. But he stumbled in the weeks that followed, as the economic crisis exploded. In September, when Lehman Brothers collapsed, he maintained that "the fundamentals of our economy are strong," before backtracking and making the ill-advised decision to suspend his campaign for a few days.[35]

Obama ran his campaign around the vague but appealing slogan, "Change We Can Believe In." Surrounding himself with talented advisers, he raised more money than any candidate to date and ran a sophisticated campaign, pioneering the use of new technologies to identify voters and bring them to the polls on election day. Obama's campaign events drew enormous crowds, and his supporters—younger and more racially diverse than the population as a whole—were highly motivated. He won election with a clear majority of the electorate and a greater percentage of the vote than any Democratic presidential candidate since 1964.

OBAMA AND THE WORLD

Obama's rise to the presidency seemed to herald the emergence of a new Democratic majority and a fundamental reorientation of U.S. domestic and international politics. He promised to reverse the previous administration's foreign policy, its penchant for secrecy, and its expansion of executive powers. In large part because of this promise, Obama won the 2009 Nobel Peace Prize, even though to that date, he had virtually no experience in international relations.

President Obama promised to withdraw American troops from Iraq. In December 2011, the last American troops would leave a country that was still ravaged by sectarian civil war, ruled by a corrupt, unstable regime, and crippled by a dysfunctional economy. The war, launched eight years earlier, had utterly failed in all its goals, other than toppling Saddam Hussein. Everyday life in Baghdad was still punctuated with car bombings. Iraq was a haven for terrorist organizations.

Obama attempted to tread a fine line between all-out war for regime change and limited interventions. He kept some key Bush administration programs in place. Breaking from a campaign pledge, he failed to close the American detention facility at Guantánamo Bay in Cuba. He continued the war on terror, authorizing the use of drones to assassinate "enemy combatants" in nonwar zones, even some who were American citizens. He continued the Bush administration's expansion of surveillance against dissenters and suspected terrorists at home and abroad. His administration fought efforts, pushed by civil liberties organizations, to restrict a National Security

Agency program to mine data from cell phone companies and Internet providers. The president also dramatically escalated the war in Afghanistan, at the same time pledging to withdraw American forces by late 2014. He deployed American troops in Libya in 2011, assisting rebels during a bloody civil war to overthrow dictator Muammar Gaddafi. But after the "regime change" occurred, he pulled American troops out. Post-Gaddafi Libya remained unstable and terror-ridden.

OBAMA AND THE LIMITS OF "CHANGE"

Taking office in the midst of the Great Recession, Obama pledged to undo the Bush administration's tax and regulatory policies that favored big business and banking. Yet he appointed a team of economic advisers who were comfortable in the world of high finance. His treasury secretary, Timothy Geithner, had run the New York Federal Reserve during the lead-up to the 2008 crash, and had close relationships to major bankers, financiers, and hedge fund managers. The head of Obama's National Economic Council, the economist Larry Summers, had played a crucial role in deregulating the financial sector as secretary of the treasury during the Clinton administration, and had worked as a consultant for a major hedge fund. Obama created a Council on Jobs and Competitiveness, headed by former General Electric chief executive Jeffrey Immelt, who had overseen a downsizing of his company's employment in the United States and massive investment in China. Obama resisted calls for the prosecution of bankers and financiers whose investment strategies—and whose illegal manipulations of the mortgage market—had led to the financial collapse in 2008. To do so, he and his advisers argued, would be divisive.[36]

Faced with a strong Republican opposition and divisions within his own Democratic Party in Congress, Obama's policy options were limited. And he was also fundamentally cautious, unwilling to engage in the messy deal making and horse trading that had allowed past presidents like Lyndon Johnson to push controversial legislation through a reluctant Congress. In early 2009 he signed the American Recovery and Reinvestment Act (also known as the stimulus package), an $800 billion program to launch "shovel ready" infrastructure projects and provide additional funds to states for education, public works, and other job creation programs. The stimulus funds were well below what mainstream economists believed was necessary to spark growth in the stagnant economy, but Obama did not have the political clout to push through anything larger.

Obamacare

Obama's signature program was health insurance reform, a longtime Democratic Party goal. About 15 percent of the population, many of them low-wage workers, had no health insurance. An injury or serious illness could be catastrophic. Many on the party's left hoped for a national health care system like those in Britain or Canada, but Obama forged a program that incorporated Republican ideas. His policy team, learning lessons from Clinton's failed reform in the 1990s, reached out to potential opponents. Obama won the support of the insurance industry, big pharmaceutical companies, and major corporations. His plan was modeled heavily on one first devised by conservative policy analysts at the Heritage Foundation and implemented in Massachusetts under Republican governor Mitt Romney, Obama's future Republican challenger.

By 2010, when the administration drafted the legislation, it faced a disciplined and unwavering Republican Party. Pulling the GOP rightward was the Tea Party, a conservative insurgency that had challenged Obama's legitimacy almost from his first day in office. Tea Party activists tarred him as un-American, a crypto-Muslim, or a black power activist. Many believed that he was an illegitimate president on the false charge that he had been born outside the United States.

The Tea Party's biggest target was health care, which they branded as "Obamacare." They charged that the president's program would create "death panels" that would decide whether to provide health care to elderly patients or let them die. Reprising themes from the Cold War, they charged that Obama was a "socialist" or a "communist" who was using health care reform as the first step to creating a totalitarian government. The Tea Party also targeted Republican officials whom they saw as insufficiently conservative, labeling them as Republicans in Name Only (RINOs) and supporting insurgent candidates in congressional races.

Obama's health care program passed Congress with no Republican votes. Still, many Republicans who opposed "Obamacare" faced angry Tea Party opponents during the 2010 primaries. Establishment Republicans, including those who had long supported presidents Reagan and Bush, lost to primary challengers from the right. In Utah, Mike Lee, a Tea Party favorite, unseated the establishment Republican senator Robert Bennett. In Kentucky, Rand Paul, a longtime libertarian, defeated a once-popular Republican secretary of state and went on to win a Senate seat. In the House, far-right Republicans formed the Tea Party caucus, using their clout to pull their colleagues even further rightward, For the next several years, House and Senate Republicans would do everything in their power to torpedo health care reform, passing dozens of resolutions calling for its appeal and filing lawsuits challenging parts of the bill in federal courts. Still Obamacare survived the sustained challenges. In late 2013, despite serious problems in the online enrollment system, nearly 7.3 million Americans enrolled in the insurance program, more than the law's backers had predicted.

The Budget

No issue generated greater partisan struggle than the federal budget. Republicans fought the Obama administration on nearly every aspect of federal spending, reprising arguments dating back to the 1980s that Democrats were profligate spenders. In 2010, Republicans forced an economic crisis over raising the federal debt ceiling, something that had been raised routinely, with little political controversy, under past Republican and Democratic presidents. Obama reached out to congressional Republicans and accepted a compromise that incorporated almost all Republican demands for dramatic cuts in federal spending while not increasing taxes, even on the richest Americans.

By 2010, Obama had turned his attention away from programs to stimulate the economy to an emphasis on deficit reduction. Many economists, notably Nobel Prize winner and *New York Times* columnist Paul Krugman, argued that the country would recover from the recession more quickly if the federal government spent more on public works and job creation, as it had during the Great Depression and World War II. But after thirty years of austerity and deficit reduction policies—under Democrats and Republicans alike—building political will for Keynesian interventions was close to impossible.

The Limits of Bipartisanship

Throughout his first term, Obama continued to hope that he could somehow bridge the deep partisan divide—just as he had back in his days as a law student at Harvard—by treating his political opponents with respect and conceding to at least some of their demands.[37] But his efforts yielded few victories. Despite an economic policy that continued to favor big business, his staunchest critics came from the right. His military policy, his commitment to "nation building" in Libya, his authorization of the assassination of Osama bin Laden, and his expansion of drone attacks were criticized by some left-leaning intellectuals, but not even the most bellicose foreign policy satisfied vast sections of the political right.

Although the recession officially ended in mid-2009, many Americans struggled to make ends meet. Obama had presided over a gradual improvement in the economy. Unemployment rates slowly fell beginning in 2009. The mortgage market remained tight, but housing prices leveled off, and in some parts of the country, they rose. Obama's policies, however, did little to address the pressing question of inequality. The economic recovery exacerbated the pattern of growing gaps between the rich, whose incomes steadily rose, in large part because of a booming stock market, and the middle and working classes, who faced a sluggish job market and falling wages. Between 2009 and 2012, incomes of the top 1 percent grew by 31.4 percent. But for the remaining 99 percent, incomes grew by only 0.4 percent.[38]

Persistent economic inequality sparked discontent on the political left. On September 17, 2011, a small group of protesters set up an encampment in Zuccotti Park, a small plaza in the heart of New York's financial district. They called themselves Occupy Wall Street (OWS) and vowed to hold major banks responsible for the ongoing economic crisis. Within weeks, a few hundred people had set up tents, and thousands more joined regular protests on the surrounding streets. In mid-November, the city of New York evicted the protesters, but Occupy movements took over public spaces in several other big cities and some college campuses throughout the fall and winter.

The Occupy movement took its inspiration from 1960s campus teach-ins and civil rights sit-ins, but also took advantage of new social media to spread their message worldwide. In Zuccotti Park, protestors set up a generator to power computers that they used to post photos, videos, and documents on Twitter, Tumblr, and Facebook. OWS activists did not, however, speak with a single voice—some wanted bank reform, others encouraged Americans to support small local businesses, some called for a repeal of austerity measures, and others demanded the overthrow of capitalism. For all of their differences—and their lack of a coherent program—OWS activists claimed to speak for the vast majority of people, versus the wealthiest one percent of the population. Their slogan, "We are the 99 percent," gave voice to those discontented at the persistence of inequality. By early 2012, the Occupy movement had dispersed, but it had succeeded in focusing attention on the widening wealth and income gaps in early twenty-first-century America.

In 2012, Obama handily won reelection against Republican Mitt Romney, who launched his political career after running Bain Capital, an investment firm that bought, restructured, and sold companies, a process that often left workers unemployed. Obama depicted Romney as an out-of-touch elitist. But even after Obama's decisive reelection, his second term would be full of unresolved challenges. Republicans continued to control the House of Representatives, using their position to block many of the president's key initiatives. After gaining control of the Senate in the 2014 midterm elections—benefiting from a low turnout among Democratic-leaning younger and minority voters—the Republicans vowed to continue to obstruct Obama's domestic initiatives. In the meantime, the administration struggled with ongoing instability in Egypt and Syria and worsening conditions in Iraq. Even with Bin Laden dead and Al Qaeda hobbled, new extremist organizations emerged in the Middle East, most prominently the Islamic State of Iraq and Syria (ISIS), which led brutal attacks on non-Muslim villages and towns in Kurdistan and western Iraq. In 2014, Obama announced that he would step up military assistance to Iraqi troops fighting ISIS. During each of these foreign policy crises, the president took a more cautious approach than Bush—unwilling to embroil the United States in another prolonged war but also unwilling to stand aside.

THE BURDEN OF HISTORY

Obama was not a transformational president, as his most fervent supporters hoped and as his staunch enemies feared he would be. He was ultimately constrained by a past that was not of his own making. The United States had been moving toward greater economic inequality since the 1970s. The grim plight of workers whose wages stagnated was the result of the collapse of organized labor, the rise of right-to-work policies, the massive flight of capital to low-wage regions around the world, and the emergence of a low-wage service sector economy at home. The Great Recession was the consequence of thirty years of financial deregulation under Democratic and Republican administrations alike.

In the Obama years, Americans intensely debated the nation's place in the world. At a moment of extreme partisanship, both parties showed signs of division over centuries-old questions about internationalism and isolation. Should the United States support regime change in places like Syria, torn by civil war? Or should it keep its distance, avoiding entanglement in another Iraq, another Vietnam? Should American foreign policy continue to be shaped by a moral vision of the United States as a global beacon of freedom? Or should the United States define its interests narrowly and act only when directly threatened? American foreign policy was still shaped, in fundamental ways, by the moral absolutism of the Cold War, an approach that was reinvigorated during the war on terror. But a countercurrent—not the majority—was chastened by the excesses of Abu Ghraib and Guantánamo and called for a reinvigoration of a lost American commitment to human rights.

Obama embodied one of the most enduring legacies of the long twentieth century, the growing recognition of African Americans in American politics. It is impossible to imagine the rise of a black president without considering the black freedom struggle of the post–World War II years. Obama looked up to civil rights leaders like U.S. representative John Lewis, who had begun his career sitting-in at movie theaters and lunch counters. Many commentators argued that Obama's election marked the rise of a "postracial" America, the dawn of a "post-civil-rights era."

But it was not so easy to overcome America's long history of racial injustice. By every measure, racial gaps remained vast, leaving people like Patricia Thompson with few opportunities for upward mobility. At the beginning of Obama's second term in office, 73 percent of whites but only 43 percent of blacks and 46 percent of Hispanics owned their own homes. The typical black household had only $5,677 in wealth (including savings accounts, real estate, and stock market investments); Hispanics had $6,325 in wealth. The comparable measure for white households was $113,149. The typical white household was twenty times wealthier than the typical black or Hispanic household.[39] Black unemployment rates have remained one and a half to two times that of whites since the 1950s—regardless of the state of the economy. And Hispanics, now 16 percent of the nation's population, comprise 28 percent of Americans living beneath the poverty line. One of the most pressing unresolved problems—the overrepresentation of blacks among those stopped by the police, arrested, and jailed—exploded in protests in 2014 after a police officer in Ferguson, Missouri, shot an unarmed black man, and when New York City police officers attempted to arrest a man for selling loose cigarettes and in the process choked him to death.

Well into the twenty-first century, the promises of the twentieth—equality, opportunity, and justice—remained only partially fulfilled. Martin Luther King, Jr., memorably stated that "the arc of the moral universe bends toward justice." But just as often, as modern American history shows, that arc veers off course. Modern America was shaped by the struggles of countless ordinary men and women, seeking to improve their communities, to achieve age-old ideals of equality and justice. But it was also shaped by a relentless drive toward self-interest. That struggle between individual interest and social responsibility remains the enduring contradiction of modern American history.

ACKNOWLEDGMENTS

The authors are grateful to Steve Forman, our editor at Norton, who brought us together, and who encouraged us, cajoled us, edited us, and enabled us to see this project through. Steve's colleague Justin Cahill masterfully shepherded us through crunch time.

Our readers saved us from embarrassing errors, gave us tips, pointed out gaping holes, and forced us to reevaluate our emphasis and approach in each chapter. The book is more correct, balanced, and comprehensive thanks to them. Some read more chapters than others, but everyone's reading proved invaluable. We are proud to be their colleagues.

James Anderson, Michigan State University
Kathryn Brownell, Purdue University–West Lafayette
Cindy Hahamovitch, The College of William & Mary
Shane Hamilton, University of Georgia
Michael Marino, The College of New Jersey
Norman Markowitz, Rutgers University
Craig Pascoe, Georgia College
Allison Perlman, University of California, Irvine
Kim Philips-Fein, New York University
Jonathan Rees, Colorado State University
Paul Rubinson, Bridgewater State University
Mark Sample, Monroe Community College
Matthew Sutton, Washington State University, Pullman
Gregory Wood, Frostburg State University

• • •

Glenda Gilmore is indebted to Lauren Pearlman, Sam Schaffer, Ashley Tallevi, Stephon Richardson, and Emily Yankowitz for their invaluable research assistance. Since I began this book, Lauren and Sam earned Ph.D.'s, and Ashley is in graduate school. Emily is a Yale undergraduate history major. Stephon began working on this book when he was in high school; he is now writing his senior thesis at Clark University. All of them showed great patience while chasing down facts, verifying figures, finding quotes, and powering through my repeated (and sometimes repetitious) queries. Eric Rutkow and Christopher McKnight Nichols provided sobering readings at a time when I sorely needed them. My Yale students in American Politics and Society, 1900–1945 and generations of graduate students in Readings in U.S. History in the Twentieth Century proved Jacquelyn Hall's observation when I accepted the job at Yale: "You will learn so much from your students!"

My teachers at the University of North Carolina at Chapel Hill taught me the interconnectedness of American history at a time when the profession sorted it into competitive subfields. William E. Leuchtenberg taught me the importance of political history, the significance of the New Deal, and the joy of birdwatching. William Barney's undergraduate survey represented the consummate lecture course. Jacquelyn Hall's women's history courses for undergraduates and graduates made the field central to American history. Nell Painter patiently showed me that African American history is American history.

Mia-lia, Derry, and Miles grew up and Ben wrote two books while I worked on *These United States*. Now that it's over, I promise them more bacon, more hikes, more Ireland, and one day soon, more Crete.

Glenda Elizabeth Gilmore

To an outside observer, writing seems a lonely occupation. I have spent many hours alone surrounded by books and papers, filling a blank screen with words. But for me, this book has been a collective project. Jessica Bird, Colin McGrath, and Kristian Taketomo provided timely research assistance. I have been very lucky to spend the first twenty-four years of my career at the University of Pennsylvania, where I tried out many of the ideas in these pages on enthusiastic and hardworking undergraduates in my courses on the New Deal, postwar politics and culture, civil rights, liberalism and conservatism, urban inequality, and America in the 1960s. I continue to learn from my dissertation advisees, a remarkably talented group, whose work has reshaped the field. Of my many talented Penn colleagues, let me single out a few who guided me on new paths through the twentieth century. Bruce Kuklick steered me toward power and ideas; Sally Gordon toward religion and law; Amy Offner toward economics and empire; and Michael Katz (may his memory be a blessing) toward education and welfare.

I have the world's best friends and family. Thanks to Peter Siskind for walks in the Wissahickon; Warren Breckman, Cordula Grewe, John Skrentny, Minh Phan-Ho, Greg Goldman, and Liz Hersh for standing by me in good times and bad, and especially for hosting a lot of good parties along the way; and Andrew Diamond and Caroline Rolland-Diamond for great conversation and food on both sides of the Atlantic. For all of you who have schmoozed with me over a cup of coffee, a lunch or dinner, or a late night drink, cheers. Finally, Brittany, Anna, and Jack: how can a line in my acknowledgments possibly capture all you have meant to me?

Thomas J. Sugrue

NOTES

PREFACE: "WE ARE STILL IN THE MAKING"

1   Franklin D. Roosevelt: "Radio Address on Brotherhood Day," February 23, 1936, http://bit.ly/1zpxXO6.

2   Saul Bellow, *It All Adds Up: From the Dim Past to the Uncertain Future* (New York: Penguin Books, 1995), 28.

3   Thomas Piketty, *Capital in the Twenty-first Century* (Cambridge, MA: Belknap Press of Harvard University Press, 2014), 316. The exception is the 1920s, when income disparity rose preceding the Great Depression.

4   Robert E. Gallman, "Trends in the Size Distribution of Wealth in the Nineteenth Century: Some Speculations," in Lee Soltow, ed., *Six Papers on the Size Distribution of Wealth and Income* (Washington, DC: National Bureau of Economic Research, 1969), 12; Piketty, *Capital,* 323.

5   Piketty, *Capital,* 11–15. This theory is known as the Kuznets curve, after economist Simon Kuznets who proposed it.

6   Piketty, *Capital,* 323–24.

7   Ibid., 316.

8   "U.S. Properties with Foreclosure Findings," http://bit.ly/1ARn44P.

9   "Remarks by Senator Barack Obama on Martin Luther King, Jr.," April 4, 2008, http://bit.ly/1JJJ8Vb.

10   U.S. Department of Homeland Security, Enforcement Actions, "Aliens Removed or Returned: Fiscal Years 1892 to 2012," http://1.usa.gov/1JJJcnE.

11   Blanche Wiesen Cook, *Eleanor Roosevelt,* vol. 1, *1884–1933* (New York: Penguin, 1993), 338.

12   Center for American Women and Politics, Eagleton Institute of Politics, Rutgers, the State University of New Jersey, "Gender Differences in Voter Turnout," http://bit.ly/1weOJZ9.

13   U.S. Bureau of Labor Statistics, "Women in the Labor Force: A Databook," http://1.usa.gov/1AYtpv7; Claudia Goldin, "The Female Labor Force and American Economic Growth, 1890–1980," http://bit.ly/1sQXwQL.

14 U.S. Bureau of Labor Statistics, "Women in the Labor Force: A Databook," http://1.usa.gov/1AYtpv7.

CHAPTER 1: ORIGINS OF THE AMERICAN CENTURY

1 Richard Harding Davis, "The Last Days of the Fair," *Harper's Weekly*, October 19, 1893.

2 G. L. Dybwad and Joy V. Bliss, eds., *White City Recollections: A Young Man's World's Fair Adventure with His Father* (Albuquerque, NM: Book Stops Here, 2003), 13–14.

3 Quoted in Robert Anderson Naylor, *Across the Atlantic* (London: Roxborough Press, 1893), 149.

4 Bertha Honoré Palmer, "Closing Address," in Mary Kavanaugh Oldham Eagle, ed., *The Congress of Women: Held in the Women's Building, World's Columbian Exposition, Chicago, U.S.A. 1893* (Chicago: Monarch Book Co., 1894), 820–24, http://bit.ly/PalmerClosing.

5 Lillie West Brown Buck, *Amy Leslie at the Fair* (Chicago: W. B. Conkey Co., 1893), 101.

6 Dybwad and Bliss, *White City Recollections*, 166.

7 Ibid., 150–51.

8 Quoted in Elliott M. Rudwick and August Meier, "Black Man in the 'White City': Negroes and the Columbian Exposition, 1893," *Phylon* 26 (1965): 359.

9 Ida B. Wells, ed., *The Reason Why the Colored American Is Not in the World's Columbian Exposition*, http://bit.ly/WellsReasonWhy.

10 Quoted in David B. Chesebrough, *Frederick Douglass: Oratory from Slavery* (Westport, CT: Greenwood Press, 1998), 79.

11 Richard Fink, ed., *Ragged Dick: And Mark the Match Boy: Two Novels by Horatio Alger* (New York: Collier Books, 1962), 6.

12 Quoted in Albro Martin, *Railroads Triumphant: The Growth, Rejection, and Rebirth of a Vital American Force* (New York: Oxford University Press, 1961), 201. See also Richard White, *Railroaded: The Transcontinentals and the Making of Modern America* (New York: W. W. Norton, 2012).

13 "Andrew Carnegie's Ode to Steelmaking," accessed at http://historymatters.gmu.edu/d/5750/, quoted from Harold Livesay, *Andrew Carnegie and the Rise of Big Business* (Boston: Little Brown, 1975), 189.

14 Ibid., 189, 166.

15 Quoted in James Howard Bridge, *The Inside History of the Carnegie Steel Company: A Romance of Millions* (New York: Aldine Book Co., 1903), 195.

16 Tim McNeese, *The Robber Barons and the Sherman Antitrust Act: Reshaping American Business* (New York: Chelsea House, 2008), 61.

17 Quoted in Howard Zinn, *A People's History of the United States* (New York: HarperPerennial Modern Classics, 2005), 260.

18 William Graham Sumner, *"Earth-Hunger" and Other Essays* (New Haven, CT: Yale University Press, 1913), 234.

19 Hamlin Garland, "Homestead and Its Perilous Trades—Impressions of a Visit," *McClure's Magazine* 3, no. 1 (June 1894).

20 Michael McGerr, *A Fierce Discontent: The Rise and Fall of the Progressive Movement in America, 1870–1920* (New York: Oxford University Press, 2005), 138.

21 Erika Lee and Judy Yung, *Angel Island: Immigrant Gateway to America* (New York: Oxford University Press, 2010), 30.

22 Marie Ganz and Nat J. Ferber, *Rebels: Into Anarchy and Out Again* (New York: Dodd, Mead, 1920), 73.

23 Quoted in Massachusetts Bureau of Statistics of Labor, *Thirteenth Annual Report*, 1883.

24 "To one he rents, to another he gives a contract for working on shares, to another he pays wages in money, and with another he swaps work, and so *ad infinitum.*" Quoted in C. Vann Woodward, *Origins of the New South* (Baton Rouge: Louisiana University Press, 1981), 206.

25 Elizabeth Sanders, *Roots of Reform: Farmers, Workers, and the American State, 1877–1917* (Chicago: University of Chicago Press, 1999), 102.

26 Historians differ on their interpretations of *Oz* as a Populist parable. For two differing views, see Henry M. Littlefield, "The Wizard of Oz: Parable on Populism," *American Quarterly* 16 (1964): 47–58, and William R. Leach, "The Clown from Syracuse: The Life and Times of L. Frank Baum," and Leach, "A Trickster's Tale: L. Frank Baum's *The Wonderful Wizard of Oz*," in L. Frank Baum, *The Wonderful Wizard of Oz* (Belmont, CA: Wadsworth Publishing Company, 1991).

27 L. Frank Baum, *The Wonderful World of Oz* (New York: Signet Classics, 2006), chap. 2.

28 Lawrence Goodwyn, *The Populist Moment* (New York: Oxford University Press, 1978), 58.

29 Ibid., 133–34.

30 Woodward, *Origins of the New South*, 204–5.

31 Robert McMath, *American Populism: A Social History 1877–1898* (New York: Hill & Wang, 1993), 177–79.

32 William Jennings Bryan, "Cross of Gold," http://historymatters.gmu .edu/d/5354.

33 Ibid.

34 Sanders, *Roots of Reform*, argues for Populism's role in Progressive-era reform.

35 Eugene V. Debs, "Present Conditions and Future Duties," circular to the American Railway Union, *Chicago Railway Times*, January 1, 1897.

36 Samuel P. Orth, "Is Socialism Upon Us?" *World's Work* 24 (May–October 1912), 453. For agrarian socialism, see James Green, *Grass-Roots Socialism: Radical Movements in the Southwest, 1895–1943* (Baton Rouge: Louisiana State University Press, 1978).

37 James Green, *World of the Worker: Labor in Twentieth-Century America* (Champaign: University of Illinois Press, 1998), 48; Stuart Bruce Kaufman, *Samuel Gompers and the Origins of the American Federation of Labor, 1848–1896* (Westport, CT: Greenwood Press, 1973), 38.

38 Green, *World of the Worker*, 48.

39 David Montgomery, *The Fall of the House of Labor: The Workplace, the State, and American Labor Activism, 1865–1925* (Cambridge, U.K.: Cambridge University Press, 1987), 308.

40 Zinn, *People's History*, 32.

41 Melvyn Dubofsky, *"Big Bill" Haywood* (Manchester, U.K.: Manchester University Press, 1987), 238–39.

42 William D. Haywood, speech in Cooper Union, *International Socialist Review*, February 1913, quoted in William English Walling et al., *The Socialism of To-day* (New York: Henry Holt, 1916), 224.

43 Quoted in Gibbs M. Smith, *Joe Hill* (Layton, UT: Gibbs Smith, 2009), 173.

44 McGerr, *Fierce Discontent*, 137.

45 John Fabian Witt, "The Transformation of Work and the Law of Workplace Accidents, 1842–1910," *Yale Law Review* 107, no. 5 (March 1998); Witt, *The Accidental Republic: Crippled Workingmen, Destitute Widows, and the Remaking of American Law* (Cambridge, MA: Harvard University Press, 2004).

46 C. Vann Woodward, *The Strange Career of Jim Crow* (New York: Oxford University Press, 2001), 38.

47 All Fonvielle quotations are from William Frank Fonvielle, "The South As I Saw It," *A.M.E. Zion Church Quarterly* 4 (January 1894): 149–58.

48 For Jim Crow legal history, see Michael J. Klarman, *From Jim Crow to Civil Rights: The Supreme Court and the Struggle for Racial Equality* (New York: Oxford University Press, 2004).

49 *Lynching in America: Statistics, Information, Images*, http://bit.ly/Lynching Stats, accessed June 23, 2008.

50 Kenneth Ng, "Wealth Distribution, Race, and Southern Schools, 1880–1910," *Education Policy Analysis Archives* 9, no. 16 (May 13, 2001), http://epaa.asu.edu/epaa/v9n16/, accessed June 23, 2008.

51 Keith Medley, *We As Freemen: Plessy v. Ferguson* (New York: Pelican, 2003), 4.

52 For state disenfranchisement, see Michael Perman, *Struggle for Mastery: Disfranchisement in the South* (Chapel Hill: University of North Carolina Press, 2001).

53 Quoted in Glenda Gilmore, *Gender and Jim Crow: Women and the Politics of White Supremacy, 1896–1920* (Chapel Hill: University of North Carolina Press, 1996), 109.

54 Quoted ibid., 113.

CHAPTER 2: "TO START TO MAKE THIS WORLD OVER"

1 *National Tribune*, May 19, 1898, 1. Elijah Banning Tunnell was born in February 1873, per Beth Fridley, *Accomack County, Virginia Births, 1866–1873* [database online] (Provo, UT: Generations Network, 2000); U.S. Census 1880, Atlantic District, Accomack County.

2 W. C. Payne to *Colored American*, August 13, 1898, in Willard Gatewood, *"Smoked Yankees": Letters from Negro Soldiers* (Fayetteville: University of Arkansas Press, 1987), 53–54.

3 Edward A. Johnson, *History of Negro Soldiers in the Spanish-American War and Other Items of Interest* (1899; reprint Project Gutenberg, 2004), 12. See also "Report of Lt. J. B. Bernadou, Commanding the *USS Winslow* in Action in Cardenas Harbor, Cuba, on May 11, 1898," http://www.spanamwar.com/winslow2.htm; and Clerk of Joint Committee on Printing, *The Abridgement of Message from the President of the United States to the Two Houses of Congress* (Washington, DC: U.S. Government Printing Office, 1899).

4 William Fitzhugh Brundage, *Where These Memories Grow: History, Memory, and Southern Identity* (Chapel Hill: University of North Carolina Press, 2000), 151.

5 "George B. Meek Monument," http://bit.ly/1DIAAgL.

6 "Report of the Secretary of the Navy, 1898, Asiatic Squadron," *Selected Naval Documents: Spanish-American War*, http://www.history.navy.mil/wars/spanam/sn98-3.htm.

7 General Basilio Augustin Davila, quoted in "Stories of American Heroes," http://bit.ly/BattleManila.

8 Theodore Roosevelt, *The Rough Riders: An Autobiography* (New York: Library

of America, 2004), quoted in Kathleen Dalton, *Theodore Roosevelt: A Strenuous Life* (New York: Vintage, 2004), 6.

9   Rayford Logan, *The Betrayal of the Negro, from Rutherford B. Hayes to Woodrow Wilson* (Boston: Da Capo Press, 1997), 337.

10 Albert Beveridge, in *Congressional Record*, 56th Cong., 1st sess. (January 9, 1900), 704–12.

11 Emily Rosenberg, *Spreading the American Dream: American Economic and Cultural Expansion, 1890–1945* (New York: Hill & Wang, 1982), 18.

12 Quoted in Patrick Brantlinger, "Kipling's 'The White Man's Burden' and Its Afterlives," *English Literature in Transition* 50, no. 2 (2007): 172.

13 Ibid.

14 *McClure's Magazine* 12, no. 4 (February 1899), 290.

15 "Teller and Platt Amendments," Library of Congress, http://www.loc.gov/rr/hispanic/1898/teller.html.

16 Quoted in Louis A. Perez, Jr., *Cuba Between Empires, 1878–1902* (Pittsburgh: University of Pittsburgh Press, 1998), 277.

17 Quoted in John Taliaferro, *All the Great Prizes: The Life of John Hay, from Lincoln to Roosevelt* (New York: Simon & Schuster, 2013), 341.

18 William Jennings Bryan, "Imperialism," speech to the Democratic National Convention, August 8, 1900, at http://bit.ly/Bryan_Imperialism.

19 Abraham Lincoln, "The Injustice of Slavery," in Clifton M. Nichols, *Life of Abraham Lincoln: Being a Biography of His Life from His Birth to His Assassination, also a Record of His Ancestors, and a Collection of Anecdotes Attributed to Lincoln* (New York: Mast, Crowell & Kirkpatrick, 1896), 206.

20 American Anti-Imperialist League, "Platform of the American Anti-Imperialist League," in Carl Schurz, *The Policy of Imperialism*, Liberty Tract No. 4 (Chicago, 1899).

21 H. T. Johnson, "The Black Man's Burden," *Voice of Missions* (Atlanta, April 1899), in Willard B. Gatewood, Jr., *Black Americans and the White Man's Burden, 1898–1903* (Champaign: University of Illinois Press, 1975), 183–84.

22 Paul Kramer, *The Blood of Government: Race, Empire, the United States, and the Philippines* (Chapel Hill: University of North Carolina Press, 2006), 157.

23 Edmund Morris, *The Rise of Theodore Roosevelt* (New York: Ballantine Books, 1980), and Nathan Miller, *Theodore Roosevelt: A Life* (New York: William Morrow, 1992), 30, 49, 82, 156, 161, 282.

24 Thomas Collier Platt, *The Autobiography of Thomas Collier Platt* (New York: B.W. Dodge & Co., 1910), 541.

25 Theodore Roosevelt to Anna Roosevelt Cowles, September 7, 1901, quoted in

"Theodore Roosevelt's Reaction to McKinley's Assassination," http://www
.roosevelt.nl/home/mckinley.

26 Quoted in "A Belated Confession," *New York Times*, March 25, 1911.

27 Theodore Roosevelt, "Fourth Annual Message," December 6, 1904, http://
www.presidency.ucsb.edu/ws/?pid=29545.

28 Bryan, "Imperialism."

29 Quoted in Raymond-Leopold Bruckberger, *Images of America: A Political, Social,
and Industrial Portrait* (Livingston, NJ: Transaction Publishers, 2009), 179.

30 Glenda Gilmore, *Who Were the Progressives?* (New York: Bedford Books,
2002), 6.

31 Frederick Winslow Taylor, *Shop Management* (New York: Harper & Brothers,
1911), 110.

32 John Dewey, *My Pedagogic Creed* (New York: E.L. Kellogg & Co., 1897), 18.

33 Morris Dickstein, "Introduction," in Upton Sinclair, *The Jungle* (New York:
Bantam, 1981), vi.

34 Theodore Roosevelt, "The Man with the Muck-rake," April 14, 1914, http://
bit.ly/TRMuck-rake.

35 Mara L. Keire, "The Vice Trust: A Reinterpretation of the White Slavery
Scare in the United States, 1907–1917," *Journal of Social History* 35 (2001):
5–41.

36 "The Houses in Our Midst," *Atlanta Constitution*, June 15, 1912, 3.

37 Gail Bederman, "'The Women Have Had Charge of the Church Work Long
Enough': The Men and Religion Forward Movement of 1911–1912 and the
Masculinization of Middle-Class Protestantism," *American Quarterly* 41,
(September 1989): 432–65.

38 Douglas F. Ottati, foreword to Walter Rauschenbusch, *Christianity and the
Social Crisis* (1907; reprint Louisville, KY: Westminster John Knox Press,
2007), xi.

39 Quoted in Bederman, "'Women Have Had Charge,'" 444–45.

40 Lincoln Steffens, *The Shame of the Cities* (1904; reprint New York: Dover,
2012), 2–3.

41 Ibid., 3.

42 Leitrim Association of People with Disabilities, http://www.lapwd.com;
David Paul Nord, "The Paradox of Municipal Reform in the Late Nineteenth
Century," *Wisconsin Magazine of History* 66, no. 2 (Winter 1982–83):
128–42.

43 California Constitution, http://www.leginfo.ca.gov/.const/.article_2; Elizabeth V. Burt, *The Progressive Era: Primary Documents on Events from 1890–
1914* (Westport, CT: Greenwood Press, 2004), 5–6.

44   Theodore Roosevelt, *An Autobiography* (New York: Macmillan, 1913), vi.

45   Theodore Roosevelt, *Selected Letters* (1951; reprint Lanham, MD: Rowman & Littlefield, 2007), 334.

46   "Confidence in Financial Circles," and "Leaders of Finance Amazed," *New York Times*, September 7, 1901, 3.

47   Michael P. Malone, *James J. Hill: Empire Builder of the Northwest* (Norman: University of Oklahoma Press, 1997), 221; Edmund Morris, *Theodore Rex* (New York: Modern Library, 2001), 92.

48   Morris, *Theodore Rex*, 92.

49   *Northern Securities Co. v. United States*, 193 U.S. 197 (1904).

50   "The Supreme Court on Railway Regulation," *Outlook* 82 (March 3, 1906), 493.

51   "Alcohol in 'Patent Medicines,'" *California State Journal of Medicine* 2, no. 6 (1904): 185.

52   Michael McGerr, *A Fierce Discontent: The Rise and Fall of the Progressive Movement in America, 1870–1920* (New York: Free Press, 2003), 163.

53   Linnie Marsh Wolfe, *Son of the Wilderness: The Life of John Muir* (New York: Alfred A. Knopf, 1945), 291–92, quoted in Michael P. Cohen, *The Pathless Way: John Muir and the American Wilderness* (Madison: University of Wisconsin Press, 1984), 303.

54   Gifford Pinchot, *Breaking New Ground* (Washington, DC: Island Press, 1998), 505.

55   Roosevelt Film Library, *T.R.'s Return from Africa, 1910,* part 1, https://www.youtube.com/watch?v=lPt_a6oCY1Q.

56   Quoted in Louis Gould, *Theodore Roosevelt* (New York: Oxford University Press, 2012), 57.

57   "Theodore Roosevelt Speaks During the Presidential Campaign of 1912," http://www.eyewitnesstohistory.com/votr.htm.

58   Theodore Roosevelt, "A Confession of Faith," speech to the Progressive Party Convention, Chicago, August 6, 1912, at http://bit.ly/RooseveltFaith.

59   Christopher Klein, "Shot in the Chest 100 Years Ago, Teddy Roosevelt Kept Talking," *History in the Headlines*, October 12, 2012, http://bit.ly/TRShotInChest.

CHAPTER 3: REFINING AND EXPORTING PROGRESSIVISM

1   Louis Auchincloss, *Woodrow Wilson* (New York: Viking, 2000), 8.

2   Thomas Woodrow Wilson, "First Inaugural Address," March 4, 1913, http://www.bartleby.com/124/pres44.html.

3   Woodrow Wilson, "Leaders of Men," June 17, 1890, http://bit.ly/LeadersOfMen.

4   Inez Haynes Irwin, *The Story of the Woman's Party* (New York: Harcourt, Brace & Co., 1921), 13.

5   Quoted in Christine A. Lunardini and Thomas Knock, "Woodrow Wilson and Woman Suffrage: A New Look," *Political Science Quarterly* 95, no. 4 (Winter 1980), 655.

6   "Alice Paul Talks," in *Votes for Women: Selections from the National American Woman Suffrage Association Collection, 1848–1921*, http://1.usa.gov/1xqtZ71.

7   Edith Phelps, ed., *Debater's Handbook Series: Selected Articles on Woman Suffrage* (New York: H.W. Wilson Co., 1912), 73.

8   Ellen Carol DuBois and Vicki L. Ruiz, eds., *Unequal Sisters: A Multicultural Reader in U.S. Women's History* (New York: Routledge, 2000), 242.

9   California, 1911; Kansas, Oregon, Arizona, 1912. Montana, Nevada, 1914, paired with Wyoming, Utah, Colorado, and Idaho.

10 "President Ignores Suffrage Pickets," *New York Times*, January 11, 1917, 13.

11 Quoted in John Milton Cooper, *Woodrow Wilson: A Biography* (New York: Vintage, 2011), 234.

12 James R. Green, *World of the Worker: Labor in Twentieth-Century America* (Champaign: University of Illinois Press, 1980), 85; Melvin Dubofsky, *We Shall Be All: A History of the Industrial Workers of the World* (New York: Quadrangle, 1969), 228.

13 Quoted in Bruce Watson, *Bread and Roses: Mills, Migrants, and the Struggle for the American Dream* (New York: Viking, 2005), 88.

14 James Oppenheim, "Bread and Roses," *American Magazine* (December 1911).

15 Joe Hill, "Rebel Girl," *Little Red Songbook* (March 1916).

16 Quoted in David Brody, *Labor Embattled: History, Power, Rights* (Champaign: University of Illinois Press, 2005), 32.

17 Quoted in Samuel Schaffer, "New South Nation: Woodrow Wilson's Generation and the Rise of the South, 1884–1920," Ph.D. diss., Yale University, 2010, 298.

18 Quoted in Bruce Bartlett, *Wrong on Race: The Democratic Party's Buried Past* (New York: Palgrave Macmillan, 2008), 102.

19 James Grossman, *Land of Hope: Chicago, Black Southerners, and the Great Migration* (Chicago: University of Chicago Press, 1991), 1.

20 Anne Scott and Andrew Scott, *One Half the People: The Fight for Woman Suffrage* (Urbana: University of Illinois Press, 1982), 34.

21 David Kennedy, *Over Here: The First World War and American Society* (New York: Oxford University Press, 1980), 3–4, 174–75.

22 Wilfred Owen, "Dulce et Decorum Est," in *Poems* (New York: Viking Press, 1921).

23 Patrick O'Sullivan, *The Lusitania: Unravelling the Mysteries* (Staplehurst, Kent: Spellmount, 2000), 59.

24 *New York Times Current History: The European War*, vol. 10, *January–March, 1917* (New York: New York Times Co., 1917), 996–97.

25 "Notice!" *New York Times*, May 1, 1917, 12.

26 "Sails, Undisturbed by German Warning," *New York Times*, May 2, 1915, 1.

27 O'Sullivan, *Lusitania;* Immigrants Groups Transcribers Guild: RMS Lusitania, passenger list, http://bit.ly/1rH15dq; information on Rosina Leverich from Ancestry.com, U.S. Census, and passports.

28 "Roosevelt Calls It An Act of Piracy," *New York Times*, May 8, 1915, 1.

29 "U.S. Protest over the Sinking of the *Lusitania,*13 May 1915," http://bit .ly/1IZ37Pb.

30 Quoted in William E. Leuchtenburg, *The Perils of Prosperity, 1914–1932* (1958; reprint Chicago: University of Chicago Press, 1993), 18.

31 Henry F. Pringle, *Theodore Roosevelt: A Biography* (New York: Harcourt, Brace, & Co., 1932), 410.

32 Emily Rosenberg, *Spreading the American Dream: American Economic and Cultural Expansion, 1890–1945* (New York: Hill & Wang, 1982), 67; Ronald E. Powaski, *Toward an Entangling Alliance: American Isolationism, Internationalism, and Europe, 1901–1950* (Westport, CT: Greenwood Press, 1991), 10.

33 German telegram received by the German ambassador, Record Group 59, General Records of the Department of State, 1756–1979, National Archives and Records Administration.

34 "Plot Awakens Congress," *New York Times*, March 2, 1917, 1.

35 "Must Exert All Our Power," *New York Times*, April 3, 1917, 1.

36 Rhodri Jeffries-Jones, *Changing Differences: Women and the Shaping of American Foreign Policy, 1917–1994* (New Brunswick, NJ: Rutgers University Press, 1995), 17.

37 "Debate Lasted 16 ½ Hours," *New York Times*, April 6, 1917, 1.

38 Quoted in David Kennedy, *Over Here: The First World War and American Society* (New York: Oxford University Press, 2004), 384.

39 Quoted ibid., 24.

40 Quoted ibid., 26.

41 W. E. B. Du Bois, "The Crisis of Europe," *Crisis* 12 (September 1916), 217–18.

42 W. E. B. Du Bois, "The Perpetual Dilemma," *Crisis* 14 (April 1917), 270–71.

43 W. E. B. Du Bois, "Close Ranks," *Crisis* 16 (July 1918), 111.

44 "U.S. Espionage Act, 15 June 1915," http://bit.ly/1sBsule; Kennedy, *Over Here*, 26, 75–76.

45   Woodrow Wilson, "Address to Congress Requesting a Declaration of War Against Germany," April 2, 1917, http://bit.ly/WilsonDeclaration.

46   Quoted in Katherine H. Adams and Michael L. Keene, *Alice Paul and the American Suffrage Campaign* (Champaign: University of Illinois Press, 2008), 183.

47   Letter to the President, *Official Bulletin*, Committee on Public Information, May 11, 1917, 4.

48   Quoted in Melvyn Dubofsky, *"Big Bill" Haywood* (Manchester, U.K.: Manchester University Press, 1987), 66.

49   Oliver Wendell Holmes, *Schenck v. United States*, 249 U.S. 47 (1919).

50   Woodrow Wilson, "Fourteen Points," January 8, 1918, http://bit.ly/Fourteen Points.

51   Ibid.

52   *The Treaty of Peace and the Covenant of the League of Nations* (Philadelphia: John C. Winston Co., 1920), https://archive.org/details/treatypeaceandc00treagoog.

53   Quoted in John Arthur Garraty, *Henry Cabot Lodge: A Biography* (New York: Alfred A. Knopf, 1968), 365.

54   *Treaty of Peace and Covenant of League of Nations*.

55   "Put Up or Shut Up," *Chicago Daily Tribune*, September 5, 1919, 1.

56   "Lodge Reservations," *Congressional Record*, 66th Cong., 1st sess. (1919), 8768–69, 8777–78, 8781–84.

57   Woodrow Wilson, "Final Address in Support of the League of Nations," September 25, 1919, http://bit.ly/WilsonLeague.

58   Norman A. Graebner and Edward M. Bennett, *The Versailles Treaty and Its Legacy: The Failure of the Wilsonian Vision* (Cambridge, U.K.: Cambridge University Press, 2014), 64.

CHAPTER 4: PROSPERITY'S PRECIPICE

1   "Normalcy" is Warren G. Harding's term; see Alan Brinkley and Davis Dyer, eds., *The American Presidency* (Boston: Houghton Mifflin, 2004), 315.

2   W. E. B. Du Bois, "Returning Soldiers," *Crisis* 28 (May 1919), 13–14.

3   James Dykeman and Wilma Stokely, *Seeds of Change: The Life of Will Alexander* (Chicago: University of Chicago Press, 1962), 56–57.

4   David M. Kennedy, *Over Here: The First World War and American Society* (New York: Oxford University Press, 2004), 288.

5   Paul Vincent Murphy, *The New Era: American Thought and Culture in the 1920s* (Lanham, MD: Rowman & Littlefield, 2011), 181.

6   "Has the Negro Gone Bolshevik?" *World Outlook* 5 (October 1919), 12–13.

7   Constitution of the United States, Amendment 19, http://bit.ly/1xquH4k.

8   "'Remember the Ladies!' Women Struggle for an Equal Voice," Tennessee State Library and Archives, http://1.usa.gov/1uWaTzL.

9   Brinkley and Dyer, *American Presidency*, 315.

10   Samuel T. McSeveney, "Ethnic Groups, Ethnic Conflicts, and Recent Quantitative Research in American Political History," *International Migration Review* 7, no. 1 (Spring 1973): 14–33.

11   Edward Behr, *Prohibition: Thirteen Years that Changed America* (1996; reprint New York: Arcade, 2011), 113.

12   Laton McCartney, *The Teapot Dome Scandal: How Big Oil Bought the Harding White House and Tried to Steal the Country* (New York: Random House, 2008), 159.

13   Senator Ellison DuRant Smith, April 9, 1924, *Congressional Record*, 68th Cong., 1st sess. (1923), 65, 5961–62.

14   Ibid.

15   Leonard J. Moore, *Citizen Klansmen: The Ku Klux Klan in Indiana* (Chapel Hill: University of North Carolina Press, 1997), 76, 77.

16   Quoted in Wyn Craig Wade, *The Fiery Cross: The Ku Klux Klan in America* (New York: Oxford University Press, 1987), 217.

17   Kathleen Blee, *Women of the Klan: Racism and Gender in the 1920s* (Berkeley and Los Angeles: University of California Press, 1991), 17.

18   Nathan Miller, *New World Coming: The 1920s and the Making of Modern America* (Boston: Da Capo Press, 2004), 142.

19   "Canada Also Stirred," *New York Times*, April 6, 1924, 20; "Klan Organizers," *New York Times*, May 4, 1924, 2, 7; "Mexico City Editor Seized," *New York Times*, August 28, 1923, 19; "Report 1,000 in New Zealand Klan," *New York Times*, August 28, 1923, 19.

20   "Japan on American Lynching," *Messenger* 3 (August 1921), 225.

21   Quoted in Glenda Elizabeth Gilmore, *Defying Dixie: The Radical Roots of Civil Rights* (New York: W. W. Norton & Co., 2009), 26.

22   Rev. R. A. Torrey, "The Certainty and Importance of the Bodily Resurrection of Jesus Christ from the Dead," in R. A. Torrey and Charles A. Feinberg, eds., *The Fundamentals: The Famous Sourcebook of Foundational Biblical Truths* (1958; reprint Grand Rapids, MI: Kregel Publications, 1990), 295–309.

23   "Annual Review of the Cost of Living, 1940," Conference Board, January 30, 1940, 3.

24   "Our Peaceful Revolution," *New York Times*, January 20, 1924, E6.

25   Calvin Coolidge, Address to the American Society of Newspaper Editors, January 17, 1925, http://bit.ly/CoolidgeEditors.

26 "Says Consumer Credit Has Aided Prosperity," *Sun* (Baltimore), December 5, 1926.

27 J. H. Tregoe, "Consumers Credit Dangerous," *American Jeweler*, March 1, 1926, 46, 3.

28 Mark H. Haller, "Organized Crime in Urban Society: Chicago in the Twentieth Century," *Journal of Social History* 5, no. 2 (Winter 1971–72), 210–34.

29 Quoted in Manning Marable, *Let Nobody Turn Us Around: An African American Anthology* (Lanham, MD: Rowman & Littlefield, 2009), 221.

30 Marcus Garvey, "Declaration of Rights of the Negro Peoples of the World," ibid., 241.

31 W. C. Handy, *Father of the Blues: An Autobiography* (Boston: Da Capo Press, 1969), 1, 15.

32 Bessye Bearden, "New York Society," *Chicago Defender*, March 13, 1932, 11; Countee Cullen, "She of the Dancing Feet Sings," http://allpoetry.com /She-Of-The-Dancing-Feet-Sings.

33 David Levering Lewis, *W. E. B. Du Bois, 1919–1963: The Fight for Equality and the American Century* (New York: Macmillan, 2000), 225.

34 Zora Neale Hurston, "How It Feels to Be Colored Me," *World Tomorrow* 11 (May 1928), 215–16.

35 Scrapbook, "Music-Art, September 1927–July 1928," *New York World*, March 11, 1928, James Weldon Johnson Collection, Beinecke Library, Yale University.

36 Eva Taylor, *Complete Recorded Works*, vol. 1, *1922–23* (1966).

37 Blanche Wiesen Cook, *Eleanor Roosevelt*, vol. 1, *1884–1933* (New York: Penguin, 1993), 107.

38 Ibid., 185.

39 Ibid., 228.

40 Ibid., 338.

41 Ibid., 352.

42 Ibid., 376–77.

43 Calvin Coolidge, Announcement that He Will Not Run for President in 1928, http://bit.ly/CoolidgeWontRun.

44 Donald Critchlow and Charles H. Parker, *With Us Always: A History of Private Charity and Public Welfare* (Lanham, MD: Rowman & Littlefield, 1998), 7.

45 Samuel Crowther, "Everybody Ought to Be Rich: An Interview with John. J. Raskob," *Ladies' Home Journal* (August 1929).

46 Herbert Hoover, News Conference, October 25, 1929, http://bit.ly /HooverNewsConf.

47 Maury Klein, "The Stock Market Crash of 1928: A Review Article," *Business History Review* 75 (2001): 325–51.

48 Herbert Hoover, News Conference, November 15, 1929, http://bit.ly /Hoover_19291115.

49 John Kenneth Galbraith, *The Great Crash 1929* (New York: Pelican, 1954), 106.

50 Herbert Hoover, March 8, 1930, quoted in "Oh Yeah? Herbert Hoover Predicts Prosperity," http://historymatters.gmu.edu/d/5063/.

51 Herbert Hoover, May 1, 1930, quoted ibid.

52 "At Odds on Amount Germany Has Paid," *New York Times*, April 27, 1924, E7; Herbert Hoover, *The Memoirs of Herbert Hoover: The Great Depression, 1929–1941* (New York: Macmillan, 1952), 16.

53 William H. Young and Nancy K. Young, *The 1930s* (Westport, CT: Greenwood Press, 2002), 18.

54 William Foster, quoted in Arthur M. Schlesinger, *The Crisis of the Old Order, 1919–1933* (1957; reprint Boston: Houghton Mifflin Harcourt, 2003), 187.

55 September 1932. "A Tour through *Fortune's* Past," March 26, 1990, archive.fortune.com/magazines/fortune/fortune_archive/1990/03/26/73201 /index.htm.

56 Herbert Hoover, "Address Accepting the Republican Presidential Nomination," August 11, 1932, http://bit.ly/Hoover1932Accept.

57 Franklin Delano Roosevelt, "Nomination Address," July 2, 1932, http://bit .ly/FDR1932NomAddress

58 Ibid.

59 Ibid.

60 Herbert Hoover, "Message to the House of Representatives," reprinted in *Time*, March 9, 1931.

61 Brig. Gen. Pelham D. Glassford, "Calling of Troops to Evict Bonus Army Without Justification," http://bit.ly/1IZ4Hk7.

62 Herbert Hoover, "Letter to the Commissioners of the District of Columbia Providing Federal Troops to Deal with Bonus Marchers," http://bit.ly /bonus-marchers.

63 Quoted in Mark Perry, *The Most Dangerous Man in America: The Making of Douglas MacArthur* (New York: Basic Books, 2014), xv. The account of William Hushka's life is compiled from Ancestry Library Edition searches of the birth, death, and marriage records of Cook County, Illinois, the 1920 U.S. Census, Hushka's naturalization papers, and the 1930 U.S. Census; Paul Dickson and Thomas Allen, *The Bonus Army: An American Epic* (New York: Walker & Co., 2004); John W. Killigrew, "The Army and the Bonus Incident," *Military Affairs* 26, no. 2 (Summer 1962), 59–65.

64   Quoted in Wendy L. Wall, *Inventing the "American Way": The Politics of Consensus from the New Deal to the Civil Rights Movement* (New York: Oxford University Press, 2009), 20.

65   Quoted in Dickson and Allen, *Bonus Army*, 184.

66   Tim Lehman, *Public Values, Private Lands: Farmland Preservation Policy, 1933–1985* (Chapel Hill: University of North Carolina Press, 1995), 17.

67   Democratic Party Platform of 1932, June 27, 1932, http://www.presidency .ucsb.edu/ws/?pid=29595.

68   Franklin D. Roosevelt, "Campaign Address on Railroads at Salt Lake City, Utah," September 17, 1932, http://www.presidency.ucsb.edu/ws/?pid=88397.

69   Franklin D. Roosevelt, "Speech at San Francisco," http://bit.ly/FDR-SF-1932.

70   James MacGregor Burns, *Roosevelt: The Lion and the Fox* (1956; reprint Boston: Mariner Books, 2002), 1:140.

71   Quoted in "Biography of Eleanor Roosevelt," http://www.fdrlibrary.marist .edu/education/resources/bio_er.html.

CHAPTER 5: A TWENTIETH-CENTURY PRESIDENT

1   Walter Matthau, "Hello to Montanans" (videorecording), 1998, http://nwda .orbiscascade.org/ark:/80444/xv0584.1.

2   Ona Hill, *Raymond Burr: A Film, Radio, and Television Biography* (Jefferson, NC: McFarland, 1999), 8.

3   Lee Server, *Robert Mitchum: "Baby, I Don't Care"* (New York: Macmillan, 2001), 34–35.

4   Quoted in David Kennedy, *Freedom from Fear: The American People in Depression and War, 1929–1945* (New York: Oxford University Press, 1999), 109.

5   Birdie Farr, Grand Island, NB, www.livinghistoryfarm.org.

6   William L. Silber, "Why Did FDR's Bank Holiday Succeed?" *FRBNY Economic Policy Review*, July 2009, http://nyfed.org/1uPN7Vb.

7   Raymond E. Moley, *After Seven Years* (New York: Harper & Brothers, 1939), 146–48; Kennedy, *Freedom from Fear*, 133.

8   Franklin Delano Roosevelt, "'Only Thing We Have to Fear is Fear Itself': FDR's First Inaugural Address," http://historymatters.gmu.edu/d/5057/

9   Quoted in James MacGregor Burns, *Roosevelt: The Lion and the Fox* (1956; reprint Boston: Mariner Books, 2002), 157.

10   Roosevelt, "First Inaugural Address."

11   Franklin D. Roosevelt, "Address of the President Delivered by Radio from the White House," March 12, 1933, http://www.mhric.org/fdr/chat1.html.

12   Silber, "Why did FDR's Bank Holiday Succeed?" 20.

13   Ibid., 23.

14   "Many Cities Celebrate: Cheering Crowds Hail Beer Trucks Distributing New Brew," *New York Times*, April 7, 1933, 1.

15   Franklin D. Roosevelt, "Three Essentials for Relief," March 21, 1933, http://newdeal.feri.org/cccmem/1933.htm.

16   John Thomas Flynn, *The Roosevelt Myth* (1948; reprint Old Greenwich, CT: Devin-Adair, 1956), 73.

17   Moley, *After Seven Years*, 11–14.

18   Alan Brinkley, *Voices of Protest: Huey Long, Father Coughlin, and the Great Depression* (New York: Vintage, 1983), 58.

19   Moley, *After Seven Years*, 11.

20   "Louis McHenry Howe (1871–1936)," http://bit.ly/1BTl2lH.

21   "A Birthday Posie," *New York Times*, January 15, 1935, 18.

22   Blanche Wiesen Cook, *Eleanor Roosevelt*, vol. 1, *1884–1933* (New York: Penguin, 1993), 495–500; Curtis Roosevelt, interview by Glenda Gilmore, 1999.

23   Molly Dewson, quoted in Susan Ware, *Partner and I: Molly Dewson, Feminism, and New Deal Politics* (New Haven, CT: Yale University Press, 1987), 190.

24   Cook, *Eleanor Roosevelt*, 1:500.

25   Kirstin Downey, *The Woman Behind the New Deal: The Life and Legacy of Frances Perkins—Social Security, Unemployment Insurance, and the Minimum Wage* (New York: Anchor, 2010).

26   Harry Hopkins annotation, "Federal Relief," in Richard Polenberg, ed., *The Era of Franklin D. Roosevelt, 1933–1945: A Brief History with Documents* (New York: Bedford Books, 2000), 83–84; Franklin D. Roosevelt, "Address before the Federal Council of Churches of Christ in America," December 6, 1933, at http://www.presidency.ucsb.edu/ws/?pid=14574.

27   "Rural Electrification," http://bit.ly/RuralElectr.

28   Kennedy, *Freedom from Fear*, 252.

29   William E. Leuchtenburg, "The New Deal and the Analogue of War," *The FDR Years: On Roosevelt and His Legacy* (New York: Columbia University Press, 1995), 35–75.

30   Quoted in Downey, *Woman Behind the New Deal*, 183.

31   Colin Gordon, *New Deals: Business, Labor, and Politics in America, 1920–1935* (New York: Cambridge University Press, 1994), 175.

32   Downey, *Woman Behind the New Deal*, 177.

33   Ted Selander, "Toledo Auto Lite Strike," June 3, 1984, http://bit.ly/1zoAQNN.

34   Jonathan Holloway, *Confronting the Veil: Abram Harris Jr., E. Franklin Fra-

zier, and Ralph Bunche, 1919–1941 (Chapel Hill: University of North Carolina Press, 2002), 66–75.

35   *Guide to the Microfilm Edition of the Papers of Mary McLeod Bethune, 1923–1948* (Wilmington, DE: Scholarly Resources, 2005), 7.

36   Nancy Joan Weiss, *Farewell to the Party of Lincoln: Black Politics in the Age of FDR* (Princeton, NJ: Princeton University Press, 1983), 144.

37   Joyce Ann Hanson, *Mary McLeod Bethune and Black Women's Political Activism* (Columbia: University of Missouri Press, 2003), 147.

38   Garth E. Pauley, *The Modern Presidency and Civil Rights: Rhetoric on Race from Roosevelt to Nixon* (College Station: Texas A&M University Press, 2001), 24–25.

39   Patricia Sullivan, *Days of Hope: Race and Democracy in the New Deal Era* (Chapel Hill: University of North Carolina Press, 1996).

40   Anne O'Hare McCormick, *The World at Home: Selections from the Writings of Anne O'Hare McCormick*, ed. Marion Turner Sheehan (New York: Alfred A. Knopf, 1956), 224.

41   Anonymous to Franklin D. Roosevelt, October 23, 1933, in Robert S. McElvaine, ed., *Down and Out in the Great Depression: Letters from the Forgotten Man* (Chapel Hill: University of North Carolina Press, 2008), 56.

42   Mrs. I. H. to Franklin D. Roosevelt, February 1, 1934, ibid., 57.

43   Mrs. E. L. to Franklin D. Roosevelt, ibid., 60–61.

44   Angelo Herndon, *Let Me Live: The Autobiography of Angelo Herndon* (New York: Random House, 1937), 15.

45   Quoted in Glenda Elizabeth Gilmore, *Defying Dixie: The Radical Roots of Civil Rights* (New York: W. W. Norton, 2009), 170–71.

46   Klaus P. Fischer, *Hitler and America* (Philadelphia: University of Pennsylvania Press, 2011), 47–51.

47   Gilmore, *Defying Dixie*, 169.

48   Jean Edward Smith, *FDR* (New York: Random House, 2008), 149.

49   Richard Breitman and Allan J. Lichtman, *FDR and the Jews* (Cambridge, MA: Belknap Press, 2013), 75.

50   Henry C. Dethloff, *Huey P. Long: Southern Demagogue or American Democrat?* (Lexington, MA: D.C. Heath, 1963), 76–93, quoted in Brinkley, *Voices of Protest*, 29.

51   Brinkley, *Voices of Protest*, 57.

52   Ibid., 114.

53   Kennedy, *Freedom from Fear*, 197–98.

54   Kennedy argues that "surely what the world eventually came to know as

'Keynesianism' grew as much from the jumble of circumstance, politics, and adaptation as it did from the pages of textbooks." *Freedom from Fear*, 358.

55   Just a Friend to Franklin D. Roosevelt, November 27, 1935, in McElvaine, *Down and Out in the Great Depression*, 126.

56   For an extended treatment of southern white Democrats' congressional power and its deleterious effects, see Ira Katznelson, *Fear Itself: The New Deal and the Origins of Our Time* (New York: Liveright, 2014); Gilmore, *Defying Dixie*, 180.

57   Gilmore, *Defying Dixie*, 367.

58   Quoted in Kennedy, *Freedom from Fear*, 328.

59   Robert F. Wagner, "The National Labor Relations Act," February 21, 1935, in Polenberg, *Era of Franklin D. Roosevelt*, 71.

60   Quoted in Frances Fox Piven and Richard Cloward, *Poor People's Movements: Why They Succeed, How They Fail* (New York: Vintage, 1979), 132.

61   Downey, *Woman Behind the New Deal*, 243.

62   Ibid., 236.

63   Quoted ibid., 243.

64   Quoted in Brinkley, *Voices of Protest*, 81.

65   Quoted in Gilmore, *Defying Dixie*, 171.

66   Quoted ibid., 192.

67   Quoted in David Levering Lewis, *W. E. B. Du Bois, 1919–1963: The Fight for Equality and the American Century* (New York: Holt, 2001), 398.

68   Franklin D. Roosevelt, Memorandum for AAA File, January 24, 1936, quoted in William J. Barber, *Designs Within Disorder: Franklin D. Roosevelt, the Economists, and the Shaping of American Economic Policy, 1933–1945* (New York: Cambridge University Press, 2006), 77.

69   Franklin D. Roosevelt, "Acceptance Speech for the Renomination for the Presidency," June 27, 1936, http://bit.ly/FDR1936RenomSpeech.

CHAPTER 6: A RENDEZVOUS WITH DESTINY, 1936–1941

1   Genealogical research on Peggy Olsson, Phil Rasmussen, Lew Sanders, Gordon Sterling, and Dorris Miller through Ancestry.com, the U.S. Census, Social Security Death Index, obituaries online, military records, and family trees.

2   Franklin D. Roosevelt, "Acceptance Speech for the Renomination for the Presidency," June 27, 1936, http://bit.ly/FDR1936RenomSpeech.

3   Franklin D. Roosevelt, "'One Third of a Nation': FDR's Second Inaugural Address," January 20, 1937, at http://historymatters.gmu.edu/d/5105/.

4   Quoted in David Kennedy, *Freedom from Fear: The American People in*

Depression and War, 1929–1945 (New York: Oxford University Press, 1999), 330.

5   Quoted in Kirstin Downey, *The Woman Behind the New Deal: The Life and Legacy of Frances Perkins—Social Security, Unemployment Insurance, and the Minimum Wage* (New York: Anchor, 2009), 259.

6   Franklin D. Roosevelt, "Fireside Chat on Reorganization of the Judiciary," in Richard Polenberg, ed., *The Era of Franklin D. Roosevelt, 1933–1945: A Brief History with Documents* (New York: Bedford Books, 2000), 58–64.

7   "Princeton Head Warns against Court Packing," *Chicago Tribune*, March 25, 1937.

8   Kennedy, *Freedom from Fear*, 333; "Burton K. Wheeler, Isolationist Senator, Dead at 92," *New York Times*, January 8, 1974, 40.

9   Burton K. Wheeler, "First Member of the Senate to Back the President in '32," *Chicago Forum*, March 10, 1937, http://bit.ly/1zWMHDa.

10   "What Court Packing Means to Senator Glass," *Hartford Courant*, March 31, 1937, 12; Ira Katznelson, *Fear Itself: The New Deal and the Origins of Our Time* (New York: Liveright, 2014), 356–57; Kennedy, *Freedom from Fear*, 338–42.

11   William E. Leuchtenburg, *The Supreme Court Reborn: The Constitutional Revolution in the Age of Roosevelt* (New York: Oxford University Press, 1995), 146–47.

12   William E. Leuchtenburg, "FDR's Court-Packing Plan: A Second Life, A Second Death," *Duke Law Journal* 1985, no. 3 (1985): 673–89.

13   Downey, *Woman Behind the New Deal*, 394.

14   Kenneth D. Roose, "Federal Reserve Policy and the Recession of 1937–1938," *Review of Economics and Statistics* 32, no. 2 (May 1950): 177–83.

15   Harold Ickes quoted in Alan Brinkley, *The End of Reform: New Deal Liberalism in Recession and War* (New York: Vintage, 1996), 30.

16   Ibid., 29.

17   Franklin Delano Roosevelt, "Message to the Conference on Economic Conditions of the South," July 4, 1936, http://bit.ly/FDR1936SouthEconomy.

18   *Report of the Special Committee on Investigation of the Munitions Industry* (Nye Report), U.S. Senate, 74th Cong., 2nd sess. (February 24, 1936), 3–13.

19   "Big Fascist Party Forming in Japan," *New York Times*, June 6, 1937.

20   "Wolf Children on Prowl," *Boston Globe*, May 1, 1938, 44; James A. Mills, "In the Wake of War: War—Through a Child's Eyes," *Christian Science Monitor*, December 23, 1937.

21   Lawrence B. Glickman, *Buying Power: A History of Consumer Activism in America* (Chicago: University of Chicago Press, 2009), 225–27.

22   Kennedy, *Freedom from Fear*, 462.

23   Sander A. Diamond, *The Nazi Movement in the United States, 1924–1941* (Ithaca, NY: Cornell University Press, 1974), 69. The survey's title translates to "Ethnic Group Law in the United States of America."

24   Lynne Olson, *Those Angry Days: Roosevelt, Lindbergh, and America's Fight over World War II, 1939–1941* (New York: Random House, 2013), 16–17.

25   Kennedy, *Freedom from Fear*, 415–16; quotations from "Berlin Raids Reply to Death of Envoy," *New York Times*, November 10, 1938, 1.

26   Kennedy, *Freedom from Fear*, 483.

27   Olson, *Those Angry Days*, 83–84.

28   "Germany Grasps Rich Czech Booty," *New York Times*, March 16, 1939, 1.

29   "London News: From Private Correspondence, Russia's Amazing Decision," *Scotsman*, August 22, 1939, 8.

30   "Fateful Sessions of Parliament," *Scotsman*, September 4, 1939, 4.

31   Olson, *Those Angry Days*, 54.

32   Ibid., 91.

33   Ibid., 71–72.

34   Quoted ibid., 126–27.

35   Kennedy, *Freedom from Fear*, 445.

36   Olson, *Those Angry Days*, 103.

37   "Swastika in Paris," *New York Times*, June 16, 1940, E1.

38   Kennedy, *Freedom from Fear*, 450.

39   Eleanor Roosevelt, "Address to the 1940 Democratic Convention," July 18, 1940, http://bit.ly/ER1940DemConvAddress.

40   Quoted in Olson, *Those Angry Days*, 216.

41   Quoted in Jennifer Kaylin, "Lindbergh Lands in New Haven," *Yale Alumni Magazine* (May 2002), http://bit.ly/1v9mxGP.

42   Olson, *Those Angry Days*, 222.

43   Phil Rasmussen, speech delivered aboard the *USS Arizona* memorial, April 19, 2003, at http://bit.ly/1CwzmRm.

44   John W. Lambert, *Pineapple Air Force: Pearl Harbor to Tokyo* (Atglen, PA: Schiffer, 1990), 6–7; Leatrice R. Arakaki and John R. Kuborn, *7 December 1941: The Air Force Story* (Washington, DC: U.S. Government Printing Office, 1991), 44.

45   Quoted in Glenda Elizabeth Gilmore, *Defying Dixie: The Radical Roots of Civil Rights* (New York: W. W. Norton, 2008), 356.

46   Franklin D. Roosevelt, "Campaign Address at Boston, Massachusetts," October 30, 1940, http://bit.ly/FDR1940Boston.

47   Franklin D. Roosevelt, Fireside Chat, December 29, 1940, http://bit.ly/FDR19401229.

48 Olson, *Those Angry Days*, 276; Kennedy, *Freedom from Fear*, 468–69.

49 Franklin D. Roosevelt, State of the Union Address, January 6, 1941, http://bit.ly/FDR1941_SOTU.

50 "'I Am an American Fête to Feature Ethel Waters," *Chicago Defender*, May 10, 1941, 2; "Quash Youth Message," *Chicago Defender*, May 18, 1941, 14.

51 A. Philip Randolph, "Call to March," *Black Worker*, January 1941, at http://www.aasp.umd.edu/chateauvert/mowm.htm.

52 Olson, *Those Angry Days*, 346.

53 Ada Margaret Olsson, interview by Ronald Marcello, December 7, 1978, Interview 461, North Texas State University Oral History Project.

54 Charles Lindbergh, speech delivered at Des Moines, IA, September 11, 1941, at http://www.charleslindbergh.com/americanfirst/speech.asp.

55 Olsson interview.

56 Rasmussen speech.

57 Ibid.; Philip Rasmussen, "Pearl Harbor Eyewitness" (video), http://vimeo.com/33762776.

58 "He Didn't Expect to Make It Home," *Hartford Courant*, May 27, 2002.

59 Joe Treen, "Bloody Sunday: Fifty Years after the Attack on Pearl Harbor, Survivors from Both Sides," *People*, December 9, 1991.

60 "Lt. Phillip Rasmussen and His P-36A," National Museum of the U.S. Air Force, http://1.usa.gov/1yWE336.

61 Rasmussen, "Pearl Harbor Eyewitness"; Rasmussen speech.

62 Rasmussen speech.

63 "Pacific Historic Parks," http://www.pacifichistoricparks.org; Bob Kinzler, "Pearl Harbor Eyewitness" (video), http://vimeo.com/33771263.

64 Treen, "Bloody Sunday."

65 Ibid.

66 Pearl Harbor Survivors Association, http://www.pearlharborsurvivorsonline.org.

67 Robert K. Chester, "'Negro's Number One Hero': Doris Miller, Pearl Harbor, and Retroactive Multiculturalism in World War II," *American Quarterly* 65, no. 1 (March 2013): 31–61. Dorris Miller is generally referred to as "Doris" or "Dorie," but the Waco, Texas, census lists his name as Dorris.

68 Laager quoted in Treen, "Bloody Sunday"; Olsson interview.

69 Franklin D. Roosevelt, "'A Date Which Will Live in Infamy': FDR Asks for a Declaration of War," December 8, 1941, http://bit.ly/FDR1941Declaration.

70 Quoted in Goodwin, *No Ordinary Time*, 292.

CHAPTER 7: THE WATERSHED OF WAR

1 Kimiko Igawa, born December 22, 1907, U.S. Census, 1930, Hawaii; genealogical research on Stan Igawa and Chiye Mori through Ancestry.com, the U.S. Census, Social Security Death Index, obituaries online, military records, immigration and travel, passenger lists, and family trees. See also "Stanley Igawa—WWII Relocation Record," http://bit.ly/1ztKT2Z.

2 Doris Kearns Goodwin, *No Ordinary Time: Franklin and Eleanor Roosevelt: The Home Front in World War II* (New York: Simon & Schuster, 1995), 297.

3 Ibid., 303–12; Alonzo Fields, *My 21 Years in the White House* (New York: Fawcett, 1961).

4 Hanson W. Baldwin, "The Coral Sea Battle: Engagement is Viewed as the Opening Clash in the Decisive Phase of the War," *New York Times*, May 10, 1942, 4.

5 Captain Takahisa Amagi, Interrogation NAV no.1, USSBS no .6, "Battle of Midway, Interrogations of Japanese Officials," Navy Department Library, http://1.usa.gov/1DIGwGA.

6 R. L. McClellan, "Lewis Sanders, Obituary," *Independent* (Robertsdale, AL), January 25, 2001.

7 Franklin D. Roosevelt, "Executive Order 9066: The President Authorizes Japanese Relocation," http://historymatters.gmu.edu/d/5154.

8 "*Korematsu v. United States*: The U.S. Supreme Court Upholds Internment," http://historymatters.gmu.edu/d/5151.

9 "Stanley Igawa—WWII Relocation Record."

10 Eleanor Roosevelt, "Race, Religion, and Prejudice," *The New Republic*, May 11, 1942, 630, in Richard Polenberg, ed., *The Era of Franklin D. Roosevelt, 1933–1945: A Brief History with Documents* (New York: Bedford Books, 2000), 224–25.

11 *Caerulea* (school yearbook), Long Beach Polytechnic High School, 1932, Ancestry.com; "Japanese American," in Josephine G. Hendin, ed., *Concise Companion to Postwar American Literature and Culture* (Oxford, U.K.: Blackwell, 2004), 374.

12 Harry Ferguson, "Manzanar Nice Place—It Better Than Hollywood," http://www.sfmuseum.org/hist8/manzanar1.html.

13 Sue Kunitomi Embrey, interview by Arthur A. Hansen, David A. Hacker, and David J. Bertagnli, August 24 and November 15, 1973, Japanese American World War II Evacuation Oral History Project, Part 1: Internees, University of California, California Digital Library; Greg Robinson, *A Tragedy of Democracy, Japanese Confinement in North America* (New York: Columbia

University Press, 2009). An issue of the *Manzanar Free Press* is online at http://home.comcast.net/~eo9066/1942/42-06/IA199.html. See also "Violence at Manzanar on December 6, 1942: An Examination of the Event, Its Underlying Causes, and Historical Interpretation," http://www.nps.gov/history/history/online_books/manz/hrs11.htm; Harry Ueno et al., "Dissident Harry Ueno Remembers Manzanar," *California History* 64, no. 1 (Winter 1985): 58–64; and Danny Serna, "Plain Utopia: The *Manzanar Free Press* and the Suppression of the Internment Narrative," *Yale Historical Review* 2, no. 3 (Spring 2013): 24–36.

14   Eric Muller, *Free to Die for Their Country: The Story of the Japanese American Draft Resisters in World War II* (Chicago: University of Chicago Press, 2001); Norihiko Shirouzu, "Decades on, a Legacy of War Still Haunts Japanese-Americans," *Wall Street Journal*, June 25, 1999, at http://www.resisters.com/news/WSJ.htm.

15   Quoted in Goodwin, *No Ordinary Time*, 388.

16   Phillip Morgan, *The Fall of Mussolini: Italy, the Italians, and the Second World War* (New York: Oxford University Press, 2007), 128.

17   Shifre Zamkov, November 30, 2005, File no. 125, New Haven Oral History Project, Manuscripts and Archives, Sterling Library, Yale University.

18   Joseph E. Persico, *Roosevelt's Secret War: FDR and World War II Espionage* (New York: Random House, 2001), 224–25.

19   Nelson quoted in Richard R. Lingeman, *Don't You Know There's a War On? The American Home Front, 1941–1945* (New York: G. P. Putnam's Sons, 1971), 126.

20   Sarah Jo Peterson, *Planning the Home Front: Building Bombers and Communities at Willow Run* (Chicago: University of Chicago Press, 2013), 72.

21   Jason Ward, "Nazis Hoe Cotton: Planters, POWs, and the Future of Farm Labor in the Deep South," *Agricultural History* 81, no. 4 (Fall 2007): 471–92.

22   Consuelo Espinosa, "Crispin G. Espinosa . . . La Entrada a USA de Bracero," Bracero History Archive, Item no. 3205, http://braceroarchive.org/items/show/3205 (accessed January 5, 2014).

23   Quoted in Nina Lerman, Ruth Oldenziel, and Arwen P. Mohun, eds., *Gender and Technology: A Reader* (Baltimore, MD: Johns Hopkins University Press, 2003), 316.

24   H. Dewey Anderson and Percy E. Davidson, *Trends in American Labor: A Supplement to Occupational Trends in the United States* (Stanford, CA: Stanford University Press, 1945), 5–6.

25   Lingeman, *Don't You Know There's a War On?*, 149–50.

26   *World's Finest Comics* 8 (Winter 1942–43).

27 Lingeman, *Don't You Know There's a War On?*, 357.

28 Clayton R. Koppes, *Hollywood Goes to War: How Politics, Profits, and Propaganda Shaped World War II* (Berkeley and Los Angeles: University of California Press, 1987), 48.

29 Superman quoted in "Superman Gets Enlisted into the Army," May 31, 2010, http://scans-daily.dreamwidth.org/1985582.html.

30 Quoted in John W. Dower, *War without Mercy: Race and Power in the Pacific War* (New York: Pantheon, 1987), 65.

31 Robert K. Chester, "'Negroes' Number One Hero': Doris Miller, Pearl Harbor, and Retroactive Multiculturalism in World War II Remembrance," *American Quarterly* 65, no. 1 (March 2013): 31–54.

32 Langston Hughes, *Jim Crow's Last Stand* (New York: Negro Publication Society of America, 1943).

33 "Hitler Invades America," quoted in Glenda Gilmore, *Defying Dixie: The Radical Roots of Civil Rights* (New York: W. W. Norton, 2008), 373.

34 "Nazi Pogroms Tame to Texas Rioters," *Afro-American* (Baltimore), June 26, 1943, 1.

35 Jason Ward, "'No Jap Crow, Japanese Americans Encounter the World War II South," *Journal of Southern History* 73 (February 2007): 97, 104.

36 Quoted in Persico, *Roosevelt's Secret War*, 217.

37 "For Sale to Humanity, 70,000 Jews" (advertisement), *New York Times*, February 16, 1943, 11.

38 Josiah DuBois, Jr., interview by Richard D. McKinzie, June 29, 1973, Truman Presidential Library; "Report to the Secretary [of the Treasury] on the Acquiescence of This Government in the Murder of the Jews, January 13, 1944," in Richard Polenberg, ed., *The Era of Franklin D. Roosevelt, 1933–1945: A Brief History with Documents* (New York: Bedford Books, 2000), 219–20. Polenberg credits the memo to Randolph Paul, but DuBois was the author.

39 Owen Brown, "Black Soldiers in Tuscany During World War II," http://bit.ly/BlackSoldiersTuscany.

40 Goodwin, *No Ordinary Time*, 381.

41 Persico, *Roosevelt's Secret War*, 288–89.

42 Andrew Roberts, *The Storm of War: A New History of the Second World War* (New York: Harper, 2009), 457.

43 Letters between John W. Pehle and John J. McCloy, "Debate about the Bombing of Auschwitz," July–November 1944, in Polenberg, *Era of Franklin Roosevelt*, 221–23.

44 Persico, *Roosevelt's Secret War*, 335, 339–40.

45 Ibid., 434.

46 Quoted in Paul F. Boller, *Presidential Wives* (New York: Oxford University Press, 1998), 300; Eleanor Roosevelt, *This I Remember* (New York: Harper & Bros., 1949), 349.

47 Quoted in David McCullough, *Truman* (New York: Simon & Schuster, 1992), 436.

48 Vincent Tubbs, "Inside View of a Nazi Horror Camp," *Afro-American*, May 19, 1945, 14.

49 Gilmore, *Defying Dixie*, 403.

50 Ben Kiernan, *Blood and Soil: A World History of Genocide and Extermination from Sparta to Darfur* (New Haven, CT: Yale University Press, 2007), 484–85; James Brooke, "Okinawa Suicides and Japan's Army: Burying the Truth?" *The New York Times*, June 20, 2005.

51 For quote and previously classified assessments of the cost of invading the home islands, see Douglas J. MacEachlin, *The Final Months of the War with Japan: Signals Intelligence, U.S. Invasion Planning, and the A-Bomb Decision*, Central Intelligence Agency, July 7, 2008, http://bit.ly/FinalMonths.

52 Quoted in William Lanquette, "Ideas by Szilard, Physics by Fermi," *Bulletin of the Atomic Scientists* 48, no. 10 (December 1992), 21.

53 Quoted in Kennedy, *Freedom from Fear*, 839.

54 Ibid., 843.

55 Sidney Shallett, "New Age Ushered," *New York Times*, August 7, 1945, 1.

56 "Parley Nears End," *New York Times*, July 24, 1945, 1.

57 Evelyn Webb, interview by Glenda Gilmore, Greensboro, NC, September 1965.

58 Truman quoted in David Rees, *The Defeat of Japan* (New York: Praeger, 1997), 156; Shallett, "New Age Ushered."

59 Shallett, "New Age Ushered"; and Hanson W. Baldwin, "The Atomic Weapon," *New York Times*, August 7, 1945, 1, 22, 10.

60 Quoted in Geoffrey E. Hill, *Ghosts of '45: Japan's War Legacy and National Purpose* (Abbott Press, 2013), 149.

61 Quotations in Richard Tanter, "Voice and Silence in the First Nuclear War: Wilfred Burchett and Hiroshima," in Ben Kiernan, ed., *Burchett: Reporting the Other Side of the World, 1939–1983* (London: Quartet Books, 1986), 19, 23.

62 Kay Raftery, "47 Years Later, Japanese Besiege Pearl Harbor," *Philadelphia Inquirer*, December 4, 1988; "Stan Igawa," in *U.S., Final Accountability Rosters of Evacuees at Relocation Centers, 1942–46*, Ancestry.com Library Edition.

CHAPTER 8: A RISING SUPERPOWER, 1944–1954

1   Merle Miller, *Plain Speaking: An Oral Biography of Harry S. Truman* (New York: Berkeley, 1974), 33.

2   Joshua B. Freeman, *American Empire: The Rise of a Global Power, The Democratic Revolution at Home, 1945–2000* (New York: Penguin, 2012), 52.

3   Elizabeth Borgwardt, *A New Deal for the World: America's Vision for Human Rights* (Cambridge, MA: Belknap Press, 2005), 122.

4   Harry S. Truman, "First Speech to Congress," April 16, 1945, http://bit.ly /1wzTAZA.

5   Harry S. Truman, "Address to the United Nations Conference in San Francisco," April 25, 1945, http://bit.ly/1wbs9p4.

6   United Nations Charter, Preamble, http://www.un.org/en/documents/charter /preamble.shtml.

7   Cynthia Soohoo, Catherine Albisa, and Martha F. Davis, eds., *Bringing Human Rights Home: A History of Human Rights in the United States* (Philadelphia: University of Pennsylvania Press, 2009), 80.

8   Natalie Kaufman, *Human Rights Treaties and the Senate: A History of Opposition* (Chapel Hill: University of North Carolina Press, 1990), 17.

9   Susan L. Carruthers, "'Produce More Joppolos': John Hersey's *A Bell for Adano* and the Making of the 'Good Occupation,'" *Journal of American History* 100 (2014), 1086–1113.

10   Joint Chiefs of Staff, "Directive to Commander-in-Chief of United States Forces of Occupation Regarding the Military Government in Germany," April 1945.

11   "Stalin Sets a Huge Output Near Ours in 5-Year Plan; Expects to Lead in Science," *New York Times,* February 10, 1946.

12   Deborah Larson, *The Origins of Containment: A Psychological Explanation* (Princeton, N.J.: Princeton University Press, 1985), 252.

13   Melvyn P. Leffler and David S. Painter, eds., *Origins of the Cold War: An International History* (New York: Routledge, 1994), 27.

14   Martin J. Medhurst and H. W. Brands, eds., *Critical Reflections on the Cold War: Linking Rhetoric and History* (College Station: Texas A&M University Press, 2000), 50.

15   George F. Kennan, *The Kennan Diaries,* ed. Frank Costigliola (New York: W. W. Norton, 2014), 105.

16   George F. Kennan, "The Charge in the Soviet Union (Kennan) to the Secretary of State," February 22, 1946, http://bit.ly/10Fhztv.

17   "Divorce—the Postwar Wave," *Newsweek,* October 7, 1946.

18 Harry S. Truman, "Radio Address to the American People on Wages and Prices in the Reconversion Period," October 30, 1945, http://www.presidency.ucsb.edu/ws/?pid=12391.

19 Olivier Zunz, Leonard Schoppa, and Nobuhiro Hiwatari, eds., *Social Contracts Under Stress: The Middle Classes of America, Europe, and Japan at the Turn of the Century* (New York: Russell Sage Foundation, 2002), 136.

20 James T. Sparrow, *Warfare State: World War II Americans and the Age of Big Government* (New York: Oxford University Press, 2011), 249.

21 Ibid., 250.

22 Nelson Lichtenstein, *State of the Union: A Century of American Labor* (Princeton, NJ: Princeton University Press, 2002), 103.

23 Kimberly Phillips-Fein, "American Counterrevolutionary: Lemuel Ricketts Boulware and General Electric, 1950–1960," in Nelson Lichtenstein, ed., *American Capitalism: Social Thought and Political Economy in the Twentieth Century* (Philadelphia: University of Pennsylvania Press, 2006), 252–53.

24 Melvyn Dubofsky and Foster Rhea Dulles, *Labor in America: A History,* 8th ed. (Wheeling, IL: Harland Davidson, 2010), 322.

25 Ibid., 319.

26 Harry S. Truman, "Radio Address to the American People on the Railroad Strike Emergency," May 24, 1946, http://www.presidency.ucsb.edu/ws/?pid=12406.

27 *Congressional Record,* 79th Cong., 1st sess. (1945), 12,512.

28 John Patrick Diggins, *The Proud Decades: America in War and Peace, 1941–1960* (New York: W. W. Norton, 1988), 102.

29 T.R.B., "Neanderthal Men," *The New Republic* 117, no. 5 (August 1947): 3.

30 Harry S. Truman, "Annual Message to the Congress on the State of the Union," January 6, 1947, http://www.presidency.ucsb.edu/ws/?pid=12762.

31 Elizabeth Tandy Shermer, *Sunbelt Capitalism: Phoenix and the Transformation of American Politics* (Philadelphia: University of Pennsylvania Press, 2013), 147.

32 Michelle Brattain, *The Politics of Whiteness: Race, Workers, and Culture in the Modern South* (Athens: University of Georgia Press, 2004), 143.

33 James T. Patterson, *Grand Expectations: The United States, 1945–1974* (New York: Oxford University Press, 1996), 127.

34 Ibid., 128.

35 Stephen E. Ambrose and Douglas G. Brinkley, *Rise to Globalism: American Foreign Policy Since 1938* (New York: Penguin Books, 1997), 81.

36 "The Sources of Soviet Conduct," *Foreign Affairs* 25, no. 4 (July 1947): 566–82.

37 George C. Marshall, "Marshall Plan Speech," address, Harvard University, Cambridge, MA, June 5, 1947.

38 Walter A. McDougall, *Promised Land, Crusader State: The American Encounter with the World Since 1776* (New York: Houghton Mifflin, 1997), 164.

39 Ambrose and Brinkley, *Rise to Globalism,* 91.

40 Freeman, *American Empire,* 52.

41 Henry Luce, "The American Century," *Life* (February 17, 1941), 63.

42 Freeman, *American Empire,* 75.

43 Joseph Crespino, *Strom Thurmond's America* (New York: Hill & Wang, 2012), 71.

44 Geoffrey Kabaservice, *Rule and Ruin: The Downfall of Moderation and the Destruction of the Republican Party, from Eisenhower to the Tea Party* (New York: Oxford University Press, 2012), 8.

45 *To Secure These Rights: The Report of the President's Committee on Civil Rights,* October 1947, http://bit.ly/137GHtW.

46 Harry S. Truman, Executive Order 9980, July 26, 1948, https://www.truman library.org/9980a.htm; and Executive Order 9981, July 26, 1948, https://www.trumanlibrary.org/9981a.htm.

47 Patterson, *Grand Expectations,* 191.

48 Alien Registration Act of 1940, 18 U.S.C § 2683 (1940).

49 Quoted in Thomas Sugrue, *Sweet Land of Liberty: The Forgotten Struggle for Civil Rights in the North* (New York: Random House, 2008), 22.

50 Arthur Schlesinger, *The Vital Center: The Politics of Freedom* (Boston: Houghton Mifflin, 1949), xviii.

51 Stephen Whitfield, *The Culture of the Cold War* (Baltimore: Johns Hopkins University Press, 1991), 172.

52 Greg Mitchell, *Tricky Dick and the Pink Lady: Richard Nixon vs. Helen Gahagan Douglas* (New York: Random House, 1998), 168.

53 Martin Halpern, "'I'm Fighting for Freedom': Coleman Young, HUAC, and the Detroit African American Community," *Journal of American Ethnic History* 17 (Fall 1997): 29.

54 Harry S. Truman, *Memoirs,* vol. 2, *Years of Trial and Hope* (Garden City, NY: Doubleday, 1956), 333.

55 "McCarthy Charges Reds Hold U.S. Jobs," *Wheeling Intelligencer,* February 10, 1950.

56 Thomas Rosteck, *"See It Now" Confronts McCarthyism: Television Documentary and the Politics of Representation* (Tuscaloosa: University of Alabama Press, 1994), 55.

57 "Have You No Sense of Decency?" June 9, 1954, U.S. Senate, Senate History, 1941–63, http://1.usa.gov/1wUhH7w.

58 *Investigation of Communist Activities, New York Area—Part VII (Entertainment), Hearings Before the Committee on Un-American Activities, House of Representatives,* 84th Cong., 1st sess. (August 17 and 18, 1955).

59 Ambrose and Brinkley, *Rise to Globalism,* 128.

CHAPTER 9: IN AT LEAST MODEST COMFORT

1 The account of Friedan draws from Daniel Horowitz, *Betty Friedan and the Making of "The Feminine Mystique": The American Left, the Cold War, and Modern Feminism* (Amherst: University of Massachusetts Press, 1998); and Sylvie Murray, *The Progressive Housewife: Community Activism in Suburban Queens, 1945–1965* (Philadelphia: University of Pennsylvania Press, 2003).

2 Donald Pisani, *From the Family Farm to Agribusiness: The Irrigation Crusade in California and the West* (Berkeley and Los Angeles: University of California Press, 1984), 451.

3 Julia Grant, *Raising Baby by the Book: The Education of American Mothers* (New Haven, CT: Yale University Press, 1998), 222.

4 Ibid.

5 Kevin Kruse, *White Flight: Atlanta and the Making of Modern Conservatism* (Princeton, NJ: Princeton University Press, 2005), 60.

6 Ibid., 61.

7 U.S. Bureau of the Census, *1960 Census of Housing,* vol. 1, *States and Small Areas* (Washington, DC: U.S. Bureau of the Census, 1963), xxxix.

8 Thomas Doherty, *Cold War, Cool Medium: Television, McCarthyism, and American Culture* (New York: Columbia University Press, 2003), 51.

9 Richard Butsch, *The Citizen Audience: Crowds, Publics, and Individuals* (New York: Routledge, 2008), 104.

10 John Reese, "The Air-Conditioning Revolution," *Saturday Evening Post,* July 9, 1960, 100, quoted in Raymond Arsenault, "The End of the Long Hot Summer: The Air Conditioner and Southern Culture," *Journal of Southern History* 50 (1984): 597–628.

11 Elizabeth Tandy Shermer, *Sunbelt Capitalism: Phoenix and the Transformation of American Politics* (Philadelphia: University of Pennsylvania Press, 2013).

12 Christopher W. Wells, *Car Country: An Environmental History* (Seattle: University of Washington Press, 2012), 279.

13   Robert Lifset, ed., *American Energy Policy in the 1970s* (Norman: University of Oklahoma Press, 2014), 165.

14   T.R.B., "Washington Wire," *The New Republic* 127, no. 24 (December 15, 1952): 3.

15   "Stresses 'Business Climate,'" *New York Times,* December 2, 1952, 34.

16   *Hearings Before the Senate Committee on Armed Services on Nominee Designates: Charles E. Wilson, etc.,* 83rd Cong., 1st sess. (1953) [statement of Charles E. Wilson].

17   "Ike vs. Democratic Party," *Life,* October 29, 1956, 130.

18   President Eisenhower to Edgar Eisenhower, November 8, 1954, in *Dwight D. Eisenhower: Papers as President of the United States, 1953–1961,* National Archives, http://research.archives.gov/description/186596.

19   Nelson Lichtenstein, *American Capitalism: Social Thought and Political Economy in the Twentieth Century* (Philadelphia: University of Pennsylvania Press, 2006), 251.

20   Kim Phillips-Fein, *Invisible Hands: The Businessmen's Crusade Against the New Deal* (New York: W. W. Norton, 2010), 99.

21   Kevin Kruse, "For God So Loved the 1 Percent . . . ," *New York Times,* January 18, 2012.

22   U.S. Department of Justice, *Justice and Crime Atlas, 2000* (Washington, D.C.: Justice Research and Statistics Association, 2000), 36–38, http://www.jrsa.org/projects/Crime_Atlas_2000.pdf.

23   *Juvenile Delinquency (Comic Books): Hearings Before the Subcommittee to Investigate Juvenile Delinquency,* 83rd Cong., 2nd sess. (1954) [statement of Fredric Wertham].

24   *Employment of Homosexuals and Other Sex Perverts in Government,* 81 S. Rep. No. 241, (1950): 4.

25   David Johnson, *The Lavender Scare: The Cold War Persecution of Gays and Lesbians in the Federal Government* (Chicago: University of Chicago Press, 2004), 98.

26   Isabel Wilkerson, *The Warmth of Other Suns: The Epic Story of America's Great Migration* (New York: Random House, 2010), 208.

27   Thomas J. Sugrue, *Sweet Land of Liberty: The Forgotten Struggle for Civil Rights in the North* (New York: Random House, 2008), 32.

28   Ibid., 150.

29   "The First Freedom Ride: Bayard Rustin on His Work with CORE," interview by Ed Edwin, September 9, 1985, http://historymatters.gmu.edu/d/6909/.

30   Claudia Goldin and Lawrence F. Katz, *The Race Between Technology and Education* (Cambridge, MA: Harvard University Press, 2008), esp. 194–246.

31 *Brown v. Board of Education*, 347 U.S. 483 (1954).

32 *The Southern Manifesto: Declaration of Constitutional Principles*, 84th Cong., 2nd sess. (March 12, 1956).

33 Mary Dudziak, *Cold War Civil Rights* (Princeton, N.J.: Princeton University Press, 2000), 130.

34 James Patterson, *Brown v. Board of Education: A Civil Rights Milestone and Its Troubled Legacy* (New York: Oxford University Press, 2001), 60.

35 Dudziak, *Cold War Civil Rights*, 128.

36 Jeff Woods, *Black Struggle, Red Scare: Segregation and Anti-Communism in the South, 1948–1968* (Baton Rouge: Louisiana State University Press, 2004), 69.

37 Andrew Hartman, *Education and the Cold War: The Battle for the American School* (New York: Palgrave Macmillan, 2008), 172.

38 Harvard Sitkoff, *The Struggle for Black Equality, 1954–1992* (New York: Hill & Wang, 1993), 36.

39 Stephen E. Ambrose and Douglas G. Brinkley, *Rise to Globalism: American Foreign Policy Since 1938* (New York: Penguin, 1997), 149.

40 Greg Grandin, *Empire's Workshop: Latin America, the United States, and the Rise of the New Imperialism* (New York: Metropolitan Books, 2006), 45.

CHAPTER 10: A SEASON OF CHANGE

1 John Lewis with Michael D'Orso, *Walking with the Wind: A Memoir of the Movement* (New York: Simon & Schuster, 1998), 127.

2 Ibid., 124.

3 Ibid., 115.

4 C. Wright Mills, "Letter to the New Left," *New Left Review* 1, no. 5 (September–October, 1960).

5 Shaun Casey, *The Making of a Catholic President: Kennedy vs. Nixon, 1960* (New York: Oxford University Press, 2009), 113, 139.

6 John F. Kennedy, "Address to Greater Houston Ministerial Association," September 12, 1960, in James T. Fisher, ed., *Communion of Immigrants: A History of Catholics in America* (New York: Oxford University Press, 2007), 135.

7 John F. Kennedy, "Inaugural Address," January 21, 1961, http://www.presidency.ucsb.edu/ws/?pid=8032.

8 John F. Kennedy, "Remarks to Members of the White House Conference on National Economic Issues," May 21, 1962, http://www.presidency.ucsb.edu/ws/?pid=8670.

9   Irving Bernstein, *Promises Kept: John F. Kennedy's New Frontier* (New York: Oxford University Press, 1991), 124.

10   Lewis, *Walking*, 124.

11   Raymond Arsenault, *Freedom Riders: 1961 and the Struggle for Racial Justice* (New York: Oxford University Press, 2006), 164.

12   "Anger that Inflamed Route 40 Yields to Common Sense," *Life,* December 8, 1961, 32.

13   Marc Trachtenberg, *History and Strategy* (Princeton, N.J.: Princeton University Press, 1991), 245–46.

14   John F. Kennedy, "Radio and Television Report to the American People on the Soviet Arms Buildup in Cuba," October 22, 1962, http://bit.ly/1GybLD1.

15   Lewis, *Walking*, 124.

16   Martin Luther King, Jr., "Letter from Birmingham Jail," April 16, 1963, http://stanford.io/1u78SUq.

17   Philip A. Klinkner and Rogers M. Smith, *The Unsteady March: The Rise and Decline of Racial Equality in America* (Chicago: University of Chicago Press, 1999), 267.

18   Thomas J. Sugrue, *Sweet Land of Liberty: The Forgotten Struggle for Civil Rights in the North* (New York: Random House, 2008), 294.

19   George C. Wallace, "Inaugural Address," January 15, 1963, http://1.usa .gov/10z7aPJ.

20   Martin Luther King, Jr., *All Labor Has Dignity,* ed. Michael K. Honey (Boston: Beacon Press, 2011), 79.

21   Martin Luther King, Jr., *A Call to Conscience: The Landmark Speeches of Dr. Martin Luther King, Jr.,* ed. Clayborne Carson and Kris Shephard (New York: Warner Books, 2001), 85.

22   William Jones, *The March on Washington: Jobs, Freedom, and the Forgotten History of Civil Rights* (New York: W. W. Norton, 2013), 193.

23   Eric Sundquist, *King's Dream* (New Haven, CT: Yale University Press, 2009), 46.

24   Sugrue, *Sweet Land of Liberty*, 313–14.

25   Malcolm X, "Message to the Grassroots," in *Malcolm X Speaks: Selected Speeches and Statements,* ed. George Breitman (New York: Grove Press, 1994), 12.

26   Ibid., 9.

27   Thomas Cowger and Sherwin Markman, eds., *Lyndon Johnson Remembered: An Intimate Portrait of a Presidency* (Lanham, MD: Rowman and Littlefield, 2003), 37.

28   Robert Caro, *The Years of Lyndon Johnson,* vol. 2, *Means of Ascent* (New York: Random House, 1990), 344.

29 Civil Rights Act of 1964, http://1.usa.gov/10Fk2nG.

30 "The National Organization for Women's 1966 Statement of Purpose," October 29, 1966, http://now.org/about/history/statement-of-purpose.

31 James Cobb, *The South and America Since World War II* (New York: Oxford University Press, 2012), 89.

32 "Individual Property Owners Are Given Bill of Rights by Realtors," *Washington World* 3 (1963): 25.

33 John Andrew, *The Other Side of the Sixties: Young Americans for Freedom and the Rise of Conservative Politics* (New Brunswick, NJ: Rutgers University Press, 1997), 222.

34 Barry Goldwater, *The Conscience of a Conservative* (Princeton, N.J.: Princeton University Press, 2007), xxii.

35 Ibid., 4.

36 Ibid., 49.

37 Ibid., 10.

38 Nancy MacLean, *Freedom Is Not Enough: The Opening of the American Workplace* (Cambridge, MA: Harvard University Press, 2008), 46.

39 Rick Perlstein, *Before the Storm: Barry Goldwater and the Unmaking of the American Consensus* (New York: Hill & Wang, 2001), 364.

40 MacLean, *Freedom Is Not Enough,* 62.

41 Ed Cray, *Chief Justice: A Biography of Earl Warren* (New York: Simon & Schuster, 1997), 386.

42 Matthew Lassiter and Joseph Crespino, eds., *The Myth of Southern Exceptionalism* (New York: Oxford University Press, 2010), 296.

43 Lucas Powe, Jr., *The Supreme Court and the American Elite, 1789–2008* (Cambridge, MA: Harvard University Press, 2009), 265.

44 Goldwater, *Conscience,* 75.

45 Perlstein, *Before the Storm,* 391.

46 Ibid., 374.

47 Kathleen Hall Jamieson, *Packaging the Presidency: A History and Criticism of Presidential Campaign Advertising* (New York: Oxford University Press, 1984), 220.

48 Richard Hofstadter, "A Long View: Goldwater in History," *New York Review of Books* (October 8, 1964): 20.

49 Rick Perlstein, *Nixonland: The Rise of a President and the Fracturing of America* (New York: Simon & Schuster, 2008), 6.

50 Lyndon B. Johnson, "Annual Message to the Congress on the State of the Union," January 8, 1964, http://www.presidency.ucsb.edu/ws/?pid=26787.

51 Thomas J. Sugrue, *Origins of the Urban Crisis: Race and Inequality in Postwar Detroit* (Princeton, NJ: Princeton University Press, 2005), 126.

52   Maurice Isserman and Michael Kazin, *America Divided: The Civil War of the 1960s* (New York: Oxford University Press, 2000), 109.

53   John Morton Blum, *Years of Discord: American Politics and Society, 1961–1974* (New York: W. W. Norton, 1991), 178.

54   Lyndon B. Johnson, Annual Message to Congress on the State of the Union, January 8, 1964, http://www.presidency.ucsb.edu/ws/?pid=26787.

55   Larry Dewitt and Edward Berkowitz, "Health Care," in Mitchell Lerner, ed., *A Companion to Lyndon B. Johnson* (New York: Wiley-Blackwell, 2012), 167.

56   Daniel Béland and Alex Waddan, *The Politics of Policy Change: Welfare, Medicare, and Social Security Reform* (Washington, DC: Georgetown University Press, 2012), 81.

57   William McCord, *Mississippi: The Long Hot Summer* (New York: W. W. Norton, 1965), 18.

58   Fannie Lou Hamer, *Testimony Before the Credentials Committee, Democratic National Convention,* August 22, 1964, transcript and audio, http://bit.ly/1BQRjws.

59   Lewis, *Walking,* 291.

60   Voting Rights Act of 1965, http://www.ourdocuments.gov/doc.php?flash=true&doc=100.

61   Martin Luther King, Jr., *Why We Can't Wait* (Boston: Beacon Press, 2010), 164.

62   Peniel E. Joseph, *The Black Power Movement: Rethinking the Civil Rights–Black Power Era* (New York: Routledge, 2006), 344.

CHAPTER 11: MAY DAY

1   On Merschel, the narrative draws from Virginia Merschel, interview by Thomas J. Sugrue, October 8, 1996; "Lawrence James Merschel," Vietnam Veterans Memorial Fund, http://bit.ly/LJMerschel; obituary, *Philadelphia Inquirer,* May 4, 1968; and "Merschel, Lawrence James, PFC," http://bit.ly/PFCMerschel.

2   Gabriel Kolko, *Anatomy of a War: Vietnam, the United States, and the Modern Historical Experience* (New York: Pantheon, 1994), 117.

3   David L. DiLeo, *George Ball, Vietnam, and the Rethinking of Containment* (Chapel Hill: University of North Carolina Press, 1991), 52.

4   Ibid., 53.

5   McNamara quoted in Michael H. Hunt, ed., *Crises in U.S. Foreign Policy: An International History Reader* (New Haven, CT: Yale University Press, 1996), 333.

6   Larry Berman, *Planning a Tragedy: The Americanization of the War in Vietnam* (New York: W. W. Norton, 1982), 144.

7   Maurice Isserman and Michael Kazin, *America Divided: The Civil War of the 1960s* (New York: Oxford University Press, 2000), 115.

8   Robert David Johnson, *Ernest Gruening and the American Dissenting Tradition* (Cambridge, MA: Harvard University Press, 1998), 253.

9   Fredrik Logevall, *The Origins of the Vietnam War* (New York: Routledge, 2013), 117.

10   David Levy, *The Debate Over Vietnam* (Baltimore: Johns Hopkins University Press, 1991), 103.

11   Stanley Karnow, *Vietnam, a History* (New York: Penguin, 1997), 361.

12   Kim McQuaid, *The Anxious Years: America in the Vietnam-Watergate Era* (New York: Basic Books, 1989), 73.

13   Michael H. Hunt, *Lyndon Johnson's War: America's Cold War Crusade in Vietnam, 1945–1968* (New York: Hill & Wang, 1996), 105.

14   Ibid., 91.

15   Michael S. Foley, *Confronting the War Machine: Draft Resistance During the Vietnam War* (Chapel Hill: University of North Carolina Press, 2003), 39.

16   Ward Just, "Vietnam Notebook (April 1968)," in Katharine Whittemore, Ellen Rosenbush, and Jim Nelson, eds., *The Sixties: Recollections from the Decade from "Harper's Magazine"* (New York: Franklin Square Press, 1995), 143.

17   DiLeo, *George Ball*, 53.

18   Ibid., 64.

19   David L. Anderson, ed., *The Columbia Guide to the Vietnam War* (New York: Columbia University Press, 2002), 267.

20   Randall B. Woods, *LBJ: Architect of American Ambition* (New York: Free Press, 2006), 677.

21   "Ho Chi Kennedy: An Editorial," *Chicago Tribune,* February 21, 1966.

22   Max Frankel, "Demonstrators Decorous—3 White House Aides Meet with Leaders: Thousands Join Antiwar March," *New York Times,* November 28, 1965.

23   Mary Hershberger, *Traveling to Vietnam: American Peace Activists and the War* (Syracuse, NY: Syracuse University Press, 1998), 16.

24   Shawn Francis Peters, *The Catonsville Nine: A Story of Faith and Resistance in the Vietnam Era* (New York: Oxford University Press, 2012), 35.

25   Michael S. Neiberg, *Making Citizen-Soldiers: ROTC and the Ideology of American Military Service* (Cambridge, MA: Harvard University Press, 2000).

26   Students for a Democratic Society, "Port Huron Statement of the Students for a Democratic Society," 1962, http://bit.ly/1u7a4Hl.

27   Francesca Polletta, *Freedom Is an Endless Meeting: Democracy in American Social Movements* (Chicago: University of Chicago Press, 2002), 205.

28   Todd Gitlin, *The Sixties: Years of Hope, Days of Rage* (New York: Bantam Books, 1989), 427.

29   Jay Sand, "The Radio Waves Unnamable," Senior Honors Thesis, Department of History, University of Pennsylvania, 1994.

30   Paul Krassner, "Revolution for the Hell of It: Reason Let Us Come Together," *Realist* (August 1967), 20, http://www.ep.tc/realist/76/20.html.

31   Christian G. Appy, *Working-Class War: American Combat Soldiers and Vietnam* (Chapel Hill: University of North Carolina Press, 1993), 6.

32   Ibid., 42.

33   Simon Hall, *Peace and Freedom: The Civil Rights and Antiwar Movements in the 1960s* (Philadelphia: University of Pennsylvania Press, 2005), 8.

34   David Remnick, *King of the World: Muhammad Ali and the Rise of an American Hero* (New York: Random House, 1998), 267; Fred Shapiro, ed., *The Yale Book of Quotations* (New Haven: Yale University Press, 2006), 14.

35   Martin Luther King, Jr., "Beyond Vietnam," April 4, 1967, http://stanford .io/1tIZogG.

36   "A Tragedy," *Washington Post,* April 6, 1967.

37   Peniel Joseph, *Waiting 'Til the Midnight Hour: A Narrative History of Black Power in America* (New York: Henry Holt, 2006), 193.

38   Stokely Carmichael, "Black Power," October 29, 1966, http://voicesof democracy.umd.edu/carmichael-black-power-speech-text.

39   Peniel Joseph, *Dark Days, Bright Nights: From Black Power to Barack Obama* (New York: Basic Books, 2010), 134.

40   Seth Rosenfeld, *Subversives: The FBI's War on Student Radicals, and Reagan's Rise to Power* (New York: Farrar, Straus & Giroux, 2012), 302.

41   "McCarthy Statement on Entering the 1968 Primaries," *New York Times,* December 1, 1967.

42   Lyndon B. Johnson, *Public Papers of the Presidents of the United States: Lyndon B. Johnson,* book 2, *1968–1969* (Washington, DC: Government Printing Office, 1970), 2.

43   Ed. Pham Van Son, trans. J5/JGS Translation Board, *The Viet Cong "Tet" Offensive* (Saigon: RVNAF, 1968), 47.

44   Larry Berman, *Lyndon Johnson's War: The Road to Stalemate in Vietnam* (New York: W. W. Norton, 1989), 175.

45   Ibid., 197.

46   Lyndon B. Johnson, *Public Papers of the Presidents of the United States: Lyndon B. Johnson,* book 2, *1968–1969* (Washington, DC: Government Printing Office, 1970), 469–76.

47   Gitlin, *Sixties,* 307.

48 Che Guevara, *Global Justice: Liberation and Socialism*, ed. Ernesto Guevara (New York: Ocean Press, 2002), 62.

49 Christian G. Appy, *Patriots: The Vietnam War Remembered from All Sides* (New York: Penguin, 2003), 425.

CHAPTER 12: WHICH SIDE ARE YOU ON?

1   Material on Carmen Roberts can be found in Carmen Roberts Papers (hereafter CRP), Michigan Historical Collections, Bentley Historical Library, University of Michigan, Ann Arbor.

2   Heather Ann Thompson, *Whose Detroit?: Politics, Labor, and Race in a Modern American City* (Ithaca, NY: Cornell University Press, 2001), 78.

3   Quotes from "Biographical Field Notes," August 15, 1986, CRP, and "Detroit School Board Member Says: 'I Have a Dream Too . . . ,'" *Wisconsin Report* in CRP, Folder: Clippings 1977.

4   Robert F. Kennedy, "Statement on Assassination of Martin Luther King, Jr.," April 4, 1968, http://bit.ly/112NULA.

5   Evan Thomas, *Robert Kennedy: His Life* (New York: Simon & Schuster, 2002), 390.

6   Todd Gitlin, *The Sixties: Years of Hope, Days of Rage* (New York: Bantam Books, 1993), 54.

7   David Farber, *Chicago '68* (Chicago: University of Chicago Press, 1988), 200.

8   Louis Gould, *1968: The Election that Changed America*, 2nd ed. (Chicago: Ivan Dee, 2010), 125.

9   Richard Nixon, "Address Accepting the Presidential Nomination at the Republican National Convention in Miami Beach, Florida," August 8, 1968, http://www.presidency.ucsb.edu/ws/?pid=25968.

10 Ronald Reagan, "A Time for Choosing," October 27, 1964, http://bit.ly/1zZqB2m.

11 Seth Rosenfield, *Subversives: The FBI's War on Student Radicals, and Reagan's Rise to Power* (New York: Farrar, Straus & Giroux, 2012), 324.

12 Ibid.

13 Marisa Chappell, *The War on Welfare: Family, Poverty, and Politics in Modern America* (Philadelphia: University of Pennsylvania Press, 2010), 66.

14 Max Frankel, "A Team of Moderates," *New York Times,* December 12, 1968.

15 Max Johnson, "Agnew Insults Leaders: Guests Quit Meeting in Bitterness," *Baltimore Afro-American,* April 13, 1968.

16 Rick Perlstein, *Nixonland: The Rise of a President and the Fracturing of America* (New York: Simon & Schuster, 2008), 526.

17   Weathermen—First Communiqué, July 31, 1970, Pacifica Radio/UC Berkeley Social Activism Sound Recording Project, http://bit.ly/1wCco9j.

18   Thomas J. Sugrue, "Affirmative Action from Below: Civil Rights, the Building Trades, and the Politics of Racial Equality in the Urban North, 1945–1969," *Journal of American History* 91, no. 1 (June 2004): 146.

19   Dean J. Kotlowski, *Nixon's Civil Rights: Politics, Principle, and Policy* (Cambridge, MA: Harvard University Press, 2001), 177.

20   Richard Scammon and Ben Wattenberg, *The Real Majority* (New York: Coward-McCann, 1970), 46.

21   "Man and Woman of the Year: The Middle Americans," *Time,* January 5, 1970.

22   Pete Hamill, "The Revolt of the White Lower Middle Class," *New York Magazine,* April 14, 1969.

23   Ibid., 26.

24   Perlstein, *Nixonland,* 495.

25   Ibid., 498.

26   Christopher Bonastia, *Knocking on the Door: The Federal Government's Attempt to Desegregate the Suburbs* (Princeton, NJ: Princeton University Press, 2006), 106.

27   Ibid., 107.

28   Ibid., 130.

29   Quoted in Walter Mondale, "Retreat on Civil Rights," *Congressional Record,* 91st. Cong., 1st sess. (1969), S31810.

30   J. Todd Moye, *Let the People Decide: Black Freedom and White Resistance Movements in Sunflower County Mississippi, 1945–1986* (Chapel Hill: University of North Carolina Press, 2004), 178.

31   George H. Gallup, *The Gallup Poll: Public Opinion, 1935–1971,* 3 vols. (New York: Random House, 1972), 3:2329.

32   Thomas J. Sugrue, *Sweet Land of Liberty: The Forgotten Struggle for Civil Rights in the North* (New York: Random House, 2008), 483.

33   Kotlowski, *Nixon's Civil Rights,* 39.

34   Sugrue, *Sweet Land of Liberty,* 484.

35   Paul R. Dimond, *Beyond Busing: Reflections on Urban Segregation, the Courts, and Equal Opportunity* (Ann Arbor: University of Michigan Press, 1985), 76.

36   Richard Nixon, "Remarks to Reporters About Nominations to the Supreme Court," April 9, 1970, http://www.presidency.ucsb.edu/ws/?pid=2455.

37   John C. Jeffries, Jr., *Justice Lewis F. Powell, Jr., A Biography* (New York: Scribner, 1994), 238.

38   Richard Kluger, *Simple Justice: The History of Brown v. Board of Education and Black America's Struggle for Equality* (New York: Knopf, 1975), 606.

39   *Milliken v. Bradley* 418 U.S. 717 (1974), at 741–42, 815.

40   Beth L. Bailey, *Sex in the Heartland* (Cambridge, MA: Harvard University Press, 1999), 139.

41   Robin Morgan, "Good-Bye to All That," in Rosalyn Baxandall and Linda Gordon, eds., *Dear Sisters: Dispatches from the Women's Liberation Movement* (New York: Basic Books, 2000), 53.

42   John D'Emilio and Estelle B. Friedman, *Intimate Matters: A History of Sexuality in America*, 2nd ed. (Chicago: University of Chicago Press, 1997), 311.

43   Robert O. Self, *All in the Family: The Realignment of American Democracy Since the 1960s* (New York: Hill & Wang, 2012), 191.

44   Steve Estes, *I Am a Man! Race, Manhood, and the Civil Rights Movement* (Chapel Hill: University of North Carolina Press, 2006), 82–83, 165.

45   Morgan, "Good-Bye to All That," 53.

46   Carol Hanisch, "The Personal Is Political," in Shulamith Firestone and Anne Koedt, eds., *Notes from the Second Year: Women's Liberation* (New York: Radical Feminism, 1970), http://www.carolhanisch.org/CHwritings/PIP.html.

47   Molly Ginty, "*Our Bodies, Ourselves* Turns 35 Today," *Women's eNews,* May 4, 2004, http://bit.ly/1GyeLPQ.

48   Marc Stein, *Sexual Injustice: Supreme Court Decisions from Griswold to Roe* (Chapel Hill: University of North Carolina Press, 201), 142.

49   Ibid.

50   Lucian Truscott IV, "Gay Power Comes to Sheridan Square," *Village Voice,* July 2, 1969.

51   Jeffrey O. G. Ogbar, *Black Power: Radical Politics and African American Identity* (Baltimore: Johns Hopkins University Press, 2005), 102.

52   Huey P. Newton, *The Huey P. Newton Reader,* ed. David Hilliard and Donald Weise (New York: Seven Stories Press, 2002), 159.

53   Susan J. Douglas, *Where the Girls Are: Growing Up Female with the Mass Media* (New York: Three Rivers Press, 1995), 162.

54   Dorothy Sue Cobble, *The Other Women's Movement: Workplace Justice and Social Rights in Modern America* (Princeton, NJ: Princeton University Press, 2004), 3.

55   *Equal Rights 1970: Hearings Before the Committee on the Judiciary,* 91st Cong., 2nd sess. (September 1970) [testimony of Myra K. Wolfgang], http://history matters.gmu.edu/d/7018/.

56   "Equal Rights Amendment Passed by Congress," *New York Times,* March 22, 1972.

57   Donald T. Critchlow, *Phyllis Schlafly and Grassroots Conservatism: A Woman's Crusade* (Princeton, NJ: Princeton University Press, 2005), 121.

58   Ibid., 217.

59   "Housewives Protest 'Equal Rights Bill,'" *Sarasota Herald-Tribune,* April 2, 1972.

60   Carol Frances Cini, "Making Women's Rights Matter: Diverse Activists, California's Commission on the Status of Women, and the Legislative and Social Impact of a Movement, 1962–1976," Ph.D. diss., University of California, Los Angeles, 2007, 437.

61   "Diary of a Glad Housewife," *Detroit Free Press*, February 4, 1974.

62   *Northeast Detroiter*, October 4, 1973.

63   John David Skrentny, *The Minority Rights Revolution* (Cambridge, MA: Harvard University Press, 2009), 318.

64   Kotlowski, *Nixon's Civil Rights*, 234.

65   *Roe v. Wade*, 410 U.S. 113 (1973).

66   David J. Garrow, *Liberty and Sexuality: The Right to Privacy and the Making of Roe v. Wade* (Berkeley: University of California Press, 1994), 483.

67   Jefferson Cowie, *Stayin' Alive: The 1970s and the Last Days of the Working Class* (New York: New Press, 2010), 105.

68   John Morton Blum, *Years of Discord: American Politics and Society, 1961–1974* (New York: W. W. Norton, 1991), 417.

69   "Caught on Tape: The White House Reaction to the Shooting of Alabama Governor and Democratic Presidential Candidate George Wallace," http://nixontapes.org/wallace.html.

70   Perlstein, *Nixonland*, 615.

71   Ibid., 652.

72   Carl Bernstein and Bob Woodward, *All the President's Men* (New York: Simon & Schuster, 1974), 132; also quoted in David von Drehle, "FBI's No. 2 Was Deep Throat," *Washington Post*, June 1, 2005.

73   Bart Barnes, "John Sirica, Watergate Judge, Dies," *Washington Post*, August 15, 1992.

74   Peter Baker, "Newly Released Tapes Show Nixon Maneuvering as Watergate Unfolds," *New York Times,* August 21, 2013.

75   *United States v. Nixon*, 418 U.S. 683 (1974).

CHAPTER 13: "A SEASON OF DARKNESS"

1   The material in this and the following paragraphs on Ksionska's life history draws from Henry Goldman, "A Way of Life Ends with Fairless Decline," *Philadelphia Inquirer,* April 10, 1983: "Obituary: John F. (Book) Ksionska, Sr.," *Bucks County-Courier Times,* August 10, 2003; Thomas Dublin and

Walter Licht, *The Face of Decline: The Pennsylvania Anthracite Region in the Twentieth Century* (Ithaca, NY: Cornell University Press, 2005).

2   Julian E. Zelizer, *Arsenal of Democracy: The Politics of National Security—From World War II to the War on Terrorism* (New York: Basic Books, 2010), 217.

3   Richard Nixon, "Address to the Nation on the War in Vietnam," November 3, 1969 , http://bit.ly/1vab2VI.

4   Gerald S. Strober and Deborah H. Strober, *Nixon: An Oral History of His Presidency* (New York: Harper Perennial, 1996), 178.

5   Eric Pace, "Le Duc Tho, Top Hanoi Aide, Dies at 79," *New York Times*, October 14, 1990.

6   Larry Berman, *No Peace, No Honor: Nixon, Kissinger, and Betrayal in Vietnam* (New York: Free Press, 2001), 172.

7   Geoffrey Kabaservice, *Rule and Ruin: The Downfall of Moderation and the Destruction of the Republican Party, from Eisenhower to the Tea Party* (New York: Oxford University Press, 2012), 174.

8   Henry Kissinger, *White House Years* (New York: Simon & Schuster, 1979), 745.

9   Memorandum of Conversation, Beijing, July 10, 1971, document 140 in *Foreign Relations of the United States, 1969–1976*, vol. 17, *China, 1969–1972*, http://1.usa.gov/1GXNVRh.

10   Kissinger, *White House Years*, 750.

11   H. W. Brands, *American Dreams: The United States Since 1945* (New York: Penguin, 2010), 173.

12   Kabaservice, *Rule and Ruin*, 328.

13   Donald T. Critchlow, *The Conservative Ascendancy: How the GOP Right Made Political History* (Cambridge, MA: Harvard University Press, 2007), 95.

14   Brands, *American Dreams*, 172.

15   Campbell Craig and Fredrik Logevall, *America's Cold War: The Politics of Insecurity* (Cambridge, MA: Harvard University Press, 2009), 281–82.

16   Rick Perlstein, *Nixonland: The Rise of a President and the Fracturing of America* (New York: Simon & Schuster, 2008), 469.

17   Judith Stein, *Pivotal Decade: How the United States Traded Factories for Finance in the Seventies* (New Haven, CT: Yale University Press, 2010), 28.

18   Geir Lundestad, *The United States and Western Europe Since 1945* (New York: Oxford University Press, 2003), 159.

19   Richard Nixon, "Annual Message to the Congress on the State of the Union," January 22, 1971, http://bit.ly/11oEXwi.

20   Jefferson Cowie, *Stayin' Alive: The 1970s and the Last Days of the Working Class* (New York: New Press, 2010), 150.

21 Leonard Silk, *Nixonomics* (New York: Praeger Publishers, 1972), 99.

22 Mark Fiege, *The Republic of Nature: An Environmental History of the United States* (Seattle: University of Washington Press, 2012), 377.

23 Norman Podhoretz, "Now, Instant Zionism," *New York Times,* February 3, 1974.

24 Richard Nixon, "Address to the Nation About Policies to Deal with the Energy Shortages," November 7, 1973, http://bit.ly/1uuJ05e.

25 Chad M. Kimmel, "'No Gas, My Ass!': Marking the End of the Postwar Period in Levittown," in Dianne Harris, ed., *Second Suburb: Levittown, Pennsylvania* (Pittsburgh: University of Pittsburgh Press, 2010), 344.

26 Michael J. Graetz, *The End of Energy: The Unmaking of America's Environment, Security, and Independence* (Cambridge, MA: MIT Press, 2011), 36.

27 Fiege, *Republic of Nature*, 381.

28 Meg Jacobs, "The Conservative Struggle and the Energy Crisis," in Bruce J. Schulman and Julian E. Zelizer, ed., *Rightward Bound: Making America Conservative in the 1970s* (Cambridge, MA: Harvard University Press, 2008), 198.

29 C. W. McCall, "Convoy," *Black Bear Road*, MGM Records, 1975.

30 Gerald R. Ford: "Remarks on Signing a Proclamation Granting Pardon to Richard Nixon," September 8, 1974, http://bit.ly/1vabfZ2.

31 Gerald Ford, "Whip Inflation Now" speech, October 8, 1974, http://bit.ly/1sNYsFk.

32 Alan Greenspan, interview by Richard Norton Smith, December 17, 2008, http://bit.ly/1Br70Lu.

33 Leslie H. Gelb, "Poll Finds U.S. Isolationism on Rise, Hope at Ebb," *New York Times,* June 16, 1974.

34 Marilyn Bender, "The Energy Trauma at General Motors," *New York Times,* March 24, 1974.

35 Alexandra Orchard, "The 1972 Lordstown Strike," *Walter P. Reuther Library* (blog), August 12, 2013, http://reuther.wayne.edu/node/10756.

36 Cowie, *Stayin' Alive,* 48.

37 Judson Gooding, "Blue-Collar Blues in the Assembly Line," *Fortune,* July 1970; Agis Salpukas, "G.M.'s Toughest Division 'Binbuster?'," *New York Times,* April 16, 1972.

38 Jefferson Cowie, *Capital Moves: RCA's Hundred Year Quest for Cheap Labor* (Ithaca, NY: Cornell University Press, 2001), 102.

39 Rachel Carson, *Silent Spring* (Boston: Houghton Mifflin, 1962), 17.

40 Christopher C. Sellers, *Crabgrass Crucible: Suburban Nature and the Rise of Environmentalism in Twentieth Century America* (Chapel Hill: University of North Carolina Press, 2012), 223, 236.

41   Joni Mitchell, "Big Yellow Taxi," *Ladies of the Canyon*, Reprise Records, 1970.

42   Adam Rome, *The Genius of Earth Day: How a 1970 Teach-In Unexpectedly Made the First Green Revolution* (New York: Hill & Wang, 2013), 161.

43   Bruce J. Schulman, *The Seventies: The Great Shift in American Culture, Society, and Politics* (Cambridge, MA: Da Capo, 2002), 30.

44   David Sibley, *Geographies of Exclusion* (New York: Routledge, 1995), 61.

45   "The Crime Wave," *Time,* June 30, 1975.

46   U.S. Department of Justice, FBI, Uniform Crime Reporting Statistics, http://www.ucrdatatool.gov/index.cfm.

47   Heather Ann Thompson, "Why Mass Incarceration Matters: Rethinking Crisis, Decline, and Transformation in Postwar American History," *Journal of American History* 97 (2010): 708.

48   Ruth Wilson Gilmore, *Golden Gulag: Prisons, Surplus, Crisis, and Opposition in Globalizing California* (Berkeley: University of California Press, 2007), 101.

49   Norman Miller, "The Transformation of Gary Hart," *Wall Street Journal,* October 28, 1974.

50   Laura Kalman, *Right Star Rising: A New Politics, 1974–1980* (New York: W. W. Norton, 2010), 255.

51   Jimmy Carter, "Inaugural Address," January 20, 1977, http://bit.ly/1wAlz7n.

52   Thomas J. Sugrue, "Carter's Urban Policy Crisis," in Gary M. Fink and Hugh Davis Graham, eds., *The Carter Presidency: Policy Choices in the Post–New Deal Era* (Lawrence: University Press of Kansas, 1998), 139–40.

53   U.S. Bureau of Labor Statistics, *Labor Force Statistics from the Current Population Survey, 1947–2014,* http://1.usa.gov/1vdVGis.

54   Melvyn Dubofsky, "Jimmy Carter and the End of the Politics of Productivity," in Fink and Graham, *Carter Presidency,* 99.

55   U.S. Bureau of Labor Statistics, *Labor Force Statistics from the Current Population Survey, 1947–2014,* http://1.usa.gov/1vdVGis.

56   Stephen B. Reed, "One Hundred Years of Price Change: The Consumer Price Index and the American Inflation Experience," *Monthly Labor Review* (April 2014), http://1.usa.gov/1EFOawC.

57   Jimmy Carter, "Airline Industry Regulation Message to the Congress," March 4, 1977, http://bit.ly/1xA5e5H.

58   Phillip J. Cooper, *The War Against Regulation: From Jimmy Carter to George W. Bush* (Lawrence: University Press of Kansas, 2009), 28.

59   Ralph Blumenthal, "Reflections of Alfred Kahn: He Won Some Battles But Lost the War," *New York Times,* November 9, 1980.

60   Jimmy Carter, "Acceptance Speech at the Democratic National Convention," August 14, 1980, http://bit.ly/1uuJnwz.

61   Graetz, *End of Energy,* 140.

62   David Farber, *Taken Hostage: The Iran Hostage Crisis and America's First Encounter with Radical Islam* (Princeton, NJ: Princeton University Press, 2005), 26.

63   Ibid.

64   Kimmel, "No Gas, My Ass," 340.

65   George F. Will, "Levittown Revisited," *Newsweek,* July 9, 1979.

66   Jimmy Carter, "Address to the Nation on Energy and National Goals," July 15, 1979, http://bit.ly/1xA5kdJ.

67   Farber, *Taken Hostage,* 176.

68   Jefferson Cowie, "'Vigorously Left, Right, and Center': The Crosscurrents of Working-Class America in the 1970s," in Beth Bailey and David Farber, eds., *America in the Seventies* (Lawrence: University Press of Kansas, 2004), 76.

69   Camper Van Beethoven, "Ambiguity Song," Telephone Free Landslide Victory, I.R.S. Records, 1985.

CHAPTER 14: THE NEW GILDED AGE, 1980–2000

1   Material on Dukes comes from Liza Featherstone, *Selling Women Short: The Landmark Battle for Workers' Rights at Wal-Mart* (New York: Basic Books, 2005) and Rick Radin, "Pittsburg Woman Back at Work After Star Turn at Supreme Court," *Contra Costa Times,* April 21, 2011. Material on Wal-Mart comes from Bethany Moreton, *To Serve God and Wal-Mart: The Making of Christian Free Enterprise* (Cambridge, MA: Harvard University Press, 2009); and Nelson Lichtenstein, *The Retail Revolution: How Wal-Mart Created a Brave New World of Business* (New York: Metropolitan Books, 2009).

2   Carter-Reagan Presidential Debate, October 28, 1980, http://bit.ly/1xFtWmi.

3   Ronald Reagan, "Inaugural Address," January 20, 1981, http://bit.ly /1yqtxCD.

4   Ronald Reagan, "Message to the Congress Transmitting the Proposed Package on the Program for Economic Recovery," February 18, 1981, http://bit.ly /16tkEA8.

5   Ronald Reagan, "Remarks to Reporters on Releasing an Audit of the United States Economy," February 12, 1981, http://www.presidency.ucsb.edu/ws/?pid =43376.

6   Meg Jacobs and Julian Zelizer, *Conservatives in Power: The Reagan Years, 1981–1989* (New York: Bedford Books, 2011), 21.

7   Romain D. Huret, *American Tax Resisters* (Cambridge, MA: Harvard University Press, 2014), 231.

8   Ronald Reagan, "White House Report on the Program for Economic Recovery," February 18, 1981, http://bit.ly/1xYjMLG.

9   William Greider, "The Education of David Stockman," *Atlantic Monthly*, December 1981.

10   Jacob S. Hacker and Paul Pierson, *Winner-Take-All Politics: How Washington Made the Rich Richer and Turned Its Back on the Middle Class* (New York: Simon & Schuster, 2010), 23.

11   Martha Derthick and Steven M. Teles, "Riding the Third Rail: Social Security Reform," in W. Elliott Brownlee and Hugh Davis Graham, eds., *The Reagan Presidency: Pragmatic Conservatism and Its Legacies* (Lawrence: University Press of Kansas, 2003), 194.

12   U.S. Bureau of the Census, Historical Poverty Tables, Table 2, http://1.usa.gov/1xp7RK8.

13   *New York Times*, February 15 and 29, 1976, and December 27, 1983; *Chicago Defender*, November 14 and 30, 1974, and February 19, 1975.

14   *Roger Biles, The Fate of Cities: Urban America and the Federal Government, 1945–2000* (Lawrence: University Press of Kansas, 2011), 285.

15   Joseph A. McCartin, *Collision Course: Ronald Reagan, the Air Traffic Controllers and the Strike that Changed America* (New York: Oxford University Press, 2011), 292.

16   U.S. Bureau of Labor Statistics, *Major Work Stoppages, 2013*, http://1.usa.gov/1xA5uSm.

17   Nelson Lichtenstein, "Wal-Mart, John Tate, and Their Anti-Union America," in Nelson Lichtenstein and Elizabeth Tandy Shermer, eds., *The Right and Labor in America: Politics, Ideology, and Imagination* (Philadelphia: University of Pennsylvania Press, 2012), 263.

18   Robert O. Self, *All in the Family: The Realignment of American Democracy Since the 1960s* (New York: Hill & Wang, 2012), 345–56.

19   John G. Turner, *Bill Bright and the Campus Crusade for Christ* (Chapel Hill: University of North Carolina Press, 2008), 118.

20   Jon Butler, Grant Wacker, and Randall Balmer, *Religion in American Life: A Short History*, 2nd ed. (New York: Oxford University Press, 2011), 394.

21   James T. Patterson, *Restless Giant: The United States from Watergate to Bush v. Gore* (New York: Oxford University Press, 2005), 139.

22   Joseph Crespino, "Civil Rights and the Religious Right," in Bruce J. Schulman and Julian Zelizer, eds., *Rightward Bound: Making America Conservative in the 1970s* (Cambridge, MA: Harvard University Press, 2008), 104.

23   Gary Scott Smith, *Faith and the Presidency from George Washington to George W. Bush* (New York: Oxford University Press, 2006), 345.

24 Self, *All in the Family*, 370.

25 Stanley K. Henshaw and Kathryn Kost, *Trends in the Characteristics of Women Obtaining Abortions, 1974 to 2004* (New York: Guttmacher Institute, 2008), 7.

26 Stephen Waldmann, "Stuart's Table," Belief.net, http://bit.ly/1zpwtQO.

27 Aydin Tözeren, *A New Life: Being a Gay Man in the Era of HIV* (Lanham, MD: University Press of America, 1997), 140–62.

28 Leslie Maitland Werner, "Education Chief Presses AIDS Tests," *New York Times*, May 1, 1987.

29 Philip M. Boffey, "Reagan Names 12 to Panel on AIDS," *New York Times*, July 24, 1987.

30 Sheldon Goldman, *Picking Federal Judges: Lower Court Selection from Roosevelt Through Reagan* (New Haven, CT: Yale University Press, 1997), 348, 353.

31 *Bowers v. Hardwick*, 478 U.S. 186 (1986).

32 John Patrick Diggins, *Ronald Reagan: Fate, Freedom, and the Making of History* (New York: W. W. Norton, 2007), 316.

33 Ronald Reagan, "Remarks at the Annual Convention of the National Association of Evangelicals in Orlando, Florida," March 8, 1983, http://bit.ly/1xYhRGR.

34 All figures from National Research Council, *Funding a Revolution: Government Support for Computing Research* (Washington, DC: National Academies Press, 1999), http://bit.ly/1qJ1PfY.

35 Margaret Pugh O'Mara, *Cities of Knowledge: Cold War Science and the Search for the Next Silicon Valley* (Princeton, NJ: Princeton University Press, 2005).

36 Sean Wilentz, *The Age of Reagan: A History, 1974–2008* (New York: Harper, 2009), 159.

37 Ronald Reagan, "Remarks of Reporters Announcing the Deployment of United States Forces in Beirut, Lebanon," August 20, 1982, http://bit.ly/1wFtDI3.

38 Ronald Reagan, "Radio Address to the Nation on the Budget Deficit, Central America, and Lebanon," February 4, 1984, http://bit.ly/1wgPLsk.

39 Greg Grandin, *Empire's Workshop Latin America, the United States, and the Rise of the New Imperialism* (New York: Macmillan, 2006), 100.

40 Ronald Reagan, "Remarks on Central America and El Salvador at the Annual Meeting of the National Association of Manufacturers," March 10, 1983, http://bit.ly/1BY7vsQ.

41 Ronald Reagan, "Address Before a Joint Session of Congress on Central America," April 27, 1983, http://bit.ly/1wFtNzj.

42 Ronald Reagan, "Address to the Nation on the Iran Arms and Contra Aid Controversy," November 13, 1986, http://bit.ly/1uSRyyB.

43 Ronald Reagan, "Remarks on East-West Relations at the Brandenburg Gate in West Berlin," June 12, 1987, http://bit.ly/1wgPUw1.

44 Julian E. Zelizer, *Arsenal of Democracy: The Politics of National Security from World War II to the War on Terrorism* (New York: Basic Books, 2010), 351.

45 Ibid., 370.

46 U.S. Bureau of Labor Statistics, *Spotlight on Statistics: Fashion*, June 2012, http://1.usa.gov/1ubi6hb.

47 Steve Striffler, *Chicken: The Dangerous Transformation of America's Favorite Food* (New Haven, CT: Yale University Press, 2007), 22.

48 Daniel J. Tichenor, *Dividing Lines: The Politics of Immigration Control in America* (Princeton, NJ: Princeton University Press, 2002), 262.

49 Joseph Rosenbloom, "Victims in the Heartland," *American Prospect*, June 16, 2003.

50 The Third Clinton-Bush-Perot Presidential Debate, October 19, 1992, http://bit.ly/16JUedv.

51 Kenneth S. Baer, *Reinventing Democrats: The Politics of Liberalism from Reagan to Clinton* (Lawrence: University Press of Kansas, 2000), 64.

52 Jon F. Hale, "Making the New Democrats," *Political Science Quarterly* 110 (1995), 217, 220.

53 Baer, *Reinventing Democrats*, 166.

54 Democratic Leadership Council, "The New Orleans Declaration," March 1, 1990, http://bit.ly/1ARCtSC.

55 Hale, "Making the New Democrats," 226.

56 Jacob S. Hacker and Paul Pierson, *Winner-Take-All Politics: How Washington Made the Rich Richer and Turned Its Back on the Middle Class* (New York: Simon & Schuster, 2010), 232.

57 Paul Pierson, "The Deficit and the Politics of Domestic Reform," in Margaret Weir, ed., *The Social Divide: Political Parties and the Future of Activist Government* (Washington, DC: Brookings Institution, 1998), 136.

58 Mark A. Peterson, "The Politics of Health Care Policy," in Weir, *Social Divide*, 183.

59 Ibid., 194.

60 The Contract with America, 1994, http://bit.ly/1ulRvzy.

61 Lawrence Mead, *The New Politics of Poverty: The Nonworking Poor in America* (New York: Basic Books, 1992), 15, 57.

62 Michael B. Katz, *The Price of Citizenship: Redefining the American Welfare State* (New York: Metropolitan Books, 2001), 339.

63 Ibid., 339–40.

64 U.S. Census Bureau, *Current Population Reports, P60-213, Money Income in*

the United States: 2000 (Washington, DC: U.S. Government Printing Office, 2001).

65 Hacker and Pierson, *Winner-Take-All Politics*, 22.

66 Sheldon A. Pollock, *Refinancing America: The Republican Antitax Agenda* (Albany: State University of New York Press, 2003), 141.

67 Dan Roberts, "Wall Street Deregulation Pushed by Clinton Advisors, Documents Reveal," *Guardian*, April 17, 2014, http://bit.ly/1Br5YPH.

68 William J. Clinton, "Remarks on the National Homeownership Strategy," June 5, 1995, http://bit.ly/1xYibpd.

69 Charles A. Kupchan, "Hollow Hegemony or Stable Multipolarity," in G. John Ikenberry, ed., *America Unrivaled: The Future of the Balance of Power* (Ithaca, NY: Cornell University Press, 2002), 83.

70 "The Year 2000: Keeping Watch: With Fears of Terrorism, Precautions Will Continue," *New York Times*, January 2, 2000.

71 William J. Clinton, "The President's Radio Address," January 1, 2000, http://bit.ly/1vdUStU.

CHAPTER 15: UNITED WE STAND, DIVIDED WE FALL, SINCE 2000

1 This account of Patricia Thompson is drawn from her oral history in Lolla Vollen and Chris Ying, eds., *Voices from the Storm: The People of New Orleans on Hurricane Katrina and Its Aftermath* (San Francisco: McSweeney's Books, 2006).

2 The First Gore-Bush Presidential Debate, October 3, 2000, http://bit.ly/1wegwc3.

3 Kevin M. Kruse, "Compassionate Conservatism: Religion in the Age of George W. Bush," in Julian Zelizer, ed., *The Presidency of George W. Bush: A First Historical Assessment* (Princeton, NJ: Princeton University Press, 2010), 229.

4 George W. Bush, "GOP Nomination Acceptance Address," August 3, 2000, http://bit.ly/1E2RW8b.

5 Robert Johnston, *The Radical Middle Class: Populist Democracy and the Question of Capitalism in Progressive Era Portland, Oregon* (Princeton, NJ: Princeton University Press, 2006), 273.

6 George W. Bush, "Remarks on Signing Executive Orders With Respect to Faith-Based and Community Initiatives," January 29, 2001, http://bit.ly/13wlAC2.

7 Sean Wilentz, *The Age of Reagan: A History, 1974–2008* (New York: Harper Collins, 2008), 438.

8   Stephen P. Miller, *The Age of Evangelicalism: America's Born-Again Years* (New York: Oxford University Press, 2014), 127.

9   George W. Bush, "Address to the Nation on Stem Cell Research," August 9, 2001, http://bit.ly/1x3dEm6.

10   Richard Land, interviewed in "The Jesus Factor," PBS *Frontline*, April 29, 2004, http://to.pbs.org/1wW0gl1.

11   James T. Patterson, "Transformative Economic Policies: Tax Cutting, Stimuli, and Bailouts," in Zelizer, ed., *Presidency of George W. Bush*, 130.

12   *Final Report of the National Commission on Terrorist Attacks Upon the United States,* Executive Summary (Washington, DC: U.S. Government Printing Office, 2004), http://1.usa.gov/1wBG7kk.

13   Timothy Naftali, "George W. Bush and the 'War on Terror,'" in Zelizer, ed., *Presidency of George W. Bush*, 66.

14   Mary L. Dudziak, "A Sword and a Shield: The Uses of Law in the Bush Administration," in Zelizer, ed., *Presidency of George W. Bush*, 43–44.

15   U.S. Senate, Select Committee on Intelligence, *Committee Study of the CIA's Detention and Interrogation Program, Findings and Conclusions*, December 2014, 2, http://1.usa.gov/13w3hwE.

16   George W. Bush, "Address Before a Joint Session of the Congress on the State of the Union," January 29, 2002, http://www.presidency.ucsb.edu/ws/?pid=29644.

17   Ibid.

18   George W. Bush, "Commencement Address at the United States Military Academy in West Point, New York," June 1, 2002, http://www.presidency.ucsb.edu/ws/?pid=62730.

19   Fredrik Logevall, "Anatomy of an Unnecessary War: The Iraq Invasion," in Zelizer, ed., *Presidency of George W. Bush,* 101.

20   Lloyd C. Gardner, *The Long Road to Baghdad: A History of U.S. Foreign Policy from the 1970s to the Present* (New York: New Press, 2008), 141.

21   Bob Woodward, "Cheney Was Unwavering in Desire to Go to War; Tension Between Vice President and Powell Grew Deeper as Both Tried to Guide Bush's Decision," *Washington Post*, April 20, 2004.

22   Logevall, "Anatomy of an Unnecessary War," 109.

23   George W. Bush, "Address to the Nation on Iraq from the *U.S.S. Abraham Lincoln*," May 1, 2003, http://www.presidency.ucsb.edu/ws/index.php?pid=68675.

24   Amy Belasco, *Troop Levels in the Afghan and Iraq Wars, FY 2001–FY 2012: Cost and Other Potential Issues* (Washington, DC: Congressional Research Service, 2009), figs. 6 and 7.

25 Hedrick Smith, *Who Stole the American Dream* (New York: Random House, 2011), 357–58.

26 Mark Sandalow, "Bush Claims Mandate, Sets 2nd-Term Goals," *San Francisco Chronicle*, November 5, 2004.

27 Nelson Lichtenstein, "Ideology and Interest on the Social Policy Home Front," in Zelizer, ed., *Presidency of George W. Bush*, 190.

28 Romain Huret, "Explaining the Unexplainable: Hurricane Katrina, FEMA, and the Bush Administration," in Romain Huret and Randy J. Sparks, eds., *Hurricane Katrina in Transatlantic Perspective* (Baton Rouge: Louisiana State University Press, 2014), 39.

29 U.S. Department of Health and Human Services, Office of Human Services Policy, *The Role of Faith Based and Community Organizations in Providing Relief and Recovery Services After Hurricanes Katrina and Rita*, September 2008, http://urbn.is/1x309mB.

30 *A Fresh Start for New Orleans' Children: Improving Education after Katrina*: *Hearing Before the Subcommittee on Education and Early Childhood Development,* Committee on Health, Education, Labor, and Pensions, U.S. Senate, 109th Cong., 2nd. sess. (July 14, 2006).

31 Louis Hyman, *Borrow: The American Way of Debt* (New York: Vintage Books, 2012), 236.

32 Debbie Gruenstein Bocian, Wei Li, Carolina Reid, and Roberto G. Quercia, *Lost Ground, 2011: Disparities in Mortgage Lending and Foreclosures* (Durham, NC: Center for Responsible Lending, 2011), 8.

33 Sheila Bair, *Bull By the Horns: Fighting to Save Main Street from Wall Street and Wall Street from Itself* (New York: Free Press, 2012).

34 Barack Obama, "Address to the Democratic National Convention," *Washington Post,* July 27, 2004.

35 Michael Cooper, "McCain on U.S. Economy: From 'Strong' to 'Total Crisis' in 36 Hours," *New York Times,* September 17, 2008.

36 The best overviews of Obama's economic policy to date are Ron Suskind, *Confidence Men: Wall Street, Washington, and the Education of a President* (New York: Harper, 2011), and Noam Scheiber, *The Escape Artists: How Obama Fumbled the Recovery* (New York: Simon & Schuster, 2012).

37 Among the overviews of Obama's policy initiatives and the constraints that he faced, the most useful is Theda Skocpol and Lawrence Jacobs, eds., *Reaching for a New Deal: Ambitious Governance, Economic Meltdown, and Polarized Politics in Obama's First Two Years* (New York: Russell Sage Foundation, 2011). On Obama's penchant toward moderation and bipartisanship, see

James Kloppenberg, *Reading Obama* (Princeton, NJ: Princeton University Press, 2010).

38 Emanuel Saez, "Striking it Richer: The Evolution of Top Incomes in the United States," University of California, Berkeley, Department of Economics, September 2013, http://bit.ly/13VZUQx.

39 Rakesh Kochhar, Richard Fry, and Paul Taylor, *Twenty-to-One: Wealth Gaps Rise to Record Highs Between Whites, Blacks and Hispanics* (Pew Research Center, Social and Demographic Trends, July 26, 2011), http://pewrsr.ch/13r5FVn.

PHOTOGRAPH CREDITS

INDEX

Page numbers in *italics* refer to illustrations.